HANDBOOK OF INSTITUTIONAL APPROACHES TO INTERNATIONAL BUSINESS

Handbook of Institutional Approaches to International Business

Edited by

Geoffrey Wood and Mehmet Demirbag
School of Management, University of Sheffield, UK

Edward Elgar
Cheltenham, UK • Northampton, MA, USA

Published by
Edward Elgar Publishing Limited
The Lypiatts
15 Lansdown Road
Cheltenham
Glos GL50 2JA
UK

Edward Elgar Publishing, Inc.
William Pratt House
9 Dewey Court
Northampton
Massachusetts 01060
USA

A catalogue record for this book
is available from the British Library

Library of Congress Control Number: 2011942546

ISBN 978 1 84980 768 5 (cased)

Typeset by Servis Filmsetting Ltd, Stockport, Cheshire
Printed and bound by MPG Books Group, UK

Contents

Contributors

Maria L. Aldred is a Senior Lecturer in International Business, Manchester Metropolitan University Business School.

Franklin Allen is the Nippon Life Professor of Finance and Professor of Economics at the Wharton School of the University of Pennsylvania. He is a past President of the American Finance Association and a Fellow of the Econometric Society. He received his doctorate from Oxford University.

Matthew M.C. Allen is a Senior Lecturer in Organization Studies, Manchester Business School, The University of Manchester. His research covers comparative employment relations, business systems, multinational corporations, employment relations and firm performance, and institutional theory.

Ahmad Arslan is Post-doctoral Researcher at the Department of Marketing, Faculty of Business Studies, University of Vaasa, Finland. His research interests include FDI strategies of MNEs especially in emerging economies, impacts of institutional environments, institutional theory and new institutional economics.

Bradley R. Barnes is Professor of International Management and Marketing at the University of Sheffield Management School. Prior to that he was the Hong Kong Endowed Chair of International Management at the University of Kent. His research is mainly in the area of international business relationships, focusing on Chinese economies. Prior to his academic career, Dr Barnes worked for over ten years in an international marketing context.

Nic Beech, Professor of Management Dean of Arts, at the School of Management University of St Andrews. His primary research focuses on the study of identity.

Jack A. Clampit is a PhD Candidate and research assistant at the Wang Center for International Business Education and Research (CIBER), where he studies the link between institutions and MNE conduct and performance (including distal relationships, e.g., institutional antecedents and societal outcomes).

David G. Collings is Professor of HRM at Dublin City University. His research interests focus on the management of MNEs with an emphasis on staffing and talent issues. He is a co-editor of *Human Resource Management Journal*.

Kieran M. Conroy is a Doctoral researcher in the discipline of Management at the National University of Ireland Galway. His research focus includes an interest in the strategic management of MNE subsidiaries with a particular emphasis on the application of an institutional perspective to this domain.

Richard Croucher is Professor of Comparative Employment Relations and Associate Dean Research at Middlesex University Business School and Visiting Professor at Cranfield School of Management. He is the author with Elizabeth Cotton of *Global Unions, Global Business* (2nd edition published by Libri Publishing, 2011).

Alvaro Cuervo-Cazurra is Associate Professor of International Business and Strategy at Northeastern University. His research focuses on international strategy, with a special focus on developing country multinational firms, and governance, with a special interest on corruption. He received a PhD from the Massachusetts Institute of Technology.

Mehmet Demirbag is Professor of International Business in the School of Management at the University of Sheffield. His current research interest focuses around MNEs from emerging markets, offshore R&D activities of MNEs, impact of institutional factors on MNEs' operations. Dr Demirbag also has extensive experience in policy development having served as principal advisor for the Turkish Ministry of Industry and Trade.

Dilek Demirbas is a Reader in Strategic Management International Business subject group at Newcastle Business School, Northumbria University. She teaches International Business and Economics.

Fragkiskos Filippaios is the Director for Postgraduate Development and Accreditations and a Senior Lecturer in International Business at Kent Business School, University of Kent. His research interests are on the roles of subsidiaries of Multinational Enterprises, the location strategies of multinationals' subsidiaries, the role of technology in the multinational group and the empirical assessment of Foreign Direct Investment.

Marc Fovargue-Davies is a Strategy Consultant and Research Associate of the London Centre for Corporate Governance and Ethics at Birkbeck, University of London.

Nolan T. Gaffney is a PhD Candidate and research assistant at the Wang Center for International Business Education and Research (CIBER), where he studies the impact of institutions on EMNEs involved in mergers and acquisitions.

Mehmet Erdem Genc is an Assistant Professor of Management at Montclair State University. His research focuses on how country institutional environments affect the strategic behavior and performance of multinational firms. Originally a native of Turkey, he holds a PhD in Strategic Management from the University of Minnesota.

Axèle Giroud is a Senior Lecturer in International Business at Manchester Business School. She has conducted several research projects on Asian and multinational firms' activities in the region. She is interested in issues of knowledge transfer, multinational firms' linkages in host economies and multinational strategies in Asia.

John Godard is a professor at the University of Manitoba. His main interest is in the implications of work and employment for broad issues of economy and society, and how these implications vary in accordance with national institutional environments.

Gail Greig is a lecturer in the School of Management at the University of St Andrews. Her PhD focused on the role of context in organisational learning from an activity theoretical perspective. Current research interests concern relations between management practice and professional/other core work practices.

Nigel Haworth is Professor of Human Resource Development in the University of Auckland in New Zealand.

Jasper J. Hotho is Assistant Professor at the Copenhagen Business School's Department of Strategic Management and Globalization. His main research interests include the internationalization process of firms, MNE knowledge processes and the effects and measurement of institutional differences.

Steve Hughes is Professor of International Organisations at the Newcastle University Business School.

Bahattin Karademir is Assistant Professor of Management and Organizations at Cukurova University, Adana, Turkey. His research interests include business groups in emerging markets, internationalization of emerging market firms, and emerging market multinationals.

Ben L. Kedia is the Robert Wang Chair of Excellence in International Business, and the Director of the Wang Center for International Business

Education and Research (CIBER) at the University of Memphis. His research interests include Cross-Cultural Management and International Business Strategy.

Gilton Klerck is Associate Professor in Industrial and Economic Sociology at Rhodes University in Grahamstown, South Africa.

Sue Konzelmann is a Reader in Management and Director of the London Centre for Corporate Governance and Ethics at Birkbeck, University of London; she is also a Research Associate of the Centre for Business Research at Cambridge University and the Higgins Labor Research Centre at the University of Notre Dame.

Jorma Larimo is Professor of International Marketing and Vice Dean of Faculty of Business Studies at the University of Vaasa, Finland and part-time Professor at the Faculty of Economics and Business Administration at the Tartu University, Estonia. His research interests include FDI, market entry and divestment strategies of MNEs, internationalization of SMEs, Management and Marketing Strategies in Central and Eastern Europe, International Retailing and Role of Culture in International Business Operations of Firms.

Martina McGuinness is a lecturer in the Management School at the University of Sheffield. Her research interests include risk and organisational resilience with a particular focus on the impact of environmental uncertainty upon international business. She is currently involved in an ESRC funded project on risk, resilience and governance which seeks to create links between academics and practitioners working in this field.

Brendan McSweeney is Professor of Management at Royal Holloway College, University of London and Visiting Professor at Stockholm University.

Hafiz Mirza is Professor of International Business at the University of Bradford School of Management and a Chief in Division on Investment, at the United Nations Conference on Trade and Development, Geneva.

Glenn Morgan is Professor of International Management at Cardiff University, Cardiff Business School. His current research interest centres around comparative management and the impact of globalization, institutional change, institutions and markets, particularly the regulation of financial markets.

Claudio Morrison is Senior Research Fellow at Middlesex University Business School. Previously based at Warwick University, his research focuses on management change, labour relations and more recently migration in the CIS.

Holly Patrick is a doctoral candidate at the School of Management, University of St Andrews. Her primary research focuses on the epistemological construction of legitimacy in cultural industries, primarily the theatre industry.

Torben Pedersen is Professor at SMG, Copenhagen Business School. He has published over 100 articles and books concerning the managerial and strategic aspects of globalization. He is co-editor of *Global Strategy Journal* and *Advances in International Management*.

Roman Stepanov is a senior lecturer in Accounting and Financial Management subject group at Newcastle Business School, Northumbria University. He teaches Accounting, International Financial Management and Corporate Governance.

Carmen Stoian is a Lecturer in International Business at Kent Business School, University of Kent. Her research interests are on the institutional determinants of foreign direct investment in Central and Eastern Europe, the location decisions by multinationals expanding in post-communist economies and the cultural differences and their impact on international business.

Zita Stone is an Assistant Lecturer at Kent Business School, University of Kent. Zita's research interests are on the equity culture creation in Central and Eastern Europe as well as the broader areas of International Business and Strategic Management.

Martin Upchurch is Professor of International Employment Relations at Middlesex University, London, UK. Prior to becoming an academic he worked for the Department of the Environment and then for a public sector trade union in the UK as a researcher and journalist. He serves on the National Executive Committee of the British Universities Industrial Relations Association and is a member of the editorial board of Work, Employment and Society.

Kee Hwee Wee is Economic Affairs Officer at the United Nations Conference on Trade and Development, Geneva.

Geoffrey Wood is Professor of HRM in the School of Management, University of Sheffield, and Associate Dean of the School. He is also Visiting Professor at Nelson Mandela Metropolitan University and Honorary Professor of the University of Witwatersrand. Geoff's research interests centre on the relationship between institutional setting, corporate governance, firm finance, and firm level work and employment relations. Whilst much of the contemporary institutional literature draws distinctions between national contexts based on stylized ideal types, macroeconomic trends and/or limited panels of case studies, his work brings to bear systematic comparative firm level evidence. At a broader theoretical level, his work encompasses explorations of the bounded nature of internal diversity within national capitalist archetypes, and, more recently, institutional crises and change. In his recent work, he has linked broader systemic crises with energy transitions, and the extent to which the latter favours owners of more fungible assets.

Attila Yaprak is Professor of Marketing and International Business at Wayne State University, Detroit, Michigan, USA and a Network Faculty in Marketing at Sabanci University, Istanbul, Turkey. He is a winner of many teaching awards, including the 2007 Outstanding Marketing Teacher Award given by the Academy of Marketing Science, and the President's Award for Excellence in Teaching given by Wayne State University.

Dorothy A. Yen is a Lecturer in Marketing and International Business, at Brunel University. She completed her master's degree and PhD at the University of Leeds. Her research area is in Chinese business relationships. Dr Yen has several years of business experience having worked in industry in both Taiwan and the UK before moving into academia.

Andrey Yukhanaev is a Lecturer in Strategic Management and International Business subject group at Newcastle Business School, Northumbria University. He teaches International Business, Strategic Management and Economics.

Introduction

Geoffrey Wood and Mehmet Demirbag

There is a growing interest on the effects of institutions on how firms manage, and how differences in embedded institutional configurations force firms to adapt how they do business according to context in different parts of the world.

Institutions may be conceived of in rational-hierarchical or relationship terms (Goergen et al. 2009). The former, grounded in rational choice economics assumes that the choices rational actors make is framed by specific institutional incentives and disincentives (North 1990; Peters 2005); it is held that, above all, of central importance is private property rights. Such approaches are dominant in the economics and finance literature (North 1990; La Porta et al. 1999).

In contrast, relationship or socio-economic approaches to institutions reject the view that a single relationship (e.g. private property rights) will overcode all others. Rather, what firms do reflects complex webs of ties, involving not just owners, but also employees, associations, wider society, and directly or indirectly, the state (Peters 2005). The literature on comparative capitalism suggests that the manner in which firms manage – and indeed, conduct other social and economic relations within and beyond the firm – will depend on specific institutional configurations, and the particular complementarities made possible in a particular space and place (Hall and Soskice 2001; Whitley 2005; Hall and Thelen 2009). What in practical terms this means is that a range of different combinations of relationships may prove equally functional: the relative strength of property rights are not necessarily the most important institutional feature in every context, and indeed, there are contexts where weaker property rights may prove more functional than stronger ones (ibid.). Such approaches (most notably the 'varieties of capitalism' literature; Hall and Soskice 2001) has been influential in both the literature on comparative political economy, and increasingly within management studies.

Institutional impacts on international business assume many different forms. While institutions in a country affect domestic firms' strategies, structure and processes, they are equally important for multinationals enterprises' (MNEs) operation in the country (Whitley 2010). While home country institutions influence MNEs (the way they are created, developed, structured, and governed), host country institutions also determine the effectiveness of MNEs and their subsidiaries, alliance partners, supply chain providers etc. This is not a one way influence, rather, it reflects the multiple and complex relationship between structure and social action. Depending on national institutional configurations, industrial organisations and their relationship with other actors, in terms of degree of influence and interdependency, role of institutions and institutional factors vary significantly between countries, regions and triad blocks.

Such institutional impacts on international business, which may create liability of foreignness and therefore transaction costs for MNEs and their partners (Demirbag et al., 2007) should be examined for every stage of international business operations and transactions including location choice, entry mode, creating alliances, organizational structure and diversification, internal processes, outsourcing, supply chain and logistics, environment management and CSR, managing innovation.

Despite the influence of each school of thought, there has been remarkably little dialogue between each camp, and indeed, few systematic attempts to compare differences and build on common ground. And, the bulk of the literature within both camps has focused on the most prosperous countries of Western Europe, North America and the Far East. There has been relatively less attention devoted to understanding the nature of Mediterranean capitalism and transitional economies. Finally, there has been increasing attention on the affects of social action on institutional structures.

The present collection brings together the work of leading scholars from a range of different starting points, present recent synthetic work and institutionally-informed accounts from transitional and emerging markets, as well as mature economies.

THE STRUCTURE OF THE BOOK

The book is explicitly multi-disciplinary, encompassing perspectives from a range of the functional areas of management studies. However, all have in common a rootedness in the broad political economy tradition and an interest in the relationship between spatial and temporal differences in institutional framework and firm-level outcomes. The book consists of three parts. Part I contains 11 theoretical chapters examining various institutional approaches. Part II consists of three chapters of more general and developed-country-oriented perspectives, while Part III contains nine chapters related to emerging and developing economies.

In Chapter 1, the editors locate the comparative analysis of business within recent directions in institutional analysis. The editors accord particular attention to the nature of internal diversity within national institutional archetypes, the open-ended, experimental and sidereal nature of institutional change, and the role of supranational institutions and actors. Finally, they argue that any comparative institutional analysis is incomplete without taking into account structural changes in global capitalism. In particular, they highlight the relationship between the present crisis and a long-term energy transition, with fundamental implications for the deployment of capital.

Morgan, in Chapter 2, focuses on the interaction between multinationals and national business systems. Morgan examines both varieties of capitalism and international business literature and takes a closer look at the interaction between internationalization and national business systems within different types of capitalism. This chapter pays special attention to institutional duality problems and implications of institutional duality and conflicts for standardization, efficiency and learning at subsidiary level.

Allen, in Chapter 3, explores the role of institutions in financing in different countries. The author examines issues of investment and saving, growth, risk sharing, information provision and corporate governance for financial institutions in five different countries. The chapter is particularly path-breaking in its firm foundations in the discipline of finance, but with its broadly encompassing nature, providing a vision and perspective that will enrich the analysis of those working in different subdisciplines of business and management studies.

In Chapter 4, Konzelmann and Fovargue-Davies explore the question of why the four main Anglo-Saxon countries experienced the 2008 financial crisis in different ways. The authors argue that despite their similar cultural attributes, legal origins and institutional configurations, the four main Anglo-Saxon countries experienced the 2008 financial crisis in different ways. This chapter goes on to analyse how political, ideational and historical factors led to different approaches to the regulation of the financial sector, economic liberalization policies and their effect on the evolution of corporate governance. Again, this chapter is path-breaking in that it firmly dispels the view that liberal markets constitute a monolithic and coherent category.

In Chapter 5, Godard contributes to institutional environment approaches and human resource management (HRM) debates and focuses on cross-national variation in HRM practice and the context. The main argument in this chapter is based on the new institutional literature and its relevance to cross-national variation in HRM. Godard develops a framework from an institutional perspective for studying cross-national differences in HRM. The framework developed in this chapter includes the role of history in shaping variations in the national institutional environments of HRM. What is particularly welcome in this chapter is its nuanced conceptualization of the law that transcends the view that the most important legal function is the protection of private property rights.

In Chapter 6, McSweeney examines the role of subjective culture (values) as the shaper of environments. McSweeney challenges the overarching power of singular cultural classifications and non-diversity arguments. He focuses on three types of imagined communities, namely: civilizations, countries and subnational monocultural groups. McSweeney develops a counterargument and critically examines claims about the cultural unity of these communities. This chapter is particularly valuable for all those scholars who have felt vaguely unhappy with comparative accounts that narrowly focus on culture, but have lacked access to a clear, concise and eloquent critique to disabuse cultural-perspective fanatics.

In Chapter 7, Kedia et al. criticize the treatment of institutions in some of the international business literature and develop a holistic framework exploring the links between institutions, multinational enterprises (MNEs) and levels of economic development. Kedia et al. draw on the works of Douglass North and John Dunning and synthesize both streams of literature via development of a model that explores the rich relationship between institutions and levels of economic development around the world.

In Chapter 8, Haworth and Hughes examine the International Labour Organization (ILO). They focus on the concept of Decent Work by identifying key ILO responses to pressures posed by globalization and market liberalization. The authors also examine the role of Decent Work in the ILO's continuing attempts to influence other supranational institutions such as the World Bank, World Trade Organization and the G20. This account imparts a welcome nuance to counter those who see these bodies as narrowly monolithic.

In Chapter 9, Cuervo-Cazurra and Genc provide depth to the concept of distance in the international business literature. The authors separate dimensions of environment and their associated distances into three types, namely: obligatory, pressuring and supporting dimensions of environment. Cuervo-Cazurra and Genc argue that the classification developed in this chapter challenges the assumption that distance is symmetric and always has a negative impact on the MNE.

In Chapter 10, Hotho and Pedersen analyse institutional approaches to international business and critically examine the value of these approaches for understanding different aspects of international business activities. First, the authors focus on comparing and contrasting three dominant institutional approaches in international business studies, namely: new institutional economics, new organizational institutionalism and comparative institutionalism. Then the authors test the explanatory power of two of these approaches by using two types of institutional distance which were derived from new institutional economics and comparative institutionalism.

In Chapter 11, McGuinness and Demirbag examine corruption and its impact on MNEs. The authors explore the impact of corruption on MNEs' strategies by looking at, first, the central role of institutions and institutional environment in the form and functioning of the MNE. This is followed by a review of institutional perspectives and implications for MNEs facing corruption in different institutional contexts.

Part II of the book contains three chapters. In Chapter 12, Conroy and Collings chronicle the application of institutional theory to the MNE and examine its usefulness as a lens for conceptualizing innovation at the subsidiary level. Conroy and Collings focus on the MNE subsidiary environment and argue that there is a diminishing view on the role of headquarters (HQ) in subsidiary innovation. The authors also highlight the institutional duality problem faced by MNE subsidiaries and develop recommendations for improving innovativeness in dual institutional contexts.

Chapter 13 by Arslan and Larimo examines the impact of institutional factors on full or partial acquisition decisions of MNEs when entering emerging and developing economies. Arslan and Larimo operationalize the impact of both formal and informal institutions in their analysis. The empirical setting of this chapter is based on acquisitions made by the Finnish MNEs in the emerging economies of Central and Eastern Europe (CEE), Asia and Latin America during the period of 1990–2006.

One of the recurrent debates within institutionalist analysis has been the relationship between structure and social action. Whilst the latter can range from coherent attempts at institutional redesign to serendipitous discoveries, Chapter 14 by Patrick et al. alerts us to an important dimension of action: improvisation. Based on case study evidence, this chapter offers vital insights into improvisation and the danger of using the term 'social action' as a catch-all phrase designed to patch up any shortcomings in institutional analysis.

Part III of this book contains nine chapters which conceptually and empirically examine institutions at emerging regional or country level.

In Chapter 15, Giroud et al. examine the key role of institutions in South–South foreign direct investment (FDI). This chapter focuses on the drives and motives of emerging and developing country MNEs for investing in other developing and emerging economies. Drawing on the recent literature on South–South FDI, and by utilizing various data sources, the authors analyse the constraints and support of the institutional environment on South–South FDI decisions.

In Chapter 16, Allen and Aldred examine the extent to which any one set of institutions is associated with the macroeconomic performance of the new member states of the European Union (EU) in CEE. The authors present a critical analysis of institutional approaches used in the international business and comparative capitalism literature. This chapter is based on country-level data from the new EU member states in CEE and identifies a great deal of institutional diversity between these countries. The findings presented in this chapter indicate that there are no clusters of countries around a specific variety of capitalism or an economic model.

In Chapter 17, Stone et al. examine equity culture in the CEE countries. The authors graphically display ten CEE countries and four benchmarks in terms of their institutional characteristics, and portray the status of their financial system developments and equity culture creation.

In Chapter 18, Croucher and Morrison examine the sources and nature of union functional diversity in Moldova. Croucher and Morrison criticize regulationist accounts and argue that they tend to overstate coherence and overlook contradictions. The authors highlight the lack of coherence in the post-socialist context, and point out that current institutional arrangements in the trade union case are unstable, dysfunctional, fragile and heterogeneous.

In Chapter 19, Upchurch reviews post-Communist transformation and focuses on the persistence of dysfunction and divergence. Upchurch argues that the persistence of dysfunction is a consequence of the adoption of a particular model of labour exploitation. Upchurch further argues that the convergence predicted by neoliberals has not occurred, and that there is a persistence of features of 'wild' capitalism such as cronyism, corruption, crime and informal and illegal working in post-Communist transformation.

In Chapter 20, Karademir and Yaprak examine the internationalization of Turkish MNEs. The authors adopt a co-evolutionary perspective and examine the internationalization of these firms in parallel with the co-evolution of the institutional environment in Turkey. Karademir and Yaprak argue that while international business scholars anchored internationalization of emerging market firms in various theories including institutional theory, studying these firms' internationalization in their co-evolutionary context may provide a better understanding and explanation.

In Chapter 21, Yen and Barnes examine *guanxi* and provide a comparative overview of this paradigm from Chinese and Western literature. The authors compare Western theories on buyer–supplier relationships with the Chinese *guanxi* paradigm by highlighting similarities and differences in terms of their origins, concepts and area of focus. Yen and Barnes also outline key constructs that are used in the Chinese *guanxi* and Western relationship management literature.

In Chapter 22, Demirbas et al. explore antecedents of corporate governance development in Russia with a specific focus on the structure, roles and functions of Russian boards of directors. The authors focus on the institutional environment in Russia and critically examine legal aspects of Russian corporate governance in light of pertinent institutional changes and recent macroenvironmental characteristics.

In the final chapter, Chapter 23, Klerck presents a powerful essay on the relevance of regulation theory for operations of firms and markets in sub-Saharan Africa. A key focus of Klerck's chapter is the notion that there is a simple and direct correlation between labour market regulation and the proliferation of market-determined employment. Klerck examines post-independence Namibia and draws out some of the relevance of the Namibian case for the broader sub-Saharan region.

CONCLUSION

We believe that not only the comparative analysis of what firms do in different settings, but also the specific and changing relationship between embedded yet dynamic rules, and firm-level outcomes, represent the principal research agenda for international and comparative business studies today. The chapters in this volume represent a wide range of different perspectives. However, what they all have in common is not only scholarly rigour, but also pragmatism in attempting to understand the key characteristics of different national institutional frameworks, and the continued viability of alternative models of capitalism.

REFERENCES

Demirbag, M., K. Glaister and E. Tatoglu (2007), 'Institutional and transaction cost influences on MNE's ownership strategies of their affiliates: evidence from an emerging market', *Journal of World Business*, **42** (4), 418–434.

Goergen, M., C. Brewster and G. Wood (2009), 'Corporate governance regimes and employment relations in Europe', *Industrial Relations/Relations Industrielles*, **64** (6), 620–640.

Hall, P. and D. Soskice (2001), 'An introduction to the varieties of capitalism', in P. Hall and D. Soskice (eds), *Varieties of Capitalism: The Institutional Basis of Competitive Advantage*, Oxford: Oxford University Press, pp. 1–70.

Hall, P. and C. Thelen (2009), 'Institutional change in varieties of capitalism', *Socio-Economic Review*, **7** (1), 7–34.

La Porta, R., F. Lopez-de-Silanes and A. Shleifer (1999), 'Corporate ownership around the world', *Journal of Finance*, **54** (2), 471–517.

North, D.C. (1990), *Institutions, Institutional Change and Economic Performance*, Cambridge: Cambridge University Press.

Peters, G. (2005), *Institutional Theory in Political Science: The New Institutionalism*, London: Continuum.

Whitley, R. (2005), 'How national are business systems? The role of states and complementary institutions in standardizing systems of economic coordination and control at the national level', in R. Whitley, G. Morgan and E. Moen (eds), *Changing Capitalisms?* Oxford: Oxford University Press, pp. 190–234.

Whitley, A. (2010), 'The institutional construction of firms', in G. Morgan, J. Campbell, C. Crouch, O.K. Pederson and R. Whitley (eds), *The Oxford Handbook of Comparative Institutional Analysis*, Oxford: Oxford University Press, pp. 453–496.

PART I

INSTITUTIONS AND COMPARATIVE BUSINESS STUDIES: THE STATE OF THE ART

1 Institutions and comparative business studies: supranational and national regulation

Geoffrey Wood and Mehmet Demirbag

1.1 INTRODUCTION

Through the 2000s, institutional approaches have been particularly influential amongst comparative studies of business. What institutional approaches suggest is that embedded social structures and rules mould and are remoulded by the choices made by firms. In practice, this means that within specific national contexts, there will emerge a dominant way of doing things, which may have the beneficial effects of imparting pre-dictability and lowering transaction costs. Critics have charged that this emphasis on the national has in many respects led to a discounting of regional and sectoral differences, and indeed, supranational trends and pressures. In the international domain, there are three possible critiques. The first centres on a discounting of the effects of supranational institutions; the second on a neglect of the role of multinational or transnational companies; and the third on an overattention to comparison and insufficient attention to the wider nature of capitalism itself.

1.2 SUPRANATIONAL INSTITUTIONS AND NATIONAL INSTITUTIONAL FRAMEWORKS

1.2.1 Supranational Institutions: The Limits of Europeanization

As Boyer and Hollingsworth (1997) note, institutions are nested within each other. Whilst a single institutional level – most commonly the national – may have particularly strong effects, the impact of other levels of institutional concentration at both the subnational and supranational levels should not be neglected. In practical terms, there are two major sets of supranational institutions that may affect what nations and firms do. The first are regional coordinative and coop-erative bodies such as the European Union; whilst the second include bodies with a global brief, most controversially international financial institutions such as the International Monetary Fund (IMF) and the World Bank.

Through the 1990s, there were both optimistic and pessimistic accounts of the effects of the European Union. The former saw the Union as the agent for dissemination of a common European social model, infusing many of the features of the coordinated markets into more peripheral regions (Masters 1998). Through the Lisbon process, the intention was to promote 'better jobs and social cohesion', whilst ensuring that Europe becomes both competitive and dynamic through a reliance on knowledge-based activities (Tausch 2006). The process fell short of predictions: up until the economic crisis, liberal markets such as the United States (US) outperformed European coordinated markets (Tausch 2006). In its after-math, mature European coordinated markets appear to be faring much better than the US model, highlighting the continued viability of the European social model; this would highlight the continued relevance of the more social dimensions of the Lisbon agenda, failings in the process notwithstanding.

In contrast, more pessimistic accounts depicted the European Union (EU) as an agent for liberalization, eroding the capabilities of individual governments to restrain firms and markets (O'Hagan 2002). As Grahl and Teague (1989) argued:

> In most cases, the intention is not to substitute Community versions for existing national regulatory systems but merely to outlaw any impact of the latter on the free movement of commodities, services and factors of production: a veritable 'bonfire of controls' which will eclipse the minor relaxations first covered by that slogan.

In practice the process has been revealed to be more complex than suggested by either side. As Scharpf (2002) notes, whilst there have been broad directives towards marketization, social policy choices have remained clustered at national level, albeit through efforts to promote common policy initiatives through performance evaluation and benchmarking.

Within accession countries, the process has been mixed: there has been no uniform convergence to either social or market models. At least one relatively recent accession state has indeed moved close to the coordinated archetype (Slovenia), and another (Slovakia) has infused many aspects of this model (Lane and Myant 2007). Again, there is at least one country that has come close to a liberal market ideal (Estonia), with others adopting aspects of this model. A third group of countries have continued to follow a distinct trajectory, liberalizing in many respects, but also retaining features of the past, and adopting certain features of European coordination, a good example being Hungary. Finally, on the peripheries of the EU

– Romania, Bulgaria and, perhaps, Greece – aspects of 'wild capitalism', more common in the non-EU Balkans (Upchurch and Zivkovic forthcoming), may be encountered. Above all, this would include the presence of a very large and poorly regulated underground economy. Hence, whatever the predictions of convergence – whether of liberalization or the diffusion of a social model – the evidence to date is of difference and divergence.

A second dimension is that institutional coverage is not always as even or as effective as commonly assumed. Within peripheral areas of the EU there is, as noted above, a large underground economy, composed of black market trading (that is, the illegal import and unregulated selling of goods), reciprocal bartering of goods and services and, finally, the sale of services and legally obtained goods and the hiring of labour unofficially and 'off the books' in order to escape taxation and labour standards (Schneider and Enste 2002). Williams (2010, 226) argues that a trend has been for workers to engage in underground work increasingly out of necessity, rather than as a means of supplementing formal incomes.

In practical terms, this makes for a progressive erosion of labour standards, as compliant firms lose competitive advantage to less principled competitors. Not only does unregulated work make for poor terms and conditions of service for those employed, but in weakening the fiscal base of the state and debilitating the regulatory base, it may both corrupt the body politic and contribute to national debt crises. Whilst it can be argued that it is common for developing economies to have both an internationally linked sector and a 'stagnant, miserable' sector that is irrelevant to international capitalism (Gourevitch 1979, 889), this discounts the interlinked nature of the sectors, the extent to which one may undermine the other, and variations in the extent to which national political institutions may mediate this mismatch.

In theoretical terms, all this highlights the only partial nature of institutional coupling not only between supranational and national institutions, but also between the national and the local, a phenomenon particularly pronounced in peripheral EU states. Institutions are both polyvalent and multilayered (Ferguson 1990, 17). Structures and associated rules do not always work in the manner intended, either in economic or social terms (ibid.). In part, this may reflect specific historical legacies. Vested interests may have very different agendas to the official one, and may actively thwart even the most powerful and determined government (Ferguson 1990, 17). Ironically, this process of contestation and opportunism may result in undesirable or unpredictable outcomes for all parties; the pursuit of predetermined agendas and their subsequent thwarting may preclude meaningful trade-offs and the bedding down of mutually acceptable rules and conventions. And, whilst the existing literature focuses on the role of vested economic interests undermining national – and, potentially, supranational – institutions, an interesting development has been the role that popular protest may play in thwarting both. Notable recent examples have been Iceland (Wade and Sigurgeirsdottir, 2010) and, even more recently (2011), Greece.

1.2.2   Supranational Institutions: The World Bank and the IMF

Existence of supranational institutions facilitates collective action where there may be market failures (Stiglitz 2002). It is also argued that provision of global public goods provides part of the logic for global collective action. That is to say, global problems in security, economic stability, knowledge, environment, humanitarian assistance and health require supranational institutions which can facilitate collective action (Stiglitz 2002; Simmons and Martin 2005). Therefore the Bretton Woods institutions of the World Bank and International Monetary Fund can be examined from the perspective of global public goods and externalities.

The regulatory architecture of the global financial system was created soon after the Second World War at an international conference at Bretton Woods, New Hampshire. At the end of the conference two supranational institutions of the IMF and the World Bank came into being, and since then these two institutions have continued to affect what nations and firms do. While the initial remits of the institutions have changed since their establishment (Dicken 2011), these two supranational institutions have continued to affect both the policies and the institutions of member nations, particularly those using the Bank's and the Fund's facilities (Stiglitz 2002). Crises from 1970s to date have forced these two institutions to reorient their activities.

In particular, the Fund's role changed dramatically after the collapse of the Bretton Woods system in 1971. The Fund has been criticized for exerting to much interference (Stiglitz 2002), particularly in developing country policies, yet without any political accountability. While the Fund was not a major lender too industrial nations after 1976, its position became more prominent during the recent financial crises. In supporting the Fund's central role in the global financial system, Truman (2009) argues that:

> It is ironic that a year ago it was fashionable to argue that the IMF was irrelevant as a lender and marginalized in its surveillance of the global economy and financial system. Benign economic and financial conditions were projected to continue indefinitely. Moreover, the prevailing view was that the systemically important countries either had guaranteed access to international financial markets or had effectively self-insured against future external financial crises by amassing huge stocks of foreign exchange reserves. (Truman 2009, 3)

More recently however criticism shifted to 'Where has the Fund been? The IMF is not discharging its duty to protect the international financial system. We must remake the international financial architecture with the IMF at the center.' (Truman 2009, 4)

This raises an interesting contradiction. At the time of the onset of the financial crisis, increasing numbers of Latin American countries had returned to growth largely through ignoring the IMF's strictures. A number of leading Asian nations and Russia had indeed stockpiled foreign exchange, simply to avoid having to turn back to the IMF in the event of a repeat of the Asian financial crisis. However, the IMF regained a lot of its former power during the 2010 crisis within the eurozone periphery; this time, developed economies were forced to turn to the IMF. Interestingly, South Africa set as a condition for its 2011 bailout of Swaziland that the unhappy country should adhere to strict IMF prescriptions, indicative of the body's continued influence on the continent. The IMF appears to have learned little and forgotten nothing from its recent history, and the policies imposed in Southern Europe and elsewhere remain the same formula of strict austerity, despite their poor track record elsewhere.

Similarly there have been questions raised as to whether the World Bank was really needed (Stiglitz 2002). While in terms of capital investment a small proportion of capital spending goes to the least-developed nations of Africa, supporters argue that the World Bank's role of expanding knowledge (that is, facilitating knowledge transfer for policy development to attract capital inflow) is more important than actual investment.

As Chapter 8 in this volume alerts us, it would be wrong to consider both bodies as monolithic, or incapable of amending their agendas to circumstance; there are, indeed, specific interventions that have had positive effects. At the same time, a focus on austerity, government spending cuts and the payback of debt leads, as Keynes alerted us, to the 'paradox of thrift', with domestic demand being depressed, delaying recovery, and making debt payback even harder. Moreover, over-hasty privatizations have, from Africa to Russia, led to corruption and asset stripping, the emergence of an overly powerful class of oligarchs, and the accumulated wealth of generations being frittered away on speculative activity or squirrelled away offshore. Such tendencies may 'crowd out' more orthodox forms of economic activity, making the rewards of conventional entrepreneurship appear meagre. Whilst there are immediate savings to be made through cutting back on basic education and health care, the costs are borne by individuals and firms into the medium and long terms; ultimately, firms face being locked into low-cost production paradigms, or facing significant upfront costs in correcting the failings of the system.

1.2.3   Supranational Institutions: Competing Agendas

Second image reversed (SIR) approaches concern themselves with the relative decline of the national state and how international developments mould and remould national choices. In contrast to traditional theories of international relations, which explore the impact of national politics on international relations, SIR approaches assume that domestic politics may represent the result of international pressures (Gourevitch 1979). As Gourevitch (1979, 882) notes: 'instead of being a cause of international politics, domestic structure may be a consequence of it. International systems, too, become causes instead of consequences.'

Central to the dominant liberal market model has been the rise of unrestrained global finance; ironically, whilst national governments are the final line of defence in regulating it, unrestrained global finance itself undermines the autonomy of national governments (Grahl 2011).

Nor is the effect of the supranational confined to specific structures: dominant ideologies may impact on domestic agendas as may external threats of force (Gourevitch 1979, 883). More peripheral countries face the challenge of dealing with evolved supranational economic structures and ties. Gourevitch (1979) argues that the Mediterranean European economies are in a particularly difficult position. On the one hand, their lower labour costs than North-Western Europe makes them an attractive locale for specific types of manufacturing. On the other hand, they 'lack the matured strength to hold on [to this type of investment] for good, and consequently face the constant danger of being thrown off' (Gourevitch 1979, 888). Over 20 years after the Gourevitch paper was written, this still holds true not only for the peripheral Mediterranean economies, but also for much of Eastern Europe. Competiveness based on low labour costs opens up the omnipresent threat of even cheaper labour being available elsewhere, whilst low-cost production precludes the investment in higher-value-added (and more spatially rooted) production paradigms (see Ebner 2008). In turn, in the absence of the latter, supporting institutional networks are likely to be weaker, and complementarities based on systemic strengths less likely.

As Thatcher (2007, 23) notes, whilst a strength of SIR approaches is their recognition that international pressures impact on domestic choices, there are many dimensions to internationalization – political, economic and technological – which are bundled together, when in fact their impacts may be diverse. Furthermore, SIR approaches assume that internationalization is an exogenous approach, beyond the control of national governments (ibid.). In practice, national governments do retain autonomy in meeting external pressures: the above-mentioned example of Iceland contrasts sharply with that of Greece and Ireland. Whilst the latter are, of course, more heavily constrained by European institutions, the specific contours of the present (2008–) financial crisis highlight not only supranational pressures, but also shifting domestic responses.

1.2.4 Supranational Institutions and Complementarity

A relatively neglected area has been the role of supranational and national institutions in making for interlocking complementarities. Analyses of supranational regulation often assume that they make for homogenizing outcomes, when they may in fact support complementarities within and between states. Such complementarities may build on systemic strengths and compensate for weaknesses. In simple terms, it would not be possible for every European state to export at the same level as Germany; specific lower-wage economies play a similarly important role in providing production sites for the supply of lower-cost, lower-value-added components. Finally, common markets allow for the interchange of goods and services not always in an equal manner, but in one that allows for the redress of systemic imbalances. It is a something of a truism to say that Europe can only accommodate one mega-exporter on the scale of Germany; but even more true that, at best, more than one City of London would spell ruin for Europe.

Although complementarity is often depicted as mutually supportive practices and rules that build on systemic strengths, complementarity may also be rules and regulated practices that compensate for systemic weaknesses (Crouch 2005). What is further key to the understanding of complementarity is that of embeddedness. There is little doubt that emerging complementarities within Europe have been shaken through systemic shocks as part of the ongoing financial crisis, and as yet it remains unclear whether systemic patching up and 'tinkering' will suffice (see Boyer 2006) or whether a further round of restructuring and institutional rebuilding will be necessary, a process that may involve a degree of institutional denesting. In other words, meta-institutional failings may not necessarily be compensated for through redesign, but through adjustment to, and a greater emphasis on, component parts.

The response of the establishment to the crisis has been to push through new waves of neoliberal reforms aimed at further weakening institutional mediation, whether at national or supranational levels (Grahl 2011). Does this mean the end of the European project? Whilst we remain optimistic, it is evident that the direction of the EU as an enabler or a constrainer and mediator of markets needs revisiting. As poorly regulated markets have directly caused the financial crisis, it is scarcely logical to argue that more deregulation will fix it, either through fresh rounds of forced liberalization at member state level, whether or not forced by speculative activity, or as a condition of central bailouts. This leads us on to two central questions. Firstly, are we on the brink of a Polanyian 'double movement'? And, secondly, how closely are institutions coupled, not only at the supranational but also at the national levels?

1.2.5   Polanyian Double Movements and the Angel of History

In his classic writings on political economy, Polanyi (1944) argued that there was a natural long-term fluctuation between periods of statism and periods of unregulated markets. There is certainly an element of truth to this. Unrestrained markets bring about excesses that will ultimately need restraining. Again, state mediation involves compromises between parties brought about by the very real threat of systemic collapse and the absence of viable alternatives; over time, such compromises will be open to revisiting and contestation, with economically dominant interests gradually picking themselves free from state restraints. However, there are also limitations. Firstly, there is an element of epochalism; this assumes that a long move in one direction will be countered by one in another. After three decades of liberalization, this may appear a comforting antidote to a constant flow of news on market excesses. However, a long historical review will reveal that there have been very lengthy periods of growth – albeit interrupted – and others of long decline; one simply needs to compare the birth of the modern era with the long decline experienced within parts of the Middle Ages.

In his recent writings, Streeck (2009) has pointed to the non-linear path of historical development. There may be swerves towards or away from deregulated markets, but each swerve is in a different place (ibid.). History may repeat itself, but never in the same place and in the same way; any state-mediated compromises will be fundamentally different to those experienced in the past. Here one is reminded of Walter Benjamin's notion of the 'Angel of History' that moves ever onward, leaving 'rubble' behind (Benjamin 1978). One may indeed build new structures out of the rubble, or seek to reconstruct aspects of previous regimes, but the resultant structure will never be the same.

Interestingly, the 1920s economic crisis coincided with a major energy transition, away from coal and to oil and gas. Whilst ultimately this allowed for cheap energy inputs for many years, it fundamentally changed the allocation of capital, favouring owners of more fungible assets over those with less (Wood and Lane 2011). It also had the long-term effect of undermining the competitiveness of those industrial centres whose

competitive advantage was founded on rich coal deposits in close proximity, although this would not become immediately apparent. Since the
1970s, oil has gradually become more expensive (the drops in the 1980s
notwithstanding), and today, although oil usage continues to rise, the proportion of oil as part of the global energy mix is declining. Again, this is
having the gradual effect of fundamentally changing input costs, a process
which favours speculative activity, and those less productive sectors
of capital with highly fungible assets (see Wood and Lane 2011). The
outcome may be a new period of growth once the energy transition is complete, but equally it could be a long decline, as the basis of much economic
activity is undermined. And, an increasing proportion of oil extracted is
unconventional, with costs to the ecosystem which are yet fully clear, yet
doubtlessly great costs will be posed on future generations. It should be
noted that whilst the literature on comparative capitalism accords much
attention to the institutional underpinnings of industrial capitalism, rather
less is accorded to that of rentiers (Krippner 2005).

1.2.6   The Closeness of Institutional Coupling

Recent work on internal diversity within national varieties of capitalism has highlighted the extent to which institutions are considerably less
closely coupled than previously presumed. Whilst this is particularly true
of the relationship between supranational and national institutions, it
is also true within nations. We have seen this in the case of peripheral
Europe. However, even within mature economies there may be divergences between the national and the regional, with the latter sometimes providing frameworks for growth that are more effective than the
national. An obvious example would be the north Italian industrial dis-
tricts (e.g. Whitley 1999), but examples can be found in most developed
countries. Within the United Kingdom (UK), a good example would be
North-Western England, where the developmental trajectory has been
rather more statist than that encountered elsewhere in England (Hudson
2011). Of course, a lack of close coupling can also have negative effects;
regional institutions may serve local elites whilst impeding orthodox
business activity and undermining labour standards (not that the two are
always compatible).

1.2.7   Bringing Political Economy Back In: Growth Regimes and
Ecosystems

If crude theories of globalization as an homogenizing force are mistaken,
a limitation of the 'varieties of capitalism' literature is that it is too much

about variety, and too little about capitalism (Jessop 2011; Thompson and Vincent 2010). In his recent work, Jessop (2011) draws a distinction between the wider capitalist ecosystem, and specific types of national institutional arrangement. The lead-up to the crisis, and the policy responses to it, have in both instances reflected the transnational hegemony of neoliberalism, with debates around mechanisms rather than desirable ends (Grahl 2011).

Inherent contradictions across capitalism do not vanish simply because specific spatial and temporal fixes appear to work (Jessop 2011). Jessop (2011) argues that at specific times, one particular variety of capitalism may assume ecological dominance, 'shaping the development of other varieties'. Since the 1970s, this has been the liberal market model, even if, as Jessop (2011) notes, it retains a 'pathological dependence' on other varieties, most notably as sources of raw materials and manufactured goods, and inward capital flows to plug structural balance of payments deficits. At the political level, 'crony capitalism' is not the preserve of developing markets (ibid.); mature capitalism can incorporate pathology.

1.3   SOCIAL ACTORS

Within debates surrounding institutional effects, there has been growing interest in the role of social action vis-à-vis structure. The somewhat mechanistic notions of structuration theory (Giddens 1984) have given way to an interest in action within historical context, and the impact of formative choices at times of institutional fluidity (Sorge 2005). Moreover, as Simmel (1981) alerts us, the choices and actions of individuals and associations reflect not just responses to objective circumstances, but also subjective reinterpretations thereof. In considering the supranational, there are two particularly relevant sets of actors: multinationals and the precariate.

1.3.1   Multinationals

It is particularly significant that many of the more influential texts on comparative capitalism, most notably Hall and Soskice (2001), Amable (2003) and Streeck and Thelen (2005), make no reference to multinational or transnational companies. Yet, as Thompson and Vincent (2010) note, whilst national institutions are important, the spatial embeddedness of firm-level work and employment practices is less likely when global firms can gain advantages through replicating practices. Indeed, it can be argued that, contrary to much of the literature on comparative capitalism, contrary to the 'varieties of capitalism' (VOC) literature, global capitalist production is increasingly likely via global networks (Thompson and Vincent 2010, 58).

In an attempt to enlarge the 'varieties of capitalism' framework, Nolke and Vliegenthart (2009) classified a particular form of capitalism: dependent market economies (DMEs). Countries in Central and Eastern Europe are considered as DMEs, as they are heavily dependent on multinational investments and prosper by being an active and credible link of the supply chains of large multinational corporations (MNCs). When foreign direct investment and multinationals play a central role in an economic system, inevitably there will be coordinated efforts to imitate what works in subsidiaries in different countries. Thus the MNC starts to become a change agent and integrate national production systems with global networks (Dunning and Lundan 2008; Dicken 2011). While the international business and 'varieties of capitalism' approaches to institutions have their differences in terms of theoretical assumptions, Jackson and Deeg (2008) demonstrate that there is a strong potential for cross-fertilization between these two approaches.

Whitley (2010a, 384) argues that the internationalization of share ownership of large firms may reduce employer–employee commitment. More remote shareholders may find it more difficult to price accurately the benefits flowing from investment in training and moving to higher-value-added production paradigms; actual choices are likely to vary between industries and according to the market for corporate control. Vogel (2005, 149) argues that increased capital mobility 'allows firms to exit from long term relations with workers' by moving operations abroad, and for firms to move from local to overseas financing. Moreover, regulatory competition between countries seeking to attract foreign direct investment (FDI) can mould both policy choices and the actual practices adopted by firms (Thatcher 2007, 262).

As Whitley (2010a, 384) notes, there is growing coordination across national boundaries, but the integration of MNCs into regional and national governance frameworks is variable. In some contexts, MNCs seek, *inter alia*, to access low-cost labour, and in others markets and/or specific skills sets and knowledge (ibid.). The general effect of this has been to make it harder for national regulatory authorities and industry associations to rein in free-riding and organize markets on a collective basis (Whitley 2010a, 384). However, where the presence of firms is on the basis of accessing skills and technologies, firms will become increasing embedded in local governance regimes (ibid., 385). In those cases where markets are large, rich and/or highly significant, MNCs will be in a weaker bargaining position, and may simply have to fit in (ibid., 385). Indeed, MNCs can seek to build on the combination of strengths that come from fitting into many different settings, allowing for the development of new transnational organizational capacities (Whitley 2010b, 480). If, however, there is little central direction, and local units are simply allowed to adapt, then there can be little move forward to building such capabilities. Transnational commitment based on complementary contributions of different settings requires genuine authority sharing (ibid., 481); the basis of efficiency gains may dilute the capacity of the MNC to act as an autonomous and lightly committed actor across national boundaries.

1.3.2   Precariate and Protest

One of the features of the global capitalist ecosystem is the growth of the precariate, a large underclass, disproportionately composed of the young, who are condemned to a lifetime of insecure working with poor terms and conditions of service (Standing 2011). A defining feature of the precariate is a lack of occupational and spatial rootedness. It is not simply about working in poor jobs, but of forced moving between occupations, and often migration, simply in order to survive (Standing 2011). Whilst amongst the precariate are citizens of every country, a feature of this process has been large-scale migration within and between countries, often with the end destination seeing burgeoning slums (Davis 2006).

Although the rise of the precariate is undeniably political destabilizing, the political consequences are not necessarily progressive (see Standing 2011). For example, within contemporary Britain, economically powerful interests have been able to secure the compliance of much of the working class through systematically engendering fear of the underclasses, an agenda painfully visible through a scrutiny of the overwhelmingly Conservative print media. Similar trends are visible elsewhere, from the United States to Berlusconi's Italy. Amongst the underclasses themselves, the certainties of religious fundamentalism – be it of the Pentacostal or Islamic variety – may displace emerging progressive agendas (Davis 2006).

This does not deny the possibility of progressive alternatives. Examples would include protest movements across Europe, from the town square occupations in Spain to the mass demonstrations in Iceland. Nor are progressive outcomes impossible, as the case of the latter will evince. Nonetheless, the fear of the underclasses, be they immigrants or simply undeserving poor, is one area where the Right have managed to gain traction, despite the bankrupcy of the neoliberal policies they espouse. To date, a progressive alternative response to precariatization, centring on the defence of labour standards, remains only partially formed, and marginalized in the mass media.

1.4   CONCLUSION

Whilst institutional frameworks offer effective analytical tools to understanding the differences in what firms do between nations, much of the literature on comparative capitalism fails to take account of the articulation between embedded rules and real practices, the often weak nature of institutional coupling, and structural changes in global capitalism. The challenges of institutional analysis involve not only taking account of such issues, but also a closer understanding of the impact both of transnational institutions and, indeed, actors. The latter range from multinational corporations through to the spatially and occupationally uprooted underclasses.

Within any theoretical project, there is always a trade-off between rigour and parsimony. However, comparisons of practice between context need a more systematic understanding of the transnational and the ecosystemic. Subsequent chapters in this volume seek to grapple with such issues and, indeed, what really defines national difference.

REFERENCES

Amable, B. (2003), *The Diversity of Modern Capitalism*, Oxford: Oxford University Press.

Benjamin, W. (1978), *Reflections*, New York: Harcourt Brace Jovanovich.

Boyer, R. (2006), 'How do institutions cohere and change', in G. Wood and P. James (eds), *Institutions and Working Life*, Oxford: Oxford University Press, pp. 13–61.

Boyer, R. and R. Hollingsworth (1997), 'From national embeddedness to spatial and institutional nestedness', in J. Hollingsworth and R. Boyer (eds), *Contemporary Capitalism: The Embeddedness of Institutions*, Cambridge, UK and New York, USA: Cambridge University Press, pp. 433–484.

Crouch, C. (2005), 'Three meanings of complementarity', *Socio-economic Review,* **3** (2), 359–63.

Davis, M. (2006), *Planet of Slums*, London: Verso.

Dicken, P. (2011), *Global Shift: Mapping the Changing Contours of the World Economy*, 6th edn, London: Sage.

Dunning, J. and S.M. Lundan (2008), *Multinational Enterprises and the Global Economy*, Cheltenham, UK and Northampton, MA, USA: Edward Elgar.

Ebner, A. (2008), 'Institutional evolution and the political economy of governance', in A. Ebner and N. Beck (eds), *The Institutions of the Market – Organizations, Social Systems and Governance*, Oxford: Oxford University Press, pp. 287–308.

Ferguson, J. (1990), *The Anti-Politics Machine*, Cambridge: Cambridge University Press.

Giddens, A. (1984), The *Constitution of Society*, Cambridge: Polity.

Gourevitch, P. (1979), 'The second image reversed: the international sources of domestic politics', *International Organization*, **32** (4), 881–912.

Grahl, J. (2011), 'A capitalist contrarian', *New Left Review*, **69**, 35–59.

Grahl, J. and P. Teague (1989), 'The cost of neoliberal Europe', *New Left Review*, **174**, 33–50.

Hall, P. and D. Soskice (2001), 'An introduction to the varieties of capitalism', in P. Hall and D. Soskice (eds), *Varieties of Capitalism: The Institutional Basis of Competitive Advantage*, Oxford: Oxford University Press, pp. 1–70.

Hudson, R. (2011), 'Regions, varieties of capitalism and the legacies of neo-liberalism', in C. Lane and G. Wood (eds), *Capitalist Diversity and Diversity Within Capitalism*, London: Routledge.

Jackson, G. and R. Deeg (2008), 'Comparing capitalisms: Understanding institutional diversity and its implications for international business', *Journal of International Business Studies*, **39**, 540–561.

Jessop, B. (2011), 'Rethinking the diversity and variability of capitalism: On variegated capitalism in the world market', in C. Lane and G. Wood (eds), *Capitalist Diversity and Diversity Within Capitalism*, London: Routledge, pp. 209–237.

Krippner, G. (2005), 'The financialization of the American economy', *Socio-Economic Review*, **3** (2), 173–208.

Lane, D. and M. Myant (eds) (2007), *Varieties of Capitalism in Post-Communist Countries*, London: Palgrave.

Masters, M. (1998), 'Public sector employment in a time of transition', *Industrial and Labor Relations Review*, **51** (4), 705–706.

Nolke, A. and A. Vliegenthart (2009), 'Enlarging the varieties of capitalism: the emergence of dependent market economies in East Central Europe', *World Politics*, **61** (4), 670–702.

O'Hagan, E. (2002), *Employee Relations in the Periphery of Europe: The Unfolding of the European Social Model*, London: Palgrave.

Polanyi, K. (1944), *The Great Transformation: The Political and Economic Origins of Our Time*, Boston, MA: Beacon Press.

Scharpf, W. (2002), 'The European social model: coping with the challenges of diversity', *Journal of Common Market Studies*, **40** (4), 645–670.

Schneider, F. and D. Enste (2002), 'Hiding in the shadows: the growth of the underground economy', *International Monetary Fund Economic Issues*, **30**, www.imf.org/External/Pubs/FT/issues/issues30/chi/issue30c.pdf.

Simmel, G. (1981), *On Individuality and Social Forms*, Chicago, IL: University of Chicago Press.

Simmons, B.A. and L.L. Martin (2005), 'International organizations and institutions', in Walter Carlsnears and Beth A. Simmons (eds), *Handbook of International Relations*, London: Sage, pp. 192–211.

Sorge, A. (2005), *The Global and the Local*, Oxford: Oxford University Press.

Standing, G. (2011), *Precariat: A New Dangerous Class*, New York: Bloomsbury.

Stiglitz, J.E. (2002), 'Globalization of the logic of international collective action: re-examining the Bretton Woods institutions', in Deepak Nayyar (ed.), *Governing Globalization: Issues and Institutions*, Oxford: Oxford University Press, pp. 238–253.

Streeck, W. (2009), *Reforming Capitalism: Institutional Change in the German Political Economy*, Oxford: Oxford University Press.

Streeck, W. and K. Thelen (2005), 'Introduction: institutional change in advanced political economies', in W. Streeck and K. Thelen, (eds), *Beyond Continuity: Institutional Change in Advanced Political Economies*, Oxford: Oxford University Press, pp. 1–39.

Tausch, A. (2006), 'The Lisbon process revisited', Paper presented at Conference on Economic Relations in the Enlarged EU, Warsaw.

Thatcher, M. (2007), *Internationalisation and Economic Institutions: Comparing Economic Experiences*, Oxford: Oxford University Press.

Thompson, P. and S. Vincent (2010), 'Labour process theory and critical realism', in P. Thompson and C. Smith (eds), *Working Life: Renewing Labour Process Analysis*, London: Palgrave, pp. 47–69.

Truman, E. (2009), 'The IMF, the global crises: role and reform', Paper delivered to the Tulsa Committee on Foreign Relations on 22 January and to the Dallas Committee on Foreign Relations on 23 January Peterson Institute for International Economics.

Upchurch, M. and A. Zivkovic (forthcoming), 'Wild capitalism, privatisation and employment relations in Serbia', *Employee Relations*.

Vogel, S. (2005), 'Routine adjustment, bounded innovation', in W. Streeck and K. Thelen (eds), *Beyond Continuity: Institutional Change in Advanced Political Economies*, Oxford: Oxford University Press, pp. 145–168.

Wade, R. and S. Sigurgeirsdottir (2010), 'Lessons from Iceland', *New Left Review*, **65** (Sept–Oct), 5–29.

Whitley, R. (1999), *The Diversity of Modern Capitalism*, Oxford: Oxford University Press.

Whitley, R. (2010a), 'Changing competition models in market economies', in G. Morgan, J. Campbell, C. Crouch, O.K. Pederson and R. Whitley (eds), *The Oxford Handbook of Comparative Institutional Analysis*, Oxford: Oxford University Press, pp. 363–398.

Whitley, R. (2010b), 'The institutional construction of firms', in G. Morgan, J. Campbell, C. Crouch, O.K. Pederson and R. Whitley (eds), *The Oxford Handbook of Comparative Institutional Analysis*, Oxford: Oxford University Press, pp. 453–496.

Williams, C. (2010), 'Evaluating the nature of undeclared work in South Eastern Europe', *Employee Relations*, **32** (3), 216–226.

Wood, G. and C. Lane (2011), 'Institutions, change and diversity', in C. Lane and G. Wood (eds), *Capitalist Diversity and Diversity Within Capitalism*, London: Routledge, pp. 1–31.

2 International business, multinationals and national business systems

Glenn Morgan

2.1 INTRODUCTION

This chapter is concerned with the interaction between multinationals and national business systems. It draws on the extensive literature which has developed comparing different forms of capitalism (Whitley 1999, 2007; Hall and Soskice 2001). In relation to the study of multinational corporations (MNCs), this perspective provides one fundamental insight which in turn gives rise to two broad interconnected research streams. The fundamental insight is that firm organization, strategy and structure is shaped by the national institutional context in which the firm exists. When a firm internationalizes in the sense of locating offices, branches, subsidiaries, production facilities in other countries, it enters a new institutional context. Kostova describes this as a situation of institutional duality (Kostova 1999; see also Morgan and Kristensen 2006). The MNC subsidiary in the locality creates a co-presence of two institutional logics. The first is conformity to the rules of its home context; the second is conformity to the host context. This gives rise to the two research themes. The first is primarily concerned with the adaptations and learning which the multinational undergoes in a specific institutional context. Does it structure the subsidiary in accordance with its home-based practices or the practices of its host context? How does this affect the overall strategy and structure of the multinational? This is increasingly described in terms of the micro-politics of the MNC and its subsidiaries. The second considers more explicitly how the MNC relates to the host institutional context. In particular, how far does it seek to alter that context by reshaping institutions to fit its own requirements? This can be labelled as the macro-politics of the MNC.

This chapter consists of three main sections. In section 2.2, the main themes of the national business systems approach are developed and linked to issues of multinationals and their strategies. In section 2.3, the micro-politics of multinationals and their relationship to institutional differences is examined. In section 2.4, the influence of the MNC on the host institutional context is the focus of attention. Section 2.5 concludes.

2.2   MULTINATIONALS AND NATIONAL BUSINESS SYSTEMS

The national business systems approach together with linked perspectives (such as variety of capitalisms) emphasizes that the strategies and structures of firms are shaped by their home institutional context. The key institutions that are examined are the labour system (in particular the nature of the skills and training regime in a particular country and the form of trade union organization and participation in the workplace that has emerged); the system of capital provision (in particular whether capital is provided primarily by banks in the form of loans or capital markets in the form of shares and bonds); the system of interfirm relationships (in particular the degree to which formal and informal rules set boundaries on the degree of opportunism which can be exercised in these relationships); and the political system (the degree to which the state intervenes in economic relations to facilitate the coordination of activities between employees and managers, or the degree to which it sets up markets as the main form of coordination). These institutions set the framework within which firms put together key resources of capital, labour and supply inputs, and within which forms of competition and cooperation evolve.

So, for example, Hall and Soskice (2001) argue that in what they term coordinated market economies (which are characterized by high levels of cooperation between employees, managers, the providers of capital and the state), firms tend to be highly effective in industries where the technology paradigm and the basic parameters of the market are predictable and stable. In such contexts, competitiveness is primarily determined by the ability to improve product and process incrementally. This in turn is best done where there are relatively high levels of skills, employee involvement in the work process is high, and the provision of capital is stable, encouraging employees and employees to invest in firm-specific assets, further increasing the level of quality and incremental improvement which occurs in the firm. This model is seen as particularly effective in engineering manufacturing, particularly around the production of cars but also in white goods manufacture (fridges, washing machines and so on) and larger consumer electronics products (such as TVs, though given the gradual integration of telecoms, the internet and 'viewing platforms' where TV is one of many, the centre of gravity of such production has shifted somewhat).

By contrast, liberal market economies are highly responsive to changing market conditions in terms of their use of labour and capital. For labour, the incentives to invest in skills and training, and in particular the development of firm-specific skills, are low since they may be subject to frequent interruptions in their employment as firms respond to market downturns by making employees redundant. Insofar as employees acquire skills, they will be at a general level and portable between firms and sectors. This tends to create on the one hand a relatively unskilled labour force (working in low-level manufacturing or services), and on the other hand a minority of highly educated employees suited to the development of, firstly, professional and creative services, and secondly, in some contexts to the development of sectors where recent scientific knowledge is being commercialized. Capital flows from liquid financial markets where exit from declining industries can be managed rapidly even if losses are taken. There are also possibilities for new risky industries to be funded by venture capital. Since the 1980s, dependence on capital markets has also been associated with a shift away from conglomerate and unrelated diversification structures towards firms focused on particular sets of competences, as shareholders prefer to manage their own portfolio diversification rather than leave this in the hands of managers (Davis 2009). Firms are generally isolated from each other, with competition law often discouraging strong forms of cooperation and favouring market relations over closer ties. Network ties are therefore loose and temporary.

These sorts of approaches tend to favour a view of global competition as one in which institutional differences create sector specialization at the level of countries. For example, the coordinated market economies (CMEs) produce firms which are globally competitive in sectors where the key advantages lie in incremental improvement; liberal market economies (LMEs) produce firms which are globally competitive in sectors characterized by radical innovation. Whilst the basic model of CME–LME contrast is helpful in identifying some key issues about how firms from different institutional contests are positioned in global competition, it is also rather limiting. Whitley, for example, identifies a range of 'competition models' which combine the basic radical–incremental distinction from Hall and Soskice with other characteristics, most notably the speed and the scale of innovation and production (Whitley 2010). The most familiar competition models are Fordism, craft production, flexible specialization and diversified quality production (DQP). To these he adds three other competition models. The opportunistic model refers to activities characterized by low skill and low investment in fixed plant or technology which enables the firm to switch between different markets and products quickly and at low cost; it is a model which firms pursue in producing cheap novelty and seasonal goods, for example toys, tourist goods, cheap clothes. The flexible mass production of differentiated goods and services (FMPDG) competition model focuses on the rapid development and commercialization of new improved goods, based on a combination of existing skills, targeted research and development investments, and high-impact marketing, for example in consumer electronics. The discontinuous innovation competition model focuses on generating and commercializing disruptive technologies that radically change markets; it requires the acquisition and use of new scientific and technological knowledge through networked forms of research and development (R&D) and through the provision of high-risk investment capital, for example internet businesses and biotechnology. Whitley argues that each of these competition models depends on particular sorts of labour, particular sets of knowledge and particular types of capital. He shows the sorts of institutional features which are conducive to being successful in producing the appropriate elements that can be combined into a particular competition model.

In this approach, therefore, firms evolve particular sorts of competences and capabilities within their national contexts and these give them a certain position on the global market. Early discussion within this approach paid little attention to different ways of competing in global markets, and in particular the shift from export-led strategies to strategies based on location in other countries and the development of multinationals. As these issues of relocation and MNCs came into focus, a new set of concepts were developed, moving the study of national business systems closer to the sphere generally studied under the heading of international business (see, for example, Morgan et al. 2001; for a more detailed account of these theoretical developments, see Morgan 2007; Collinson and Morgan 2009).

This can be seen, for example, in the issue of liabilities of foreignness. In her formulation of this, Zaheer pointed to the problems which MNCs face in entering foreign contexts and the liabilities which any multinational carried into new institutional spaces (Zaheer 1995). From the point of view of national business systems, the liabilities of foreignness are affected by the degree to which the normal practices of the firm in its home context are dependent on the specific institutional configuration in which it is located. Where the firm has built practices which depend strongly on its institutional context, for example in terms of using skills that are highly dependent on a specific structure of training (as in Germany or Denmark), then transferring its usual pattern of organization to another environment involves bridging a substantial institutional gap. The more deeply dependent and socially embedded a firm is in a particular institutional context, the more difficult it will be for it to internationalize its production facilities and become a multinational. Setting up a foreign production facility for a manufacturing firm from a coordinated market economy is likely to be high risk, particularly in terms of managing a labour force and organizing supply chains of firms from a different context. This is not the same problem for firms from liberal market economies which are used to short-term, highly specified relationships with workers and suppliers, whereas in more coordinated forms of capitalism these relationships are longer term, more asset specific and based on more cooperation and trust between the various actors. It is not therefore surprising from this perspective that firms from coordinated market economies such as Germany and Japan initially preferred export models of internationalization and only reluctantly began to build up their international production facilities from the 1980s, whereas US and UK firms had a history of internationalization of production from the late nineteenth century.

Becoming internationalized, therefore, has a different meaning and significance for firms depending on their home institutional context. When they internationalize, firms from coordinated market economies will aim to protect their firm-specific advantages as strongly as they can by creating as much as possible what may be termed 'functional equivalences' to the key aspects of their home-based system. Thus a Japanese MNC is not going to offer Japanese-style lifetime employment with a seniority-based wage system and a comprehensive rotation form of training inside the firm when it enters a context such as the United States (US) or the United Kingdom (UK), but nor is it simply going to reproduce a US or UK-style employment system. It will seek for ways which will reproduce the model it uses in Japan but through different means, accepting necessary adaptations and changes in the process (Whitley et al. 2003; Elger and Smith 2005). One such route to functional equivalence involves setting up a greenfield operation, copying as closely as possible the production technology existing in Japan. A greenfield plant also means that the workforce can be chosen carefully and introduced to the working practices which the Japanese management want to institute without having to deal with a legacy of previous industrial relations. Sharpe, for example, has shown how problematic managing a brownfield operation taken over from British owners proved to be for the new Japanese owners, because of this legacy (Sharpe 2001).

It is relevant to note here that an MNC from a coordinated market economy may not necessarily seek to establish functional equivalences to the institutions in its home base when it enters other contexts. On the contrary, it may decide that it actually wants to learn from being in a new context about how to manage market relations. In the case of a German multinational, for example, it may want to learn about managing in contexts which lack such strong embedded power of trade unions, both because it may want to investigate new models of managing that it may try at home, and because it recognizes that in most of its overseas operations, managing through the market rather than through coordination is going to be quicker, easier and more flexible (Ferner and Varul 2000; Lane 2000,

2005; Geppert and Mayer 2006; Streeck 2009; Dörrenbächer and Geppert 2011).

The liability of foreignness is also affected by the national business system. Coordinated market economies are characterized by strong relationships between key actors that have been produced and reproduced over long periods of time. In general, these may be characterized as insider systems with strong barriers to outsiders. Such barriers are constructed across a wide front. Thus it is difficult to instigate an overseas takeover of either a German or a Japanese firm as part of an MNC's strategy of merger and acquisition (on Germany, see Höpner and Jackson 2006; Halsall 2008 on Japan, see Aoki et al. 2007). In the rare cases where such acquisitions are made or greenfield operations are set up, the danger is that the foreign MNC remains isolated from key parts of the system, unable to access high-level skills or knowledge because they are effectively locked into certain companies or networks. By contrast, in liberal market economies, takeover rules tend to allow foreign acquisitions without much difficulty, and resources in the society are available through market transactions and not locked away. This makes it much easier in general for MNCs to enter liberal market economies than to enter coordinated market economies.

Since coordinated market economies differ substantially in the nature of their institutions, a firm with experience in one coordinated market economy brings no particular advantage if it internationalizes into another. The institutional distance may be equally as great as moving from its home base into a liberal market economy. By contrast, firms from liberal market economies where there is less dependence on local social institutions and more emphasis on the market will find it relatively easy to adapt in other liberal market contexts. They too will find barriers in coordinated market economies, but they may find space to develop market-like relations within even this institutional context, particularly where there have been other internal and external pressures for a society to become more market-like. Thus the locked-in character of resources within insider systems such as Germany and Japan may be breaking down and allowing in some (limited) arenas the presence of foreign MNCs (see for example the discussion of the impact of the entry of foreign banks on the Japanese financial system in Morgan and Kubo 2005).

The national business systems approach, therefore, suggests that we need to be aware of the home context of the MNC and how it shapes the approach of the firm to internationalization. We also need to be aware of how national business systems facilitate or constrain the entry of foreign MNCs (a point discussed in more detail in section 2.4).

2.3   MANAGING THE MULTINATIONAL AND INSTITUTIONAL DUALITY

Having developed the broad outlines of the national business systems approach, however, it is useful to go into more detail in relation to the central concepts of micro-politics and institutional duality. Previously, I have discussed the broad pressures from the head office and the host context on the organization of subsidiaries within the MNC. In a situation of institutional duality, actors are presented with two pressures. On the one hand, senior managers from the head office may seek to transfer to subsidiaries practices and processes that conform with the institutional practice of the home base; local subsidiaries are therefore pressured to confirm to head office practices. On the other hand, actors in local subsidiaries have to engage with other actors in the local context and with the institutions that are taken for granted in that context. Thus the pressure towards institutional isomorphism comes from different sources and has profoundly different impacts on local subsidiaries. Both these pressures are in an institutionalist sense 'legitimate'; that is, they derive from embedded expectations about appropriate forms of behaviour that are accepted in their different social contexts as legitimate claims on how business and management 'should' be done. Since Weber, the claim to legitimate authority (and the source of that claim) has been central to understanding organizational relations. The distinctiveness of the MNC lies in the existence of multiple competing forms of legitimate authority and the impact that this has on the internal and external relations of the MNC. The study of multinationals is therefore about how organizations are impacted on by the process of managing in multiple institutional contexts. What does this mean for the traditional questions about the forms and structures of control and coordination that exist amongst different MNCs?

The national business systems approach suggests that in order to answer this question it is necessary to understand, firstly, the sorts of pressures which are being exerted by headquarters, and secondly, the institutional resources on which local actors call when confronted by these pressures. In relation to the former, we can distinguish three broad pressures that will vary in intensity and significance depending on the sector and the nature of competition. The first is the pressure for standardization, the second is the pressure for efficiency and productivity in use of capital employed, and the third is the pressure for innovation and learning. Although these pressures are obviously tied together, it is helpful as a heuristic device to treat them separately.

2.3.1   The Pressure for Standardization

Standardization as a process refers to the development and application of shared management systems across the multinational. An obvious such system relates to the way in which performance of units in the MNC are assessed. What are the key metrics (financial, manpower, productivity, innovation measures) which the MNC headquarters aims to collect? Other forms of standardization may include the application of particular human resources policies, in terms of appraisal systems, training systems, equal opportunities and diversity policy, global talent management systems and so on.

From the perspective of the national business systems approach, this raises a number of questions. Firstly, how do MNCs from different forms of capitalism diverge in terms of the sorts of standardization of policies and processes which they prioritize? For example, there is substantial evidence that US MNCs are the most focused on creating common HR policies across all their subsidiaries. Further, these policies very much reflect the US environment in that they are highly individualistic, generally seek to avoid trade unions, are strongly performance oriented and emphasize equal opportunities (Ferner et al. 2005; Almond and Ferner 2006; Tempel et al. 2006). US MNCs are also most focused on short-term financial outcomes, a characteristic that fits with their national origins and the dominance of capital markets in shaping managerial orientations.

The second question which this raises is how far these practices diverge from those of the host society. In some contexts, such practices are not particularly divergent from those already existing, for example the presence of US multinationals in the UK does not tend to lead to much clash on the ground of distinctive national practices. On the other hand, anti-trade-union policies are difficult to implement in an environment like Germany where legal regulation as well as informal expectations about the organization of work and the nature of the participation of the workforce in the organization would be substantially different. Similarly in Japan, where individual performance-based payment systems are still only one component of a person's salary, status and position, the imposition of a performance-based system is problematic.

Thirdly, how do these policies actually get implemented in the local context? There is always a process of translation when practices and policies move from one environment to another. There have to be a group of 'brokers' or intermediaries who do the translation and implementation in the local context (on the modalities of translation see Czarniawska-Joerges and Sevon 1996, 2005; Czarniawska-Joerges 2002). Who are these brokers and what interests do they have? National business systems analysis point to the important distinction between expatriate managers and local managers in this context. Expatriate managers are specifically brought into subsidiaries to ensure that practices conform as closely as possible to what headquarters expects. Where their career is essentially an international one, either staying in the MNC or moving around to other MNCs in a similar expatriate capacity, then these managers are likely to be supportive of head office and implementation. However, where local managers predominate in the subsidiary, they may become not so much brokers as barriers to head office efforts to introduce standardization because they are closer to local expectations and local institutions (see the discussions of this issue in Kristensen and Zeitlin 2005; Morgan and Kristensen 2006).

Finally, there is the issue of the degree to which the local employees 'translate' these expectations or conform to them. There are multiple studies of this process of translation which indicate that there are very different degrees of resistance and conformity. In particular, the stronger the social embeddedness of the subsidiary in local institutions, the more unwilling local employees are to simply follow headquarters' practices, for example in terms of training, knowledge development, attitudes towards trade unions and employee participation in the work process. They will therefore tend to resist these forms of imposition.

2.3.2   Enforcing and Monitoring Efficiency in the Subsidiary

These processes are also seen in relation to the second main area of relations between subsidiaries and head office, which is over issues of efficiency and productivity in relation to capital employed. Birkinshaw (2000) identified this in terms of the development of three different sorts of internal markets in which subsidiaries competed against each other:

1.   intermediate products or services. Competition with internal and external providers over the delivery of products or services to the next stage in the value chain (which could be an internal or external customer).
2.   Charter. Birkinshaw refers to this as: 'most visible in cases of new investments – a new production plant, an R&D centre or a logistics centre. While new investments are almost always actively competed for . . . existing charters are increasingly deemed to be mobile and therefore open to competition' (Birkinshaw 2000, 119).
3.   Capability or practice. This refers to the transfer of best practices between sites and is dependent on internal benchmarking processes. Birkinshaw states that this is not overtly 'competitive', but the consequences of such transfers may be complex. On the one hand, a

subsidiary that engages in transfer gains a reputation for its expertise in particular processes and this may give it a strong position in winning charters or positions in internal markets. On the other hand, the transfer process potentially dilutes this power by diffusing knowledge across to other subsidiaries. Thus competition exists, but the rules of the game and how one wins such a competition and with what consequences are unclear.

The MNC in the current era is defined by an increasingly rigorous application of the rules of the market to the allocation of resources and status to subsidiaries. Recent work has suggested that subsidiary managers recognize this and engage in positioning themselves in these processes. They do this in a number of ways. The most important of these is to engage in their own initiatives and evolve their own strategies. Again Birkinshaw (2000, Ch. 2) provided a useful typology of forms of initiative which could be undertaken at subsidiary level:

- Local market initiatives: building and developing products, services and linkages in the host context.
- Global market initiatives: 'driven by unmet product or market needs among non-local suppliers and customers', subsidiaries may attempt to develop initiatives that have broader implications.
- Internal market initiatives: 'geared towards reconfiguring and rationalizing the activity system in the MNC', internal market initiatives are 'symptomatic of an overall shift towards geographical concentration by value-adding function in MNCs'.
- Global–internal hybrid initiatives: Birkinshaw states that 'the locus of the market opportunity is outside the subsidiary's home market. But like internal initiatives, the locus of *pursuit* is internal in that it involves convincing head office managers, not external customers' (ibid, 28).

A crucial aspect of this process has been identified in further work. Ling et al. refer to this as 'issue-selling by subsidiary managers' (Ling et al. 2005) whilst Bouquet and Birkinshaw discuss 'how foreign subsidiaries gain attention from corporate headquarters' (Bouquet and Birkinshaw 2008). Ling et al. define 'issue-selling' as the discretionary behaviour used to direct top management's attention toward or increase their understanding of, strategic issues. Bouquet and Birkinshaw develop a similar theme from a slightly different perspective. They are interested in the strategies that organizational units deploy to attract headquarters (HQ) attention as a key question becomes how they gain the necessary levels of HQ attention to deliver on their potential and contribute to the MNC's long-term success. From their empirical studies, they argue that:

> initiative taking and profile building constitute important drivers of HQ attention . . . To be successful in shaping the perception that they are reliable, credible and trustworthy actors of the MNC organization, our findings suggest that subsidiaries will not only need to maintain a basic track-record of success, but also reaffirm their commitment to the parent's objectives and, then finally, [*sic*] take deliberate steps to manage impressions with powerbrokers at head office.

The stream of research by Birkinshaw and his colleagues demonstrates how subsidiaries have become much more active inside MNCs and that they work in various ways to protect themselves. From a national business systems perspective, what are crucial are the resources which the subsidiaries and the headquarters deploy in these contexts. The main resources of the headquarters derive from strategic power, the power to close and the power to invest; these powers are utilized within the context of the power to manage the subsidiary effectively through standardization procedures and monitoring of performance, both on a continuous basis and through one-off tournaments over investments. Key translators of these powers are managers in local subsidiaries and the degree to which their careers and identity are embedded in the head office of the MNC or in the local subsidiary.

The main resources of the subsidiary derive from, firstly, the degree of asset specificity, stickiness of the investment and importance of the subsidiary to the MNC's overall strategy. Where the subsidiary brings distinctive strengths because it is embedded in a local context with distinctive and valuable skills and expertise – for example, it is embedded in a highly dynamic industrial district or cluster where high-quality standards permeate through the area through various institutions of training, knowledge creation and knowledge diffusion – then the head office is less likely to withdraw its investment than if it can replicate the skills easily elsewhere. The second main resource of the subsidiary is where employees in the subsidiary are capable of acting together collectively (which in turn is shaped by institutional features such as trade unions, labour market regulation, laws on the participation of employees in decisions). The third resource is where local institutions, for example local governments and other actors in the local sector, offer strong support to employees in the subsidiary. Thus locations with strong employee representation embedded in an active and powerful local governance system that can support upskilling and upgrading are better able to resist demands than in contexts where trade unions are weak and local agencies relatively powerless (see the case studies in Kristensen and Zeitlin 2005 for clear illustrations of how these factors affect the ability of subsidiaries to develop their own strategies). There are now a large range of case studies and analyses of how these relationships work out in different sectors, in different locations and between social actors from different forms of capitalism (Morgan et al. 2001; Almond and Ferner 2006; Geppert and Mayer 2006; Dörrenbächer and Geppert 2009, 2011; Dörrenbächer and Gammelgard 2011). These studies show that how subsidiaries work in practice, the degree to which they implement head office standards and improve productivity and efficiency through following head office practices, is highly variable. It is affected by the sorts of standards and practices which are being transferred, and the degree to which these practices 'fit' the host institutional context. It is also affected by the different powers that exist in the head office and in the host location.

2.3.3 Multinationals and Learning

Increasingly, multinationals perceive the internationalization process from the point of view of learning. This can vary from learning different management practices as a result of being in a different context, through to accessing specific knowledge and innovation expertise by locating in a particular industrial district or cluster. The first process has been labelled one of 'reverse diffusion' (Edwards 1998; Edwards et al. 2005; Edwards and Tempel 2010). Reverse diffusion refers to the degree that the MNC aims to bring back to the home base practices and processes which it has learned in other contexts. As already discussed, this has been of particular interest in terms of German multinationals where the experience of working in liberal market economies, particularly in relation to managing the workforce, has been relevant as they have struggled to reduce costs and to shift the German system away from national and sectoral forms of wage bargaining towards more plant-level agreements (see for example the discussions in Doellgast and Greer 2007; Streeck 2009). By contrast, studies of Japanese multinationals have revealed that they engage in very little that can be described as reverse diffusion; in fact they seem positively to try to avoid any influence from overseas operations permeating the organization (Morgan et al. 2003; Whitley et al. 2003).

In relation to more specific forms of learning and innovation, key issues that have been identified in the wider literature concerning differences between formal knowledge and informal knowledge, and between explicit and tacit knowledge, reveal the difficulties of accessing particular forms of knowledge and expertise (Nooteboom 2000). From the perspective of the multinational, a key element in being able to access knowledge is having the absorptive capacity to make sense of the information which is available (Cohen and Levinthal 1990). Absorptive capacity is partly a function of expertise and partly a function of scale; in other words, if the subsidiary is going to be able to access the knowledge creation processes in a certain area it has to have a staff that is knowledgeable enough and large enough to be able to recognize significant developments. As has already been discussed, it is much easier to build up this absorptive capacity quickly in market-based systems where expertise is both visible outside the firm (e.g. by personal reputation building, citation indices, patent data) and accessible on the marketplace to be purchased. Thus it is relatively simple for an MNC to set up a subsidiary in Silicon Valley and staff it with locals who are embedded in the local networks of knowledge and information, but in other areas where large firms predominate this becomes more difficult, as Saxenian shows in her comparison of Silicon Valley in the early 1990s with the Boston area (Saxenian 1994). Even in liberal market contexts, firms from coordinated market economies may find it difficult to enter local networks and may fail to gain any innovation advantage, as Lam found in her studies of Japanese pharmaceutical firms in the UK (Lam 2003), because their practices are so deeply embedded in their home context and incapable of being opened up to outside influences.

In conclusion, therefore, learning and innovation processes across MNCs are shaped by distinctive features of the national business systems. As Tregaskis et al. point out from their empirical research on MNCs in the UK, firms can attempt to deal with the barriers which result through developing stronger internal procedures in terms of human resource management (HRM) policies that reward cooperation, particularly amongst R&D personnel (Tregaskis et al. 2010). However, their ability to do so will depend greatly on the sorts of learning and the sorts of expertise with which the firm is dealing, as well as the influence of the home national business system.

2.4   MULTINATIONALS AND INSTITUTIONS

In this section, the objective is to study how multinationals may seek to change national business systems. It shifts the focus from micro-politics within the firm to macro-politics between the firms and the institutions of the national business system. How do MNCs seek to change these institutions as part of their strategies? As much recent research from authors in the national business systems and comparative capitalism research tradition has argued, institutions are not immutable. On the contrary, they are susceptible to change and being reshaped in significant ways by actors on the basis of small, incremental, often invisible changes. This is in part because institutions are also not necessarily homogenous within a national business system; there are often alternative institutions, alternative inter-pretations of what institututions mean and how they should be enacted, as well as different sorts of institutions perhaps based in a particular region or district, or perhaps in the sense of historical legacies which can be revived (Crouch 2005; Streeck and Thelen 2005; Lane and Wood 2009; Morgan et al. 2010; Almond 2011). MNCs play a particularly important role in this (Morgan 2009). In this section, I explore this through using a framework developed by John Dunning (2001). Dunning noted that MNCs sought different things from their internationalization activity. He identified three broad strategies which MNCs followed: efficiency seeking, market seeking and strategic asset seeking. Whilst it is clear that most MNCs are likely to pursue a combination of these approaches, there is heuristic and analytical value in identifying them separately, because using the national business systems approach it is possible to see how each strategy is embedded in distinctive sets of social relationships and has particular consequences for how those are organized and how national business systems change.

2.4.1 The Efficiency-Seeking Strategy

Beginning with what Dunning describes as the efficiency-seeking MNC strategy, this is where the firm aims to reduce costs in the value chain by accessing cheaper factors of production and producing on a larger scale. Usually this means reducing labour costs, but it also refers to reducing other costs, for example in terms of land as well as organizing production in a way which maximizes economies of scale and scope through intensive use of labour and technology.

Both land and labour are relatively immobile, certainly compared to capital which most MNCs can access in international markets. In prin-ciple, this could also mean accessing more productive workforces, and this does point to an issue for the MNC which relates to balancing the cost of labour with the quality and broader productiveness of labour. For the purposes of this discussion, however, we can assume that efficiency-seeking strategies look to reduce labour costs as a proportion of final costs and to maximize the utilization of machinery and technology.

This can be achieved through subcontracting or through the setting up of MNC subsidiaries. Where efficiency-seeking strategies involve the acquisition or setting up of subsidiaries, they are potentially high cost for the MNC in terms of the capital outlay. Achieving the efficiency benefits therefore requires, as previously suggested, the ability to hold down labour costs. In an efficiency-seeking strategy, therefore, we are likely to see the MNC particularly focused on the issue of labour, its utilization, its cost, its quality and its control. This is the *locus classicus* of MNC micro-politics as discussed in the previous section, because it engenders a struggle within the MNC at the point of production between the MNC head office and its representatives in the subsidiary who are trying to maximize production through imposing their own rules and expectations, and the employees in the local context with their own institutionally predetermined understandings of the nature of work and organization. From the perspective of the multinational, this struggle within the firm also depends on and links to wider struggles about labour markets and labour market regulation, and from there into issues of institutional change more broadly. Even if it is not explicitly mobilizing to change law and regulation on labour and the environment it can, given the right combination of circumstances, become visible in such debates, a process which can have dangers if the legitimacy of the MNC as a 'foreign' entrant into these arguments is challenged. For this reason, MNCs often prefer to hide behind the rhetoric of 'Market forces' articulated by insiders; that is, the argument that foreign direct investment (FDI) will cease coming and MNCs will depart if the institutions do not reinforce the efficiency-seeking objectives of the firm. In coordinated market economies, therefore, the entry of MNCs from liberal market contexts has particular dangers if such firms do not participate in industry-or sector-level bargaining or contribute to skills training; which is what Streeck argues has begun to happen in the German context, with consequences that undermine the broader institutional context (Streeck 2009).

2.4.2   The Market-Seeking Strategy

In Dunning's analysis, the openness of markets is broadly taken for granted. What the national business systems approach emphasizes, however, is that the degree of opennesss of markets is variable because of the institutional context. Thus Japan has for a long time been seen as a relatively closed market, not just to foreign direct investment which is very low compared to the level of FDI between other industrialized countries, but also in terms of imports, where in spite of formal commitment to free trade norms there are multiple formal and informal barriers to the entry of foreign goods and services. Similarly in the 1980s, threats by the European Union (EU) and the US to put formal trade barriers in place against Japanese imports were eventually counteracted by Japanese firms agreeing to increase their FDI and produce inside those contexts, thus providing employment where this had previously been shrinking due to competition from Japan. Market seeking and market access is therefore often a response to fear of being locked out of important or growing markets.

However, market seeking is also a process of reshaping institutions, particularly in contexts such as coordinated market environments where large parts of economic activity have been kept away from the market. Since the 1980s, therefore, MNCs have become engaged with and have responded to, on the one hand, government restrictions on free markets; and on the other hand, the increasingly powerful discourse of neoliberalism with its pressure on states to create more markets and more deregulated markets, for example in the public sector, the financial sector, professional services and so on. Historically, this is relatively novel (Blyth 2002; Prasad 2006). Up to the 1970s and later, some industrialized countries maintained formal and informal trade barriers in the sphere of manufactured goods, for example Japan and Korea. The General Agreement on Tariffs and Trade (GATT) and later the World Trade Organization (WTO) were set up to provide a shared framework for open trade across developed and developing countries. Membership of the Organisation for Economic Co-operation and Development (OECD) was also linked to a commitment to free trade, and of course the EU pushed this agenda selectively from its beginnings (Duina 2006; Jabko 2006; Abdelal 2007).

There are a number of points arising from this. Firstly, the ability of MNCs to benefit from open markets is not pre-given. Such markets have to be constructed, and MNCs play a crucial role in lobbying national governments and international organizations to make markets, either by deregulating existing areas or by allowing market competition in areas previously protected such as public services. Secondly, there remain substantial restrictions on free markets in spite of their strong support in policy circles. For example, negotiations continue in the WTO and elsewhere on agriculture; on mutual recognition of professional qualifications and the right to practice in different countries, which remains restricted; the role of market competition in public services remains controversial in many countries. Making markets is therefore an ongoing process, not something that has been achieved. Thirdly, open markets need institutional support within the society, not just from international bodies such as the WTO. In particular, they require forms of competition law that prevent anti-competitive practices, whether emerging from inside (from governments or nationalized industries) or from large private sector groups. MNCs therefore have to work hard to get markets made open and accessible to themselves.

To make an open market is an institution-building task. Furthermore it is one which has been increasingly monopolized by certain forms of MNCs and certain types of policy-making networks. The multinational professional service companies – the lawyers, management consultants, accountants and bankers – have played a key part. These firms have multiple gains from the process of opening markets. They are employed by governments to construct the open markets in areas such as utilities, health and other public services. They advise on the regulatory and legal structures required, the sorts of contracts which can achieve public interests as well as private profitability, and the monitoring mechanisms required to set, measure and assess performance standards. Once they have engaged in these tasks, they are in a prime position to advise MNCs wishing to participate in the new markets about how the system works. These groups are also represented on the international bodies such as the International Monetary Fund (IMF), the World Bank, the WTO, the EU and the OECD, which have pushed forward this agenda as well as creating multiple forms of international networks to exchange information and ideas on this process (Djelic 2002, 2006; Djelic and Kleiner 2006).

Making markets is obviously a political task in many cases (see, for example, Halliday and Carruthers 2009 which reveals in detail how firms, international bodies and governments developed and implemented a global framework for bankruptcy laws which were deemed essential to FDI and market making). It therefore requires building relationships into government which may require turning insiders into partial outsiders (hiring former government employees or ministers to open up doors in ministries which adjudicate on market opening processes) and turning outsiders into partial insiders (giving them access to decision-makers). These processes have shaded from legitimate lobbying activities into forms of corruption and bribery.

For Dunning, market seeking was a simple economic act that any rational firm would undertake. From a sociological perspective, however, making markets in order to construct them as capitalist markets has to be investigated. How does it occur? The argument here is that MNCs, and particularly professional services firms (PSF), have been crucial. Their main institutional focus is not therefore labour regulation but the construction and regulation of markets per se. Thus MNCs engage in changing national business systems in order to produce markets that offer them opportunities to expand and develop.

2.4.3   Strategic Asset Seeking

Dunning also describes a third strategy which he describes as strategic asset seeking. In the previous subsection the micro-politics of acquiring knowledge assets was discussed. In this subsection, the focus is on securing access to raw materials and commodities. Here technological expertise embedded in the MNC, and the ability to access large amounts of capital to make the investments required, go along with the need for political connections in order to access these assets. These sorts of assets are highly fixed, and although there may be alternative sources there are also a large number of competitors seeking such assets. Therefore strategies tend to focus on a combination of identifying resources and the technological and capital resources required to make them profitable on the one hand, and on the other hand managing the politics of such processes, and particularly issues around the degree of national control of such assets and the terms and conditions under which they can be extracted. As with some forms of market seeking, this may shade over into illegality, a process that when revealed can lead to substantial problems both with the home government – for example in terms of the strong laws against bribery which exist in the US and, now, the UK – and with global social movements that campaign against such activities.

In these contexts, the MNC may become explicitly politicized. This is obvious in areas like oil which have been predominantly nationalized by governments over the last few decades and where major oil MNCs have had to engage in joint ventures or to work as subcontractors to government-owned companies (as in Venezuela). In other contexts where states are failing and there is a violent struggle between war lords to capture control of valuable raw materials (such as the notorious 'blood diamonds' of Southern Africa), MNCs become drawn into the local politics to such an extent that they becomes the main builders of institutions, filling the gap that has emerged from state failure (Crouch 2006; Hall 2010).

In conclusion, MNCs are fundamentally involved in reshaping national business systems. They do this in a variety of ways depending on their main strategies. Although there is no guarantee that they will be successful, in many areas of the world where neoliberalism has become the predominant mode of analysis of markets, MNCs have been able to join with external and internal actors in pushing this agenda forward through deregulation and marketization. Even some of the coordinated market economies have succumbed to this, in part through international pressure and regulation via institutions such as the WTO, the OECD and the EU. Where states are weaker and national business systems more fragile (as in many parts of Central Europe and Latin America), MNCs have been powerful agents in the diffusion of free markets. This does, however, potentially carry a price because it loosens existing institutional structures, in some cases to such an extent that they completely collapse – in which case the MNC may have to become one of the central actors in rebuilding the society if it is going to have the predictability and stability which it requires to develop its business.

2.5 CONCLUSIONS

The national business systems approach has much to contribute to the study of international business. In particular, it is an important way of illuminating how multinationals work. The home origins of MNCs affect the particular structure of competences and capabilities which they develop. This creates a form of sectoral specialization so that companies from particular national business systems tend to concentrate on particular areas of business. The distinction between liberal market economies and coordinated market economies developed by Hall and Soskice (2001) is relevant for understanding how competitive advantage is created. Where institutions support the development of firm-specific skills, and long-term commitment to the firm on the part of labour, capital and suppliers, then firms became very effective at patterns of incremental innovation, meaning that in sectors defined by a basic technological paradigm and a relatively stable market structure, they could do well in global competition. Where industries are more unstable and there is discontinuous change and innovation, flexibility in the labour and capital markets as well as in supplier relationships facilitates better the development of globally competitive companies.

These patterns also help to explain the speed and nature of internationalization. Firms strongly embedded in their own institutional context would find higher liabilities of foreignness than firms which were predominantly organized through market contracts. Therefore firms from coordinated market economies tend to rely on export strategies for longer than firms from liberal market economies, and only gradually do they internationalize their production. One strategy to protect themselves from liabilities of foreignness has been to build greenfield plants, copying home-based models, and to select a workforce which as far as possible would conform to expectations of the home-based managers. Alternatively, the MNC might use the international experience as a way of innovating and bringing change into the firm, as some German MNCs seem to have done, with consequences for the reproduction of the home national business system.

The management of subsidiaries is also well explained by the national business systems approach. The conflict between two institutional logics (that of the head office and of the host context) varies in its extent. Within the subsidiary, these tensions are played out over processes of standardization, of efficiency and of learning. Practices cannot simply be imposed; they have to be translated and adapted to contexts. The degree to which the local context contests and forces forms of adaptation depends on the degree of collective identity in the subsidiary and also the degree to which managers in the subsidiary are local or expatriates. Local managers are more likely to work with local employees in adapting and translating in ways which do not cut across the institutional logic of the home context, whereas expatriate managers are much more likely to be loyal to the head office of the firm and therefore more pressing in terms of implementing decisions from there. There are now many case studies which reveal the interesting interactions and micro-politics which occur at the subsidiary level, and which are revealed by the use of the national business systems perspective.

The MNC, however, also engages in macro-politics; in other words, it engages in changing national business systems in ways which enable it to work more effectively and profitably. In an era when neoliberal policy prescriptions of open and deregulated markets have dominated in international organizations and in many national contexts, MNCs have been silent partners in extending markets and establishing them in new areas. The marketization process that has occurred has been led particularly by large multinational professional service companies, such as lawyers, accountants and management consultants, who have advised governments on how to make markets work. In the process, they have reshaped national business systems that have previously worked along more coordinated lines. Whilst large powerful coordinated markets such as Japan have been able to resist, many others have found it more difficult. Germany, in particular, has been reconstructed from inside and outside, and from some perspectives its coordinated system is slowly collapsing. More fragile national business systems have been permeated more easily by neoliberal markets and MNCs with consequences that are yet to be fully understood. In still other contexts, where institutions have broken down partly as a result of the inability to sustain a functioning state, multinationals have found themselves increasingly responsible for building new institutions and taking on a sort of political function.

In conclusion, the national business systems perspective can contribute a lot to the understanding of international business. It constitutes an ongoing stream of research that draws together researchers in business and management, political economists, sociologists and political scientists in the exploration of the way in which institutions shape economic life. As multinationals have grown more significant, the interaction of these firms with institutions both in the home base and in host countries has become more important and more researched. This opens up a space for interaction between international business and comparative institutional analysis that should be highly productive in future years.

REFERENCES

Abdelal, R. (2007), *Capital Rules: The Construction of Global Finance*, Cambridge, MA, Harvard University Press.

Almond, P. (2011), 'The sub-national embeddedness of international HRM', *Human Relations*, **64** (4), 531–551.

Almond, P. and A. Ferner (2006), *American Multinationals in Europe: Managing Employment Relations across National Borders*, Oxford: Oxford University Press.

Aoki, M., G. Jackson and H. Miyajima (2007), *Corporate Governance in Japan: Institutional Change and Organizational Diversity*, Oxford: Oxford University Press.

Birkinshaw, J. (2000), *Entrepreneurship in the Global Firm*, London: Sage.

Blyth, M. (2002), *Great Transformations: Economic Ideas and Institutional Change in the Twentieth Century*, Cambridge: Cambridge University Press.

Bouquet, C. and J. Birkinshaw (2008), 'Weight versus voice: how foreign subsidiaries gain attention from corporate headquarters', *Academy of Management Journal*, **51** (3), 577–601.

Cohen, W.M. and D.A. Levinthal (1990), 'Absorptive capacity: a new perspective on learning and innovation', *Administrative Science Quarterly*, **35**, 128–152.

Collinson, S. and G. Morgan (2009), *The Multinational Firm*, Chichester, UK and Hoboken, NJ: Wiley.

Crouch, C. (2005), *Capitalist Diversity and Change: Recombinant Governance and Institutional Entrepreneurs*, Oxford: Oxford University Press.

Crouch, C. (2006), 'Modelling the firm in its market and organizational environment: methodologies for studying corporate social responsibility', *Organization Studies*, **27**, 1533–1551.

Czarniawska-Joerges, B. (2002), *A Tale of Three Cities: Or the Glocalization of City Management*, Oxford: Oxford University Press.

Czarniawska-Joerges, B. and G. Sevon (1996), *Translating Organizational Change*, Berlin: Walter de Gruyter.

Czarniawska-Joerges, B. and G. Sevon (2005), *Global Ideas: How Ideas, Objects and Practices Travel in a Global Economy*, Malmö: Liber & Copenhagen Business School Press.

Davis, G.F. (2009), *Managed by the Markets: How Finance Reshaped America*, Oxford: Oxford University Press.

Djelic, M.-L. (2002), 'Does Europe mean Americanization? The case of competition', *Competition and Change*, **6** (3), 233–250.

Djelic, M.-L. (2006), 'Marketization: from intellectual agenda to global policy-making', in M.-L. Djelic and K. Sahlin-Andersson (eds), *Transnational Governance: Institutional Dynamics of Regulation*, Cambridge: Cambridge University Press, pp. 53–73.

Djelic, M.-L. and T. Kleiner (2006), 'The international competition network: moving towards transnational governance', in M.-L. Djelic and K. Sahlin-Andersson (eds), *Transnational Governance: Institutional Dynamics of Regulation*, Cambridge: Cambridge University Press, pp. 287–307.

Doellgast, V. and I. Greer (2007), 'Vertical disintegration and the disorganization of German industrial relations', *British Journal of Industrial Relations*, **45** (1), 55–76.

Dörrenbächer, C. and J. Gammelgard (2011), 'Subsidiary power in multinational corporations: the subtle role of micro-political bargaining power', *Critical Perspectives on International Business*, **7** (1), 30–47.

Dörrenbächer, C. and M. Geppert (2009), 'A micro-political perspective on subsidiary initiative-taking: evidence from German owned subsdiaries in France', *European Management Journal*, **27**, 100–112.

Dörrenbächer, C. and M. Geppert (2011), *Politics and Power in the Multinational Corporation: The Role of Institutions, Interests and Identities*, Cambridge: Cambridge University Press.

Duina, F.G. (2006), *The Social Construction of Free Trade: The European Union, NAFTA, and MERCOSUR*, Princeton, NJ and Oxford, UK: Princeton University Press.

Dunning, J.H. (2001), 'The key literature on IB activities', in A.M. Rugman and T.L. Brewer (eds), *The Oxford Handbook of International Business*, Oxford: Oxford University Press, pp. 36–68.

Edwards, T. (1998), 'Multinationals, labour management and the process of reverse diffusion: a case study', *International Journal of Human Resource Management*, **9** (4), 696–709.

Edwards, T., P. Almond, I. Clark, T. Colling and A. Ferner (2005), 'Reverse diffusion in US multinationals: barriers from the American business system', *Journal of Management Studies*, **42** (6), 1261–1286.

Edwards, T. and A. Tempel (2010), 'Explaining variation in reverse diffusion of HR practices: evidence from the German and British subsidiaries of American multinationals', *Journal of World Business*, **45** (1), 19–28.

Elger, T. and C. Smith (2005), *Assembling Work: Remaking Factory Regimes in Japanese Multinationals in Britain*, New York: Oxford University Press.

Ferner, A., P. Almond and T. Colling (2005), 'Institutional theory and the cross-national transfer of employment policy: the case of "workforce diversity" in US multinationals', *Journal of International Business Studies*, **36** (3), 304–321.

Ferner, A. and M. Varul (2000), '"Vanguard" subsidiaries and the diffusion of new practices: A case study of German multinationals', *British Journal of Industrial Relations*, **38** (1), 115–140.

Geppert, M. and M. Mayer (2006), *Global, National and Local Practices in Multinational Companies*, New York: Palgrave Macmillan.

Hall, J. (2010), 'State Failure', in G. Morgan, J.L. Campbell, C. Crouch, O.K. Pedersen and R. Whitley (eds), *The Oxford Handbook of Comparative Institutional Analysis*, Oxford: Oxford University Press, pp. 587–600.

Hall, P.A. and D. Soskice (2001), *Varieties of Capitalism: The Institutional Foundations of Comparative Advantage*, Oxford: Oxford University Press.

Halliday, T. and B. Carruthers (2009), *Bankrupt: Global Lawmaking and Systemic Financial Crisis*, Stanford, CA: Stanford University Press.

Halsall, R. (2008), 'Intercultural mergers and acquisitions as "legitimacy crises" of models of capitalism: a UK–German case study', *Organization*, **15** (6), 787–809.

Höpner, M. and G. Jackson (2006), 'Revisiting the Mannesmann takeover: how markets for corporate control emerge', *European Management Review*, **3** (3), 142–155.

Jabko, N. (2006), *Playing the Market: A Political Strategy for Uniting Europe, 1985–2005*, Ithaca, NY and London, UK: Cornell University Press.

Kostova, T. (1999), 'Transnational transfer of strategic organizational practices: a contextual perspective', *Academy of Management Review*, **24**, 308–324.

Kristensen, P.H. and J. Zeitlin (2005), *Local Players in Global Games: The Strategic Constitution of a Multinational Corporation*, Oxford: Oxford University Press.

Lam, A. (2003), 'Organizational learning in multinationals: R&D networks of Japanese and US MNEs in the UK', *Journal of Management Studies*, **40** (3), 673–703.

Lane, C. (2000), 'Globalization and the German model of capitalism: erosion or survival?', *British Journal of Sociology*, **51** (2), 207–234.

Lane, C. (2005), 'Institutional transformation and system change: changes in the corporate governance of German corporations', in G. Morgan, R. Whitley and E. Moen (eds), *Changing Capitalisms? Internationalization, Institutional Change and Systems of Economic Organization*, Oxford: Oxford University Press, pp. 78–109.

Lane, C. and G. Wood (2009), 'Capitalist diversity and diversity within capitalism', *Economy and Society*, **38** (4), 531–551.

Ling, Y., S.W. Floyd and D.C. Bladridge (2005), 'Toward a model of issue-selling by subsidiary managers in multinational organizations', *Journal of International Business Studies*, **36**, 637–654.

Morgan, G. (2007), 'National business systems research: progress and prospects', *Scandinavian Journal of Management*, **23** (2), 127–145.

Morgan, G. (2009), 'Globalization, multinationals and institutional diversity', *Economy and Society*, **38** (4), 580–605.

Morgan, G., J.L. Campbell, C. Crouch, O.K. Pedersen and R. Whitley (2010), *The Oxford Handbook of Comparative Institutional Analysis*, Oxford: Oxford University Press.

Morgan, G. and P.H. Kristensen (2006), 'The contested space of multinationals: varieties of institutionalism: varieties of capitalism', *Human Relations*, **59** (11), 1467–1490.

Morgan, G., P.H. Kristensen and R. Whitley (2001), *The Multinational Firm: Organizing across Institutional and National Divides*, Oxford: Oxford University Press.

Morgan, G. and I. Kubo (2005), 'Beyond path dependency? Constructing new models for institutional change: the case of capital markets in Japan', *Socio-Economic Review*, **3** (1), 55–82.

Morgan, G., R. Whitley, D. Sharpe and W. Kelly (2003), 'Global managers and Japanese multinationals', *International Journal of Human Resource Management*, **14** (3), 389–407.

Nooteboom, B. (2000), *Learning and Innovation in Organizations and Economies*, Oxford: Oxford University Press.

Prasad, M. (2006), *The Politics of Free Markets: The Rise of Neoliberal Economic Policies in Britain, France, Germany and the United States*, Chicago, IL: University of Chicago Press.

Saxenian, A. (1994), *Regional Advantage: Culture and Competition in Silicon Valley and Route 128*, Cambridge, MA: Harvard University Press.

Sharpe, D. (2001), 'Globalization and change: organizational continuity and change within a Japanese multinational in the UK', in G. Morgan, P.H. Kristensen and R. Whitley (eds), *The Multinational Firm: Organizing across Institutional and National Divides*, Oxford: Oxford University Press, pp. 196–221.

Streeck, W. (2009), *Re-Forming Capitalism: Institutional Change in the German Political Economy*, Oxford: Oxford University Press.

Streeck, W. and K.A. Thelen (2005), *Beyond Continuity: Institutional Change in Advanced Political Economies*, Oxford: Oxford University Press.

Tempel, A., T. Edwards, A. Ferner, M. Muller-Camen and H. Wächter (2006), 'Subsidiary responses to institutional duality: collective representation practices of US multinationals in Britain and Germany', *Human Relations*, **59** (11), 1543–1570.

Tregaskis, O., T. Edwards, P. Edwards, A. Ferner and P. Marginson (2010), 'Transnational learning structures in multinational firms: organizational context and national embeddedness', *Human Relations*, **63** (4), 471–499.

Whitley, R. (1999), *Divergent Capitalisms: The Social Structuring and Change of Business Systems*, Oxford: Oxford University Press.

Whitley, R. (2007), *Business Systems and Organizational Capabilities: The Institutional Structuring of Competitive Competences*, Oxford, UK and New York, USA: Oxford University Press.

Whitley, R. (2010), 'Changing competition models in market economies', in G. Morgan, J.L. Campbell, C. Crouch, O.K. Pedersen and R. Whitley (eds), *The Oxford Handbook of Comparative Institutional Analysis*, Oxford: Oxford University Press, pp. 363–397.

Whitley, R., G. Morgan, W. Kelly and D. Sharpe (2003), 'The changing Japanese multinational: application, adaptation and learning in car manufacturing and financial services', *Journal of Management Studies*, **40** (3), 643–672.

Zaheer, S. (1995), 'Overcoming the liability of foreignness', *Academy of Management Journal*, **5** (38), 2.

3 Financing firms in different countries
Franklin Allen

3.1 INTRODUCTION

In the traditional literature, there have been two approaches to the role of institutions in the financing of firms. The first is to consider how agents interact through financial markets. The second looks at the operation of financial intermediaries such as banks and insurance companies. Sixty years ago, the financial system could be neatly bifurcated in this way. Rich households and large firms used the equity and bond markets, while less wealthy households and medium and small firms used banks, insurance companies and other financial institutions. Table 3.1, for example, shows the ownership of corporate equities in 1950. Households owned over 90 per cent. By 2010 it can be seen that the situation had changed dramatically. By then households held around 36 per cent; non-bank intermediaries, primarily pension funds and mutual funds, held over 40 per cent. This change illustrates why it is no longer possible to consider the role of financial markets and financial institutions separately. Rather

Table 3.1   Holdings of corporate equities in the US (%)

Sector	1950	1970	1990	2010
Private pension funds	0.8	8.0	16.8	8.8
State & local pension funds	0.0	1.2	7.6	7.8
Life insurance companies	1.5	1.7	2.3	6.1
Other insurance companies	1.8	1.6	2.3	1.0
Mutual funds	2.0	4.7	6.6	20.7
Closed-end funds	1.1	0.5	0.5	0.4
Bank personal trusts	0.0	10.4	5.4	–
Foreign sector	2.0	3.2	6.9	13.3
Household sector	90.2	68.0	51.0	35.9
Other	0.6	0.6	0.7	6.0
Total equities outstanding (billions of dollars)	142.7	841.4	3543	22 962

Source: Federal Reserve Board 'Flow of funds', http://www.federalreserve.gov/releases/z1/current/accessible/l213.htm. Figures are for the end of period.

than intermediating directly between households and firms, financial institutions have increasingly come to intermediate between households and markets on the one hand, and between firms and markets on the other.

There are some historical instances where financial markets and institutions have operated in the absence of a well-defined legal system, relying instead on reputation and other implicit mechanisms. However, in most financial systems the law plays an important role. It determines what kinds of contracts are feasible, what kinds of governance mechanisms can be used for corporations, the restrictions that can be placed on securities and so forth. Hence, the legal system is an important component of the institutional basis of a financial system.

A financial system is much more than all of this, however. An important prerequisite of the ability to write contracts and enforce rights of various kinds is a system of accounting. In addition to allowing contracts to be written, an accounting system allows investors to value a company more easily and to assess how much it would be prudent to lend to it. Accounting information is only one type of information (albeit the most important) required by financial systems. The incentives to generate and disseminate information are crucial features of a financial system.

This chapter considers the role of institutions in the financing of firms in different countries. In particular, financial institutions and markets are considered. Sections 3.2 to 3.6 focus on issues of investment and saving, growth, risk sharing, information provision and corporate governance, respectively. Section 3.7 contains concluding remarks.

3.2   INVESTMENT AND SAVING

One of the primary purposes of the financial system is to allow savings to be invested in firms. In a series of important papers, Mayer (1988, 1990) documented how firms obtained funds and financed investment in a number of different countries. Table 3.2 shows the results based on data from 1970 to 1989, using Mayer's methodology. The figures use data obtained from statements of sources and uses of funds. For France, the data are from Bertero (1994), while for the United States (US), United Kingdom (UK), Japan and Germany they are from Corbett and Jenkinson (1996). It can be seen that internal finance is by far the most important source of funds in all countries. Bank finance is moderately important in most countries and particularly important in Japan and France. Bond finance is only important in the US and equity finance is

Table 3.2   Unweighted average gross financing of non-financial enterprises 1970–1989 (% of total)

	US	UK	Japan	France	Germany
Internal	91.3	97.3	69.3	60.6	80.6
Bank finance	16.6	19.5	30.5	40.6	11
Bonds	17.1	3.5	4.7	1.3	−0.6
New equity	−8.8	−10.4	3.7	6	0.9
Trade credit	−3.7	−1.4	−8.1	−2.8	−1.9
Capital transfers	–	2.5	–	1.9	8.5
Other	−3.8	−2.9	−0.1	−6.5	1.5
Statistical adjustment	−8.7	−8	0	2.5	0

Sources: Bertero (1994) and Corbett and Jenkinson (1996).

either unimportant or negative (that is, shares are being repurchased in aggregate) in all countries. Mayer's studies and those using his methodology had an important impact because they raised the question of how important financial markets are in terms of providing funds for investment. It seems that, at least in the aggregate, equity markets are unimportant while bond markets are important only in the US. These findings contrast strongly with the emphasis on equity and bond markets in the traditional finance literature. Bank finance is important in all countries, but not as important as internal finance.

Another perspective on how the financial system operates is obtained by looking at savings and the holding of financial assets. Table 3.3 shows the relative importance of banks and markets in the US, UK, Japan, France and Germany. It can be seen that the US is at one extreme and Germany at the other. In the US, banks are relatively unimportant: the ratio of assets to gross domestic product (GDP) is only 80 per cent, about a quarter of the German ratio of 338 per cent. On the other hand, the US ratio of equity market capitalization to GDP is 118 per cent, almost three times the German ratio of 43 per cent. The UK is an international banking centre and this is why its bank assets to GDP ratio is so high: 465 per cent. Its equity market capitalization to GDP is also high, though, at 161 per cent. In France and Japan banking assets are high relative to the US, and equity market capitalizations are significantly lower. The US and the UK are often referred to as market-based systems, while Germany, Japan and France are often referred to as bank-based systems.

Table 3.3   An international comparison of banks and markets in 2010 ($ billions)

	GDP	Total banking assets	BA/GDP (%)	Equity market capitalization	EMC/GDP (%)
US	$14658	$11733	80	$17283	118
UK	$2247	$10454	465	$3613	161
Japan	$5459	$9782	179	$3828	70
France	$2583	$8642	335	$1888	73
Germany	$3316	$11195	338	$1430	43

Notes:
Data for US and Japan are as at the end of 2010. Data for UK, France and Germany are as at the end of June 2010.
'Banking assets' is defined as follows:
● US: total assets of commercial banks in the United States;
● Japan: the total assets of domestically licensed banks;
● UK, Germany and France: total assets of all domestic banks.
Domestic 'equity market capitalization' is defined as follows:
● US: the total market cap of NYSE and NASDAQ;
● Japan: the total market cap of Tokyo Stock Exchange;
● UK: the total market cap of London Stock Exchange;
● France: the total market cap of French domestic shares on Euronext Exchange;
● Germany: the total market cap of Deutsche Börse.

Sources: IMF, Bank of Japan, Federal Reserve Board, European Central banks, CEIC database and http//:www.world-exchanges.org.

3.3   GROWTH AND FINANCIAL STRUCTURE

The relationship between the growth rate of an economy and its financial structure is a long-debated issue. On the one hand, Bagehot (1962 [1873]) and Hicks (1969) argue that the UK's financial system played an important role in the Industrial Revolution. On the other hand, Robinson (1952) suggests that the causation goes the other way, and the financial system developed as a result of economic growth.

In a pioneering study using cross-country data, Goldsmith (1969) found a relationship between growth and financial development. However, his study was based on limited data and did not control in a satisfactory way for other factors affecting growth. In a series of studies King and Levine (1993a, 1993b, 1993c) consider data for 80 countries over the period 1960–1989, and carefully control for other factors affecting growth. They find a strong relationship between growth and financial development and also find evidence that the level of financial development is a good predictor of future economic growth. In an innovative study, Rajan and Zingales (1998) use data from the US to find which industries rely on external finance, and investigate whether these industries grow faster in countries with better-developed financial systems. They find a positive correlation between growth rates and financial development, suggesting that finance is important for growth. Demirgüç-Kunt and Maksimovic (1996) consider firm-level data from 30 countries and argue that access to stock markets leads to faster growth. In an influential contribution, McKinnon (1973) did case studies of Argentina, Brazil, Chile, Germany, Korea, Indonesia and Taiwan in the period after the Second World War. His conclusion from these cases is that better financial systems support faster economic growth. Allen et al. (2010) consider the historical experiences of the UK, US, Germany and Japan. They argue that in the case of the UK and US there is clear evidence that the financial system developed prior to the start of high growth rates. For Germany and Japan the evidence is less clear. Taken together, these studies provide some support for a relationship between finance and growth.

A large number of theoretical studies consider the growth–finance relationship. Hicks (1969) and Bencivenga et al. (1995) argue that the liquidity provided by capital markets was key in allowing growth in the UK Industrial Revolution. Many of the products produced early in the Industrial Revolution had been invented some time before, but lack of long-term finance delayed their manufacture. Liquid capital markets allowed the projects to be financed by savers with short time horizons and/or uncertain liquidity needs. Similarly, Bencivenga and Smith (1991) argue that intermediaries may be able to enhance liquidity, while at the same time funding long-lived projects. Greenwood and Jovanovic (1990) point out that intermediaries that can effectively process information about entrepreneurs and projects can induce a higher rate of growth. King and Levine (1993c) suggest that intermediaries can also do a better job of choosing innovations. Another avenue for increasing growth is the higher expected returns that can be achieved if risk is reduced through diversification (Saint-Paul 1982). Boyd and Smith (1996, 1998) suggest that banks are important at low levels of development while markets become more important as income rises. Rajan and Zingales (2001) suggest that banks are less dependent than markets on the legal system. Hence, banks can do better when the legal system is weak and markets do better when the legal system is more developed.

Another important element of the debate concerns the relative contributions of banks and financial markets in spurring growth. This debate was originally conducted in the context of German and UK growth in the late nineteenth and early twentieth centuries. Gerschenkron (1962) argues that the bank-based system in Germany allowed a closer relationship between bankers providing the finance and industrial firms than was possible in the market-based system in the UK. Goldsmith (1969) pointed out that although manufacturing industry grew much faster in Germany than the UK in the late nineteenth and early twentieth centuries, the overall growth rates were fairly similar. More recently Levine (2002) uses a broad database covering 48 countries over the period 1980–1995. He finds that the distinction between bank-based and market-based systems is not an interesting one for explaining the finance–growth nexus. Rather, elements of a country's legal environment and the quality of its financial services are most important for fostering general economic growth. In contrast, in a study of 36 countries from 1980 to 1995, Tadesse (2002) does find a difference between bank-based and market-based financial systems. For underdeveloped financial sectors, bank-based systems outperform market-based systems, while for developed financial sectors market-based systems outperform bank-based systems. Levine and Zervos (1998) show that higher stock market liquidity or greater bank development lead to higher growth, irrespective of the development of the other. There is some evidence that financial markets and banks are complements rather than substitutes. Demirgüç-Kunt and Maksimovic (1998) show that more developed stock markets tend to be associated with increased use of bank finance in developing countries.

Allen and Gale (1999; 2000a, Ch. 13) ask whether financial markets or banks are better at providing finance for projects where there is diversity of opinion, for example in the development of new technologies. Diversity of opinion arises from differences in prior beliefs, rather than differences in information. The advantage of financial markets is that they allow people with similar views to join together to finance projects. This will be optimal provided that the costs necessary for each investor to form an opinion before investment decisions are made are sufficiently low. Finance can be provided by the market even when there is great diversity of opinion among investors. Intermediated finance involves delegating the financing decision to a manager who expends the cost necessary to form an opinion. There is an agency problem in that the manager may not have the same prior knowledge as the investor. This type of delegation turns out to be optimal when the costs of forming an opinion are high and there is likely to be considerable agreement in any case. The analysis suggests that market-based systems will lead to more innovation than bank-based systems.

3.4 RISK SHARING

One of the most important functions of the financial system is to share risk, and it is often argued that financial markets are well suited to achieve this aim. However, market-based financial systems can actually create risk through changes in asset values. In the US and the UK stock markets are relatively more important, as we have seen, so these changes in asset values adversely affect people. In contrast, in the other countries more wealth is held in banks and this exposes the population to less risk. How can one explain these differences in the amount of risk households are apparently exposed to in different financial systems? Standard financial theory suggests that the main purpose of financial markets is to improve risk sharing. How can it be that households are exposed to more risk in the US and UK than in Japan, France and Germany?

Allen and Gale (1997; 2000a, Ch. 6) have provided a resolution to this paradox. They point out that traditional financial theory has little to say about hedging non-diversifiable risks. It assumes that the set of assets is given, and theory focuses on the efficient sharing of these risks through exchange. For example, the standard diversification argument requires individuals to exchange assets so that each investor holds a relatively small amount of any one risk. Risks will also be traded so that more risk-averse people bear less risk than people who are less risk-averse. This kind of risk sharing is termed cross-sectional risk sharing, because it is achieved through exchanges of risk among individuals at a given point in time. However, importantly, these strategies do not eliminate macroeconomic shocks that affect all assets in a similar way.

Departing from the traditional approach, Allen and Gale focus on the intertemporal smoothing of risks that cannot be diversified at a given point in time. They argue that such risks can be averaged over time in a way that reduces their impact on individual welfare. One hedging strategy for non-diversifiable risks is intergenerational risk sharing. This spreads the risks associated with a given stock of assets across generations with heterogeneous experiences. Another strategy involves asset accumulation in order to reduce fluctuations in consumption over time. Both are examples of the intertemporal smoothing of asset returns.

Allen and Gale show that the opportunities for engaging in intertemporal smoothing are very different in market-based and bank-based financial systems. They demonstrate that incomplete financial markets, on the one hand, may not allow effective intertemporal smoothing. Long-lived financial institutions such as banks, on the other hand, can achieve intertemporal smoothing, as long as they are not subject to substantial competition from financial markets. In fact, competition from financial markets can lead to disintermediation and the unravelling of intertemporal smoothing provided by long-lived institutions. In good times, individuals would rather opt out of the banking system and invest in the market, thus avoiding the accumulation of reserves from which they may not benefit. Therefore, in the long run, intertemporal smoothing by banks is not viable in the presence of direct competition from markets.

This theory provides a framework for thinking about the role of risk management in different financial systems. In bank-based systems, such as those in Japan, France and Germany, risk management could be achieved through intertemporal smoothing, in which financial intermediaries eliminate risk by accumulating low-risk, liquid assets. Cross-sectional risk sharing through markets is less important, and the importance of other forms of risk management is reduced correspondingly.

In market-based financial systems, on the other hand, intertemporal smoothing by intermediaries is ruled out by competition from financial markets. Here, cross-sectional risk sharing becomes correspondingly more important. As a result, individuals and institutions acting on their behalf need to trade and manage risk in a very different way. They need to ensure that those who are most tolerant of risk end up bearing most of the risk.

The Allen–Gale theory thus predicts that as financial systems become more market oriented, risk management through the use of derivatives and other similar techniques will become more important. The theory is thus consistent with the fact that these particular forms of risk management are more important in the US and UK than they are in less market-oriented economies such as Japan, France and Germany.

The Allen–Gale theory points to clear opportunities for improving welfare through intertemporal risk sharing when markets are incomplete, but it leaves open the question of whether financial institutions will have the right incentives to offer this kind of risk sharing. In fact, there is as yet no adequate theory of long-lived financial institutions. In some cases, we can obviate this gap in the theory by assuming that competitive institutions maximize the welfare of their depositors. However, when depositors are heterogeneous as, for example, in an overlapping generations economy, this device breaks down. One of the important questions posed by the behaviour of financial institutions in different countries is, what is the objective function of a financial institution?

3.5   INFORMATION PROVISION

The acquisition and use of information to allocate resources efficiently is one of the most important functions of a financial system. In market-based systems, such as the US, the large number of publicly listed firms, together with extensive disclosure requirements, means that a great deal of information about firms' activities is released. In addition to this publicly available information, there are many analysts working for mutual funds, pension funds and other intermediaries who gather private information. The empirical evidence on efficient markets suggests that much of this information is reflected in stock prices. On the other hand, in some countries with bank-based systems, such as Germany and other continental European countries, relatively few companies are listed so only limited private information is incorporated into stock prices. Although the financial markets have more information available in market-based financial systems like the US than in bank-based systems like Germany, the reverse is true for intermediaries. The greater prevalence of long-term relationships in bank-based systems means that the banks are able to acquire considerable amounts of information about the firms they lend to, more than is released to the market. This can be used to allocate resources more efficiently.

Corresponding to these two perspectives are two traditional approaches to the role of information in financial systems. The first comes from the general equilibrium and rational expectations literatures on the role of prices in resource allocation. The second comes from the intermediation literature and is concerned with the role of banks as delegated monitors. I will consider each in turn. Based on the first approach, it is sometimes argued that since market-based financial systems have many more prices that are publicly observed, they allocate resources better than bank-based systems. Similarly, based on the second approach it is sometimes argued that bank-based systems do better. As will be seen, these simplistic arguments ignore many important factors.

3.5.1 Prices and Information

The standard neoclassical view of prices, which originated with Adam Smith's 'invisible hand', is that they are indicators of scarcity and value. The modern version of this theory is captured in the Arrow–Debreu–Mackenzie (ADM) model and the fundamental theorems of welfare economics. If markets are complete and certain other restrictions are satisfied, markets allow a Pareto-efficient allocation of resources.

The neoclassical theory of resource allocation, which culminated in the ADM theory, was initially developed under the assumption of certainty. Under these conditions, decision-making is relatively simple. How firms should make investment decisions to maximize their value is the subject of capital budgeting. Over the years, it has become a mainstay of the curriculum in most business schools. It has been expounded in numerous textbooks (see, e.g., Brealey et al. 2011). According to the methodology outlined in these books, managers first need to derive the stream of cash flows that will accrue to shareholders over time, including the initial cost of the investment. This is done using various types of information. Projections based on accounting data generated within the firm usually play an important part. Once the cash flows have been calculated, they are discounted at the opportunity cost of capital for each period. Net present value (NPV) is obviously maximized by accepting positive NPV projects and rejecting negative NPV projects. There are a number of other capital budgeting methods such as internal rate of return (IRR) and profitability index (PI) which are widely used and are equivalent to NPV if correctly applied. I will focus on NPV below.

The discount rates that should be used are found from the term structure of interest rates. Since there is no uncertainty, markets are complete if every agent can borrow and lend at these rates. Then there is unanimous agreement among the shareholders about the optimal policy for the firm. Shareholders should simply tell the managers to follow the NPV rule (or an equivalent). If all managers follow this rule, the allocation of resources within the economy will be Pareto efficient. Furthermore, the actual mechanics of decentralizing decisions from shareholders to managers are particularly simple. The information that shareholders need to convey to managers is minimal. The shareholders do not need to tell the managers anything except 'Maximize NPV'. In particular, they do not need to tell the managers their preferences or the discount rates that should be used. The managers can observe the term structure of interest rates themselves.

The assumption of certainty on which this whole theory is based is, of course, unrealistic. However, all the important elements of the theory carry through with uncertainty provided markets are complete. In other words, provided there are markets at the initial date for all goods and services contingent on every possible state of nature, the introduction of uncertainty has no effect as far as firms are concerned. A firm buys all its inputs and sells all its outputs on a contingent basis, before any uncertainty is resolved. Consequently, the firm's profits and market value are known for sure at the initial date when all decisions are made.

In the case of certainty the main informational role of financial markets is to provide the term structure of interest rates. Stock markets are informationally redundant since the value of the firm can easily be calculated from the prices of inputs and outputs and interest rates. Since both market-based and bank-based financial systems have a term structure of interest rates that can be publicly observed by all agents, there is essentially no difference between them. The fact that bank-based systems do not have stock market prices available is of no consequence for resource allocation. A similar argument can be made in the case where there is uncertainty and markets are complete.

The weakness of this argument is that, in practice, markets are not complete. How can firms make decisions in this case? Corporate finance textbook expositions of capital budgeting techniques suggest a simple method of calculating the effect of an investment decision on the value of the firm in this situation. The stream of certain cash flows is replaced with a stream of expected cash flows and the present value is calculated using a discount rate from an asset pricing model estimated from historical price data. The model that is typically used is the capital asset pricing model (CAPM). In order to calculate the discount rate using the CAPM, it is necessary to have historical data from the stock market on the covariance of returns for the firm's stock with the market portfolio (a value-weighted portfolio consisting of all the stocks in the market). It is possible to show that if firms adopt this method, there will be an efficient allocation of resources in a stock market economy provided some firms are listed in every industry (see, e.g., Allen and Gale 2000a, Ch. 7). Thus, a stock market provides the information that is necessary for efficient decentralization. Stock market prices provide information in the sense that they allow the asset pricing model to be estimated. They are no longer redundant.

In the frameworks discussed so far, information is public. An important issue in the literature has been the process by which private information becomes reflected in prices; in other words, their role as aggregators of information. One of the questions that received considerable attention in the 1960s and 1970s is the extent to which stock markets are informationally efficient and reflect all the available information. The notion implicit in much of this research is that if stock prices are informationally efficient, they would provide a good mechanism for allocating investment resources. This view is well exposited by Fama (1976, p. 133) who wrote:

> An efficient capital market is an important component of a capitalist system. In such a system, the ideal is a market where prices are accurate signals for capital allocation. That is, when firms issue securities to finance their activities they can expect to get 'fair' prices, and when investors choose among the securities that represent ownership of firms' activities, they can do so under the assumption they are paying 'fair' prices. In short, if the capital market is to function smoothly in allocating resources, prices of securities must be good indicators of value.

Extensive evidence was provided during the 1960s and 1970s that markets are efficient in the sense that investors pay 'fair' prices and it is not possible to make excess returns above the reward for bearing risk using information that is publicly available. This is termed 'semi-strong form efficiency'. There was some evidence that even using apparently private information, it is not possible to make excess returns. This is termed 'strong form efficiency'. More recently, studies have been less supportive. For coverage of the empirical literature on efficient markets see Fama and French (2008).

Grossman (1976) developed a theoretical model based on rational expectations to show how private signals obtained by investors could become incorporated in prices, so that apparently private information became public. If an investor has favourable information, they will buy the security and bid up its price, while if they have unfavourable information they will sell and bid down the price. Grossman was able to show that, under certain conditions, prices aggregate all the economically relevant private information. This result provides a theoretical underpinning for the notion of prices as aggregators of information and led to a large literature on information revelation, including Grossman and Stiglitz (1980), Hellwig (1980) and Diamond and Verrecchia (1981). For surveys see Admati (1989).

An important point, which is often disregarded in discussions of financial systems, is that informational efficiency and welfare (Pareto) efficiency are different things (see, e.g., Dow and Gorton 1997; Allen and Gale 2000a, Ch. 7). In special cases, full revelation of information through market prices or in some other way can lead to the first-best, as the above quote from Fama suggests. In other words, informational efficiency is equivalent to Pareto efficiency. However, this need not be true in general. For example, in order to reveal information, prices have to fluctuate with changes in underlying information; but price fluctuations themselves are costly to the extent that they impose risk of uninsured changes in wealth on investors. There is therefore a trade-off between allocative efficiency and risk sharing. This is similar to the point made by Hirshleifer (1971) that the public release of information can destroy valuable risk-sharing opportunities.

3.5.2   Delegated Monitoring and Banks

One of the arguments that is often put forward in favour of bank-based systems is that banks form long-term relationships with firms and thus allow various informational problems to be solved. In Japan this is called the main bank system, while in Germany it is called the *hausbank* system. The problem that is of particular interest here is that borrowers must take some action to make proper use of the funds they have borrowed. This action could be the level of effort, or choice of project from among various different risky alternatives. The borrower can always claim that a low outcome is due to bad luck rather than from not taking the correct action. Lenders cannot observe the borrower's action unless they pay a fixed cost to monitor the borrower. In a financial market with many lenders, there is a free-rider problem. Each lender is small, so it is not worth paying the fixed cost. Everybody would like to free-ride, leaving it to someone else to bear the monitoring cost. As a result, no monitoring will be done.

A possible solution is to hire a single monitor to check what the borrower is doing. The problem then becomes one of monitoring the monitor, to make sure they actually monitor the borrowers. Diamond (1984) develops a model of delegated monitoring to solve this problem. Intermediaries have a diversified portfolio of projects for which they provide finance. They precommit to monitor borrowers by promising lenders a fixed return. If the intermediary does not monitor, then it will be unable to pay the promised return to lenders. Diamond's model thus illustrates how intermediaries and, in particular, banks have an incentive to act as a delegated monitor and produce the information necessary for an efficient allocation of resources.

Boot and Thakor (1997a) develop a model of financial system architecture that builds on this view of banks as delegated monitors. They assume there are three types of information problem. The first is that there is incomplete information about the future projects a firm has available to it. Outside investors can gather information about this type of information. The second problem is that lenders cannot observe whether borrowers invest the funds in a risky or safe project. The third problem is the likelihood that borrowers will have the opportunity to invest in a risky project. Boot and Thakor are able to show that the first problem can best be solved by a financial market, and the second and third problems can best be solved by intermediaries. They argue that banks will predominate in an emerging financial system, while the informational advantages of markets may allow them to develop in a mature financial system.

Boot and Thakor (1997b) compare various aspects of different financial systems. The important characteristic of financial markets in their models is that prices reveal information. This is what differentiates financial markets from financial institutions. They show that financial innovation occurs more often in a system where commercial and investment banking are separated, than in a system with universal banking.

3.6　CORPORATE GOVERNANCE

In most countries, including the US, the UK, Japan and France, managers of corporations are ultimately responsible to the shareholders. However, the details of corporation law differ across countries. The common origins of company law in the US and UK have led to a similar structure. In both countries, managers have a fiduciary duty; that is, they have a strong legal requirement to act in the interests of shareholders. The official channel through which shareholders influence company affairs is the board of directors, elected by the shareholders, typically on the basis of one share, one vote. The board of directors is a mixture of outside and inside directors, the latter being the top executives in the firm. The role of management is to implement the policies determined by the board. Shareholders have very little say beyond electing directors. For example, it is the directors who decide their own compensation without any input from shareholders. A committee of outside directors determines the senior management's compensation. Except in unusual circumstances, such as a proxy fight, the outside directors are nominated by the incumbent management and thus typically owe their allegiance to the chief executive officer (CEO).

Japan resembles the US in terms of the legal form of corporations because of the heavy influence of the US Occupation Forces on the legal system and the structure of institutions after the Second World War. Some important differences do exist, however. In the past, non-financial corporations faced elaborate restrictions that prevented them from establishing holding companies. The rights of Japanese shareholders are in theory greater than those of shareholders in the US and UK. For example, in Japan it is easier for shareholders to nominate and elect directors.

Germany has a very different type of governance structure than the US, the UK or Japan. The system of co-determination, which has a long history, arose in the late nineteenth century from an attempt to overcome the contradiction between the reality of industrialization and liberal ideas about the self-determination and the rights of individuals (Pistor 1996). Currently the most important legislation governing it is the Co-determination Act (*Mitbestimmungsgesetz*) of 1976. This generally applies to companies with more than 2000 employees.

Firms to which it applies have two boards: the supervisory board and the management board. The supervisory board is the controlling body. As outlined in Prowse (1995), half of the representatives are elected by shareholders and the other half by the employees. The shareholders' general meeting elects the shareholder representatives. Two-thirds of the employee representatives work for the company, while the other third are trade union representatives. The supervisory board elects a chairman and deputy chairman from its members. The chairman is usually from the shareholder side, while the deputy chairman is from the employee side. In the event of a tie in the voting of the supervisory board, the chairman has a casting vote. It is in this sense that shareholders have ultimate control.

However, members of the supervisory board legally represent the interests of the company as a whole and not just the groups they represent.

The German system provides an interesting contrast to the Anglo-American and Japanese systems. It is often argued that the dual board system better represents outside shareholders and ensures management must take account of their views. In addition, employees' views are also represented and their bias is presumably to ensure the long-run viability of the firm.

France has a system which contains elements of both the Anglo-American and the German systems. Firms can choose between two types of boards of directors. The first type, which is more common, is single-tiered as in the Anglo-American system. The board elects the *président directeur-général* (PDG) who is like a CEO but more powerful. He or she has the sole right to 'represent' the company and is the only person who can delegate this power. Single-tiered boards mostly consist of outside directors who are shareholders and representatives from financial institutions with which the firm has transactional relationships. As in the Anglo-American model, the board determines business policies which are then carried out by the PDG and management.

The second type of board has two tiers, as in Germany. The *conseil de surveillance* is like the German supervisory board except that employees do not have the right to representation. However, one unique feature of the French system which makes it more akin to the German one is that with single-tiered and two-tiered boards workers' representatives have the right to attend board meetings as observers, in all companies with at least 50 employees. The *conseil de surveillance* appoints the *directoire* who have responsibility for the management of the company. One of the members of the *directoire* is designated *président de directoire* by the others.

In their seminal book, Berle and Means (1932) argued that, in practice, managers pursued their own interests rather than the interests of shareholders. The contractual aspect of the firm together with the problem highlighted by Berle and Means led to the development of the agency approach to corporate governance by, among others, Coase (1937), Jensen and Meckling (1976), Fama and Jensen (1983a, 1983b) and Hart (1995). An excellent account of the literature is contained in Goergen (2012). The literature describes a number of corporate governance mechanisms that encourage managers to act in the interests of the shareholders.

3.6.1   The Board of Directors

The board of directors is, in theory at least, the first mechanism that shareholders have to control managers and ensure the company is run in their interest. As discussed above, the way that boards are chosen and structured differs significantly across countries. Although the structure of boards is different across countries, the limited empirical evidence available suggests that they are equally effective (or ineffective) at disciplining management. Mace (1971), Weisbach (1988) and Jensen (1989) document the weakness of US boards in disciplining managers. Bhagat and Black (1998) survey the literature on the relationship between board composition and firm performance. The evidence indicates that boards with a majority of independent directors do not perform better than firms without such boards.

However, it does seem that having a moderate number of inside directors is associated with greater profitability. Kaplan (1994a, 1994b) has conducted studies of the relationship between management turnover and various performance measures in Japan, Germany and the US. His findings indicate a similar relationship in each of the countries. Kang and Shivdasani (1995) confirm these results for Japan and also provide evidence on the effectiveness of different types of governance mechanisms. Among other things, they find that the presence of outside directors on the board has no effect on the sensitivity of top executive turnover to either earnings or stock-price performance. In contrast, concentrated equity ownership and ties to a main bank do have a positive effect. For Germany, Franks and Mayer (2001) find a strong relationship between poorly performing companies and turnover on management boards, but not with turnover on supervisory boards.

3.6.2   Executive Compensation

An additional method of ensuring that managers pursue the interests of shareholders is to structure compensation appropriately. Diamond and Verrecchia (1982), Holmstrom and Tirole (1993) and Dow and Gorton (1997) have developed models where compensation is conditioned on the firm's stock price and this reflects information gathered by analysts. Stock prices are not the only contingency that can be used to motivate managers. Accounting-based performance measures are also frequently used. Managers who perform extremely well may be bid away at higher compensation levels to other companies. The managerial labour market thus also plays an important part in providing incentives to managers. There has been some debate about the optimal sensitivity of executive compensation to stock price in practice. Jensen and Murphy (1990) confirm previous findings of a positive relationship between executive pay and performance in the US, and estimate that CEO compensation varies by about $3 for every $1000 change in firm value. They suggest that this figure is much too small. Haubrich (1994) has calibrated an appropriately designed principal–agent model which takes into account risk aversion, and argues that a small sensitivity is optimal for reasonable parameter values. For other countries, the number of empirical studies is small. Kaplan (1994a, 1994b) considers the sensitivity of pay and dismissal to performance in Germany and Japan. He finds that they are similar to the US in this respect.

3.6.3   The Market for Corporate Control

Manne (1965) has argued that an active market for corporate control is essential for the efficient operation of capitalist economies. It allows able management teams to gain control of large amounts of resources in a small amount of time. Inefficient managers are removed and replaced with people who are better able to do the job. The existence of a market for corporate control also provides one means of disciplining managers. If a firm is pursuing policies which do not maximize shareholders' wealth it can be taken over and the managers replaced.

The market for corporate control can operate through proxy contests, friendly mergers and hostile takeovers. Theoretical analyses of proxy fights, which throw some light on why they do not work well, are contained in Bhattacharya (1997) and Maug and Yilmaz (2002).

The third way in which the market for corporate control can operate is through hostile takeovers. This mechanism is potentially very important in ensuring an efficient allocation of resources in the way Manne (1965) suggested. However, Grossman and Hart (1980) have pointed to a problem with the operation of this mechanism of corporate governance. Existing shareholders will have a strong incentive to free-ride on raiders who plan to increase the value of the firm. On the one hand, if the price offered by the raider is below the price that the new policies will justify and the shareholder believes the offer will succeed, then there is no point in tendering. However, in that case the offer will not succeed. On the other hand, if the raider offers a price above the current value and the shareholder believes that the offer will not succeed, then it will be worth tendering his shares. But then the offer will succeed. In both cases, the shareholder's beliefs are inconsistent with equilibrium. The only equilibrium is one in which the raider's offer price is equal to the price the new policies will justify. In that case, the raider's profit will be zero, before allowing for any costs incurred in undertaking the bid. If these costs are included, the profit will be negative and there will be no incentive to attempt a takeover.

A number of solutions to the free-rider problem have been suggested. Grossman and Hart's (1980) solution is that corporate charters should be structured so that raiders can dilute minority shareholders' interests after the takeover occurs. This means the raider can offer a price below the post-takeover value of the firm to him, and the bid still succeeds. Existing shareholders will know that if they retain their shares the raider will dilute their interest. Shleifer and Vishny (1986) pointed out that if the raider can acquire a block of stock before attempting a takeover at the low pre-takeover price, there will be a profit on this block even if all the remaining shares are purchased at the full price justified by the raider's plans. Burkart (1995) shows that it is privately optimal for a large shareholder to overbid, and this can lead to possible losses and inefficiencies.

In addition to the Grossman and Hart free-rider problem there are a number of other problems with the operation of the market for corporate control. One is that once a takeover bid is announced, other raiders will realize it is an attractive target and will bid. This will mean that it is not possible for the initial firm to recoup any fixed costs from identifying the target in the first place. The third problem in the operation of the market for corporate control is the possibility of management entrenchment. Managers may be incompetent and want to prevent a takeover to preserve their jobs.

Why do these differences in the number of hostile takeovers between the US and UK and other countries exist? A standard explanation for the difference in the occurrence of takeovers across countries is the prevalence of cross-shareholdings in Japan and the structure of holding companies and cross-shareholdings in Germany and France that make it difficult to acquire the necessary number of shares.

3.6.4   Concentrated Holdings and Monitoring by Financial Institutions

Stiglitz (1985) has argued that one of the most important ways that value maximization by firms can be ensured is through concentrated ownership of the firm's shares. Shleifer and Vishny (1986), Huddart (1993) and Admati et al. (1994) all model equity-financed firms which have one large shareholder and a fringe of smaller ones. In all these models, more wealth commitment by owners increases monitoring and firm performance. Shleifer and Vishny find that firm value increases with the large shareholder's holding, but this need not be true. In Huddart (1993) and Admati et al. (1994) the reverse can occur because the large shareholder is risk-averse.

A number of theoretical analyses have reconsidered important aspects of concentrated ownership. Burkart et al. (1997) consider the costs and benefits of monitoring by large shareholders. They show that such monitoring may restrict the misuse of resources *ex post*, but may also blunt *ex ante* managerial initiative. There is a trade-off between control and initiative. Bolton and von Thadden (1998a, 1998b) develop a framework to analyse the trade-off between liquidity and control. Large blocks result in incentives to monitor but also lead to a lack of liquidity. Pagano and Röell (1998) consider the trade-off between public and private ownership and monitoring. With private ownership there is monitoring because of shareholder concentration but no liquidity. Going public is costly and public ownership results in less monitoring but greater liquidity.

The importance of equity ownership by financial institutions in Japan and Germany, and the lack of a market for corporate control in these countries, have led to the suggestion that the agency problem in these countries is solved by financial institutions acting as outside monitors for large corporations. In Japan, this system of monitoring is known as the main bank system. The characteristics of this system are the long-term relationship between a bank and its client firm, the holding of both debt and equity by the bank, and the active intervention of the bank should its client become financially distressed. It has been widely argued that this main bank relationship ensures that the bank acts as delegated monitor and helps to overcome the agency problem between managers and the firm. Hoshi et al. (1990a, 1990b, 1991) provide evidence that the main bank system helps firms by easing liquidity constraints, and reduces agency costs. They also document that firms reduced their bank ties in the 1980s as access to the bond market became easier.

In Germany, the data on concentration of ownership probably understate the significance of the banks' effective position. The reason is that many bank customers keep their shares on deposit at banks and allow banks to exercise proxies on their behalf. As a result, banks control a higher proportion of voting equity and have more representation on boards of large industrial enterprises than their direct holdings suggest. A 1978 Monopoly Commission study found that, of the top 100 corporations, banks controlled the votes of nearly 40 per cent of the equity and were represented on two-thirds of the boards. German banks thus tend to have very close ties with industry and form long-run relationships with firms. This is the *hausbank* system. A number of studies have provided evidence on the effectiveness of the outside monitoring of German banks. Cable (1985) and Gorton and Schmid (2000) find evidence that firms with a higher proportion of equity controlled by banks have better performance. This evidence is consistent with the hypothesis that bank involvement helps the performance of firms, but it is also consistent with the hypothesis that banks are good at picking winners.

3.6.5 Debt

An important strand of the corporate governance literature has focused on the role of debt as a means of disciplining managers. Grossman and

Hart (1982) were the first to argue that managers could precommit to work hard by using debt rather than equity. Similarly, Jensen's (1986) free cash flow theory suggested that debt could be used to prevent managers from squandering resources. In the late 1980s and early 1990s it was widely argued that leveraged buyouts (LBOs), whereby managers or other groups purchased firms using a large proportion of debt financing, were a response to agency problems. However, debt can have undesirable as well as desirable effects on managers' behaviour. Jensen and Meckling (1976) pointed out that managers have an incentive to take risks and may even accept projects that destroy value if significant amounts of debt are used. Myers (1977) pointed to the debt overhang problem where firms may forego good projects if they have significant debt outstanding. The reason is that for a firm facing financial distress, a large part of the returns to a good project go to bondholders.

Perhaps the most important weakness of the argument that debt is important for ensuring managerial discipline in corporations is the fact that retained earnings are the most important source of finance for corporations, as Table 3.2 indicates. In most countries, debt is much less important than retained earnings. Typically, large corporations can service their debt without difficulty, that is, without constraining their operations or investment plans.

3.6.6   Product Market Competition

It has been argued (see, e.g., Alchian 1950; Stigler 1958) that competition in product markets is a very powerful force for solving the agency problem between owners and managers. If the managers of a firm waste or consume large amounts of resources, the firm will be unable to compete and will go bankrupt. There is little doubt that competition, particularly internationally, is a powerful force in ensuring effective corporate governance.

Competition between different organizational forms may be helpful in limiting efficiency losses. If a family-owned business has the sole objective of maximizing share value, it may force all the corporations in that industry to do the same thing. Hart (1983) develops a model based on this idea. Unobservable effort leads to 'managerial slack'. Using the assumption that managers are infinitely risk-averse at a particular level of income, Hart is able to show that aggregate output is lower and price is higher than in the first-best, where every action is contractible. Scharfstein (1988) shows that if the manager's marginal utility of income is strictly positive, increased competition can increase rather than reduce managerial slack. Schmidt (1997) addresses a related question in a model without hidden information. He observes that increased competition may threaten the survival of a firm by forcing it into bankruptcy, and asks what effect this may have on managerial slack. As in Scharfstein (1988), he demonstrates that increased competition does not necessarily reduce managerial slack.

Allen and Gale (2000b) depart from the agency approach and argue that motivating managers is not the main problem in the modern corporation. They view the top management of firms as being 'entrepreneurial' in that they choose the direction of the firm and assign crucial tasks to subordinates. Shareholders' concern is not whether managers work hard but whether they have the 'right stuff'. If product markets are competitive, then good firms can push out bad firms and capture the market. This contrasts with the standard story in which companies with underperforming managements are taken over by corporate raiders.

3.7 CONCLUDING REMARKS

This chapter has considered the role of financial intermediaries and markets in allocating finance to firms in different countries. The US and UK have rather different institutions than France, Germany and Japan. Which system is superior is not at all clear cut. Each system has different advantages and disadvantages.

REFERENCES

Admati, A. (1989), 'Information in financial markets: the rational expectations approach', in S. Bhattacharya and G.M. Constantinides (eds), *Financial Markets and Incomplete Information: Frontiers of Modern Financial Theory*, Volume 2, Totowa, NJ: Rowman & Littlefield, pp. 139–152.

Admati, A., P. Pfleiderer and J. Zechner (1994), 'Large shareholder activism, risk sharing, and financial market equilibrium', *Journal of Political Economy*, **102**, 1097–1130.

Alchian, A. (1950), 'Uncertainty, evolution, and economic theory', *Journal of Political Economy*, **58**, 211–221.

Allen, F., F. Capie, C. Fohlin, H. Miyajima, R. Sylla, G. Wood and Y. Yafeh (2010), 'How important historically were financial systems for growth in the UK, US, Germany, and Japan?' Working Paper 10-27, Wharton Financial Institutions Center, University of Pennsylvania.

Allen, F. and D. Gale (1997), 'Financial markets, intermediaries, and intertemporal smoothing', *Journal of Political Economy*, **105**, 523–546.

Allen, F. and D. Gale (1999), 'Diversity of opinion and the financing of new technologies', *Journal of Financial Intermediation*, **8**, 68–89.

Allen, F. and D. Gale (2000a), *Comparing Financial Systems*, Cambridge, MA: MIT Press.

Allen, F. and D. Gale (2000b), 'Corporate governance and competition', in X. Vives (ed.), *Corporate Governance: Theoretical and Empirical Perspectives*, Cambridge: Cambridge University Press, pp. 23–94.

Bagehot, W. (1962 [1873]), *Lombard Street*, Homewood, IL: Irwin.

Bencivenga, V. and B. Smith (1991), 'Financial intermediation and endogenous growth', *Review of Economic Studies*, **58**, 195–209.

Bencivenga, V., B. Smith and R. Starr (1995), 'Transactions costs, technological choice, and endogenous growth', *Journal of Economic Theory*, **67**, 53–177.

Berle, A. and G. Means (1932), *The Modern Corporation and Private Property*, Chicago, IL: Commerce Clearing House.

Bertero, E. (1994), 'The banking system, financial markets, and capital structure: some new evidence from France', *Oxford Review of Economic Policy*, **10**, 68–78.

Bhagat, S. and B. Black (1998), 'The uncertain relationship between board composition and firm performance', in K. Hopt, M. Roe and E. Wymeersch (eds), *Corporate Governance: The State of the Art and Emerging Research*, New York: Oxford University Press, pp. 281–306.

Bhattacharya, U. (1997), 'Communication costs, information acquisition, and voting decisions in proxy contests', *Review of Financial Studies*, **10**, 1065–1097.

Bolton, P. and E. von Thadden (1998a), 'Blocks, liquidity, and corporate control', *Journal of Finance*, **53**, 1–25.

Bolton, P. and E. von Thadden (1998b), 'Liquidity and control: a dynamic theory of corporate ownership structure', *Journal of Institutional and Theoretical Economics*, **154**, 177–223.

Boot, A. and A. Thakor (1997a), 'Financial system architecture', *Review of Financial Studies*, **10**, 693–733.

Boot, A. and A. Thakor (1997b), 'Banking scope and financial innovation', *Review of Financial Studies*, **10**, 1099–1131.

Boyd, J. and B. Smith (1996), 'The co-evolution of the real and financial sectors in the growth process', *World Bank Economic Review*, **10**, 371–396.

Boyd, J. and B. Smith (1998), 'The evolution of debt and equity markets in economic development', *Economic Theory*, **12**, 519–560.

Brealey, R., S. Myers and F. Allen (2011), *Principles of Corporate Finance*, 10th edn, New York: McGraw Hill Irwin.

Burkart, M. (1995), 'Initial shareholdings and overbidding in takeover contests', *Journal of Finance*, **50**, 1491–1515.

Burkart, M., D. Gromb and F. Panunzi (1997), 'Large shareholders, monitoring, and the value of the firm', *Quarterly Journal of Economics*, **112**, 693–728.

Cable, J. (1985), 'Capital market information and industrial performance', *Economic Journal*, **95**, 118–132.

Coase, R. (1937), 'The nature of the firm', *Economica*, **4**, 386–405.

Corbett, J. and T. Jenkinson (1996), 'The financing of industry, 1970–1989: an international comparison', *Journal of the Japanese and International Economies*, **10**, 71–96.

Demirgüç-Kunt, A. and V. Maksimovic (1996), 'Stock market development and financing choices of firms', *World Bank Economic Review*, **10**, 341–370.

Demirgüç-Kunt, A. and V. Maksimovic (1998), 'Law, finance, and firm growth', *Journal of Finance*, **53**, 2107–2137.

Diamond, D. (1984), 'Financial intermediation and delegated monitoring', *Review of Economic Studies*, **51**, 393–414.

Diamond, D. and R. Verrecchia (1981), 'Information aggregation in a noisy rational expectations economy', *Journal of Financial Economics*, **9**, 221–235.

Diamond, D. and R. Verrecchia (1982), 'Optimal managerial contracts and equilibrium security prices', *Journal of Finance*, **37**, 275–287.

Dow, J. and G. Gorton (1997), 'Stock market efficiency and economic efficiency: is there a connection?', *Journal of Finance*, **52**, 1087–1129.

Fama, E. (1976), *Foundations of Finance*, New York: Basic Books.

Fama, E. and K. French (2008), 'Dissecting anomalies', *Journal of Finance*, **63**, 1653–1678.

Fama, E. and M. Jensen (1983a), 'Separation of ownership and control', *Journal of Law and Economics*, **26**, 301–325.

Fama, E. and M. Jensen (1983b), 'Agency problems and residuals claims', *Journal of Law and Economics*, **26**, 327–349.

Franks, J. and C. Mayer (2001), 'Ownership and control in Germany', *Review of Financial Studies*, **14**, 943–977.

Gerschenkron, A. (1962), *Economic Backwardness in Historical Perspective*, Cambridge, MA: Harvard University Press.

Goergen, M. (2012), *International Corporate Governance*, Harlow: Prentice Hall.

Goldsmith, R. (1969), *Financial Structure and Development*, New Haven, CT: Yale University Press.

Gorton, G. and F. Schmid (2000), 'Universal banking and the performance of German firms', *Journal of Financial Economics*, **58**, 29–80.

Greenwood, J. and B. Jovanovic (1990), *Journal of Political Economy*, **98**, 1076–1107.

Grossman, S. (1976), 'On the efficiency of competitive stock markets where traders have diverse information', *Journal of Finance*, **31**, 573–585.

Grossman, S. and O. Hart (1980), 'Takeover bids, the free-rider problem, and the theory of the corporation', *Bell Journal of Economics*, **11**, 42–64.

Grossman, S. and O. Hart (1982), 'Corporate financial structure and managerial incentives', in J. McCall (ed.), *The Economics of Information and Uncertainty*, Chicago, IL: University of Chicago Press, pp. 107–140.

Grossman, S. and J. Stiglitz (1980), 'On the impossibility of informationally efficient markets', *American Economic Review*, **70**, 393–408.

Hart, O. (1983), 'The market mechanism as an incentive scheme', *Bell Journal of Economics*, **14**, 366–382.

Hart, O. (1995), *Firms, Contracts and Financial Structure*, Oxford: Clarendon Press.

Haubrich, J. (1994), 'Risk aversion, performance pay, and the principal–agent problem', *Journal of Political Economy*, **102**, 258–276.

Hellwig, M. (1980), 'On the aggregation of information in competitive markets', *Journal of Economic Theory*, **22**, 477–498.

Hicks, J. (1969), *A Theory of Economic History*, Oxford: Clarendon Press.

Hirshleifer, J. (1971), 'The private and social value of information and the reward to inventive activity', *American Economic Review*, **61**, 561–574.

Holmstrom, B. and J. Tirole (1993), 'Market liquidity and performance monitoring', *Journal of Political Economy*, **101**, 678–709.

Hoshi, T., A. Kashyap and D. Scharfstein (1990a), 'Bank monitoring and investment: evidence from the changing structure of Japanese corporate banking relationships', in R.G. Hubbard (ed.), *Asymmetric Information, Corporate Finance and Investment*, Chicago, IL: Chicago University Press, pp. 105–126.

Hoshi, T., A. Kashyap and D. Scharfstein (1990b), 'The role of banks in reducing the costs of financial distress in Japan', *Journal of Financial Economics*, **27**, 67–68.

Hoshi, T., A. Kashyap and D. Scharfstein (1991), 'Corporate structure, liquidity and investment: evidence from Japanese industrial groups', *Quarterly Journal of Economics*, **106**, 33–60.

Huddart, S. (1993), 'The effect of a large shareholder on corporate value', *Management Science*, **39**, 1407–1421.

Jensen, M. (1986), 'Agency costs of free cash flow, corporate finance, and takeovers', *American Economic Review*, **76**, 323–329.

Jensen, M. (1989), 'The eclipse of the public corporation', *Harvard Business Review*, **67**, 60–70.

Jensen, M. and W. Meckling (1976), 'Theory of the firm: managerial behavior, agency costs and ownership structure', *Journal of Financial Economics*, **3**, 305–360.

Jensen, M. and K. Murphy (1990), 'Performance pay and top-management incentives', *Journal of Political Economy*, **98**, 225–264.

Kang, J. and A. Shivdasani (1995), 'Firm performance, corporate governance, and top executive turnover in Japan', *Journal of Financial Economics*, **38**, 29–58.

Kaplan, S. (1994a), 'Top executives, turnover, and firm performance in Germany', *Journal of Law, Economics, and Organization*, **10**, 142–159.

Kaplan, S. (1994b), 'Top executive rewards and firm performance: a comparison of Japan and the United States', *Journal of Political Economy*, **102**, 510–546.

King, R. and R. Levine (1993a), 'Financial intermediation and economic development', in C. Mayer and X. Vives (eds), *Financial Intermediation in the Construction of Europe*, London: Center for Economic Policy Research, pp. 156–189.

King, R. and R. Levine (1993b), 'Finance and growth: Schumpeter might be right', *Quarterly Journal of Economics*, **108**, 717–738.

King, R. and R. Levine (1993c), 'Finance, entrepreneurship, and growth: theory and evidence', *Journal of Monetary Economics*, **32**, 513–542.

Levine, R. (2002), 'Bank-based or market-based financial systems: which is better?' *Journal of Financial Intermediation*, **11**, 398–428.

Levine, R. and S. Zervos (1998), 'Stock markets, banks and economic growth', *American Economic Review*, **88**, 537–558.

Mace, M. (1971), *Directors, Myth and Reality*, Boston, MA: Harvard Business School Press.

Manne, H. (1965), 'Mergers and the market for corporate control', *Journal of Political Economy*, **73**, 110–120.

Maug, E. and B. Yilmaz (2002), 'Two-class voting: a mechanism for conflict resolution?' *American Economic Review*, **92**, 1448–1471.

Mayer, C. (1988), 'New issues in corporate finance', *European Economic Review*, **32**, 1167–1188.

Mayer, C. (1990), 'Financial systems, corporate finance, and economic development', in R.G. Hubbard (ed.), *Asymmetric Information, Corporate Finance and Investment*, Chicago, IL: University of Chicago Press, pp. 307–332.

McKinnon, R. (1973), *Money and Capital in Economic Development*, Washington, DC: Brookings Institution.

Myers, S. (1977), 'Determinants of corporate borrowing', *Journal of Financial Economics*, **5**, 147–175.

Pagano, M. and A. Röell (1998), 'The choice of stock ownership structure: agency costs, monitoring and the decision to go public', *Quarterly Journal of Economics*, **113**, 187–225.

Pistor, K. (1996), 'Co-determination in Germany: a socio-political model with governance externalities', Conference on Employees and Corporate Governance, Columbia Law School, 22 November.

Prowse, S. (1995), 'Corporate governance in an international perspective: a survey of corporate control mechanisms among large firms in the US, UK, Japan and Germany', *Financial Markets, Institutions and Instr*uments, **4**, 1–63.

Rajan, R. and L. Zingales (1998), 'Financial dependence and growth', *American Economic Review*, **88**, 559–586.

Rajan, R. and L. Zingales (2001), 'Financial systems, industrial structure and growth', *Oxford Review of Economic Policy*, **17**, 467–482.

Robinson, J. (1952), 'The generalization of the General Theory', *The Rate of Interest and Other Essays*, London: Macmillan, pp. 67–142.

Saint-Paul, G. (1982), 'Technological choice, financial markets and economic development', *European Economic Review*, **36**, 763–781.

Scharfstein, D. (1988), 'Product market competition and managerial slack', *RAND Journal of Economics*, **19**, 147–155.

Schmidt, K. (1997), 'Managerial incentives and product market competition', *Review of Economic Studies*, **64**, 191–214.

Shleifer, A. and R. Vishny (1986), 'Large shareholders and corporate control', *Journal of Political Economy*, **94**, 461–488.

Stigler, G. (1958), 'The economies of scale', *Journal of Law and Economics*, **1**, 54–71.

Stiglitz, J. (1985), 'Credit markets and the control of capital', *Journal of Money, Credit and Banking*, **17**, 133–152.

Tadesse, S. (2002), 'Financial architecture and economic performance: international evidence', *Journal of Financial Intermediation*, **11**, 429–454.

Weisbach, M. (1988), 'Outside directors and CEO turnover', *Journal of Financial Economics*, **20**, 431–460.

4   Anglo-Saxon capitalism in crisis? Models of liberal capitalism and the preconditions for financial stability
Sue Konzelmann and Marc Fovargue-Davies

4.1   INTRODUCTION

The comparative capitalism literature sees national business systems as 'configurations of institutions', where different socio-economic institutions are interconnected in coherent, non-random ways (Jackson and Deeg 2008). From a comparative perspective it is argued that different countries cluster into a limited number of 'models' (Albert 1993; Whitley 2000; Hall and Soskice 2001; Amable 2003). Whilst different classifications exist, virtually all of them group the six Anglo-Saxon countries into the same category of market-based, shareholder-oriented or 'liberal market economies' (LMEs).

The similarities in the institutional configuration of the Anglo-Saxon economies would lead us to predict similar conditions for doing business and comparable economic trajectories. However the 2008 financial crisis has demonstrated that the broad categorizations of models of capitalism may conceal important differences among these LMEs. Indeed, the Anglo-Saxon variety of capitalism groups some of the worst-hit countries with countries whose financial systems were remarkably stable during the crisis. As evident in the *Financial Times* ranking of the 50 largest banks by market capitalization (*Financial Times* 2009), between 1999 and 2009, American and British banks had lost considerable ground whilst those of the two other main Anglo-Saxon countries, Canada and Australia, clearly gained. This casts doubt on the conclusion that the 2008 crisis represents a crisis of Anglo-Saxon capitalism as such.

This chapter examines the question of why the four main Anglo-Saxon countries experienced the 2008 financial crisis in such divergent ways, despite their similar cultural attributes, legal origins (La Porta et al. 1997) and institutional configuration (Hall and Soskice 2001). Of particular interest are the reasons behind the rise to dominance of the British and American financial sectors – and the resulting shift in the balance of the economy in their favour. This is in sharp contrast to the Canadian and Australian systems, where greater restraint prevented a similar outcome.

We explore how political, ideational and historical factors led to different approaches to the regulation of the financial industry, focusing on the influences shaping the process of economic liberalization in each country and their effect on the evolution of corporate governance. Our analysis reveals a clear division in the interpretation of liberal economic theory and the way it was applied. This gave rise to more than just the 'fundamentalist' neoclassical incarnation, characteristic of both British and American capitalism; by contrast, the Canadian and Australian systems evolved in a more balanced way, producing an apparently more stable result. From this, it is hard to escape the conclusion that there is in fact no such a thing as 'Anglo-Saxon capitalism', and consequently, no general failure of liberal capitalism per se. Instead, the 2008 crisis suggests the failing of a particular variety of economic liberalism, where the balance between the state and the private sector had become unsustainable.

We begin by examining the similarities among the four main Anglo-Saxon economies, and why, at first glance, they might have been expected to respond to a general crisis in comparable ways. We then consider the influences that caused the interpretation of liberal economic theory and its translation into policy to diverge – ultimately producing the two varieties discerned in our analysis. Finally we examine the role of regulation – deregulation and re-regulation – in the 2008 crisis before turning to our conclusions.

4.2   ONE CRISIS, TWO OUTCOMES

The United States (US), United Kingdom (UK), Canada and Australia, along with Ireland and New Zealand, constitute the 'Anglosphere' and are all within the LME variety of capitalism (Hall and Soskice 2001).[1] The four share a variety of features, stemming from their common historical and cultural heritage, that distinguish them from other advanced economies, notably continental Europe and Japan.

Yet, although many have interpreted the recent financial crisis as one of Anglo-Saxon capitalism, there are compelling differences in the relative resilience of the four countries' financial systems during the crisis. As evident in Table 4.1, compared with a decade earlier, the largest Canadian and Australian banks gained ground in terms of market capitalization whilst American and British banks lost heavily.[2] The contrast is even starker when the magnitude of bank bailouts is considered. By March 2009, American rescue packages amounted to 6.8 per cent of gross domestic products (GDP) and the UK's a staggering 19.8 per cent (Stewart 2009). By contrast, Australia used only 0.1 per cent of GDP to help struggling banks and Canada, nothing at all.[3]

Table 4.1   Change in bank market capitalization

	Change 1999–2009 ($bn)
Australia	+85.6
Canada	+97.5
UK	−211.4
USA	−633.0

Source: Financial Times (2009, 9). 1999 values are as of 31 May 1999; 2009 values are as of 17 March 2009.

From a comparative capitalism point of view, these differences are surprising. If the global financial crisis was a crisis of neoliberal, market-based capitalism, then Australia and Canada should have been equally vulnerable. Moreover, the macroeconomic imbalances, to which the recent crisis has been widely attributed (FSA 2009), were present in all four countries, to varying degrees.[4] Capital account liberalization combined with imbalances in household savings rates between Asia and the West, contributing to the availability – and uptake – of cheap and plentiful debt. In the largely post-industrial Anglo-Saxon economies, this money found its way into the consumer sector, inflating a property bubble and significantly increasing the ratio of mortgage debt to GDP.[5] Consumer leverage also rose; and mortgages were made at ever higher initial loan-to-value ratios, as borrowers and lenders assumed that debt burdens would ultimately fall as a result of continued house price appreciation. Asset bubbles are significantly associated with financial crises (Reinhart and Rogoff 2009), particularly when inflated prices are used as collateral to raise further debt.

Economic liberalization and deregulation since the early 1970s have also been identified as contributing factors in the crisis (FSA 2009; Reinhart and Rogoff 2009). But recent studies suggest that the four countries' trajectories were comparable and that they have all become considerably more 'liberal',[6] especially since the early 1980s. They were the four most liberalized of the Organisation for Economic Co-operation and Development (OECD) countries in 1980, a position they maintained in 2000, although the UK had overtaken Australia as the second most liberal after the US (Höpner et al. 2009). The effect of economic liberalization was particularly apparent in the four countries' financial sectors, which rapidly replaced manufacturing as the driver of employment and growth (Boyer 2000; Peters 2011). In 1970, the value added by banks, real estate and other business services accounted for 14.6 per cent of total value added in Australia, 17 per cent in Canada, 15.9 per cent in the UK and 17.5 per cent in the US. By the early 2000s, it had risen to 29.1 per cent in

Australia, 25.6 per cent in Canada, 30.1 per cent in the UK and 32.1 per cent in the US, whilst services as a proportion of employment represented 74.9 per cent in Australia, 74.7 per cent in Canada, 73.6 per cent in the UK and 77.5 per cent in the US (OECD 2009).

However, whilst Reinhart and Rogoff (2009) identify financial market liberalization as an important determinant of financial crises, the resilience of the Canadian and Australian banking systems suggests that this is not always the case, and that liberalization can be achieved without necessarily creating major instabilities.

4.3   CHANGING THE CONVENTIONAL WISDOM

In his book *The Affluent Society*, Galbraith argued that the 'conventional wisdom' in economics is inherently conservative and gives way not so much to new ideas as to 'the massive onslaught of circumstances with which [it] cannot contend' (Galbraith 1999, 17). This creates the environment in which different ideas find favour and reconstitute the conventional wisdom. Friedman (1982 [1962]) articulated the process by which new conventional wisdom becomes embedded in policy. In his view:

> Only a crisis – actual or perceived – produces real change. When that crisis occurs, the actions that are taken depend on the ideas that are lying around. That, I believe, is our basic function: to develop alternatives to existing policies, to keep them alive and available until the politically impossible becomes politically inevitable.

Once crisis had struck, Friedman believed that it was crucial to act swiftly, before the moment was overtaken by the 'tyranny of the status quo' (Friedman and Friedman 1984, 3).[7]

One example of this was the replacement of laissez-faire economic liberalism by Keynesian conventional wisdom, triggered by the mass unemployment and poverty of the interwar years, which eventually led to the state's management of the economy. The growing inflationary crisis of the 1970s also constituted a 'massive onslaught of circumstance'. But this time, the 'ideas lying around' were those of Friedman and the Chicago School economists and the conventional wisdom reverted to pre-Keynesian, liberal economic ideas, in which combating inflation depends on controlling the money supply, whilst efficiency in the use of resources is most effectively secured by markets. Similar developments can be observed in the evolution of theory and policy relating to corporate governance, with the efficient market hypothesis emerging to provide the orthodox explanation for – and justification of – the role of the stock market in reorganizing industry and its ownership.[8]

We are now potentially in the midst of another 'Galbraithian episode', giving rise to doubts about the conventional wisdom of economic liberalism, and debate about the future direction of theory and policy. However, the apparently sustainable economic liberalism evolved in Canada and Australia suggests that some incarnations of liberal theory may in fact be able to contend with that 'massive onslaught' after all.

In the following sections, we examine the underlying theories behind economic liberalism, the reasons for its ascendancy during the decades leading up to the 2008 financial crisis, and most crucially the varying processes of economic liberalization in the US, UK, Canada and Australia. We focus on the way that economic liberalism was understood and translated into policy; and we argue that this would define the relationship between the private sector and the state, the nature and extent of regulation, the relative position of the financial sector in the broader economy and, ultimately, the relative resilience of the system as a whole.

4.3.1 Keynesianism Displaced by the Promises of Economic Liberalism

Contemporary economic liberalism, particularly in Britain and America, was strongly influenced by the work of Friedrich von Hayek, Milton Friedman and the Chicago School economists. John Ranelagh tells an anecdote of a Tory Party meeting during the 1970s when Margaret Thatcher took a copy of Hayek's *Constitution of Liberty* from her handbag. She brandished it at a speaker who had argued for a pragmatic middle way between right and left, declaring '*This* is what we believe!' (quoted in Gamble 1996).

Milton Friedman, too, was an influential figure in the emergence of the British and American 'new right'. As prices and unemployment rose together despite counter-inflationary measures, he revived pre-Keynesian monetary theory and argued that inflation is purely a monetary phenomenon, caused by an increase in the money supply in excess of real growth at the natural level of unemployment (non-accelerating inflation rate of unemployment, NAIRU). From this perspective, there is a level of unemployment at which prices are stable, a natural level determined by inflexibilities and imperfections in the labour market. Thus, excesses in monetary expansion generate inflation; and unemployment stems not from an insufficiency of effective demand but from labour market imperfections resulting from state and trade union intervention, overly generous welfare benefits that discourage work, and the poor quality and low motivation of those without work which makes them unemployable at the prevailing wage. As such factors were considered to be determinants of the natural rate of unemployment, attempts by government to increase employment beyond this level were theorized either to increase inflation or to squeeze out employment elsewhere in the economy (Friedman 1977).[9]

During the 1970s, as inflation appeared to be out of control, these alternative theories displaced Keynesianism as the conventional wisdom in economics and were progressively incorporated into government policy. But deep recessions during the early 1980s and 1990s undermined confidence in Monetarism, which was ultimately replaced by 'rational expectations' theory.[10] Meanwhile, the task of dealing with employment and competitiveness was delegated to market reforms. Markets and business were deregulated; large sections of the public sector were privatized; and taxes on the rich were cut to encourage enterprise. Trade unions were weakened; legal control of labour standards was relaxed; out-of-work benefits were reduced and made subject to more onerous conditions; and wage subsidization was introduced with the express purpose of lowering NAIRU and generating higher levels of employment. In the interest of freeing-up global financial markets, exchange rate controls were removed, encouraging banks and other financial institutions to move offshore. As a consequence, attempts to regulate the banking and financial sector became increasingly futile; and any remaining control over the money supply was lost.

Thus, in contemporary economic liberalism, the focus of theory and policy centred on the monetary causes of inflation and the efficiency and welfare benefits associated with free markets. The central bank was assigned responsibility for controlling inflation by means of interest rate policy while the central government assumed responsibility for maintaining market freedom. This effectively severed the theoretical and policy link between the dynamics of financial markets and those of other markets.

4.3.2   Economic Liberalism in Theory

The underlying assumption of the neoclassical model of economic liberalism is that self-regulating markets transform the inherent selfishness of individuals into general economic well-being. The market is seen as providing opportunities and incentives for individuals to exploit fully their property (labour in the case of workers), whilst preventing them from exploiting any advantages that ownership might afford by throwing them into competition with others similarly endowed. By these means, markets are assumed to provide a forum in which the values of individual contributions are collectively determined by the choices of buyers and sellers. Judgements are delivered as market prices, which guide labour and other resources to their most efficient use. Competitive markets should therefore function as equilibrating mechanisms, delivering both optimal economic welfare and distributional justice. Neoclassical economic liberals therefore assert that man-made laws and institutions need to conform to the laws of the market if they are not to be in restraint of trade and by extension economically damaging. From this logic follows a radical anti-government rhetoric, best expressed in Ronald Reagan's assertion that: 'Government is not the solution to our problem. Government *is* the problem.' From this perspective, the effective functioning of markets was best assured by 'rolling back the state'.

In addition to the claim of minimal state intervention, neoclassical economic liberalism also has a perspective on how the state should intervene in the economy when required. One of the central aims is that the state should regulate economic activity; but it should not intervene as an economic actor (Gamble 1996). It should 'steer', but not 'row'. In other words, the state should not concern itself with the outcome of the economic game; it should instead make sure that there is room for the 'game' to be played.

Whilst this describes the interpretation and implementation of economic liberalism in the US and UK, the process of economic liberalization in Canada and Australia does not appear to have stemmed from such a narrow doctrinal root. There is no policy agenda in either country that could be branded with the name of its champion in the same way that 'Reaganomics' or 'Thatcherism' have been. This is largely a result of the political and economic power of the provinces, states and territories relative to central government as well as the range of participants in the economic policy-making process. The result is a more even balance of power between the state and the private sector, which seems to have curbed the excesses of both and produced a more stable political and economic system. It is worth noting, however, that this more balanced outcome is a result of the interplay of responses to events during the process of economic liberalization rather than of a deliberate approach to liberal economic policy.

4.3.3 Economic Liberalization in the US and the UK

The return to economic liberalism was strongly influenced by the political and economic climate of the 1970s and early 1980s. Whilst in the US and the UK it is associated with the rise to power of the politically conservative governments of Ronald Reagan and Margaret Thatcher, its origins can be traced to the early 1970s and the liberal responses of the Nixon and Heath governments to the economic challenges of that decade.

During the 1960s, especially in America, the emphasis in economic policy had shifted – from maintaining full employment and a high level of aggregate demand to a 'new economics' focused on economic growth (Perry and Tobin 2000). In 1961, confronted with recession, the newly elected Kennedy–Johnson administration's expansionary policy response reflected the view that rising unemployment was caused by cyclical as opposed to structural factors. The resulting strong growth seemed to justify this perspective and boosted confidence in the direction of economic policy at the time. Real interest rates remained low and investment strong, largely due to confidence about future profits. Yet Johnson's chief economic strategist, Gardner Ackley, was quoted in a 1965 article in *Time Magazine* as saying: 'We're learning to live with prosperity and frankly, we don't know as much about managing prosperity as getting there.'

As it turned out, he was right. The prosperity of the 1960s masked growing imbalances (Marglin and Schor 2007). With production scraping up against the economy's capacity limits, productivity growth began to slow and by 1965, the economy was beginning to show signs of strain. Labour costs rose faster than productivity; consumer and wholesale price inflation accelerated sharply and the federal budget was increasingly strained by the war in Viet Nam (Clark 1979). As the newly rebuilt Japanese and European production systems began to come online, manufacturing imports surged and the US balance of trade deteriorated. In 1971, in response to its first trade deficit since before the First World War, and under pressure to devalue the currency, President Nixon took Milton Friedman's advice and announced that the US would no longer provide gold backing for the American dollar (Helleiner 1994, 115–121).[11] This effectively lifted the capital controls that had been introduced in 1944 under the Bretton Woods Agreement. Although Japanese and Western European governments lobbied for voluntary capital controls in an effort to maintain a degree of policy autonomy, the US refused, urging other countries to follow its lead (Helleiner 1994). With the collapse of Bretton Woods, international capital movement restrictions and fixed currency relationships were eliminated.

It is important to note that during the Nixon and Ford administrations, advocates of neoliberal economic thought held influential positions on the Council of Economic Advisors and in the Treasury (Helleiner 1994, 115). After Nixon's resignation, there was a brief return to the use of Keynesian tools by the Democratic Carter administration, in an effort to mitigate the effects of the first oil shock. But the Iranian revolution in 1979 set off another oil shock; and with inflation and unemployment rising sharply and American hostages being taken by Islamist militants in Tehran, in 1980 Ronald Reagan was elected President, by a landslide.

In the UK, the overriding problem during the 1960s had been the plight of sterling, causing the International Monetary Fund (IMF) to put pressure on the government to address the problem through monetary policy (Marglin and Schor 2007, 139). In 1971, the Heath government introduced a policy of 'Competition and Credit Control', in an effort to liberalize the money markets and stimulate competition among banks. Quantitative limits on bank lending were removed, liquidity requirements reduced, and interest rates were allowed to play a more central role in credit allocation. In response to rising unemployment, the Heath government also made a 'dash for growth'.[12] Fiscal and monetary expansion and macroeconomic growth were accelerated by increased bank lending. However, against a backdrop of international inflationary conditions during the 1970s, speculation inflated a property bubble resulting in the Secondary Banking Crisis of 1973–1975. The Bank of England quickly provided emergency liquidity, averting a wider collapse. But these policies did not have the desired longer-term effect.

The elections in 1974 eventually resulted in the Labour Party's James Callaghan becoming Prime Minister. Confronted with a sterling crisis and fiscal deficit, he was persuaded by the promises of Monetarism; and in a speech at the 1976 Labour Party Conference, he warned that: 'you could not spend your way out of recession. It only fuelled problems by injecting inflation into the economy. The result was higher inflation, followed by higher unemployment. That is the history of the last 20 years' (Smith 2006). But Callaghan would not get the chance to put this policy into practice. In 1979, Britain returned to a Conservative government, led by Margaret Thatcher.

In Britain and America, the 1980s ushered in a strengthening commitment to the neoliberal political and economic agenda. What came to be known as 'Reaganomics' and 'Thatcherism' are associated with laissez-faire, supply-side economics, shifting the policy focus from aggregate demand to the economy's productive capacity. 'Business-friendly' policies included tax cuts, weakening of trade unions and reduction of the government's role in the economy, whilst monetary policy – manipulating the money supply – was used to combat inflation. In the UK, public industries were privatized and people were encouraged to buy property (Skidelsky 1990; Johnson 1991). In the US, the economy was deregulated and the defence industry modernized (Boskin 1987). Throughout the 1980s, despite strong pressure from organized labour and their Democratic and Labour party allies to protect domestic industry and employment, both Reagan and Thatcher believed that protectionism would only create inefficiency and competitive weakness; unions were seen to have caused wage inflation and industrial disruption. Both leaders thus remained committed to allowing free market ideology to determine the winners and losers in industry, and they challenged the legitimacy of organized labour. In the US, Reagan's success in shaping policy was aided by the fact that for the first time in 28 years, Republicans gained control of the Senate; and although the Democrats retained a narrow majority in the House, Republicans and conservative Democrats accounted for an effective majority.

The apparent return to economic prosperity during the 1980s boosted confidence in neoliberal economic theory and policy. However, by the end of the decade, both the US and UK had high levels of fiscal debt; and responsibility for social welfare had been largely individualized. A less obvious effect was that in both countries a significant shift in relative power had also taken place, with the private sector – finance in particular – increasing its influence, at the expense of the state. Both Reagan and Thatcher had begun their administrations with enough political clout to push through a narrow political and economic vision; but that vision would ultimately result in less clout for future governments.

4.3.4 Economic Liberalization in Canada and Australia

The challenges of the 1970s also encouraged a return to economic liberalism in Canada and Australia. However, the process assumed a more balanced form than it did in the US and UK, due in large part to the existence and relative strength of countervailing political and economic forces that mitigated against the imposition of a narrow policy agenda by a dominant central government. There was to be no Thatcher or Reagan in either country and no central government with the power to do as it wished. The process was also overseen by mostly liberal or labour – rather than conservative – governments.

In Canada, confidence in Keynesianism remained strong during the 1970s, despite the turbulence of that era and a concerted effort by political and business coalitions to mobilize support for neoliberal economic policies (Enoch 2007). Distrust of big business and the free market system was reinforced by the 1973 oil crisis, when Canadian oil companies seemed to profit at the expense of consumers; and in 1974, in an attempt to stabilize inflation, Trudeau was forced to introduce controversial wage and price controls. In his view, this 'amounted to a massive intervention in the decision-making power of economic groups, and it's telling Canadians that we haven't be able to make it work, the free market system' (Clarke 1997, 11).

Nevertheless, the difficulties of the 1970s and early 1980s put pressure on the fiscal budget and challenged faith in economic management. In

1984, after 12 years of Trudeau's liberal government, the Progressive Conservative government of Brian Mulroney came to power. But the constitutionally based economic powers of the Canadian provinces and the relative strength of organized labour meant that economic liberalism had to reflect the interests of a broad range of constituencies. According to Norrie and Owram (1991, 620), taken as a package, Canada's liberal reforms: 'constitute a consistent policy agenda, with the twin themes of increasing reliance on market signals to guide the allocation of resources and a desire to accommodate the diverse regional nature of the Canadian economy and society more formally in the formulation of economic and social policy'.

In Australia, economic liberalism was incorporated into policy by the Labor governments of Bob Hawke (1983–1991) and Paul Keating (1991–1996), under the banner of 'economic rationalism'. Economic rationalists had a mainstream post-war view, blending Keynesian macroeconomic theory with neoclassical microeconomics, based on a simple model of perfect competition that allowed for market failure, market imperfection and externalities (Quiggin 1997). From this perspective, government intervention was justified in order to correct market failures and stabilize the level of employment and output (Patience and Head 1979).

Rather than being imposed by the government and economic rationalists, however, the process of economic liberalization in Australia was a negotiated one that sought a balance between the concerns of business, markets and the broader community (Argy 2001). Following its election, the Hawke government held a politically successful national economic summit, creating a tripartite system that extended the accord between government and organized labour to include business interests (Quiggin 1998). It also continued the social democratic policy of earlier liberal governments. The expansionary fiscal policy inherited from the Fraser government was maintained and extended; social welfare benefits were raised and a national health insurance system was introduced.

Thus, as in Canada, economic liberalization in Australia did not result in a dismantling of the welfare state; and it was not accompanied by deregulation. Instead, it involved a range of relevant stakeholders and was accompanied by regulation designed to ensure that markets operated effectively and that the private sector profit motive did not impede the provision of public services or the public good (Argy 2001). According to Berg (2008): 'the most striking attribute of the last few decades is how Australian governments have matched privatisations and liberalisations with regulatory expansion, rather than retreat. Governments have shifted away from the direct provision of services, to the regulation of those services.'

4.4   COUNTERVAILING POWER IN THE ANGLO-SAXON WORLD

The above narratives tracing the evolution of different interpretations of liberal capitalism demonstrate that the frameworks of national financial systems are determined in complex, ongoing processes, where different events and actors influence the outcome. An important element, which seems to explain in part why the British and American financial systems were particular vulnerable, is the lack of willingness on the part of governments and regulators to oppose the industry's desire for ever more far-reaching liberalization. Both Australia and Canada had much more determined governments that reined in the industry's options and created a more stable structure. This state capacity can in turn be related to certain features of the state in the two countries. Here, the presence and relative strength of countervailing powers in the policy-making process is important. The more 'veto players' or 'veto points' there are – that is, those who can block or modify a given policy – the more difficult it becomes for any single actor to get what they want (Tsebelis 2000). Such players in the countries in our study include electoral, corporate governance and industrial relations systems, which served to shape relations within and between actors in the political system, industry and organized labour. It is to these that we now turn.

4.4.1   Electoral Systems

The US, UK, Canada and Australia are all liberal, constitutional democracies in which the decision-making power of elected representatives is moderated by a constitution that emphasizes protection of individual liberties and minority rights within society. The US is a constitutional republic with a presidential system of government in which executive, legislative and judicial powers are separated in order that no individual or group has absolute power. Thus, whilst the President's ability to implement policy is ultimately dependent on the support of Congress, the system is set up to limit the power of the executive, whose party may or may not control the Senate and the House of Representatives. During the first six years of the Reagan government, the conservatives' control over the House and Senate effectively lifted the electoral constraint on the President's ability to implement radical changes in policy, with very significant knock-on effects. These early changes would effect a shift in power away from central government and towards the private sector, paving the way for an increasingly powerful lobbying base which would, in time, help put in place the preconditions for a major financial crisis.

The UK, Canada and Australia are constitutional monarchies with a parliamentary system of government in which the British monarch is head of state and an elected Prime Minister is head of government. The executive and legislative branches of government are not separate, but the prime minister is dependent on the support of Parliament.[13] As a result, a Prime Minister is on the face of it, less likely than an American President to face strong opposition to the policy agenda of central government. This was the case under Thatcher; and the apparent success of the neoliberal policy agenda meant that New Labour did little to reverse the current of policy when it came to power in the late 1990s. In Canada and Australia, however, the political and economic strength of the provinces, states and territories and the more collective approach to the formulation of policy served as a moderating force within the system, highlighting the importance of the nature and structure of the relationship between central and regional government.

Whilst the UK is a unitary state, with a centralized national government, it has devolved some powers to Northern Ireland, Scotland and Wales; but the Prime Minister still has considerable influence over the direction of policy. By contrast, the US, Canada and Australia are federal states, with partially self-governing regions and states, united by a central government. In the US, the diffuse nature of political power and reliance on the support of Congress, with representation from each of the 50 states, serves to limit the President's influence over the direction of policy; and this acts as an impediment to major shifts in the direction of policy from one administration to the next. However, with 50 states, as opposed to the much smaller number of provinces and territories in Canada and Australia, strong opposition to central government policy is harder to crystallize. Yet as we saw during the 1980s, the nature and structure of the electoral system had a clear influence on the ability of the executive to push forward an economic and policy agenda. In both Britain and America, a single vision was implemented, by and large, as intended. Ronald Reagan had, perhaps unusually, the benefit of Republican and conservative Democratic control of Congress to help pass a raft of liberalizing legislation during his first term in office. This helped to shift the balance of power, as the state gave ground to the private sector, which only made it easier to pass further legislation in the future. In the same way, opposition to the Thatcher programme was also weak and relatively ineffective. The British system tends to allow a Prime Minister with a large majority in the House of Commons and a relatively united party to implement their policy agenda with very little moderating influence.

In Canada and Australia, on the other hand, the political and economic strength of the provinces, states and territories not only limits the extent to which central government can unilaterally impose a policy agenda; it also means that policy is determined through a process of negotiation and compromise involving a range of stakeholder groups from various competing geographical constituencies and both sides of industry. This also contributes to a cultural divide with regard to perceptions about the balance between the state and the private sector. In Britain and America, where the state has withdrawn in favour of the private sector over the last 30 years, there is frequently a presumption of the primacy of the private sector. In both Canada and Australia, government has played a much stronger part and, if anything, the presumption is in favour of the state. This difference was a significant contributor to moderating the process of liberalization.

4.4.2   Corporate Governance and 'the Market for Corporate Control'

The effect of the presence or otherwise of countervailing power was especially clear in the evolution of corporate governance and the financial sector. From the 1960s onwards, finance assumed a progressively larger role in both the British and American economies.

In Britain, corporate raiders such as Tiny Rowland, James Goldsmith and Jim Slater of Slater Walker showed what could be done with leveraged finance (BBC 1999). They then passed the baton to the Americans, like Michael Milkin and Ivan Bosky, and to the mutual fund managers, who by and large continued the process in the US and UK. The motivation for the bankers, shareholders and investors was the realization of large, short-term profits and the creation of funds with which to carry on the process, targeting ever larger businesses and selling off acquired assets to finance the debt (Bluestone and Harrison 1982; Reich 2008). The benefits for the businesses involved, however, were transitory at best, often amounting to little more than a brief spike in the share price. Many were left without the resources to sustain their productive activities; and the large numbers of job losses involved – both from announcements of lay-offs (that served to excite the markets) and from the industrial restructuring that typically followed hostile acquisitions – did little to improve the relationship between unions and the governments of the day (Bluestone and Harrison 1982; Deakin and Singh 2008; Reich 2008). This was particularly the case in the US and UK, where many of the corporate raiders were political insiders. Nevertheless, the short-term increase in share price convinced some that the combination of leveraged finance and asset stripping was delivering results, while others saw it as economic cannibalism.

Whilst the tactics of corporate raiding were exported wholesale from Britain to America, with similar effect, takeovers in Australia had only a brief heyday during the 1980s and in Canada they were never really a factor. The reasons for this are both cultural and structural, and are a significant part of the story of finance in the Anglo-Saxon economies.

Anglo-Saxon corporate governance is typically characterized by widely dispersed equity ownership among individuals and institutions, prioritization of shareholder interests in company law and the protection of minority shareholder interests by securities law and regulation. Hall and Soskice (2001) argue that rather than being based on bank finance, financial systems in LMEs are centred on the financial markets. This is a result of the relaxation or even lack of capital flow regulation that also tends to be a feature of these economies. In LMEs, stock markets are well developed and play a central role. A similar argument, based on different assumptions, can be found in the law and finance literature. La Porta et al. (1997), for example, posit that common law countries in the Anglo-Saxon world have more developed financial markets than do civil law countries. Nevertheless, the role played by the stock market in the US and UK differs sharply from that in Canada and Australia, particularly with respect to the restructuring of industry and the economy during economic liberalization.

In the US and UK, the leveraged buyouts of the 1980s effectively dismantled the heavy industrial sectors in both countries. Unions were weakened and opportunities for longer-term investment in manufacturing curtailed. During the 1990s, this process was carried on in America by institutional investors, reacting to the enormous loss of (long-term) shareholder value that had resulted from the poor performance, or in many cases failure, of the productive organizations previously targeted by the corporate raiders. Investor activism took a variety of forms in the US and UK, but it demonstrated the increasing power of the shareholder – and the will to use it.

Liberal economic theorists lauded the stock exchange as an 'efficient market' for managerial control in which the value of a company's shares reflected the value of the underlying productive enterprise (Fama 1970).[14] The stock market boom was taken as evidence of overall industrial strength while the short-term increase in share prices, resulting from cost cutting in companies that had been taken over, served to reinforce these assumptions. However, the reality was that the 'profits' generated by hostile takeovers were derived from asset stripping (Bluestone and Harrison 1982; Lazonick and O'Sullivan 2000), and consequently a one off 'blip', as opposed to enhanced sustainable output and productivity in the organizations involved.

The structure in much of corporate Canada and Australia, however, for the most part mitigated against a similarly extended frenzy of leveraged buyouts. Both Canada and Australia have well-developed stock markets and many listed companies with dispersed shareholder ownership. But this form of ownership is not the norm. In Canada, only a minority (just under 16 per cent) of the 550 largest companies had a widely dispersed shareholder base in 1989 (Morck et al. 1998); and in more than 75 per cent of Canadian companies, a single shareholder – often a wealthy family – controlled at least 20 per cent of the voting shares (Rao and Lee-Sing 1995). In Australia, too, share ownership tends to be concentrated; and there is a much higher incidence of founding family and intercompany control than in the US and UK. According to Clarke (2007, 145): 'all the evidence suggests that Australian business has maintained an unusually high degree of block-holder control'. In 1999, only 11 of the 20 largest public quoted companies did not have a shareholder that held 10 per cent or more of the equity, with a similar pattern among smaller companies (Stapledon 1998; Clarke 2007).

It is unsurprising, then, that in both Canada and Australia the takeover market is not particularly active. Dignam and Galanis (2004, 20) conclude that the discipline mechanism of the American and British market for corporate control 'is absent from the Australian listed market' and that 'block-holders exercise control over key decisions as to the sale of the company'. Similarly, a 2008 study of Canadian companies found that: 'a significant share of Canadian firms is largely immune to hostile takeover attempts' (Secor 2008, 6).

4.4.3   Labour Relations

In most industrialized countries, organized labour and trade union movements were broadly accepted by the 1970s, and their relative power seemed secure, especially in countries with social democratic governments (Fairbrother and Griffin 2002). During the 1980s and 1990s, however, there was a sharp reversal. The widespread acceptance of neoliberalism undermined the pluralist political ideology upon which the justification of union involvement in economic, social and political activity was based; and the legitimacy of unions and existing labour market structures was seriously challenged.

Corporate governance played a part by allowing investor interests to trump those of industry and labour particularly in the US and UK. Electoral systems in the four countries also played a role through their influence on relations between the state and organized labour and, indeed, attitudes towards labour generally. Canada and Australia have a much stronger tradition of liberal or labour governments, and with the exception of the period in power of the Progressive Conservatives in Canada, the process of liberalization was carried out by these centre-left parties. The result was thus a far less confrontational process, involving labour;

Table 4.2   Trade union density (% of employed wage and salary earners)

	1960	1970	1980	1990	1995
Canada	28.3	29.8	36.0	36.0	37.0
Australia	49.1	44.4	48.0	41.0	35.2
UK	44.3	48.6	52.8	40.1	32.2
US	28.9	25.9	22.0	16.0	14.2

Sources: Visser (1993), ILO (1997) and OECD (1997).

and there were relatively few scenes of industrial strife in the media. The situation in America, and especially Britain, could hardly have been more different.

Already severely weakened by the industrial restructuring and dein-dustrialization triggered by the corporate raiders, trade unions in the US and UK resisted further concessions. Bitter and violent disputes between organized labour, big business and the state were widely publicized; and throughout the 1980s and 1990s, a series of laws and legal rulings further eroded union power, marginalizing them in political and economic policy (Fairbrother 2002; Jarley 2002). As is evident in Table 4.2, whereas trade union density in the UK peaked in 1980 at 52.8 per cent, by 1995 it had declined to 32.2 per cent. In the US, organized labour was much weaker, with trade union density falling steadily from 1960, to 14.2 per cent in 1995.

In Australia, too, the ability of organized labour to participate effec-tively in political and economic policy debates was seriously eroded during the 1980s and 1990s (see Table 4.2), although not as a result of a concerted effort on the part of government. Despite the election of a Labor govern-ment in the early 1980s and a return to centralized wage determination in which unions assumed a major role, from 1987 onwards this accord was gradually eroded; and in the early 1990s, a system of enterprise bargaining was introduced and extended (Griffin and Fairbrother 2002, 246). According to Griffin and Svensen (2002), the centralized nature of Australian trade union governance was unable to cope effectively with the decentralization of collective bargaining, undermining the relative strength of the union movement.

In sharp contrast, the Canadian trade union movement retained much of its membership and density during the 1980s and 1990s. Table 4.2 shows density increasing steadily throughout the period of economic liberalism. This is in large part due to the central role that provincial-level political action and law play in union–state relations and the traditional strength of the relationship between the local and national levels within Canadian unions (Murray 2002). Thus, even in an environment of employer opposition and periodic hostility on the part of state governments and policy, Canadian trade union strength was not eroded during the 1980s and 1990s, providing a voice for labour in economic, social and political policy debates that continues to the present.

In short, whilst Canadian labour maintained its voice in the political and economic policy arena, the process of economic liberalization in the other three countries seriously undermined organized labour's relative position, skewing the balance between the two sides of industry and removing or weakening an important countervailing force within the system.

4.4.4   Financial Market Liberalization and Regulation in the Anglo-Saxon World

Although the more obvious beginnings of financial market liberalization can be located in the 1970s, when international capital flow restrictions were removed, its roots can be traced much earlier, to the 1950s and the emergence of euromarkets, regulation-free markets where banks deal in currencies other than their own.

Following the Second World War, the enormous increase in the quantity of US dollars held by foreign banks, companies and countries, including the Soviet Union, gave rise to the need for a market in which to exchange them; and during the Cold War this made London (rather than New York) an attractive centre for eurodollar activities, which expanded rapidly during the 1960s, with the strong support of both the US and the UK (Helleiner 1994, 81–100). This huge increase in available funds not only increased the importance of the City of London as a centre for international finance; it also gave rise to the first cross-border hostile takeover (by Siegmund Warburg) and marked the beginning of the return to dominance of the American and British financial sectors (Ferguson 2010).

4.5   THE UK AND US: LIGHTLY REGULATED FINANCIAL MARKETS AND INSTITUTIONS

Following the 1929 stock market crash, both sentiment and policy in the US and UK had taken a more cautious turn and the Treasury assumed greater influence over monetary affairs. Since the financial community was held responsible for the chaos, reform focused on stricter control of domestic financial markets and monetary policy and on limiting the power of the central bank and financiers (Helleiner 1994, 32).

4.5.1 American Financial Markets: Regulatory Fragmentation

The American financial system has historically been a fragmented one. The Constitution gives the federal government control over the money supply but is silent about control of banks, so bank regulation was left to the states (Gordon 2004). After the Civil War, the 1863 National Bank Act offered federal charters to banks with sufficient capital that were willing to submit to strict regulation by the newly created Office of the Comptroller of the Currency. But they were prohibited from branching across state lines or from branching within states that did not allow it. Despite the establishment of national banks, state banks proliferated. In states that did not permit branching, they were small and vulnerable to the economic performance of the local community in which they were located. In 1913, the Federal Reserve System (Fed) was established to regulate state banks, secondary national banks and bank holding companies. But instead of one, 12 reserve banks were created, located in major financial centres across the country.

During the Great Depression, one-third of all American banks failed (Richardson 2007). In response, Congress made sweeping reforms: the Federal Reserve System was reorganized and the Federal Deposit Insurance Corporation (FDIC) was set up. The Glass–Steagall Act separated commercial and retail banking from investment banking. By preventing institutions that were 'principally engaged' in banking from underwriting or dealing in securities, and vice versa, Glass–Steagall resolved the conflict of interest between those wanting a safe place for their money and those prepared to speculate. This was reinforced by the 1956 Bank Holding Act that applied the same separation to bank holding companies. Glass–Steagall's Regulation Q prohibited the payment of interest on demand deposits and put a ceiling on interest rates on deposit accounts in order to encourage local banks to lend instead of holding balances with larger banks that used these funds for speculative purposes (Gilbert 1986).

But there remained thousands of banks, along with thrifts (savings and loans associations), bank holding companies and credit unions, regulated by different authorities at both the state and federal levels. According to Pan (2011, 837): 'the United States has the dubious distinction of having one of the most complex and arguably least coordinated regulatory structures in the world'.[15] Nevertheless, the system was stable during the prosperous post-war period, when the memory of the financial crisis and Great Depression was fresh. But it began to break down during the 1960s and 1970s as inflation accelerated and the economy confronted increasing structural challenges. As regulation was progressively loosened, it began to show serious failings – with drastic consequences.

4.5.2   The American Savings & Loans Crisis: A Warning Goes Unheeded

A clear example of the potential consequences of insufficient prudential oversight was the American savings and loans institution (S&L) crisis. During the 1970s, when inflation caused interest rates to rise above those set by Regulation Q, investors sought alternatives to traditional deposit accounts and funds flowed out of depository institutions in search of higher yields. This caused particular distress for the tightly regulated S&L industry, which specialized in taking short-term deposits and making long-term mortgage loans. Because of the risk of large numbers of S&L failures, the industry was quickly deregulated. The Depository Institutions Deregulation and Monetary Control Act of 1980 eliminated many of the distinctions between S&Ls and banks and removed the interest rate cap on deposit accounts. But further inflation and competitive pressures pushed up the interest rates that S&Ls had to pay, causing large losses and some failures. No large-scale action was taken, however, as the Federal Savings and Loan Insurance Corporation (FSLIC) had insufficient funds to bail out insolvent S&Ls and the Federal Home Loan Bank Board (FHLBB) provided lax supervision (Sherman 2009).

The Garn–St Germain Depository Institutions Act of 1982 allowed federal S&Ls to own projects funded by their loans. This resulted in a mass conversion of S&Ls from state to federal status and fuelled a commercial real estate boom. However, poor lending decisions and excessive leverage laid the foundations for the S&L crisis. This leverage was partly facilitated by Drexel Burnham Lambert, an investment bank which wrote the first collateralized debt obligation (CDO) for the Imperial Savings Association in 1987. In this, loans were bundled together and sold on the securities market, permitting Imperial to remove assets from its balance sheet and generate cash for additional loans, with leverage increasing as the process continued. The fatal weakness was dependency on continually rising, or at least stable, property prices and cheap debt. A downturn, or an increase in interest rates, would burst the bubble.

During the early 1980s, rising interest rates cut off the cheap funding upon which many S&Ls relied; and with the disappearance of real estate tax shelters, funds dried up, causing the failure of 747 S&Ls in 'the greatest collapse of US financial institutions since the Great Depression' (Curry and Shibut 2000, 33). As the total cost exceeded the Federal Savings and Loan Insurance Corporation's (FSLIC) ability to pay insured depositors, US taxpayers and the industry were required to contribute to the insurance coverage at a total cost of approximately $210 billion. (Curry and Shibut 2000). In 1989, the newly elected Bush administration signed into law a bailout plan for the S&L industry. The Financial Institutions

Recovery and Enforcement Act (FIRREA) abolished the FSLIC and transferred assets to the FDIC. The FHLBB was abolished and the Office of Thrift Supervision was created to regulate the S&Ls; and the Resolution Trust Corporation was created to dissolve and merge troubled institutions.

Whilst many contributors to the S&L crisis bear comparison to that of 2008, a crucial difference was its limitation to one sector of the American banking industry, whose survival was not considered critical to confidence in the national or global financial system. As a result, the S&L crisis did not shock America into reforming its system of financial regulation. Ultimately, the response was further deregulation, in spite of the voices calling for reform. In a 1996 address, delivered in Tokyo, Japan, L. William Seidman, former Chairman of the FDIC and the Resolution Trust Corporation (RTC),[16] said that during the 1980s and 1990s, the US had experienced 'a banking, S&L and credit union problem of major proportions – clearly the worst difficulties since the Great Depression'. He went on to say that 'given the extent of the problems, we in the US are "long" on experience and if we don't learn a lot from these experiences, we will surely repeat our problems' (Seidman 1997, Volume II, 55–56). In the wake of the recent financial market crisis, it would appear that the important lessons were not learned.

4.5.3   British Financial Markets: A Tradition of Regulatory Informality

After the Second World War, HM Treasury assumed responsibility for monetary policy and regulating building societies, friendly societies and trustee savings banks; the Department of Trade and Industry (DTI) had responsibility for securities and insurance regulation; and the Bank of England was nationalized and given responsibility for regulating banks.

The Bank of England's approach to financial supervision has historically been informal (Goodhart 2004), with regulation largely entrusted to the industry itself, through the Financial Intermediaries, Managers and Brokers Regulatory Association (FIMBRA). Until the 1970s, the system seemed to work well. During the early 1970s, however, a number of fringe banks found themselves in trouble, triggering the 'Secondary Banking Crisis'. Precipitated by a property bubble, cheap debt and excessive leverage, the crisis was met with a financial 'lifeboat', swiftly launched by the Bank to provide emergency liquidity. Following the crisis, the Treasury put banking regulation on a statutory footing. The 1979 Banking Act gave the Bank legal powers to underpin its supervisory authority; it also created a two-tier system of 'recognized banks' and 'licensed institutions' and introduced a scheme to protect small depositors in the event of bank failure. But the Treasury retained ongoing responsibility for the legal framework of banking supervision and the performance of its regulator.

The 1984 collapse of Johnson Matthey Bankers (JMB) revealed flaws in the 1979 Act and fault lines in the regulatory system itself. To prevent a loss of confidence in the City of London's gold bullion market, where JMB was a key player, the Bank acted once again. The Banking Act of 1987 significantly increased the Bank's supervisory capacity. But this time, the Conservative Chancellor, Nigel Lawson, felt that the Bank had acted without keeping him informed. A public rift ensued, straining relations between the government and the Bank, with obvious implications for the effectiveness of the tripartite system. This political tension appears to have contributed to pressures that were already mounting for a change in the structure of regulation; in particular, regulation of securities, financial markets and insurance. In 1981, a review of the role and functioning of financial institutions and investor protection for securities and other property produced the 1986 Financial Services Act, the first UK legislation to regulate comprehensively the securities industry and markets. The Securities and Investments Board (SIB) was set up to oversee the various self-regulatory organizations (SROs); and City firms conducting business in the UK were required to seek membership in an SRO or direct supervision by the SIB. Since the SIB's members were appointed by the Treasury, the changes served to erode further the regulatory authority of the Bank.

Throughout the 1980s, the supervision of securities and insurance remained the responsibility of the DTI. But as the lines between financial institutions became blurred, the Treasury assumed responsibility for regulating financial services in 1993, and insurance in 1998. In 1998, the Bank of England was granted operational independence and assigned responsibility for the implementation of monetary policy. The 2000 Financial Services and Markets Act created the Financial Services Authority (FSA), as a single, unified regulator for financial services. The Treasury has no operational or financial control over the FSA, which was established as a private company, limited by guarantee, to emphasize its independence. There was no formal legislation setting out the respective responsibilities of the three financial authorities; but a Memorandum of Understanding was established, fitting the tradition at the Bank of England, of flexibility in the banking system and avoiding the red tape and restrictions found in other systems. The Memorandum delineated the responsibility of the Treasury as being responsible for the legal framework; the Bank for the stability of the financial system as a whole; and the FSA for the supervision of individual firms.

4.5.4 Stock Market Liberalization in the US and UK and 'Light-Touch' Regulation

During the late 1920s and early 1930s, both London and New York were considered the epicentres of the global financial crisis. As US Treasury Department Secretary, Henry Morgenthau, told the conference at Bretton Woods, the objective was: 'to drive the usurious money-lenders from the temple of international finance . . . [and] move the financial centre of the world from London and Wall Street to the US [and HM] Treasury' (quoted in Gardner 1980, 76).

However, as memories of the stock market crash and Great Depression faded, so did the atmosphere of caution; and increasing concern about restoring the attractiveness of London and New York to global capital gradually overwhelmed concerns about domestic financial market regulation. During the 1970s and 1980s, 'competitive deregulation' accelerated the process of liberalization (Helleiner 1994, 12). In 1974, the US removed the capital controls it had introduced during the 1960s. Britain followed by abolishing its 40-year-old capital controls in 1979; and others were forced to follow suit or lose business and capital to New York and London.

On 1 May 1975, 'Mayday', the New York Stock Exchange deregulated its commission structure, allowing competition, opening stock trading to market forces of supply and demand, and driving down commissions. The result was reduced profitability of trades, and the incentive to make up the loss by increasing volume and economizing on market research, shifting the focus from 'research and analysis' to 'sales'. Britain followed in 1986, with the 'big bang'. However, these developments also gave rise to a governance question of a similar nature to that addressed by the Glass–Steagall Act in 1933: are Chinese walls between differing sets of interests in the same organization a sufficient guarantee of probity?

4.5.5 USA: Progressive Loosening of Regulation

In the US, bankers had been lobbying Congress as early as the 1960s to loosen the restrictions of Glass–Steagall. With money market mutual funds and other complex financial instruments that blurred the lines between deposits and securities, the banking industry complained that the Glass–Steagall restrictions were becoming obsolete. Regulators were sympathetic on some accounts. There was always a fear that financial deregulation in other countries would entice firms to take their capital abroad; and many in government shared the free market ideology of deregulation.

In 1986–7, the Fed loosened the Glass–Steagall restrictions and allowed banks to derive up to 5 per cent of gross revenues from investment banking business and to handle, among other things, commercial paper, municipal bonds and mortgage-backed securities. In 1987, Greenspan was appointed Chairman of the Federal Reserve Board; and early in his tenure, Glass–Steagall was reinterpreted to allow banks to deal in certain debt and equity securities, up to 10 per cent of gross revenues. In 1996, this was raised to 25 per cent, which effectively rendered Glass–Steagall obsolete. In 1994, the Reagle–Neal Interstate Banking and Branching Efficiency Act eliminated restrictions on interstate banking and branching, and in 1999 the Gram–Leach–Bliley Act repealed all restrictions on the combination of banking, securities and insurance operations for financial institutions.

After the 'big bang' deregulation in the City of London, US financial institutions had seen the potential to circumvent Glass–Steagall by means of overseas subsidiaries beyond its jurisdiction. This encouraged the growth of multinational financial conglomerates, with a keen focus on profits and share price by both investors and management. It also made risk management more difficult, an effect magnified by the individualization of computer technology. Thus, the final repeal of Glass–Steagall in 1999 under President Clinton's administration seemed a relatively insignificant event. In reality, though, it helped to inflate the subprime bubble by speeding up the process of securitizing increasingly risky mortgages, as well as allowing mergers such as that of Citibank and Traveler's Group, continuing the growth of the financial behemoths.

4.5.6   The Emergence of Financial Behemoths in London

By the mid-1980s, London had fallen behind New York as a financial centre. Attributing this to excessive regulation and the 'old boys' network', the Thatcher government set out to remove both. In 1986, 'big bang' liberalization ushered in radical cultural changes and a period of rapid internationalization, with profound effects on the UK financial sector, and by extension, the wider economy. Prior to 1986, the City had been composed of small, specialist companies, largely immune from takeover. The roles of buying and selling were separated by intermediaries, or stockjobbers, through whose books every transaction went, on a fixed-fee basis.

On 27 October 1986, this regime was swept away; the buy and sell sides of brokerage were united and the modern trader was born. At the same time, City firms found themselves vulnerable to international competition and hostile takeover. Computerized trading, and a time zone ideally placed between New York and Tokyo, put London at the centre of the global financial network. This and the easing of regulation attracted overseas banks, resulting in a wave of acquisitions, many by non-British institutions. This was not restricted to specialist City firms. By 1992 the Hong

Kong Shanghai Bank (HSBC) had acquired the Midland Bank – then the UK's biggest high street bank by market capitalization – and moved its headquarters to London to take advantage of 'light-touch' regulation.

British banks also pursued growth through acquisition. In 1986, Lloyds acquired the Continental Bank of Canada, adding the Trustee Savings Bank and the Cheltenham & Gloucester Bank in 1995. RBS acquired the Citizens Financial Group, which itself had made acquisitions, becoming the eighth-largest bank in America and giving RBS significant representation in the US market. RBS also aquired NatWest in the 1990s, and not long before the crisis, the Dutch bank ABN Amro. By this process, the 'Big Four' UK domiciled banks were created.

Whilst superficially this might appear similar to the Australian 'four-pillar' policy or Canada's system dominated by six large banks, the reality could not be more different. Not only were the large London-based banks highly internationalized in their business, and consequently much less 'British' than Australian banks were 'Australian' or Canadian banks 'Canadian'; they were also much more diversified in terms of share ownership and vastly more complex in terms of management systems.

Indeed, in 1981, when Standard Chartered attempted to acquire the Royal Bank of Scotland (RBS), against RBS's expressed wishes, HSBC put in a counter-bid. Both were referred to the Monopolies and Mergers Commission and blocked. The failure of the HSBC bid was based on a persuasive argument by RBS that a large overseas-owned UK bank might be less willing to be 'leant on' in the national interest than a 'native' bank, or feel a conflict between public demands (that is, to help out in a troubled situation) and its owner's interests. 'We find', the Commission reported 'that the transfer of ultimate control of a significant part of the clearing system outside the United Kingdom would have the adverse effect of opening-up possibilities of divergence of interest which would not otherwise arise' (Reid 1988).

4.5.7 Summing Things Up

In both Britain and America, the return to dominance of the London and New York financial centres was aided by 'light-touch' regulation. However, the British and American systems are at opposite ends of the spectrum. The UK takes an 'integrated' approach, where a single universal regulator ensures consumer and investor protection, as well as the health and stability of financial institutions in all sectors of the financial services industry. By contrast, the US system is diffuse, with a plethora of institutions regulated by an equally complex system of federal and state regulatory agencies. Both systems have been criticized for their inability to provide supervisory oversight of financial institutions offering an ever-expanding range of services. But whilst 'modernization' of the financial services industry has been welcomed, regulatory reform has met with opposition from powerful industry insiders, lobbyists and political activists (Gordon 2004).

In short, in New York and London, regulators are charged with responsibility for regulating a dynamic and innovative marketplace, populated by highly internationalized financial institutions and dependent on global capital for the financial sector's economic performance. An international footprint brings the ability to span jurisdictions, arbitrage regulatory systems and quickly relocate if necessary. There is thus a potential conflict of interest for the financial market regulators: while light-touch regulation is attractive to global capital, it also increases the risk of instability.

4.6   CANADA AND AUSTRALIA: FINANCIAL MARKET LIBERALIZATION – BUT WITH REGULATORY REFORM

In both Canada and Australia, prior to adoption of the current 'twin peaks' model of regulation, the approach to financial market regulation was institutional, with the firm's legal status determining the regulator responsible for overseeing its activities. As the boundaries between financial institutions became increasingly blurred by the diversification of services provided, in stages, financial market regulation evolved into a 'twin peaks' system in which the central bank is responsible for monetary policy and market stability, and a separate regulator is responsible for safety and stability and for conduct of business. Both Canada and Australia also take a 'principles-based' approach to regulation in which financial institutions are required to ensure that they meet both the intent and the prescription of legislation; this approach (in contrast to a 'rules-based' approach) is believed to encourage competition and innovation as well as to make the financial market more attractive to international financial institutions (Pan 2011).

In both Canada and Australia, financial markets are seen as integral to the performance of the economy as a whole, rather than being an end in themselves (Courchene and Purvis 1993; Nieuwenhuysen et al. 2001). The core of the financial services industry is a branch banking system in which a few large banks provide retail, commercial and investment banking services nationwide. Branching and diversification of financial services are seen as contributing to reduced vulnerability to regional and market shocks, significant economies of scale for the banks involved and, hence, market stability. At the same time, competition among the banks is considered to be in the public interest (Department of Industry 1997).

In Canada, the government's commitment to maintaining a balance between the public interest and the commercial interests of Canadian business is enforced by the Competition Bureau Canada (CBC), whose mandate is to: 'ensure that Canada has a competitive marketplace and that all Canadians enjoy the benefits of low prices, product choice and quality service' (Competition Bureau Canada 1998). Consequently, all proposed mergers are subject to review. In 1998, with the objective of improving their competitiveness in the global financial market, the Royal Bank and the Bank of Montreal proposed merging, as did the Canadian Imperial Bank of Commerce (CIBC) and the Toronto Dominion Bank. However, the mergers were blocked on the grounds that they would work against the best interests of Canadians by concentrating economic power, reducing competition and restricting the government's ability to address future prudential concerns (Lott 2005).

A similar balance was achieved in Australia by the government's 'six-pillar' policy, initiated by Paul Keating in 1990 when he blocked the merger between the ANZ Bank and the National Mutual insurance company and extended the ban to any merger between the four largest banks (Commonwealth Bank – CBA, Westpac, NAB and ANZ) and the two largest insurance companies (AMP and NatMut). The six-pillar policy was maintained until the 1996 Wallis investigation into financial system reform, which exposed the largest banks and insurance companies to the same level of takeover pressure as other publicly listed companies. Thus, in 1997, the merger ban was lifted for the two insurance companies, but not the four largest banks, resulting in the present 'four-pillar' policy.

4.6.1 Canada's Banking 'Pillars': a Change of Architecture

Traditionally, the 'four pillars' of Canadian banking – chartered banks, trust and loan companies, insurance companies and securities dealers – were distinct in terms of ownership, market function and legislative control, with regulations that enforced an institutional separation of activities and prohibited cross-ownership. During the 1950s, however, financial innovation by 'near banks', beyond the jurisdiction of regulation, caused a gradual blurring of the institutional lines differentiating financial institutions. This, in a context of growing concern about capital market liberalization with the decline of the Bretton Woods Arrangement, uncertainty about the eurodollar market, and competition from newly rebuilt Europe and Japan, led to the establishment of the Royal Commission on Banking and Finance in 1961. The resulting 1964 Porter Commission

Report produced the Bank Act of 1967, which loosened controls on interest rate ceilings and reserve requirements, to allow financial institutions in Canada greater flexibility in responding to market opportunities. It also introduced rules maintaining a clear separation between banks and their customers and established the Canada Deposit Insurance Corporation (CDIC) to guarantee deposits of up to $60 000 Canadian (now $100 000 Canadian).

During the 1970s, in response to the financial uncertainty created by soaring inflation, the 1980 Bank Act relaxed restrictions on ownership and entry. In response to this and the Mulroney government's 1987 Deregulation Bill, by the end of the 1980s all of the major Canadian banks had entered into the brokerage and investment banking business by acquiring existing firms or building their own (Krysanowski and Ursel 1993). This emergence of universal banking was met with the 1987 establishment of the Office of the Superintendent of Financial Institutions (OSFI) – the first of the 'twin peaks' – as a centralized regulator of banks, insurance companies and pension funds.

In 1988, concerns about the globalization of finance, markets and production, cross-border competition in corporate and government finance, and global financial consolidation led to the formation of the MacKay Task Force. One of its key findings was an information and power imbalance between financial institutions and their consumers and investors. In response, the Financial Consumer Agency of Canada (FCAC) – the second of the 'twin peaks' – was founded in 2001 to consolidate and strengthen consumer protection regulation.

Another concern of the Task Force was the tension between federal and provincial government in the regulation of the financial services industry. The Canadian constitution assigns national government the authority to regulate 'the business of banking' but it does not define what that means (Brean et al. 2011). This ambiguity has impeded the establishment of a pan-Canadian regulatory framework, particularly with respect to securities regulation. At present, securities regulation is entirely in the hands of the provinces, with cross-border regulation coordinated by the Canadian Securities Administrators (CSA), whose membership includes the chairs of the 13 provincial commissions. Despite efforts to centralize securities regulation, it continues to be met with strong opposition from provincial government.

4.6.2   Australia's 'Corporate Cowboys' Bite the Dust

In Australia, as in Canada, the institutional lines between financial firms began to blur during the 1950s. While major banks were tightly regulated by the Reserve Bank of Australia, by 1960 every big bank had acquired an equity stake in a major finance company, operating in the profitable fringe banking sector beyond the jurisdiction of central bank controls. The finance companies began in hire purchase but became increasingly entrepreneurial, and by the 1960s and 1970s were heavily engaged in property speculation with the 'corporate cowboys' of the day (Sykes 1994). Although the banks extended very little finance to the speculators, their finance companies were less cautious. This fuelled a property bubble that burst in 1974, causing a devastating string of corporate and financial failures.

In 1979, amid growing concern about the effectiveness of existing regulations, the government commissioned a review of the financial system, the Campbell Inquiry. Although the 1981 Campbell Report noted that Australian banks had become significantly involved in non-banking business activities through their ownership of equity stakes in finance companies, money market companies, superannuation funds and insurance brokers (Bain and Harper 2000), its recommendations resulted in the introduction of an institutional system of regulation, composed of four main regulators: the Reserve Bank of Australia (RBA) was responsible for banks; the Insurance and Superannuation Commission (ISC) for insurers and superannuation funds; the Australian Securities Commission (ASC) for securities market conduct and disclosure; and the state and territory based State Supervisory Authorities for the building societies, friendly societies and credit unions. The Report also paved the way for liberalization of the financial system.

In 1983, Australia's new Labor government was welcomed into office by a major currency crisis, brought about by speculators fearful of the change in government. The government's leaders 'immediately realized that long-term stability depended on reassuring a wary business community' (Helleiner 1994, 165), and in 1984 the Australian Financial System Review recommended further deregulation. However, the result was instability and scandals in both the corporate and financial sectors of the economy; and in 1990, Australia entered a severe recession, dominated by financial failure (MacFarlane 2006). According to Sykes (1994):

> The corporate booms and busts of the 1980s were the greatest ever seen in Australian history. The boom saw a bunch of corporate cowboys financed to dizzying heights by greedy and reckless bankers. Large sectors of Australian industry changed hands. (p. 1)

In 1991, the Martin Inquiry into the effects of deregulation and the extent of bank competition was followed by the 1996 Wallis Inquiry, whose objective was to reduce the potential for regulatory arbitrage and increase neutrality within the Australian financial system. In particular, it explored the idea of a 'twin peaks' regulatory model, favoured by the Treasury Department, and ultimately recommended it to the Howard government (Bakir 2003). The result was the 1998 creation of a new single prudential regulator, the Australian Prudential Regulatory Authority (APRA) and the Australian Securities and Investment Commission (ASIC). APRA took over prudential regulatory powers from the RBA, ISC and the Australian Foundation Investment Company (AFIC); and ASIC took over responsibility for consumer protection and market integrity from the ASC, ISC and Australian Consumer and Competition Committee (ACCC). To coordinate financial regulation among the different branches of government, the Council of Financial Regulators was set up, composed of representatives from the RBA, APRA, ASIC and the Treasury. In March 2001, the failure of Australia's second-largest insurance company, HIH Insurance, prompted further prudential regulation, bringing most insurance companies, previously only lightly regulated, under the jurisdiction of APRA.

4.6.3   Summing Things Up

In both Canada and Australia, the financial sector is predominantly composed of a relatively small number of domestic and largely immobile banks and financial institutions, subject to 'twin peaks' regulation, in which separate regulators have responsibility for soundness and for conduct of business oversight. In both Australia and Canada, financial market liberalization was matched by flexible regulation designed to ensure that markets were stable and operated effectively. The continuous development of prudential regulation in response to the challenges of liberalization and shifting market conditions reflects the strong tradition of respect for government and for the public interest, which is well summarized in the credo of both countries' Constitutions: 'peace, order and good government'.[17]

The relative strength of Canadian and Australian regulation – and its regulators – may also reflect popular opinion about banks and financial interests. According to Harris (2004, 167): 'Bank bashing . . . is a favourite pastime in Canada, participated in by both politicians and bureaucrats'; and in Australia, Malcolm Maiden famously commented that: 'banks are bastards; bigger banks are bigger bastards' (Maiden 2008).[18] Perhaps this helps to keep the banks, and the bankers, in their proper place within the political and economic system.

4.7 REACTIONS TO REGULATION IN THE ANGLO-SAXON WORLD: CONFORM OR CONFIGURE?

Getting around regulation, getting it changed, or simply fending it off, became something of an art form for the international investment banks in London and New York, as indeed it had for the British 'fringe' banks prior to the Secondary Banking Crisis of the 1970s and the American S&Ls during the 1980s – each time with similar results.

Canadian and Australian banks, however, did not join the international party. They were less dependent on the money markets than their American and British counterparts. Canadian banks are funded mainly through deposits, reducing exposure to capital markets (Booth 2008, 43), and changes in interest rates or availability of funds. As evident in Table 4.3, in December 2008, domestic and foreign deposits accounted for 77 per cent of total funding in the Canadian banking sector. This contrasts sharply with America, where deposits accounted for only 56 per cent of total funding.[19] Low savings rates, resulting from increased consumer leverage, necessitated funding through the financial markets.

In Australia and the UK, the use of foreign and domestic deposits as a source of funding is somewhere between the two, accounting for 60 and 61 per cent, respectively. This was one reason for disintermediation and the creation of special investment vehicles (SIVs), especially by US banks (Booth 2008, 43). SIVs are 'virtual banks' – essentially shell companies, with a line of credit from the parent bank which it was assumed would never be required; the SIV would fund itself via the short-term money markets at low interest rates. SIVs would borrow money (by issuing short-term securities at low rates of interest) and lend it (by buying long-term securities at a higher rate of interest), making a profit for investors from

Table 4.3 Share of domestic and foreign deposits in total funding, December 2008

	%
Canada	77
Australia	61
United Kingdom	60
United States	56

Note: Deposits include CDs. Total funding includes total liabilities, excluding derivative liabilities.

Source: Battellino (2009) based on data from the Royal Bank of Australia and banks' financial statements.

the difference. By buying new assets as the old ones matured, SIVs were envisaged to have an indefinite lifespan, offering a means by which regulatory capital requirements could be reduced, and the money invested for profit instead.

In response to the increasing ease with which financial institutions could practise regulatory arbitrage, the US, UK, Canada and Australia were all signatories to the Basel II Accord. Basel II represented an attempt to extend consistent, international regulatory criteria to banks, especially those that had outgrown national jurisdictions. Among its recommendations was specification of the amount of capital to be held against assets on banks' balance sheets, which included a risk weighting criteria on differing asset classes.

Although the US and UK were signatories to Basel II, the large internationalized banks in New York and London looked for ways around it. The carnage of the S&L crisis had not lived long in America's corporate memory: excessive leverage, poor lending decisions, flawed risk models and off-balance-sheet accounting gymnastics would all be back. L. William Seidman, Chairman of the FDIC at the time of the S&L Crisis, in an address to Nikkin in Tokyo, had noted the potentially devastating effect of derivatives and off-balance-sheet transactions a decade earlier, in September 1996:

> Technology can create soundness or hinder it. Many have identified the globalization created by new technology as a threat to the world financial system. Its speed does create the potential for panic. Another danger is that technology also gives institutions the ability to create infinitely complex financial instruments. These new contracts are a two edged sword, giving the banks and regulators the ability to hedge risk and also misjudge it. The challenge is to use technology to develop systems that will aid safety and soundness knowing all the while that it also has the potential to destroy. (Seidman 1997)

The Basel II Accord was also circumvented in other ways. Firstly, it applied to banks only; and as SIVs that were trading securitized products were not technically banks, their relationship to regulation was unclear. Secondly, because risk models could apparently demonstrate a very high level of safety for super-senior debt, only 20 per cent of the full regulatory capital against these assets was required. In America, regulation of the derivatives market had also been avoided through successful lobbying on the part of the banks (Tett 2009). Instead of operating in the open via an exchange, transactions were private, 'over-the-counter' deals; and there was a clear conflict of interest resulting from the issuer (rather than the investor) paying the fees associated with the rating of derivative products.

In quite the opposite approach, Australian and Canadian banks chose to match, or preferably exceed, the capital reserve requirement recommendations of Basel II. Both countries voluntarily opted for a higher ratio of capital against assets, which although not adding to returns or growth, contributed positively to financial stability.

4.8 THE ANGLO-SAXON VARIETIES OF LIBERALISM ARE PUT TO THE TEST

The conditions that produced the long consumer boom preceding the 2008 financial crisis confronted the internationalized banks in New York and London with problems. Low interest rates and the large volume of Asian savings in the market had not only depressed returns, but also increased pressure from investors for higher yields, which could be generated in essentially two ways: higher risk and higher leverage. Many opted for both, using the booming property markets as fuel.

The desired returns were initially provided by collateralized debt obligations (CDOs), derivative vehicles cherry-picking higher-risk (and hence, higher-yield) loans from conventional asset-backed securities (ABSs). Advances in computing meant that ever more complex CDOs could be constructed by individuals on desktop machines and traded privately – without an exchange as an intermediary. When demand from investors for these 'over-the-counter' products (SIVs were a popular mechanism for investing in them) proved insatiable, erosion of initial profit margins through the increased cost of the underlying loans produced further creativity. The resulting 'synthetic' CDOs were constructed from the riskier parts of traditional CDOs, adding another layer of complexity and risk to achieve the desired returns.

A governance challenge also arose in organizations with widely dispersed shareholder ownership, hungry for returns. The perceived risk of hostile action by shareholders or the markets impeded the board's ability to take decisions relating to risk independently of the sector – a major contributor to a build-up of systemic risk. JP Morgan, one of the more cautious players on Wall Street, paid the price for its individual view on derivative risk through a hostile takeover by Chase Manhattan in December 2000 (Tett 2009, 92–3) and was subsequently forced again to defend its continued conservative stance on derivatives to shareholders.

A fundamental building block of CDOs were mortgage-backed securities (MBSs), mostly created in the US. However, despite recent *bête noire* status, mortgage securitization is far from new.[20] In the US, the structured financing of mortgage pools has its origins in the 1970s, when MBSs were used to help the American banking sector keep up with growing demand for housing credit. Prior to this, banks held loans to maturity. The first MBS was created by the US Department of Housing and Urban Development (HUD) in 1970; and the Government National Mortgage Association (Ginnie Mae) was set up to sell these securities with a guarantee of timely repayment on principal and interest.

In the UK, where mortgage securitization in Europe was pioneered, the first MBS was issued in 1985 and the market grew rapidly during the housing boom (ODPM 2003). However, it declined equally rapidly with the recession of the late 1980s and remains relatively small. More recently, despite some growth in the subprime market, consumer leverage was fuelled by other forms of questionable lending, notably the extraction of equity from homes to fund additional investment in property or consumer goods, and the issuance of mortgages with improbable loan-to-value ratios of up to 125 per cent. During the boom, the conventional wisdom again assumed that these conditions would continue, eroding debt levels – until the bubble burst.

Mortgage securitization is even less significant in the Canadian and Australian financial markets, where concern about maintaining high-quality assets means that banks tend to operate an 'originate to hold' strategy – holding loans to maturity, rather than selling them on. Between 2003 and 2006, MBSs as a proportion of outstanding residential loans averaged 20.1 per cent in the US, significantly higher than in the other three countries, accounting for 7.9 per cent of residential loans in Australia, 6.4 per cent in the UK and 3.6 per cent in Canada (IMF 2008, 107).

4.8.1   Fuelling the Bubble: Residential Financing in the Anglo-Saxon World

The securitization of risky American subprime mortgages was key to the high returns of the CDOs they populated; it also precipitated the crisis. Whilst subprime mortgages provided the raw material for risky derivative products created in the US, the system of home financing in the UK, Australia and Canada prevented the proliferation of such risky loans in these countries. Thus, while home ownership patterns are comparable, the systems of home financing gave rise to very different outcomes with respect to mortgage lending, playing a role in their experience of the crisis. Nevertheless, the high returns on these derivative products encouraged many to invest in them, exposing investors around the world to the American subprime bubble. It is thus useful to examine the systems of home financing in the main Anglo-Saxon countries.

The Great Depression created both mass unemployment and industrial unrest amongst those still working.[21] One response was to create incentives encouraging more American households to own their homes, and in 1938 the Federal National Mortgage Association (Fannie Mae) was set up to purchase mortgages from their originators, freeing up their capital to make additional loans. American home ownership is also encouraged by tax policy: interest payments on mortgage loans are tax deductible and up to $500000 in capital gains from the sale of a house is tax exempt. At the same time, ease of obtaining a mortgage and limited liability in the case of default provide incentives to purchase houses using debt. When mortgage affordability is assessed, other debts are typically not taken into account; car loans, for example, are specifically excluded. Mortgage loans are 'non-recourse', meaning that a homeowner's liability is limited to the amount invested in the mortgage. If the mortgage debt exceeds the value of the house, it is possible to turn in the keys and walk away from the loan. Mortgage insurance is optional; and high loan-to-value ratios normal, especially during a boom.

The effect was spectacular: between 1940 and 1960, home ownership in the US rose from 43.6 to 61.9 per cent (US Census Bureau 2004). By 2000, 66.2 per cent of American households owned their homes. This figure peaked in 2004 at 69.0 per cent before declining slightly to 67.4 per cent in 2009 (US Census Bureau 2010). However, whilst the 'easy in' policies encouraged rapid growth in home ownership, their counterpart, 'easy out' options, also built in a much higher degree of volatility than in the other three systems.

In the UK many homes were rented, but from 1980, under the Thatcher government's 'right to buy' legislation, there was a rapid expansion in home ownership. As with America during the interwar period, a political agenda lay behind this: increasing the rate of home ownership by offering more and cheaper mortgages and privatizing government-owned housing was part of a wider strategy, which included encouraging people to buy shares in newly privatized businesses and expand Conservative Party support.

Under the 1980 Housing Act, UK public sector tenants were encouraged to purchase the properties they occupied, at heavily discounted prices. In 1981, 56 per cent of British households lived in owner-occupied accommodation; by 2003 the figure had risen to 68 per cent, and by 2007 it was 70 per cent (ONS 2010). In contrast to the American system, however, the Conservative government soon began to cut back on income support for mortgage interest and withdraw mortgage interest tax relief, which by 2000, under New Labour, was completely abolished. Thus, from the mid-1990s, there was a steady reduction in government support for home ownership, as measured by income support for mortgage interest, mortgage income tax relief, stamp duty and inheritance tax (Williams and

Pannell 2007). As increasing house prices outpaced earnings growth and affordability, and with growing interest in strengthening public services, attention has been refocused on housing policy in favour of home owner-ship (Williams and Parnell 2007, 5). The 2001 Starter Home Initiative and the 2004 Key Worker Living Scheme were introduced to help key public sector workers – particularly nurses, teachers and police – to buy or rent homes in the communities in which they serve. Mortgage support schemes have also been set up to provide assistance to first-time home buyers and to those experiencing difficulty paying their mortgage due to unemploy-ment or a short-term decline in income.

British – and especially American – home ownership and financing systems stand in sharp contrast with those of Australia and Canada. In these countries, mortgage insurance is mandatory and lending criteria more stringent. The regulator's emphasis on the quality of assets means that instead of securitizing mortgages, banks hold onto them until they are paid off. Adjustable-rate and interest-only mortgages are virtually unheard of. There are no non-recourse loans, and mortgage interest is not tax deductible. The subprime market is thus relatively insignificant in both countries.

Whilst, ironically – given the retreat of the state in most other areas – the American system is a product of heavy and ongoing government intervention, the Australian mortgage system is a product of minimal intervention, the last of which was phased out during the early 1990s with the collapse of the New South Wales government-owned equivalent to Fannie Mae (Stapledon 1998). In Australia, mortgages have tradition-ally been limited to a level where debt servicing accounts for less than 30 per cent of a borrower's gross income. More recently, this was adjusted such that income above the 'costs of living' serves as the basis for assess-ing mortgage affordability (Laker 2004, 6). As the costs of living can be considered independent of income level, wealthier individuals can expand debt further than others. As a result, only those who can afford to take on the debt can secure mortgage loans. Mortgage debt is insured by Lenders' Mortgage Insurance (LMI), which covers 100 per cent of mort-gage debt, transferring the risk of credit exposure to the insurer. Although there was some securitization of mortgages during the 1990s and 2000s, a strong ownership culture combined with non-deductibility of inter-est and no capital gains tax on owner-occupied property provide strong incentives for Australians to build equity in their homes. At the same time, high property market transparency and the predominance of Listed Property Trusts (LPTs) as issuers of mortgage-backed securities contrib-utes to the relative stability of the MBS market in Australia (Australian Securitization Forum 2008). LPTs are legally required to report their activities and underlying collateral performance to the regulators, the Australian Securities Exchange (ASX) and ASIC.

In Canada, too, the mortgage market is highly restrictive. The vast majority of mortgages are originated by banks to hold, thereby providing a strong incentive not to lend where there is a high risk of default. All mortgages with less than a 20 per cent down payment must be insured by the Canadian Mortgage and Housing Corporation (CMHC), backed by government guarantee. As a result, Canadian mortgages are much less leveraged, translating to lower risk for the lender. Established in 1945, the CMHC insures the principal and interest on Canadian mortgage loans, backed by its borrowing power under federal government legislation, the National Housing Act (NHA). High credit standards on eligibility for mortgage insurance, imposed by government regulators, were recently tightened to guard against a US-style housing bubble (CBC News 2010). As a result, only those who can demonstrate an ability to repay the loan are able to secure mortgages in Canada. In 1985, the CMHC introduced the National Housing Act Mortgage Backed Securities (NHA MBS) programme in response to rising mortgage costs. In 1987, following investors' complaints about the lengthy payment period on defaulted loans during the 1980s, the NHA MBS programme added a 'guarantee of timely payment'. This effectively removed risk from the equation. With a defaulted mortgage, the payments would be kept up until the principal was repaid by the guarantor, the CMHC. The stability of the Canadian MBS market was further strengthened and liquidity increased in 2001, when the CMHS introduced the three- and five-year Canada Mortgage Bond (CMB), guaranteed by the CMHC.

Thus, although MBSs are present in the British, Australian and Canadian financial systems, they do not account for a significant proportion of the market. Further, given the nature of house financing in these countries – especially Australia and Canada – there has been little or no growth in the volatile subprime sector, which remains very small outside of the US.

4.8.2 Neoclassical Liberalization Finally Goes too Far

By the mid-2000s, the housing boom in America was cooling, so the search for yield by the internationalized banks intensified. An apparent solution was found in ever more extreme parts of the American subprime sector. Here, heightened risk meant higher returns in the securitized products built from these mortgages. However, exploiting these highly risky segments would require nearly complete relaxation of lending criteria, which in turn created pressure to securitize subprime loans more quickly, before they went bad. Closer examination of the criteria for subprime lending reveals the reason why: all that was required was a willingness to sign up for an adjustable-rate mortgage (ARM). No proof of income, no documentation and no insurance was required. However, a very low initial rate – and many could barely afford even that – quickly increased to unaffordable levels. Even when the initial rate was being paid, under Generally Accepted Accounting Practices (GAAP) lenders could show the full amount in their books, so by the time the mortgage defaulted, it would be someone else's problem. So popular were these products that between 2000 and 2005 subprime mortgage-backed bonds exploded from $80 billion, or less than a tenth of the market, in 2000 to $800 billion, or almost half, by 2005 (Tett 2009).

For the ARM loan holders, though, things were even worse; the sub-prime bubble had lengthened the property boom, so they had bought at the very top of the market. Not only could they not afford their loans, there was no incentive even to try. With non-recourse loans, they could easily walk away; so they did exactly that – in their droves. But when default rates outpaced expectations, investor confidence collapsed, as did liquidity in the money markets and the ability of many SIVs to fund themselves.

The relaxation of lending criteria, however, also required relaxation by other regulators – in particular the Federal Department of Housing and Urban Development (HUD). Whilst the Clinton administration had set targets to help more low-income and minority families own their own homes, it had also charged HUD with curbing predatory lending. By not allowing Fannie Mae and Freddie Mac to get involved with the riskiest subprime loans, it was expected that the worst excesses of the lenders would be limited. However, in spite of warnings by HUD researchers in 2001 that default rates were rising, little action was taken. By the time HUD targets were next revised, in 2004 under the Bush administration, the affordable housing goal was raised from 50 to 56 per cent, and Freddie and Fannie's purchases of subprime securities had risen by a factor of ten; between 2004 and 2006 they purchased an additional $434 billion of subprime loans, exposing borrowers to exploitation and the securities market to extreme volatility. HUD has since been severely criticized for poor policy implementation and weak regulation. According to Senator Jack Reed:

> We need to focus on putting families in homes they can truly afford, not just getting a sale, packaging the loan into a sophisticated financial security and walking away to the next closing. Today people are wondering, 'why weren't the regulators and the industry probing these loans more deeply?' (Leonnig 2008)

By contrast, in response to continuing house price inflation in Australia, the Australian Prudential Regulatory Authority (APRA), well aware that house prices could not increase forever, warned that competition for a share of a slowing house lending market should not lead to an easing of credit standards. Instead, banks were advised to consider alternative investment opportunities, in particular a return to corporate lending (Laker 2004, 9). This more cautious approach may have prevented a further increase in investment – at lower lending standards – in the housing sector, ultimately contributing to gentle deflation of the Australian housing bubble and avoiding the destruction of a burst.

With hindsight, the American subprime bubble appears to be the inevitable result of successful lobbying for successive and specific loosening of regulation in order to allow predatory mortgage lending practices and toothless housing policy. The securitization of subprime mortgages encouraged risk-taking in lending; the predominance of non-recourse loans encouraged risk-taking in borrowing; and housing policy designed to promote subprime lending, in a system where there is little regulation or supervision of the market for derivative products, both legislated and legitimated risk-taking on the part of all involved. The failure of policy-makers to address the obvious problem of risk that is inherent in the American house financing system however suggests that political influences and vested interests may be at play, hinting at undue private sector influence over the state. This, in many ways, is the underlying principle defining the 'varieties of liberalism' approach – the relative balance of power between the state and the private sector, and the character of that relationship.

4.9   CONCLUSIONS

The return to economic liberalism in the Anglo-Saxon world was motivated by the apparent failure of Keynesian economic management to control the stagflation of the 1970s and early 1980s. In this context, the theories of economic liberalism, championed by Friederich von Hayek, Milton Friedman and the Chicago School economists, provided an alternative. However, the divergent experience of the US, UK, Canada and Australia reveals two distinct 'varieties' of economic liberalism: the 'neoclassical' incarnation, which describes American and British liberal capitalism; and the more 'balanced' economic liberalism that evolved in Canada and Australia. In large part, these were a product of the way that liberal economic theory was understood and translated into policy, which in turn shaped the evolving relationship between the state and the private sector, and the relative position of the financial sector within the broader economic system. Together, these determined the nature and extent of financial market regulation and the system's relative stability during the 2008 crisis.

4.9.1   The 'Neoclassical' and more 'Balanced' Varieties of Economic Liberalism

In the US and the UK, 'Reaganomics' and 'Thatcherism' represented a conscious rejection of Keynesian theory and a reorientation of policy, away from reducing unemployment and boosting growth, towards improving the productivity of individual sectors within the economy. In both countries a strong central government, led by a charismatic leader, was able to effect a radical change in policy, emphasizing the merits of free markets, private sector provision, withdrawal of the state and individualization of social welfare.

In Canada and Australia, however, whilst the challenges of the 1970s undermined confidence in the state's ability to manage the economy, it did not weaken support for the social welfare state. Canadian and Australian economic liberalism thus emphasized the merits of competition in markets (rather than focusing purely on market freedom); it sought to limit the role of the state in the provision of services, but without compromising access to basic health, education and income security. Economic liberalization was therefore accompanied by regulation designed to permit the market to function effectively; and to the degree that public services were privatized, the state assumed a strong role in regulation in the public interest.

In both Canada and Australia, economic liberalism was interpreted and implemented by successive Liberal and/or Labour governments, in an incremental process that involved the cooperation of economic liberals and modernizing social democrats; and those policies that were seen to best serve the interests of society were evolved through a process that encouraged learning to take place when challenges were encountered. The existence of countervailing forces, including strong regional governments and effective mechanisms for the participation of a range of stakeholders, including citizens and representatives from both sides of industry, resulted in a more 'balanced' approach to economic liberalism that in some respects served to enhance the capacity of the Canadian and Australian states.

Despite the logical coherence of economic liberalism in Australia and Canada, however, the process of incorporating it into policy was evolutionary, rather than consciously planned. It is thus possible to argue the existence of a third – more deliberate – variety of liberalism: 'ordoliberalism'. Whilst ordoliberalism contains many of the features that distinguish the Australian and Canadian varieties of economic liberalism from their American and British counterparts, the crucial difference is that far from being accidental, ordoliberalism represents an overall vision of economic liberalization. The theory was championed by Walter Eucken and Alexander Rüstow and arises from Germany, a nation with very strong regional governments as well as institutions for joint consultation and collective participation in debates about social and economic policy – all powerful veto players.

4.9.2 The Theoretical and Historical Roots of 'Ordoliberalism'

'Ordoliberalism'[22] was originally conceptualized by the economists of the German Freiburg School during the interwar period (Boas and Gans-Morse 2009). Drawing on the concept of *ordo*, the Latin word for 'order', ordoliberalism refers to an ideal economic system that would be more orderly than the laissez-faire economy advocated by classical liberals (Oliver 1960, 133–34). Following the 1929 stock market crash and Great Depression, while Franklin Roosevelt was pledging a 'New Deal' for Americans and John Maynard Keynes was writing *The General Theory*, intellectuals of the German Freiburg School were proposing a pragmatic revision of liberal economic policy. They argued that for the free market to function effectively, the state should assume an active role, supported by a strong legal system and appropriate regulatory framework. Without a strong government, they argued, private interests, in a system characterized by differences in relative power, would serve to undermine competition (Oliver 1960; Boarman 1964; Gerber 1994). The German ordoliberals were concerned that the rules of the game not favour the powerful and wealthy (Gerber 1994, 38). However, they opposed full-scale Keynesian employment policies and an extensive welfare state. Instead, the ordoliberals believed that liberalism – the freedom of individuals to compete in markets – should be separated from laissez-faire: the freedom of markets from government intervention.

Walter Eucken, one of the founding fathers and most influential representatives of the Freiburg School, criticized classical laissez-faire liberalism for its 'naturalistic naivety', which finds expression in the US and UK varieties of liberalism. These systems hold onto the belief that the market is a 'natural given', a natural order which occurs spontaneously if the state does not hamper its emergence (Foucault 2004). On the contrary, Eucken's understanding of the market and of competition is very much at odds with the classical (and neoclassical) liberal notion that markets constitute some sort of natural order, which requires protection from excessive state interference. In Eucken's view, the market and competition can only exist if a strong state establishes an economic order. The state's role must be clearly delimited; but in the area where the state has a role to play, it needs to be powerful and active. It is this theory of order that distinguishes German ordoliberalism most clearly from its American neoclassical cousin. For ordoliberals, government is the solution to the problem, so long as it is the right kind of government. Only specific conditions, created by the state, can establish competitive markets. It is not about rolling back the state to free the underlying natural market order. Rather, it is about a strong state creating a functioning and humane economic order (Eucken 1932; Rüstow 1953, 1957; Goldschmidt and Rauchenschwandtner 2007).

This humane economic order has the principle of competition at its heart; and it is through this principle that the state constitutes its *raison d'être*. This perspective was expressed by Alexander Rüstow, a prominent German ordoliberal, in a 1932 essay entitled 'Free economy – strong state'. In the words of Hartwich (2009, 14):

> Rüstow blamed excessive interventionism for the economic crisis. He also warned of burdening the state with the task of correcting all sorts of economic problems. His speech was the clear rejection of a state that gets involved with economic processes. In its place, Rüstow wanted to see a state that set the rules for economic behaviour and enforced compliance with them. It was a limited role for the state but it required a strong state nonetheless. Apart from this task, however, the state should refrain from getting too engaged in markets. This meant a clear 'no' to protectionism, subsidies, cartels – or what today we would call 'crony capitalism,' 'regulatory capture,' or 'corporate welfare.' However, Rüstow also saw a role for a limited interventionism as long as it went 'in the direction of the market's laws.'

Conversely, as the state had to be powerful, but limited, markets were similarly not seen as an absolute principle, but as one that had to be confined within a given economic order. According to Wilhelm Röpke, another major figure in ordoliberalism:

> [W]e must stress most emphatically that we have no intention to demand more from competition than it can give. It is a means of establishing order and exercising control in the narrow sphere of a market economy based on the division of labor, but no principle on which a whole society can be built. From the sociological and moral point of view it is even dangerous because it tends more to dissolve than to unite. If competition is not to have the effect of a social explosive and is at the same time not to degenerate, its premise will be a correspondingly sound political and moral framework. There should be a strong state, aloof from the hungry hordes of vested interests, a high standard of business ethics, and undegenerated community of people ready to co-operate with each other, who have a natural attachment to, and a firm place in society. (Röpke 1950, 181)

In other words, for ordoliberals it was not the state but private monopolies that were the main enemy of a free society. In order to preserve a free society, the state had to be strong and impose a rigorous competition policy. Another central claim of the ordoliberal school was the importance of creating an economy where production is decentralized and takes place in relatively small units (Röpke 1950, 1981; Rüstow 1953, 1957). Achieving this implied a role for the state in preventing powerful actors from concentrating their economic power. Hayek, who early on in his career was a link between the German ordoliberals and the US neoliberals (Foucault 2004), defended similar views regarding decentralization (Gamble 1996). But, in the more libertarian views of Milton Friedman, the free play of markets overwhelmed concerns about concentration of economic power in certain industries.

To what extent it would be possible to have deliberately imposed such a wide-ranging system on another economy is a moot point; and much would depend upon the scale of Galbraith's 'massive onslaught of circumstance' and the nature of Friedman's 'ideas lying around at the time'. In the final analysis, it is time to engage in a debate about the true nature of the varieties that exist within economic liberalism. Only then will we be able to understand the type that has failed, and in so doing to identify ways out of the current crisis of contemporary capitalism.

NOTES

1. According to Hall and Soskice (2001), LMEs rely on market mechanisms to solve the problem of coordination, both among firms and between firms and their various stakeholder groups, including employees, customers, suppliers and capital providers. LMEs have open and competitive markets that are protected by strict anti-trust and competition legislation. Levels of regulation, taxation and government intervention in the macroeconomy are comparatively low. Labour markets are flexible; and in comparison with the coordinated market economies (CMEs), employment protection and welfare spending are relatively low.
2. Table 4.1 reports the change in cumulated market value of each country's largest banks, that is, those among the world's 50 largest banks.
3. It should be noted however that the Harper government in Canada decided in the autumn of 2008 to make available a bailout and stimulus package of C$75 billion, corresponding to 4.3 per cent of GDP. Yet this package can by no means be compared to the US or UK rescue packages. The Canadian 'bailout plan' consisted of the government's commitment to buy 'good' – as opposed to 'toxic' – assets from the banks so as to inject liquidity into the banking system and, ultimately, the real economy. These funds were thus made available to prevent a slowdown in economic growth rather than to support failing banks. Nevertheless, a proportion of these funds was used to acquire parts of foreign banks that were in trouble and to make strategic acquisitions in attractive markets such as Brazil (Chossudovsky 2009; Heinrich 2009).
4. Canada appeared somewhat less vulnerable (in terms of its current account balance and

mortgage debt to GDP ratio). See Konzelmann et al. (2010b), especially section 2, for a further discussion.

5. In 2008, the mortgage debt to GDP ratio was 71 per cent in the US, 86.3 per cent in the UK and 85 per cent in Australia (Vorms 2009; Keen 2009). This is in contrast to the much lower ratio of 45.6 per cent in Canada (Keen 2009).

6. Höpner et al. (2009, 5–6) single out three defining principles of a liberal economic order: individual responsibility, decentralized decision-making and competition.

7. Research on the role of ideas in economic change in the field of political science largely supports this view: external shocks and economic crises challenge and destabilize the existing orthodoxy which did not manage to prevent or was even the very cause of the crisis. As the dominant view is weakened, 'policy entrepreneurs' use existing ideas or reactivate old ones in order to propose alternatives to the failed existing orthodoxy (Hall 1993; Blyth 2002).

8. For a further discussion, see Konzelmann et al. (2010a).

9. By contrast, New Keynesians attributed stagflation to the presence of union monopoly that served to increase wages above their market clearing rate, thereby causing unemployment to rise. From this perspective, attempts to increase employment beyond the 'non-accelerating inflation rate of unemployment' (NAIRU), would merely fuel inflation (Meade 1982). Thus, for both liberal and New Keynesian economists, there was a simple choice between higher real wages and more jobs.

10. Rational expectations theory posits that outcomes do not differ systematically from what people rationally expect.

11. Under the Bretton Woods system, most countries sought to maintain an overall balance of trade, settling international trade balances in US dollars, with the US's agreement to redeem other central banks' dollar holdings for gold at a fixed rate of $35 per ounce. The US, however, had not been not overly concerned about maintaining a balance in trade since it could pay its export deficits in dollars. Nor had it taken action to prevent the steady loss of American gold. By 1971, under pressure to devalue its currency, due to the decline in US gold reserves, instead of devaluing the dollar, President Nixon removed gold backing from the dollar.

12. Pressures contributing to unemployment during this period were in part a result of the (not yet evident) hollowing-out of the British manufacturing sector through leveraged buyouts which continued into the 1970s. See also Konzelmann et al. (2010a).

13. The American, British and Canadian voting systems are plurality systems in which seats are awarded to the person with the most votes, even if it is not a majority. This is in contrast with the Australian system, which seeks to resolve the concern about balancing plurality with proportional representation. In Australia, seats are awarded in the upper house on the basis of proportional representation by states and territories, and in the lower house on the basis of preferential voting. This system is argued to produce a more stable government while having better diversity of parties to review its actions (Morelli 2004; Calvo 2009).

14. The efficient markets theory of financial securities prices, which is rooted in rational expectations theory, asserts that the price of an asset reflects all relevant available information about its value.

15. Five different US federal agencies share responsibility for regulating depository institutions: the Federal Reserve, Federal Deposit Insurance Corporation (FDIC), National Credit Union Administration (NCUA), Office of the Comptroller of the Currency (OCC) and Office of Thrift Supervision (OTS). Depending on its legal structure, a depository institution may be subject to regulation by up to three of these federal agencies as well as a state regulator. State authorities are also responsible for regulating the insurance industry. The national securities markets being regulated by the Securities Exchange Commission (SEC) and the futures markets are regulated by the Commodities Futures Trading Commission (CFTC), individual derivatives and commodities exchanges and the National Futures Association (a self-regulating organization or SRO).

16. The RTC was established and assigned responsibility for winding up the failed S&Ls.
17. It is interesting to note the contrast with the American credo: 'Life, liberty and the pursuit of happiness'.
18. Malcolm Maiden is business editor for *The Age*.
19. One explanation for this pattern is the existence of caps on deposit rates in the US. Since banks could only promise a limited return on bank accounts, savings were channelled away from them, leading to lower levels of deposits, further increasing incentives for banks to rely on money markets (Booth 2008, 43).
20. Prior to the first CDO created for Imperial Savings & Loans, MBSs had a successful track record. Corporate debt also has a history of securitization, but is much easier for investors to assess than mortgage debt. Aside from broad indications of the source of the mortgages in the securitized product, the system's stability is reliant on solid lending criteria for a low rate of default. America however, evolved the least stringent lending criteria of the four countries in our study – and carried out the vast majority of securitizations of the resulting loans.
21. In the US, a strike at Ford's Detroit plant in 1938 resulted in the strikers being summarily fired. This triggered the events leading up to the 'Ford Massacre' and the deaths of four workers. The ensuing public outrage resonated with then current events in China and Germany and with the revolution in Russia 15 years earlier. As a result, one of the aims of the Roosevelt Administration's New Deal was to foster cooperation among workers, industry and government and in so doing to avoid the likelihood of more radical social change (Ferguson 2002).
22. For further discussion of the historical development of 'ordoliberalism', see Hartwich (2009) and Boas and Gans-Morse (2009), who trace the origin of the term – originally used synonymously with 'neoliberalism' – to interwar Germany and the intellectual writing of the Freiburg School. In this context, 'neoliberalism' means quite the opposite of its contemporary usage. Hence, in the discussion here, we use the term 'ordoliberalism' to avoid confusion with the more classical economic liberalism associated with contemporary 'neoliberalism'.

REFERENCES

Albert, M. (1993), *Capitalism vs. Capitalism: How America's Obsession with Individual Achievement and Short-Term Profit has Led It to the Brink of Collapse*, New York: Four Walls Eight Windows.

Amable, B. (2003), *The Diversity of Modern Capitalism*, Oxford: Oxford University Press.

Argy, F. (2001), 'Liberalism and economic policy', in J. Nieuwenhuysen, P. Lloyd and M. Mead (eds), *Reshaping Australia's Economy: Growth with Equity and Sustainability*, Cambridge: Cambridge University Press, pp. 67–85.

Australian Securitization Forum (2008), *The Financial Services and Credit Reform Green Paper Submission by the Australian Securitization Forum*, available at http://securitisation.com.au/docs/press/ASF_Financial_Services_and_Credit_Reform_Green_Paper_Submission__by_the_Australian_Securitisation_Forum.pdf (accessed 14 June 2011).

Bain, E. and I. Harper (2000), 'Integration of financial services: evidence from Australia', *North American Actuarial Journal*, **4** (3), 1–19.

Bakir, C. (2003), 'Who needs a review of the financial system in Australia? The case of the Wallis Inquiry', *Australian Journal of Political Science*, **38** (3), 511–534.

Battellino, R. (2009), 'Some comments on bank funding. Remarks to the 22nd Australian Finance and Banking Conference', available at http://www.rba.gov.au/speeches/2009/sp-dg-161209.html (accessed 31 May 2011).

BBC (1999), 'Mayfair Set', available at http://www.archive.org/details/AdamCurtis_TheMayfairSet (accessed 14 June 2011).

Berg, C. (2008), 'Regulation and the regulatory burden', available at http://www.ipa.org.
au/news/1630/regulation-and-the-regulatory-burden/category/1 (accessed 31 May 2011).
Bluestone, B. and B. Harrison (1982), *The Deindustrialization of America: Plant Closings,
Community Abandonment and the Dismantling of Basic Industry*, New York: Basic Books.
Blyth, M. (2002), *Great Transformations. Economic Ideas and Institutional Change in the
Twentieth Century*, Cambridge: Cambridge University Press.
Boarman, P. (1964), *Germany's Economic Dilemma: Inflation and the Balance of Payments*,
New Haven, CT: Yale University Press.
Boas, T. and J. Gans-Morse (2009), 'Neo-liberalism: from new liberal philosophy to anti-
liberal slogan', *Studies in Comparative International Development*, **44** (2), 137–161.
Booth, L. (2008), 'Subprime, market meltdown, and learning from the past', in K.
Ambachtsheer (ed.), *Financial Crisis and Rescue. What Went Wrong? Why? What Lessons
Can Be Learned?* Toronto: Toronto University Press, pp. 17–53.
Boskin, Michael (1987), *Reagan and the Economy: The Successes, Failures and Unfinished
Agenda*, San Francisco, CA: International Center for Economic Growth.
Boyer, R. (2000), 'Is a finance-led growth regime a viable alternative to Fordism? A prelimi-
nary analysis', *Economy and Society*, **29** (1), 111–145.
Brean, D., L. Kryzanowski and G. Roberts (2011), 'Canada and the United States: different
roots, different routes to financial sector regulation', *Business History*, **53** (2), 249–269.
Calvo, E (2009), 'The competitive road to proportional representation: partisan biases
and electoral regime change under increasing party competition', *World Politics*, **61** (2),
254–295.
CBC News (2010), 'Flaherty tightens mortgage taps', available at http://www.cbc.ca/money/
story/2010/02/16/mortgage-flaherty.html (accessed 31 May 2011).
Chossudovsky, M. (2009), 'Canada's 75 billion dollar bank bailout', available at http://www.
globalresearch.ca/index.php?context=va&aid=12007 (accessed 31 May 2011).
Clark, P. (1979), 'Issues in the analysis of capital formation and productivity growth',
Brookings Papers on Economic Activity, **10** (2), 423–446.
Clarke, T. (1997), *Silent Coup: Confronting the Big Business Takeover of Canada*, Ottowa:
CCPA.
Clarke, T. (2007), *International Corporate Governance. A Comparative Approach*, Oxford:
Routledge.
Competition Bureau Canada (1998), 'Backgrounder: the Competition Bureau and bank
mergers', available at http://www.competitionbureau.gc.ca/eic/site/cb-bc.nsf/eng/00825.
html (accessed 14 June 2011).
Courchene, Tom and Douglas Purvis (1993), 'Productivity growth and Canada's interna-
tional competitiveness', Kingston, Ontario: Bell Canada Papers on Economic and Public
Policy.
Curry, T. and L. Shibut (2000), 'The cost of the savings and loan crisis: truth and conse-
quences', *FDIC Banking Review*, **13** (2), 26–35.
Deakin, S. and A. Singh (2008), 'The stock market, the market for corporate control and
the theory of the firm: legal and economic perspectives and implications for public policy',
Cambridge Centre for Business Research Working Paper, 365.
Department of Industry (1997), *Merger Enforcement Guidelines as Applied to a Bank Merger*,
Ottawa: Supply and Services Canada.
Dignam, A. and M. Galanis (2004), 'Australia inside out: the corporate governance system of
the Australian listed market', *Melbourne University Law Review*, **28** (3), 623–653.
Enoch, S. (2007), 'Changing the ideological fabric? A brief history of (Canadian) Neo-
liberalism', *State of Nature: An Online Journal of Radical Ideas*, available at http://www.
stateofnature.org/changingTheIdeological.html (accessed 30 May 2011).
Eucken, W. (1932), 'Staatliche Strukturwandlungen und die Krisis des Kapitalismus',
Weltwirtschaftliches Archiv, **36**, 297–323.
Fairbrother, Peter (2002), 'Unions in Britain: towards a new unionism?' in Peter Fairbrother
and Gerrard Greffin (eds), *Changing Prospects for Trade Unionism: Comparisons Between
Six Countries*, New York: Continuum, pp. 56–89.

Fairbrother, Peter and Gerrard Griffin (eds) (2002), *Changing Prospects for Trade Unionism: Comparisons Between Six Countries*, New York: Continuum.

Fama, E. (1970), 'Efficient capital markets: a review of theory and empirical work', *Journal of Finance*, **25** (2), 383–417.

Ferguson, N. (2002), *The Ascent of Money: A Financial History of the World*, London: Allen Lane.

Ferguson, N. (2010), *High Financier: The Lives and Time of Siegmund Warburg*, London: Reed Elsevier.

Financial Services Authority (FSA) (2009), *The Turner Review. A Regulatory Response to the Global Banking Crisis*, London: Financial Services Authority.

Financial Times (2009), 'The fearsome become the fallen', 23 March, p. 9.

Foucault, M. (2004), *Naissance de la biopolitique: Cours au collège de France (1978–1979)*, Paris; Gallimard-Seuil.

Friedman M. (1977), 'Unemployment and inflation', Institute of Economic Affairs, Occasional Paper 51.

Friedman, M. (1982 [1962]), *Capitalism and Freedom*, Chicago, IL: University of Chicago Press.

Friedman, Milton and Rose Friedman (1984), *Tyranny of the Status Quo*, San Diego, CA: Harcourt Brace Jovanovich.

Galbraith, John (1999), *The Affluent Society*, London: Penguin Books.

Gamble, Andrew (1996), *Hayek. The Iron Cage of Liberty*, Boulder, CO: Westview Press.

Gardner, Richard (1980), *Sterling–Dollar Diplomacy in Current Perspective: The Origins and the Prospects of our International Economic Order*, New York: Columbia University Press.

Gerber, D. (1994), 'Constitutionalizing the economy: German neo-liberalism, competition law and the "new" Europe', *American Journal of Comparative Law*, **42** (1), 25–84.

Gilbert, G. (1986), 'Requiem for Regulation Q: what it did and why it passed away', *Federal Reserve Bank of St Louis Review*, February, 22–37.

Goldschmidt, N. and H. Rauchenschwandtner (2007), 'The philosophy of social market economy: Michel Foucault's analysis of ordoliberalism', *Freiburg Discussion Papers on Constitutional Economics*, **7** (4), 1–30.

Goodhart, C. (2004), 'The Bank of England: 1970–2000,' in R. Michie and R. Williamson (eds), *The British Government and the City of London in the Twentieth Century*, Cambridge: Cambridge University Press, pp. 340–371.

Gordon, John (2004), *An Empire of Wealth: The Epic History of American Economic Power*, New York: Harper Collins.

Griffin, Gerrard and Peter Fairbrother (2002), 'Conclusions: the state of unions', in Peter Fairbrother and Gerrard Griffin (eds), *Changing Prospects for Trade Unionism: Comparisons Between Six Countries*, New York: Continuum, pp. 238–256.

Griffin, Gerrard and S. Svensen (2002), 'Unions in Australia: struggling to survive', in Peter Fairbrother and Gerrard Griffin (eds), *Changing Prospects for Trade Unionism: Comparisons Between Six Countries*, New York: Continuum, pp. 21–55.

Hall, P. (1993), 'Policy paradigms, social learning and the state: the case of economic policy-making in Britain', *Comparative Politics*, **25** (3), 275–296.

Hall, Peter and David Soskice (2001), 'An introduction to varieties of capitalism', in Peter Hall and David Soskice (eds), *Varieties of Capitalism. The Institutional Foundations of Comparative Advantage*, Oxford: Oxford University Press, pp. 1–70.

Harris, S. (2004), 'Financial sector reform in Canada: interests and the policy process', *Canadian Journal of Political Science*, **37** (1), 161–84.

Hartwich, O. (2009), 'Neo-liberalism: the genesis of a political swearword', CIS Occasional Paper 114.

Heinrich, E. (2009), 'What Obama can learn from Canada on bank bailouts', *Time Magazine*, 19 February.

Helleiner, Eric (1994), *States and the Reemergence of Global Finance*, Ithaca, NY: Cornell University Press.

Höpner, M., A. Petring, D. Seikel and B. Werner (2009), 'Liberalisierungspolitik. Eine Bestandsaufnahme von zweieinhalb Dekaden marktschaffender Politik in entwickelten Industrieländern', MPIfG Discussion Paper 09/7.
ILO (1997), *World Labour Report*, Geneva: ILO.
IMF (2008), World Economic Outlook (April), 'Housing and the business cycle', New York: International Monetary Fund.
Jackson, G. and R. Deeg (2008), 'From comparing capitalisms to the politics of institutional change', *Review of International Political Economy*, **15** (4), 680–709.
Jarley, P. (2002), 'American Unions at the start of the 21st century: going back to the future?' in P. Fairbrother and G. Griffin (eds), *Changing Prospects for Trade Unionism: Comparisons Between Six Countries*, New York: Continuum, pp. 200–237.
Johnson, Christopher (1991), *The Economy Under Mrs Thatcher*, London: Penguin Books.
Keen, S. (2009), 'Household debt: the final stage in an artificially extended Ponzi bubble', *Australian Economic Review*, **42** (3), 347–357.
Konzelmann, S., F. Wilkinson, M. Fovargue-Davies and D. Sankey (2010a), 'Governance, regulation and financial market instability: the implications for policy and reform', *Cambridge Journal of Economics*, **34** (5), 929–954.
Konzelmann, S., M. Fovargue-Davies and G. Schnyder (2010b), 'Varieties of liberalism: Anglo-Saxon capitalism in crisis?' Cambridge Centre for Business Research, Working Paper No. 403.
Kryzanowski, L. and N. Ursel (1993), 'Market reactions to announcements of legislative changes and Canadian bank takeovers of Canadian investment dealers', *Journal of Financial Services Research*, **7** (2), 171–185.
La Porta, R., F. Lopez-de-Silanes, A. Shleifer and R. Vishny (1997), 'Legal determinants of external finance', *Journal of Finance*, **52** (3), 1131–1150.
Laker, J. (2004), 'The Australian banking system – building on strength', Paper presented at the Business Banking 2005 Conference, Sydney, 10 November.
Lazonick, W. and M. O'Sullivan (2000), 'Maximizing shareholder value: a new ideology for corporate governance', *Economy and Society*, **29** (1), 13–35.
Leonnig, C. (2008), 'How HUD mortgage policy fed the crisis', *Washington Post*, 10 June, A01, http://www.washingtonpost.com/wp-dyn/content/article/2008/06/09/AR20080 60902626.html.
Lott, Susan (2005), *Bank Mergers and the Public Interest*, Ottawa: Public Interest Advocacy Centre.
MacFarlane, I. (2006), 'The real reasons why it was the 1990s recession we had to have', *Age*, 2 December.
Maiden, M. (2008), 'Westpac–St George merger won't topple four-pillars', *Age*, 15 May.
Marglin, Stephen and Juliet Schor (2007), *The Golden Age of Capitalism: Re-interpretting the Post-War Experience*, Oxford: Clarendon Press.
Meade, James (1982), *Wage Fixing*, London: Allen & Unwin.
Morck, R., D. Strangeland and B. Yeung (1998), 'Inherited wealth, corporate control and economic growth: the Canadian disease?' NBER Working Paper, 6814.
Morelli, M. (2004), 'Party formation and policy outcomes under different electoral systems', *Review of Economic Studies*, **71** (3), 829–853.
Murray, G. (2002), 'Unions in Canada: strategic renewal, strategic conundrum', in P. Fairbrother and G. Griffin (eds), *Changing Prospects for Trade Unionism: Comparisons Between Six Countries*, New York: Continuum, pp. 93–136
Nieuwenhuysen, J., P. Lloyd and M. Mead (2001), *Reshaping Australia's Economy: Growth with Equity and Sustainability*, Cambridge: Cambridge University Press.
Norrie, K. and D. Owram (1991), *A History of the Canadian Economy*, Toronto: Harcourt Brace Javonovich Canada.
OECD (1997), *Employment Outlook*, OECD: Paris.
OECD (2009), *Factbook*, OECD: Paris, available at: www.oecd.org/publications/factbook.
Office of the Deputy Prime Minister (ODPM) (2003), 'The mortgage backed securites market in the UK: overview and prospects', Housing Research Summary, 201.

Office for National Statistics (ONS) (2010), 'Housholds – savings ratios' available at: http://www.statistics.gov.uk/CCI/nscl.asp?ID=5927 (accessed 30 May 2011).

Oliver, H. (1960), 'German neo-liberals', *Quarterly Journal of Economics*, **74** (1), 117–149.

Pan, E. (2011), 'Structural reform of financial regulation in Canada', *Transnational Law and Contemporary Problems*, **19**, 796–867.

Patience, Allan and Brian Head (1979), *From Whitlam to Fraser: Reform and Reaction in Australian Politics*, Melbourne: Oxford University Press.

Perry, George and James Tobin (eds) (2000), *Economic Events, Ideas and Policies: The 1960s and After*, Washington, DC: Brookings Institution.

Peters, J. (2011), 'The rise of finance and the decline of organized labour in the advanced capitalist countries', *New Political Economy*, **16** (1), 73–99.

Quiggin, J. (1997), 'Economic rationalism', *Crossings*, **2** (1), 3–12.

Quiggin, J. (1998), 'Social democracy and market reform in Australia and New Zealand', *Oxford Review of Public Policy*, **14** (9), 79–109.

Rao, P. Someshwar and Clifton Lee-Sing (1995), 'Governance structure, corporate decision-making and firm performance in North America', in Ronald Daniels and Randall Morck (eds), *Corporate Decision-Making in Canada*, Alberta: University of Calgary Press, pp. 43–104.

Reich, Robert (2008), *Supercapitalism: The Battle for Democracy in an Age of Big Business*, Cambridge: Icon Books.

Reid, Margaret (1988), *All Change in the City: The Revolution in Britain's Financial Sector*, London: Macmillan Press.

Reinhart, Carmen and Kenneth Rogoff (2009), *This Time is Different. Eight Centuries of Financial Folly*, Princeton, NJ: Princeton University Press.

Richardson, G. (2007), 'The collapse of the US banking system during the Great Depression, 1929 to 1933: new archival evidence', *Australasian Accounting, Business and Finance Journal*, **1** (1), 39–50.

Röpke, Wilhelm (1950), *Ist die deutsche Wirtschaftspolitik richtig? Analyse und Kritik*, Stuttgart: Kohlhammer.

Röpke, Wilhelm (1981), 'Richtpunkte des liberalen Gesamtprogramms', in W. Stützel, C. Watrin, H. Willgerodt and H. Wünsche (eds), *Grundtexte zur Sozialen Marktwirtschaft: Zeugnisse aus 200 Jahren ordnungspolitischer Diskussion, Vol. 1*, Stuttgart: Ludwig-Erhard-Stiftung e.V, pp. 227–232.

Rüstow ([1932] 1963), 'Die Staatspolitischen Vorraussetzngen des Wirtschaftspolitischien Liberalismus' (Free economy – strong state); in *Rede und Antwort*, Ludwigsburg: Hoch.

Rüstow, Alexander (1953), 'Soziale Marktwirtschaft als Gegenprogramm gegen Kommunismus und Bolschewismus', in Albert Hunold (ed.), *Wirtschaft ohne Wunder*, Erlenbach-Zurich: E. Rentsch, pp. 97–108.

Rüstow, Alexander (1957), 'Vitalpolitik gegen Vermassung', in Albert Hunold (ed.), *Masse und Demokratie, Voksvirtschaftliche Studien für das Schweizer Institut für Auslandsforschung*, Erlenbach-Zurich: E. Rentsch, pp. 215–238.

Secor Consulting (2008), *Positioning Canadian Firms in the Global Market for Corporate Control,* available at http://www.secorgroup.com/files/pdf/SECOR_final_report_on_Canadas_MA_competitiveness.pdf (accessed 30 May 2011).

Seidman, L. William (1997), *History of the Eighties: Lessons for the Future*, Washington, DC: Federal Deposit Insurance Corporation.

Sherman, Matthew (2009), *A Short History of Financial Deregulation in the US*, Washington, DC: Centre for Economic and Policy Research.

Skidelsky, Robert (1990), *Thatcherism*, Oxford: Blackwell Publishers.

Smith, D. (2006), 'The Chicago boy who gave monetarism to the world', *Sunday Times*, 19 November.

Stapledon, N. (1998), 'Housing and the global financial crisis: US versus Australia', *Economic and Labour Relations Review*, **19** (2), 1–16.

Stewart, H. (2009), 'IMF: Fifth of Britain's GDP spent so far on bank bailouts', *Guardian*, 6 March.

Sykes, Trevor (1994), *The Bold Riders: Behind Australia's Corporate Collapses*, Sydney: Allen & Unwin.

Tett, Gillian (2009), *Fool's Gold: How Unrestrained Greed Corrupted a Dream, Shattered Global Markets and Unleashed a Catastrophe*, London: Little Brown.

Time Magazine (1965), 'We are all keynesians now', available at http://www.time.com/time/magazine/article/0,9171,842353,00.html (accessed 30 May 2011).

Tsebelis, G. (2000), 'Veto players and institutional analysis', *Governance*, **4**, 441–474.

US Census Bureau (2004), Housing and Household Economic Statistics Division, available at http://www.census.gov/hhes/www/housing/census/historic/owner.html (accessed 30 May 2011).

US Census Bureau (2010), Housing and Household Economic Statistics Division, available at http://www.census.gov/hhes/www/housing/hvs/historic/index.html (accessed 30 May 2011).

Visser, J. (1993), 'Union organization: why countries differ', *International Journal of Comparative Labour Law and Industrial Relations*, **9** (Fall), 206–225.

Vorms, B. (2009), 'After the crisis: what kind of home ownership policies?' available at http://www.anil.org/fileadmin/ANIL/Etudes/2009/ownership_policies.pdf (accessed 30 May 2011).

Whitley, Richard (2000), *Divergent Capitalisms: The Social Structuring and Change of Business Systems*, Oxford: Oxford University Press.

Williams, P. and B. Pannell (2007), 'Home ownership at the cross-roads?' *Housing and Finance*, **2**, 1–14.

5 Framing human resource management: the importance of national institutional environments to what management does (and should do)
John Godard

5.1 INTRODUCTION

The study of labour and employment practices has a long history, dating at least to the early 20th century (Kaufman 2008, 36ff). Yet the term 'human resource management' (HRM) did not enter popular usage until the 1980s. The emergence of this term and the practices associated with it reflected a unique set of historical conditions – conditions that portended a major shift in academic ideologies. Whether it also portended the emergence of a new field or simply the transformation of an old one – in substance as well as name – is unclear.[1] But there can be little question of a major break between the study of labour and employment practices prior to the 1980s and the study of these practices subsequently. There can also be little question that the received wisdom changed, especially in liberal market economies, and that this was reflected not only in academic work, but also (to some degree) in what employers did. In effect, the accommodative, pluralistic practices advocated in the post-Second World War era came to be viewed as obsolete, to be replaced by the more unitary, managerialist practices of the 'new' HRM, with its emphasis on aligning employee goals with those of the employer through values-based selection, 'soft' skills training, performance management and financial incentives.

Underlying this shift was an important set of unstated assumptions – assumptions that reflected the broader ideologies and conditions of the time (see Godard and Delaney 2000). In a nutshell, these assumptions were those of a neoliberal world, one defined by a weakening of labour and its institutions, a strengthening of employers and, concomitant with both, little if any accepted role for either the state or labour organizations in shaping employer practices. Not all proponents of the new HRM explicitly adhered to a neoliberal ideology. Instead, many likely saw themselves as neutral social scientists studying new management techniques and seeking to elevate their status in business schools by claiming that these practices were of 'strategic' importance and hence the key to competitive advantage. Moreover, some advocated a collaborative, support role for unions. Nonetheless, the assumption was generally one of virtually unconditioned managerial unilateralism, which in turn assumes an ideal-typical neoliberal world, with little substantive role for governments, unions or other forms of legal representation.

These assumptions meant a dearth of institutional analysis and, more importantly, an almost total lack of attention to the role of the state in shaping what it is that employers do and ultimately the consequences of what they do. In the United States in particular, researchers often proceeded from an institutionally blind, social-psychological approach, under which the question came to be not one of why management does as it does or even what it actually does, but rather how various practices can be expected to affect performance and ultimately what management should do in order to maximize that performance. Some researchers applied economic models to the analysis of HRM (see Grimshaw and Rubery 2007), but with the exception of those concerned specifically with the implications of established laws (an important but understudied aspect of HRM), their analyses tended to suffer from a similar institutional blindness.

Not only was little attention paid to the actual practice of HRM, little attention was also paid to the persistence of cross-national variation in this practice – despite claims about globalization and its implications for convergence (Godard 2004a). The assumption seems to have been that this has little to do with what does or does not constitute 'best' practice. Rather, the problem is that employers in some nations have been slower to adopt this practice than have their counterparts in other nations. Where scholars did attempt to explain this variation, they often turned to cultural explanations (e.g., Jackson 2002; see De Cieri 2008), typically adopting some variant of the Hofstede model and using this more as a defence than as a basis for fully coming to terms with institutional complexities and norms that underpin cross-national variation (Aycan 2005).

The underlying problem has been that HRM, and management in general, do not occur in an institutional vacuum. Instead, they are substantially conditioned by the institutional environment within which they are practised. This means not only that the sorts of practices that are likely to be adopted vary, but also that both the way in which they are understood and their likely effectiveness vary. Thus any attempt to establish 'best' practice is likely to be misguided if it does not account for the institutional conditions under which this practice is to be implemented, as is any attempt to establish why it is that management adopts some practices and not others. But even more fundamentally, any attempt to understand

HRM or employment relations in general is likely to be partial at best if it does not take into account the institutional conditions and environment within which they are embedded. In other words, the problem is not just one of understanding variation in the adoption and effectiveness of specific HRM practices across different contexts, but also one of realizing that these practices are institutionally embedded and cannot be fully studied or understood within a given institutional environment unless they are viewed in institutional terms.

This chapter thus advances an institutional environments approach to the study of HRM, with a particular emphasis on cross-national variation in both the context and practice of HRM and the role played by the state in shaping this variation. I begin by discussing the new institutionalist literature and its relevance to the study of cross-national variation in HRM. I then develop a framework for analysing the importance of national institutional environments. Finally, I address the significance of national institutional paradigms and traditions for understanding these environments.

5.2   THE NEW INSTITUTIONALISM, VARIETIES OF CAPITALISM AND HRM

Attempts to define the new institutionalism are now widespread and do not bear repeating here. For present purposes, it can be defined to include all contemporary literature addressing how formal and informal rules (including norms and understandings) embodied in economic, social and political institutions account for substantive questions of economy and society, with a particular focus on the relations between the economic, the social and the political. Although this definition masks considerable variation within and across disciplines in both topic area and theoretical emphasis (Godard 2002, 253), common to all versions is recognition that actors do not behave in an institutional vacuum but are instead part of a broader community of actors subject to (and constitutive of) common rules and the institutions in which they are embedded.

These rules are generally argued not just to constrain and facilitate behaviour, but also to shape the power resources of actors and provide cognitive and normative templates for interpretation and ultimately strategic interaction (Godard 2002; Scott 1995, 43; Hall and Taylor 1996, 939). They do so indirectly as well as directly, becoming embedded in economic, social and political structures that form the broader socio-economic environment within which parties act and ultimately shaping not just how they seek to achieve goals, but also the goals they appear to have, how one course of action comes to be viewed as more rational to the attainment of these goals than another, and how, indeed, what is rational comes to be defined (e.g., Chang 2001). Thus, in analysing HRM, the question is not just whether employers pursue a particular policy or practice, but also what identities or orientations underlie the adoption of that policy or practice (e.g., Locke and Thelen 1995), what taken-for-granted rules and assumptions guide it, and what purpose it is expected to serve – all questions that are too often taken for granted in the HRM literature, and the answers to which may in considerable measure reflect the institutional environment within which HRM is practised.

Perhaps the best illustration of how institutional environments matter is to be found in the 'varieties of capitalism' (VofC) literature. This literature is most closely associated with the work of Hall and Soskice, particularly the introductory chapter to their 2001 edited volume, *Varieties of Capitalism: The Institutional Foundations of Comparative Advantage*. Although the Hall and Soskice contribution is no longer 'new' and is concerned primarily with the economic performance of nations, it is a useful starting point for demonstrating the importance of national institutional environments to the practice of HRM, and ultimately to explaining cross-national variation in this practice.

A central argument advanced by Hall and Soskice is that there are complementarities between the various characteristics of national economies, making it possible to identify different varieties of capitalism, each with its own logic. Hall and Soskice indentify two distinctive such varieties: liberal market economies (LMEs) and coordinated market economies (CMEs). LMEs are most exemplified by the United States of America (USA). They are characterized by competitive markets and weak associational structures, extensive stock market financing, a weak vocational training system, weak social and labour market protections, and only limited legal representation at work, whether this involves collective bargaining or consultation and co-decision rights. CMEs are most exemplified by Germany. They are characterized by coordinated market relations and strong associational structures (e.g., employer associations), extensive bank financing, a strong vocational training system, strong social and labour market protections, industry-wide collective agreements, and extensive worker representation through unions, works councils and/or worker directors.

Although Hall and Soskice do not specifically address HRM, their analysis, coupled with the broader VofC literature, suggests that these varieties give rise to different employer values, beliefs and strategies, and ultimately different work and HRM regimes (Godard 2004a). In LMEs, investor control and short-term pressures imposed by financial markets mean that employers are more likely to adopt a short-term, shareholder-value orientation, in which they view employees largely as resources to be deployed in accordance with immediate shareholder interests. In addition, highly competitive markets and an absence of industry-level collective bargaining mean that employers are under pressure to adopt a cost minimization strategy, one that includes minimization of labour costs and minimal investment in human resources. These conditions, coupled with a lack of participatory rights at work and weak labour market protections, result in a bias towards low-trust labour–management relations and low-skill, low-pay, low-quality jobs in which workers receive little hard skill training, are provided with little job security and have little meaningful representation in employer decisions.

In CMEs, employers are more likely to proceed from a long-term stakeholder orientation, because banks tend to have a longer-term orientation and to view themselves more as 'social' institutions than as agents of shareholders. Coordinated markets mean that they are subject to less direct competitive pressure, and the existence of industry-wide collective agreements means that they do not compete on the basis of labour costs. Although they operate in a higher-cost environment, strong training institutions ensure that they have more highly skilled employees, thus enabling them to adopt a high-quality strategy. This, coupled with strong participatory rights for employees, means that they view employees largely as partners, and that there is a bias towards high-trust labour–management relations and high-skill, high-pay, high-quality jobs in which workers are highly trained, provided with extensive job security, and have strong representation and voice in employer decisions (e.g., Streeck 1992, 1997).

The implication is that the sorts of HRM practices often viewed as best practice in LMEs (e.g., the United States) may not be readily transferable to CMEs (e.g., Germany), resulting in different adaptations to the developments associated with globalization. In LMEs, there are few barriers to the adoption of values-based selection, 'soft' skills training, performance management and financial incentives. Moreover, these both appeal to employees, who tend to have an instrumental orientation and are happy to work in an organization that enables them to maximize their outcomes; and to employers, because they (in theory) facilitate a workforce that is obeisant and committed to achieving measurable performance targets over the short term, even if for instrumental reasons. In CMEs, there are substantial barriers to these practices, and the orientations of employees differ significantly. Because employees possess recognized (and typically rigorous) skill qualifications, they tend to view US-style practices as degrading. Selection and advancement tend to be based on objective qualifications (values-based selection is actually illegal in Germany), and both performance appraisal and performance-based pay are limited, as is 'soft' skills training. The result is a workforce that is less obeisant yet more committed to quality, which although often difficult to measure over the short term, is consistent with long-term success – especially in view of the high-quality emphasis fostered by the broader institutional environment.

These two ideal types are overstylized, and neither fully exists in contemporary reality. Although the USA may come the closest to the ideal-typical LME, and Germany to the ideal-typical CME, both economies are more complex and diverse than the LME–CME distinction suggests (e.g., Allen 2004). Moreover, they tend to be oversimplified, glossing over important differences between individual nations. For example, Canada, the USA and Britain are all identified as LMEs, yet their institutional environments differ in a number of important respects, and what works in one does not necessarily do so in another (Godard 2008, 2009b). Nonetheless, the VofC approach provides a useful starting point for illustrating the importance of national institutional environments to understanding not just variation in HRM practices and outcomes across nations, but also why US-style 'best' practices and outcomes may in fact not be best within a particular nation, and why it may be necessary for transnational firms to adapt their HRM practices accordingly.

Despite the potential of the VofC approach, and the new institutionalism in general, scholars have yet to develop a specific 'institutional environments' approach to HRM. Below I draw on, yet go beyond this literature in an attempt to do so, developing an analytical foundation and framework for understanding and analysing how institutional environments shape HRM. Following Hall and Soskice and other analyses in the VofC literature, my focus is on the national level. Not only is this focus in keeping with the purposes of this volume, but as Hall and Soskice note (2001, 16): 'so many of the institutional factors conditioning the behaviour of firms remain nation-specific', largely due to 'nationally specific processes of development' but also to nationally specific state policies and paradigms that shape institutional environments, both of which are addressed more fully below. This is not to suggest that these environments are monolithic or that variation within nations does not matter, but only that to consider them is outside of the scope of this chapter. Also following Hall and Soskice, I adopt a relational approach, considering the institutional environment of HRM as an environment that shapes the relationships between employees and employers, and HRM policies and practices as reflective of this relationship.

5.3   THE INSTITUTIONAL ENVIRONMENT OF HRM[2]

One problem with much of the new institutionalist literature has been a tendency to define rules (and norms) so broadly that they become little more than a sensitizing construct, one that serves as a catch-all for just about everything but the kitchen sink. Institutional theorists often seem to be intent on establishing that only institutional environments matter to explaining systematic variation, and so are constrained to define rules to include virtually everything but pure agency (which is often just unexplained variation). However, we can for present purposes distinguish between rules that comprise an established form of relationship or institution (e.g., employment), rules that are specific to particular relationships, and general cultural rules. Although all three types are interrelated and the distinctions between them can be blurred, the first is of primary interest here.

These rules may be constitutive, in the sense that they define or constitute a particular form of relationship or institution and the rights of various parties within it; or regulative, in the sense that they regulate how the parties act within that relationship/institution. Constitutive and regulative rules may be seen to form the constitutive and regulative contexts that are specific to the employment relationship, and they generally shape the interactions between the parties in that form of relationship. However, these interactions also occur within a broader web of institutional arrangements and relationships, also characterized by constitutive and regulative rules. In the case of HRM, these arrangements and relationships form the broader socio-economic context within which employees and employers interact.

In combination these three contexts comprise the institutional environment of HRM. They have important implications not just for how managers act, but also for the motives and identities that underlie that action. This may be the case even where management is subject to different structural conditions (e.g., ownership or market structure) than those that predominate in these three contexts, because as part of a broader community of actors, managers are both susceptible to dominant ways of thinking and expected to 'play by the rules' that have come to be established within that community.[3] In effect, therefore, these 'indirect' implications may be expected to reduce variation between firms in the HRM practices adopted. They may also become so embedded as to be relatively immune to changes in predominant structural conditions, at least over the short term. As such, they may also reduce variation over time. Below, I consider the three contexts and their potential implications more fully.

5.3.1 The Constitutive Context

Constitutive rules undergird and effectively shape the way in which the employment relation is constituted, effectively taking the form of rights.

These rights are often so basic to the structure of the employment relation within a given national context that they are taken for granted and hence overlooked, even though they may be the most important aspect of the institutional environment. States play a critical role in this respect, not only through specific legislation, but also through legal doctrines and rulings that reinforce or interpret established arrangements, often based on judicial assumptions and ideologies (Woodiwiss 1990; Atleson 1995). Both may not only shape but also affirm concepts, definitions and rights that come to underpin and define the nature of the employment relation over time, with implications for how employers and employees view the relationship between them. A common distinction in this respect is between common law and civil law regimes, the latter of which tends to be more reflective of social expectations and public norms than does the former, and hence tend to be more conducive than the former to court rulings favouring worker rights (Botero et al. 2004; Goergen et al. 2009).

To understand the constitutive role of law and its importance to HRM, it is useful to return to the distinction between liberal market economies from coordinated market economies. In liberal market economies, such as the US, Britain and Canada (all of which have common law regimes), the employment relation is legally constituted as a contract of service rather than of partnership or cooperation (Arthurs et al. 1993, 131), and as such it is considered distinct from ordinary contracts under property law (see Hepple 1986, 11). Unlike a contract between two legal equals, in which legal rights and obligations not jointly determined by the parties derive from implicit understandings and norms that have developed over time, the employment contract is interpreted as providing employers with broad residual authority over virtually all matters not formally specified in contractual form (see Hepple 1986; Block 1994, 701–702; Godard 1998). Employees are generally deemed to be in positions of subordination to managerial authority,[4] with little if any say over how this authority is exercised. As John R. Commons phrased it:

> As a bargainer, the modern wage-earner is deemed to be the legal equal of his employer, induced to enter the transaction by persuasion or coercion; but once he is permitted to enter the place of employment he becomes legally inferior, induced by commands which he is required to obey. (Commons 1961, 60–1, cited in Rowlinson 1997, 120)

Not only does the employment relation become asymmetrical once entered into, but also managers are typically under a fiduciary obligation to owners (if they are not themselves owners). To the extent that this is the case, the result is that capital–labour interest conflicts become internalized within the employment relation, as managers seek to manage the firm in accordance with ownership interests, unelected by and with little direct accountability to employees. This fundamentally shapes both how employers conceive of their rights and obligations with respect to the exercise of authority, and the 'problem' which drives the way in which it is exercised, that is, the problem of control and commitment. This in turn has defining implications for what employers do and why what they do varies (Godard 1998). Elsewhere, for example, I have argued that the limited adoption and effectiveness in the USA of the high-performance model, which emphasizes self-directed teams and extensive employee participation systems, is attributable to the high costs of overcoming problems of employee trust and 'buy-in' arising from the structure of the employment relation, which have meant that only a limited number of employers have found it in their interests to adopt this model fully (Godard 2004b; Godard and Delaney 2000).

In coordinated market economies (which typically have civil law regimes), employees are also in positions of subordination. However, they may be granted a number of rights that bring the employment relation closer to a partnership conception of contractual relations, with implications for employer orientations towards employees. These rights can include representation on boards of directors, union representation rights, and workplace information-sharing, consultation and co-decision rights. To the extent that these rights are strong, employers are likely to consider employee interests as of equivalent importance to those of investors. This likelihood is in turn likely to be enhanced to the extent that investor pressures are weak due to cross-share holdings or bank ownership, and workers possess the level of resources and organization necessary to exercise their rights effectively. Under these circumstances, a 'stakeholder' orientation is likely to replace the 'shareholder value' orientation dominant within liberal market economies. Indeed, the ability of employers unilaterally to determine HRM policies and practices can be substantially limited. The result is higher levels of trust and partnership. Returning to the earlier example, attempts to implement high-performance practices are less likely to suffer from problems of trust and 'buy-in' and hence are more likely to be adopted, albeit in somewhat different form due to different institutional conditions (Godard 2004b).

In addition, although laws and court decisions may normally be critical to how the employment relation is constituted, it is possible to conceive of an environment in which laws matter less than normative rules. For example, it is sometimes argued that in Japan employees have truly been viewed as 'members', and that the system of selection and managerial advancement has been such that the senior management identifies more with fellow employees than with investors (Kuwahara 2004). The result is a deeply embedded 'obligational' orientation, in which employers believe that their first obligation is to employees and make decisions accordingly. This orientation may have weakened over the past decade or more, and has no doubt been facilitated by the broader socio-economic context of Japanese firms, but it nonetheless illustrates the role that can be played by constitutive norms. Returning again to the high-performance example, the result is that trust and buy-in are again less likely to be a problem, resulting in high levels of adoption.

5.3.2   The Regulative Context

Because constitutive laws and norms have implications for the orientations of management towards employees, they also have important implications for employer policies and practices. However, these implications are filtered through the regulative context in which HRM is practised. When considering this context, the tendency has been to focus on legal regulations, often ignoring the importance of normative and cognitive rules to which employers adhere, and the relationships between these rules and the effectiveness of legal regulations. Thus, although I address both, I focus on the latter.

Legal regulation
In considering legal regulation, it is common to distinguish between labour law and employment law. The former involves laws designed to regulate the processes by which workers exercise their collective rights relative to their employer. Particularly important in this respect, especially in LMEs, are laws regulating employer and union behaviour in the union-recognition process and in collective bargaining. The latter involves laws pertaining more to rights and protections regulating the relationship between employers and their employees in general. These laws principally include: (1) employment standards, such as minimum wage levels, holiday entitlements, employee leave allowances and working hours; (2) health and safety; (3) human rights; (4) employment equity; and (5) job security, including laws that regulate dismissal and lay-offs.

Labour and employment laws can be of major if not defining importance to the practice of HRM. This may be especially evident with respect to employment law, which directly restricts what employers can do and can substantially alter employer practices. For example, research finds that the strengthening of these laws in the US in the 1960s and 1970s substantially enhanced the role and importance of the HRM function, because these laws required the implementation of more legalistic internal procedures and due process mechanisms (Dobbin et al. 1988; Edelman 1990; Dobbin et al. 1993). Yet labour laws can also have major, albeit less direct, implications (see Verma 2005). For example, to the extent that they facilitate strong unions, employers are more likely to find themselves having to negotiate rules and procedures governing training, promotion, pay, performance appraisal and even selection – all of which may be seen to represent the 'core' of HRM. Indeed, recent research suggests that in Canada, unionized workplaces are much more likely to adopt 'bureaucratic' and in some senses traditional HRM practices, characterized by more objective criteria for promotion, discipline and lay-offs than is typical of non-union workplaces (Godard 2009a). Yet this was not found to be the case in England, where labour laws have been much weaker and differ in a number of respects (see below).

Because labour and employment laws often restrict the exercise of employer authority, they tend to generate employer resistance. However, the extent to which they do may vary, depending on the broader institutional environment in which they operate. For example, in CMEs they may be only weakly resisted by employers, because although they restrict authority and flexibility, they are believed to reflect and affirm legitimate stakeholder rights. They can also serve as important means of coordinating employer HRM practices across firms and sectors, thus in effect ensuring that similar policies are adopted and that employers who adopt positive policies do not find themselves at a disadvantage. In LMEs (especially the USA), they tend to be more highly resisted, because they restrict not only authority and flexibility, but also ultimately the ability to maximize shareholder returns. Flexibility in the management of human resources is seen to be especially critical in these economies, because the ability to adapt to changing market conditions is more important, and because employers are more likely to compete on the basis of labour costs. Thus, not only may the strength of labour and employment laws vary by nation, but so may their implications for employers and the way in which employers respond to them.

Cognitive and normative rules
Cognitive and normative rules can serve as useful supplements to, or even replacements for, legal regulation. Their importance is especially apparent with respect to employer practices toward unions. For example, American employers have long resisted the right of workers to form unions, in part because of the nature of the US economy, but largely because union representation is seen as an infringement on management's right to manage – a right which derives from a Lockean conception of private property. The National Labor Relations Act was, therefore, passed in 1935 in order to provide workers with protections against employer resistance and to ensure that they could form unions of their own choice and engage in

meaningful bargaining. Yet employers have increasingly had little compunction about circumventing and even breaking the law where able to do so. Where a union has become organized, they have also had little compunction about engaging in hard bargaining, pushing workers into a lengthy strike and then hiring permanent replacements for them (see Human Rights Watch 2000). These activities have on occasion met with some backlash. But generally speaking, they have come to be viewed as normal if not acceptable business practice (Godard 2004c).

In contrast, British employers have a long history of voluntarily recognizing and bargaining with unions. This history is partly attributable to unique economic considerations (Howell 2005), but it also reflects different conceptions of the rights and obligations that attach to property and how they translate into HRM practices. The result has been that, where strong laws have seemed necessary to protect worker rights in the USA, this has traditionally not been the case in the UK. Instead, employers have traditionally been much more subject to strong norms and to various sanctions (often from the state) should they violate these norms.

These different norms have applied, however, not just to union representation, but also to HRM practices in general. In the US, laws designed to regulate management practices so as to protect employees have almost always been hotly resisted by employer groups, and employers typically resist or abuse efforts to regulate them through alternative means. Yet, in the UK, similar efforts have often (though certainly not always) been seen as acceptable if consistent with established norms of 'fairness' and serving to regulate deviant employers. Often, they have involved the establishment of codes of practice (most notably with respect to appropriate disciplinary procedures) rather than explicit laws. Violation of these codes can provide a basis for legal action from an aggrieved employee (e.g., for violation of natural justice), but they allow for substantial amounts of flexibility – largely because employers have traditionally believed that they represent the 'rules of the game' and that they have a moral obligation to play by these rules.

The relation between legal and cognitive and normative regulation
Normative and cognitive rules can serve not only as alternatives for legal regulation, but they may also serve as the basis for such regulation in the event that some actors seem unwilling to adhere to them and alternative measures fail. In this regard, it should already be apparent that, to the extent that the parties subject to regulation view this regulation to be legitimate or justified, they are more likely to accept and adhere to it, other things being equal.[5] Yet attempts to regulate employer practices are likely to be even more effective to the extent that they are designed and implemented in conjunction with processes conducive to these rules and

accompanied by a deliberate strategy to reshape them. Under such conditions, the law may function as much through its implications for expectations and norms as through the specific rights and regulations it embodies (see Hyde 1994). This is generally consistent with what has variously been referred to as a 'reflexive', a 'decentred' or a 'new governance' approach, under which the function of law changes from 'an authoritative instrument of control into a facilitative instrument for mutual recognition of self-regulation' (Rogowski 1994, 90); also see Lobel, 2008.

The statutory union recognition laws implemented in the UK under the Blair government (Wood and Godard 1999; Godard and Wood 2000) would appear to exemplify such an approach, for they were intended not just to build on a history of moderate employer attitudes and voluntary recognition, but also to strengthen this tradition and in so doing encourage the development of a new workplace culture. In Prime Minister Blair's words, they are based on the premise that: 'a change in law can reflect a new culture, can enhance its understanding and support its development', and were intended to 'change the culture of relations at work' through 'the promotion of partnership' (DTI 1998, 3). Although these laws provide for formal statutory recognition, they are designed to encourage voluntary recognition and partnership, in considerable part by providing unions with only weak (if any) rights (Smith and Morton 2001), thus lessening the threat and likelihood of union intransigence, which is believed to be a major source of employer resistance. Initially, they appear to have met with some success, both in increasing the rate of voluntary union recognition (Gall 2004) and in altering culture, at least in some workplaces (e.g., Oxenbridge et al. 2003). However, their success now appears to have fallen short of Prime Minister Blair's stated ambitions for it.[6]

Employment laws can also have implications for employer norms and practices. For example, US research found that civil rights mandates indirectly helped to create a normative environment characterized by a general expectation of due process and equitable treatment that, if not met, could result in internal morale and external reputational costs for employers (Sutton et al. 1994). This, in combination with the growth of legal constraints on employers during the 1960s and 1970s, induced employers to adopt more legalistic selection and discipline procedures, thereby strengthening the role of specialized HRM departments (Dobbin et al. 1988; Edelman 1990; Dobbin et al. 1993).

5.3.3 The Socio-Economic Context

The socio-economic context of HRM can be complex, reflecting a wide array of institutions and the relationships they engender. For present purposes, however, it may be seen to consist of four main components: (1) financial markets and firm ownership structures; (2) product market structures and conditions; (3) labour market policies and programmes; and (4) labour and employer organizations.

Financial markets and firm ownership structures

The structure of financial markets and of the principal–agent relation between managers and owners are both believed to have important implications for employer orientations, through their implications for employer incentive structures (Berglof 1990; Porter 1992; Roe 1994; Hutton 1995, 2002; Gospel and Pendleton 2006). As noted earlier, firms in CMEs typically rely on long-term bank financing and/or are characterized by extensive cross-holdings, with firms owning substantial portions of each other's shares. The result is that firm performance tends to be measured more by long-term growth and stability and there are few immediate pressures to maximize shareholder returns. Although profits are important, other goals can at any point in time take equal or even greater priority, with firms tending to adopt a stakeholder rather than a shareholder value model.

In contrast, firms in LMEs are primarily controlled by stock market investors. The nature and extent of this control can vary depending on the type of investor involved (e.g., pension funds, insurance companies, trusts or mutual funds, as well as individual investors) and the extent to which ownership is concentrated in one or a few investors (Gospel and Pendleton 2006). However, it is generally argued that because of their legal fiduciary duties and various pressures to which they may be subject, these investors are likely to place greater pressure on management not just to maximize returns, but also to do so over the short term. As a result, employers tend to adopt a short-term orientation to HRM, as reflected in higher lay-offs, lower worker pay levels, lower investment in training and ultimately lower levels of firm-specific skill. They may also be less willing to accommodate unions, especially if this means increased costs over the short term or a reduction in the speed with which they can adjust to market developments (Gospel and Pendleton 2006). These implications may be especially strong in the USA, where mutual funds play a comparatively larger role. Managers of these funds may often have limited knowledge of the firms in which they invest, and they are subject to often intense short-term competition from other funds. As such, they may not adequately value investments in human resources, because they are difficult to measure, and they may also be less likely to care about them because they typically involve longer-term pay-backs (Blair 1995). They may also undervalue the potential long-term benefits that accrue to positive relations between unions and management (Gospel and Pendleton 2006).

Product market structures and conditions
In LMEs, economic relations between employers tend to be highly opportunistic and competitive, and states adopt policies that are designed to
foster such competitiveness, including strong competition laws, free
trade policies and/or restrictive monetary policies. As a result, employers
can generally be expected to face heightened competitive pressures. In
contrast, employers in coordinated market economies tend to engage in
strategic interaction and to develop long-term relations, and states adopt
policies designed to support these arrangements, including substantial
regulations restricting competitive behaviours, managed trade policies
and/or expansionary monetary policies.

Under conventional economic theory, the former strategy is most
conducive to competitiveness. The resulting competitive pressures are
believed to have a 'disciplinary' function, inducing employers to engage in
a continuous search for productivity-enhancing technologies and innovations. However, they also limit an employer's willingness and ability to
grant more favourable terms and conditions of employment, and can be a
further source of short-termism, with employers adopting policies directed
at short-term cost minimization and work intensification, and forsaking
the kind of long-term policy commitments associated with a well-trained,
experienced and loyal workforce (e.g., Soskice 1990; Hutton 1995; Gospel
and Pendleton 2006). In contrast, employers in coordinated market
economies are able to provide employees with higher-quality, long-term
employment, investing more fully in employee training and development,
providing good wages and benefits, and creating a more trusting and
secure labour force, as has traditionally been the case in Japan. However,
they are less likely to achieve the level of flexibility and dynamism of their
LME counterparts.

Labour market policies and programmes
Two types of labour market programme are typically identified: passive
and active. Passive programmes include benefits or social assistance that
offset income loss in the event of job loss. Active programmes assist the
unemployed through retraining, job search and relocation assistance.
Where both are strong, employees are less likely to fear job loss, and
hence are less likely to experience labour market coercion or acquiesce
to employer actions that they consider to be in violation of their interests
or expectations. Where they are not, the opposite is likely to be the case –
especially if unemployment levels are high. High unemployment and weak
support programmes effectively solve the problem of control for employers, rendering more expensive 'high-performance' policies unnecessary, as
may have been the case in Canada and the UK during the 1980s and 1990s

(Godard 1997). Conversely, low unemployment and active labour market policies (e.g., high unemployment benefits, generous training and relocation programmes) create conditions conducive to a 'high-commitment', socio-technical systems approach, as appears to have been the case in Sweden in the 1970s and 1980s.

There may be important interactions between labour market conditions and the degree of legal regulation of the employment relation. For example, Burawoy (1985, 126) argues that improved state social insurance programmes and legislation have historically meant a shift from 'despotic' employer practices, based on coercion, to 'hegemonic' practices, in which employers seek to win 'consent' or voluntary cooperation from their employees. He also argues that the degree and form of state regulation has played an important role in explaining differences in the form of hegemonic practices to emerge. Comparing Britain to the US, he argues that in Britain a lack of state regulation of industrial relations helped give rise to a system of informal or 'fractional' bargaining in the workplace, or what others have referred to as 'mutuality' (Hyman 1995), and might even be viewed as a form of partnership. In the US, the Wagner Act and related legislation helped give rise to more bureaucratic practices (Burawoy 1985, 138–148). Burawoy also explicitly incorporates a role for trade policy, arguing that, coupled with a lack of state control over the movement of capital, the free trade policies that began to be adopted in the 1980s have been giving rise to a new set of practices, which he labels 'hegemonic despotism' because although they entail consent, this consent is coerced by the fear of job loss (Burawoy 1985, 148–152). These practices appear essentially to be what has come to be viewed as 'best' HRM practice.

Burawoy's analysis may overemphasize the importance of labour market policies and programmes, and in so doing underestimate the importance of other aspects of the institutional environment. But it provides an illustration of the potential role of these programmes within institutional environments, and how they may serve as a further source of variation in HRM practices across nations and over time.

Finally, training and educational institutions have important implications for the level and types of skills offered by workers. In particular, considerable attention has been paid to the dual system adopted in Germany, under which trainees undergo both theory-based classroom training and on-the-job training, and develop specific occupational credentials that are recognized throughout the country (see Thelen 2004). As of 2008, more than half of the labour force had some form of vocational skills qualification (OECD 2008). This not only allows for the production of high-quality products, but it also means that the training needs and policies of employers differ markedly from those of their counterparts in liberal market economies, where there is little organized vocational skills training, thereby requiring employers either to rely on low-paid, low-skilled workers, or to invest substantially in worker training. Moreover, because well-trained employees can be subject to poaching by other employers, much of the training that does take place is firm- and job-specific, with important implications for the type of skills employees have and ultimately for the design of the workplace. Finally, strong vocational skills qualifications can mean not only that employees are capable of producing higher-quality products and services, but also that they possess greater pride and stronger occupational identity, both of which foster a commitment to high-quality standards.

Labour and employer organizations
Although labour and employer organizations are relatively weak in LMEs, they play a critical role in CMEs, not just directly shaping, regulating or negotiating HRM practices, but also assisting in the coordination of these practices across employers, through the negotiation of industry or even nationwide settlements governing wages, benefits and related terms and conditions of employment. Labour and employer organizations may also play an important role in shaping other aspects of the institutional environment. This may be especially true with respect to the regulative environment, in which they may not only influence and participate in the development of law, but also establish norms and standards to regulate the conduct of their members and how the law is understood and interpreted. But it is also true with regard to the broader socio-economic environment. In Germany, for example, the 'social partners' (labour and employer organizations) have traditionally played an active role not just in designing, implementing and even administering social and labour market programmes, but also in shaping broader social and economic policies, with critical implications for national institutional conditions.

5.4   NATIONAL INSTITUTIONAL PARADIGMS AND VARIETIES OF INSTITUTIONAL ENVIRONMENT

As should be apparent to this point, the various components of the institutional environment within which HRM is conducted should not be viewed in isolation. Indeed, the extent to which they are consistent (or inconsistent) with each other likely has critical implications for the effective functioning of an economy. Yet attempts to identify specific types of capitalism, as does the VofC literature, do not adequately capture national differences. In this regard, it is useful to consider the role of national institutional paradigms.

National institutional paradigms may be thought of as logic systems or ways of thinking about policy formation and implementation as they apply to institutional design. Although they extend beyond the formal purview of national governments, they generally form the basis for policy directives and hence help to ensure some level of consistency between various elements of national institutional environments. Because institutional environments are complex and contingent on the actions of various actors, and because state policies are ultimately subject to both political processes and political constraints, the extent to which consistency is achieved can vary considerably over time and across nations, as can the specific policies associated with it. In this regard, these paradigms are often sufficiently 'loose' so as to allow considerable room for policy variation, and both their interpretation and implementation tend to be contested (e.g., by competing political actors). Moreover, nations may move either closer to or further away from the core precepts of a particular paradigm, even potentially shifting towards a new paradigm. Nonetheless, these paradigms may be seen to play an important role in establishing and reinforcing national institutional environments, and ultimately in understanding these environments and differences between them.[7] For the present, six such paradigms can be identified: neoliberal, liberal managerialist, liberal pluralist, managerial corporatist, democratic corporatist and social democratic. These are not exhaustive of all existing (or possible) paradigms, but each is relatively representative of at least one developed nation, and each suggests a significantly different variety of institutional environment.

The neoliberal paradigm is most dominant in the USA. In general, it is based on the assumption that unbridled competition between firms and individuals is the key to a successful and dynamic economy and that such an economy invariably provides an improved standard of living for all. Under this paradigm, problems of fairness and equality are addressed largely by market forces, provided that there are no artificial barriers (e.g., racial discrimination). Thus, the main role of the state is to ensure that market forces are allowed to operate to their fullest, intervening only where artificial barriers are believed to exist. Employees as individuals are assumed to have sufficient power and opportunity in the labour market to be able to obtain fair and equitable terms and conditions of employment. Thus, social or labour market programmes tend to be weak, as are labour and employment laws. Employers are free to act unilaterally and are under little normative constraint, treating their employees as 'resources' towards which they have little legal or moral obligation.

The liberal managerialist paradigm has perhaps been most dominant in the UK (especially under the Blair administration in the late 1990s and early 2000s), although it has been popular in some academic and policy circles in the USA and Canada (Godard 2003). It is generally based on the assumption that competition and flexibility are critical to a successful economy, but that this competition should be limited by 'rules of the game' that ensure all parties are treated fairly and equitably. These rules generally entail cognitive and normative rather than legal regulation, although the latter is believed to help foster and sustain the former, as discussed earlier. To the extent that they are adhered to, the parties are able to develop higher levels of trust, which ultimately results in higher levels of economic performance for all. Social and labour market programmes can play an important role in ensuring that the disadvantaged can enjoy a minimal standard of living and have the opportunity to develop skills and abilities that are in demand in the labour market. In this regard, there is some recognition that employees and employers can have conflicting goals and that employees can find themselves at a disadvantage as individuals. Labour unions are thus considered to play a legitimate role in the economy. However, an underlying assumption is that both employees and employers benefit if they work together as partners, and the role of unions is in considerable measure to help foster this partnership, albeit not as an equal to management.

The liberal pluralist paradigm is at present difficult to identify in practice, although it was generally believed to be dominant in the United States and Canada in the immediate post-Second World War era, and may still come closest to describing the Canadian case, especially as it pertains to labour and employment law. It is generally based on the assumption that important conflicts of interest can occur within capitalist economies and that this is especially the case in the employer–employee relation, because the pursuit of efficiency by management can occur at the expense of employee goals. In this respect, equitable and fair treatment of employees may not always be in an employer's interest, and employees as individuals often find themselves at a power disadvantage in the employment relation. There is thus a need for the state to establish policies and institutional arrangements that ensure that some level of equity and fairness is achieved, balancing this goal against the goal of economic efficiency. The primary such policy is to protect the right of workers to join unions and engage in 'free' collective bargaining, under which they and their employer are free to resolve such conflicts on their own terms, thus achieving a balance that most suits their particular circumstance. The state also has a role in establishing employment laws and social and labour market programmes. But these programmes serve mostly as a last resort for those who are unable to find employment or, if employed, are for some reason or other not represented by a union. As such, they tend to be limited.

The managerial corporatist paradigm is perhaps most associated with Japan, especially as it developed prior to the 1990s. It is generally based on the assumption that cooperation between firms and individuals (especially within firms) is more critical to economic performance than is liberal-market-style competition. Equity and fairness are important not just as ends in themselves, but also as means of minimizing conflict and enhancing this cooperation. Because this is conducive to firm performance, it is in the interests of employers to ensure that employees are treated accordingly. This means that there is only limited need for state involvement or intervention, beyond helping to promote the appropriate policies and practices. Thus, the state typically provides only limited social and labour market programmes, and labour and employment laws tend to be weak and directed at fostering cooperative relations. However, the state also enacts policies that allow for only limited market competition, and for governance structures in which management enjoys a substantial amount of autonomy from financial markets, thereby facilitating a more cooperative, long-term orientation than typically observed in liberal market economies. It also develops economic policies designed to support and enhance the ability of various sectors to compete internationally. In designing these and other policies, the state consults extensively with employer groups. Finally, unions play a largely positive, integrative role, helping to ensure standard wage increases across firms and industries, fostering cooperation rather than conflict within firms. However, they are typically excluded from national policy formation processes.

The democratic corporatist paradigm is most exemplified by Germany. It generally proceeds from the assumption that liberal market economies are characterized by a power imbalance between capital and labour, and that as a result outcomes can be distorted in a way that serve the interests of the former more than the latter. This occurs not just at the level of the firm, but also within society as a whole. There is thus a need to structure and control markets so as to ensure that this does not occur, and to establish institutional arrangements that enable labour to become an equal 'partner' with capital both at the level of the firm and within the economy as a whole, through the provision of co-determination rights (e.g., works councils, representation on corporate boards), strong social and labour market programmes, strong labour and employment laws, and equal labour–management participation in the formation and (where possible) administration of social and economic policies. The ultimate result is a highly skilled workforce, with a strong commitment to quality and partnership, thereby facilitating high-value, quality products and services and ultimately high wages and benefits.

The social democratic paradigm is most reflected by the Nordic model, especially as developed in Sweden. In general, it goes a step further than the democratic corporatist paradigm, assuming not only that there is an imbalance of power in a 'pure' capitalist economy, but also that, in a true democracy, the interests of citizens (i.e., labour) must take priority, with capital serving only as a means to the attainment of these interests. In this regard, there is a need to go beyond concerns having to do with trade-offs between equity and efficiency in order to ensure high levels of equality and democracy both at the level of the firm and in society as a whole. This is accomplished through the establishment of strong labour and social programmes, strong labour and employment laws, and the provision of strong representation and voice rights for workers at both the level of the firm and the level of state policy formation. Although this may (or may not) weaken economic performance, it gives rise to much stronger social performance (e.g., lower poverty and inequality levels, higher life expectancy).

Overall, these paradigms suggest several different models of capitalism and hence varieties of institutional environment, with implications for the practice of HRM beyond those suggested by the VofC distinction. In reality, they are also oversimplified, and the developments of the 1990s and 2000s may have substantially weakened the extent to which they apply in the nations associated with them. Nonetheless, there continue to be substantial differences in the institutional environments of HRM across these nations, and these differences may be seen as continuing to reflect differences in underlying policy paradigms. The critical question, of course, is why such variation exists. Below, I briefly address this question.

5.5 UNDERSTANDING CROSS-NATIONAL VARIATION: THE ROLE OF HISTORY

Variation in the national institutional environments of HRM and the policies and paradigms associated with them can ultimately be traced to formative developments in the social, economic and political histories of nations (see Frege and Godard 2010). These developments and the discourses around them give rise to institutional norms, or beliefs, values and principles as to the role, rationale for and legitimacy of established institutions. These norms may be viewed as cultural, and it is in this sense that broader cultural values and beliefs – including those often identified in the management literature – matter. However, while institutional norms may reflect and even be intertwined with broader cultural values and beliefs, they are more institutionally specific. They give institutions (and the rules that comprise them) meaning and legitimacy. They also essentially form the basis for national institutional paradigms and ultimately economic, social and political life.

Institutional norms are thus much 'deeper' than, and underpin, the everyday formal and informal rules through which institutions of the political economy are produced and reproduced. They are drawn on in national debates and struggles around institutions (Godard 2008, 2009a), as actors respond to the ongoing conflicts and crises that arise within and across national (capitalist) economies (e.g. Jessop forthcoming). As such, how they are understood and interpreted may vary across actors and over time. But because they tend to be the product of history, and can reflect centuries of social, economic and political development, attempts to alter them in any fundamental way typically fail over the long run. So, as a result, do attempts to alter fundamentally the institutional environments and paradigms that they underpin (Godard 2009a, 83).

This means that if one is to understand cross-national variation in HRM, one must ultimately understand national histories, especially the conditions under which national economic, political and social institutions were formed and the institutional norms which were developed out of these conditions. Thus, for example, the neoliberal paradigm dominant within the United States may ultimately be attributable to the conditions under which the United States was formed, especially its individualist development, lack of formal class traditions (and conflicts), revolutionary birth and Puritanical religious traditions (see Godard 2009a; Frege and Godard 2010). These developments gave rise to norms supporting unbridled competition, a limited role for government, strong employer (property) rights and an emphasis on freedom of contract, including limited constraints on employer practices towards their employees.[8] The more restrained, liberal managerialist paradigm of the UK reflects formal class traditions derived from feudal times and the sense of *noblesse oblige* and responsibility instilled in the upper classes as a result (Jacoby 1991), thus giving rise to norms of fairness and responsibility in the treatment of employees. The democratic corporatist paradigm that has tended to be dominant in Germany may be attributable to its formation as an exercise in state-building beginning in the 1870s, its state-driven industrial development and its significant social-Catholic influences (Lehmbruch 2001, 56–57), thus giving rise to a belief that the state has a strong role to play, and norms favouring stronger employee rights and protections (Frege and Godard 2010).

These illustrations are oversimplified. Nonetheless, they suggest that national histories are the key to understanding the nature of, and variation in, the institutional environments of HRM and the national paradigms associated with them, thus ultimately explaining not only why HRM is practised differently in different nations, but also why it tends to be practised in a particular way within any given nation. Thus, they should ideally be the starting point for any attempt to understand HRM, even if this seems a very long way not just from the everyday practice of HRM, but also from conventional research in the area.

5.6   CONCLUSION

The central theme of this chapter has been that HRM is practised not in a vacuum, but instead within a broad community of actors, subject to common (informal and formal) rules and the institutions they embody. These rules and institutions comprise the institutional environment of HRM and management in general, which in turn not only regulates what management does, but also has implications for the goals and orientations underlying the practice of HRM and what is or is not viewed as rational and legitimate. To illustrate these implications, I first drew on the distinction between liberal market economies and coordinated market economies, as found in the varieties of capitalism literature. I then developed a specific institutional environments approach to the study of HRM, distinguishing between constitutive, regulative and socio-economic components of the national institutional environments within which HRM is practised. I followed this with a discussion of the importance of national institutional paradigms and identification of alternative paradigms. Finally, I discussed the importance of institutional norms and ultimately political, economic and social history in helping to account for cross-national variation in institutional paradigms, institutional environments and, ultimately, the practice of HRM. Throughout, focus has been on cross-national variation, which is in keeping with the purposes of this *Handbook*, but also reflects the predominant level at which variation in institutional environments occurs. Subsequent work in this area would be well served, however, if it also considered the importance of variation in institutional environments within nations. To this end, the present chapter can serve as a starting point.

NOTES

1. The answer varies by nation. For example, in the USA the term HRM came to replace the term 'personnel management', which was considered to be an area within the broader field of industrial relations; it generally came to be viewed as a distinct field, with industrial relations coming to be largely equated with the study of unions and collective bargaining, and to be largely dominated by psychologists. In the UK, HRM initially referred to a specific set of practices emergent in the 1980s; although it eventually came to refer to a field of study, it has been much more interdisciplinary and has continued to have considerable overlap with the field of industrial relations, in part reflecting different academic and institutional traditions in the UK. See Godard and Delaney (2000, 493–96).
2. This section draws extensively on, but goes beyond, Godard (2002).
3. In the organization theory literature these are referred to, respectively, as 'memetic isomorphism' and 'normative isomorphism' (DiMaggio and Powell 1983).
4. The tendency of economists to view restrictions on employer authority as weakening property rights does not hold with respect to the employment relation. If property rights are defined as control over assets owned by an employer (e.g., those appearing in financial statements), restrictions on the use and deployment of labour cannot be viewed as depletions of or infringements on these rights unless one views employees as the property of employers. It would therefore appear that employer authority exists as a 'residual right' deemed to derive from the employment contract as a relation of subordination (see Block 1994, 700–701 for a discussion). However, that employer authority is not restricted to what has been specified (implicitly or explicitly) would appear to be based on notions of managerial prerogative which derive from property rights. Thus, while restrictions on employer authority cannot be seen as restrictions on property rights, the nature of this authority under the law may be seen as deriving from property rights.
5. In a democracy, the very fact that such regulation has been implemented by a legally elected government may be seen as imposing a moral duty to obey, irrespective of whether the parties agree with the law. However, the extent to which this is the case may vary across nations. For example, it would appear that laws carry stronger normative weight in Britain than in the US, where employers are notorious for considering only the likely economic consequences of violating the law (not surprisingly, the 'economics of law' emerged in the US). Thus, employers are more subject to normative pressures to respect them.
6. For example, union density resumed its long decline in 2005 (the laws were implemented in 1999). It seems that although law can serve as a catalyst for normative regulation, its potential as an alternative to traditional legal regulation is limited, especially where employers are subject to conflicting norms and incentives, as is the case in a contemporary liberal market economy, and workers lack sufficient countervailing power. Nonetheless, it may represent an effective approach under the right circumstances.
7. These paradigms, and the extent to which consistency is achieved in their implementation, likely have important implications for both economic and social performance. These are outside of the purpose of this chapter.
8. Arguably, Roosevelt's New Deal may be viewed as a largely failed attempt to shift away from this paradigm towards a liberal pluralist one (see below). Any real success it may have had appears for the most part to have been of limited duration. This was especially true with regard to labour rights (Godard 2009a).

REFERENCES

Allen, Matthew (2004), 'The varieties of capitalism paradigm: not enough variety?' *Socio-Economic Review*, **2** (1), 87–108.

Arthurs, Harry, Don D. Carter, Judy Fudge, Harry J. Glasbeek and G. Trudeau (1993), *Labour Law and Industrial Relations in Canada*, Toronto: Butterworths.

Atleson, J.B. (1995), 'Law and union organizing', in C.G. Flood (ed.), *Unions and Public Policy*, Westport, CT: Greenwood Press, pp. 149–164.

Aycan, Zeynep (2005), 'The interplay between cultural and institutional/structural contingencies in human resource management practices', *International Journal of Human Resource Management*, **16** (7), 1083–1119.

Berglof, Erik (1990), 'Capital structure as a mechanism of control', in M. Aoki, B. Gustafasson and O.E. Williamson (eds), *The Firm as a Nexus of Treaties*, London: Sage, pp. 57–78.

Blair, Margaret (1995), *Ownership and Control: Rethinking Corporate Governance for the Twenty-First Century*, Washington, DC: Brookings Institution.

Block, Fred (1994), 'The roles of the state in the economy', in Neil Smelser and Richard Swedberg (eds), *Handbook of Economic Sociology*, Princeton, NJ: Princeton University Press, pp. 691–710.

Botero, J., S. Djankov and R. La Porta (2004), 'The regulation of labor', *Quarterly Journal of Economics*, **119** (4), 1339–1382.

Burawoy, Michael (1985), *The Politics of Production: Factory Regimes under Capitalism and Socialism*, London: Verso.

Chang, Ha-Joon (2001), 'Breaking the mould: an institutionalist political economy alternative to the neoliberal theory of the market and the state', Social Policy and Development Program Paper no. 6. Geneva: United Nations Institute for Social Development.

Commons, John R. (1961), *Institutional Economics: Its Place in Political Economy*, Vol. 1, Madison, WI: University of Wisconsin Press.

De Cieri, Helen (2008), 'Transnational firms and cultural diversity', in Peter Boxall, John Purcell and Patrick Wright (eds), *The Oxford Handbook of Human Resource Management*, Oxford: Oxford University Press, pp. 509–530.

DiMaggio, Paul and Walter Powell (1983), 'The iron cage revisited', *American Sociological Review*, **48** (2), 147–160.

Dobbin, Frank R., Lauren Edelman, John Meyer and W. Richard Scott (1993), 'Equal opportunity law and the construction of internal labor markets', *American Journal of Sociology*, **99**, 396–427.

Dobbin, Frank R., Lauren Edelman, John Meyer, W. Richard Scott and Ann Swidler (1988), 'The expansion of due process in organizations', in Lynn Zucker (ed.), *Institutional Patterns and Organizations*, Cambridge, MA: Ballinger, pp. 71–98.

DTI (Department of Trade and Industry, British Government) (1998), 'Fairness at work', Cm. 3968, London: Stationery Office.

Edelman, Lauren (1990), 'Legal environments and organizational governance: the expansion of due process in the American workplace', *American Journal of Sociology*, **95**, 1401–1440.

Frege, Carola and John Godard (2010), 'Institutional norms and cross-national variation in representation rights at work', in Adrian Wilkinson, Paul Gollan, Mike Marchington and David Lewin (eds), *The Oxford Handbook of Participation in Organizations*, Oxford: Oxford University Press, pp. 526–552.

Gall, Gregor (2004), 'Trade Union recognition in Britain, 1995–2002: turning a corner', *Industrial Relations Journal*, **35** (3), 249–70.

Godard, John (1997), 'Managerial strategies, labour and employment relations, and the state', *British Journal of Industrial Relations*, **35** (3), 399–426.

Godard, John (1998), 'An organizational theory of variation in the management of labor', in David Lewin and Bruce Kaufman (eds), *Advances in Industrial and Labor Relations*, Vol. 8, Stanford, CT: JAI Press, pp. 25–66.

Godard, John (2002), 'Institutional environments, employer practices, and states in liberal market economies: the US, Canada, and the UK', *Industrial Relations* (US), **41** (2), 249–286.

Godard, John (2003), 'Labour unions, workplace rights, and Canadian public policy', *Canadian Public Policy*, **29** (4), 449–467.

Godard, John (2004a), 'The new institutionalism, capitalist diversity, and industrial relations', in Bruce Kaufman (ed.), *Theoretical Perspectives on Work and the Employment Relationship*, Urbana-Champaign, IL: Industrial Relations Research Association, pp. 229–264.

Godard, John (2004b), 'A critical assessment of the high performance paradigm', *British Journal of Industrial Relations*, **42** (2), 349–378.

Godard, John (2004c), *Trade Union Recognition: Statutory Unfair Labour Practice Regimes in the USA and Canada*, Research Series, #25, London: Department of Trade and Industry Employment Relations UK Government.

Godard, John (2008), 'An institutional environments approach to industrial relations', in Charles Whalen (ed.), *Industrial Relations as an Academic Enterprise*, Northampton, MA: Edward Elgar, pp. 68–88.

Godard, John (2009a), 'The exceptional decline of the American labor movement', *Industrial and Labor Relations Review*, **63** (1), 81–107.

Godard, John (2009b), 'Institutional environments, work and human resource practices, and Unions: Canada Versus England', *Industrial and Labor Relations Review*, **62** (2), 173–199.

Godard, John and John Delaney (2000), 'Reflections on the high performance paradigm's implications for IR as a field', *Industrial and Labor Relations Review*, **53** (3), 482–502.

Godard, John, and Stephen J. Wood (2000), 'The British experiment with labour law reforms: an alternative to Wagnerism?', Proceedings of the 52nd Annual Meeting of the Industrial Relations Research Association, Madison, WI: IRRA.

Goergen, Marc, Chris Brewster and Geoffrey Wood (2009), 'Corporate governance regimes and employment relations in Europe', *Relations Industrielles*, **64** (4), 620–640.

Gospel, Howard and Andrew Pendleton (2006), 'Corporate governance, and labour management: an international comparison', in Howard Gospel and Andrew Pendleton (eds), *Corporate Governance, and Labour Management*, Oxford: Oxford University Press, pp. 1–32.

Grimshaw, Damian and Jill Rubery (2007), 'Economics and HRM', in Peter Boxall, John Purcell and Patrick Wright (eds), *The Oxford Handbook of Human Resource Management*, Oxford: Oxford University Press, pp. 68–77.

Hall, Peter and David Soskice (2001), 'An introduction to varieties of capitalism', in Peter Hall and David Soskice (eds), *Varieties of Capitalism: The Institutional Foundations of Comparative Advantage*, Oxford: Oxford University Press, pp. 1–68.

Hall, Peter and Rosemary Taylor (1996), 'Political science and the three new institutionalisms', *Political Studies*, **44**, 936–957.

Hepple, Bob (1986), 'Introduction', in Bob Hepple (ed.), *The Making of Labor Law in Europe*, London: Mansell Publishing.

Howell, Chris (2005), *Trade Unions and the State*, Princeton, NJ: Princeton University Press.

Human Rights Watch (2000), 'Unfair advantage: workers' freedom of association in the United States under international human rights standards', New York: Human Rights Watch.

Hutton, Will (1995), *The State We're In*, London: Jonathan Cape.

Hutton, Will (2002), *The World We're In*, London: Little Brown.

Hyde, Alan (1994), 'Labour law as political symbol: a critical model of labour legislation', in Ralf Rogowski and Ton Wilthagen (eds), *Reflexive Labour Law*, Boston, MA: Kluwer Law and Taxation Publishers.

Hyman, Richard (1995), 'The historical evolution of British industrial relations', in Paul Edwards (ed.), *Industrial Relations Theory and Practice in Britain*, Oxford: Blackwell, pp. 27–41.

Jacoby, Sanford (1991), 'American exceptionalism revisited: the importance of managers', in Sanford Jacoby (ed.), *Masters to Managers: Historical and Comparative Perspectives on American Employers*, New York: Columbia University Press, pp. 173–200.

Jackson, Terence (2002), *International HRM: A Cross-Cultural Approach*, London: Sage.

Jessop, Bob (forthcoming), 'Rethinking the diversity and variability of capitalism: on variegated capitalism in the world market', in Geoffrey Wood and Christel Lane (eds), *Capitalist Diversity and Diversity Within Capitalism*, London: Routledge.

Kaufman, Bruce (2008), *Managing the Human Factor*, Ithaca, NY: Cornell Press.

Kuwahara, Yasuo (2004), 'Employment relations in Japan', in G. Bamber, R. Lansbury and N. Wailes (eds), *International and Comparative Employment Relations*, London: Sage Publications, pp. 277–306.

Lehmbruch, Gerhard (2001), 'The institutional embedding of market economies: the German "Model" and its impact on Japan', in W. Streeck and K. Yamamura (eds), *The Origins of Nonliberal Capitalism: Germany and Japan in Comparison*, Ithaca, NY: Cornell University Press, pp. 39–93.

Lobel, Orley (2008), 'National regulation in a global economy: new governance approaches to 21st century work law', in K. Dau-Schmidt, S. Harris and O. Lobel (eds), Encyclopedia of Labor and Employment Law and Economics, Cheltenham: Edward Elgar.

Locke, Richard and Kathleen Thelen (1995), 'Apples and oranges revisited: contextualized comparisons and the study of comparative labor politics', *Politics and Society*, **23** (3), 337–67.

OECD (Organisation for Economic Co-operation and Development) (2008), *Education at a Glance*, Paris: OECD

Oxenbridge, Sarah, William Brown, Simon Deakin and Cliff Pratten (2003), 'Initial response to the statutory recognition provisions of the employment relations act 1999', *British Journal of Industrial Relations*, **41** (2), 315–334.

Porter, Michael E. (1992), 'Capital disadvantage: America's failing capital investment system', *Harvard Business Review*, **70** (5), 65–82.

Roe, Mark J. (1994), *Strong Managers, Weak Owners*, Princeton, NJ: Princeton University Press.

Rogowski, Ralf (1994), 'Industrial relations, labour conflict resolution and reflexive labour law', in Ralf Rogowski and Ton Wilthagen (eds), *Reflexive Labour Law*, Boston, MA: Kluwer Law and Taxation Publishers.

Rowlinson, Michael (1997), *Organizations and Institutions*, London: Macmillan Press.

Scott, W. Richard (1995), *Institutions and Organizations*, Thousand Oaks, CA: Sage.

Smith, Paul and Gary Morton (2001), 'New labour's reforms of Britain's employment law: the devil is not only in the detail but in the values and policy too', *British Journal of Industrial Relations*, **39** (1), 119–138.

Soskice, David (1990), 'Reinterpreting corporatism and explaining unemployment: co-ordinated and non-co-ordinated market economies', in R. Brunetta and Carla Dell' Aringa (eds), *Labor Relations and Economic Performance*, New York: New York University Press.

Streeck, Wolfgang (1992), *Social Institutions and Economic Performance*, London: Sage Publications.

Streeck, Wolfgang (1997), 'German capitalism: does it exist? can it survive?', in Colin Crouch and Wolfgang Streeck (eds), *Political Economy of Modern Capitalism*, London: Sage, pp. 33–54.

Sutton, John R., Frank Dobbin, John W. Meyer and W. Richard Scott (1994), 'The legalization of the workplace', *American Journal of Sociology*, **99**, 944–971.

Thelen, Kathleen (2004), *How Institutions Evolve: the Political Economy of Skills in Germany, Britain, the United States, and Japan*, Cambridge: Cambridge University Press.

Verma, Anil (2005), 'What do unions do to the workplace? Union effects on management and HRM policies', *Journal of Labor Research*, **26** (3), 415–449.

Wood, Stephen and John Godard (1999), 'The statutory recognition procedure in the Employment Relations Bill: a comparative analysis', *British Journal of Industrial Relations*, **37** (2), 203–245.

Woodiwiss, Anthony (1990), *Rights vs. Conspiracy: A Sociological Essay on the History of Labor Law in the United States*, New York: Berg.

6 Constitutive contexts: the myth of common cultural values
*Brendan McSweeney**

6.1 INTRODUCTION

A major contribution of institutional theory has been to stress that markets, organizations and individuals are deeply and essentially embedded in institutionalized contexts which do not merely influence and regulate, but also constitute (Meyer et al. 1994). The conceptualizations of such contexts vary along a number of continua including: homogeneous–heterogeneous; closed–open; static–dynamic; constraining–enabling. The processes which shape and change institutions (relatively self-activating designs for chronically repeated social activities) are complex and contested. There is no agreed account (Campbell and Pedersen 2001). Descriptions of the degree, indeed the nature, of agency exercisable in the construction, continuity, change and consequences of institutions also vary.

There is a fundamental distinction between the description of the properties and consequences of institutions, and institutionalization – the processes of such attainment (Jepperson 1991). The former is the object of much consideration, especially within the comparative political economy literature (Crouch 2005; Deeg and Jackson 2007; Lane and Wood 2009; Streeck and Thelen 2005, for instance). But institutionalization, the source(s) of, the explanations for institutions, has however not received quite as much attention. A sample of theoretical presuppositions in such explanations includes: a manifestation of domination (by class or other elites) (Dahrendorf 1958; Hancke et al. 2007); a reflection of conditions appropriate for efficiency (Williamson 1975; Hall and Soskice 2001); and an expression of deep-seated psychological orientations (Mead 1953; Hofstede et al. 2010).

This chapter considers the latter position by examining a particular notion of constitutive contexts, one which defines institutionalized environments as primarily created by coherent, self-sustaining, subjective 'culture' and within which agents are in effect relays of such culture. 'Deeply sedimented' psychological orientations 'attaching to or inhering in particular groups' (Ortner 1997, 8–9), narrowly defined as subjective values (or norms),[1] create, it is posited, enduring social uniformity and continuity. The central notion is that a general value system is instilled through socialization (e.g. Parsons 1951). This unvarying and transcendent idea of culture dominates (albeit does not monopolize) cultural analysis in management and organization theory (Tsui et al. 2007). It is argued in this chapter that this explanation of institutionalization is misleading.

6.2   CULTURE AS FOUNDATION

In common with the new institutionalism and neo-institutionalism literature, the psychological conditions literature takes it as given that the basic building blocks of social and political life empower or constrain social patterns or orders. But in that literature (hereafter: 'culture as values literature') explicit use of the term 'institution' is rare and then only as an outcome, as a dependent variable, as a 'consequence' (Hofstede 2001), which is shaped by psychological conditions. Those conditions are narrowly defined as enduring, bounded, primordial values and norms of specified groups (e.g. nations). Geert Hofstede, for instance, states that 'societal norms' or 'values' lead to the 'development and pattern maintenance of institutions in society'. He goes on to say that if institutions change, the societal 'value system patiently smoothes the new institution until their structures and ways of functioning are again adapted to the societal norms' (Hofstede 2001, 11–12). The notion of value has many definitions (Rohan 2000), but the culture as values literature uses it in the Parsonian sense[2] of deep-seated, 'standards (value orientations) that are applied in evaluative processes' (Parsons 1953, 16). Parsons defines the 'culture system' as 'a normative pattern-structure of values' (Parsons 1951, 37). Culture is conflated with values, values with norms, and meanings with values (Parsons 1951, 213–215, 263–264; 1968, 75–77; 1972). The integration of value-orientations within societies is postulated as a functional imperative. Social roles, Parsons and Shils state, are only 'institutionalised when they are fully congruous with the prevailing culture patterns and are organized around expectations of conformity with morally sanctioned patterns of value-orientations shared by members of the collectivity' (1951, 23).

6.3   CULTURE AND INSTITUTIONS

The term 'culture' is employed in the new institutionalism and neo-institutionalism[3] literature in a variety of ways. For instance, it is used interchangeably with 'institutions'; as one type of institution; as a 'carrier' of institutions; or as one of many sources of institutions.

Peter Hall and David Soskice (2001, 13) refer to 'culture' only very briefly. In contrast with the culture as values literature, they say that their notion of culture is a 'cognitive' one, broadly in line with Swidler's (1986) 'available strategies for action' and DiMaggio and Powell's (1991) 'shared understandings'. Swidler (1986, 273) states that the values 'model used to understand culture's effects on action is fundamentally misleading'. Even more specifically, Hall and Soskice say that in their view the role which 'culture can play in strategic interactions of the political economy is similar to the one Kreps (1996) accords it in organizations faced with problems of incomplete contracting' (Hall and Soskice 2001, 13). Kreps locates his view of culture within the 'new institutional economics' (or rational choice institutionalism) tradition initiated by Coase (1937, 1960) and reinvigorated by Oliver Williamson (1975, 1985). A transaction is the primary unit of analysis in this tradition (Kreps 1996). As DiMaggio and Powell say of this perspective:

> The parties to an exchange wish to economize on transaction costs in a world in which information is costly, some people behave opportunistically and rationality is bounded . . . institutions reduce uncertainty by providing dependable and efficient frameworks for economic exchange. (DiMaggio and Powell 1991, 4)

Subjective culture has no place within this tradition. Whilst 'optimistic functionalism' (Kuran 1988), the view that particular institutions are formed and survive because they are useful, dominates new institutionalism, the alternative view – that institutions may persist even when they are collectively suboptimal – has also been advanced. George Akerlof (2005), for instance, argues that the caste system is not economically efficient and yet it persists. But his explanation does not include a role for cultural values.

The term 'culture' also appears in the literature of 'neoinstitutionalism'. Wolfgang Streek and Kathleen Thelen (2005, 15), for instance, urge the avoidance of an '"over socialized" conception of human actors as is often implied in normative, or cultural [values], concepts of institution'. Hall and Thelen (2009, 10) make reference to 'culture' in just one sentence. They see a potential influence of culture (not defined) on institutions, but they reject the notion that it has a deterministic role or that it necessarily has a major role. Paul DiMaggio and Walter Powell (1991, 12), who draw somewhat from the new institutionalism literature, state that institutionalism 'stresses the role culture in shaping organizational reality' but whilst 'old institutionalism' emphasized the constitutive roles of subjective values, the new institutionalism/neo-institutionalism, they say, tends 'to reject socialization theory . . . [n] ot norms and values but taken-for-granted scripts, rules, and classifications are the stuff of which institutions are made' (1991, 14–15). Colin Crouch (2005, 14) rejects the relegation of institutional analysis to 'the study of norms'. Bruno Amable makes a few references to culture. Like DiMaggio and Powell, he uses it in the sense of something 'cognitive' but also stresses its 'hegemonic' (in a Gramscian sense) role. He is critical of the overuse and underspecification of culture: 'after all', he states, 'culture is used as a last resort in many comparative studies' (Amable 2003, 8).

Although Ronald Dore (1997, 27) states that analysts of institutions 'fear' the word 'culture', John Meyer and colleagues frequently use it. They 'conceptualize Western society as essentially a cultural project'; they state that 'institutionalized cultural rules define the meaning and identity of the individual and the pattern of appropriate economic, political, and cultural activity engaged in by those individuals' (Meyer et al. 1994, 9); and they define institutions as 'cultural rules giving collective meaning and value to particular entities and activities, integrating them into larger schemes' (ibid., 10). They refer to 'cultural accounts', 'cultural systems' and 'cultural forms' (ibid., 10, 11, 15, 24). Although they contend that there are normative (as well as other) sources of institutions, they do not conceive of culture predominantly, if at all, in the psychological sense of values. A notion of 'abstract values internalized by individuals through socialization', they state, 'simply leaves out too much' and is given 'too much reified inevitability'. They describe as 'primitive' the notion of culture as 'a cluster of consensual general values' (Meyer et al. 1994, 11–12, 17) and they explicitly reject the Parsonian idea of a general value system into which individuals are socialized (ibid., 12).

Thus, overall in the new institutionalism/neo-institutionalism literature the specific and narrow notion of culture (as values) is either ignored, dismissed or is seen as sometimes having a comparatively minor part in much more complex processes. Explicitly, or implicitly, the privileging of deeply sedimented psychological values over the ideational and the material is rejected. The explanatory ability even of wider notions of culture has also been rejected. Immanuel Wallerstein (1990, 34), for instance, states that he is 'skeptical that we can operationalize the concept of culture in any way that enables us to use it for statements that are more than trivial'. Jeffrey Sachs (2000, 43) argues that the influence of culture is usually insignificant; and Ronald Dore (1997, 27) explicitly avoids using the 'protean concept' of 'culture'.

6.4   THE CULTURAL TURN

And yet, for a variety of complex reasons the idea of 'culture' as a/the key social driver, or as a window into social processes, has gained immense popularity across a range of academic disciplines – from literary studies to international relations (Weeden 2002; Jacobs and Spillman 2005). This is also the case beyond the academy. As Henrietta Moore and Todd Sanders (2006, xv) observe: 'International agencies, local civil society groups, management consultants, consumer researchers, and a host of other groups and institutions [have] embraced it'. Culture is said to be shaping 'social, economic and political transformations . . . [it is] a major force for change in the world' (Held and Moore 2008, 2). It is also said to be a major source of resistance to, neutralization of, and repulsion of change. The current financial problems of the Greek state have, for instance, been attributed by some commentators to 'Greek culture'; the 'culture' of London's Metropolitan Police is said to be 'too white'; the US government is spending tens of millions of dollars trying to identify indigenous 'cultures' in Afghanistan; and so on. But the label 'culture' has multiple, often underspecified meanings. As early as the 1950s, Alfred Kroeber and Clyde Kluckhohn (1952) estimated – in a survey of English language sources only – that there were already over 160 definitions of culture ('and its near-synonym civilization') in use. Raymond Williams observed that culture was 'one of the two or three most complicated words in the English language' (in Weeden 2002).

In the psychological conditions literature, culture has a very narrow meaning: the supposedly enduring, ordered and common subjective values of specific partitioning of people. 'Culture', Hofstede et al. (2010, 5) state, is 'mental programming'. Furthermore, within that literature, 'culture' is seen as having immense influence. It is posited as the determinant, or in other words the independent variable, of social action. According to David Hickson and Derek Pugh (1995, 17), it: 'lie[s] beneath [a society's] characteristic arts, clothes, food, ways of greeting and meeting, ways of working together, ways of communicating, and so on'. Similarly, David Landes (2000, 2) states that: 'culture makes almost all the difference'. In the tradition of Talcott Parsons (1951, 37), culture is conceived of as 'normative pattern-structuring values' which act as a hierarchically superordinated control system (Schmid 1992). As in some new economic institutionalism and neo-institutionalism literature, deterministic path-dependencies are supposed, but in the subjective culture literature that ongoing power is seen as fundamentally a capability and consequence of subjective culture.

The assumption of cultural determinism alone does not exclude the possibility of social diversity and innovation. What the subjective culture model also supposes is that for each specific arena or category of actors (civilization, country, ethnic group, or whatever) culture is coherent, that is: uniform, non-contradictory. The assumption of monopolistic cultural coherence (and the neglect or peripheralization of non-cultural influences) necessarily leads to assertions of the complementarity of the logics of action. Conceiving culture as characterized by some diversity at least – rather than by pure uniformity – would imply variety of logics and thus both peaceful coexistence and potential conflicts between institutions.

6.5   CULTURAL COHERENCE

There is a long-standing debate about whether cultures are coherent or non-coherent. Although DiMaggio (1997) states that the coherent notion of culture has succumbed to that of culture as fragmented (non-coherent), the former retains a significant and robust presence within and outside of academia. Despite a quarter of a century, or more, of constructivist theorizing in the social sciences, critiques of reification in many disciplines, and destabilizing contributions of post-structuralist, post-modernist and other theories, the partitioning of people on the basis of subjective cultures (values) continues to be treated as a fundamental unit of social analysis in a wide range of arenas (Brubaker 2004). Such partitioning has the merit of rejecting micro-reductionism – the anorexic notion of social action as the mere aggregate of the choices of rational individuals. But the alternative it advances, it is argued, is problematic.

The notion of coherence probably has its roots in German romanticism: 'with all of the variations of the idea of the Geist (spirit) of an age or a people' (Appadurai 1988, 41). And canonized in Hegel's 'holism' and Weber's 'world image'. Claude Lévi-Strauss put forward an archipelago image of the world made up of 'peoples' each with a radically different 'culture' like a string of separate islands (in Wright 1998, 13). Pitrim Sorokin (1937), the early Ruth Benedict (1934) and Gregory Bateson (1973 [1941]), all argued that each culture has a single leitmotif, or ethos. Talcott Parsons (1951) argued that the coordination of mutual social action was the result of an ordered symbolic communality which he described as a 'common culture' which has 'logical consistency', 'pattern consistency' and 'symmetry'. In sum, as Carl Ratner (2006, 61) states: 'individuals . . . participate in a common, coherent culture that is structurally integrated at the societal level'. Some coherentists acknowledge the possibility of inconsistencies or deviances, but these are deemed to be eradicable or insignificant. If cultural determinism is supposed, then cultural coherence will be seen as inevitably creating uniform institutions and social practices.

In contrast, an example of a non-coherent view is Richard Merelman's (1984) description of culture in the US as a 'loosely bounded fabric, ill-organized, permeable, inconsistent', and tolerant of ambiguity (in Smelser 1992, 6). Edward B. Tylor (1920 [1871]) characterized culture as a thing of 'shreds and patches'. Bronislaw Malinowski (1926, 121) states that: 'human cultural reality is not a consistent or logical scheme, but rather a seething mixture of conflicting principles'. James Tully (1995) repudiated what he called the 'billiard-ball conception of culture', which represents each culture as 'separate, bounded and internally uniform'. Clifford Geertz, in harmony with what has become the accepted view in anthropology, dismissed the coherence view which he ridiculed as a: 'seamless superorganic unit within whose collective embrace the individual simply disappears into a cloud of mystic harmony' (Geertz 1965, 145). Paul DiMaggio (1997, 263) states that: 'cognitive research confirms views of culture as fragmented'. If cultural influence on social action is supposed, then cultural incoherence must logically be supposed to create social diversity. Rejection of cultural coherence does not necessarily entail rejection of some patterns within cultures. Diversity is not unbounded.

6.6   THREE TYPES

In this chapter, three types of imagined communities, each posited by their advocates as constituted by unique, shared, coherent cultural values, are discussed, namely: civilizations, countries and subnational monocultural groups. Essentialist claims about the cultural unity of each community are described. These claims are then in turn contrasted with some counter-evidence which, it is argued, points to diversity, not enduring uniformity. The overarching power of singular cultural classifications and the non-diversity supposedly produced is challenged. Each notion of culturally cohesive communities relies, it is argued, on a 'falsely homogenising reification' (Phillips 2007, 14) that greatly exaggerates both the internal unity of cultures and therefore the degree of social uniformity and continuity.

6.7   CIVILIZATIONS

Outside of the discipline of management and organization studies, Samuel Huntington's stark views about fault-lines between 'civilizations' (1993, 1996) – a term he uses interchangeably with 'culture' – has shaped much of the debate about intercultural conflict and understanding (Turner 2005). Perhaps somewhat overstating the case, but nonetheless indicative of its importance, this notion has, according to Kalevi Holsti, become the 'master explanatory variable' in world politics (in Henderson and Tucker 2001, 317). The diverse international political luminaries such as the Pakistani Prime Minister, the late Benazir Butho, and the Italian Prime Minister Silvio Berlusconi, have lauded Huntington's work which has been influential on the foreign policies of a number of governments, including that of the US (Said 2001). Having fallen somewhat out of fashion, the term 'civilization' has been resuscitated and repopularized by Huntington. Theories do not have to be true to become conventional wisdom (Abrahamian 2003).

According to Huntington, in his hugely cited article 'The clash of civilizations?' (1993), and his subsequent best-seller *The Clash of Civilizations* (1996), each civilization is constituted and motivated by a unique culture so that the 'major differences in political and economic development among civilizations are clearly rooted in their different cultures' (Huntington 1993, 22; 1996, 29). Whilst within management and organization studies the intercultural literature predominately focuses on the notion of nations (or rather states) as the primary self-bounded cultural units, the idea of much larger, transnational, culturally cohesive communities has also been advanced in that literature. Geert Hofstede (2001), for instance, depicts Arab countries as sharing a common culture and Confucianism as the basis of Asian values. The later view is also held by Huntington.

Huntington (1996, 21) identifies 'seven or eight major civilizations', namely, Sinic (Chinese), Japanese, Hindu, Islamic, Orthodox, Western and Latin American (he is unclear about whether Africa constitutes a civilization). In common with all coherent culture theories, each civilization is regarded as a coherent and self-sustaining system. Each civilization is, Huntington states, a cultural 'totality' (1996, 42). In effect, the population of each civilization is culturally predestined.

The idea of regional or transnational cultures, values or civilizations long preceded Huntington and draws its support from many other sources. Edward Said, for instance, has extensively depicted the long-standing stereotyping of the 'Orient' and the fabrication of 'Orientalism' (Said 1979). More widely there is the banal but very fashionable spatially reductive notion that the 'West' is a culturally unique and uniform cultural region. But the term 'belongs to the imagination more than to geography' (Gjerde 2004, 143). The faux cultural label, the 'West', is largely a legacy of colonialist rationalizations. A similar grand reifying idea is the essentially racist and historically bogus notion of 'Anglo-Saxon' values. Genes do not create culture, and in any event only a very small proportion of the United Kingdom's population is of Anglo-Saxon descent (Oppenheimer 2007).

In *The History of British India* (Mill 2010 [1817]), the early nineteenth century 'bible for the British Indian officer', its author James Mill states that: 'under the glossing exterior of the Hindu, lies a general disposition to deceit and perfidy', and that Hindus 'in reality made but a few of the earliest steps in the progress to civilization'; and Winston Churchill described Indians as 'the beastliest people in the world, next to the Germans' (in Sen 2007, 87). In 'civilized' circles, such pejorative generalizations are no longer acceptable, but the idea that people necessarily belong to exclusively one uniform civilization or culture retains considerable credibility in some academic, political and business circles. Breidenbach and Nyíri (2009, 262), for instance, report that the Chairman of Daimler-Chrysler decided not to appoint a Japanese person as a manager of plant in India because he was convinced that 'Shinto culture' and 'Hindu culture' 'do not go together'. A Buddhist Japanese manager with a US MBA would, it was assumed, be totally and irrevocably 'programmed' by Shinto culture, and Muslim workers in the factory would likewise be prisoners of Hindu culture. An alternative view – but also a culturally deterministic one – is that both the Japanese manager and the Indian workers shared a common 'Asian' culture (Hofstede 2001), and so it would have been appropriate to have appointed the Japanese manager to the post, but not to have appointed, say, a German.

An infatuation with the cultural notion of a singular 'Asianness' was reinvigorated by business school-led explanations for the 'economic miracles' first of Japan, then more widely of the Asian 'tiger economies', and then of China. Although Max Weber had famously argued that Confucian ethics had prevented capitalist development in China, many writers linked those ethics for economic development not only to China but also to South East Asia as a whole. Huntington asserts a fundamental opposition between 'Western' values of economic liberalism and Chinese values. And yet (with the explicit sanction of the Chinese state) the former type of values (or rather policies and practices) have been key in China's post-Maoist transformation; the notion of a monolithic Chinese (or wider Asian) culture 'obscures the immense poverty and growing social divisions . . . as a result of hyperdevelopment' in that area (Cheah 2008, 145); and there is extensive evidence of within-country, and within-region, organizational diversity, hybridity and fusions – not uniformity.

Generalizations about civilizations appeal to established prejudices and are politically useful to some interests. But they are analytically misleading. Focusing just on Huntington's work, it is inconsistent, ignores internal diversity, disregards change and is at odds with historical and contemporary records of conflict.

The basis of Huntington's categorization is inconsistent (Henderson and Tucker 2001; Magala 2005). For instance, he separates the Latin

American civilization from the Western civilization on the basis of the former's Catholic majority. Thus, his notion of a Latin American civilization relies on the implausible assumption that all Catholics share the same culture, and that the large non-Catholic minority in Latin American has the same culture as the Catholic majority, but that this Catholic Latin American culture somehow is not the same culture as that of Catholic majority countries in 'Western' Europe, which Huntington treats as identical to that in Protestant-majority countries such as Australia. With yet further inconsistency and confusion, in a paper fearful of what he calls the 'Hispanic challenge', Huntington describes 'US culture' – supposedly part of 'Western' civilization – as 'Anglo-Protestant', which he states is gravely threatened by Catholic Mexicans (Huntington 2004, 32).

Relying on the illusion of singularity within civilizations, Huntington disregards diversity within the spaces he supposes to be distinguished by a monoculture. For instance, a Swedish pacifist vegetarian is supposed to share the same socially constituting 'Western' culture as a carnivorous Spanish bull-fighting supporter, as does an Andalucian politician who wants to preserve bull-fighting with a Catalan politician who wants to ban it. Although the Prime Minister of India is Sikh, the President of the country's largest party is a Christian, and with 150 million Muslim citizens (nearly as many as in Pakistan) Huntington depicts India purely as a Hindu civilization. Furthermore, there are multiple varieties of Hinduism – the notion that it is a single religion is a colonially constructed myth (Bloch et al. 2010; Inden 1986). 'Unlike the monotheistic one-book creeds of Islam, Judaism and Christianity, Hinduism is an accretion of stories, poems and cults. It has a multiplicity of philosophies, gods . . . and sects, and has no central authority' (Beattie 2009, 140). There are at least 36 000 different Hindu gods and goddesses (Adiga 2008). In India, as well as Hindus and Muslims, there are also Sikhs, Parsis, Jews, Jains, Christians, Buddhists, atheists and agnostics. The extent and ways in which religion influences social action vary enormously, and there are many other influences. Implausibly, the millions of Muslims who fled from the newly territorially defined India to Pakistan in 1947 were, in Huntington's depiction, part of a 'Hindu civilization' before they fled, but part of an 'Islamic civilization' afterwards. The reverse is supposedly true of the millions of Hindus who hastily moved or were driven out of Pakistan to India. In Bangladesh, formerly East Pakistan, 16 per cent of the population is Hindu (CIA 2010), but they are defined as part of the 'Islamic civilization'. Although Christianity is, according to Huntington, the basis of 'Western civilization', the millions of members of the lowest castes and classes who embraced Christianity are deemed to be constituted by a 'Hindu civilization'. Huntington disregards diversity within space, which he defines as culturally uniform.

He ignores change or temporal diversity. In common with all other cultural essentialists, Huntington regards the common culture which defines a civilization as enduring for centuries. His theory supposes, for instance, that 'successive generations' (1996, 41) of Germans have been characterized by the same 'Western' culture. Such that Germans of today have been unaffected by knowledge of the Holocaust – in which the German state played the central, albeit not exclusive, role – and that contemporary Germans who successfully campaigned against nuclear power stations share the same culture as those of a previous generation who were members of the Wafen SS.

His claims are at odds with historical and contemporary evidence of conflict within 'civilizations'. For instance, the hugely destructive Thirty Years War which pitted Catholic powers in Europe against Protestant powers; the Hundred Years War which was part of the centuries-long enmity between England and France; the lengthy conflict in Northern Ireland between largely Catholic and Protestant groups; and the bloody Rwandan massacre in 1994 of Christians by Christians, are but a few examples of the multiple instances of conflicts within 'civilizations'. Richardson's study of conflicts between 1820 and 1929 found that in the main, common religion did not have a dampening effect on the incidence of war – nor did common language. Conflicts are more common between states belonging to the same 'civilization' than between different 'civilizations'. Errol Henderson and Richard Tucker's (2001, 317) study of the pre-Cold War period (1816–1945) demonstrated that: 'states of similar civilization were more likely to fight each other that those of different civilizations', and that in the post-Cold war period (1989–1992) 'civilization membership was not significantly associated with the probability of interstate war'. Almost all civil wars have been within 'civilizations', including those in England, Iraq, Ireland, Rwanda, Russia, Spain, Sri Lanka, the Congo and the US. And Huntington's claims are at odds with the record of cross- 'civilization' alliances. For example, during the Second World War, Japan (one of Huntington's civilizations) was allied with Germany against other members of the same 'civilization' as Germany. In Kosovo it was countries from within Western 'civilization' which came to the rescue of the Islamic 'civilization'. The 'Islamic' Libyan government supplied arms and funds to the 'Western' Irish Republican Army (IRA) in Northern Ireland.

With regard to Confucianism, which Huntington claims to be the source of a uniform 'Sinic [Chinese] civilization', it is not a holistic framework or a hegemonic influence. 'Confucianism' – a term invented by Jesuit missionaries – consists of a large body of work that is interpretable in multiple ways. Explaining the values of the 4 billion Asians on the basis of one person's writings is as absurd as claiming to explain the behaviour of three-quarters of a billion Europeans from the Bible (Breidenbach and Nyíri 2009). Christianity is not the same as Islam, not the same as Hinduism, and so on – and so, insofar as religion makes a social difference, the varieties of religions matter. But to make religion the source of uniform and persistent 'civilizations' presupposes that religion is the primary or exclusive influence and that each religion is a homogeneous totality. Both suppositions are false. In each there is an immense diversity of influences. Insofar as religion or quasi-religion is deemed to be influential, as Huntington deterministically does, in China there is also Taoism, Buddhism, Maoism, Christianity and Islamism, for instance, and multiple interpretations of each. Broad divisions within Buddhism include Otani, Shingon, Shinyo-en, Tendai and Tibetan. And there are many variations within each of these. Within the wider region of Asia there is an immense plurality of other traditions (Sen 2007). As Joana Breidenbach and Pál Nyíri (2009, 73) state: 'There are many different ways of being more or less Christian, or more or less Confucian, or more or less Muslim', and likewise with other religious or secular bodies of work.

The origins, extent, form, pace and consequences of changes within varieties of capitalism are objects of extensive investigation and debate within the arenas of comparative political economy. Notwithstanding its insights and the research they have stimulated, the institutional 'varieties of capitalism' models (including, but not exclusively, Hall and Soskice 2001) are criticized for conceiving national and regional institutions in an overly functional, deterministic, static and homogeneous manner (Crouch 2005; Streeck and Thelen 2005; Lane and Wood 2009, for instance). But civilization partitioning has nothing to contribute to this discussion. It stifles analysis. No differences between, or changes within, the institutional configurations (corporate governance regimes, and so forth) of, say, France, Germany and the United Kingdom are conceivable, as all are defined as belonging to the same uniform and enduring 'Western' civilization.

6.8   NATIONS

Huntington's depiction of each civilization as a monolithic cultural unity relies almost entirely on anecdotal evidence (Fox 2002). As Edward Said (2001), referring directly to Huntington's work, bluntly states: 'a great deal of demagoguery and downright ignorance is involved in presuming to speak for whole religions or civilizations'. The primary depictions of 'national cultures' are largely derived from attitude surveys. The methodology of that research and its application have been extensively critiqued (see Cooper 1982; Bock 1999; McSweeney 2002a, 2002b, 2009; Gerhart and Fang 2005; Breidenbach and Nyíri 2009 for instance) and so are not discussed here.

This notion of the world as a mosaic of distinct and enduring national cultures has a long pedigree, for instance in the eighteenth-century writings of Johann von Herder. As in the other cultural theories considered in this chapter, national culture is represented as enduring and as uniformly determinate. 'National values', Hofstede and Hofstede (2005, 13) state, are 'as hard as a country's geographic position'; and 'while change sweeps the surface, the deeper layers remain stable, and the [national] culture rises from its ashes like the phoenix' (ibid., 36). And Hofstede (2001, xix) boldly states that he has identified: 'five main dimensions along which the dominant value systems in more than 50 countries can be ordered and that [they] affect human thinking, feeling, and acting, as well as organizations and institutions, in predictable ways'. The basic idea is, as Clifford Geertz (1973, 44) critically observes, that culture is: 'a set of control mechanisms – plans, recipes, rules, instructions (what computer engineers call "programs") – for governing behaviour'.

The centrality of the nation-state as the unit of analysis is not unique to the national cultural model. 'This centrality', Colin Crouch states, 'is central in most neo-institutionalist studies' (2005, 41) (see also Strange 1996). The notion of enduring and distinct national culture is a central part of nationalistic myths about the primordiality of nations (Cubitt 1998). All are of comparatively recent origin.

But even the 'geographic position[s]' of many countries are not 'hard' (Hofstede and Hofstede 2005, 13). State boundaries may be unstable. Poland, for instance, ceased to exist as a nation-state in the late eighteenth century and was only reconstituted with quite different borders at the Treaty of Versailles in 1919 when the borders of many other European countries were radically altered. After the Second World War, the borders of Poland and many other countries were again changed. Land and people formerly in one state may be redesignated as part of another state. For example, Alsace-Lorraine was returned to France most recently in 1945 (having yo-yoed back and forth over the previous century). Whole states or parts of states may be annexed (or reclaimed), as the north of Cyprus was by Turkey. New states may be formed by seceding from other states (e.g. Bangladesh). Some multinational states are very stable (e.g. Switzerland), some are very volatile (e.g. Iraq). States may be formed by the voluntary or involuntary combination of multiple states (e.g. Germany in the late nineteenth century and again in the late twentieth century). States may fragment into multiple states, violently (e.g. the break-up of Pakistan into [West] Pakistan and Bangladesh) or peacefully (e.g. the separation of

Czechoslovakia into the Czech Republic and Slovakia). Writing about the determination of national boundaries at the Versailles Peace Conference in 1919, Arthur Balfour, the UK's Foreign Secretary, angrily observed the spectacle of 'all powerful, all ignorant men sitting there and partitioning continents', and UK diplomat Harold Nicolson despairingly said: 'How fallible one feels here! A map – a pencil – tracing paper: Yet my courage fails at the thought of the people whom errant lines enclose or exclude' (in Will 2004, 131).

Not only is a unique national culture supposed to map neatly onto often arbitrary and recently created political boundaries, but there is also confusion in the literature as to whether the uniform and causal culture is that of a nation, a nation-state, or a multi-nation-state. As Rubenstein and Crocker (1994, 122) observe:

> Of the roughly 180 states that compose the current world system, 15 at most can be called nations in the sense that a vast majority of people believe that they share a common ancestry and cultural identity. The norm for states is multinationality, with 40 per cent containing people from five or more distinct nations.

In almost than one-third of states, the largest national group does not even compose a majority of the population.

Nations may comprise part of a state or extend beyond the borders of a single state (e.g. the Kurds and the Basques). The territories supposed in the national culture model to be each characterized by a uniform, enduring, causal culture are overwhelmingly not single nations, but clusters of nations within a single state, and yet each country is treated as having just one, not multiple, national cultures. When Yugoslavia, for instance, existed as a single country, Hofstede 'measured' its supposed consequences-creating 'national culture' – as did Trompenaars (1993) (with different results). After its break-up into seven separate states, Hofstede measured the 'national cultures' of three of these new states (namely, Croatia, Serbia and Slovenia). If 'national cultures' exist and if the national culture of the initial state (Yugoslavia) had been accurately identified, then the national cultures of the seven states into which it fragmented would be very similar to each other, and to that of the initial state. But Hofstede's measurements of the 'national' cultures of three of those states show the opposite – dissimilarity (Hofstede 2001, 87, 151, 215, 286).

Attempts to define something held culturally common in the population of states or nations always fail (Gellner 1983; Cubitt 1998; Zimmer 1998; Sen 2007). Claims to have identified the unique quality of 'Englishness', or 'Frenchness', or 'Germanness', or whatever-nationality-ness, always flounder in essentialist impressionism relying on groundless stereotypes (for instance, all English people are emotionally repressed); features that

are not unique (every English person likes an 'English breakfast'); historical myths (the English have always been distinguished by their tolerance);
or national generalizations based on the preferences or dislikes of a subnational group (the English prefer sweet sherry). In every area of social action
(however small in terms of population or geographical territory), there is
evidence of diversity. Steensby's study of 'Eskimo culture', for instance,
identified 25 variants of 'economic culture', and Wuad Krake documented
two highly contrasting leadership styles in a tiny South American tribe (in
Bock 2000). Homicide rates vary not only between countries (and over
time), but they also differ immensely across locations, socio-economic,
gender and ethnic groups (Nisbett and Cohen 1996; Gaines and Kappeler
2003; McSweeney et al. 2010). Goold and Campbell (1987) describe three
different 'styles' of planning and control by UK-based, large, diversified
companies. And so on.

As in the theory of 'civilizations' discussed above, that of national
culture as values relies on an oversocialized notion of individuals. Nancy
Adler (2002, 19), for instance, states that a national 'cultural orientation
describes the attitude of most people most of the time'. And that: 'in
[Hofstede's] study, national culture explained 50 per cent of the differences
in employees' attitudes and behaviors'. And yet, based on Hofstede's own
data, Barry Gerhart and Meiyu Fang (2005) point out that: 'somewhere
between 2 and 4 per cent [only] is explainable by individuals' nationality'.[4]
Daphna Oyserman, Heather Coon and Markus Kemmelmeier's analysis
of all cross-national empirical research studies published in English on
individualism and/or collectivism (the 'dimension' of national culture
which has received the most empirical attention) found that country
explains only 1.2 per cent of the variance in individual-level individualism
scores; that is, 98.8 per cent of variance in individualism is unexplained by
country (Oyserman et al. 2002).

The characteristics of institutional change is perhaps the key issue currently being considered within the comparative political economy literature (Lane and Wood 2009). The perspective on change through the lens
of coherent national culture is stark and implausible: change very rarely
occurs; if it happens, the transformation is country-wide (not in particular
locations – regions, sectors, industries, or whatever); and because absolute
within-country cultural complementarity is posited, the source of change
cannot be internal to a country, it must necessarily come from beyond its
borders. But the national cultural perspective on change is wholly a priori:
the answers are 'known' without studying actual change. And the 'answers'
conflict with many empirical studies (see Smith et al. 2008, for instance).

Take the example of the transnationalization of the regulation of the
consolidated (that is, group) financial reports of listed companies. Until

comparatively recently, these reports were almost entirely determined by national regulations – a situation not at odds with the deterministic claims of national culturalists (Gray 1988). But today the regulations have largely been transnationalized. In more than 100 countries (including all European Union countries) these reports are required to be, or are permitted to be, based on International Financial Reporting Standards (IFRS) constructed and issued by the International Accounting Standards Board (IASB). In a number of other countries new, purportedly national regulations are, albeit without acknowledgement, largely or wholly based on IFRS. Transnational and international influences on the transformation have been widely identified (McSweeney 2010). These include competition between the European Union and the United States, the Asian financial crisis, major corporate scandals, the liberalization of cross-national capital flows, and the various roles played by a range of organizations such as the European Commission, the International Organisation of Securities Commissions, the Organisation for Economic Co-operation and Development and the World Bank.

But studies of support for, and acceptance of, the change from national to transnational regulations in individual countries also point to the significance of within-country processes as either initiators or mediators, for example lobbying and unilateral actions by top management of some factions of capital favouring transnationalization. But support is rarely, if ever, unanimous. There was also opposition as well as support from within. For instance, whilst the New York Stock Exchange has vigorously supported transnationalization of financial reporting regulations, the US Financial Accounting Standards Board has persistently opposed it; the American Accounting Association is divided on the issue; and the US Securities and Exchange Committee has, depending on who is chairing that organization, variously opposed and supported change (Sunder et al. 2007; Cunningham 2008; Hopkins et al. 2008). Contestation between interested within-country parties retarded transnationalization in some countries, but accelerated it in others.

Exclusively exogenous, or more precisely extra-national, explanations alone obscure how substate actors and interactions were essential. What happened was the consequence of deep-domestic as well as a transnational or international processes. For instance, the 'break-out' of some major continental European firms from the corporate governance traditions in their home countries via listings on the New York Stock Exchange was motivated in part by the desire to convert their shares into a more acceptable acquisition currency, and generated pressure both within their home countries and in the EU Commission. The forces which created the transformation were combinations of those external to, and internal to, countries. The theory of national culture acknowledges the former – but otherwise has no further contribution – and it denies the possibility of the latter. In fact, none of the three cultural theories considered here provide any leverage in explaining how and why the transformation occurred.

6.9   PLURAL MONOCULTURES

Demarcating groups on the grounds of their (or their ancestral) location of origin or on the basis of objective characteristics – for example, male Sikh turbans – does not require an assumption that the members of a group share a common subjective culture. But ethnic diversity has provided fuel – although not the only fuel – for the growth of 'multicultural' claims which oppose representations of a national cultural singularity with the notion of multiple cultural groups.

The term 'multicultural' indicates that what supposedly primarily differentiates subnational groups is their 'culture', but in contrast with national culture (above) the differentiator is not the water's edge, but usually the skin colour (Geertz 1985). The concept of culture is problematically fused with ethnic identity. The architect of apartheid, Werner Eiselen, stated that culture, not race, was the true basis of difference (Giliomee 2003). In the contemporary world, the 'new racism' (Barker 1981) employs cultural difference instead of inherited characteristics, but uses it to justify pejorative descriptions of particular ethnic groups. But much more influential has been the view that democratic governments should accord ethnic minority groups collective cultural autonomy on the grounds that cultural recognition is a right (Eriksen 2002). Especially since the American civil rights movement, there has been greater awareness of the harm suffered by minorities labouring under inequities or discrimination practised over decades, and in some instances over centuries (Kukathas 1992).

Defining ethnicity is problematic, and identifying specific ethnic groups is arbitrary. But in any event the idea that defined ethnic groups have distinct, identifiable and enduring cultures, that each is a 'more or less coherent cultural' entity (Matin-Asgari 2004), glosses over considerable in-group diversity and relies on crude demarcations of ethnic groups. By implication, even the majority ethnic group (however that is defined) also, implausibly, collectively shares its own unique and common culture.

The notion of 'ethnicity' is an umbrella term that embraces groups that constitute a section of a country's population and not the whole. The qualifying attributes of identification as a member of a specific group are 'restricted to genetically transmitted features or to the language, religion, place of origin, tribe, region, caste, clan, nationality, or race of one's parents and ancestors' (Chandra 2006, 400). Whilst 'ethnicity' has been the main basis of multicultural categorization, other distinctions include gender, sexual orientation and various minority groups.

The notion is often applied inconsistently. For instance, Hindus and Muslims in or from India, and similarly Muslims and Christians in Lebanon, are part of the same ethnic group if it is defined geographically, but different if religion is the demarcator. Within Pakistan, Punjabis, Sinhis, Pathans, Baluchs and Bengalis are often seen as distinct ethnic groups, but in other countries they are usually collectively defined as Pakistanis, or more widely as Asians. Many white Americans from former slave-owning families share proximate ancestors with black Americans, but the two sets are defined as belonging to two distinct ethnic groups (Chandra 2006). Max Weber (1992 [1930]) criticized the notion of ethnicity for its lack of conceptual rigour. Multiple writers have rejected primordial or essentialist notions of ethnicity (Baumann 1996; Comaroff and Comaroff 2009, for instance).

Acknowledgement of differential (positive or negative) access to material or symbolic capital by different national subgroups does not have to be predicated on acceptance of the notion of that each group has a unique, collectively shared and coherent culture. But such claims are made. *Riding the Waves of Culture* (Trompenaars and Hampden-Turner 2005, 223), for example, includes two chapters on cultures within countries, specifically South Africa and the US. Each ethnic group, for instance eight in South Africa (including Xhosa, Zulu, Tsonga and English) and five in the US (White/Caucasian, Black/African, Hispanic, Native American and Asian/Pacific Islander), and in both countries males and females, are each supposed to have their own distinct cultures: 'women . . . are capable of revealing values different yet complementary to those of men'. The source of their generalizations about the ethnic cultures of South Africa is not disclosed. The extensive literature condemning essentialist notions of ethnicity and gender is ignored. For example, studies even of supposedly isolated and 'primitive' groups by anthropologists have identified considerable internal heterogeneity: different myths, dialects, institutions, rituals and religions (Bock 1999, 2000; Kuper 1999). Malcolm X (1964) noted the differences between rural and urban blacks and between middle-class and poor blacks in the US. He observed that in New York in the 1960s, the street vocabulary of sections of Harlem was unintelligible to many middle-class blacks (in Chandra 2006, 411).

The idea of coherent national culture has also been amplified through demands from some politicians, and others, that all citizens in a country must commit themselves to unique national values (Brown 2005). In part this is a reaction to what is said to be the adverse consequences of policies founded on multicultural notions (Joppke and Morawska 2003). But this retreat from imagined coherent multiculturalism to imagined coherent national monoculturalism does not identify any national uniqueness – it merely puts national labels on generic (that is, not nationally specific) liberal democratic values (Joppke 2004).

The notion that particular minorities are united by a common coherent culture underpins many of the moral claims and political demands and responses advanced by, or on behalf of, minorities. But as Amartya Sen (2007, 157) points out, notwithstanding the common description, and justification, of such policies as 'multicultural' they are, in fact, based on the notion of 'plural monoculturalism' – the false and misleading notion that distinct cultures do, and should continue to exist in, as it were, 'secluded boxes'. Uma Narayan calls the difference or essentialist version of multiculturalism a 'package picture of cultures' in which each culture is represented as neatly wrapped up, sealed off and identifiable by core values (in Phillips 2007, 27). Gerd Baumann's study of Southall, a suburb in South-West London, describes and challenges essentialist notions of distinct cultures. The reification of culture, according to Baumann, is the defining feature of what he calls the dominant discourse of multicultural 'community' and 'identity'. The dominant discourse about each of the area's five 'communities': 'Sikhs, Hindus, Muslims, Afro-Caribbeans and Whites', is that each has a distinct culture. This notion, he argues, is reinforced and legitimated by institutions such as media, local government, community leaders and political organizations. But he also identified a 'demotic' (popular) discourse in the Southall 'communities', a discourse which is more flexible and complex, recognizing the situational and multifacteted character of individual identification and framing (in Eriksen 2002). Ken Pryce's (1979) study of West Indian immigrants in Bristol showed how different groups of West Indians pursued very different life projects.

Multiculturalist policies do not necessarily rest on the assumption of coherent culture (Phillips 2007). The notions of communal interests and communal identity (by members or outsiders), whilst often conflated with that of communal culture, are conceptually distinct. Terence Turner usefully distinguishes between 'critical' multiculturalism and 'difference' multiculturalism. The former is a dynamic notion which acknowledges diversity both within and between groups seeking to challenge hegemonic cultural claims and aiming to construct more vital, open and democratic cultures. In sharp contrast, the latter is a static notion which fetishizes cultural difference and internal homogeneity.

Arguably, the notion of collective cultures has facilitated more respect for differences and encouraged recognition of minority particularities. That in turn has perhaps helped counter racism, reduced inequality, enabled greater recognition of minority rights, led to more pluralist education; and deflated some post-imperial hubris. But on the other hand, partitioning society on the basis of supposed collective cultures legitimates and perpetuates segregation and encourages ignorance about and mistrust between each defined group. It encourages political and intellectual separatism. It elevates cultural membership above other distinctions, leading to neglect of other arguably more pertinent distinctions such as class and other asymmetrical socio-economic power relations.

This leads to the absurd policy assumption that all members of a 'cultural' group face the same inequality of circumstances. As a consequence in the UK, for example, because its Arts Council formally recognizes the former (inequality because of 'cultural' membership) but not the latter (socio-economic inequality), it is easier for a very rich member of what is defined as an ethnic group to get funding than it is for a poor person who is not seen as a member of such a group. It has allowed powerful members to codify contested practices, thereby establishing their own authoritative readings that they employ to enforce conformity among group members. It has facilitated opportunistic defences of malpractices (including the misogynistic), legitimated patriarchal practices and reinforced stereotypical representations. It has restricted the opportunities for individuals and minorities within communities to reshape those communities, whether directly or through interaction with those outside. By treating a culture as a badge of group identity it fetishizes it in ways which serve a shallow notion of 'political correctness' and put some practices of group members in organizations, in the neighbourhoods and elsewhere beyond the reach of criticism and critical analysis (Turner 1993).

For good and ill, the undertheorized notion of culture employed by many key advocates of multiculturalism is but the latest way of conceiving and explaining otherness (McGrane 1989). Todd Gitlin (1992) calls this the 'romancing of otherness'. But whatever the consequences, and they vary between contexts, the idea that defined groups share a common coherent and compelling culture is an invention that does not reflect the reality of diversity, subgroup identities, subgroup conflicts and fluidity. Policies supposedly reflective of, and protective of, distinct coherent cultures in fact perpetuate the myth of such cultures (Horowitz 1985). 'Cultural' groups are not undifferentiated wholes.

6.10   DISCUSSION AND CONCLUSIONS

The constitutive role of subjective culture (values) as the shaper of environments was questioned above. The three typologies of cultural communities discussed differed on the domain range of the determinate influence of culture but in common they conceive subjective culture as a pregiven, determinate monolith, as the uncaused cause, as the first cause. Each type of location is conceived of as a container of a blanket and undifferentiated culture which moulds the social in its supposed domain. Key claims made by each of the theories were described above and in turn the plausibility of each was questioned. Their basic building block of coherent, enduring, determinate, subjective culture forecloses consideration of the levels, properties, components, dynamics and sources of both social change and diversity. They celebrate the existence of different logics of action between, but not within, populations. Below, some suppositions common to all three cultural depictions of defined populations are further discussed and critiqued.

First, culture and causality. Each of the three theories fall into the traps of oversimplification, determinism and timelessness. Culture can be defined as causal or non-causal. The causal power of culture can be theorized on a range from the scarcely significant to the dominant driver. The coherent culture theories discussed here locate culture at the latter end. Culture creates fixed fatalism. Culture does not have to be conceived of as static and can be employed to explain both change and stability (Schmid 1992; Chabal and Daloz 2006). But not if it is defined, as in the three types of theories considered here, as a deterministic constant. In them, culture supposedly orchestrates behaviour. It is conceived of as collective 'glue' and 'fuel'. Improvization, innovation, localized practices, transportability, adoptions and piecemeal changes are effectively excluded. There is no room for conflicts within, or between, institutions as each is deemed to be the reflection of a seamless cultural web.

Even when the possibility of extraordinary change is acknowledged it can only be conceived within the theories as happening simultaneously and at every pertinent location and level. Even after change, cultural coherence and uniform consequences are somehow reachieved. For instance, Hofstede states that on the very few occasions when there is a change in a national culture, the change occurs not only across that country but also within all countries throughout the world. National cultures very rarely change, he states, but when they do, 'they change in formation' across the globe, that is to say the 'relative position or ranking' of national cultures are unaffected (Hofstede 2001, 36). The possibility of convergence, no matter how limited or incremental, is denied. An acknowledgement of the possibility of change that would not occur everywhere or not have similar consequences everywhere in the cultural location (e.g. civilization, country) would be inconsistent with the master assumption of coherent culture. What is deemed to be true of one place within a cultural location must, it is supposed, be true of everywhere in that location – otherwise the foundational assumption of a general value system would be contradicted.

Insofar as culture is influential, defining it as fragmented opens the possibility of not only exogenous but also endogenous change through conflict, contradiction, competition and ambiguity, which the notion of coherent culture excludes.

History is not just continuity; it also involves the novel formations and new events which are unaccountable on the basis of unchanging cultural forces. To define culture only as a persistent heritage of values ignores the significant element of change. A profound inconsistency is employed. At some time in the past the inhabitants of a supposedly culturally uniform location are defined as active in creating a culture, but for multiple generations the inhabitants have ceased to be creative and instead have been passive inheritors. And yet studies even of isolated 'primitive' societies have shown that their cultural history is one of flux (Boas 1982 [1940]; Brightman 1995).

Second, culture and agency. Institutional theories posit that actors and their interests are institutionally constructed. If coherent culture is posited as the fundamental influence then the constituted actors can only be uniform 'cultural dopes' – collective relays, unable to exercise any discretion or improvisation. This excludes the possibility of 'creative recombinations of institutional fragments' (Lane and Wood 2009).

But there is ample evidence that complex interdependencies, highly contingent relationships and specific context dependencies characterize life. The coherent culture theories discussed above are blind to cultural ambiguities, to cultural multiplicity, to cultural (or institutional) residues and dormancies; to contending interests, to inequalities, and differentiated access to material and symbolic resources. As Smelser (1992, 25) observes: 'any culture will present a number of contradictory adages or sayings ("look before you leap" and "he who hesitates is lost") as part of its repertoire'. Most people of a religious disposition simultaneously employ the notions of 'free will' (agency) and 'the will of God' (determinism). The tensions between the active Church engaged with the world and the monastic ideal in Christianity also illustrates non-identical orientations within a single tradition (Eisenstadt 1992). Francis Hsu writes of the deep value conflicts in the United States, for example: Christian love with religious bigotry; democratic ideals of equality and freedom with totalitarian tendencies and witch-hunting; emphasis on science, progress and humanitarianism with parochialism and racism (in Bock 1999, 102).

In addition to these and many other 'glaring inconsistencies' (Meyer et al. 1994, 12) what might appear to be unambiguous is open to interpretation by individuals. For instance, the fifth commandment, 'Thou shalt not kill', seems to some unequivocally to prohibit abortion, war and capital punishment; for others it does not. And individuals may simultaneously hold several conflicting views. Such incoherence makes space for constrained agency – for bounded free will (Slater 1970; Swidler 1986; Derné 1994). Within the notion of coherent culture there is no room for 'nonuniformity' (Wallace 1970, 35). The insistence on cultural uniformity in each of the three partitionings of populations precludes any theory of change springing from internal dynamics (Archer 1988). Logically, the component parts of any complex system can generate change – but only if some internal heterogeneity is allowed.

Third, culture and action. Each representation of an imagined community of cultural coherence makes an ontological distinction between culture and social action. In this context social action means social behaviour because little, if any, room is given for agency. Action or behaviour is seen as an expression of, and ideally predictable from, cultural profiles.

The representation of imaginary communities discussed above not only suppose cultural coherence, continuity and purity, and neglects the possible effects of cultures other than the one monopolistic culture, but it also excludes the possible independent effects of non-cultural features. Action has many ingredients other than, or additional to, culture. Their exclusion in seeking to explain or predict action is reckless and unwarranted. As Kuper (1999, 247) points out: 'unless we separate out the various processes that are lumped together under the heading of culture, and then look beyond the field of culture to other processes, we will not get very far in understanding any of it'.

Culture is conceived of in the three theories as a persistent heritage. Conservatism reigns supreme. But cultures are fusions, remixes, recombinants. They are made and remade through exchange, imitation, intersection, incorporation, reshuffling; through travel, trade, subordination. Take the example of the Russian group of painters known as the Wanderers (*Peredvizhniki*). They were dissidents who broke away from the St Petersburg Academy because of its emphasis on 'Western' art. They sought to establish a truly Russian school of art through painting Russian landscape and traditional peasant life. Yet despite this overtly nationalist stance the influence of artistic developments outside of Russia is evident in their work (Kostenevich 2008). In many cases the so-called ancient customs, stories, music, symbols and styles of dress are neither ancient nor typical. The systemic is not, contrary to the coherentists' reductive models, merely composed of a blanket and undifferentiated culture. Life is made in impurity and intermingling.

There are no gaps in the theories between the culture and conduct. There is no room for improvisation, for oscillation, for opportunism or for force. An overly culturalized conception of the person is employed. Culture and action are theoretically and empirically distinct; hence they can vary independently of one another (Geertz 1957; Allaire and Firsirotu 1984; Archer 1988; Kaufman 2004). Uniformity may result from common values, but it may not. Common action does not require such unity, nor does such action necessarily result from common values (Gregory 1983; Merelman 1984; Archer 1988; Schudson 1994). An extensive post-Parsonian literature argues on both theoretical and empirical grounds against both the conflation of values and social action and also alternatively against the treatment of one or other as the independent or merely the dependent variable (Schmid 1992). To draw a distinction between culture and social action is not necessarily to deny the effects of culture on action, but it does exclude a restricted focus on culture, even non-coherent culture, as the determining force.

The three models of coherent culture, discussed above, are examples of what Margaret Archer (1988) critically calls 'downward conflation' – the view that social action is 'engulfed' by culture. As social practices are collapsed into culture in each of the models, 'the dynamic elements in social change which arise from the failure of cultural patterns to be perfectly congruent with the forms of social organization are largely incapable of formulation' (Geertz 1957, 33). A single culture (of a civilization, nation, ethnic group, or whatever) does not create 'total institutions' (Goffman 1961). It is possible to suppose the existence of large-scale coherent cultures but without attributing deterministic powers to them. If such cultures exist they might be non-causal, or be causal outcomes not causal forces, or have limited causality, or be just one component in a fixed or varying cocktail of influences.

Views of culture as unvarying point to path-dependencies, to the present as history (but overstate the lock-in created by initial conditions). They contribute to countering atomistic views of societies (but exclude the possible strategic exercise of agency). They counter wholly rational or materialistic reductionism (but in their place offer another singularity). They focus on the particular and emphasize differences between populations (but their representations are too thin and fixed, being blind to the richness and ambiguities of the specific; blind to transformations, fluidity, fragmentations, contestations and hybridization; blind to translocalization and to border crossings in general). If 'culture' is to have a role in understanding the dynamics of institutions, and social action in general, analysis needs to discount the idea of culture as a general system of coherent, static and determining values. Such analysis needs to recognize culture as fragmented whether it be conceived of as cognitions, symbols, meanings, categories and/or practices. It needs to engage with the influence of power relations and acknowledge the influence of non-cultural forces. We need complex interactional models, not simplistic unicausal ones, but the coherent culture theories discussed above do not provide them.

NOTES

*   Comments by Sheila Duncan and Geoff Wood on an earlier version of this chapter are gratefully acknowledged.
1.   The terms 'values' and 'norms' are used with little distinction in the 'culture as values' literature and 'culture' and 'values' are conflated. An early expression of the latter is the statement of anthropologists Alfred Kroeber and Clyde Kluckhohn that: 'In fact values provide the only basis for the fully intelligible comprehension of culture, because the actual organization of all cultures is primarily in terms of their values' (in Kuper 1999, 57–58).
2.   Over decades, Parsons chronically modified his theory of culture (Schmid 1992). Broadly, and certainly in the latter period of his work, he employed the notion of consistent, non-contradictory, 'patterns of value-orientation' (Parsons 1951, 552, and elsewhere) largely as an 'ideal type', but contemporary culture as values literature treats uniform values as a social actuality. Furthermore, whilst that literature treats culture as the determining influence on social action, Parsons's ambit of influences is wider. Parsons separated 'social structure' from culture. When the Parsons team drafted the manifesto of the Parsonians *Towards a General Theory of Social Action* (Parsons and Shils 1951) the then eminent anthropologist Clyde Kluckhohn objected, arguing that: 'social structure is part of the cultural map' (in Kuper 1999, 55). In that sense, the three theories of cultural values discussed in this chapter are more 'Kluckhohnian' than 'Parsonian'. But it is the latter which has become a term of art. Kluckhohn's work does not feature in contemporary discussions in anthropology or sociology.
3.   The term 'new institutionalism' is used here to refer to work which is based on institutional economics and public-choice theories, whilst 'neo-institutionalism' refers to work which draws on theories in the sociological tradition. The latter is a more heterogeneous family of theories than the former. There are similarities and differences between and within both families of theories. New and neo-institutionalism is a division of convenience and some writers on institutions could be located in either tradition (Campbell and Pedersen 2001; Crouch 2005).
4.   Hofstede's own estimate is 4.2 per cent (2001, 50).

REFERENCES

Abrahamian, E. (2003), 'The US media, Huntington and September 11', *Third World Quarterly*, **24** (3), 529–544.

Adiga, Aravind (2008), *White Tiger*, London: Atlantic Books.

Adler, Nancy J. (2002), *International Dimensions of Organizational Behaviour*, 4th edn, Cincinnati, OH: South-Western.

Akerlof, George A. (2005), *Explorations in Pragmatic Economics*, Oxford: Oxford University Press.

Allaire, Y. and M.E. Firsirotu (1984), 'Theories of organizational culture', *Organization Studies*, **5** (3), 193–226.

Amable, Bruno (2003), *The Diversity of Modern Capitalism*, Oxford: Oxford University Press.

Appadurai, A. (1988), 'Putting hierarchy in its place', *Cultural Anthropology*, **3** (1), 36–49.
Archer, Margaret S. (1988), *Culture and Agency: The Place of Culture in Social Theory*, Cambridge: Cambridge University Press.
Barker, Martin (1981), *The New Racism: Conservatives and the Ideology of the Tribe*, London: Junction Books.
Bateson, Gregory (1973 [1941]), *Steps Towards an Ecology of Mind*, Frogmore: Paladin.
Baumann, Gerd (1996), *Contesting Culture: Discourses of Identity in Multi-ethnic London*, Cambridge: Cambridge University Press.
Beattie, Alan (2009), *False Economy: A Surprising Economic History of the World*, London: Penguin Books.
Benedict, Ruth (1934), *Patterns of Culture*, Boston, MA: Houghton Mifflin.
Bloch, Esther, Mariane Keppens and R. Rajaram Hegde (eds) (2010), *Rethinking Religion in India: The Colonial Construction of Hinduism*, London: Routledge.
Boas, Franz (1982 [1940]), *Race Language and Culture*, Chicago, IL: Chicago University Press.
Bock, Philip K. (1999), *Rethinking Psychological Anthropology*, 2nd edn, Prospects Heights, IL: Waveland.
Bock, P.K. (2000), 'Culture and personality revisited', *American Behavioral Scientist*, **44** (1), 32–40.
Breidenbach, Joana and Pál Nyíri (2009), *Seeing Culture Everywhere: From Genocide to Consumer Habits*, Seattle, WA: University of Washington Press.
Brightman, R. (1995), 'Forget culture: replacement, transcendence, relexification', *Cultural Anthropology*, **10** (4), 509–546.
Brown, G. (2005), 'Speech by the Rt Hon. Gordon Brown, Chancellor of the Exchequer, at the CBI Annual Conference in London', available at http://www.hm-treasury.gov.uk/newsroom_and_speeches/press/2005/press_99_05.cfm.
Brubaker, Rogers (2004), *Ethnicity without Groups*, Cambridge, MA: Harvard University Press.
Campbell, L. John and Ove K. Pedersen (2001), *The Rise of Neoliberalism and Institutional Analysis*, Princeton, NJ: Princeton University Press.
Chabal, Patrick and Jean-Pascal Daloz (2006), *Culture Troubles: Politics and the Interpretation of Meaning*, London: Hurst & Company.
Chandra, K. (2006), 'What is ethnic identity and does it matter?' *Annual Review of Political Science*, **9**, 397–424.
Cheah, Pheng (2008), 'Culture and religions of liberalism in a global era', in D. Held and H.L. Moore (eds), *Cultural Politics in a Global Age: Uncertainty, Solidarity and Innovation*, pp. 140–147.
CIA (2010), *CIA Factbook*, available at: https://www.cia.gov/library/publications/the-world-factbook/geos/bg.html.
Coase, R.H. (1937), 'The nature of the firm', *Economica*, **16**, 386–405.
Coase, R.H. (1960), 'The problem of social cost', *Journal of Law and Economics*, **3**, 1–44.
Comaroff, L. John and Jean Comaroff (2009), *Ethnicity, Inc.*, Chicago, IL: Chicago University Press.
Cooper, C.L. (1982), 'Review of G. Hofstede: culture's consequences', *Journal of Occupational Behaviour*, **3** (2), 202–204.
Crouch, Colin (2005), *Capitalist Diversity and Change*, Oxford: Oxford University Press.
Cubitt, Geoffrey (ed.) (1998), *Imagining Nations*, Manchester: Manchester University Press.
Cunningham, L.A. (2008), 'The SEC's global accounting vision: a realistic appraisal of Quixotic quest', *North Carolina Law Review*, **87**, 101–181.
Dahrendorf, R. (1958), 'Out of utopia: towards a reorientation of sociological analysis', *American Journal of Sociology*, **64**, 115–127.
Deeg, R. and G. Jackson (2007), 'Towards a more dynamic theory of capitalist diversity', *Socio-Economic Review*, **5** (1), 149–180.
Derné, Steve (1994), 'Cultural conceptions of human motivation and their significance for culture theory', in Diane Crane (ed.), *The Sociology of Culture*, Oxford: Blackwell, pp. 267–287.

DiMaggio, P.J. (1997), 'Culture and cognition', *Annual Review of Sociology*, **23**, 263–287.

DiMaggio, Paul J. and Walter Powell (1991), 'Introduction', in Walter Powell and Paul J. DiMaggio (eds), *The New Institutionalism in Organizational Analysis*, Chicago, IL: University of Chicago Press.

Dore, Ronald (1997), 'The distinctiveness of Japan', in Colin Crouch and Wolfgang Streeck (eds), *Political Economy of Modern Capitalism: Mapping Convergence and Diversity*, London: Sage, pp. 19–32.

Eisenstadt, S.N. (1992), 'The order-maintaining and the order-transforming dimensions of culture', in R. Münch and N.J. Smelser (eds), *Theory of Culture*, Berkeley, CA: University of California Press, pp. 64–87.

Eriksen, Thomas H. (2002), *Ethnicity and Nationalism*, 2nd edn, London: Pluto Press.

Fox, Jonathan (2002), 'Ethnic minorities and the clash of civilizations: a quantitative analysis of Huntington's thesis', *British Journal of Political Science*, **32** (3), 415–434.

Gaines, Larry K. and Victor Kappeler (2003), *Policing in America*, 4th edn, Cincinnati, OH: Anderson Publishing Co.

Geertz, C. (1957), 'Ritual and social change: a Javanese example', *American Anthropologist*, **59** (1), 32–54.

Geertz, Clifford (1965), *The Social History of an Indonesian Town*, Cambridge, MA: MIT Press.

Geertz, Clifford (1973), *The Interpretation of Cultures*, New York: Harper Collins.

Geertz, C. (1985), 'The uses of diversity: the Tanner lectures on human values', available at http://www.unsam.edu.ar/mundoscontemporaneos/pdf/12.pdf.

Gellner, Ernest (1983), *Nations and Nationalism*, Ithaca, NY: Cornell University Press.

Gerhart, B. and M. Fang (2005), 'National culture and human resource management: Assumptions and evidence', *International Journal of Human Resource Management*, **16** (6), 971–986.

Giliomee, H. (2003), 'The making of the apartheid plan, 1929–1948', *Journal of Southern African Studies*, **29** (2), 373–392.

Gitlin, Todd (1992), 'On the virtues of a loose cannon', in Patricia Aufderheide (ed.), *Beyond PC: Towards a politics of understanding*, St. Paul, MN: Greywolf Press.

Gjerde, P.F. (2004), 'Culture, power, and experience: toward a person-centered cultural psychology', *Human Development*, **47**, 138–157.

Goffman, Erving (1961), *Asylum: Essays on the Social Situation of Mental Patients and Other Inmates*, New York: Anchor Books.

Goold, Michael and Andrew Campbell (1987), *Strategies and Styles: The Role of the Centre in Managing Diversified Corporations*, Oxford: Basil Blackwell.

Gray, S.J. (1988), 'Towards a theory of cultural influence on the development of accounting systems internationally', *Abacus*, **3**, 1–15.

Gregory, K.L. (1983), 'Native-view paradigms: multiple cultures and culture conflicts in organizations', *Administrative Science Quarterly*, **28**, 359–376.

Hall, Peter A. and David Soskice (2001), 'An introduction to varieties of capitalism', in Peter A. Hall and David Soskice (eds), *Varieties of Capitalism: Institutional Foundations of Comparative Advantage*, Oxford: Oxford University Press, pp. 1–68.

Hall, P.A. and K. Thelen (2009), 'Institutional change in varieties of capitalism', *Socio-Economic Review*, **7**, 7–34.

Hancke, Bob, Martin Rhodes and Mark Thatcher (2007), 'Introduction: beyond varieties of capitalism', in Bob Hancke, Martin Rhodes and Mark Thatcher (eds), *Beyond Varieties of Capitalism*, Oxford: Oxford University Press, pp. 1–10.

Held, David and Henrietta L. Moore (2008), 'Introduction: cultural futures', in David Held and Henrietta Moore (eds), *Cultural Politics in a Global Age: Uncertainty, Solidarity and Innovation*, Oxford: Oneworld, pp. 1–20.

Henderson, E.A. and R. Tucker (2001), 'Clear and present strangers: the clash of civilizations and international conflict', *International Studies Quarterly*, **45**, 317–338.

Hickson, David J. and Derek S. Pugh (1995), *Management Worldwide: The Impact of Social Culture on Organizations Around the Globe*, London: Penguin.

Hofstede, Geert (2001), *Culture's Consequences: Comparing Values, Behaviours, Institutions and Organizations across Nations*, 2nd edn, Thousand Oaks, CA: Sage.

Hofstede, Geert H. and Gert J. Hofstede (2005), *Cultures and Organizations: Software of the Mind,* 2nd edn, New York: McGraw-Hill.

Hofstede, Geert, Gert J. Hofstede and Michael Minkov (2010), *Cultures and Organizations: Software of the Mind*, 3rd edn, New York: McGraw-Hill.

Hopkins, P.E., C. Botosan, M. Bradshaw, C. Callahan, J. Ciesielski, D. Farber, M. Kohlbeck, L. Hodder, R. Laux, T. Stober, P. Stocken and T.L. Yohn (2008), Financial Accounting and Reporting Section of the American Accounting Association (Financial Reporting Committee), 'Response to the SEC Release: Acceptance from foreign private issuers of financial statements prepared in accordance with international financial reporting standards without reconciliation to US GAAP', available at http://papers.ssrn.com/sol3/papers.cfm?abstract_id=1083679 (accessed 22 June 2010).

Horowitz, Donald L. (1985), *Ethnic Groups in Conflict*, Berkeley, CA: University of California Press.

Huntington, S.P. (1993), 'The clash of civilizations?' *Foreign Affairs*, **72** (3), 22–49.

Huntington, Samuel P. (1996), *The Clash of Civilizations and the Remaking of World Order*, London: Simon & Schuster.

Huntington, S.P. (2004), 'The Hispanic challenge', *Foreign Affairs*, **141**, 30–45.

Inden, R.B. (1986), 'Orientalist constructions of India', *Modern Asian Studies*, **20** (1), 1–46.

Jacobs, M.D. and L. Spillman (2005), 'Cultural sociology at the crossroads of the discipline', *Poetics*, **33**, 1–14.

Jepperson, R.L. (1991), 'Institution, institutional effects, and institutionalism', in Walter Powell and Paul J. DiMaggio (eds), *The New Institutionalism in Organizational Analysis*, Chicago, IL: University of Chicago Press, pp. 143–163.

Joppke, C. (2004), 'The retreat of multiculturalism in the liberal state: theory and policy', *British Journal of Sociology*, **55** (2), 237–257.

Joppke, Christian and Ewa Morawska (eds) (2003), *Towards Assimilation and Citizenship: Immigrants in Liberal Nation-States*, Basingstoke: Palgrave.

Kaufman, J. (2004), 'Endogenous explanations in the sociology of culture', *Annual Review of Sociology*, **30**, 335–357.

Kostenevich, A. (2008), 'Russia–France: a meeting at the crossroads', London: Royal Academy of Arts.

Kreps, D.M. (1996), 'Corporate culture and economic theory', in R. Coase, P.J. Buckley and J. Michie (eds), *Firms, Organizations and Contracts in Industrial Organization*, Oxford: Oxford University Press, pp. 221–275.

Kroeber, A.L. and C. Kluckhohn (1952), 'Culture: a critical review of concepts and definitions', *Papers of the Peabody Museum of American Archaeology and Ethnology*, Vol. 47. Cambridge, MA: Harvard University Press.

Kukathas, C. (1992), 'Are there any cultural rights?' *Political Theory*, **20** (1), 105–139.

Kuper, Adam (1999), *Culture: The Anthropologists' Account*, Cambridge, MA: Harvard University Press.

Kuran, T. (1988), 'The tenacious past: theories of personal and collective conservatism', *Journal of Economic Behavior and Organization*, **10**, 143–171.

Landes, David (2000), 'Culture makes almost all the difference', in Lawrence E. Harrison and Samuel P. Huntington (eds), *Culture Matters: How Values Shape Human Progress*, New York: Basic Books, pp. 2–13.

Lane, C. and G. Wood (2009), 'Capitalist diversity and diversity within capitalism', *Economy and Society*, **38** (4), 531–551.

Magala, Slawomir (2005), *Cross-Cultural Competence*, London: Routledge.

Malinowski, Bronislaw (1926), *Crime and Custom in Savage Society*, New York: Harcourt Brace.

Matin-Asgari, A. (2004), 'Islamic studies and the spirit of Max Weber: a critique of cultural essentialism', *Middle East Studies*, **13** (3), 293–312.

McGrane, Bernard (1989), *Beyond Anthropology: Society and Other*, New York: Columbia University Press.

McSweeney, B. (2002a), 'Hofstede's model of national cultural differences and their consequences: a triumph of faith – a failure of analysis', *Human Relations*, **55** (1), 89–117.

McSweeney, B. (2002b), 'The essentials of scholarship: a reply to Hofstede', *Human Relations*, **55** (11), 1363–1372.

McSweeney, B. (2009), 'Dynamic diversity: variety and variation within countries', *Organization Studies*, **39** (9), 933–957.

McSweeney, B. (2010), 'The transnationalization of financial reporting standards', School of Management, Royal Holloway, University of London, Working Paper No. 1006.

McSweeney, B., D. Brown and S. Iliopoulou (2010), 'How not to do cross cultural analysis', School of Management, Royal Holloway, University of London, Working Paper No. 1004.

Mead, Margaret (1953), 'National character', in Alfred L. Kroeber (ed.), *Anthropology Today*, Chicago, IL: University of Chicago Press, pp. 642–667.

Merelman, Richard M. (1984), *Making Something of Ourselves: On Culture and Politics in the United States*, Berkeley, CA: University of California Press.

Meyer, John. W., John Boli and George M. Thomas (1994), 'Ontology and rationalization in the Western cultural account', in W.R. Scott and J.W. Meyer, *Institutional Environments and Organizations: Structural Complexity and Individualism*, London: Sage, pp. 9–27.

Mill, James (2010 [1817]), *The History of British India*, Cambridge: Cambridge University Press.

Moore, Henrietta and Todd Sanders (eds) (2006), *Anthropology in Theory: Issues in Epistemology*, Oxford: Blackwell.

Nisbett, Dov and Richard E. Cohen (1996), *Culture of Honor: The Psychology of Violence in the South*, Oxford: Westview Press.

Oppenheimer, Stephen (2007), *The Origin of the British: A Genetic Detective Story*, London: Constable & Robinson.

Ortner, S.B. (1997), 'Introduction', *Representations*, **59** (Special Issue), 8−9.

Oyserman, D., H.M. Coon and M. Kemmelmeier (2002), 'Rethinking individualism and collectivism: evaluation of theoretical assumptions and meta-analyses', *Psychological Bulletin*, **128** (1), 3–72.

Parsons, Talcott (1951), *The Social System*, New York: Free Press.

Parsons, Talcott (1953), 'The theory of symbolism in relation to action', in Talcott Parsons, R.F. Bales and Edward Shils (eds), *Working Papers in the Theory of Action*, New York: Free Press.

Parsons, Talcott (1968), *The Structure of Social Action – Volume 2*, New York: Free Press.

Parsons, T. (1972), 'Culture and social systems revisited', *Social Science Quarterly*, **53** (2), 253–266.

Parsons, Talcott and Edward A. Shils (eds) (1951), *Towards a General Theory of Social Action*, Cambridge, MA: Harvard University Press.

Phillips, Anne (2007), *Multiculturalism without Culture*, Princeton, NJ: Princeton University Press.

Pryce, Ken (1979), *Endless Pressure: A Study of West Indian Life Styles in Bristol*, Bristol: Classic Press.

Ratner, Carl (2006), *Cultural Psychology: A Perspective on Psychological Functioning and Social Reform*, Mahwah, New Jersey: Lawrence Erlbaum Associates.

Rohan, M.J. (2000), 'A rose by any name? The values construct?' *Personality and Social Psychology Review*, **4** (3), 255–277.

Rubenstein, R.E. and J. Crocker (1994), 'Challenging Huntington', *Foreign Policy*, **96**, 113–128.

Sachs, Jeffrey (2000), 'Notes on a new sociology of economic development', in Lawrence E. Harrison and Samuel Huntington (eds), *Culture Matters: How Values Shape Human Progress*, New York: Basic Books, pp. 29–43.

Said, Edward (1979), *Orientalism*, New York: Vintage Books.

Said, E. (2001), 'The clash of ignorance', *Nation*, 22 October, available at http://www.the nation.com/article/clash-ignorance.

Schmid, M. (1992), 'The concept of culture and its place within a theory of social action: a critique of Talcott Parson's theory of culture', in Richard Münch and Neil J. Smelser (eds), *Theory of Culture*, Berkeley, CA: University of California Press, pp. 88–120.

Schudson, Michael (1994), 'Culture and the integration of national societies', Diane Crane (ed.), *The Sociology of Culture*, Oxford: Blackwell, pp. 21–43.

Sen, Amartya (2007), *Identity and Violence: The Illusion of Destiny*, London: Penguin Books.

Slater, Philip L. (1970), *The Pursuit of Loneliness*, Boston, MA: Beacon Press.

Smelser, Neil J. (1992), 'Culture: coherent or non-coherent', in Richard Münch and Neil J. Smelser (eds), *Theory of Culture*, Berkeley, CA: University of California Press, pp. 3–28.

Smith, Chris, Brendan McSweeney and Robert Fitzgerald (2008), *Re-making Management: Between Local and Global*, Cambridge: Cambridge University Press.

Sorokin, Pitrim (1937), *Social and Cultural Dynamics*, New York: American Book Company.

Strange, Susan (1996), *The Retreat of the State: The Diffusion of Power in the World Economy*, Cambridge: Cambridge University Press.

Streeck, Wolfgang and Kathryn Thelen (2005), 'Introduction: institutional change in advanced political economies', in Wolfgang Streeck and Kathy Thelen (eds), *Beyond Continuity: Institutional Change in Advanced Political Economies*, Oxford: Oxford University Press, pp. 1–39.

Sunder, S., G.J. Benston, D.R. Carmichael, K. Jamal, T.E. Christensen, R.H. Colson, S.R. Moehrle, S. Rajgopal, T.L. Stober and R.L. Watts (2007), 'A perspective on the SEC's proposal to accept financial statements prepared in accordance with international reporting standards (IFRS) without reconciliation to US GAAP', available at http://papers.ssrn.com/sol3/papers.cfm?abstract_id=1020408.

Swidler, A. (1986), 'Culture in action: symbols and strategies', *American Sociological Review*, **51**, 273–286.

Trompenaars, Fons (1993), *Riding the Waves of Culture: Understanding Cultural Diversity in Business*, London: Nicholas Brealey Publishing.

Trompenaars, Fons and Charles Hampden-Turner (2005), *Riding the Waves of Culture: Understanding Cultural Diversity in Business*, 2nd edn, London: Nicholas Brealey Publishing.

Tsui, A.S., S.S. Nifadkar and A.Y. Ou (2007), 'Cross-national, cross-cultural organizational behavior research: advances, gaps, and recommendations', *Journal of Management*, **33** (3), 426–478.

Tully, James (1995), *Strange Multiplicity: Constitutionalism in an Age of Diversity*, Cambridge: Cambridge University Press.

Turner, B.S. (2005), 'Leibniz, Islam and cosmopolitan virtue', *Theory, Culture and Society*, **22** (6), 139–147.

Turner, T. (1993), 'Anthropology and multiculturalism: what is it about anthropology that multiculturalists should be mindful of it?' *Cultural Anthropology*, **8** (4), 411–429.

Tylor, Edward B. (1920 [1871]), *Primitive Culture: Researches into the Development of Mythology, Philosophy, Religion, Languages, Art and Culture*, Boston, MA: Estes & Lauriat.

Wallace, Anthony F.C. (1970), *Culture and Personality*, New York: Random House.

Wallerstein, I. (1990), 'Culture as the ideological battleground of the modern world-system', *Theory, Culture and Society*, **7**, 31–55.

Weber, Max (1992 [1930]), *The Protestant Ethic and the Spirit of Capitalism*, London: Routledge.

Weeden, L. (2002), 'Conceptualizing culture: possibilities for political science', *American Political Science Review*, **96** (4), 713–728.

Will, G.F. (2004), 'The slow undoing: the assault on, and underestimation of, nationality', in Irwin Stelzer (ed.), *Neo-conservatism*, London: Atlantic Books, pp. 127–139.

Williamson, Oliver E. (1975), *Markets and Hierarchies: Analysis and Antitrust Implications*, New York: Free Press.
Williamson, Oliver (1985), *The Economic Institutions of Capitalism*, New York: Free Press.
Wright, S. (1998), 'The politicization of "culture"', *Anthropology Today*, **14** (1), 7–15.
Zimmer, O. (1998), 'In search of natural identity: Alpine landscape and the reconstruction of the Swiss nation', *Comparative Studies in Society and History*, **40**, 637–665.

7 The role of institutions and multinational enterprises in economic development
Ben L. Kedia, Jack A. Clampit and Nolan T. Gaffney*

7.1 INTRODUCTION

Economists have written extensively about the relationship between the institutional frameworks that govern various nations and their respective levels of economic development (e.g., Barro 1996). International business scholars have a rich tradition of examining the link between multinational enterprises (MNEs) and their effect on the standard of living of the populations they invest in (e.g., Kedia et al. 2005). While this MNE-oriented literature offers numerous studies that sometimes do explicitly take institutions into account, the inclusion of institutions in this context is often as a control variable rather than as an integral part of a holistic framework exploring the links between institutions, MNEs and levels of economic development in given societies at once (e.g., Borensztein et al. 1998). Drawing on the works of Douglass North and in the spirit of John Dunning, who often urged scholars to integrate institutions and social concerns more fully into our studies, Figure 7.1 illustrates the purpose of this chapter: to synthesize both streams of literature via the development of an integrated framework that explores the rich, interrelated nature of the relationship between institutions, MNEs and levels of economic development around the world.

According to the World Bank (WDI 2010), globalization is spurring widespread and rapid economic development, leading to a marked rise in living standards around the world. Their estimates, for example, suggest that the number of people living on $1.25 a day or less has decreased dramatically since the 1980s, falling from 1.9 billion in 1981 to 1.8 billion in 1990 to about 1.2 billion in 2010. The greatest reductions occurred in Asia, where the poverty rate declined from nearly 80 percent in the early 1980s to less than 20 percent in 2005, a decline that translates into an absolute decrease of over 750 million people. Though they still have far to go, India and China are perhaps the two countries mentioned most often in terms of poverty reduction, and for good reason: India's official poverty rate has been nearly halved, from over 50 percent in 1978 to 27.5

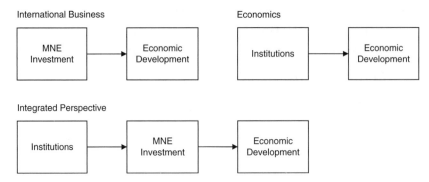

Source: Adapted from Kedia et al. (2011).

Figure 7.1   Three views of economic development

percent in 2005 (Government of India, 2007), while China's poverty rate has fallen from 84 percent to 16 percent, with some predicting that this 16 percent figure will fall to less than 1 percent by 2015 (Goodspeed 2011). It is not all good news, though. For example, the poverty rate in sub-Saharan Africa fell by just 5 percent during the same approximate time frame. And, unfortunately, the recent global financial crisis and rising food costs (due to the proliferation of biofuels) have led to predictions that up to one-third of those around the world who had escaped poverty may soon fall back below the poverty line (Oxfam 2008; World Bank 2008, 2009). Still, it must be noted that the general direction with regard to economic development and living standards worldwide is positive.

In spite of this generally positive trend, critics often charge that the relative new-found prosperity in parts of the world that have shown impressive economic gains has often come at the expense of economic equality. In other words, rises in income due to economic development must be tempered by the possibility that the gap between the rich and poor may have become larger. This concern is captured by the question of whether measures of poverty should be operationalized on an absolute or relative basis. Its recent financial troubles notwithstanding, Ireland serves as a prime example. Notten and Neubourg (2007) note that its recent ascent from the poorest to second-richest country in Western Europe (it has since dropped two places, behind Norway and Switzerland, but is still in the top ten globally) helped cut its absolute poverty rate by more than half, from 25.3 percent to 10.6 percent. At the same time, they note that relative measures showed poverty rates that were nearly twice as high as rates measured on an absolute basis. Smeeding (2006), meanwhile, points out that while absolute measures show a double-digit reduction in its poverty rate, relative measures show an increase of 5.4 percent. Examining this relationship globally, however, Gwartney and Lawson (2008) show that while the average income of the poorest 10 percent is nearly 900 percent higher in countries with growth-oriented institutions versus those lacking the most in this regard, the literature as a whole is simply mixed as to whether higher incomes and rising levels of economic development are related to inequality or not (Barro 2007; Gwartney and Lawson 2008; Nolan and Smeding 2005). It should be noted that in this chapter, when discussing economic development and subsequent poverty reduction, we are referring to absolute, rather than relative, increases in income. In other words, we adopt the view that a family earning $6000 a year today is better off than when they earned $3500 a year (constant dollars at purchasing power parity, PPP), regardless of whether the richest segment of society gained or lost relative to the poor.

The next question, then, is what the best way is to bring about rises in standards of living. A common answer is aid. Proponents often claim that a 'living wage' or redistributions of income large enough to offset the gap between actual and living wages is a fundamental human right. Furthermore, they often claim that a 'big push' is needed for countries trapped in poverty to escape, that is, aid can serve as the necessary springboard to future growth, serving as a hand-up as opposed to a handout (Krugman 1991; Sachs and Warner, 1999). Invoking the likes of Hobbes, Locke, Voltaire and Descartes, critics of aid point to the fallacy of accepting positive human rights as legitimate when they impose claims upon designated duty bearers that directly violate the negative rights of others, before then noting that aid as an economic development strategy has been tried again and again, with history proving one thing: it does not work. In fact, merely not working, according to critics, is often the best-case scenario, as in many instances aid has made matters worse by delaying needed reform, fostering a culture of dependency and facilitating corruption (Chauffour 2009). Doucouliagos and Paldam (2009, 433), meanwhile, examined the results of over 1000 regression equations in nearly 100 aid studies, concluding that despite pressure to publish results favorable to aid-based strategies, and despite recent attempts to tease out effective examples of aid by including contingencies along the lines of good host-country governance, 'a clear pattern emerges in the results: after 40 years of development aid, the evidence indicates that aid has not been effective'. (Their meta-regression, in fact, actually showed a small negative effect of aid on economic development, both with and without outliers included.) The stance of this chapter is not to endorse or disapprove of aid-based tactics to reduce poverty, but to explore an alternative mechanism (whether it is a substitute or complement): the role MNEs and institutions play with respect to economic development.

The list of scholars noting the role MNEs play in elevating living standards worldwide is long (e.g. Bhagwati 2007; Kedia et al. 2005; Krugman 1997; Lodge and Wilson 2006). While critical theorists are quick to point out negative externalities associated with MNE conduct, such as the crowding out of local businesses, MNEs also provide jobs where jobs previously did not exist, pay higher-than-market salaries when jobs do exist, often provide positive horizontal and/or vertical spillovers that spur the growth of domestic businesses, help integrate local firms into the global economy, provide political leverage for local governments to embark upon positive institutional change, invest in local infrastructure, and uplift the morale of young people who previously thought there was no hope to escape from poverty.

An example is offered by Lodge and Wilson (2006), who relay the story of a Panamanian bishop who helped farmers establish credit and marketing cooperatives. An interesting consequence was that as locals witnessed first hand that situations are not always hopeless, that positive change was, indeed, possible, they began to see the value of education and, thus, built schools teaching vocational skills. Though certain entrenched powers resisted this change and killed the priest, the movement did not die, and today runs Central America's biggest chicken factory. Meanwhile, in the neighboring province Nestlé followed the bishop's lead and actively organized farmers for the production of milk. While the bishop was a local who did not seek profit, Nestlé was an MNE which did. In both cases, culture was changed from defeatist to optimistic, and productivity and relative prosperity followed.

Bishops of a like mind and capability may be fairly rare agents of change along these lines, but MNEs uplift the standards of living of local populations every day, as evidenced by firms like Daimler which, in Brazil, constructed a factory manufacturing headrests and seats from renewable domestic fibers, a factory that employs over 5000 people that were formerly impoverished, a factory full of people who now actively participate in civic affairs and whose children now attend school. Bhagwati (2007) passionately notes that the empirical record regarding MNEs points to higher wages for local workers, better working conditions and better environmental practices, and claims that MNEs promote positive change that improves the living conditions of domestic populations, for example reduced corruption and tighter integration into global markets. Moreover, the number of empirical studies showing a link between MNE entry and subsequent economic growth, including an increase in the standard of living of the poor, is large (see Klein et al. 2002, for a review). Adam Smith (1776), then, may have been correct when suggesting that we promote societal interests most effectively by pursuing our own interests, that is:

> It is not from the benevolence of the butcher, the brewer, or the baker that we expect our dinner, but from their regard to their own interest. We address ourselves, not to their humanity, but to their self-love, and never talk to them of our own necessities, but of their advantages.

As Lodge and Wilson (2006, 21) note, MNEs 'have the unmatched power and competence to reduce global poverty', and if Smith is right, they have the motive too.

7.2   INSTITUTIONS AND DEVELOPMENT

If economic development is the goal, and MNE activity helps bring about this goal, another question surfaces: how can countries encourage MNEs to participate positively in the economic development process? As the correlations in Table 7.1 and Figure 7.2 suggest, one possible answer may be by adopting the right set of institutions. This chapter adopts North's definition of institutions as: 'the humanly devised constraints that structure human interaction', that consist of the 'formal constraints (rules, laws, constitutions), informal constraints (norms of behavior, conventions, and self-imposed codes of conduct), and their enforcement characteristics' (North 1990, 3). They are 'the rules of the game', so to speak, that dictate a society's incentive structure that, in turn, determines the decision set available to entrepreneurs (including economic entrepreneurs such as MNEs) and, thus, entrepreneurial actions and subsequent outcomes. In other words, institutions provide constraints and incentives that influence the conduct of organizations (such as MNEs), and that conduct directly influences how successful those organizations will be. Nove's (1969, 314) question of how a 'country capable of making an A-bomb (the USSR) could

Table 7.1   *Correlation matrix of institutional, economic development and foreign direct investment indicators*

	Institutions	Development	FDI
Institutions	1.00	0.72	0.42
Development	0.72	1.00	0.70
FDI	0.42	0.70	1.00

Sources: World Bank (GDP data), UNCTAD (FDI data), Heritage Foundation (Index of Economic Freedom data).

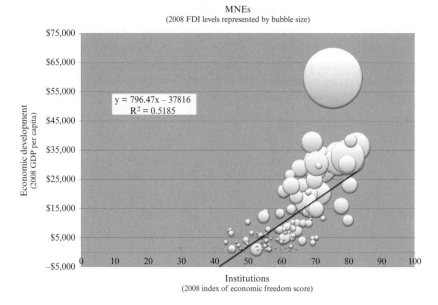

MNEs
(2008 FDI levels represented by bubble size)

$$y = 796.47x - 37816$$
$$R^2 = 0.5185$$

Institutions
(2008 index of economic freedom score)

Sources: World Bank (GDP), UNCTAD (FDI), Heritage Foundation (Index of Economic Freedom).

Figure 7.2   Institutions, MNEs and economic development

not supply its citizens with eggs' offers a pithy example of how powerful institutional incentives can be. The answer, of course, is that the institutions of the USSR rewarded conduct aimed at building A-bombs while discouraging – actually, prohibiting – the kind of decentralized planning and profit motives that would have resulted in an allocation of resources efficient enough to supply its citizens with eggs.

The exacting precision of their mathematical models notwithstanding, neoclassical economists have for years assumed a static and frictionless environment where transactions are free and the strategies of firms unconstrained by institutions. They have to all intents and purposes confined the role of institutions to that of a bit player in the background, to the extent that they are acknowledged at all. In reality, however, transactions have costs, for example negotiation costs, search costs, and costs incurred when writing and enforcing contracts (Coase 1937; Williamson 1981). In 1970 these costs represented 45 percent of United States (US) gross national product (GNP), and have only risen since then as technology reduces production costs (Wallace and North 1986). These costs, and associated incentives and constraints, are directly influenced by the institutional framework within which firms operate. The heterogeneity among the decision sets available to entrepreneurs in different countries goes a long way towards explaining their behavior and subsequent economic outcomes (Alston et al. 1996; Bruton et al. 2007; Bueno de Mesquita and Root 2000; Hill 2007; Lee et al. 2007; North 1990; Wan and Hoskisson 2003).With this in mind, and in order to position the role of institutions properly as it relates to economic development, we will next review literature that suggests institutional settings differ, and that those differences matter with respect to determining whether the people of a nation will prosper or remain poor.

7.2.1 Heterogeneous, Non-Ergodic Settings

Institutional settings differ, and their non-ergodic nature makes it more difficult for firms to predict or react to differences in those settings, as they are sometimes forced to deal with a moving target (North 1990). The following two examples (World Bank, WDI 2005, 2008) illustrate just how much this framework differs in different parts of the world: (1) it requires 124 days and costs more than 20 percent of the property value to register property in Nicaragua and Mali, while in New Zealand it takes two days and costs 0.1 percent of the property value; (2) on average it takes over 200 days and costs 153 percent of per capita income to register a new business in Haiti, while in Australia it takes two days and costs 2 percent of per capita income. On the basis of generalizations drawn from statistics like these alone, one can probably quite accurately guess which countries are more productive and, thus, have a higher standard of living.

Peng et al. (2008) implore scholars to account explicitly for the impact of institutions on MNEs via a three-legged stool metaphor, with resource, industry and institutional-based views of the firm as legs. Hoskisson et al. (2000) also suggest that institutional theory is important and is, in fact, one of the three most insightful theories that exist today when examining MNE activity in developing economies. And while they do also predict that its importance will diminish as isomorphism brings about relative convergence in institutional settings, we might argue that, as recent examples of institutional failure in the United States illustrate, institutions will still matter and important differences will still exist even between countries considered to be institutionally similar; for example France's legally mandated 35-hour work week limit stands in stark contrast to labor laws in places like America.

Drawing on research streams from political science and socio-economics, various studies suggest the existence of multiple varieties of capitalism based on heterogeneous institutional configurations resulting from different histories, cultures and goals (Albert 1993; Chandler 1990; Hall and

Soskice 2001; Redding 2005; Wade 1990; Whitley 1999). Moreover, not only are the institutional matrices different when comparing nations in different regions (for example Asian countries versus the US), but they are also different when comparing firms in the same region (for example Asian countries versus other Asian countries) (Orru 1997).

Another stream of research introduces the constructs of coordinated or liberal market economies (CMEs or LMEs). In LMEs firms adjust to environmental changes on their own, with other firms copying the practices of the more successful firms, resulting in initial heterogeneity but eventual isomorphism, In CMEs aggregate level change is voluntarily implemented or dictated by labor unions, governments, and so on (Albert 1993; Hall and Soskice 2001; Witt and Lewin 2007). This is not the same as centralization or decentralization, where a central authority in a socialist or communist country, or an authoritarian ruler, makes centralized decisions as opposed to the decentralized decision-making people are used to in the United States. For example, the US is a decentralized LME while Germany is a fairly decentralized CME. One key point to be extracted from this stream of research is the idea that CMEs are slow to adjust and prone to groupthink – thus, if the wrong kind of change is made, all firms suffer together. Witt and Lewin (2007) thus predict that as societal coordination increases, institutional misalignment – the gap between goals of the firm and what institutions promote and/or discourage – will increase.

Further evidence of differing institutional environments, and their nonergodic nature, comes from the recent 2007 FDI Confidence Index report that includes the results of surveys of managers with strategic decision-making responsibilities in the Global 1000 (representing 60 countries, 6 continents and 17 industries). In fact, not only do these surveys suggest differing institutional environments around the globe, but they also imply that opinions regarding the institutional make-up may differ even within the same country. For example, while 23 percent of respondents said they had more confidence in the United States as a potential environment for foreign direct investment (FDI) versus last year, 23 percent had less confidence (AT Kearney 2007). As always, the FDI Confidence Index report includes updates of important changes in the institutional environments of various countries around the globe. A sampling of institutional changes from a single year to the next can be found in Table 7.2, while Table 7.3 illustrates longer run changes with respect to tax levels.

7.2.2   Impact of Distinct Institutional Matrices

In order to insert institutions legitimately into our framework, we had to first show that institutional configurations at the nation-state level differ

Table 7.2   2007 institutional settings update

Country	Update
Indonesia	While rich in natural resources and possessing the 4th largest population in the world, Indonesia has had trouble attracting FDI due to institutionally related issues such as an overburden some regulatory environment and security concerns, but is now promising to improve customs rules, labor laws, taxation levels, property rights and bureaucracy levels.
Thailand	Thailand dropped completely off the 2007 index due to political stability concerns after a military coup.
Germany	In response to concerns that businesses were leaving due to institutional disadvantages, Germany cut corporate taxes from 39% to 30%. 'Union wage restraint' is mentioned as another positive development.
United Kingdom	The UK, with twice as much IFDI as its closest European rival, continues to benefit from higher transaction costs imposed on US markets by Sarbanes–Oxley, due to a more favorable regulatory environment and skilled workers.
Russia	Survey respondents noted an improved economy, large markets and skilled labor, but more than half decided to pull back or hold investment constant due to political concerns including the threat of nationalization, poor rule of law and crime.
France	Outlook improved due to promised reforms including greater labor flexibility and improved education; however the recent US financial crisis seems to have tempered reform. Protectionism concerns remain.
Africa	Concerns remain the same, with 92% mentioning bureaucracy, 80% citing political instability, 69% citing poor public infrastructure, and 58% mentioning the poorly skilled workforce as reasons to avoid Africa.

Source: AT Kearney's 2007 FDI Confidence Index Report and Kedia et al. (2011).

and, while certain aspects are remarkably stubborn, those configurations are constantly evolving. Implied in the assertion that they differ is that those differences matter. It is these differences, after all, that provide incentives and disincentives that influence the decision of MNEs to either enter or avoid a country, and its behavior if it does enter; and development prompted by MNE behavior is often a critical channel by which growth-oriented institutions in developing countries alleviate poverty.

The proposition that institutions matter is not controversial; the notion, in fact, can be found as far back as Adam Smith's magnum opus, *An*

Table 7.3   National statutory corporate tax rates (%)

Country	2011	1981	Change
Ireland	12.50	45.00	−32.50
Austria	25.00	55.00	−30.00
Portugal	19.00	47.20	−28.20
United Kingdom	26.00	52.00	−26.00
Germany	30.83	56.00	−25.18
Greece	20.00	45.00	−25.00
Canada	16.50	37.80	−21.30
Luxembourg	22.00	40.00	−18.00
Netherlands	30.00	48.00	−18.00
Finland	26.00	43.00	−17.00
New Zealand	28.00	45.00	−17.00
Australia	30.00	46.00	−16.00
France	34.43	50.00	−15.57
Denmark	25.00	40.00	−15.00
Sweden	26.30	40.00	−13.70
Italy	27.50	40.00	−12.50
Japan	30.00	42.00	−12.00
Mexico	30.00	42.00	−12.00
United States	35.00	46.00	−11.00
Spain	30.00	33.00	−3.00
Norway	28.00	29.80	−1.80
Switzerland	8.50	9.80	−1.30

Source: OECD (does not include subnational taxes).

Inquiry into the Nature and Causes of the Wealth of Nations (1776), where he plainly asserts that the state must define property rights and enforce contracts in order for a society to be able to take advantage of the gains associated with the division of labor and trade and, thus, collectively improve its material lot. Simply put, the rule of law and sound, growth-oriented institutions are a prerequisite for the invisible hand to be able to work its magic. The question to consider, then, is how, and to what degree, institutions matter.

Some have argued that a background role is sufficient in advanced market economies, where vital institutional frameworks such as the rule of law can simply be assumed and taken for granted. Increasingly, however, the direct impact of institutions on the firm has been demonstrated to be worth actively considering as more and more evidence surfaces regarding the manner and degree of the impact (Lewin and Kim 2004; Peng et al. 2005; Wan and Hoskisson 2003).

Before discussing institutional effects specifically related to MNE behavior and poverty outcomes, two brief macro-level examples should confirm that even in a country as advanced as the United States, institutions do indeed matter a great deal and are not always efficient to the point of being invisible: first, the role of the Federal Reserve before and during the Great Depression, and second, the catalogue of potential institutional missteps by various actors involved in the United States' current financial crisis.

During the Great Depression the United States' real output fell nearly 30 percent and unemployment rate rose from roughly 3 percent to nearly 25 percent (with many of the 'employed' holding part-time jobs), with recovery over a decade away (Bernanke 2004). Regarding the role of institutions, Lucas (2011, 25) endorses the empirical work of Milton Friedman and Anna Schwartz that blames the Great Depression on decisions made by the Federal Reserve. He then – in a manner reminiscent of Deirdre McCloskey (2010) – laments the subsequent demonization of business (e.g., by Franklin Delano Roosevelt) and the consequential and unfortunate effect this mindset inevitably has on the standard of living within a country. Similarly, Federal Reserve Chairman, Ben Bernanke, has on more than one occasion publicly admitted that 'we did it', that is, contrary to the image held by some of the Federal Reserve as a 'white knight' which cleaned up the mess of the greedy capitalists and speculative market forces, the Federal Reserve itself actually played a central role in causing the Great Depression (Bernanke 2002, 2004). More specifically, Bernanke (2004) offers four central policy missteps from 1923 to 1933 as the 'smoking gun' that turned what otherwise would have been a run-of-the-mill recession into the worst economic disaster in the country's history, before going on to note that the malaise – a kind depiction if ever there was one – then spread throughout the world, including to Germany where the downturn, combined with weak German political institutions, allowed the Nazis to ascend from fringe political group status, garnering just 2.6 percent of the vote four years earlier, to become Germany's ruling party (Berman 1997; Childers 1983, 1986; Falter 1991; Orlow 1969).

Institutional influence is prominently on display in modern times as well. Comments made in 2007 by the then President of the Federal Reserve Bank of St Louis notwithstanding – attesting to the prowess of today's Federal Reserve at fostering real prosperity: 'advances in knowledge permit us to say with some confidence that these gains are not just an accident of Alan Greenspan's special skills and intuition' (Poole 2007) – the actions of the Federal Reserve and other US institutional players are currently under scrutiny for their role in the subprime-induced financial crisis.

Some point fingers at institutional policy-makers which decided to promote homeownership feverishly among people with track records of not paying their debts, while others note the informal constraints preventing politically astute actors from pointing out the danger of those policies. Others point to perverted institutional incentives allowing lenders to lend with impunity as risks were transferred to entities like Fannie Mae, Freddy Mac and global investors. Still others blame 'easy money' policies of the Federal Reserve that may have helped fuel a real estate bubble, while Alan Greenspan shifts the blame towards irrational actors in financial institutions who, based on greed or a desire to placate the never-ending demands of customers for higher returns on their 'safe' investments, over-relied on math experts and finance scholars who suggested there was a new kind of alchemy enabling firms magically to transmute risky mortgages into relatively safe assets via the use of certain derivatives. Regarding these derivatives, many point to failure among regulatory institutions that allowed them to play such a prominent role in the first place, while others claim that, contrary to a lack of regulations, rules already on the books actually encouraged their use. Regardless of who is truly at fault for the economic mess the US is now in, institutional failure does seem to be squarely in the spotlight. And if perhaps the archetypical model for a sound institutional framework can let its populace down to the degree it has, should it be any surprise that institutions often fail in less established countries?

Institutions can, of course, do tremendous good. In developed countries they are the bedrock of civilization, providing law and order and the necessary ingredients for prosperity. In fact, the argument has often been made that it is precisely because of their institutions that the corporations of some countries, and thus the country as a whole, have been so prosperous; and precisely because of their lack of growth-oriented institutions that third world countries remain poor. In other words, though they certainly help, peace and prosperity do not owe their existence to a country's large population, abundant natural resources or especially intelligent people, but rather to effective institutions. Interestingly enough, democracy does not correlate as strongly with prosperity as many might suspect, with some positing a curvilinear effect, with a direct relationship that turns downward once people in mature democracies start voting themselves more and more largesse (Barro, 1996). Economic freedom, however, does correlate positively with prosperity, whether it is ensured by the government of a democracy or by the government of a market-oriented autocracy; for example Taiwan and South Korea jump-starting growth under authoritarian regimes, and Singapore as a current quasi-authoritarian state with an enviable economic record (Alston et al. 1996; Bueno de Mesquita and Root 2000; North 1990, 2005).

Employing a game-theoretic context, North (1991) illustrates the logic of institutions in a simple and intuitive fashion via a story of how transition in an old village from local exchange to regional trade was made possible by newly birthed institutions designed to minimize transaction costs. When trade was local, actors possessed accurate information regarding the reliability of others, and as those actors lived near each other and constantly repeated transactions, there was intense social pressure to keep one's bargains. The development of impersonal exchange in the form of long-distance trade, however, was characterized by: (1) buyers and sellers who knew little about each other and might never deal with one another again (that is, it was a single, rather than a repeat, game context); (2) agents hired to deliver goods from villages to faraway markets, to sell those goods at a worthy price and, finally, to return and relinquish the profits from their sale; and (3) hired protection to thwart armed bandits. Where societies developed institutions – such as rudimentary forms of contract enforcement and rule of law (e.g., agreements with local princes for protection or the formation of guilds that provided customers with the promise of a relatively standardized quality of goods) – trade flourished. Where appropriate institutions did not develop, however, economic growth never materialized, as the transaction costs in the absence of facilitating institutions quite simply exceeded the pay-off.

Empirically, Acemoglu et al. (2001) examined over 70 former European colonies and found that colonists in disease-free locales (such as Australia, New Zealand and North America) crafted strong institutions designed to protect property rights and curb the power of the state; but when they arrived in areas with high rates of malaria, yellow fever, etcetera they did not found as many permanent settlements and, thus, did not create the kinds of stable, liberty-oriented institutions that make growth possible. They go on to suggest that today's institutional and cultural setting can be traced back to decisions made by colonists back then, decisions that explain much of today's current levels of growth or lack thereof. Doucouliagos and Ulubasoglu's (2006) meta-analysis of over 40 studies (n = 6302), meanwhile, finds a strong and robust link between institutional quality as proxied by measures of economic freedom (including rule of law and various political factors) and economic growth.

7.3   CONCEPTUAL FRAMEWORK

The following model (see Figure 7.3) may serve as a useful framework to help illustrate the interrelated nature of the relationship between institutions and MNEs and global poverty.

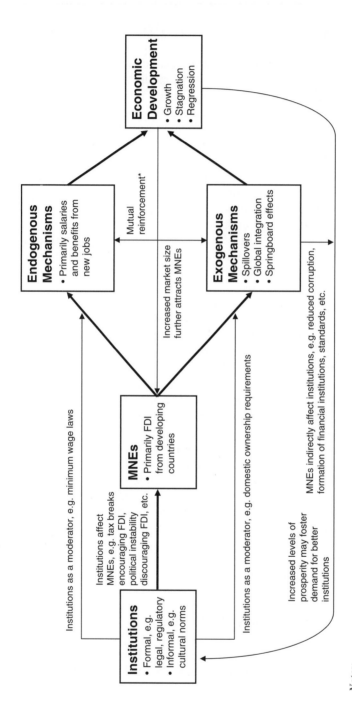

Notes:
Thick lines indicate main effects. Thin lines indicate secondary effects.
* For example, salaries may facilitate savings that may be used to start new businesses, creating upward pressure on salaries as firms compete for workers.

Figure 7.3   Integrated 'Institution → MNEs → Economic Development' framework

7.3.1   Main Effects

Institutions → MNEs
The first relationship illustrated in Figure 7.3 is the relationship between the location choice of MNEs which have made the decision to invest abroad, and the institutional framework governing potential host countries. Much of the study of institutions and MNEs examines formal institutions. Examples include assessments of the threat of government expropriation; the degree to which political and legal institutions ensure property rights and an efficient and independent judiciary system; the level of regulatory burden with regard to the opening and operation of businesses, trade barriers, tax levels and price controls; the degree of restrictions with regard to foreign exchange and capital transfers; the presence of efficient capital markets and private ownership of banks and insurers; the quality of the legal and regulatory framework of a country's labor market; levels of political risk; and corruption levels. Each of these institutions serves as an important determinant of an MNE's location choice. In fact, according to recent AT Kearney surveys of Global 1000 executives, six of the top ten most critical risks to firm operations were related to the performance of a country's institutions, and five of the top six criteria of where to locate research and development (R&D) operations were also related to institutions.

One of the most commonly studied determinants of location choice is the tax policy of potential host countries. AT Kearney (2005) reported that FDI inflows into Germany dropped from $27.2 billion in 2003 to negative $38.6 billion in 2004 after revisions to the German tax code made it less attractive for foreign companies to retain liquid assets in Germany. Meanwhile, De Mooij and Ederveen's (2005) meta-analysis (n = 427) found semi-elasticities ranging from close to zero to as high as 13.75, depending on methodology, with an overall adjusted average of 4.28, meaning FDI drops by 4.28 percent for each 1 percent increase in the tax rate.

Another commonly studied determinant, the threat of government expropriation, serves as a constant reminder of the paradox that a government strong enough to protect property rights and enforce contracts is also strong enough to expropriate assets (Haber et al. 2003). MNEs will naturally prefer to operate in countries where the risk of nationalization is low. Thus, countries able to provide credible commitments that they will protect the property rights of firms, even from the countries themselves – whether it be via the vertical checks and balances of federalism or horizontal competition among different branches of the government – are viewed as more attractive than locations where the commitment is suspect.

Brunetti and Weder (1994) and Henisz (2000) go on to note that in some cases, institutions that make it difficult for the government to enact policy changes can further serve to make governmental commitments more credible.

Regarding contract enforcement, in Burkina Faso it typically requires 41 procedures, 446 days and 95 percent of the debt to collect money owed but not paid; and worldwide, contract enforcement difficulties, crime, bureaucratic regulations and corruption cost firms up to 25 percent of revenue (World Bank, WDI 2005). Regarding corruption specifically, Stone et al. (1996) found that 90 percent of small firms, 70 percent of medium-sized firms and 60 percent of large firms in Brazil admit to paying bribes to government officials, and note that Brazil's regulatory quagmire prompts a significant percentage of firms to exit the formal economy and operate in the thriving shadow economy. Consequently, efficiencies related to economies of scale are intentionally bypassed, as firms balance profitability with conscious attempts to remain small enough not to be noticed. Firms from home countries with laws forcing them to adhere to domestic norms, for example laws that prohibit them from offering graft, face a different set of consequences, as they may find themselves at a disadvantage vis-à-vis firms which operate under different moral codes and may, thus, decide simply to avoid especially corrupt countries. Indeed, Mauro's (1995) seminal study bears that assertion out, showing how corruption cripples investment, and how lowered investment reduces growth.

Meanwhile, Globerman and Shapiro (2002) suggest that FDI inflows are directly related to good governance, while Kauffman et al. (1999) suggest that political instability and violence, large regulatory burdens, rule of law and graft all affect FDI inflows. Along similar lines, Pajunen (2008) mentions many of the same institutional determinants, while also suggesting equifinality, as different attractive institutional mixes leading to improved FDI inflows. Finally, Bénassy-Quéré et al. (2005, 4) plainly assert that: 'good institutions almost always increase the amount of FDI received'.

Informal institutions, such as culture and social norms, also affect the actions of firms. For example, in Crossland's (2007) examination of institutional effects on managerial discretion in 24 countries, he refers to Hambrick and Finkelstein (1987) and House et al.'s (2004) GLOBE dimension of institutional collectivism, while suggesting that the normative constraints on unilateral managerial discretion depend upon the acceptance of powerful stakeholders and the society each MNE is embedded in. Crossland and Hambrick (2007), meanwhile, specifically examine Japan, noting that societal tendencies embracing consensus, inclusiveness and risk-aversion help to explain their finding that executive discretion is severely constrained there as compared to Germany and, especially, the US. They then refer to Abegglen and Stalk's (1985) observation of the frequent use of terms like *ringisho* (management by consensus) and *nemawashi* (prior consultation) among Japanese managers, and to Porter's suggestion that relatively heterogeneous MNE strategies in Japan and, therefore, performance are inertial (Porter et al. 2000). Thus, according to them, if a chief executive officer (CEO) feels as if their company is operating in a competitive environment where they need to be able to make unilateral decisions quickly without having to build internal coalitions and lobby for the support of others before acting, then they may feel limited by this informal institutional constraint and may, therefore, decide to avoid entering such countries altogether.

Doh et al. (2010) offer another example of firms acting in accordance with prevailing social norms, finding that institutional endorsements of socially responsible behavior positively affects shareholder wealth, while also noting that Orlitzky's (2003) meta-analysis finds that good corporate citizens are more likely to be rewarded than punished. If firms, then, are inclined to undertake activities that go against the grain of socially acceptable behavior in their certain countries (for example stem cell research in a country opposed to such practices), then it would obviously be prudent to avoid moving related operations to these countries.

The study of institutional characteristics as determinants of MNE investment has been an especially active area of research. While, in our view, there are many institutional effects still to be tested, especially among less formal institutions, we feel that currently available evidence allows us to suggest the following:

Proposition 1: The quality of a nation's institutions is directly related to the level of MNE investment.

MNEs → endogenous/exogenous effects → poverty

The second main effect in our framework is the link from MNEs to poverty outcomes, with endogenous and exogenous mediators. The obvious example of an endogenous effect is the salary paid to a worker in a job that previously did not exist, or a higher salary paid to a worker who made less at his or her previous job. Examples of exogenous effects include spillovers along the lines of linkages with external buyers, suppliers or sources of capital, and technology externalities or productivity increases stemming from demonstration effects, movement of skilled employees and competition effects (Chauffour 2009; Dunning and Fourtanier 2007). These spillovers help domestic firms become more productive and prosperous, which has the effect of raising the standard of living in the host country, and even prompts some of the more ambitious firms to decide to internationalize themselves (Globerman and Shapiro 2002; Kedia et al. 2005; Luo and Tung 2007). For example, Easterly (2002) relays the story of Indian textile manufacturer Desh Garments, which grew from a $55 000 company (annual sales) with a handful of employees in 1980 to a $2 billion company in less than 20 years. Korean conglomerate Daewoo, seeking a manufacturing locale from which exports could evade US and European tariffs, entered into an agreement to work with Desh. Desh, an especially fast learner, cancelled this agreement after only two years and then used knowledge acquired from Daewoo to increase its share of the Bangladeshi export market from 1/10 000th of all exports to more than every other company combined. Clearly, spillovers, whether endogenous or exogenous, have the potential to help countries develop economically. Thus, we propose the following:

Proposition 2: Endogenous effects mediate the relationship between MNEs and poverty in countries where they invest.

Proposition 3: Exogenous effects mediate the relationship between MNEs and poverty in countries where they invest.

7.3.2   Secondary Effects

Institutions → MNE relationship with endogenous/exogenous effects
While MNE investment in developing nations certainly has the potential to help them grow, externalities are not automatically positive, and the question of whether spillovers are usually positive on net is an open one in the minds of many. Globerman and Shapiro (2002), for example, claim that quality institutions are not only necessary to attract FDI, but also necessary to create favorable conditions for domestic companies to emerge, learn from foreign firms and subsequently venture abroad themselves. Others, however, sometimes point to spillovers not emerging or actually having negative effects, for example the crowding-out of domestic firms and infant industries by fitter, richer foreign entrants which may also be more politically connected. In an attempt to answer this question of whether spillovers are positive on net, a meta-analysis conducted by Görg and Strobl (2001) found that 13 studies generally found support for the existence of positive spillovers, four found negative spillovers (e.g. the crowding-out of local businesses) and four were mixed. The question, then, if positive spillovers do not automatically happen, is what host-country institutions can do to moderate positively the relationship between MNEs and their endogenous and exogenous effects.

Buckley et al. (2007), finding a curvilinear relationship for some spillovers in China (with geographical proximity and the level of technology as moderators) suggest that China should not promote high inward FDI in low-technology industries. Tian (2007), meanwhile, studied 11 324 Chinese firms, finding that positive technology spillovers occurred through tangible versus intangible assets (e.g. patents, copyrights), through domestically consumed products rather than exported products, through traditional rather than new products, and through MNEs employing unskilled rather than skilled workers. Negative spillovers, however, occurred through exports and through the employment of skilled workers.

Moran et al. (2005) suggest that the main moderators are openness and absorptive capacity, suggesting that when host countries impose restrictions prompting MNEs to move operations there to jump trade barriers (forcing MNEs to partner with local firms, or requiring the use of domestic content), MNEs may still find the country profitable enough to enter, but may avoid bringing their best technologies or linking to their best sourcing networks. This suggests that while wage regulations and partner requirements may seem to encourage high wages and linkages to domestic firms that spur technology spillovers, the opposite may in fact be true. In the end, if countries are too restrictive in their quest for spillovers, spillovers may not materialize.

Proposition 4: The quality of institutions positively moderates the relationship between MNEs and endogenous effects.

Proposition 5: The quality of institutions positively moderates the relationship between MNEs and exogenous effects.

Endogenous effects ↔ exogenous effects
An example of endogenous effects interacting with exogenous effects is when employees save portions of their salary and use it to start a new business, applying techniques learned while in the employee of the MNE. An example in the other direction is when wage competition from that new firm leads to increased wages at the MNE.

Proposition 6: Endogenous effects are directly related to exogenous effects.

MNEs → institutions
The link between institutions and MNEs runs both ways. Recalling the previous study by Acemoglu et al. (2001) of the institution-building activities of colonial ventures suggests that foreigners have a long history of impacting local institutions. More recently, Dunning and Fourtanier (2007, 34) say: 'The most commonly cited example on how

MNEs may contribute to institutions is the financial sector, where for example banks and insurance companies can help establish a structure of financial incentives and thus promote entrepreneurship and enterprise creation.'

A notable corollary to the rule that secure property rights are positively related to economic growth is the following: the ability to convert property into capital is positively related to growth. As De Soto (2000) notes, while many of the poor already possess the assets, they are often in defective forms (e.g. houses but no titles, crops but no deeds). Absent the institutions needed to specify and form formal property rights, they cannot generally be used as collateral for a loan or used as a share against investment. Heitger (2004) suggests that property rights and economic growth develop simultaneously, implying a role for MNEs in the development process, possibly via political leverage, and certainly via links to external markets once property rights have been formally specified.

With respect to this leverage, Lodge and Wilson (2006, 19) say: 'Poverty reduction requires systematic change, and MNCs are the world's most efficient and sustainable engines of change'. They also note the previously mentioned effect of MNEs on informal institutions, such as changing cultural norms that previously convinced people there was no hope for a better life, before talking about how much money MNEs often spend on infrastructure and local education.

Meanwhile, Kwok and Tadesse (2006) find that MNEs are a powerful agent of change in terms of reducing institutional corruption. Oliver and Holzinger (2008) position a firm's ability to manage its external political environment as a dynamic capability that can serve as a competitive advantage. Luo (2006) invokes a structuration perspective while exploring the same topic in a strictly international context. And Havrylyshyn (2008) suggests that among Central European, Baltic, and Commonwealth of Independent States (CIS) countries, liberalization was followed by growth and, finally, real institutional reform, implicitly suggesting that MNEs positively affected institutions.

Proposition 7: There is a direct relationship between MNE investment in a country and improving institutional conditions.

Poverty → MNEs

Four commonly accepted FDI motives are: market seeking, efficiency seeking, asset seeking and strategic asset seeking. This link speaks to the first motivation. As many authors have suggested (e.g. Dunning 1998), as the standard of living in a country rises, MNEs will find it a more attractive market and, thus, be more likely to enter.

Poverty → institutions

The causal link going from institutions to economic growth is commonly accepted. The literature is mixed with regard to whether there is causation in the other direction too. Scholars who claim that there is, suggest that rising prosperity levels prompt citizens to demand higher-quality institutions, and provides them with the means to pay for them. Consistent with this hypothesis is the previously mentioned Havrylyshyn (2008) paper suggesting that among Central European, Baltic and CIS countries, liberalization was followed by growth and, finally, real institutional reform.

Proposition 8: As a country's standard of living rises, MNEs are more likely to enter.

Proposition 9: As a country's standard of living rises, the quality of its institutions will rise.

7.4 DISCUSSION

7.4.1 Getting it Right

North (2005) notes that the world's track record in terms of institutional choices is not characterized by countries 'getting it right'. The overwhelming norm, unfortunately, across both time and space, is for countries to get things wrong, assuming that the goal is to create and enact institutions that foster social order, peace within and between nations, and economic growth. Sometimes, however, we do seem to get it more right than wrong or, at least, more right than the rest of the world, for example institutional frameworks resulting in historically strong growth rates in the US and Western Europe. The conceptual framework offered explains how institutions and MNEs can interact in a manner that promotes economic development. Knowing what to do, however, is not the same thing as doing it. As Lodge and Wilson (2006, 18) note, despite the proven capacity of MNEs to raise standards of living in poor countries when working in concert with complementary institutions, and despite the wealth of examples of poverty when sound institutions and MNE investment are absent, a recent meeting of the World Economic Forum brought out a cadre of anti-globalization protestors waving signs saying, 'Our resistance is as global as your oppression'.

History is, unfortunately, no stranger to populations that embrace ideas that are not only erroneous, but harmful, for example those believing in the utopia of communism. North (2005) claims that formal institutions are the external manifestation of a society's beliefs. Experienced events and inevitable gaps between intended and actual institutional results continually alter our beliefs. Different beliefs in different societal settings produce different sets of institutions, some growth inducing and others growth hindering (Greif 1989; North 2005). The complicated nature of this world, the filtering of heterogeneous experiences through pre-existing belief systems and cognitive biases and delayed feedback loops, complicates our understanding of what works and does not work by making it more difficult accurately to discern cause and effect.

Once established, institutional change – even when institutions are of poor quality – can be difficult, due to the prevalence of stubborn belief systems or because change threatens certain powerful special interests. Some types of institutions can change more quickly than others, provided they are not in conflict with opposing institutional constraints. For example, while the addition and modification of laws can occur quite frequently, extremely ambitious programs suggested by politicians sometimes have to be phased in gradually, on a piecemeal basis, if the public is not ready to accept drastic change all at once; or even postponed entirely until a society is ready, for example the US rejecting nationalized health care when proposed by Bill Clinton in the early 1990s, while seeming more open to it today. With the exception of periodic shocks, these factors tend to make societies rigid and stifle forms of growth-inducing institutional change that goes against the cultural paradigm of the day (Coatsworth 2005; Krugman 1996; Mudambi and Navarra 2002; North 2005; Williamson 2000). Statements by the FDR (lamenting rising prosperity levels on the ground that they would undermine public justification of New Deal programs as a necessary precondition for prosperity levels to rise) and, more recently, by Barack Obama's first Chief of Staff, Rahm Emanuel (suggesting that politicians should never let a good crisis go to waste) show that politicians are acutely aware of this (Roosevelt 1937; Sieb 2008). Higgs (1997) similarly notes that crises increase the ability of politicians to enact change, and that if the crisis is deemed serious enough, constituents may actually demand change. Sometimes, however, a fever pitch on the part of constituents to 'do something' results in rash action. For example, Niskanen (2007, 34) notes that when asked whether he would have done things differently if he knew today what the real world effects of the Sarbanes–Oxley Act would have been, Oxley says: 'Absolutely . . . I would have written it differently, and he would have written it differently . . . But it was not normal times.' Along similar lines, the Dodd–Frank Act, promoted as an answer to the more recent global financial crisis, has also been criticized. Some note that the Act's authority to close financial institutions does not apply to the US's biggest banks (Johnson 2011), while others go a bit further, suggesting that it actually now encourages the very

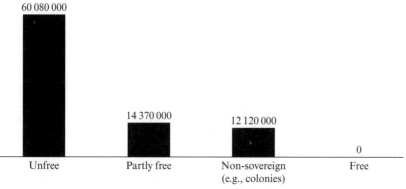

Source: Rummel (2005), Freedom House rankings.

Figure 7.4 *Example of extremely low levels of economic development: the relationship between a country's political institutions and famine (twentieth century)*

thing it is supposed to stop, that is, rather than prevent, it may have actually institutionalized 'too big to fail' policies (Calomiris 2011). Still more cynical critics, pointing to widespread interlocks and pecuniary contributions among Wall Street firms, politicians and regulators (e.g., both Dodd and Frank received contributions from Fannie Mae and Freddie Mac), suggest that regulatory capture is here to stay. Kay (2010, 1), noting that the molding of institutions for their own purposes by elites is nothing new, relates the following quote from the President of Union Pacific Railroad to a sympathetic congressman regarding regulation passed to placate the demands of common folks against robber barons: 'What is desired is something having a good sound, but quite harmless, which will impress the popular mind with the idea that a great deal is being done, when, in reality, very little is intended to be done.'

A particularly ill-fated example of harmful institutional change – that puts the milder preceding examples into perspective – is that of the Bolsheviks of 1917, who undoubtedly foresaw a much rosier future than the one that actually materialized. Another example is that of China's Great Leap Forward under Mao Tse-tung. Alluding to the consequences of Mao's policies, Rummel finds that the adoption of harmful political institutions is a direct antecedent of economic development rates so anemic that famine ensues. Figure 7.4, in fact, shows that of the roughly 87 million people that died in various famines around the world in the twentieth century, none of them occurred in a country classified as 'free' by Freedom House's survey of political and civil liberties. Sen (1999) is a bit more authoritative, stating that there has simply never been a famine in a functioning democracy supported by (classically) liberal institutions. Some ask about Ireland's great potato famine, but as noted by Sen, Ireland in the mid-1800s was not a functioning democracy but a non-sovereign country subject to harmful rules enacted by the English (e.g., rules prohibiting land ownership, voting or education). The potato blight spread throughout Northern Europe, decimating the potato stocks of Belgium, Denmark, France, Holland, Prussia, Scotland, Spain and Sweden. Yet no other country suffered like Ireland did. In Ireland, dearth turned into famine, leading Irish revolutionary John Mitchell to famously claim that: 'God sent the blight, but the English caused the famine'. The cost of institutional failure can be high, indeed.

Fast forward to the 1980s, however, and this same country, Ireland, offers a striking example of the capacity of superior institutional frameworks to facilitate economic growth. Ireland of the 1980s suffered from chronically high levels of unemployment and poverty, double-digit inflation rates, alarming levels of public debt and a mass exodus of emigrants. In order to improve their country's lot, politicians set aside their differences and charged policy-makers with the task of enacting credible institutions that fostered an openness to global markets, relatively low levels of regulation, easy taxes, reasonable levels of union influence, and investment in education. This was followed by growth that transformed their country from one of Europe's historically poorest into its second-richest, in terms of GDP per capita (Dorgan 2006). Ireland has recently, of course, taken a large step backwards, as the bursting of its real estate bubble led to large bank bailouts and, ultimately, a quest from the Irish government for financial support from the International Monetary Fund (IMF). Some claim that an overly eager attitude towards attracting FDI ushered in an era of rampant speculation within an environment characterized by excess and recklessness. Others note that a one-size-fits-all monetary policy for all of Europe deserves much of the blame, as low interest rates that may be beneficial to slow-growing countries help to create asset bubbles in countries whose economies are already on the verge of overheating. Irish voters, meanwhile, seem to be angrily asking why Irish citizens should be forced to bail out foreign creditors, on the grounds that those who would gladly reap the benefits of private profits should not be allowed to socialize losses. What nobody seems to be saying, however, is that Ireland was better off before instituting the policies that helped it grow, as even the harshest critic of neoliberalism concedes, when pressed, that despite its recent fall it is still in a better place than where it originally began. In other words, while not nearly as rich as they thought they were, the Irish are still richer than before, as having merely the fifth-highest GDP per capita in Europe and an unsustainable debt load is better than being in debt but also being back at the bottom in terms of GDP.

Baltic Tiger Estonia offers another recent example of a country that rose from relative poverty to prosperity seemingly overnight. Estonian GDP had been relatively flat from the late 1980s, when it began to assert economic independence from the Soviet Union, until 1999, generally hovering between US$4 and US$6 billion (World Bank, WDI 2011). Naively believing that its institutional prescriptions (such as flat taxes and no tariffs) had been adopted wholesale by the West, Prime Minister Mart Laar (2008) recounts using Milton Friedman's *Free to Choose* (Friedman and Friedman 1980) as a blueprint to follow when actively reforming his country's political and economic institutions. As a result, its GDP per capita rose from roughly US$2000 in the late 1980s to nearly US$21 000 in 2007 (IMF 2010), with an overall GDP of nearly US$24 billion (World Bank, WDI 2011). Due in part to the global financial crisis, Estonia's economy contracted by roughly 16 percent during 2008 and 2009, and GDP per capita fell to US$17 695; as of 2010, however, it were growing again, with a GDP per capita of US$18 274 (IMF 2010).

In short, the Irish and Estonian examples illustrates that: (1) crisis can overcome inertia and partisanship with respect to the spurring of institutional change; (2) institutional change can spur economic growth; and (3) the path is not always smooth from beginning to end, as bumps and setbacks, even in the midst of generally positive change, seem almost to be inevitable.

7.5   CONCLUSION

Prior to 1700, the world's richest countries were roughly two to three times wealthier than the poorest countries. Due in part to a global environment characterized by increasing returns, today that gap is a factor of 60 and getting bigger by the day (Parente 2008). The good news is that, as countries like Ireland and Estonia have shown, the rate at which countries can catch up to those ahead of them is faster today than ever. Botswana is yet another country that has developed especially fast, in stark contrast to its neighbor, Nigeria, which serves as a cautionary tale of institutional failure. Fortunately, Pinkovskiy and Sala-i-Martin (2010) claim that economic development in most of Africa is proceeding at a faster pace than many of us previously thought, with poverty alleviation in many countries almost perfectly mirroring growth in per capita GDP, and lower levels of income inequality. Another part of the world to keep an eye on might be Central America, as Honduras ponders the implementation of Romer's 'Charter City' idea where, like Hong Kong of the 1950s, a host country adopts

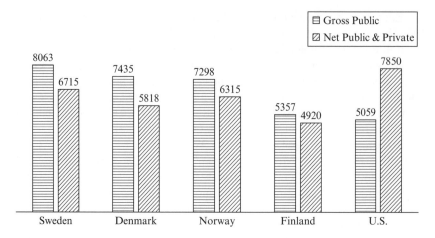

Notes: Figures assume 1990 $US at PPP (e.g., $7850 in 1990 = $13 644 in 2011). Net public and private social expenditures adjust for taxes (e.g., consumption taxes) and also for private expenditures (e.g., charitable transfers).

Source: Fishback (2010).

Figure 7.5   Social expenditures per capita

institutions designed and enforced by another country whose institutions have been shown to be relatively successful.

One further bit of good news is that as countries develop economically, it is not just the upper classes that benefit, as the correlation between incomes of a country's poorest people and those of the country as a whole is quite strong. Moreover, richer countries tend to have both the motivation and the means to construct social safety nets that benefit those in need of help. While some countries (like those of Scandinavia) are well known for their generous safety nets, as Figure 7.5 illustrates, even more classically liberal countries like the US often offer enough help to ensure that their poorest citizens are able to maintain at least a base level of subsistence.

With regard to economic development, international business scholars have written extensively about the link between MNEs and the growth rate of the countries they invest in. Economists, meanwhile, have written extensively about the link between a nation-state's institutional framework and the standard of living of its population. In this chapter we hoped to synthesize these two streams of literature by developing an integrated framework that explores the rich, interrelated nature of the relationship between institutions, MNEs and economic development. Thus, we first reviewed the current state of economic development and poverty before examining the literature regarding the role that MNEs and institutions have to play. Next, we reviewed our integrated model, explaining each link and offering testable propositions. Finally we discussed the implications of what we are suggesting. When it comes to economic development, we seem to have a pretty good idea as to what works, at least in a general sense. The Asian Tigers doubled their GDP in less than a decade. Countries like Botswana and Chile have shown how rapidly standards of living can rise when freedom-oriented institutions allow MNEs to enter and pursue growth-oriented strategies. Countries like Estonia seem to be on the right track today, while Honduras may be one to watch in the coming years. Hopefully the rest of the world will be inspired enough by the plethora of success stories to follow their lead, adopting institutional frameworks that allow them to experience the same kind of rapid economic development that has improved the material lot of those they emulate.

NOTE

*   We would like to thank Dr Francis Fabian for her comments on an earlier version of this chapter. We also wish to note that parts of this chapter (especially with regard to early background material related to institutions) were adapted from 'Institutions, MNEs, and sustainable development' (Kedia, Clampit and Gaffney, 2011).

REFERENCES

Abegglen, J. and Stalk G. (1985), *Kaisha: The Japanese Corporation*, New York: Basic Books.
Acemoglu, D., S. Johnson and J.A. Robinson (2001), 'The colonial origins of comparative development: an empirial investigation', *American Economic Review*, **91**, 1369–1401.
Albert, M. (1993), *Capitalism Against Capitalism*, London: Whurr.
Alston, L., T. Eggertsson and D. North (1996), *Empirical Studies in Institutional Change*, New York: Cambridge University Press.
AT Kearney (2003–2007), *FDI Confidence Index Report*.
Barro, R. (1996), 'Democracy and growth,' *Journal of Economic Growth*, **1**(1), 1–27.
Barro, R. (2007), 'Inequality and growth revisited', Paper presented at ADB Distinguished Visitor Forum, September.
Bénassy-Quéré, A., L. Fontagne and A. Lahreche-Revil (2005), 'How does FDI react to corporate taxation?', *International Tax and Public Finance*, **12** (5), 583–603.
Berman, S. (1997), 'Civil society and the collapse of the Weimar Republic', *World Politics*, **49** (3), 401–429.
Bernanke, B. (2002), 'On Milton Friedman's ninetieth birthday', presentation to Conference to Honor Milton Friedman, Chicago, IL, accessed from www.ferealreserve.gov.
Bernanke, B. (2004), 'Money, gold, and the Great Depression', H. Parker Willis Lecture in Economic Policy, Washington and Lee University, Lexington, Virginia, accessed from www.ferealreserve.gov.
Bhagwati, J. (2007), 'Why multinationals help reduce poverty', *World Economy*, **30** (2), 211–228.

Borensztein, E., J. Gregorio and J-W. Lee (1998), 'How does foreign direct investment affect economic growth?', *Journal of International Economics*, **45** (1), 115–135.

Brunetti, A. and B. Weder (1994), 'Political credibility and economic growth in less developed countries', *Constitutional Political Economy*, **5** (1), 23−43.

Bruton, G.D., G. Dess and J. Janney (2007), 'Knowledge management in technology focused firms in emerging economies', *Asia Pacific Journal of Management*, **24** (2), 115–130.

Buckley, P., J. Clegg and C. Wang (2007), 'Is the relationship between inward FDI and spillover effects linear? An empirical examination of the case of China', *Journal of International Business Studies*, **38**, 447–469.

Bueno de Mesquita, B. and H. Root (2000), *Governing for Prosperity: When Bad Economics is Good Politics*, New Haven, CT: Yale University Press,

Calomiris, C. (2011), 'An incentive-robust program for financial reform', *Manchester School*, **79**, 39–72.

Chandler, A.D. (1990), *Scale and Scope*, Cambridge, MA: Harvard University Press.

Chauffour, J-P. (2009), *The Power of Freedom: Uniting Development and Human Rights*, Washington DC: Cato Institution.

Childers, T. (1983), *The Nazi Voter: The Social Foundations of Fascism in Germany*, Chapel Hill, NC: University of North Carolina Press.

Childers, T. (1986), *The Formation of the Nazi Constituency*, London: Croom Helm.

Coase, Ronald H. (1937), 'The Nature of the Firm', *Economica*, **4** (16), 386–405.

Coatsworth, J. (2005), 'Structures, endowments, and institutions in the economic history of Latin America', *Latin American Research Review*, **40** (3), 126–144.

Crossland, C. (2007), 'National institutions and managerial discretion: a taxonomy of 24 countries', Academy of Management annual meeting; Philadelphia, PA, August.

Crossland, C. and D. Hambrick (2007), 'CEOs and national systems', *Strategic Management Journal*, **28**, 767–789.

De Mooij, Ruud A. and Sjef Ederveen (2005), 'Explaining the variation in empirical estimates of tax elasticities of foreign direct investment', December, Tinbergen Institute Discussion Paper No. 2005-108/3, available at http://ssrn.com/abstract=869753.

De Soto, H. (2000), *The Mystery of Capital*, New York: Bantam Press.

Doh, J., S.D. Howton and S.W. Howton (2010), 'Does the market respond to institutional endorsement of social responsibility? The role of information, institutions and legitimacy', *Journal of Management*, **36** (6), 1461–1485.

Dorgan, S. (2006), 'How Ireland became the Celtic Tiger', Backgrounder, No. 1945.

Doucouliagos, C. and M. Ulubasoglu (2006), 'Economic freedom and economic growth: does specification make a difference?' *European Journal of Political Economy*, **22** (1), 60–81.

Doucouliagos, H. and M. Paldam (2009), 'The aid effectiveness literature: the sad results of 40 years of research', *Journal of Economic Surveys*, **23**, 433–461.

Dunning, J.H. (1998), 'Location and the multinational enterprise: a neglected factor?', *Journal of International Business Studies*, **40**, 5–19.

Dunning, J.H. and F. Fourtanier (2007), 'Multinational enterprises and the new development paradigm: consequences for host country development', *Multinational Business Review*, **15** (1), 25–46.

Easterly, W. (2002), *The Elusive Quest for Growth*, Cambridge, MA: MIT Press:

Falter, J. (1991), *Hitlers Wähler*, Munich:Verlag.

Fishback, P. (2010), 'Social expenditures in the United States and the Nordic countries: 1900–2003', revised version of paper presented at International Economic History Association Congress in Utrecht, the Netherlands, August 2009.

Friedman, M. and R. Friedman (1980), *Free to Choose: A Personal Statement*, New York: Harcourt Brace Jovanovich.

Globerman, S. and D. Shapiro (2002), 'Global foreign direct investment flows: the role of governance infrastructure', *World Development*, **30** (11), 1898–1819.

Goodspeed, P. (2011), 'The end of poverty: what globalization did that aid could not', *National Post*, 28 May.

Görg H. and E. Strobl (2001) 'Multinational companies and productivity spillovers: a meta-analysis', *Economic Journal*, **111** (475), 723–739.

Government of India (2007), National Sample Survey, v. 61.

Greif, A. (1989), 'Reputation and coalition in medieval trade: evidence on the Maghribi traders', *Journal of Economic History*, **49** (4), 857–882.

Gwartney, J. and R. Lawson (2008), *Economic Freedom of the World: 2008 Annual Report*, Vancouver: Fraser Institute.

Haber, S., D. North and B. Weingast (2003), 'If economists are so smart, why is Africa so poor?' *Wall Street Journal*, 30 July.

Hall, P.A. and D. Soskice (2001), *An Introduction to Varieties of Capitalism*, New York: Oxford University Press, pp. 1–68.

Hambrick, D. and S. Finkelstein (1987), 'Managerial discretion: a bridge between polar views of organizational outcomes', in B. Staw and L.L. Cummings (eds), *Research in Organizational Behavior*, Greenwich, CT: JAI Press, pp. 369–406.

Havrylyshyn, O. (2008), 'Growth recovery in CIS countries: the sufficient minimum threshold of reforms', *Comparative Economic Studies*, **50** (1), 53–78.

Heitger, B. (2004), 'Property rights and the wealth of nations: a cross-country study', *Cato Journal*, **23** (3), 381–402.

Henisz, W.J. (2000), 'The institutional environment for multinational investment', *Journal of Law, Economics, and Organization*, **16** (2), 334–364.

Higgs, Robert (1987), *Crisis and Leviathan: Critical Episodes in the Growth of American Government*, New York: Oxford University Press.

Hill, C.W. (2007), 'Digital piracy: causes, consequences, and strategic responses', *Asia Pacific Journal of Management*, **24** (1): 9–25.

Hoskisson, R., L. Eden, C. Lau and M. Wright (2000), 'Strategy in emerging economies', *Academy of Management Journal*, **43** (3), 249–267.

House, R., P. Hanges, M. Javidan, P. Dorfman and V Gupta (2004), *Leadership, Culture, and Organizations: The GLOBE Study Of 62 Societies*, Thousand Oaks, CA: Sage.

International Monetary Fund (IMF) (2010), *2010 World Economic Outlook*.

Johnson, S. (2011), 'Too big to fail not fixed, despite Dodd–Frank: Simon Johnson', *Bloomberg View*, 9 October.

Kaufmann, D., A. Kraay and P. Zoido-Lobatón (1999),'Governance matters', World Bank Policy Research Working Paper, No. 2196.

Kay, J. (2010), 'Better a distant judge than a pliant regulator', *Financial Times*, 3 November.

Kedia, B., J. Clampit and N. Gaffney (2011),'Institutions, MNEs, and sustainable development', in S.C. Jain and B. Kedia (eds), *Enhancing Global Competitiveness through Sustainable Environmental Stewardship*, Cheltenham, UK and Northampton, MA, USA: Edward Edgar Publishing, pp. 70–108.

Kedia, B., R. Mahto and L. Nordtveldt (200), 'Role of multinational corporations in poverty reduction', in Chapter 3 S. Jain and S. Vachani (eds), *Multinational Corporations and Global Poverty Reduction*, Cheltenham, UK and Northampton, MA, USA: Edward Elgar Publishing.

Klein, M., C. Aaron and B. Hadjimichael (2002), 'Foreign direct investment and poverty reduction', in OECD (ed.), *New Horizons for Foreign Direct Investment*, Paris: OECD.

Krugman, P. (1991), 'History versus expectation', *Quarterly Journal of Economics*, **106** (2), 651–667.

Krugman, P. (1996), 'Los ciclos en las ideas dominantes con relacion al desarrollo economic', *Desarrollo Economico*, **36** (143), 715–732.

Krugman, P. (1997), 'In praise of cheap labor: bad jobs at bad wages are better than no jobs at all', Slate, 21 March.

Kwok, C. and S. Tadesse (2006), 'The MNC as an agent of change for host-country institutions: FDI and corruption', *Journal of International Business Studies*, **37**, 767–785.

Laar, M. (2008), 'The Estonian economic miracle', backgrounder #2060, available at www.heritage.org.

Lee, S., M. Peng and J. Barney (2007), 'Bankruptcy law and entrepreneurship development: a real options perspective', *Academy of Management Review*, **32** (1), 257–272.

Lewin, A. and J. Kim (2004), 'The nation state and culture as influences on organizational change and innovation', in M.S. Poole (ed.), *Handbook of Organizational Change and Development*, Oxford, UK: Oxford University Press, pp. 324–353.

Lodge, G. and C. Wilson (2006), 'Multinational corporations and global poverty reduction', *Challenge*, **49** (3), 17–25.

Lucas, R. (2011), 'The US recession of 2007–201?', presentation given at University of Washington, 19 May http://www.econ.washington.edu/news/millimansl.pdf.

Luo, Y. (2006), 'Political behavior, social responsibility, and perceived corruption: a structuration perspective', *Journal of International Business Studies*, **37**, 747–766.

Luo, Y. and R. Tung (2007), 'International expansion of emerging market enterprises: a springboard perspective', *Journal of International Business Studies*, **38**, 481–498.

Mauro, P. (1995), 'Corruption and growth', *Quarterly Journal of Economics*, **110** (3), 681–712.

McCloskey, D. (2010), *Bourgeois Dignity: Why Economics Can't Explain the Modern World*, Chicago, IL: University of Chicago Press.

Moran, T., M. Graham and M. Blomstrom (2005), *Does Foreign Direct Investment Promote Development?* Washington, DC: Peterson Institute for Economics.

Mudambi, M. and R. Navarra (2002), 'Institutions and international business', *International Business Review*, **11** (6), 635–646.

Niskanen, W. (2007), 'US capital markets may be dangerously overregulated', *World Commerce Review*, **1** (1), 32–34.

Nolan, B. and T. Smeding (2005), 'Ireland's income distribution in comparative perspective', *Review of Income and Wealth*, **51** (4), 537–560.

North, D. (1990), *Institutions, Institutional Change, and Economic Performance*, New York: Press Syndicate of the University of Cambridge.

North, D. (1991), 'Institutions', *Journal of Economic Perspectives*, **5** (1), 97–112.

North, D. (2005), *Understanding the Process of Economic Change*, Princeton, NJ: Princeton University Press.

Notten, G. and C. Neubourg (2007), 'Relative or absolute poverty in the USA and EU? The battle of the rates', MGSoG Working Paper, 2007/001, Maastricht University Maastricht.

Nove, A. (1969), *An Economic History of the USSR*, London: Allen Lane.

Oliver, C. and I. Holzinger (2008), 'The effectiveness of strategic regulatory management: a dynamic capabilities framework', *Academy of Management Review*, **33** (2), 496−520.

Orlitzky, M., F. Schmidt and S. Rynes (2003), 'Corporate social and financial performance: a meta-analysis', *Organization Studies*, **24** (3), 403–441.

Orlow, D. (1969), *The History of the Nazi Party, 1919–1933*, Pittsburgh, PA: University of Pittsburgh Press.

Orru, M. (1997), 'The institutionalist analysis of capitalist economices', in M. Orru, N. Woolsey Biggart and G. Hamitton (eds), *The Economic Organization of East Asian Capitalism*, Thousand Oaks, CA: Sage, pp. 297–310.

Oxfam (2008), 'Another inconvenient truth: biofuels are not the answer to climate or fuel crisis', 26 June.

Pajunen, K. (2008), 'Institutions and inflows of foreign direct investment: a fuzzy-set analysis', *Journal of International Business Studies*, **39** (4), 652–669.

Parente, S. (2008), 'Narrowing the economic gap in the 21st century', *2008 Index of Economic Freedom*, Washington, DC and New York: The Heritage Foundation and Dow Jones & Co.

Peng, M., S.H. Lee and D. Wang (2005), 'What determines the scope of the firm over time? A UTD/FT focus on institutional relatedness', *Academy of Management Review*, **30** (3), 622−633.

Peng, M., D. Wang and Y. Jiang (2008), 'An institution-based view of international business strategy: a focus on emerging economies', *Journal of International Business Studies*, **39** (5), 920−936.

Pinkovskiy, M. and X. Sala-i-Martin (2010), 'African poverty is falling . . . much faster than you think!' NBER Working Paper No. 15775, Cambridge, MA: NBER.

Poole, William (2007), 'Milton and money stock control', Milton Friedman Luncheon, Co-sponsored by the University of Missouri-Columbia Department of Economics, the Economic and Policy Analysis Research Center, and the Show-Me Institute.

Porter, M., H. Takeuchi and M. Sakakibara (2000), *Can Japan Compete?* Cambridge, MA: Perseus Publishing.

Redding, G. (2005), 'The thick description and comparison of societal systems of capitalism', *Journal of International Business Studies*, **36** (2), 123–155.

Roosevelt, F.D. (1937), *Second Inaugural Address*, http://www.bartleby.com/124/pres50. html.

Rummel, R.J. (2005), *Never Again: Ending War, Democide, and Famine Through Democratic Freedom*, Coral Springs, FL: Llumina Press.

Sachs, J. and A. Warner (1999), 'The big push, natural resource booms and growth', *Journal of Development Economics*, **59**, 43–76.

Sen, A. (1999), 'Democracy as a universal value', *Journal of Democracy*, **10** (3), 3–17.

Sieb, G. (2008), 'In crisis, opportunity for Obama', *Wall Street Journal*, 21 November, available at http://tinyurl.com/5n8u58.

Smeeding, T. (2006), 'Poor people in rich nations: the United States in comparative perspective', *Journal of Economic Perspectives*, **20** (1), 69–90.

Smith, Adam (1776), *An Inquiry into the Nature and Causes of the Wealth of Nations*, London: W. Sorahan and T. Cadell.

Stone, A., B. Levy and R. Paredes (1996), 'Public institutions and private transactions: a comparative analysis of the legal and regulatory environment for business transactions in Brazil and Chile', in L. Alston, T. Eggertsson and D. North (eds), *Empirical Studies in Institutional Change*, Cambridge: Cambridge University Press, pp. 95–128.

Tian, X. (2007), 'Accounting for sources of FDI technology spillovers: evidence from China', *Journal of International Business Studies*, **38** 147–159.

Wade, R. (1990), *Governing the Market*, Princeton, NJ: Princeton University Press.

Wallace, J. and D. North (1986), 'Measuring the transaction sector in the American economy', in S.L. Engerman and R.E. Gallman (eds), *Long Term Factors of Economic Growth*, Chicago, IL: University of Chicago Press, pp. 95–192.

Wan, W. and R.E. Hoskisson (2003), 'Home country environments, corporate diversification strategies, and firm performance', *Academy of Management Journal*, **46** (1), 27–45.

Whitley, R. (1999), *Divergent Capitalisms: The Social Structuring and Change of Business Systems*, New York: Oxford University Press.

Williamson, O. (1981), 'The economics of organization: the transaction cost approach', *American Journal of Sociology*, **87** (3), 548–577.

Williamson, O. (2000), 'The new institutional economics: taking stock, looking ahead', *Journal of Economic Literature*, **38** (3), 595–613.

Witt, M. and A. Lewin (2007), 'Outward foreign direct investment as escape response to home country institutional constraints', *Journal of International Business Studies*, **38**, 578–595.

World Bank (WDI 2005–2011), *World Development Indicators*, Washington, DC: World Bank.

World Bank (2008), 'Rising food prices: policy options and World Bank response', available at http://siteresources.worldbank.org/NEWS/Resources/risingfoodprices_backgroundnote_apr08.pdf.

World Bank (2009), 'E. Europe and C. Asia: crisis pushing people back into poverty', available at http://worldbank.or/html/extdr/financialcrisis.

8 The International Labour Organization
Nigel Haworth and Steve Hughes

8.1 INTRODUCTION

Since 1994, the International Labour Organization (ILO) has undergone a significant shift in focus, requiring a simultaneous reordering of the ILO's structures and priorities. At the heart of its contemporary activity is the concept of 'Decent Work', introduced under the guidance of the Director General, the Chilean Juan Somavia, following his appointment in 1999 Decent Work is, for Somavia, the mechanism by which the ILO displays its historic capacity for adaptation, renewal and change and, as we shall see, its relevance and presence in the international economic order.

In 2019 the ILO will celebrate its centenary, underlining its existence as one of the oldest international organizations. Its tripartite system of governance, providing independent votes to government, employer and worker bodies of member states, remains unique among United Nations (UN) institutions, and is the legacy of those moved by a mix of political, economic and humanitarian concerns in the aftermath of the First World War. Given its longevity, it is often a surprise that this 'firstborn' of existent international organizations is so little known, and yet its activities are central to addressing the social and economic problems of global integration and its role is increasingly prominent in debate on the reconfiguration of global governance.

When in 1975 the ILO moved its administrative headquarters to a large and imposing building in Geneva, it vacated its original home to the General Agreement on Tariffs and Trade (GATT) secretariat and, eventually, the World Trade Organization (WTO). The move reflected growing complexity in the mandate of both organizations. While globalization was being facilitated by one, it represented a fundamental challenge to the other. The international trade agenda was being driven by the ideology of market liberalism which became a dominant force behind the structural changes of the 1970s and 1980s. To the fundamentalist advocates of market liberalism, the ILO's history and emphasis were anachronistic and no longer relevant to a world of deregulated labour markets, shrinking union density and reduced welfare spending. The ILO's response, the demonstration of its relevance to the challenges and costs of globalization, and the introduction of the Decent Work agenda, are the subject of this chapter.

We begin by introducing the concept of Decent Work by identifying key ILO responses to the pressures posed by globalization and market liberalism. Second, we explain the role of Decent Work in the ILO's continuing attempts to engage with international agencies and multilateral forums such the Bretton Woods institutions, the World Trade Organization and the G20. Third, we illustrate how Decent Work, in a broader framework of international labour standards, is now a baseline for many private sector organizations in the global economy. Finally, we conclude with an assessment of the future direction of Decent Work and labour standards in the global economy.

8.2 THE RECENT HISTORY OF THE ILO

The ILO entered the 1990s in search of a renewed identity. It had survived the Cold War despite the deep internal divisions created by the East–West split. However, the new globalized world, in which the emergence of global production systems vied for priority with the growth of new production centres (particularly China), was equally challenging. The ILO had endeavoured to maintain a global presence in the 1970s and 1980s on the basis of high-quality technical analysis packaged within a development-driven framework. It had also continued its traditional role in setting labour standards, but challenges were emerging that questioned the continuation of this role. The rate of ratification of standards was an issue, as was growing concern about the number and observance of conventions that were being created.

Neoliberal policy hegemony in the 1980s challenged the tripartite model upon which the ILO was formed in 1919. Trade union density was declining in many economies as free-market policies rejected corporatist arrangements and frequently marginalized the union voice. A perennial question – is the ILO an anachronism? – was gaining ground and, particularly in the Employer Group in the ILO, a push for change grew.

Such challenges were not new. The ILO has been adept over its 90-plus years at repositioning itself in the face of changing circumstances. Early on, it had succeeded in distancing itself from the failing League of Nations by promoting membership of the ILO separate from membership of the League. It had also made itself relevant by providing high-quality advice on rising levels of unemployment during the interwar depression, and had built a respected international presence by engaging directly with countries, especially beyond Europe. To the surprise of many, it had come through the Second World War as a founder agency of the new United Nations, while its survival during the Cold War was delivered by a combination of technical relevance and political skill at the level of the organization's leadership.

The longevity of the ILO is a case study in institutional resilience, testament to those who work for it, the quality of the technical advice they offer and the relevance of their role to the tripartite partners they serve. As we have argued elsewhere, a central tenet to this longevity has been three approaches to its international relations that the ILO has developed since its inception. An emphasis on nurturing institutional and intellectual independence demonstrated autonomy of action that helped distance it from the failing League of Nations and provided a pathway into the postwar United Nations system. Crucially, this autonomy was underlined by demonstrating a relevance to the needs of its tripartite membership. From the production of data and social policy advice on mass unemployment during the 1930s (Hughes and Haworth 2008),[1] to major reports on developing a social dimension to globalization and joint reports with the WTO (WTO/ILO 2007) and the IMF (ILO/IMF 2010) on employment and social cohesion, the ILO has sought to provide topical and accessible reports on issues relevant to the needs of its tripartite members. In doing so, it has worked hard to develop a physical and intellectual presence among its membership through a global network of regional and field offices, facilitating among other activities the work of over 600 technical experts engaged in ILO-related activities each year. The emphasis on presence has two objectives: to make the ILO ideologically relevant by linking its efforts to promote social justice at the international level with activities of social reformers and trade unions at the national level; and to maintain a positive and proactive profile of the ILO in the minds and activities of those in a position to influence public opinion.

Director General Francis Blanchard recognized the new challenges facing the ILO in the 1980s. In particular, he encouraged proactive engagement with the Bretton Woods institutions. As 'structural adjustment' became established in the international lexicon, in 1987 Blanchard convened a High-Level Meeting on Employment and Structural Adjustment involving the World Bank and International Monetary Fund. The meeting called for a greater understanding and acceptance of the ILO's social and labour agenda in World Bank and IMF thinking, and paved the way for closer cooperation between the three institutions. In doing so, Blanchard recognized that the ILO would have to find its niche in a 'structurally adjusted' global economy, a significant challenge for the traditional tripartite message of the ILO.

Blanchard's initiatives were important markers for his successors. Michel Hansenne, Director General between 1989 and 1999, continued a renovation agenda. His key measure was the 1998 ILO Declaration on

Fundamental Principles and Rights at Work. At the heart of this measure was a much-contested definition of 'core' labour standards, which the ILO required as a condition of membership irrespective of the level of economic development. His desire was to establish labour standards as a fundamental dimension of a 'fair' globalization, by providing better-targeted standards with ethical and regulatory greater impact. Hansenne also recognized that further change would be needed in the operation and direction of the ILO if it was to prosper.

The focus on labour standards with greater presence and impact was continued by Hansenne's successor, Juan Somavia, who became Director General in 1999 after taking a leading role in the 1995 Copenhagen World Summit for Social Development, in which the importance of core labour standards was explicitly recognized for the first time. Somavia moved the ILO forward on four fronts. First, he drove through the 2008 Declaration on Social Justice for a Fair Globalization, which brings together ILO thinking on globalization since 1994. Second, he insti-gated internal organizational changes within the ILO to improve the quality and focus of its activities. Third, he introduced and promoted the Decent Work agenda. And, fourth, he renewed efforts to work with other international agencies, particularly the World Bank, IMF and WTO. Somavia, in an elegant metaphor, described the activities of the international agencies as an 'archipelago of unconnected islands', that is, institutions and initiatives unconnected to each other and therefore likely to contradict or duplicate their efforts, and unlikely to benefit from respective expertise. He supported, in place of the 'archipelago', a more integrated approach to policy implementation and outcomes across the multilateral agencies.

The Decent Work agenda is intended to capture, holistically and com-prehensively, concerns about the quality as well as the quantity of job creation. It is based on the understanding that importance of work is manifold and central to the well-being of the individual, the family and society. Work is a source of economic security, family stability, personal dignity and economic growth that expands opportunities for jobs and enterprise development. It is perhaps best understood in terms of its role in implementing the ILO's four strategic objectives:

1. Creating jobs – an economy that generates opportunities for invest-ment, entrepreneurship, skills development, job creation and sustainable livelihoods.
2. Guaranteeing rights at work – to obtain recognition and respect for the rights of workers. All workers, and in particular disadvantaged or poor workers, need representation, participation, and laws that work for their interests.
3. Extending social protection – to promote both inclusion and productivity

by ensuring that women and men enjoy working conditions that are safe, allow adequate free time and rest, take into account family and social values, provide for adequate compensation in case of lost or reduced income and permit access to adequate healthcare.
4. Promoting social dialogue – involving strong and independent workers' and employers' organizations is central to increasing productivity, avoiding disputes at work, and building cohesive societies. (ILO 2008)

There is also an element of 'branding' in the adoption of the term. Somavia wanted a simple, easily communicated message that captured the scope of ILO activity. Whilst some felt that there was a reductionism in its simplicity, many felt that it gave the ILO a strong communication advantage.

A particular priority for Somavia in the development of the Decent Work agenda was the search for a more effective, integrated approach to the challenges posed by globalization, a challenge delineated in another Somavia-driven project, which produced in 2004 'A fair globalization: creating opportunities for all'.[2] Moreover, Decent Work also reflected Somavia's own concerns about the performance of the ILO, in terms of both its technical capacity to deliver effectively across the four strategic objectives, and its organizational preparedness to improve that delivery.

We can see, therefore, a consistent pattern of reflection on, and strategic redirection of, the ILO across three successive Directors General since the 1980s. This is consistent with that far longer tradition of safeguarding the purpose and functions of the ILO, begun by its first Director General, Albert Thomas, in 1919 (Hughes and Haworth 2010).

8.3 DECENT WORK AND INTERNATIONAL INSTITUTIONS

Decent Work, and its associated core labour standards, has been central to the ILO's engagement with other international institutions. The 2008 global financial crisis provided an important opportunity for the ILO to establish its strategic priorities in the global responses to the crisis. In a concerted effort begun in the 1980s by Director General Blanchard, Somavia's ILO worked hard to engage with, first, the Bretton Woods organizations and, subsequently, the G20. This engagement has, on the whole, been successful, in contrast to the stalled involvement with the WTO in the 1990s around the Social Clause.[3] The ILO produced a technical overview of the employment impacts of the 2008 crisis following calls made by the G20 leaders at their April 2009 London Summit on Growth, Stability and Jobs. The ILO was invited to bring a report to the Pittsburgh G20 meeting later in that year, arguably establishing the ILO at the 'top table' of global institutions in a manner similar to its establishment as a relevant and technically competent body during the interwar depression.

Underpinning that engagement with the G20 was the ILO's development of a Global Jobs Pact in 2009 (ILO 2009). This emphasized the impacts of the crisis on labour markets, highlighting the long-term damage done by unemployment, developing Decent Work-based responses to those impacts and, simultaneously, providing a technical rationale for engagement with the G20. The principal objective of the global jobs pact is to reduce the time lag between economic recovery and recovery in the employment market. According to ILO estimates, even if a global recovery were to take hold, the global economy would need to create 440 million new jobs over the period to 2020 just to keep pace with 45 million new entrants to the global jobs market annually (ILO/IMF 2010, 59).

The Global Jobs Pact calls for an integrated response involving national, regional and multilateral institutions focused on a set of policy measures that place employment and social protection at the centre. In pursuit of this, the Pact proposes measures and policies to:

- retain women and men in employment as far as possible, and sustain enterprises, in particular small, medium-sized and micro-enterprises;
- support job creation and promote investments in employment-intensive sectors, including green jobs;
- facilitate more rapid re-entry into employment and address wage deflation;
- protect persons and families affected by the crisis, in particular the most vulnerable, and those in the informal economy by strengthening social protection systems to provide income support and sustain livelihoods as well as security of pensions;
- accelerate recovery of employment and expand opportunities by acting simultaneously on labour demand and on labour supply;
- equip the workforce with the skills needed for today and tomorrow (ILO 2009, iv).

With comparisons between the Great Depression of the 1930s and the 2007–2009 crises a recurring theme among G20 leaders, the social and political consequences of high levels of unemployment were underlined in ILO reports and helped shift the G20 toward a more coordinated response to the crisis. Now as then, high unemployment and growing income inequalities are key determinants in the deterioration of social stability (IILS 2010). Somavia saw in the wreckage of the crisis a major opportunity for Decent Work to contribute to recovery, whilst also consolidating the relevance and status of the ILO and its work.

If the 2008 global crisis offered an opportunity for the ILO to consolidate its status at the level of the G20, the Decent Work agenda also provided an opportunity for closer practical cooperation with the Bretton Woods institutions in the context of development. That opportunity derived from a twofold process. The first was the development of Decent Work Programmes (DWPs) in ILO member countries. The DWP is the mechanism at national level through which Decent Work is to be fostered. Each country, dependent on its levels of development and other circumstances such as broader development agendas, is expected to define, and act upon, appropriate Decent Work priorities. Thus DWPs are designed to give practical expression of the Decent Work agenda in member states and provide a nationally legitimized jobs and rights agenda endorsed and supported by employer and worker organizations.

Second, there is the ILO's involvement in the Poverty Reduction Strategy Papers (PRSP) process. The PRSP process was introduced in 1999 as a way of ensuring that concessional financing through the IMF's Poverty Reduction and Growth Facility (PRGF) and the World Bank group's International Development Associations (IDA) more effectively addressed poverty reduction. A number of key aims informed the process: to strengthen country ownership of the PRSP process; to broaden the representation of civil society, particularly the poor, in PRSP design and implementation; to improve coordination among development agencies; and to focus the combined resources of the international community on reducing poverty (World Bank 2000, 2). By 2008, the PRSP process had become the central platform of the multilateral financial and aid architecture that guides national development planning, budget allocation and development aid for over 70 countries.

Five core principles underlie the PRSP approach. Poverty reduction strategies should be:

- country-driven, promoting national ownership of strategies through broad-based participation of civil society;
- result-oriented, and focused on outcomes that will benefit the poor;
- comprehensive in recognizing the multidimensional nature of poverty;
- partnership-oriented, involving coordinated participation of development partners (government, domestic stakeholders and external donors); and
- based on a long-term perspective for poverty reduction (IMF 2011).

In a shift away from the traditional emphasis on dialogue with state ministries in which the local ministry of finance loomed large, an essential element of the PRSPs is that they deliver 'widely owned' outcomes, based upon extensive consultation with labour and civil society groups. With agreement around the need for greater policy coherence among multilateral institutions in place, synergies between the ILO's Decent Work agenda and the poverty reduction focus of the International Financial Institutions (IFIs) were recognized and developed. As a result, a platform for closer cooperation between poverty reduction activities and employment-intensive economic growth was established through a series of pilot projects funded by the United Kingdom (UK) government's Department for International Development (DFID) in which the ILO developed a systematic approach to the integration of the Decent Work perspective into the implementation of PRSP processes (Hughes and Haworth 2011).

The ILO strategy for integrating Decent Work with the PRSP process consists of four connected elements:

- Empowering the tripartite partners (ministries of labour, employers and worker organizations) – by strengthening their capacity to influence the drafting, implementation and monitoring of national poverty reduction strategies.
- Incorporating employment and other relevant dimensions of the Decent Work agenda into poverty reduction strategies – by identifying appropriate entry points and country-specific priorities and by articulating a visible and marketable platform for action.
- Influencing and developing partnerships through strategic communication at the country level – through seeking to influence other government ministries and departments (particularly ministries of finance and planning) driving the design and implementation of poverty reduction strategies, and development organizations (including multilaterals, bilateral and civil society organizations) to embrace the Decent Work route out of poverty.
- Maintaining critical dialogue at the global and regional levels with the IFIs, regional commissions, regional development banks and the UN Development Programme (UNDP) – by reference to the overall assessment of the content and process of poverty reduction strategies (ILO 2007).

8.4 DECENT WORK AND THE COMPANY

As a tripartite body in which employers play one of the three leading roles, the ILO has sought to bring its Decent Work and core labour standards message to the business world. Juan Somavia, for example, has attended the World Economic Forum, speaking on an array of issues and offering practical platforms on which to deliver the ILO agenda (WEF 2010). For example, the ILO established a helpdesk for business on labour standards within its Multinational Enterprises Programme (ILO 2010) which acts as a one-stop shop for companies wishing to align their practices with international labour standards. It operates under the framework laid out by the 1998 ILO Declaration on Fundamental Principles and Rights at Work and the 1977 Tripartite Declaration of Principles concerning Multinational Enterprises and Social Policy, now in a fourth edition (ILO 2006a). The Tripartite Declaration sets out principles in the fields of employment, training, conditions of work and life, and industrial enterprises are recommended to observe on a voluntary basis. It also intersects with the ILO's position on corporate social responsibility (CSR) (ILO 2006b).

The ILO's belief that Decent Work and international labour standards should be as important at company level as it is at national policy-making level is reflected in the broader UN approach to CSR, including the 2000 United Nations Global Compact. The Global Compact was a UN initiative led by Kofi Annan, designed to align businesses with ten universally accepted principles in the areas of human rights, labour, environment and anti-corruption. In terms of labour, the principles are:

- Principle 3: Businesses should uphold the freedom of association and the effective recognition of the right to collective bargaining.
- Principle 4: The elimination of all forms of forced and compulsory labour.
- Principle 5: The effective abolition of child labour.
- Principle 6: The elimination of discrimination in respect of employment and occupation.

These are, of course, the core labour standards of the ILO, brought into the Global Compact as essential principles of good business practice. The Global Compact is a voluntary arrangement, governed by a board of business, labour and civil society representatives, appointed by the UN Secretary-General in their personal capacity. The purpose of the Compact is to mainstream these ten principles, including core labour standards, across global business, whilst also acting as a means to extend other UN goals, such as the Millennium Development Goals.

Whilst the impact of the Global Compact is subject to debate, the signal to business from the UN has been that when it comes to appropriate labour market behaviour, the standards expected are those laid down by the ILO. Much as is the case for the ILO itself, the only weight behind the

Compact is moral, yet arguably it would be wrong to see such pressure as irrelevant or marginal. The establishment of international benchmarks against which, for example, non-governmental organizations (NGOs) and consumers might measure business performance is not an insignificant achievement. Moreover, corporate signatories to the Global Compact are delisted for not abiding by the annual requirement of Communication on Progress (COP), a report made public to stakeholders detailing progress in implementing the Global Compact's ten principles. From the introduction of the COP enforcement policy in 2005 to 2010, 1043 signatories have been delisted (UN 2010) as stakeholders, and pressure groups keep a watchful eye on those who view Compact membership as more a marketing exercise than a commitment to its principles.

8.5 GLOBAL PRODUCTION SYSTEMS AND LABOUR STANDARDS: THE DYNAMIC OF SOCIAL UPGRADING

The most significant contemporary context in which the relationship between labour standards and global production is being analysed is that of global production systems. As we have come to understand the networked or 'chain-based' integration of global production, we have also come to understand the array of pressures on those networks or chains as, on the one hand, efficiencies are sought in quality and cost terms, and on the other, requirements for social and environmental upgrading are imposed by buyers and consumers.

In brief, there are perhaps four main streams of network and chain thinking (Plank et al. 2009). Initially, there developed the idea of the 'commodity chain', defined as the network of labour and production processes giving rise to a finished commodity. Subsequently, the 'global commodity chain' emerged as a more developed concept, focusing on interfirm networks and the organization of global production and on production upgrading. Thereafter, the idea of the 'global value chain' emerged as a third tradition, critical of preceding traditions, and emphasizing the creation and appropriation of value, the structure and role of governance within global production systems and, again, system upgrading. Finally, the idea of 'global production networks' seeks to trump previous approaches with a focus on the entirety of network relationships (that is, beyond the linear relationships argued to be key to GVC analysis) and on the full range of networking relationships between actors in the network, rather than on narrower interfirm governance arrangements.

It is not our purpose here to rehearse the complex arguments that define this important area of scholarship. What is important is that within these debates exists a burgeoning discussion of 'social upgrading', that is, the incorporation of labour standards into these networks at the behest of the buyers and consumers, or their incorporation as a result of supplier strategy, or of government intervention (Barrientos, 2008). These stand-ards are most frequently the core labour standards defined by the ILO, reflecting the role and status of the ILO in labour standards setting, and Hansenne's championing of their definition.

The debate around social upgrading has a number of dimensions. First, there are important strategic dimensions of these chains in relation to social upgrading. Traditionally, network strategies might be placed on a continuum between 'low road' strategies, in which the advantages offered by global production arrangements derive from access to pools of cheap labour, and 'high road' strategies in which skill and quality outputs combine to produce higher value outputs. Social upgrading might traditionally be expected in high road approaches, but not in low road. However, there is also evidence that some sectors traditionally associ-ated with low road approaches (e.g. apparel), are also being required to upgrade on both social and environmental fronts, with the drive to social upgrading coming from the buyers in the chain or network.

Second, there is an interesting discussion of 'learning' in these chains. Learning, and the transfer of knowledge, within chains, is argued to be uneven and an effect primarily of the different governance arrangements that exist. However, it is agreed that different types of learning and trans-fer take place, particularly in terms of product, functional and process arrangements. Recently, it has been argued that transfers and learning associated with both environmental and social upgrading need to be better understood and the focus of empirical study.

Third, there is the 'pull–push' mechanism that promotes social upgrad-ing in these networks. Producer firms may adopt improved labour stand-ards as a means to achieve improved deals with buyers and to command associated rents. Equally, buyers with an eye to consumer expectations, may require social upgrading as a component of a contract. Another aspect of the 'push' component is the role of national governments, which are likely to be developing DWPs and may be cooperating in PRSPs, and are therefore undertaking a national 'upgrading' of labour standards as part of a broader development strategy.

From an ILO perspective, the extent and importance of these networks makes them an important target for Decent Work and labour standards activity. Equally, however, it is clear that, in the case of networks on a 'high road', the ILO is pushing at an open door, as social upgrading tends towards ILO standards and their inclusion. When one brings together the adoption of core labour standards in the CSR practices of MNEs, and a similar presence in global production systems, one might reasonably argue that the presence of the ILO has extended in tandem with the integration of global production.

8.6 CONCLUSION

An objective view of the current status of international labour standards would, we suggest, accept that they are more visible, more debated and, indeed, more controversial now than at any stage of the ILO's history. This reflects, on the one hand, the pressures produced in global production as an effect of globalization, and on the other, the repositioning of labour standards in the international debate promoted by the ILO. Moreover, in globally integrated production systems, into which the attitudes and expectations of consumers must be factored, one could argue that the constituency interested in labour standards has been expanded beyond the traditional social partners to include layers of civil society – non-governmental organizations (NGOs), consumer organizations and individual consumers. Whilst the changes introduced by successive Directors General have at times been controversial, even highly divisive, it is undeniable that this repositioning has promoted the presence and status of the ILO.

Perhaps perversely, this success brings with it serious new challenges for the ILO. If, for example, many institutions and systems now 'own' the labour standards debate, is there a risk that the purpose of the ILO will become redundant? Is it possible that another organization, or organizations, may in time usurp the historical role of the ILO? Such questions have reverberated around the ILO's 'epistemic community', who quite reasonably wish to see the ILO remain at the centre of the labour standards system.

Inevitably, then, the ILO must continue its long tradition of political deftness if it is to safeguard that central role. The repositioning begun in the 1980s is likely to continue as the labour standards discussion shifts ground. This is, of course, how the ILO has survived, and is a lesson rapidly learnt and understood by each Director General. There are some obvious areas in which the ILO must develop further. For example, its established constituency – the social partners – are recognized to be often unrepresentative of large sectors of the workforce in some member countries. Improved representivity is, then, a pressing issue for the ILO. How the ILO builds its relationship with civil society organizations beyond the established social partners is another pressing challenge. The imminence of these issues is well recognized in the ILO hierarchy, and we can expect future initiatives on these fronts.

We should not forget the DWPs, which provide another secure anchor for the ILO in member countries. Decent Work is commensurate with the desire for 'high road' development found in most modern economies. Decent Work, as an ideology and as a technical prescription, resonates across all levels of economic development, and gives the ILO a degree of certainty in its thinking as it faces the challenges previously outlined. Moreover, Decent Work, like the Global Jobs Pact, has resonated with key political and institutional constituencies. The Millennium Development Goals (MDGs) were amended in 2005 to reference the Decent Work agenda explicitly. For example, MDG 1, which aims to eradicate extreme poverty and hunger, now includes a target to 'achieve full and productive employment and decent work for all, including women and young people'. The ILO's presence at the G20 and its joint work with the IMF and WTO on the global crisis has moved Pascal Lamy, Director General of the WTO, to talk of an emerging, if still fragile, 'triangle of coherence' in global economic governance linking the G20, the United Nations and specialized institutions such as the ILO (Lamy 2010). Others have moved so far as to call for the ILO to have the same status as the IMF in the activities of the G20 (Fitoussi and Stiglitz 2011).

The Decent Work agenda has become a powerful mobilizing force both within and outside the ILO. Its success has placed significant challenges on the ILO to deliver in its attempts to influence the international policy agenda. Despite this, the future is uncertain. A hitherto key ally in the pursuit of policy coherence, Dominique Strauss Kahn, is gone. Somavia must now hope to build an equally positive relationship with new IMF Managing Director Christine Lagarde while his executive works to establish an ILO beachhead in the system of global economic governance. It remains a significant and defining challenge.

NOTES

1. The work of Tony Endres and Grant Fleming has been particularly informative in highlighting the contribution of the ILO in challenging established interwar economic orthodoxy and offering reflationary solutions to the problems of economic stagnation – ideas acknowledged by J.M. Keynes in his magnum opus *General Theory of Employment, Interest and Money*. See for example, Endres and Fleming (1996, 1999, 2002).
2. This report can be retrieved at http://www.ilo.org/public/english/wcsdg/docs/report.pdf.
3. This was an attempt to use trade sanctions, operated by the WTO, to extend the take-up of labour standards through a clause attached to multilateral trade agreements. First established in WTO debate at the Singapore Ministerial Conference 1996, and returning

in successive conferences thereafter, the call for a Social Clause was pushed by some European countries and the US, while being fiercely opposed by many developing economies that saw in the proposed measure a blatant protectionism.

REFERENCES

Barrientos, S. (2008), 'Contract labour: the "Achilles Heel" of corporate codes in commercial value chains', *Development and Change*, **39** (6), 977–990.

Endres, T. and G. Fleming (1996), 'International economic policy in the inter-war years: the special contribution of ILO economists', *International Labour Review*, **136**, 2.

Endres, T. and G. Fleming (1999), 'Public investment programmes in the interwar period: the view from Geneva', *European Journal of the History of Economic Thought*, **6** (1), 87–109.

Endres, Tony and G. Fleming (2002), *International Organisations and the Analysis of Economic Policy – 1919–1950*, Cambridge: Cambridge University Press.

Fitoussi, J.-P. and J. Stiglitz, Paris Group (2011), 'The G20 and recovery and beyond. An agenda for global governance for the twenty first century – Chairmen's summary', available at http://www.ofce.sciences-po.fr/pdf/documents/ebook2011.pdf.

Hughes, S. and N. Haworth (2008), 'The role of the ILO in the development of economic and social policies during the 1930s', International Institute of Labour Studies ILO Century Project, Geneva, May, available at http://www.ilo.org/public/english/century/informa tion_resources/papers_and_publications.htm.

Hughes, S. and N. Haworth (2010), *The International Labour Organisation. Coming in from the Cold*, London: Routledge.

Hughes, S. and N. Haworth (2011), 'Decent work and poverty reduction', *Industrial Relations/Relations Industrielles*, **66** (1), 34–53.

International Institute for Labour Studies (IILS) (2010), *World of Work Report 2010: From One Crisis to the Next*, Geneva: ILO.

International Labour Organization (ILO) (2006a), *Tripartite Declaration of Principles Concerning Multinational Enterprises and Social Policy – Fourth Edition*, Geneva: ILO.

International Labour Organization (ILO) (2006b), 'In Focus Initiative on Corporate Social Responsibility (CSR)', Governing Body Sub-committee on Multinational Enterprises, GB./295/MNE/2/1, 295th Session, March, available at http://www.ilo.org/public/english/ standards/relm/gb/docs/gb295/pdf/mne-2-1.pdf.

International Labour Organization (ILO) (2007), 'The Decent Work Agenda in Poverty Reduction Strategy Papers (PRSPs): Recent Developments', Governing Body Committee on Employment and Social Policy, GB. 300/ESP/3, ILO, Geneva, November, p. 3.

International Labour Organization (ILO) (2008), 'The Decent Work Agenda', available at http://www.ilo.org/global/about-the-ilo/decent-work-agenda/lang--en/index.htm.

International Labour Organization (ILO) (2009), *Recovering from the Crisis: A Global Jobs Pact*, ILO: Geneva.

International Labour Organization (ILO) (2010), 'ILO launches new web-based information and assistance service for business: ILO Helpdesk for Business on International Labour Standards', available at http://www.ilo.org/empent/areas/business-helpdesk/ WCMS_149775/lang--en/index.htm.

International Labour Organization (ILO) and International Monetary Fund (IMF) (2010), 'The challenges of growth, employment and social cohesion', Discussion Document, Oslo, available at http://www.osloconference2010.org/discussionpaper.pdf.

International Labour Organization (ILO) and World Trade Organization (WTO) (2007), 'Trade and employment. Challenges for policy research', WTO Secretariat, Geneva, available at http://www.ilo.org/public/english/bureau/inst/download/eddy.pdf.

International Monetary Fund (IMF) (2011), 'Poverty Reduction Strategy Papers (PRSP)', available at http://www.imf.org/external/np/exr/facts/prsp.htm.

Lamy, P. (2010), *Impact of the Financial Crisis on Global Economic Governance*, Geneva: United Nations Geneva Lecture Series.

Plank, L., C. Staritz and K. Lukas (2009), *Securing Labour Rights in Global Production Networks*, Kammer für Arbeiter und Angestellte für Wien, Wein.

United Nations (UN) (2010), 'United Nations Global Compact Annual Review – Anniversary Edition', available at http://www.unglobalcompact.org/docs/news_events/8.1/UNGC_Annual_Review_2010.pdf.

World Bank (2000), 'Partners in transforming development: new approaches to developing country-owned poverty reduction strategies', available at http://www.imf.org/external/np/prsp/pdf/prspbroc.pdf.

World Economic Forum (WEF) (2010) 'After the financial crisis: consequences and lessons learned', available at http://www.weforum.org/s?s=Juan Somavia.

World Trade Organization (WTO) and International Labour Organization (ILO) (2007), 'Trade and employment: challenges for policy research', WTO Secretariat, Geneva, available at http://www.ilo.org/public/english/bureau/inst/download/eddy.pdf.

9 Categories of distance and international business

Alvaro Cuervo-Cazurra and
Mehmet Erdem Genc*

9.1 INTRODUCTION

Distance between and within countries is a central topic of study for economic geographers (e.g. geographic clusters, agglomeration economies), trade economists (e.g. gravity models of trade) and international business researchers (e.g. location choice, competitive advantage). Curiously, distance has generally been considered an adversity in all of these literatures. For instance, in international economics gravity models predict that interaction between two entities (regions, countries, economies, and so on) is inversely related to distance between them. Thus, gravity models predict that countries that are distant from each other will trade less (e.g. Bergstrand 1985), will have fewer equity flows (e.g. Portes and Rey 2005), and will have fewer migration flows (e.g. Isard 1960; Lucas 2001). In a similar vein, the literature discusses co-location advantages and agglomeration economies, which result from companies locating at a short distance from each other to solve distance challenges (e.g. Krugman 1991; Jaffe et al. 1993; Saxenian 1994; Porter 2000; Morgan 2004).

The concept of distance also occupies a central place in international business literature and has important implications for strategic firm decisions, such as location choice (e.g. Johanson and Vahlne 1977; Xu and Shenkar 2002; Mudambi 2008; Cuervo-Cazurra 2011), transfer of organizational practices (Kostova and Roth 2002), and mode of entry (Kogut and Singh 1988; Cuervo-Cazurra 2008). The initial key contribution in this area was the work of Johanson and Vahlne (1977), which introduced and defined psychic distance as: 'the sum of factors preventing the flow of information from and to the market' (p. 24). This concept generated a long tradition of studies analyzing distance and its impact on the multinational company (MNC) (e.g. Kogut and Singh 1988; Barkema et al. 1996; Ghemawat 2001; Cuervo-Cazurra 2007; Nachum et al. 2008).

However, studies of location and distance need further development

(O'Grady and Lane 1996; Dunning 1998; Krugman 1998; Shenkar 2001; Cuervo-Cazurra 2011). In particular, studies of distance have made two simplifying assumptions about the concept. First, studies have assumed that distance is directionless, or symmetric. That is, the distance between two countries is the same, whether you move from Country A to Country B or from Country B to Country A. Therefore, firms from either country moving into the other would face the same cultural, geographic and economic challenges. Second, studies generally view distance as having an adverse effect on firms' operations. That is, the greater the distance between home and host country, the greater the difficulties the firm faces.

In this chapter we challenge these two assumptions. We do so by classifying dimensions of the firm's environment and the associated distances between countries based on two criteria: whether countries can be ranked in terms of their level of development; and if so, whether the dimension of the environment on which distance is measured supports a firm's operations or pressures the firm to continuously improve its non-market resources. These ideas build upon and extend Cuervo-Cazurra and Genc (2011) to provide a more general discussion of distance.

The classification results in three types of dimensions: obligating, supporting and pressuring. First, for some dimensions countries cannot be ranked in terms of their level of development; they can only be characterized as being more or less different from one another. For such dimensions, firms expanding into a different country are obligated to develop new non-market resources to deal with the differences. Hence, we call these the obligating dimensions. Second, on other dimensions countries can be distinguished from one another as more or less developed in their provision of non-market resources that are essential to support firms' operations. Thus, we call these supporting dimensions. Finally, on yet other dimensions countries can be classified as more or less developed in the extent to which the dimensions pressure firms to improve their non-market resources in order to deal with various stakeholder demands. We call these the pressuring dimensions.

The rest of the chapter is organized as follows. We first discuss in more detail the concept of distance, briefly reviewing studies in international business that have used the concept and the underlying assumptions these studies make. We then discuss our categorization scheme and explain the three categories of distance we propose, providing examples for each category. After this we provide a discussion of the implications of our categories of distance for international business research. We conclude with the contributions of our chapter to the literature.

9.2 DISTANCE IN THE INTERNATIONAL BUSINESS LITERATURE

In international business, distance has been hypothesized to affect country selection, market entry timing and mode of entry, all of which are crucial strategic decisions for the MNC. One of the earliest studies that dealt with the notion of distance explicitly in international business is that of Jan Johanson and Jan-Erik Vahlne of the 'Uppsala School', who were interested in explaining the process of internationalization. These authors conceptualized distance as 'psychic distance', defined as: 'the sum of factors preventing the flow of information from and to the market. Examples are differences in language, education, business practices, culture, and industrial development' (Johanson and Vahlne 1977, 24).

Although this definition of psychic distance is quite broad, most subsequent studies narrowed it and conceptualized or measured psychic distance as merely cultural distance (see reviews in Shenkar 2001, and in Tihanyi et al. 2005). While some of these studies found evidence that firms tended to go to culturally similar countries (e.g. Bilkey and Tesar 1977), others found that cultural distance did not have a significant role in explaining market entry (e.g. Benito and Gripsrud 1992). In a meta-analysis of the literature, Tihanyi et al. (2005) report that results fail to provide evidence of a significant relationship between cultural distance and market entry mode, international diversification, or firm performance.

Recent studies have returned to the original broad definition of psychic distance and proposed various dimensions on which distance can be measured. For instance, Ghemawat (2001) proposed that distance between countries can be grouped into four categories (cultural, administrative, geographic and economic) and examined these to identify the true attractiveness of host countries (as opposed to pure economic attractiveness). Perhaps not coincidentally, these dimensions correspond roughly to four major social science disciplines: sociology (culture), political science (administrative), geography and economics. Others developed broad measures of psychic distance and applied them to exporter behavior, finding a strong negative correlation between psychic distance and the likelihood of a country's selection as an export market (Dow and Karunaratna 2006; Brewer 2007).

Studies of distance in international business vary in their conceptualization, measurement and findings, but they tend to make two assumptions, which we challenge in this chapter: distance is an obstacle, and distance is symmetric. First, studies largely assume that distance between countries is an obstacle – to market entry, to serving a market profitably and to performance – even though empirical results do not fully confirm this view (e.g. Tihanyi et al. 2005). This negative view of distance as an impediment is implicit in the

222 Institutional approaches to international business

very definition of psychic distance provided by Johanson and Vahlne (1977) and dominates the literature in international business, as exemplified, for instance, by the concept of 'liability of foreignness' (Hymer 1976; Zaheer 1995; for a review see Cuervo-Cazurra et al. 2007). Even popular works such as Friedman (2005), which argues that the world is flat, is a confirmation of the difficulties that distance poses and how the 'death of distance' (Cairncross 1997) facilitates trade and development globally, although this idea has been challenged (e.g. Ghemawat 2003a, 2007; Morgan 2004).

Second, studies of distance assume that distance is symmetric or directionless. This is implicit in the concept of distance in geography, in which the spatial distance does not have a direction. As a result, studies tend to view the movement from Country A to Country B as posing the same challenges as moving from Country B to Country A.

9.3 CATEGORIZING DIMENSIONS OF THE ENVIRONMENT AND THEIR ASSOCIATED DISTANCES

In this chapter we go deeper into the concept of distance and challenge the assumptions of previous studies. These ideas build on Cuervo-Cazurra and Genc (2011) and here we provide a more general discussion; Cuervo-Cazurra and Genc (2011) focuses on competition between developing-country MNCs and advanced-economy MNCs. Thus, rather than list the multiple dimensions of the environment that can be used to measure distances between countries and explain how these distances could result in an advantage or disadvantage for the MNC, we follow and classify a country's environment into three types of dimensions – namely obligating, pressuring and supporting – and discuss how the three types of distances between home and host country impact MNC decisions. Our categorization is based on how the dimension in question affects development of firm resources at home, and the value of such resources abroad. Specifically, we categorize distances based on the following two criteria: whether countries can be ranked in terms of level of development along that dimension; and if so, whether the dimension supports the operations of the firm or pressures it to be more competitive.

9.3.1 Dimensions of the Environment on which Countries Cannot Be Ranked in Terms of Development

In order to determine the directionality of distance, we ask whether the dimension in question can be ranked in terms of level of development. We

choose level of development as the relational variable because in international business as well as in other sciences, countries are ranked mostly
by their level of development – whether this development is couched in
economic, social, educational or other terms – because a higher level of
development is seen as desirable. Level of development affects everything
from available factors of production, to demand and supply conditions, to
ease of doing business in the country. Therefore, level of development is a
natural candidate to assess directionality: moving toward a desired level
of development is different from moving away from it, even though the
absolute distance traveled may be the same.

Type 1: obligating dimensions of the environment

Obligating dimensions are those dimensions that obligate firms to
develop certain resources, market and non-market, in order to simply
operate in the country. However, these dimensions have a special additional property: they do not allow countries to be ranked qualitatively,
that is, as better or worse (Cuervo-Cazurra and Genc 2011). A firm
originating in a country develops a bundle of resources that are unique
to that country. When the firm expands abroad, if it goes to a country
that is different from the home country on these dimensions, it needs to
develop new resources to be able to operate in that country. The firm is at
a disadvantage because it cannot use its home-country resources to their
full extent (since countries are not better or worse in these dimensions,
the resources do not provide an advantage). Instead, it is obligated to
develop new resources. Thus, the larger the difference between home and
host countries is, the bigger the disadvantage. Another way to identify
obligating versus other dimensions of the environment is to ask whether
distances in that dimension are directionless (or symmetric) or directional
(asymmetric). Dimensions on which distances are directionless do not
distinguish among countries other than how 'far' they are from each
other; the only thing that can be measured is how distant two countries
are. In other words, distances are absolute in a mathematical sense: there
is no difference between negative (going from more to less) versus positive
(going from less to more) movement on the behavior of the firm; direction
of movement does not matter.

For obligating dimensions of the environment, the MNC faces the
disadvantage of operating in an environment that is different from its
home country. Furthermore, the more different the home country is from
the host country, the larger the challenge a company faces because it is
more difficult to transfer and use resources and knowledge developed in
one country into the other country. This is the view of in the incremental
internationalization model (Johanson and Vahlne 1977). Under this view,

what matters is the absolute magnitude of distance between home and host countries.

We consider some geographic and cultural variables to be dimensions that cannot be ranked in terms of development. First, geographic distance is a dimension that cannot be ranked in terms of development. Strictly speaking, it is not possible to talk about countries that are geographically more developed versus less developed. Countries can only be ranked in terms of their geographic distance to other countries. It is equally challenging to move in one direction or another. In this case, the firm faces added transportation, communication and coordination costs.

Second, culture is another dimension that cannot be ranked by development, even though it can be measured as a continuous variable that takes higher or lower values (Hofstede 1980; House et al. 2004). A country cannot be considered culturally more 'developed' than others just because a dimension of culture takes higher values in that country. For example, it is not possible to talk about a country being more developed because it has a higher or lower power distance than another country. Therefore, a firm that expands to a host country that is culturally different from the home country would experience a disadvantage in the form of not fully understanding how to operate there, independent of whether the host country is above or below the home country in that dimension. In either case, the more distant the destination country is from the origin country, the bigger the disadvantage the MNC faces.

A special case of obligating dimensions occurs when countries can be differentiated from one another but the magnitude of differences cannot be compared across countries. These dimensions of the environment result in categorical differences between home and host country, that is, distance between countries cannot be quantified. One cannot say that country B is greater than country A in this dimension, or that the difference between country A and country B is greater than the difference between country A and country C. One can only say that country A is different from country B. Distances that fall into this category can also be thought of as nominal scales: countries that have the same value or type are equal and all others are different, but it is not possible to ascertain the degree of difference.

For such dimensions of the environment, an MNC expanding abroad faces either a disadvantage or no disadvantage. If the firm is expanding into a host country that is different from its home country along that dimension, it would be at a disadvantage in the host country because it lacks the knowledge to deal with this dimension of the environment. If both home and host countries are of the same type along that dimension, the MNC would not be at a disadvantage compared to its home operations because it operates in the same dimension as it did at home.

However, it would have an advantage over MNCs whose home countries are different than the host country. Nevertheless, when comparing MNCs from two home countries both of which differ from the host country, it is not possible to compare their disadvantages.

We consider some aspects of the legal and political dimensions of the environment as falling into this group. First, the legal family of a country's laws – that is, whether the legal system has an English, French, Scandinavian, German or Islamic tradition underpinning its laws – is a discrete type. Not only are there large differences across legal families (such as common versus civil law), but there are also large differences even across countries that are in the same legal family (La Porta et al. 1998). Thus, a firm that moves to a country whose laws are based on a different legal family is obligated to develop a new resource: knowledge of that country's laws to operate there, because the new legal environment renders some of the MNC's resources useless. Until the firm develops this new resource, it will be at a disadvantage.

Second, dimensions in the political realm such as ties between countries in the form of historical relationships (e.g. colonial links) or current relationships (e.g. belonging to the same political association) are discrete types. The host country either has a political relationship with the home country or it does not. In the latter case, the firm would face a disadvantage compared to firms coming from countries that do have political ties to the host country, as those ties would facilitate operations of those MNCs. Such differences obligate the firm to develop resources to deal with this disadvantage. For example, the firm may need to hire and train more locals for managerial positions in order to be perceived as a local company, or try to develop strong relationships with decision-makers.

9.3.2 Dimensions of the Environment on which Countries Can Be Ranked in Terms of Development

The dimensions of environment we have considered thus far did not allow countries to be ranked in terms of their level of development. In this section, we consider dimensions on which countries can be distinguished qualitatively, that is, as more versus less developed. Although many dimensions of the environment are continuous and allow countries to be ranked in terms of their level of development, not all of them have the same impact on the firm. While moving from a more developed country to a less developed country could result in an advantage for the firm on certain dimensions, the opposite can be true in other dimensions. Hence, distance is directional and we need a criterion to distinguish between these two possibilities. The quality criterion we apply to make this distinction among dimensions is whether the dimension supports a firm's operations by providing comple-mentary external resources, or forces the firm to become more competitive by placing greater demands on it. This distinction builds on the dichotomy of location-specific resources that support operations of the firm, such as a well-developed institutional environment (e.g. North 1990; Fisman and Khanna 2004; Kaufmann et al. 2004; Cuervo-Cazurra 2006; Khanna and Palepu 2010); and location-specific resources that induce companies to be more competitive, such as sophisticated customers (Porter 1990; Saxenian 1994) or competitors (Cuervo-Cazurra and Dau 2009a). We now discuss each of these two categories of dimensions in more detail.

Type 2: pressuring dimensions of the environment
Pressuring dimensions of the environment are those dimensions in which countries differ in the extent to which they force firms to upgrade their resources in order to operate in that country (Cuervo-Cazurra and Genc 2011). That is, the firm faces demands in its home country that induce it constantly to invest and upgrade its resources and capabilities. These dimensions reflect higher sophistication and standards that require com-panies to improve in order to operate in the home country. If the company fails to do so, it falls behind its competition, which better responds to these demands. As a result, the company is required to improve itself in order to maintain its position in the marketplace.

For pressuring dimensions of the environment, an MNC that moves to a country that is less developed than its home country is likely to enjoy an advantage compared to its home operations, and an MNC that moves in the opposite direction suffers from a disadvantage. In the former case, the MNC is used to facing more sophisticated and demanding conditions at home, and as a result has had to improve its competitiveness. Therefore, when it moves to a country in which there are lower demands, it brings with it a level of competitiveness that is above that of most firms in the host country, thus achieving an advantage. In contrast, when the MNC moves to a country that is more developed in the dimension, the MNC is not used to the higher level of demands in the host country and cannot match the competitiveness of firms there, suffering a disadvantage.

We consider some of the economic and political dimensions of the envi-ronment to be pressuring dimensions. First, some economic dimensions pressure the firm to improve its competitiveness to be able to sell to highly demanding consumers and use sophisticated financial and technological resources in open competition with other firms. Thus, when the MNC moves to a country that is less developed in these dimensions, it brings capabilities that provide it with an advantage over domestic firms that lack the capabilities to operate in a highly competitive environment. This idea explains traditional observations that foreign products coming from developed countries tend to be perceived as superior in quality by consumers (Bilkey and Nes 1982), that developed-country MNCs have advantages in innovation and marketing over developing-country MNCs (Lall 1983; Wells 1983), and that developing-country MNCs need to upgrade their capabilities to satisfy more stringent technical and quality standards to compete in more developed countries (Bartlett and Ghoshal 2000; Aulakh 2007; Cuervo-Cazurra 2007; Cuervo-Cazurra and Dau 2009b).

Second, in the political arena, extensive political rights and civil liberties force the firm to develop capabilities to satisfy multiple, vocal stakeholders with competing interests (e.g. political parties, interest groups, non-governmental organizations, free press) that have the power to demand transparency and change in the firm. When the MNC moves to a country with a less developed political environment (that is, less pluralistic, fewer civil rights), it is at an advantage because there are fewer stakeholders whose demands have to be met, and it is more capable of meeting stakeholder demands because it already has experience in dealing with sophisticated stakeholders. In contrast, when the firm moves to a more developed political environment, it faces a disadvantage because it has not developed a capability to manage conflicting sets of demands from a variety of stakeholders. This idea is behind the observation that MNCs from developed countries are better in their environmental, labor and social relations because they are used to satisfying a more demanding environment at home (Harrison 1994; Aitken et al. 1996; Bellak 2004; Albornoz et al. 2009).

Type 3: dimensions that support firm operations

In contrast to the pressuring dimensions, supporting dimensions assist a firm's operations by providing resources that help it become more efficient and competitive without the burden of having to invest in developing such resources. In other words, supporting dimensions provide resources that are not owned by the firm. Many of these dimensions are what economists consider public goods provided by the government to help the country's development, such as a good public education system, a well-developed transportation infrastructure and a high-quality regulatory system.

On supporting dimensions, firms suffer a disadvantage when they move from more to less developed countries, and they gain an advantage when they move in the other direction. When the firm moves to a less developed country it suffers from a disadvantage because it does not have the supporting resources it took for granted in its home country. Since these resources are external to the firm, it cannot take them abroad. As a result, the firm has to invest in developing those resources itself, which is costly and beyond its expertise. On the other hand, if the MNC moves into a more developed country in these dimensions, it achieves an advantage compared to its home operations because it gains access to more sophisticated resources to support its operations, and does not have to invest in developing them. However, the MNC will not have an advantage over MNCs coming from other more developed countries, because they all have access to the same resources. In other words, moving to a more developed country levels the playing field by offering all firms the same external resources. All of this is in contrast to the obligating dimensions we have discussed, which involve suffering a disadvantage as long as the firm is expanding into a country that is different from its home country on that dimension.

We consider some of the legal, institutional, social and infrastructure dimensions of the environment to be supporting dimensions. First, as part of a well-functioning legal system, the efficiency and independence of courts supports the operations of the firm by decreasing uncertainty and reducing the cost of contract writing, monitoring and enforcement. Thus, the firm can engage in relationships with others without the fear of opportunism, and is able to make long-term investments due to reduced uncertainty.

Second, high-quality public goods, prudential regulations that apply equally to all, well-protected private property rights, prevailing rule of law and control of corruption are all elements of a well-developed institutional environment that support the operations of the firm in the country by facilitating its contracting and economic exchanges (Kaufmann et al. 2004).

Third, in the social dimension the availability of a well-educated, healthy and skilled workforce supports the operations of the firm (World Bank 2002). With a better-educated, healthier and more skilled workforce, the MNC can be more efficient because it does not have to invest in the education and healthcare of its workers.

Finally, the infrastructure dimension also supports firm operations in the country because the firm relies on it to obtain and send information and physical goods (Porter 1990). If the firm moves to a less developed country, it will face a disadvantage because it is not used to operating with poorly developed, unreliable telecommunication systems or poorly developed road networks, which would all reduce the value of its other, more firm-specific resources.

9.4   IMPLICATIONS FOR INTERNATIONAL BUSINESS

The categorization of distance dimensions into three types based on their characteristics has important implications for international business.

We discuss the implications for two major research areas that we have been hinting at throughout the discussion: selection of countries in which to expand abroad, and outcomes of competition among MNCs from different home countries competing in the same host country.

First, our framework suggests that a firm choosing among multiple host countries to enter has to compare the distances of the host countries to the home country, but will not always choose the least distant country. The traditional view has been that a more distant country would be more detrimental, and therefore the firm should select a proximate country (Johanson and Vahlne 1977). However, under our classification of environment dimensions into three distinct types, the predictions of which country to choose differ depending on the type of dimension analyzed. First, the traditional implication that firms should choose the least distant countries (e.g. Johanson and Vahlne 1977; Ghemawat 2001) hold for obligating dimensions of the environment. It is important to note, however, that for certain dimensions (categorical dimensions) the disadvantage is not comparable across potential host countries as long as they are all different from the home country. Second, for pressuring dimensions of the environment, distance along that dimension results in a relative disadvantage when the firm expands into countries that are more developed than its home country, but a relative advantage when it enters countries that are less developed. Hence, the selection of the country is affected by the direction of movement. Third, for supporting dimensions of the firm, distance causes a disadvantage when the firm expands to countries that are less developed than its home country, but a relative advantage when it expands to countries that are more developed. Thus, as for pressuring dimensions, the selection of the country is affected by both distance and direction of movement, but now the implications are reversed.

In sum, the selection of the country to enter is more complex than traditionally thought. It is not determined only by the institutional characteristics of the host country (e.g. Meyer 2001) or by the institutional (or other) distance between a home and host country dyad (e.g. Ghemawat 2001; Kostova and Roth 2002). Whereas distance in some dimensions results in a relative disadvantage as discussed in previous models, distance in others results in a relative advantage. Similarly, whereas distance in some dimensions can be compared across countries, such a comparison is not possible for other dimensions. The overall impact on the firm therefore depends on the combination of the advantages and disadvantages provided by each dimension of the environment, and the relative magnitude of such advantages and disadvantages. Furthermore, all advantages and disadvantages are relative to other firms operating in the host country; therefore advantage and disadvantage also depends on who else operates in the host country, and where those firms originate. Thus, this framework provides a more fine-grained way of comparing countries the firm can enter. The ranking of countries will vary depending on which environmental dimensions are used to compare them. In this sense, our work builds on others who have suggested that distance can be a source of advantage through exploiting differences (that is, arbitrage) across countries (e.g., Kogut 1985; Porter 1986; Ghemawat 2003b). However, these authors focused mostly on exploiting differences in individual value chain activities, such as labor costs, which in many cases do not require multinationalization (Hennart 2007) and can be quickly imitated. Our work goes beyond this by showing how home-based ownership advantages can become more valuable when the MNC competes in more distant countries, providing it with a sustained advantage.

Second, foreign firms competing in the same host country have to consider all types of distances when evaluating the relative advantages of firms coming from different home countries. The dominant view in the literature has been that companies can be classified as those that come from developed countries and those that come from developing countries (Bartlett and Ghoshal 2000; Ramamurti and Singh 2009), and that each group of firms enjoys certain advantages over the other when both operate in a third country (Lall 1983; Wells 1983; Khanna and Palepu 2006; Cuervo-Cazurra and Genc 2008). However, under our classification of distances into three types, the relative advantage and disadvantage of firms coming from different home countries and operating in the same host country vary depending on the dimension analyzed. For obligating dimensions, firms suffer a disadvantage if they come from a country that differs from the host country in that dimension, and firms coming from more distant countries suffer a larger disadvantage than firms coming from less distant countries if it is possible to compare the differences between countries. For pressuring dimensions, firms from less developed countries than the host country face a disadvantage, while firms coming from more developed countries than the host country enjoy an advantage. Finally, for supporting dimensions, companies coming from less developed countries than the host country enjoy an advantage, while firms coming from more developed countries than the host country face a disadvantage.

The implication of this comparison is that the classification of firms into developing- or developed-country MNCs needs more careful thought: the developing- versus developed-country MNC dichotomy breaks down under our view of distance. Presumably, these two groups are different because firms in the latter group originate in different institutional contexts. However, in our view the separation of firms into developed- and developing-country MNCs loses significance in many instances. First, some of the dimensions of the environment cannot be ranked in terms of development (obligating dimensions). In such cases, it is not possible to classify countries as developed or developing. Second, even for dimensions that can be ranked by development, the same country can be classified as developed in one dimension and developing in another. Third, developed and developing are relative notions, as the level of development depends not only on the characteristics of the home country, but also on the characteristics of the host country it is being compared to. The dichotomy of developed versus developing is not absolute as most studies assume, but instead varies depending on the dimension in which countries are compared.

9.5 CONCLUSIONS

In this chapter, we take a fresh look at the concept of distance that underpins many studies of international business and economic geography. The traditional view of distance assumes that it is directionless, harmful to the operations of foreign firms, and that the larger the distance, the larger the harm. In contrast, we build on Cuervo-Cazurra and Genc (2011) and classify dimensions of the environment into three types (obligating, supporting, pressuring), and argue that for many of these dimensions, the direction of movement does matter, and that for some dimensions distance actually can provide an advantage. This classification has important implications for the selection of countries to enter and for the analysis of competition among MNCs from different countries operating in the same host country.

This categorization of distance into three types contributes to the literature in several ways. First, we refine the concept of distance and its impact on MNCs. We challenge the assumptions of symmetry and adversity and explain how not all types of distance have a negative impact on the firm, and how the direction of movement matters for other types. More importantly, the proposed classification has predictive power and can accommodate any dimension of the environment, going beyond most studies that have focused on particular dimensions. Second, the view of distance presented here provides depth to the analyses of the selection of countries to enter (e.g. Johanson and Vahlne 1977; Cuervo-Cazurra 2008, 2011). Separating distances into three types, based on how they affect the firm's resources and its use of those resources abroad, not only alters the attractiveness of countries but also alters the way in which the firm can evaluate such attractiveness. Third, our view provides depth to the studies of competition among firms from different home countries in the same host country (e.g. Tallman 1991; Rangan and Drummond 2004; Cuervo-Cazurra and Genc 2008, 2011). The classification of distances we propose challenges the notion that firms coming from a particular home country will always be at an advantage over firms from another home country. The advantage will depend on which dimensions carry the most weight in that particular industry. Advantage in one dimension can be negated or even overwhelmed by disadvantage in an even more important dimension.

In sum, our chapter provides a novel and richer conceptualization of distance, outlines the influences of distance on the firm, and discusses the main implications for two important areas of international business research. This classification can influence other areas of inquiry, where the classification can be adapted to the particular dimensions considered.

NOTE

*   We thank Mehmet Demirbag for useful suggestions for improvement. The first author thanks the Center for International Business Education and Research at the University of South Carolina for financial support. The second author thanks Zicklin School of Business and Baruch College Fund for financial support. Any errors are ours.

REFERENCES

Aitken, B.J., A.E. Harrison and R.G. Lipsey (1996), 'Wages and foreign ownership: a comparative study of Mexico, Venezuela, and the United States', *Journal of International Economics*, **40**, 345–371.
Albornoz, F., M.A. Cole, R.J.R. Elliott and M.G. Ercolani (2009), 'In search of environmental spillovers', *World Economy*, **32** (1), 136–163.
Aulakh, P.S. (2007), 'Emerging multinationals from developing economies: motivations, paths and performance', *Journal of International Management*, **13** (3), 235–240.
Barkema, H.G., J.H.J. Bell and J.M. Pennings (1996), 'Foreign entry, cultural barriers, and learning', *Strategic Management Journal*, **17**, 151–166.
Bartlett, C.A., and S. Ghoshal (2000), 'Going global: lessons from late movers', *Harvard Business Review*, **78** (2), 132–142.
Bellak, C. (2004), 'How domestic and foreign firms differ and why does it matter?' *Journal of Economic Surveys*, **18** (4), 483–514.
Benito, G.R. and G. Gripsrud (1992), 'The expansion of foreign direct investment: discrete rational location choices or a cultural learning process?' *Journal of International Business Studies*, **23** (3), 461–476.
Bergstrand, J.H. (1985), 'The gravity equation in international trade: some microeconomic foundations and empirical evidence', *Review of Economics and Statistics*, **71** (1), 143–153.
Bilkey, W.J. and E. Nes (1982), 'Country-of-origin effects on product evaluations', *Journal of International Business Studies*, **13** (1), 89–99.
Bilkey, W.J. and G. Tesar (1977), 'The export behavior of smaller-sized Wisconsin manufacturing firms', *Journal of International Business Studies*, **8** (1), 93–98.
Brewer, T. (2007), 'Operationalizing psychic distance: a revised approach', *Journal of International Marketing*, **15** (1), 44–66.

Cairncross, F. (1997), *The Death of Distance*, Cambridge, MA: Harvard Business School Press.

Cuervo-Cazurra, A. (2006), 'Who cares about corruption?', *Journal of International Business Studies*, **37** (6), 803–822.

Cuervo-Cazurra, A. (2007), 'Sequence of value-added activities in the internationalization of developing country MNEs', *Journal of International Management*, **13** (3), 258–277.

Cuervo-Cazurra, A. (2008), 'The multinationalization of developing country MNEs: the case of Multilatinas', *Journal of International Management*, **14** (2), 138–154.

Cuervo-Cazurra, A. (2011), 'Selecting the country in which to start internationalization: the non-sequential internationalization argument', *Journal of World Business*, **46** (4), 426–437.

Cuervo-Cazurra, A. and L.A. Dau (2009a), 'Pro-market reforms and firm profitability in developing countries', *Academy of Management Journal*, **52** (6), 1348–1368.

Cuervo-Cazurra, A. and L.A. Dau (2009b), 'Structural reform and firm exports', *Management International Review*, **49** (4), 479–507.

Cuervo-Cazurra, A. and M. Genc (2008), 'Transforming disadvantages into advantages: developing country MNEs in the least developed countries', *Journal of International Business Studies*, **39**, 957–979.

Cuervo-Cazurra, A. and M. Genc (2011), 'How context matters: non-market advantages of developing-country MNEs', *Journal of Management Studies*, **48** (2), 441–445.

Cuervo-Cazurra, A., M. Maloney and S. Manrakhan (2007), 'Causes of the difficulties in internationalization', *Journal of International Business Studies*, **38** (5), 709–725.

Djankov, S., R. La Porta, F. Lopez-De-Silanes and A. Shleifer (2002), 'The regulation of entry', *Quarterly Journal of Economics*, **117** (1), 1–37.

Dow, D. and A. Karunaratna (2006), 'Developing a multidimensional instrument to measure psychic distance stimuli', *Journal of International Business Studies*, **37**, 578–602.

Dunning, J.H. (1998), 'Location and the multinational enterprise: a neglected factor?' *Journal of International Business Studies*, **29** (1), 45–66.

Fisman, R. and T. Khanna (2004), 'Facilitating development: the role of business groups', *World Development*, **32** (4), 609–628.

Friedman, T. (2005), *The World is Flat: A Brief History of the Twenty-First Century*, New York: Farrar Straus & Giroux.

Ghemawat, P. (2001), 'Distance still matters', *Harvard Business Review*, **79** (8), 137–145.

Ghemawat, P. (2003a), 'Semiglobalization and international business strategy', *Journal of International Business Studies*, **34** (2), 138–152.

Ghemawat, P. (2003b), 'The forgotten strategy', *Harvard Business Review*, **81** (11), 76–84.

Ghemawat, P. (2007), 'Why the world isn't flat', *Foreign Policy*, **159**, 54–60.

Harrison, A. (1994), 'The role of multinationals in economic development: the benefits of FDI', *Columbia Journal of World Business*, **29** (4), 6–11.

Henisz, W.J. (2000), 'The institutional environment for multinational investment', *Journal of Law, Economics and Organization*, **6** (2), 334–364.

Hennart, J.M.A. (2007), 'The theoretical rationale for a multinationality performance relationship', *Management International Review*, **47** (3), 423–452.

Hofstede, G. (1980), *Culture's Consequences: International Differences in Work-Related Values*, Beverly Hills, CA: Sage.

House, R.J., P.J. Hanges, M. Javidan, P.W. Dorfman and V. Gupta (2004), *Culture, Leadership, and Organizations: The Globe Study of 62 Societies*, Thousand Oaks, CA: Sage Publications.

Hymer, S.H. (1976), *The International Operations of National Firms: A Study of Foreign Direct Investment*, Cambridge, MA: MIT Press.

Isard, W. (1960), *Methods of Regional Analysis*, Cambridge, MA: MIT Press.

Jaffe, A., M. Trajtenberg and R. Henderson (1993), 'Geographic localization of knowledge spillovers as evidenced by patent citations', *Quarterly Journal of Economics*, **63** (3), 577–598.

Johanson, J. and J.E. Vahlne (1977), 'The internationalization process of the firm: a model of knowledge development and increasing foreign market commitments', *Journal of International Business Studies*, **8** (1), 23–32.

Kaufmann, D., A. Kraay and M. Mastruzzi (2004), 'Governance Matters III: Governance Indicators for 1996, 1998, 2000, and 2002', *World Bank Economic Review*, **18** (2), 253–287.

Khanna, T. and K. Palepu (2006), 'Emerging giants: building world-class companies in developing countries', *Harvard Business Review*, **84** (10), 60–69.

Khanna, T. and K. Palepu (2010), *Winning in Emerging Markets: A Road Map for Strategy and Execution*, Boston, MA: Harvard Business Press.

Kogut, B. (1985), 'Designing global strategies: profiting from operating flexibility', *Sloan Management Review*, Fall, 27–38.

Kogut, B. and H. Singh (1988), 'The effect of national culture on the choice of entry mode', *Journal of International Business Studies*, **19** (3), 411–432.

Kostova, T. and K. Roth (2002), 'Adoption of an organizational practice by subsidiaries of multinational corporations: institutional and relational effects', *Academy of Management Journal*, **45** (1), 215–233.

Krugman, P. (1991), 'Increasing returns and economic geography', *Journal of Political Economy*, **99** (3), 483.

Krugman, P. (1998), 'Space: the final frontier', *Journal of Economic Perspectives*, **12**, 161–174.

La Porta, R., F. Lopez-de-Silanes, A. Shleifer and R.W. Vishny (1998), 'Law and finance', *Journal of Political Economy*, **106** (6), 1113–1155.

Lall, S. (1983), *The New Multinationals: The Spread of Third World Enterprises*, New York: Wiley.

Lucas, R.E.B. (2001), 'The effects of proximity and transportation on developing country population migrations', *Journal of Economic Geography*, **1** (3), 323.

Meyer, K.E. (2001), 'Institutions, transaction costs and entry mode choice in Eastern Europe', *Journal of International Business Studies*, **31**, 357–367.

Morgan, K. (2004), 'The exaggerated death of geography: learning, proximity and territorial innovation systems', *Journal of Economic Geography*, **4** (1), 3–21.

Mudambi, R. (2008), 'Location, control and innovation in knowledge-intensive industries', *Journal of Economic Geography*, **8** (5), 699–725.

Nachum, L., S. Zaheer and S. Gross (2008), 'Does it matter where countries are? Proximity to knowledge, markets and resources, and MNE location choices', *Management Science*, **54** (7), 1252–1265.

North, D.C. (1990), *Institutions, Institutional Change, and Economic Performance*, New York: Cambridge University Press.

O'Grady, S. and H. Lane (1996), 'The psychic distance paradox', *Journal of International Business Studies*, **27** (2), 309–334.

Porter, M.E. (1986), *Competition in Global Industries*, Cambridge, MA: Harvard Business School Press.

Porter, M.E. (1990), *The Competitive Advantage of Nations*, New York: Free Press.

Porter, M.E. (2000), 'Location, clusters and company strategy', in G. Clark, M. Gertler and M. Feldman (eds), *Oxford Handbook of Economic Geography*, Oxford: Oxford University Press, pp. 253–274.

Portes, R. and H. Rey (2005), 'The determinants of cross-border equity flows', *Journal of International Economics*, **65** (2), 269–296.

Ramamurti, R. and J.V. Singh (eds) (2009), *Emerging Multinationals from Emerging Markets*, New York: Cambridge University Press.

Rangan, S. and A. Drummond (2004), 'Explaining outcomes in competition among foreign multinationals in a focal host market', *Strategic Management Journal*, **25** (3), 285–293.

Saxenian, A. (1994), *Regional Advantage: Culture and Competition in Silicon Valley and Route 128*, Cambridge, MA: Harvard University Press.

Shenkar, O. (2001), 'Cultural distance revisited: towards a more rigorous conceptualization and measurement of cultural differences', *Journal of International Business Studies*, **32**, 519–535.

Tallman, S.B. (1991), 'Strategic management models and resource-based strategies among MNEs in a host market', *Strategic Management Journal*, **12** (4), 69–82.

Tihanyi, L., D.A. Griffith and C.J. Russell (2005), 'The effect of cultural distance on entry mode choice, international diversification, and MNE performance: a meta-analysis', *Journal of International Business Studies*, **36**, 270–283.

Wells, L.T. (1983), *Third World Multinationals*, Cambridge, MA: MIT Press.

World Bank (2002), *World Development Report: Institutions for Markets*, New York: Oxford University Press.

Xu, D. and O. Shenkar (2002), 'Institutional distance and the multinational enterprise', *Academy of Management Review*, **27** (4), 608–618.

Zaheer, S. (1995), 'Overcoming the liability of foreignness', *Academy of Management Journal*, **38**, 341–363.

10 Beyond the 'rules of the game': three institutional approaches and how they matter for international business
Jasper J. Hotho and Torben Pedersen

10.1 INTRODUCTION

A recurring question in international business (IB) research is how institutions matter for IB activity (Henisz and Swaminathan 2008; Eden 2010). The value of institutional thought to understanding international business is increasingly recognized and the use of institutional arguments has risen considerably in recent years. Yet what institutions are and how they impact upon the behaviour of international firms often remains unclear. This is partially because terms such as 'institutions', 'institutional distance' and 'institutional theory' mask the wide variety of institutional approaches that are currently used in international business research. In line with its interdisciplinary nature, international business research draws on institutional approaches from various disciplines, such as economics, sociology and political economy. However, the IB field often seems to lack awareness of the differences among the various takes on institutional theory and their respective explanatory powers.

This is problematic because the various institutional approaches differ considerably in terms of their conceptualizations of institutions, their levels of analysis and, ultimately, their explanations of how institutions matter for international business. For instance, views on whether and how institutions affect international firm behaviour differ greatly depending on whether institutions are conceived of as formal rules and regulations, or as shared regulative, normative and cognitive frames. In other words, a discussion of institutions without further specification almost guarantees confusion, at least in an international business context. The implication is that to further our understanding of 'how institutions matter' for international business, it is important to be explicit about the institutional 'theory-in-use', and to establish a credible link between that theory and the phenomenon to be explained.

Our aim in this chapter is to clarify some of the institutional approaches in international business research and to illustrate their value for understanding different aspects of international business activities. We do so, first, by comparing and contrasting three dominant institutional approaches in international business: new institutional economics, new organizational institutionalism and comparative institutionalism. We subsequently highlight the differential explanatory power of two of these approaches using an empirical illustration. Specifically, we examine the effects of two types of institutional distance – one derived from new institutional economics and the other from comparative institutionalism – on the development of local knowledge by foreign firms, which is a key construct in the internationalization process literature (e.g. Johanson and Vahlne 1977; Eriksson et al. 1997).

As we argue and illustrate, the different institutional approaches are largely complementary, as they address and explain different facets of international firm behaviour. For instance, whereas new institutional economics draws attention to the implications of the functioning or effectiveness of home- and host-country institutions, comparative institutionalism highlights the implications of differences in the structure and organization of economies for multinational enterprises (MNEs). Thus, the ways in which institutions matter for international business are to a great extent dependent on how institutions are conceptualized and measured.

For instance, our empirical example illustrates that whereas differences in the effectiveness or quality of institutions predominantly affect firms' perceived lack of host-country knowledge, such as knowledge of laws, standards and practices, comparative institutional differences – or differences in national business systems (Whitley 1999, 2007) – impact upon firms' perceived lack of business knowledge, or knowledge of the local industry structure. Furthermore, it appears that while the impact of differences in institutional effectiveness disappears with experience, comparative institutional differences increase in importance. This is presumably because such subtle but more substantive institutional differences only become apparent over time and are more difficult to overcome. However, despite their relevance for explaining international firm behaviour, such comparative institutional differences are often overlooked in quantitative analyses of IB activity, partially due to the difficulties of obtaining appropriate indicators. As our analysis illustrates, the inclusion of institutional distance measures that capture comparative institutional differences, rather than mere differences in institutional quality and effectiveness, offers considerable promise in terms of further enriching our understanding of how institutions affect IB activity.

In the section that follows, we review the three dominant institutional approaches in international business research. Our aim is not to present an exhaustive analysis but rather to outline the differences in how institutions are conceptualized within each approach, and the value and implications of each approach for international business research. We then set the stage for our empirical illustration of the explanatory power of different institutional distance measures on IB activity. We introduce our data and methods, and present our results, before we discuss the implications for future research.

10.2   INSTITUTIONAL APPROACHES IN INTERNATIONAL BUSINESS RESEARCH

Scholars focused on economics, sociology, political science and organizational studies often rely on vastly different conceptions of institutions and their effects. These differ, for instance, in whether institutions are primarily perceived as regulative, normative or cultural-cognitive systems, as well as in the level of analysis (Scott 1995). As a result, scholars with an interest in institutions focus on such diverse topics as economic growth and development (North 1990; Glaeser et al. 2004), the spread of organizational forms and practices (DiMaggio and Powell 1991; Greenwood and Hinings 1996) and the diversity of contemporary forms of capitalism (Amable 2003; Hancké et al. 2007; Whitley 1999). This often makes it difficult to refer to institutions in a more general sense. The variety of notions about what institutions are also implies that institutional approaches differ in their explanatory power, in the sense that they address and explain fundamentally different facets of social life. Thus, as Aoki (2001, 10) concludes: 'which definition of an institution to adopt is not an issue of right or wrong; it depends on the purpose of the analysis'.

As IB is a field that draws on several disciplines and is concerned with multiple levels of analysis (Dunning 1989; Shenkar 2004; Toyne and Nigh 1998), it is only natural that different strands of institutional theory have come to inform IB research. For instance, the contributions included in a recent *Journal of International Business Studies* special issue on institutions draw on institutional arguments from economic sociology (Jackson and Deeg 2008b), organizational sociology (Orr and Scott 2008) and institutional economics (e.g. Clougherty and Grajek 2008; Pajunen 2008). However, because institutional approaches differ in their explanatory potential, it is important to be aware of the differences between them if we are to improve our understanding of institutions.

For instance, whether an institutional distance measure is appropriate depends on whether the type of institutional indicators included in the measure match the mechanisms through which institutions are believed to have an impact. A country's degree of institutional development, for instance, has little explanatory value if the perceived legitimacy and subsequent adoption of a practice is largely driven by normative differences. Given the differences in explanatory power of different institutions and institutional approaches, therefore, it is important that the selection of institutional indicators is theoretically informed, rather than driven by convenience. This requires awareness of the different types of institutional approaches in international business research.

In the following subsections, we first compare and contrast the three most dominant institutional perspectives in IB: new institutional economics, new organizational institutionalism and comparative institutionalism.[1] While the aim is not to be exhaustive – a rare feat when one attempts to discuss the many (and heterogeneous) strands and substrands of institutional theory – an attempt is made to highlight their disciplinary origins and their value for international business research.

10.2.1 New Institutional Economics

The first dominant institutional approach in international business research, new institutional economics, is strongly rooted in microeconomics. New institutional economic arguments have been widely applied in, for example, studies of economic history (North 1990, 1991), and in game-theoretic approaches to the formation of and changes in macroeconomic institutions (Aoki 2001). New institutional economic thought is also evident in the subfields of international business in which the effectiveness of country-level institutions is paramount. The kernel of new institutional economics is perhaps best understood when contrasted with the view of institutions taken by the 'old' institutional economists, such as Thorstein Veblen, John Commons and Gunnar Myrdal.

The origins of new institutional economics
At the beginning of the twentieth century and, in particular, during the interwar period, a group of economists rebelled against the neoclassical view of the economy as a relatively closed model. The central principle of what became known as institutional economics was that because the institutional features of societies (including individual preferences) are interdependent, analyses of economic problems should take the dynamics of the entire social system into account (Myrdal 1978). As indicated by Veblen's (1909, 626) definition of institutions as 'settled habits of thought', institutional economists recognized that institutions and their interdependencies are closely intertwined with habits and cultures (Hodgson 2006). However, this recognition also severely complicated their institutional analyses. Such analyses tended to result in 'tentative generalizations and mere plausible hypotheses' (Myrdal 1978, 775), which appeared to contribute little

to theory formation (Coase 1998). After the Second World War, the role of institutional economics was therefore largely marginalized in favour of neoclassical economics (Hodgson 2007; Lowndes 1996).

Widespread appreciation for the role of institutions in economics returned in the 1970s and 1980s, most notably through the work of Douglass North and Oliver Williamson. The renewed interest in institutions – under the header of new institutional economics (NIE) – was largely a reaction to the neoclassical view of markets as frictionless allocation mechanisms driven by rational agents with perfect information (Ménard and Shirley 2005; North 1991). New institutional economics suggests that the nature of exchange processes and the amount of 'friction' are dependent on the institutional context in which they take place. For instance, the extent to which the institutional environment guarantees property rights and facilitates the enforcement of contracts affects the level of transaction costs (Coase 1937; Williamson 1975). Furthermore, institutionalized rules and regulations 'dictate the margins at which organizations operate' (North 1990, 110), or the boundaries of tolerated behaviour, particularly with regard to competition, collaboration and corruption. Rules and regulations, therefore, also affect whether the behaviour of organizations has negative or beneficial effects on an economy's overall productivity. In new institutional economics, therefore, the effectiveness or quality of the institutional framework is believed to have a direct bearing on the functioning and form of markets and organizations, and on economic performance.

To new institutional economists, 'institutions are the rules of the game in a society or, more formally, are the humanly devised constraints that shape human interaction' (North 1990, 3). Although they acknowledge the existence of both formal and informal institutions, new institutional economists focus mainly on formal rules and regulations (Williamson 2000; Joskow 2008), and how those rules and regulations affect the choice of governance arrangements through which economic activity is organized. Thus, an important distinction between old institutional economics and new institutional economists is that the latter largely view institutions as (relatively adaptable) constraints, rather than as conditioners of individual choice. Norms and customs are treated largely as givens (Williamson 2000), and individuals are assumed to create and shape institutions relatively independently of cultural preferences (Mayhew 1989). Thus, from the perspective of new institutional economics, institutions affect which governance arrangements are most efficient, but they have little impact on how the game is played other than through the establishment of rules and regulations.

In economics, discussions on institutions have moved beyond the simple dichotomy of old and new institutional economics. Aoki (2001) and Greif (1998), among others, adopt a more game-theoretical approach to understanding the emergence of institutions. While their work remains strongly rooted in new institutional economics, it pays particular attention to the interdependencies among the outcomes of games in various economic domains (Aoki 2001). There is also a renewed interest in old institutional economic thought, especially in the evolutionary work of Veblen and the notion of endogenous preferences, in relation to understanding socio-economic evolution (e.g. Brette 2006; Hodgson 1998, 2003, 2007; Potts 2007). Similarly, new institutional economists are increasingly acknowledging and exploring the cognitive implications of institutions (e.g. Denzau and North 1994; Dequech 2002; Hodgson 2007) as well as the interdependencies among institutions (e.g. Ostrom 2005).

New institutional economics in international business research

From the perspective of new institutional economics, institutions matter for international business because host countries' institutional frameworks have a considerable impact on the costs and uncertainty MNEs face when setting up local operations, and on their access to local resources. Strong and stable host-country institutions lower transaction costs and the level of policy uncertainty (Delios and Henisz 2003; Henisz 2000; Meyer 2001), and they contribute to efficient markets for local resources (Khanna et al. 2005; Meyer et al. 2009). Therefore, the quality of the institutional framework affects not only the performance of local investments (Treviño and Mixon 2004; Wan and Hoskisson 2003) but also the appropriateness of alternative governance forms. For instance, MNEs are more likely to enter through wholly owned subsidiaries in host countries with developed institutions than in countries with less developed institutions (Henisz 2000; Meyer 2001; Meyer et al. 2009). In addition, developed institutions reduce the risks and complexities of acquisitions (Dikova and Van Witteloostuijn 2007), and allow entrants to devote less effort to understanding the policy environment (Delios and Henisz 2003).

International business scholars' increasing interest in institutions coincides with the rise of several key emerging markets, such as India and China, which offers new opportunities to extend our understanding of how institutions matter (Meyer and Peng 2005) and has 'pushed the institution-based view to the cutting edge of strategy research' (Peng et al. 2008, 923). The rise of large emerging economies also gives rise to new questions. For instance, an increasing amount of attention is being paid to how firms can overcome the absence of a strong institutional framework and the lack of intermediaries, known as 'institutional voids', in emerging markets (e.g. Chakrabarty 2009; Khanna et al. 2005; Mair and Marti 2009). Variation in the ability of MNEs to manage such institutional idiosyncrasies may

explain why foreign affiliates' performance in developing market economies varies widely (Henisz 2003; Chan et al. 2008). In addition, a growing
stream of literature seeks to explain the internationalization of MNEs
from emerging markets, especially the ways in which such MNEs may
internationalize despite the disadvantages of coming from countries with
weak institutions and inefficient market mechanisms (e.g. Aulakh 2007;
Child and Rodrigues 2005; Luo and Tung 2007). While these MNEs
often lack more sophisticated strategic resources, which may necessitate
the acquisition of such assets from more mature MNEs (Luo and Tung
2007), their ability to operate in difficult institutional environments also
gives emerging-market MNEs a relative advantage when entering other
less developed market economies (e.g. Cuervo-Cazurra and Genc 2008).

In line with the focus of new institutional economics on institutional
effectiveness, measures of institutional distance that build on new institutional economics typically capture the quality, strength or level of
development the institutional framework. For instance, the widely applied
World Bank Governance Indicators (Kaufmann et al. 2009) encompass
six categories that reflect the strength of the legal and political environment, such as the degree of government effectiveness, regulatory quality,
the rule of law and the control of corruption (for applications in IB, see for
example Cuervo-Cazurra and Genc 2008; Dikova and Van Witteloostuijn
2007; Pajunen 2008; Rao et al. 2005). A comparable data source is the
World Competitiveness Yearbook (see, e.g., Chan et al. 2008; Delios et al.
2008; Gu and Lu 2011; Wan and Hoskisson 2003; Yiu and Makino 2002).
Other measures capture more specific aspects of the quality of the institutional environment, such as Henisz' (2000) POLCON indices of political
constraints or the EBRD transition indices, which measure the extent of
institution building (see, e.g., Meyer 2001).

Thus, applications of new institutional economics in international business generally conceptualize institutions on the country level (e.g. rules
and regulations). Such institutions are believed to affect transaction costs
and to constrain the actions of actors in the pursuit of their interests.
However, they are assumed to have no or little effect on the interests that
actors pursue or on the preferences of actors other than what the rules
of the game exclude. For example, as Aguilera and Jackson (2003) note,
agency approaches to comparative corporate governance tend successfully to characterize different governance mechanisms, but they provide
little or no explanation for the observed differences in governance. In
addition, institutions and their effects are implicitly assumed to be relatively unrelated rather than interdependent. This has translated into what
Jackson and Deeg (2008b) term a 'variable-based approach' to institutions, in which institutions are conceived of as factors that independently

'constrain or impact . . . the cost of IB activity' (Jackson and Deeg 2008b, 542). Recent fuzzy-set analyses highlight the dangers of this approach. For instance, Pajunen (2008) illustrates that the mere presence or absence of a single institutional factor may have little impact on the perceived costs of operation and, hence, on the attractiveness of a location. Similarly, Schneider et al. (2010) illustrate that single institutional characteristics do not sufficiently explain export performance in high-tech industries.

10.2.2 New Organizational Institutionalism

The second dominant institutional approach within international business is new organizational institutionalism (e.g. Meyer and Rowan 1977; DiMaggio and Powell 1983; Powell and DiMaggio 1991). New organizational institutionalism, which is rooted in sociology and organization theory, focuses on organizational forms and organizational practices (Powell and DiMaggio 1991) rather than 'the rules of the game'. Just as new institutional economics is best understood when contrasted with old institutional economics, so new organizational institutionalism is best understood when compared with 'old' organizational institutionalism, although the difference between the latter two is less pronounced (Lowndes 1996).

The coming of age of new organizational institutionalism

The phrase 'old organizational institutionalism' is somewhat deceptive, as it may suggest that the institutionalisms originally developed in sociology and organizational studies were relatively homogeneous. This was not the case, as Scott (1987) illustrates in a seminal review of the 'many faces of institutional theory' (1987, 493). The 'old' organizational institutionalism against which the 'new' positioned itself is the strain of organizational institutionalism for which Philip Selznick has been singled out as the main proponent (see Powell and DiMaggio 1991), not the least because of his hallmark definition of organizational institutions.

The focus of old organizational institutionalists, such as Selznick (1949, 1957; Broom and Selznick 1955) and Clark (1960, 1972), was on explaining the distinctiveness or 'character' of individual organizations. They argued that organizations develop distinctive characteristics, such as distinctive practices (Clark 1960) and distinctive competences (Selznick 1952), because some practices become institutionalized in the interplay between internal interests and the external environment. Such practices persist even when conditions change because they become '*infuse*[d] *with value* beyond the technical requirements of the task at hand' (Selznick 1957, 17). Although power and influence are often emphasized in depictions of the old organizational institutionalism (e.g. Powell and DiMaggio 1991; Greenwood and Hinings 1996), old organizational institutionalists view institutionalization as a neutral adaptive mechanism of organizations (Selznick 1996) that promotes stability by creating 'orderly, stable, socially integrating patterns out of unstable, loosely organized, or narrowly technical activities' (Broom and Selznick 1955, 238).

The notion of institutionalization in old and new organizational institutionalism differs primarily in whether institutionalization is argued to occur within individual organizations, or within particular domains or fields. In old organizational institutionalism, institutions are viewed as intra-organizational patterns and activities, which makes the organization the primary unit of analysis (Greenwood and Hinings 1996). In contrast, in new organizational institutionalism, institutionalized elements are part of more widely shared belief systems (Scott 1987). This implies that the old organizational institutionalist idea of institutionalization can be used to explain differences between organizations, while new organizational institutionalism uses institutionalization to explain homogeneity in organizational forms and practices across organizations (Powell and DiMaggio 1991).

Broadly speaking, in new organizational institutionalism, 'institutions are taken for granted ways of acting, which derive from shared regulative, cognitive and normative frames' (Morgan and Kristensen 2006, 1470). Such rules, beliefs and norms are shared across organizations, and institutionalized organizational forms and conventions often differ by organizational field rather than by individual organization (Powell and DiMaggio 1991). Organizations conform to such institutionalized behaviour because it is rewarding: conformity increases organizational legitimacy, access to resources and, ultimately, organizational survival (Meyer and Rowan 1977). In contrast with new institutional economics, new organizational institutionalism suggest that social behaviour is not only restricted through formal institutions, but also guided and encouraged by normative pressures and cultural-cognitive systems (DiMaggio and Powell 1983; Scott 1995, 2008). These isomorphic pressures, in turn, explain convergence in organizational structures and practices.

Due to its emphasis on how organizational forms and practices are shaped by their environment – particularly in early contributions (Scott 2008) – new organizational institutionalism runs the risk of being overly deterministic (DiMaggio 1988). This raises the paradox of embedded agency, or the question of how actors influence and change the institutional fields in which they themselves are strongly embedded (Holm 1995; Seo and Creed 2002). Subsequent work has lead to a more dynamic view of new organizational institutionalism by arguing, for instance, that contradictory institutional logics provide actors with opportunities for choice (Emirbayer and Mische 1998; Friedland and Alford 1991), and by illustrating that institutionalized forms and practices need to be actively maintained if they are to persist (Dacin et al. 2010; Oliver 1992). In addition, new organizational institutionalism suggests that actors may respond to institutional pressures in different ways. Instead of conforming to institutional expectations, they may defy or manipulate them (Oliver 1991). Thus, in unstable or heterogeneous institutional environments, actors with favourable social positions may act as 'institutional entrepreneurs' and successfully influence which organizational forms and practices are perceived as legitimate (Battilana et al. 2009; DiMaggio 1988; Garud et al. 2007).

New organizational institutionalism in international business research
In international business research, new organizational institutionalism has been predominantly developed, applied and refined in the work of Kostova, Zaheer and Roth (Kostova 1997, 1999; Kostova and Zaheer 1999; Kostova and Roth 2002). When applied to international business, new organizational institutionalism suggests that the greater the differences between the institutional environments of the home and host countries, the more challenging it will be for MNEs to establish and maintain internal and external legitimacy (Kostova and Zaheer 1999), and to transfer organizational practices to foreign subsidiaries (Kostova 1999; Kostova and Roth 2002). In other words, the larger the institutional differences between the home and the host contexts, the larger the institutional duality experienced by local subsidiaries (Kostova and Roth, 2002) and the greater the complexity faced by MNEs.

Such arguments are widely used to explain variation in the work practices of foreign operations, such as those in the human resource practices and staffing strategies of foreign affiliates (Rosenzweig and Nohria 1994; Gaur et al. 2007), corporate social responsibility (CSR) practices and corruption (Husted and Allen 2006; Rodriguez et al. 2005), or staffing issues, such as expatriate adjustment and the organizational identification of subsidiary managers (Ramsey 2005; Vora and Kostova 2007). Others link variations in pressures for internal and external legitimacy to variations in entry mode decisions (Chan and Makino 2007; Davis et al. 2000; Haveman 1993; Rozenweig and Singh 1991), while Xu and Shenkar (2002) suggest that the regulative, normative and cognitive distances between the home and the host country may also affect the location strategy of MNEs. In addition, the ways in which the presence of MNEs may shape the institutional host environment, for instance with respect to such elements as norms regarding corruption (Kwok and Tadesse 2006), are also the subject of increasing attention.

In terms of the measurement of institutional pressures, various contributions demonstrate how the institutional environment can be decomposed into regulative, normative and cultural-cognitive dimensions (Kostova 1997; Busenitz et al. 2000; Kostova and Roth 2002), which can be used to compile institutional country profiles. These can then be used as fine-grained distance measures. However, an important limitation of this method is that the higher the level of aggregation, the more difficult it is to identify and segregate the relevant regulative, normative and cultural-cognitive institutional elements. This is especially true when researchers rely on secondary data rather than on tailor-made surveys. Therefore, measures of institutional distance that build on new organizational institutionalism are best suited to analyses of the legitimacy and transferability of particular practices, and should be applied with caution in analyses of firm-level international business phenomena.

In general, new organizational institutionalism has helped international business research become more attentive to variation in national environments, and has contributed to a more differentiated view of the MNE as a 'nexus of differentiated practices' (Rozenzweig and Nohria 1994, 230). However, as with the agency discussion in new organizational institutionalism, international business and management scholars increasingly recognize the difficulty of viewing MNE practices as the product of isomorphic pressures, as MNEs are embedded in multiple, evolving institutional systems at different levels of analysis (Kostova et al. 2008; Szyłowics and Galvin 2010). A promising avenue for future research lies in explaining how MNEs handle the multiplicity of internal and external pressures, which shifts the locus of attention from the effects of institutional differences to how MNEs can manage them.

10.2.3   Comparative Institutionalism

The third dominant institutional approach in international business research is comparative institutionalism, which has its origins in political science, the sociology of work and comparative political economy. Similar to new institutional economics, it deals predominantly with country-level institutions (Whitley 2005), although institutions on the subnational level are increasingly in focus (Lane and Wood 2009). However, whereas new institutional economics predominantly focuses on the institutional effectiveness of rules and regulations, comparative institutional approaches seek to explain differences in socio-economic organization between countries. For instance, although Germany, Denmark and the United Kingdom (UK) are all relatively similar in terms of the effectiveness of their institutional framework (see, e.g., the World Bank's

Worldwide Governance Indicators; Kaufmann et al. 2010), comparative institutionalism highlights the considerable differences in how economic activities are organized and controlled in these three countries. In other words, comparative institutionalism shows that large intrinsic differences exist among market economies, and that these differences may have a considerable impact on the structures and practices adopted by firms operating across national borders (Ferner 1997; Harzing and Sorge 2003; Whitley 1999).

An introduction to comparative institutionalism
Comparative institutionalism seeks to describe, compare and explain the diversity, change and persistence of distinct systems of economic coordination and control in developed-market economies. Although comparative institutionalism comes in various guises (Jackson and Deeg 2008a), a central feature is that institutions in different societal domains, such as the education system, the financial system and market relations, are considered to be reciprocally constituted and path-dependent. That is, comparative institutionalism suggests that societal institutions often develop in an interdependent and mutually reinforcing way (e.g. Hall and Soskice 2001; Whitley 1992, 1999). As a result, institutions in developed market economies often form relatively stable and complementary configurations that help reproduce a distinctive economic logic, or particular 'strategies, routine approaches to problems and shared decision rules that produce predictable patterns of behaviour by actors within the system' (Jackson and Deeg 2008b, 557). This explains why there are significant differences in business structures and processes between, for instance, the relatively market-oriented United States (US) and the relatively state-guided France (e.g., Redding 2005; Hancké 2001), or among Germany, Italy and South Korea (e.g., Amable 2003; Whitley 1992, 1999).

Comparative institutionalism recognizes that there are distinct differences in the ways in which economic activities are organized in market economies. Institutions are not seen as independent constraints but as part of interrelated, culturally informed solutions for resolving economic coordination problems (Whitley 1999). As a result, developed market economies often differ considerably in terms of the dominant type of firm, their organizational capabilities and interests, and their relations with other economic actors (Whitley 1999, 2003, 2007). Thus, the forms, practices, structures and capabilities of firms resonate with the institutional context in which they are embedded. For this reason, there are considerable differences between, for instance, the types of innovations that are developed in societies that are more liberal and those that are more coordinated (e.g., Casper 2000; Hall and Soskice 2001; Whitley 2003, 2007), and institutional contexts may give economies a comparative advantage in some activities but not in others.

Comparative institutionalists have traditionally relied on 'thick' qualitative analyses to characterize the interplay between institutions and economic activity (Maurice 2000; Redding 2005). Although they are insightful, such descriptions often tend to be relatively particularistic, and extensive systematic characterizations of large groups of countries are sparse. A well-known exception is the empirical work of Hall and Soskice (2001), which relies on the distinction between liberal and coordinated market economies to characterize and classify Anglo-Saxon and continental European economies. However, although this parsimonious classification is insightful, the reduction of modern capitalism into two categories overlooks the diversity of institutional arrangements that is evident among more coordinated market economies, such as France, Germany and Japan (see, e.g., Amable 2003; Hancké et al. 2009; Whitley 1999).

Perhaps the most elaborate and systematic attempt to classify market economies is found in Whitley's comparative business systems framework (Whitley 1992, 1994, 1999). Whitley's characterization and classification of different business system types, or distinctive patterns of economic organization, therefore serves as an important analytical tool (Morgan 2007; Morgan et al. 2005). As in comparative institutionalism in general, the key notions of the business systems framework are that the way in which economic activities in countries are organized is often internally consistent and that the characteristics of market economies are closely related to the dominant type of institution (Whitley 1994, 1999). Market economies are argued to differ mainly in terms of the dominant type of ownership relations, in how the relations between economic actors are coordinated and in the nature of employment relations (Whitley 1998). Whitley argues that the form of a particular market economy is largely dependent on four key institutional dimensions: the role assumed by the state, the characteristics of the financial system, the skill development system, and the norms and values that resonate in work relations (Whitley 1998, 1999). The more specific and coherent the institutions, the more distinctive and cohesive the business systems that arise. Whitley subsequently identifies six distinct 'business system types', which range from market-oriented compartmentalized business systems to more coordinated types, such as state-organized and collaborative business systems.

Comparative institutionalism in international business research
In international business research, insights from comparative institutionalism have been used to understand the effect of both home and host-country institutions on the strategies, structures and organizational

practices of MNEs (Kristensen and Zeitlin 2001). Such applications of comparative institutionalism illustrate that MNEs' operations abroad are subject to considerable home-country effects. For example, Harzing and Sorge (2003) find that the country of origin impacts upon the type of corporate control mechanisms that MNEs employ. Matten and Geppert (2004) suggest that substantive characteristics of the home and host institutional contexts affect subsidiary work-system designs, while Saka (2004) relates such differences to the transfer of knowledge. Similarly, the institutional home context may have a significant bearing on how MNEs respond to industry pressures, such as their propensity to outsource or diversify, as Djelic and Ainamo (1999) illustrate in their study on MNEs in the luxury fashion industry. Thus, comparative institutionalism demonstrates that internationalization processes may 'bear traces of institutional legacies' (Morgan and Quack, 2005, 1780), although firms may also reinterpret and redefine their institutional contexts in order to position themselves better for internationalization.

Authors drawing on comparative institutionalism also consider how MNEs affect the host country's institutional context (e.g. Hancké et al. 2007; Kristensen and Morgan 2007; Morgan 2009). Kristensen and Morgan (2007) argue that the impact of MNEs on a host country's institutional competitiveness depends on the MNE's investment motives and the strength of the institutional complementarities of the host context. In addition, an increasing amount of attention is being paid to the impact of the interplay between home and host institutional contexts for MNEs (Sorge 2005). For instance, recent work in comparative institutionalism explores how the institutional duality faced by MNE subsidiaries may lead to micro-political games and power struggles (Dörrenbächer and Geppert 2006, 2009) in terms of such activities as the standardization of practices and policies (Ferner et al. 2005; Morgan and Kristensen 2006), or the internal division of resources (Morgan and Kristensen 2006).

Thus, from the perspective of comparative institutionalism, institutions matter for international business because societal institutions affect the competences and practices of MNEs, and because the specificity of the institutional host environments affects the specific challenges MNEs face in setting up operations and establishing local linkages. However, despite the interest of international business scholars in the effects of inherent country differences on the nature of the MNE (as demonstrated by the considerable amount of literature on the effects of cultural differences), comparative institutionalism remains relatively underrepresented in international business research (Jackson and Deeg 2008b; Redding 2005). Although this is partially because international business scholars are unfamiliar with comparative institutional thought, the lack of data also often makes it difficult to construct an adequate comparative institutional distance measure. This is especially true when compared with institutional distance measures that focus on institutional development, quality or effectiveness, for which excellent data are readily available. As a result, while the many qualitative studies that draw on comparative institutional thought demonstrate the importance of inherent institutional differences and characteristics to our understanding of the MNE, such differences are seldom taken into account in quantitative studies in international business.

10.3 AN ILLUSTRATION OF THE EXPLANATORY POWER OF DIFFERENT INSTITUTIONAL DISTANCE MEASURES FOR IB ACTIVITY

The preceding discussion illustrates that the focus, the level of analysis and the application of the different institutional approaches in IB vary considerably. For instance, both new institutional economics and comparative institutionalism focus on the country level. But while new institutional economics focuses on governance in the form of formal rules and regulations, the focus of comparative institutionalism is on how institutions are configured. Instead, new organizational institutionalism differs in terms of both its level of analysis, which is more disaggregated; and its broader view of institutions, which includes normative, cognitive and regulative institutions. These differences have important implications for how the institutional approaches are applied in IB, as outlined in Table 10.1.

Studies based on new institutional economics typically consider the quality, development and effectiveness of institutions in a country. These can be measured in many different ways using a range of variables. As a result, a myriad of different indices exist that measure the overall quality, development and effectiveness of institutions in a given country, such as the World Bank Governance Indicators, the POLCON index and the Freedom House indices.[2] Such institutional indicators reflect the level of effectiveness of the institutional frameworks of countries, but are less attentive to differences in how the institutional framework is organized. Comparative institutionalism, on the other hand, acknowledges that there are different ways of configuring institutions. Therefore, in quantitative studies, comparative institutionalists tend to rely more on measures of the coordination and interaction of activities in a country in order to capture the interplay between institutions and the workings of the system (e.g. Hall and Gingerich 2009).

Below, we aim to illustrate empirically that the choice of institutional approach, and the corresponding choice of institutional distance measure,

Table 10.1 Features of the three dominant institutional approaches in IB

	Focus	Level of analysis	Typical measures	Typical applications in IB	Study examples
New institutional economics	Formal rules and regulations	Country level	Institutional quality, development and effectiveness	Governance modes, location decisions and performance	Delios and Henisz (2003), Dikova and Van Witteloostuijn (2007), Meyer (2001), Meyer et al. (2009), Treviño and Mixon (2004), Wan and Hoskisson (2003)
New organizational institutionalism	Regulative, normative and cultural-cognitive systems	Organizational and practice levels	Survey-based regulative, normative and cognitive profiles	Subsidiary work practices, knowledge transfer and adoption, and institutional duality	Busenitz et al. (2000), Davis et al. (2000), Gaur et al. (2007), Kostova and Zaheer (1999), Kostova and Roth (2002), Vora and Kostova (2007), Xu and Shenkar (2002)
Comparative institutionalism	Socio-economic differences and the configuration of societal institutions	Country level	The degree of coordination (LME-CME); qualitative assessments	Home-country effects on MNE control mechanisms, work practices and organizational capabilities, and interaction with host-country specificities	Aguilera and Jackson (2003), Djelic and Ainamo (1999), Harzing and Sorge (2003), Kristensen and Morgan (2007), Kristensen and Zeitlin (2005), Matten and Geppert (2004), Redding (2005), Sorge (2005), Whitley (1999, 2007)

therefore has considerable implications for when and how institutions matter for international business. To this end we apply two contrasting institutional distance measures: one based on new institutional economics; and a new measure derived from comparative institutionalism, on a key construct in IB, namely the knowledge gap perceived when entering new markets. Specifically, we explore the extent to which different types of institutional differences shape the perception of the knowledge gap when firms go abroad. Our focal question therefore is the following: what is the explanatory power of these institutional approaches relative to the knowledge gap foreign entrants perceive when entering new markets?

Institutions and Perceived Knowledge Gaps

Perceived knowledge gaps occur when current knowledge is not, or no longer, deemed sufficient to achieve expected performance. That is, it implies a gap between the knowledge possessed and the knowledge needed to solve a problem in a specific situation. The recognition of a knowledge gap can be triggered by various factors, such as environmental and technological changes, new strategies or decreasing resources, and it often initiates further learning (March 1999).

Firms may also experience considerable knowledge gaps when entering new markets, between the knowledge needed to succeed in the new context and firms' actual understanding of the new host context (Petersen et al. 2008). The internationalization process view promotes the idea that such knowledge gaps constitute a key source of uncertainty, and therefore are a major impediment to internationalization (Johanson and Vahlne 1977). As Forsgren and Johanson (1992, 10) highlight: '[i]nternational expansion is inhibited by the lack of knowledge about foreign markets and such knowledge can mainly be acquired gradually through experience from practical operations abroad'. Thus, firms' increasing resource commitments to foreign markets are contingent upon diminishing knowledge gaps, which are therefore a central factor in determining the pace and character of internationalization.

With respect to foreign market entries, the perception of knowledge gaps can be divided into two distinct dimensions: a perceived gap in host-country knowledge and a perceived gap in business knowledge (Eriksson et al. 1997, 2000). Host-country knowledge comprises a firm's general understanding of the foreign host context, such as in terms of laws, regulations and practices. Instead, business knowledge refers to knowledge on the business level, such as the firms' understanding of local consumers, suppliers and competitors. Previous research suggests that firms learn gradually about country-specific institutions (Chetty et al. 2006). Below, we therefore explore whether the kind of institutional distance between two host countries has a bearing on the perception of knowledge gaps when a firm enters a foreign country. As shown in Figure 10.1, we expect both types of institutional distance to widen the perceived knowledge gaps. The greater the institutional distance, the less familiar the new context, and the larger is the perception of a gap between the possessed and necessary knowledge related to the foreign country.

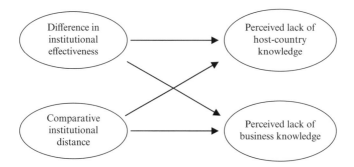

Figure 10.1   Basic model of the relationship between knowledge gaps and institutional distance

10.4   DESCRIPTIONS OF DATA AND METHOD

The data for this study were gathered through a mail survey undertaken in four countries: Denmark, Finland, New Zealand and South Korea. A pilot study was conducted in 1997 in which ten managers were asked to answer the questionnaire in an interview situation. The final standardized questionnaire was sent out in August–September 1998 to firms that were involved in international operations, that is, those involved in exports or with subsidiaries abroad.

The target firms in each country were identified through secondary sources. The population comprised firms in various industries (manufacturing and services firms were included) with different international locations. This population was chosen due to the active involvement of these firms in foreign markets, an involvement that exposed them to a possible knowledge gap. The four countries were selected in order to reflect diversity in both the effectiveness and the configuration of host-country institutions. The countries vary considerably in terms of the quality of institutions and the systemic workings of the institutions. The substantial variation in the institutional set-ups between South Korea, the two Nordic countries of Denmark and Finland, and New Zealand provides an excellent setting in which to test the explanatory power of institutional distance.

The questionnaires were mailed to company chief executive officers (CEOs), and a reminder and a new questionnaire were sent three weeks later. Most questionnaires were completed by the CEO or another high-level executive, and 385 useable responses were received across all four countries: 152, 93, 76 and 64 from Denmark, Finland, New Zealand and South Korea, respectively. At the beginning of the questionnaire, respondents were asked to select one recent business venture or operation in a foreign market, such as the firm's entrance into a new market or a considerable expansion of an existing business in a foreign market. The operation was to be important to the firm and its international expansion. Furthermore, the operation was to be well under way in the foreign location. Most of the subsequent questions in the questionnaire were related to this self-selected foreign market operation. Each firm provided responses for only one foreign market operation.

The questionnaire provided information on the perceived knowledge gap and a number of other variables related to the particular foreign operation. As described below, the institutional distance between the home and host countries was measured using secondary sources.

10.4.1   Operationalization of Variables

Difference in institutional effectiveness
To measure differences in institutional effectiveness, we adopted the widely used Worldwide Governance Indicators (Kaufmann et al. 2007), which are based on World Bank data. We used data for the year 1998 for each country with respect to six variables: voice and accountability, political stability, government effectiveness, regulatory quality, the rule of law, and control of corruption. The differences among each pair of countries across the six variables were calculated as the bilateral Euclidian distance in institutional effectiveness between the two countries. The mean value of this variable is 1.3 and the standard deviation is 1.1.

Comparative institutional distance
To capture comparative institutional differences, we constructed a measure based on the institutional features associated with differences in national business systems, as identified by Whitley (1999). We used data on 30 Organisation for Economic Co-operation and Development (OECD) countries gathered from the *Global Competitiveness Report* (Porter et al. 2000), which contains data collected in 1999. We matched Whitley's institutional features with the indicators from the Global Competitiveness Report that best captured the intended institutional characteristics (see Appendix). We then calculated the Euclidean distance among the country pairs. The mean value is 3.2 and the standard deviation is 1.3.

Appendix Table 10A.2 lists the number of observations (in brackets) and the institutional distance measures for all country pairs. The dataset includes a total of 69 country pairs. For each of these 69 pairs, the institutional distance measure is given, with the measure of the difference in institutional effectiveness presented first, followed by the measure of comparative institutional distance. The values of the two institutional distance measures are strikingly different. In fact, the correlation between the two institutional distance measures is negative with a coefficient of −0.38, which indicates that they measure different aspects of institutional distance.

A few examples serve as illustrations. For instance, the difference in institutional effectiveness between Denmark and New Zealand is rather low at 0.4 (only one-third of the mean value). This indicates a small distance, as Denmark and New Zealand achieve rather similar scores on the six variables that form our measure of differences in institutional effectiveness. At the same time, however, the comparative institutional distance measure returns a value of 3.4, which is above the mean and indicates a substantial institutional distance. Another example is found in the institutional distance between South Korea and France, where the difference in institutional effectiveness (2.1) is well above the mean of 1.3, while the comparative institutional distance (1.9) for these two state-organized economies (Whitley, 2000) is clearly below the mean of 3.2. Therefore, the descriptive data reinforce the point that the two measures of institutional distance are clearly distinct and that they reflect different types of institutional differences.

Perceived knowledge gap
This measures the perceived lack of knowledge in relation to the particular foreign business operation. Respondents were asked to indicate the extent to which a lack of various kinds of local knowledge constituted an obstacle to the success of the foreign business operation. Following Eriksson et al. (1997), the foreign knowledge was categorized as either 'host-country knowledge' or 'business knowledge'. Respondents were informed that 'host-country knowledge' consisted of knowledge of business laws and practices, financial practices, and technology and quality standards, and that 'business knowledge' comprised knowledge of counterparts (customers, suppliers and competitors) in the host country. The respondents were then asked to use a seven-point Likert scale (1 = highly disagree and 7 = highly agree) to indicate whether: 'A lack of the following type knowledge is an obstacle to the conduct of the local business operation abroad'. The following three types of knowledge informed our measure of 'host-country knowledge':

-   knowledge of laws on technology, product and quality standards;
-   knowledge of business laws; and
-   knowledge of financial practice and currency laws.

The following three types of knowledge formed our measure of 'business knowledge':

- knowledge of customers in the foreign market;
- knowledge of suppliers in the foreign market; and
- knowledge of competitors in the foreign market.

In addition, a number of control variables were added in order to obtain information on: (1) the experience of the firm in the focal country (that is, the time span of the particular assignment, whether the firm had previous assignments in the country and whether the assignment was outsourced to an independent firm); (2) internationalization experience (that is, the number of countries in which the firm had sales or previous business experience); and (3) characteristics of the product (that is, level of standardization).

10.5   RESULTS

The model shown in Figure 10.1 was analysed using ordinary least square (OLS) regressions. Two OLS models – one with the perceived lack of host-country knowledge and one with the perceived lack of business knowledge as dependent variables – were used. The results are provided in Table 10.2, columns 2 and 3, for all foreign assignments. They include the two independent variables and the control variables. The models are highly significant with F-values of 7.61 ($p < 0.001$) and 6.19 ($p < 0.001$), respectively. The R-squareds of 0.15 (for host-country knowledge) and 0.13 (for business knowledge) are also satisfactory, as they explain 15% and 13% of the variation in perceived lack of knowledge in these models, respectively. The coefficients for the two independent variables of institutional distance are included in Figure 10.2.

All four relations shown in Figure 10.2 appear to be significant at the 5 per cent level. Both institutional distance measures affect the perceived lack of knowledge when conducting business abroad: The greater the institutional distance, the more respondents perceive a lack of knowledge about the foreign market. However, the difference in institutional effectiveness has a stronger impact on the perceived lack of host-country knowledge (0.37, $p < 0.001$), while comparative institutional distance has the largest impact on the perceived lack of business knowledge (0.28, $p < 0.001$).

In order to explore this finding further, we conducted two split-sample analyses. In the first analysis, the sample was split along the median for

Table 10.2   OLS regressions model on lack of host-country knowledge and lack of business knowledge for all assignments and split samples (N = 385)

	All assignments		Short time span		Long time span		Sales in few countries		Sales in many countries	
	Lack of host-country knowledge	Lack of business knowledge	Lack of host-country knowledge	Lack of business knowledge	Lack of host-country knowledge	Lack of business knowledge	Lack of host-country knowledge	Lack of business knowledge	Lack of host-country knowledge	Lack of business knowledge
Difference in institutional effectiveness	0.37*** (0.08)	0.18* (0.09)	0.46** (0.16)	0.28 (0.17)	0.21* (0.09)	0.16 (0.10)	0.47** (0.14)	0.32* (0.15)	0.32** (0.11)	0.11 (0.12)
Comparative institutional distance	0.21** (0.07)	0.28*** (0.08)	0.21 (0.13)	0.32** (0.15)	0.15 (0.08)	0.29*** (0.09)	0.20 (0.10)	0.27* (0.11)	0.24* (0.10)	0.31** (0.11)
Time span of assignment	-0.01* (0.005)	0.005 (0.005)					-0.02* (0.01)	0.01 (0.01)	-0.01 (0.01)	0.01 (0.01)
Previous assignments in country (dummy)	-0.05 (0.15)	-0.14 (0.17)	-0.19 (0.29)	0.06 (0.32)	0.19 (0.19)	0.20 (0.20)	0.04 (0.23)	0.11 (0.25)	0.08 (0.21)	0.22 (0.23)
Assigned to a third-party (dummy)	-0.42** (0.16)	-0.13 (0.17)	-0.34 (0.27)	-0.22 (0.30)	-0.41* (0.20)	0.27 (0.21)	-0.48* (0.23)	0.14 (0.25)	-0.42 (0.22)	0.06 (0.24)
Number of countries with sales	-0.07 (0.17)	-0.04 (0.18)	-0.30 (0.29)	-0.17 (0.32)	-0.02 (0.21)	0.18 (0.22)				

Table 10.2 (continued)

	All assignments		Short time span		Long time span		Sales in few countries		Sales in many countries	
	Lack of host-country knowledge	Lack of business knowledge	Lack of host-country knowledge	Lack of business knowledge	Lack of host-country knowledge	Lack of business knowledge	Lack of host-country knowledge	Lack of business knowledge	Lack of host-country knowledge	Lack of business knowledge
Level of product standardization	−0.04 (0.04)	−0.07 (0.04)	0.01 (0.07)	0.01 (0.07)	0.07 (0.05)	0.10 (0.05)	0.01 (0.06)	0.07 (0.06)	0.08 (0.05)	0.06 (0.06)
Previous business experience	−0.34*** (0.07)	−0.39*** (0.07)	−0.26* (0.12)	−0.26* (0.13)	−0.38*** (0.08)	−0.43*** (0.09)	−0.37*** (0.10)	−0.31** (0.11)	−0.29*** (0.09)	−0.44*** (0.10)
Previous international experience	−0.19** (0.07)	−0.07 (0.08)	−0.21 (0.13)	−0.16 (0.15)	−0.17 (0.09)	−0.03 (0.10)	−0.32*** (0.10)	−0.12 (0.10)	0.01 (0.12)	0.03 (0.13)
Intercept	4.57*** (0.49)	3.90*** (0.53)	4.66*** (0.84)	4.32*** (0.90)	4.67*** (0.62)	3.62*** (0.66)	5.39*** (0.69)	3.79*** (0.75)	3.17*** (0.77)	3.67*** (0.85)
F-value	7.61***	6.19***	3.29***	2.12*	5.22***	5.79***	5.22***	2.35*	3.98***	4.89***
R-squared	0.15	0.13	0.17	0.10	0.15	0.16	0.19	0.10	0.14	0.17

Note: ***, ** and *indicate significance levels of 0.1%, 1% and 5%, respectively.

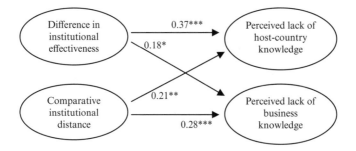

Note: ***, ** and * indicate significance levels of 0.1%, 1% and 5%, respectively.

Figure 10.2 The results of the OLS model for all assignments

the variable 'time span of assignment' to test whether the experience of the firm in the particular foreign market made a difference. In the second analysis, the sample was split along the variable 'number of countries with sales' in order to test the impact of internationalization experience outside the specific market. The results for the two analyses are shown in Table 10.2, columns 4–7 and 8–11. The key results are also shown in Figure 10.3, which demonstrates the relationship between the two independent variables of institutional distance and the two dependent variables of perceived lack of knowledge for the two split samples.

The supplementary analyses reinforce the observation that differences in institutional effectiveness mainly affect the perceived lack of host-country knowledge, while comparative institutional differences are mainly associated with a perceived lack of business knowledge. These relations are significant at the 5 per cent level in all of the tested cases. However, differences in institutional effectiveness only significantly affect the lack of business knowledge in the case of sales to a few countries, or in the case with little international experience. Similarly, comparative institutional distance only affects the lack of host-country knowledge in the case of sales to many countries, or with more extensive international experience.

In addition, the impact of differences in institutional effectiveness on the perceived lack of knowledge seems to decrease as experience increases. This is true both in terms of experience within the focal market (the coefficient drops from 0.46 to 0.21 when moving from a short to a long time span) and in terms of general internationalization experience (the coefficient drops from 0.47 to 0.32 when moving from sales in a few countries to sales in many countries). The effect of comparative institutional distance, on the other hand, is not affected by an increase in experience. In fact, the effect size of comparative institutional distance increases from 0.27 to 0.31 when moving from sales in a few countries to sales in many countries,

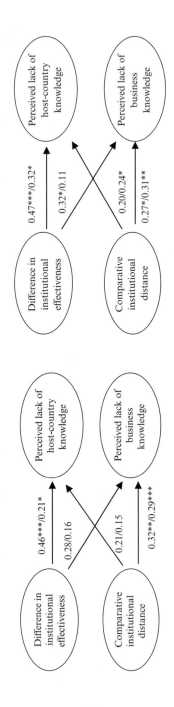

Figure 10.3 OLS results for split-sample models

which indicates that it remains important in determining the perceived lack of knowledge even when the firm acquires more experience.

In general, the results suggest that both types of institutional distance affect the perceived lack of knowledge in the foreign market but that they influence the two types of knowledge gaps in different ways. In particular, the factors captured by the comparative institutional distance measure seem to be much more persistent, as they remain even when experience increases, while the effects of differences in institutional effectiveness diminish with increasing experience.

10.6 DISCUSSION AND CONCLUSION

As we noted at the outset of this chapter, the growing general interest in institutions has fuelled a debate on how institutions matter for international business. Our objective in this chapter was to contribute to this debate by highlighting the plurality of institutional approaches that are currently used in international business research, and to sketch out how these approaches address and explain different aspects of international firm behaviour, and how they translate into different measures of institutional distance. Specifically, we have tried to highlight that whether and how institutions matter for international business depends on one's view of what constitutes 'institutions'. For instance, new institutional economics highlights the quality or effectiveness of countries' institutional frameworks and how those qualities affect such factors as the appropriateness of alternative governance forms. In contrast, new organizational institutional and comparative institutional perspectives highlight more substantive institutional differences among countries, albeit on different levels of analysis. This has implications for the appropriateness of alternative institutional distance measures and their explanatory powers.

We illustrated this point using an empirical illustration of the effects of two types of institutional distance measures – one that draws on new institutional economics and another that draws on comparative institutionalism – on a key construct in the internationalization literature, namely managers' perceived understanding of foreign host contexts (e.g. Eriksson et al. 1997; Johanson and Vahlne 1977). As our findings illustrate, the different types of institutional differences affect the development of local market knowledge in different ways. Differences in institutional effectiveness predominantly affect managers' perceived lack of host-country knowledge, while comparative institutional differences have a larger bearing on managers' perceived lack of business knowledge. Furthermore, while the effect of institutional effectiveness on such knowledge gaps diminishes with experience, comparative institutional differences, or differences in national business systems, gain in importance. This suggests that although differences in national business systems, or how economic activities are organized and controlled, may be less apparent to foreign entrants initially, in the long run they may pose larger challenges than differences related to the effectiveness of the institutional framework, such as governmental effectiveness and the level of corruption.

Although our empirical illustration is restricted to the analysis of a specific IB phenomenon, we hope it serves to highlight several important issues related to applying institutional theory to international business research. First, different institutional approaches differ considerably in their explanatory power. As international business research draws on multiple disciplines and addresses phenomena at different levels of analysis, different institutional approaches may have value in their own right. In other words, in exploring how institutions and institutional differences matter for IB, it may be worthwhile to move beyond conceptualizations of institutions as 'the rules of the game' to draw on other institutional traditions as well, such as comparative institutionalism or institutional ecology (see, e.g., Zhou and Van Witteloostuijn 2010). This may help to explain a broader range of international business phenomena or, as our analysis of comparative institutional differences and the development of local knowledge illustrates, lead to new insights into how institutions affect well-studied international business phenomena.

Second, although we favour institutional pluralism in international business research, the selection of institutional distance measures should not be driven by convenience. Rather, the selection of such measures must be explicitly justified in relation to the phenomenon to be explained. For instance, as work drawing on new organizational institutionalism suggests, the relative impact of rules, norms and values differs considerably from practice to practice. For example, US firms in Spain experience larger normative differences in entrepreneurship than in quality management (Busenitz et al. 2000; Kostova and Roth 2002). This means that while we can compile institutional profiles for individual practices, doing so for more general firm-level phenomena, which comprise practices from multiple domains, is less appropriate. Similarly, the use of secondary country-level data sources may fail to capture the normative and regulative pressures that affect the adoption of a particular practice.

Finally, our contribution supports repeated calls for the IB research community to consider comparative institutional differences more fully (e.g. Jackson and Deeg 2008b; Redding 2005). Although the literature on comparative institutionalism is extensive, intrinsic differences between developed market economies, such as France, the US and Germany, are rarely considered in quantitative IB studies. This may be the result of both a lack of familiarity with comparative institutionalism and the difficulty of obtaining appropriate indicators. In recent years, the use of measures derived from one strand of comparative institutionalism, the 'varieties of capitalism' approach (Hall and Soskice 2001; Hall and Gingerich 2004), has been on the rise (e.g. Fenton-O'Creevy et al. 2008; Witt and Lewin 2007). Although such measures are susceptible to the critique that there is considerable variety among more coordinated market economies (e.g. Amable 2003; Hancké et al. 2009), the increasing use of such measures reflects the growing recognition that the effects of comparative institutional differences remain underexplored. As our analysis illustrates, the development and inclusion of institutional distance measures that capture more subtle comparative institutional differences may hold considerable promise in further enriching our understanding of how institutions affect IB activities.

NOTES

1. The institutional approaches that are considered most dominant are, of course, dependent on the issue at hand, and on where the line is drawn between international business and other domains. Morgan and Kristensen (2006), for example, distinguish between organizational institutionalism and comparative institutionalism, which suits their discussion on the institutional duality within multinational enterprises (MNEs).
2. See for instance Vitold Henisz's website for a brief overview of different indices and resources, http://www.management.wharton.upenn.edu/henisz/.

REFERENCES

Aguilera, R.V. and G. Jackson (2003), 'The cross-national diversity of corporate governance: dimensions and determinants', *Academy of Management Review*, **28** (3), 447–465.
Amable, B. (2003), *The Diversity of Modern Capitalism*, New York: Oxford University Press.
Aoki, M. (2001), *Toward a Comparative Institutional Analysis*, Cambridge, MA: MIT Press.
Aulakh, P.S. (2007) 'Emerging multinationals from developing economies: motivations, paths and performance', *Journal of International Management*, **13** (3), 235–240.
Battilana, J., B. Leca and E. Boxenbaum (2009), 'How actors change institutions: towards a theory of institutional entrepreneurship', *Academy of Management Annals*, **3** (1), 65–107.
Brette, O. (2006), 'Expanding the dialogue between institutional economics and contemporary evolutionary economics: Veblen's methodology as a framework', *Journal of Economic Issues*, **40** (2), 493–500.
Broom, L. and P. Selznick (1955), *Sociology: A Text with Adapted Readings*, New York: Row, Peterson.
Busenitz, L.W., C. Gómez and J.W. Spencer (2000), 'Country institutional profiles: unlocking entrepreneurial phenomena', *Academy of Management Journal*, **43** (5), 994–1003.
Casper, S. (2000), 'Institutional adaptiveness, technology policy, and the diffusion of new business models: the case of German biotechnology', *Organization Studies*, **21** (5), 887–914.

Chakrabarty, S. (2009), 'The influence of national culture and institutional voids on family ownership of large firms: a country level empirical study', *Journal of International Management*, **15** (1), 32–45.

Chan, C.M., T. Isobe and S. Makino (2008), 'Which country matters? Institutional development and foreign affiliate performance', *Strategic Management Journal*, **29** (11), 1179–1205.

Chan, C.M. and S. Makino (2007), 'Legitimacy and multi-level institutional environments: implications for foreign subsidiary ownership structure', *Journal of International Business Studies*, **38**, 621–638.

Chetty, S., K. Eriksson and J. Lindbergh (2006), 'The effect of specificity of experience on a firm's perceived importance of institutional knowledge in an ongoing business', *Journal of International Business Studies*, **37** (5), 699–712.

Child, J. and S.B. Rodrigues (2005), 'The internationalization of Chinese firms: a case for theoretical extension?', *Management and Organization Review*, **1** (3), 381–410.

Clark, B.R. (1960), *The Open-Door Colleges: A Case Study*, New York: Prentice Hall.

Clark, B.R. (1972), 'The organizational saga in higher education', *Administrative Science Quarterly*, **17**, 178–184.

Coase, R.H. (1937), 'The nature of the firm', *Economica*, **4** (16), 386–405.

Coase, R. (1998), 'The new institutional economics', *American Economic Review*, **88** (2), 72–74.

Clougherty, J.A. and M. Grajek (2008), 'The impact of ISO 9000 diffusion on trade and FDI: a new institutional analysis', *Journal of International Business Studies*, **39** (4), 613–633.

Cuervo-Cazura, A. and M. Genc (2008), 'Transforming disadvantages into advantages: developing-country MNEs in the least developed countries', *Journal of International Business Studies*, **39**, 957–979.

Dacin, M.T., K. Munir and P. Tracey (2010), 'Formal dining at Cambridge colleges: linking ritual performance and institutional maintenance', *Academy of Management Journal*, **53** (6), 1393–1418.

Davis, P.S., A.B. Desai and J.D. Francis (2000), 'Mode of international entry: an isomorphism perspective', *Journal of International Business Studies*, **31** (2), 239–258.

Delios, A. and W.J. Henisz (2003), 'Political hazards, experience, and sequential entry strategies: the international expansion of Japanese firms, 1980–1998', *Strategic Management Journal*, **24** (11), 1153–1164.

Delios, A., D. Xu and P. Beamish (2008), 'Within-country product diversification and foreign subsidiary performance', *Journal of International Business Studies*, **39**, 706–724.

Denzau, A.T. and D.C. North (1994), 'Shared mental models: ideologies and institutions', *Kyklos*, **47** (1), 3–31.

Dequech, D. (2002), 'The demarcation between the "old" and the "new" institutional economics: recent complications', *Journal of Economic Issues*, **36** (2), 565–572.

Dikova, D. and A. van Witteloostuijn (2007), 'Foreign direct investment mode choice: entry and establishment modes in transition economies', *Journal of International Business Studies*, **38** (6), 1013–1033.

DiMaggio, P. (1988), 'Interest and agency in institutional theory', in L.G. Zucker (ed.), *Institutional Patterns and Organizations: Culture and Environment*, Cambridge, MA: Ballinger, pp. 3–21.

DiMaggio, P.J. and W.W. Powell (1983), 'The iron cage revisited: institutional isomorphism and collective rationality in organizational fields', *American Sociological Review*, **48** (2), 147–160.

DiMaggio, P.J. and W.W. Powell (1991), 'Introduction', in W.W. Powell and P.J. DiMaggio (eds), *The New Institutionalism in Organizational Analysis*, Chicago, IL: University of Chicago Press, pp. 1–38.

Djelic, M.L. and A. Ainamo (1999), 'The coevolution of new organizational forms in the fashion industry: a historical and comparative study of France, Italy, and the United States', *Organization Science*, **10** (5), 622–637.

Dörrenbächer, C. and M. Geppert (2006), 'Micro-politics and conflicts in multinational corporations: current debates, re-framing, and contributions of this special issue', *Journal of International Management*, **12** (3), 251–265.

Dörrenbächer, C. and M. Geppert (2009), 'A micro-political perspective on subsidiary initiative-taking: evidence from German-owned subsidiaries in France', *European Management Journal*, **27** (2), 100–112.

Dunning, J.H. (1989), 'The study of international business: A plea for a more interdisciplinary approach', *Journal of International Business Studies*, **20** (3), 411–436.

Eden, L. (2010), 'Letter from the editor-in-chief: lifting the veil on how institutions matter in IB research', *Journal of International Business Studies*, **41**, 175–177.

Emirbayer, M. and A. Mische (1998), 'What is agency?' *American Journal of Sociology*, **103** (4), 962–1023.

Eriksson, K., J. Johanson, A. Majkgård and D.D. Sharma (1997), 'Experiential knowledge and cost in the internationalization process', *Journal of International Business Studies*, **28** (2), 337–360.

Eriksson, K., J. Johanson, A. Majkgård and D.D. Sharma (2000), 'Effect of variation on knowledge accumulation in the internationalization process', *International Studies of Management and Organization*, **30** (1), 26–44.

Fenton-O'Creevy, M., P. Gooderham and O. Nordhaug (2008), 'Human resource management in US subsidiaries in Europe and Australia: centralisation or autonomy?' *Journal of International Business Studies*, **39**, 151–166.

Ferner, A. (1997), 'Country of origin effects and HRM in multinational companies', *Human Resource Management Journal*, **7** (1), 19–37.

Ferner, A., P. Almond and T. Colling (2005), 'Institutional theory and the cross-national transfer of employment policy: the case of "workforce diversity" in US multinationals', *Journal of International Business Studies*, **36** (3), 304–321.

Forsgren, M. and J. Johanson (1992), 'Managing internationalization in business networks', in M. Forsgren and J. Johanson (eds), *Managing Networks in International Business*, Philadelphia, PA: Gordon & Breach, pp. 1–16.

Friedland, R. and R.R. Alford (1991), 'Bringing society back in: symbols, practices, and institutional contradictions', in W.W. Powell and P.J. DiMaggio (eds), *The New Institutionalism in Organizational Analysis*, Chicago, IL: University of Chicago Press, pp. 232–263.

Garud, R., C. Hardy and S. Maguire (2007), 'Institutional entrepreneurship as embedded agency: An introduction to the special issue', *Organization Studies*, **28** (7), 957–969.

Gaur, A.S., A. Delios and K. Singh (2007), 'Institutional environments, staffing strategies, and subsidiary performance', *Journal of Management*, **33** (4), 611–636.

Glaeser, E.L., R. La Porta, F. Lopez-de-Silanes and A. Shleifer (2004), 'Do institutions cause growth?' *Journal of Economic Growth*, **9**, 271–303.

Greenwood, R. and C.R. Hinings (1996), 'Understanding radical organizational change: Bringing together the old and new institutionalism', *Academy of Management Review*, **21** (4), 1022–1054.

Greif, A. (1998), 'Historical and comparative institutional analysis', *American Economic Review*, **88** (2), 80–84.

Gu, Q. and J.W. Lu (2011), 'Effects of inward investment on outward investment: the venture capital industry worldwide 1985–2007', *Journal of International Business Studies*, **42**, 263–284.

Hall, P.A. and D.W. Gingerich (2004), 'Varieties of capitalism and institutional complementarities in the macroeconomy: an empirical analysis', Max-Planck-Institut für Gesellschaftsforschung Discussion Paper 04/5.

Hall, P.A. and D.W. Gingerich (2009), 'Varieties of capitalism and institutional complementarities in the political economy: an empirical analysis', *British Journal of Political Science*, **39**, 449–482.

Hall, P. and D. Soskice (2001), 'An introduction to varieties of capitalism', in P. Hall and D. Soskice (eds), *Varieties of Capitalism: The Institutional Foundations of Comparative Advantage*, Oxford: Oxford University Press, pp. 1–68.

Hancké, B. (2001), 'Revisiting the French model: coordination and restructuring in French industry', in P.A. Hall and D. Soskice (eds), *Varieties of Capitalism, The Institutional Foundations of Comparative Advantage*, Oxford: Oxford University Press, pp. 307–334.

Hancké, B., M. Rhodes and M. Thatcher (2007), 'Introduction: beyond *Varieties of Capitalism*', in B. Hancké, M. Rhodes and M. Thatcher (eds), *Beyond Varieties of Capitalism*, Oxford: Oxford University Press, pp. 3–39.

Hancké, B., M. Rhodes and M. Thatcher (2009), 'Beyond varieties of capitalism', in B. Hancké (ed.), *Debating Varieties of Capitalism: A Reader*, Oxford: Oxford University Press, pp. 273–300.

Harzing, A.-W. and A.M. Sorge (2003), 'The relative impact of country of origin and universal contingencies on internationalization strategies and corporate control in multinational enterprises: worldwide and European perspectives', *Organization Studies*, **24** (2), 187–214.

Haveman, H.A. (1993), 'Follow the leader: mimetic isomorphism and entry into new markets', *Administrative Science Quarterly*, **38** (4), 593–627.

Henisz, W.J. (2000), 'The institutional environment for multinational investment', *Journal of Law, Economics, and Organization*, **16** (2), 334–364.

Henisz, W.J. (2003), 'The power of the Buckley and Casson thesis: the ability to manage institutional idiosyncrasies', *Journal of International Business Studies*, **34** (2), 173–184.

Henisz, W. and A. Swaminathan (2008), 'Institutions and international business', *Journal of International Business Studies*, **39** (4), 537–539.

Hodgson, G.M. (1998), 'The approach of institutional economics', *Journal of Economic Literature*, **36** (1), 166–192.

Hodgson, G.M. (2003), 'Darwinism and institutional economics', *Journal of Economic Issues*, **37** (1), 85–97.

Hodgson, G.M. (2006), 'What are institutions?' *Journal of Economic Issues*, **40** (1), 1–255.

Hodgson, G.M. (2007), 'The revival of Veblenian institutional economics', *Journal of Economic Issues*, **41** (2), 325–340.

Holm, P. (1995), 'The dynamics of institutionalisation: transformation processes in Norwegian fisheries', *Administrative Science Quarterly*, **40**, 398–422.

Husted, B.W. and D.B. Allen (2006), 'Corporate social responsibility in the multinational enterprise: Strategic and institutional approaches', *Journal of International Business Studies*, **37**, 838–849.

Jackson, G. and R. Deeg (2008a), 'From comparing capitalisms to the politics of institutional change', *Review of International Political Economy*, **15** (4), 680–709.

Jackson, G. and R. Deeg (2008b), 'Comparing capitalisms: understanding institutional diversity and its implications for international business', *Journal of International Business Studies*, **39**, 540–561.

Johanson, J. and J.-E. Vahlne (1977), 'The internationalization process of the firm: a model of knowledge development and increasing foreign market commitments', *Journal of International Business Studies*, **8** (1), 23–32.

Joskow, P.L. (2008), 'New institutional economics: a report card', in É. Brusseah and J.-M. Glachant (eds), *New Institutional Economics: A Guidebook*, Cambridge: Cambridge University Press, pp. 1–19.

Kaufmann, D., A. Kraay and M. Mastruzzi (2005), 'Governance Matters IV: Governance Indicators for 1996–2004', World Bank Policy Research Working Paper #3630.

Kaufmann, D., A. Kraay and M. Mastruzzi (2007), 'Governance Matters VI: Aggregate and Individual Governance Indicators 1996–2006', World Bank Policy Research Working Paper #4280.

Kaufmann, D., A. Kraay and M. Mastruzzi (2009), 'Governance matters VIII: Aggregate and individual governance indicators 1996–2008', World Bank Policy Research Working Paper #4978.

Kaufmann, D., A. Kraay and M. Mastruzzi (2010), Worldwide Governance Indicators, http://info.worldbank.org/governance/wgi/index.asp.

Khanna, T., K.G. Palepu and J. Sinha (2005), 'Strategies that fit emerging markets', *Harvard Business Review*, **83** (6), 63–76.

Kostova, T. (1997), 'Country institutional profiles: concept and measurement', *Academy of Management Proceedings*, pp. 180–184.

Kostova, T. (1999), 'Transnational transfer of strategic organizational practices: a contextual perspective', *Academy of Management Review*, **24** (2), 308–324.

Kostova, T. and K. Roth (2002), 'Adoption of an organizational practice by subsidiaries of multinational corporations: institutional and relational effects', *Academy of Management Journal*, **45** (1), 215–233.

Kostova, T., K. Roth and M.T. Dacin (2008), 'Institutional theory in the study of multinational corporations: a critique and new directions', *Academy of Management Review*, **33** (4), 994–1006.

Kostova, T. and S. Zaheer (1999), 'Organizational legitimacy under conditions of complexity: the case of the multinational enterprise', *Academy of Management Review*, **24** (1), 64–81.

Kristensen, P.H. and G. Morgan (2007), 'Multinationals and institutional competitiveness', *Regulation and Governance*, **1** (3), 197–212.

Kristensen, P.H. and J. Zeitlin (2001), 'The making of a global firm: pathways to multinational enterprises', in G. Morgan, P.H. Kristensen and R. Whitley (eds), *The Multinational Firm: Organizing Across Institutional and National Divides*, Oxford: Oxford University Press, pp. 172–195.

Kristensen, P.H. and J. Zeitlin (2005), *Local Players in Global Games*, Oxford: Oxford University Press.

Kwok, C.C.Y. and S. Tadesse (2006), 'The MNC as an agent of change for host-country institutions: FDI and corruption', *Journal of International Business Studies*, **37** (6), 767–785.

Lane, C. and G. Wood (2009), 'Capitalist diversity and diversity within capitalism', *Economy and Society*, **38** (4), 531–551.

Lowndes, V. (1996), 'Varieties of new institutionalism: a critical appraisal', *Public Administration*, **74** (2), 181–197.

Luo, Y. and R.L. Tung (2007), 'International expansion of emerging market enterprises: a springboard perspective', *Journal of International Business Studies*, **38**, 481–498.

Mair, J. and I. Marti (2009), 'Entrepreneurship in and around institutional voids: a case study from Bangladesh', *Journal of Business Venturing*, **24** (5), 419–435.

March, J.G. (1999), *The Pursuit of Organizational Intelligence*, Oxford: Blackwell.

Matten, D. and M. Geppert (2004), 'Work systems in heavy engineering: the role of national culture and national institutions in multinational corporations', *Journal of International Management*, **10** (2), 177–198.

Maurice, M. (2000), 'The paradoxes of societal analysis: a review of the past and prospects for the future', in M. Maurice and A.M. Sorge (eds), *Embedding Organizations: Societal Analysis of Actors, Organizations, and Socio-Economic Content*, Amsterdam: John Benjamins, pp. 13–36.

Mayhew, A. (1989), 'Contrasting origins of the two institutionalisms: the social science context', *Review of Political Economy*, **1** (3), 319–333.

Ménard, C. and M.M. Shirley (2005), *Handbook of New Institutional Economics*, Dordrecht: Springer.

Meyer, K.E. (2001), 'Institutions, transaction costs, and entry mode choice in Eastern Europe', *Journal of International Business Studies*, **32** (2), 357–368.

Meyer, K., S. Estrin, S.K. Bhamik and M.W. Peng (2009), 'Institutions, resources, and entry strategies in emerging economies', *Strategic Management Journal*, **30** (1), 61–80.

Meyer, K.E. and M.W. Peng (2005), 'Probing theoretically into Central and Eastern Europe: transactions, resources, and institutions', *Journal of International Business Studies*, **36** (6), 600–621.

Meyer, J.W. and B. Rowan (1977), 'Institutionalized organizations: formal structure as myth and ceremony', *American Journal of Sociology*, **83** (2), 340–363.

Morgan, G. (2007), 'National business systems research: progress and prospects', *Scandinavian Journal of Management*, **23** (2), 127–145.

Morgan, G. (2009), 'Globalization, multinationals and institutional diversity', *Economy and Society*, **38** (4), 580–605.

Morgan, G. and P.H. Kristensen (2006), 'The contested space of multinationals: varieties of institutionalism, varieties of capitalism', *Human Relations*, **59** (11), 1467–1490.

Morgan, G. and S. Quack (2005), 'Institutional legacies and firm dynamics: the internationalisation of British and German law firms', *Organization Studies*, **26**, 1765–1785.

Morgan, G., R. Whitley and E. Moen (2005), *Changing Capitalisms? Internationalization, Institutional Change, and Systems of Economic Organization*, Oxford: Oxford University Press.

Myrdal, G. (1978), 'Institutional economics', *Journal of Economic Issues*, **12** (4), 771–783.

North, D.C. (1990), *Institutions, Institutional Change and Economic Performance*, Cambridge: Cambridge University Press.

North, D.C. (1991) 'Institutions', *Journal of Economic Perspectives*, **5** (1), 97–112.

Oliver, C. (1991), 'Strategic responses to institutional processes', *Academy of Management Review*, **16** (1), 145–179.

Oliver, C. (1992), 'The antecedents of deinstitutionalization', *Organization Studies*, **13** (4), 563–588.

Orr, R.J. and W.R. Scott (2008), 'Institutional exceptions on global projects: a process model', *Journal of International Business Studies*, **39**, 562–588.

Ostrom, E. (2005), *Understanding Institutional Diversity*, Princeton, NJ: Princeton University Press.

Pajunen, K. (2008), 'Institutions and inflows of foreign direct investment: a fuzzy-set analysis', *Journal of International Business Studies*, **39** (4), 652–669.

Peng, M.W., D.Y.L. Wang and Y. Jiang (2008), 'An institution-based view of international business strategy: a focus on emerging economies', *Journal of International Business Studies*, **39** (5), 920–936.

Petersen, B., T. Pedersen and M. Lyles (2008), 'Closing knowledge gaps in foreign markets', *Journal of International Business Studies*, **39**, 1097–1113.

Porter, M.E., J.D. Sachs, A.M. Warner, P.K. Cornelius, M. Levinson and K. Schwab (eds) (2000), *The Global Competitiveness Report 2000*. New York: Oxford University Press for World Economic Forum.

Potts, J. (2007), 'Evolutionary institutional economics', *Journal of Economic Issues*, **41** (2), 341–350.

Powell, W.W. and P.J. DiMaggio (1991), 'Introduction', in P.J. DiMaggio and W.W. Powell (eds), *The New Institutionalism in Organizational Analysis*, Chicago, IL: University of Chicago Press, pp. 1–38.

Ramsey, J.R. (2005), 'The role of other orientation on the relationship between institutional distance and expatriate adjustment', *Journal of International Management*, **11** (3), 377–396.

Rao, A.N., J.L. Pearce and K. Xin (2005), 'Governments, reciprocal exchange and trust among business associates', *Journal of International Business Studies*, **36** (1), 104–118.

Redding, G. (2005), 'The Thick description and comparison of societal systems of capitalism', *Journal of International Business Studies*, **36**, 123–155.

Rodriguez, P., K. Uhlenbruckand and L. Eden (2005), 'Government corruption and the entry strategies of multinationals', *Academy of Management Review*, **30** (2), 383–396.

Rosenzweig, P.M. and N. Nohria (1994), 'Influences on human resource management practices in multinational corporations', *Journal of International Business Studies*, **25** (2), 229–251.

Rosenzweig, P.M. and J.V. Singh (1991), 'Organizational environments and the multinational enterprise', *Academy of Management Review*, **16** (2), 340–361.

Saka, A. (2004), 'The cross-national diffusion of work systems: translation of Japanese operations in the UK', *Organization Studies*, **25** (2), 209–228.

Schneider, M.R., C. Schulze-Bentrop and M. Paunescu (2010), 'Mapping the institutional capital of high-tech firms: a fuzzy-set analysis of capitalist variety and export performance', *Journal of International Business Studies*, **41** (2), 246–266.

Scott, W.R. (1987), 'The adolescence of institutional theory', *Administrative Science Quarterly*, **32**, 493–511.

Scott, W.R. (1995), *Institutions and Organizations*, Thousand Oaks, CA: Sage.

Scott, W.R. (2008), 'Approaching adulthood: the maturing of institutional theory', *Theory and Society*, **37** (5), 427–442.

Selznick, P. (1949), *TVA and the Grass Roots*, Berkeley, CA: University of California Press.

Selznick, P. (1952), *The Organizational Weapon*, New York: McGraw-Hill.

Selznick, P. (1957), *Leadership in Administration*, New York: Harper & Row.

Selznick, P. (1996), 'Institutionalism "old" and "new"', *Administrative Science Quarterly*, **41**, 270–277.

Seo, M.-G. and W.E.D. Creed (2002), 'institutional contradictions, praxis, and institutional change: a dialectical perspective', *Academy of Management Review*, **27** (2), 222–247.

Shenkar, O. (2004), 'One more time: international business in a global economy', *Journal of International Business Studies*, **35**, 161–171.

Sorge, A.M. (2005), *The Global and the Local: Understanding the Dialectics of Business Systems*, Oxford: Oxford University Press.

Szyłowics, D. and T. Galvin (2010), 'Applying broader strokes: extending institutional perspectives and agendas for international entrepreneurship research', *International Business Review*, **19** (4), 317–332.

Toyne, B. and D. Nigh (1998), 'A more expansive view of international business', *Journal of International Business Studies*, **29** (4), 863–875.

Treviño, L.J. and F.G. Mixon (2004), 'Strategic factors affecting foreign direct investment decisions by multi-national enterprises in Latin America', *Journal of World Business*, **39** (3), 233–243.

Veblen, T. (1909), 'The limitations of marginal utility', *Journal of Political Economy*, **17** (9), 620–636.

Vora, D. and T. Kostova (2007), 'A model of dual organizational identification in the context of the multinational enterprise', *Journal of Organizational Behavior*, **28** (3), 327–350.

Wan, W.P. and R.E. Hoskisson (2003), 'Home country environments, corporate diversification strategies, and firm performance', *Academy of Management Journal*, **46** (1), 27–45.

Whitley, R. (1992), *European Business Systems; Firms and Markets in Their National Contexts*, London: Sage.

Whitley, R. (1994), 'Dominant forms of economic organization in market economies', *Organization Studies*, **15** (2), 153–182.

Whitley, R. (1998), 'Internationalization and varieties of capitalism: the limited effects of cross-national coordination of economic activities on the nature of business systems', *Review of International Political Economy*, **5** (3), 445–481.

Whitley, R. (1999), *Divergent Capitalisms: The Social Structuring and Change of Business Systems*, Oxford: Oxford University Press.

Whitley, R. (2000), 'The institutional structuring of innovation strategies: business systems, firm types and patterns of technical change in different market economies', *Organization Studies*, **21** (5), 855–886.

Whitley, R. (2003), 'From the search of universal correlations to the institutional structuring of economic organization and change: the development and future of organization studies', *Organization*, **10** (3), 481–501.

Whitley, R. (2005), 'How national are business systems? The role of states and complementary institutions in standardising systems of economic co-ordination and control at the national level', in G. Morgan, R. Whitley and E. Moen (eds), *Changing Capitalisms? Internationalization, Institutional Change, and Systems of Economic Organization*, Oxford: Oxford University Press, pp. 190–231.

Whitley, R. (2007), *Business Systems and Organizational Capabilities: The Institutional Structuring of Competitive Competences*, Oxford: Oxford University Press.

Williamson, O.E. (1975), *Markets and Hierarchies: Analysis and Antitrust Implications*, New York: Free Press.

Williamson, O.E. (2000), 'The new institutional economics: taking stock, looking ahead', *Journal of Economic Literature*, **38** (3), 595–613.

Witt, M.A. and A.Y. Lewin (2007), 'Outward foreign direct investment as escape response to home country institutional constraints', *Journal of International Business Studies*, **38**, 579–594.

Xu, D. and O. Shenkar (2002), 'Institutional distance and the multinational enterprise', *Academy of Management Review*, **27** (4), 608–618.

Yiu, D. and S. Makino (2002), 'The choice between joint venture and wholly owned subsidiary: an institutional perspective', *Organization Science*, **13** (6), 667–683.

Zhou, C. and A. Van Witteloostuijn (2010), 'Institutional constraints and ecological processes: evolution of foreign-invested enterprises in the Chinese construction industry, 1993–2006', *Journal of International Business Studies*, **41**, 539–556.

APPENDIX

Table 10A.1   Key institutional features and indicators

Key institutional features	Indicators*
The state	
Dominance of the state and its willingness to share risk	Independence of government policies from elites and special interest groups (3.05)
	The extent to which government subsidies promote competition (3.03)
State antagonism to collective intermediaries	The pervasiveness of industrial clusters and specialized institutions (10.16)
Extent of formal regulation of markets	The burden of regulation (3.01)
Financial systems	
Capital market or credit based	Access to external finance (8.04)
	The use of the stock market (8.11)
Skill development and control system	
Strength of public training system	The difference in the quality of schools available to rich and poor children (6.02)
Strength of independent trade unions	The extent of union power and influence (6.10)
Trust and authority relations	
Trust in formal institutions	Public trust of politicians (4.16)
Predominance of paternalistic authority relations	The willingness to delegate authority to subordinates (11.13)
	The extent to which management-worker relations are cooperative (6.09)

Notes: The institutional distance scores are based on data from the *Global Competitiveness Report* (Porter et al. 2000) and matched with the key institutional features of business systems identified by Whitley (1999). All scores range from 1 and 7. We invert the scores on union power for interpretation. We identified suitable indicators for all institutional subfeatures except the dominant organizing principle of unions, the extent to which bargaining is centralized and the extent to which communal norms govern authority relations.
*   Corresponding items in the Global Competitiveness Report 2000 are in parentheses.

Table 10A.2   Number of observations and calculated institutional distances for pairs of countries

Host country	Home country			
	Denmark	Finland	South Korea	New Zealand
Australia	0.3–3.2 (2)		3.1–2.7 (3)	0.6–2.2 (25)
Austria		0.6–3.8 (4)		
Belgium				1.4–3.8 (2)
Canada		0.5–4.3 (1)		
Czech Republic	2.6–6.0 (3)	2.7–7.2 (1)		2.7–4.7 (1)
Denmark		0.3–3.1 (4)		0.4–3.4 (1)
Finland				0.3–5.0 (3)
France	1.4–5.0 (7)	1.6–5.8 (1)	2.1–1.9 (2)	1.6–3.9 (3)
Germany	0.5–4.3 (38)	0.7–4.9 (14)		0.8–4.7 (1)
Greece	2.5–6.0 (2)	2.6–7.1 (1)	1.0–3.1 (2)	2.6–4.7 (1)
Holland	0.4–1.6 (1)	0.3–3.2 (5)	3.7–4.4 (2)	
Hungary	2.2–5.3 (1)	2.3–6.6 (4)		2.2–2.9 (1)
Ireland		0.8–5.4 (1)		
Italy	2.3–5.7 (2)	2.4–6.5 (1)	1.3–2.2 (2)	2.3–5.2 (2)
Japan	1.9–4.8 (5)	2.0–5.9 (4)	1.9–3.2 (6)	2.0–3.8 (8)
Mexico			1.6–3.4 (3)	
New Zealand			3.5–4.0 (1)	
Norway	0.3–2.5 (6)	0.5–4.2 (11)	3.4–4.8 (1)	
Poland	2.6–6.2 (12)	2.7–7.3 (6)	1.0–2.6 (2)	2.7–4.9 (1)
Portugal		1.4–6.1 (1)		

Table 10A.2 (continued)

Host country	Home country			
	Denmark	Finland	South Korea	New Zealand
South Korea	3.4–5.4	3.6–5.9		3.5–4.0
	(3)	(4)		(3)
Spain	1.4–4.4		2.2–2.2	1.5–2.8
	(5)		(4)	(1)
Sweden	0.3–2.7	0.5–4.2		
	(16)	(9)		
Switzerland	0.3–2.7	0.3–4.2	3.5–5.1	
	(2)	(5)	(1)	
Turkey	5.0–6.1	5.1–7.2		
	(2)	(2)		
UK	0.5–4.6	0.6–5.8	3.3–3.9	0.6–2.4
	(17)	(8)	(8)	(7)
US	0.7–4.8	0.8–6.1	2.8–3.7	0.8–3.1
	(21)	(6)	(28)	(20)
Total number of observations	152	93	64	76

Note: The difference in institutional effectiveness is listed first, the comparative institutional distance second. The number of observations is reported in parentheses.

11 The multinational enterprise, institutions and corruption

Martina McGuinness and Mehmet Demirbag

11.1 INTRODUCTION

Why should we be interested in examining institutions in international business research? Quite simply, institutions matter. Institutions are central features of the context within which firms make decisions about every aspect of organizational life. Organizations are not hermetically sealed entities. More problematically, but also more interestingly, they represent open systems existing within a wider environmental context comprising of a range of institutions, influences and actors which often exert different, and sometimes conflicting pressures upon the organization. The focus for this chapter is upon institutions from the perspective of the multinational enterprise (MNE). Specifically, we explore the topic of corruption and the impact that this has upon the MNE. It is impossible to address the issue without understanding corruption as an attribute of the institutional environment within which the MNE operates. As such, any discussion of corruption must first begin by reviewing institutional perspectives. In this way, it shall be made clear to the reader why, exactly, institutions matter and what might be the implications for the MNE facing the challenge posed by corruption.

11.2 INSTITUTIONAL THEORY AND THE MNE

The influence that institutions exert upon international business activity has long been recognized (Hymer 1976; North 1991, 1990). The actions of actors, particularly state actors, can affect the structure and operation of the markets within which firms operate. Institutions are 'the rules of the game' (North 1990, 3). More specifically:

> Institutions provide the framework within which human beings interact. They establish the cooperative and competitive relationships which constitute a society and more specifically an economic order . . . [They] are a set of rules, compliance procedures, and moral and ethical behavioural norms designed to

constrain the behaviour of individuals in the interests of maximizing the wealth or utility of principals. (North 1981, 201–202)

At a practical level, the domestic institutional context sets parameters which influence the structures, strategies and activities of business. This context can either add costs to the activities of the firm, or can facilitate organizational efficiencies, that is: 'institutions play a key role in the costs of production' (North 1990, 61). Stable and transparent institutions are significant in facilitating efficiencies in the internal leveraging of the heterogeneous organizational resources (Barney 1991; Wernerfelt 1984) together with the firm's external interactions with other actors (Porter 1981, 1980). There is a fundamental dynamic between institutions and the costs of doing business. As North himself states:

> My theory of institutions is constructed from a theory of human behaviour combined with a theory of the costs of transacting. When we combine them we can understand why institutions exist and what role they play in the functioning of societies. If we add a theory of production we can then analyse the role of institutions in the performance of economies. (North 1990, 27)

Having said that, reconciling the dual imperatives from institutions and costs can result in conflicts for the organization. For example, problems can arise when organizational attempts to promote efficiencies through coordination and control conflict with perceptions of institutional legitimacy (Meyer and Rowan 1977). This picture becomes yet more complex by virtue of the nature of the MNE itself, that is, an organization which operates multiple units in multiple environments (Westney and Zaheer 2003, 349) and which therefore must adapt simultaneously to these diverse institutional environments (Ghoshal and Bartlett 1990; Meyer et al. 2011; Nelson et al. 2007; Scott 1992).

Why does a firm engage in international production and invest in foreign territories; that is, what leads it to become a MNE? A range of different views have been espoused, including product lifecycle (Vernon 1966), oligopolistic interaction (Hymer 1976), knowledge management (Kogut and Zander 1993) and experiential learning (Johanson and Vahlne 1990). A dominant overarching perspective for explaining this process has been the search for efficiencies through the effective management of transaction costs:

> Transaction cost economics poses the problem of economic organization as a problem of contracting. A particular task is to be accomplished. It can be organized in any of several alternative ways. Explicit or implicit contract and support apparatus are associated with each. What are the costs? (Williamson 1985, 20)

Transaction cost theory is predicated upon the belief that firms operate within imperfectly structured markets. Consequently, firms organize their activities and interdependencies within these market structures in the manner which best enhances efficiencies and decreases transaction costs. Williamson (1979) points out that if transaction costs are negligible then the organization of economic activity is irrelevant. However, the reality is that the cost of any transaction is determined by the method chosen to organize it. Some methods offer greater efficiencies than others and therefore the associated transaction costs are less. One example of these includes hierarchical governance modes, typical of the MNE. These enhance efficiencies where the transaction costs of markets are high (Hoskisson et al. 2000). Through internalization, the MNE structure offers certain competitive advantages:

> the exploitation of firms' knowledge-based assets across national boundaries is often most efficiently undertaken internally within the hierarchical structure of the multinational enterprise. (Buckley and Strange 2011, 460)

Hennart (2003, 132) observes that MNEs prosper when they are more efficient than markets and contracts in organizing interdependencies between agents in different countries. In other words, MNES are able to internalize these exchanges rather than engaging in external market transactions, and thereby avoid additional transaction costs resulting from imperfect markets. However, this source of competitive advantage is not unfettered; certain constraints are imposed at the institutional level. Dunning and Rugman (1985, 230) capture, in a concise fashion, the double-edged sword faced by the MNE:

> The great advantage of being an MNE is the ability to use internal markets across nations. The MNE can use transfer prices, manoeuvre liquid assets, move around production facilities, and so on. In this way the MNE has greater degrees of freedom than a uni-national firm confined to one country. Yet, as an offset, the MNE faces environmental uncertainty as foreign governments can change the political, cultural, and social factors which determine its economic efficiency.

Internalization is one of the variables comprising the eclectic paradigm (Dunning 1988, 1980a, 1980b), one of the most influential models of the MNE. Dunning posits that a firm's propensity for foreign direct investment (FDI) lies in the interaction between internalization, location and ownership variables, that is:

> first, the extent to which it possesses (or can acquire, on more favourable terms) assets which its competitors (or potential competitors) do not possess; second,

whether it is in its interest to sell or lease these assets to other firms, or make use of – internalise – them itself; and third, how far it is profitable to exploit these assets in conjunction with the indigenous resources of foreign countries rather than those of the home country. (Dunning 1980b, 9)

Any examination of the eclectic paradigm soon reveals similarities with North's integrative approach. Dunning incorporates institutions as a variable that both influences, and is influenced by, the extent, content and quality of the resources, capabilities and market opportunities available. Thus, the specific ownership advantages possessed by the MNE can be characterized in terms of particular assets (ownership or exclusive access), the ability of the firm to coordinate efficiently the utilization of those assets and institutionally related competitive advantages, for example structural incentives (Dunning 2006). To illustrate, the eclectic paradigm recognizes the influence of both structural and transactional market imperfections on MNE location decisions (Dunning 1988). An example of structurally based market distortion which may act as an incentive or disincentive for FDI is government policy (Brewer 1993). The MNE can utilize internal markets to exploit positive structural imperfections, but its ability to moderate negative structural imperfections may be limited, dependent upon its asset-specific advantages. In certain cases involving significant structural upheaval, even these resource-based advantages may be to no avail. Structural upheavals, or unfamiliarity with institutional infrastructure across national boundaries, may lead the MNE to experience knowledge voids, or 'institutional exceptions' which interfere with its business activities and which require a response which is beyond the existing knowledge or experience of the organization (Orr and Scott 2008). This creates environmental uncertainty for the organization (Kobrin 1976, 1982; Miller 1992) which may necessitate ad hoc problem-solving resulting in additional transaction costs for the business. This places the MNE at a disadvantage vis-à-vis local competitors who do not encounter the same information vacuum due to their host-country knowledge or embeddedness.

Although MNEs possess certain firm-specific advantages which allow them to compete successfully with local firms, they are competing against firms which are in possession of greater knowledge of local markets, consumer preferences and business practices (Blomström and Sjöholm 1999). So, simply by virtue of operating in an alien locale, MNEs are subject to disadvantages which result in additional costs to the business, which local incumbents do not suffer. Attempts have been made to understand these disbenefits and cost implications more fully. Some commentators have focused upon market related costs of doing business abroad (CDBA) whilst others argue that there are more significant, and less easily quantifiable, costs associated with the social and institutional dimensions which result in a liability of foreignness (LOF) for the MNE (Eden and Miller 2004; Zaheer 2002, 1995).

Consequently, MNE survival and long-term success lies not simply in reconciling the sometimes contrary dynamics of transaction costs and institutional pressure, but doing so across national borders with the accompanying differences in institutional structures (Ghemawat 2007). It would be a mistake to view the MNE as a passive actor in a unidirectional relationship with institutional actors. MNEs are not simply reactive to institutional influence; through their activities they can also alter the institutional domain within which they operate (Dunning 2006). Although FDI can bring a direct financial injection to an economy, the longer-term benefits are of greater importance, particularly for less developed economies. These boons relate primarily to spillovers from FDI, and particularly technology spillovers (Blomström and Kokko 1998; Eden et al. 1997). It is this proprietary technology that provides the MNE's competitive advantage and which it seeks to exploit further through entry into a new territory. The impact of FDI spillover depends upon certain institutional factors, including the host-country policy context and the technology gap between home and host. One illustration of the former can be seen in ownership structures for MNEs, that is, requirements for MNEs to enter joint ventures with local partners (Blomström and Sjöholm 1999). Alternatively, some have argued that open trade policies encourage motivation and learning capabilities on the part of local incumbents in the face of foreign competition (Meyer and Sinani 2009). Ultimately, neither of these approaches may lead to seamless spillover where the technology gap between home and host is too large and consequently host firm learning is inhibited (Blomström and Sjöholm 1999; Meyer and Sinani 2009). However, what is clear from this discussion is that MNE investment has the potential to shape the institutional environment itself, that is, the MNE is moulded to a degree by the host domain, but so too is the local institutional environment shaped by FDI.

So far we have identified that the MNE is a particular form of business organization; a firm that crosses borders making foreign direct investment (Wilkins 2010, 641). At its heart is a specific type of business activity – international production. The MNE engages in FDI in order best to exploit ownership, location and internalization advantages over its competitors. This discussion has shown that a complete understanding of the business activity, and therefore the MNE itself, is only possible within an integrated framework which encompasses institutional and transaction cost theory. We shall now move on to examine this integrated framework in greater depth, using corruption as a vehicle to explore some of the complexities that arise as a result of this dynamic relationship and concomitant implications for MNE strategy, structure and decision-making.

11.3 INSTITUTIONS AND GOVERNANCE

MNEs play an important role in the economic growth of countries, particularly developing economies where they can stimulate a model of industrialization (Ozawa 2009). Although global FDI flows decreased drastically in 2009, FDI inflows still accounted for $1114 billion and FDI outflows $1101 billion. World Bank forecasts project growth in FDI inflows to $1.2 trillion, $1.3–1.5 trillion and $1.6–2 trillion in 2010, 2011 and 2012, respectively (UNCTAD 2010). Empirical work shows that the quality of institutional infrastructure impacts upon FDI flows (Kolstad and Villanger 2008; Mmieh and Owusu-Frimpong 2004; Stoian and Filippaios 2008). Institutions are socially constructed in nature and can be disaggregated into different dimensions – normative, regulative and cognitive-cultural – which facilitate and constrain social behaviour (Scott 2008, 1992).

Whilst these different institutional pillars may have different bases of compliance, order and legitimacy, these interrelating elements impact directly upon the behaviour of the organization. Some of these influences may be clearly defined and explicitly articulated, such as rules, laws and sanctions (regulative), but others are less transparent including values and norms (normative) and shared conceptions of social reality (cultural-cognitive).

Relating institutional perspectives explicitly to the MNE, Dunning stresses the importance of institutions in framing the ethos, attitudes and governance of the organizations responsible for resource and capability creation and utilization (Dunning 2006, 197). More particularly, Dunning and Lundan (2008) explicitly outline how institutions influence the MNE by outlining the relationship between institutional infrastructure and the ownership, location and internalization (OLI) paradigm. Formal institutions such as laws, regulations, conventions and discipline of economic markets directly impact on the organizational and governance aspect of the OLI framework. Similarly, both formal (laws, regulations, conventions) and informal institutions (traditions, social mores and civil society) affect the social capital aspect of location-specific advantages.

There is a clear synthesis of regulative, normative and cultural-cognitive perspectives in the OLI analytical framework presented by Dunning and Lundan (2008). The MNE is subject to a range of formal and informal influences. Some of these, for example laws and regulations, are more easily identifiable than others, for example culture, tradition and social mores. If regulative institutions are robust, they are more likely to be transparent and therefore the FDI decision is driven with less uncertainty (Miller 1993, 1992). However, this is more problematic with respect to the normative and cultural-cognitive institutional dimensions, which are less overt from the MNE perspective and may contribute to greater levels of uncertainty in the FDI decision.

11.3.1   The State

The state is critical to any understanding of institutions, as 'the basic services it provides are the underlying rules of the game' (North 1981, 24). It is the backbone of regulative governance. Or, as Hall and Soskice assert (2001a, 4):

> many of the most important institutional structures – notably systems of labour market regulation, of education and training, and of corporate governance – depend on the presence of regulatory regimes that are the preserve of the nation-state.

North distinguishes between contract and predatory (exploitation) theories of the state. The former emphasizes the state as the enhancer of efficient exchanges between agents (thus maximizing wealth for society), whilst the latter views the state as agent of a particular group of actors who seek to extract rents from constituents (thus maximizing the wealth of the group in control). However, these two viewpoints are not incompatible:

> It is the distribution of violence potential that reconciles them. The contract theory assumes an equal distribution of violence potential amongst the principals. The predatory theory assumes an unequal distribution. (North 1981, 22)

This typology places the security of property rights at the heart of institutional theory and the state. Property rights are 'the rights individuals appropriate over their own labour and the goods and services they possess' (North 1990, 33), and regulative institutions are at the forefront of ensuring property rights at all levels of society, from the individual to the corporate.

Any considerations of property rights leads to an assessment of the political, legal and economic institutions. Policy is a key determinant for FDI flows and the state is the pre-eminent actor directing political, legal and economic policy. Less developed countries have high market growth potential and this tends to be accompanied by less robust institutions with lower levels of property rights protection and enforcement mechanisms, lack of sophisticated intermediaries, and lower levels of political and financial stability (Makino et al. 2004). Through government policy these constraints can be ameliorated. Some less developed states, for example Hungary, have actively counteracted such institutional limitations through liberalizing policies and laws which explicitly secure property rights, and have managed to grow FDI successfully as a result (Akbar and McBride 2004). At the most basic level, state policy determines whether FDI is allowed into the host country. For example, it is possible to discern patterns of MNE investment in foreign manufacturing as a result of trade barriers (Dunning 2000, 1988). Incentives can be offered to encourage FDI. The *World Investment Report* (UNCTAD 1998) noted that during 1997, 151 changes in FDI regulatory regimes were made by 76 countries, 89 per cent of them in the direction of creating a more favourable environment for FDI, that is, attempts to encourage MNEs to invest. From the MNE point of view:

> the wider the attractions of a foreign rather than a home country production base, the greater the likelihood that an enterprise, given the incentive to do so, will engage in international production. (Dunning 1980b, 9)

The operative words above are 'given the incentive to do so'. As illustrated above, countries can attract FDI through a range of different institutionally based incentives. Conversely, the threat of state intervention can act as a disincentive to FDI through, for example expropriation (Durnev et al. 2010).

11.3.2 Varieties of Capitalism

The state paradigm can take a variety of forms with consequential diversity in the nature of the political economy. Hall and Soskice's (2001b) book, *Varieties of Capitalism*, was a watershed in debates around the nature and rationale of different forms of political economy. The authors moved beyond traditional interpretations of comparative capitalism such as modernization, neo-corporatism and social systems to offer 'a new framework for understanding the institutional similarities and differences among developed economies', with the firm at its centre (Hall and Soskice 2001a, 1). Arguing that firms are successful only if they can develop core competencies (Hamel and Prahalad 1996, 1993) or dynamic capabilities (Teece 1998; Teece et al. 1997), and that these capabilities are ultimately relational in nature, Hall and Soskice (2001a, 6–7) argue that there are a number of areas (industrial relations, vocational training and education, corporate governance, interfirm relations and employees) in which the firm must develop relationships in order to resolve coordination problems that can hamper these capabilities. The means by which firms coordinate these activities will vary according to the kind of market economy within which they operate, ranging across a continuum of liberal market to coordinated market economies, with different market economies characterized by different forms of institutional arrangements and actors. Consequently, at the heart of the 'varieties of capitalism' (VoC) framework:

> Institutions, organizations, and culture enter this analysis because of the support they provide for the relationships firms develop to resolve coordination problems. (Hall and Soskice 2001a, 9)

This support is primarily through facilitating cooperative behaviour among firms and actors through the exchange of information, monitoring, sanctioning of defection (from cooperative endeavour) and deliberation (pp. 10–12). These behaviours vary across different forms of political economies with their institutional diversity. Heterogeneity means different sets of coordinating institutions and consequential opportunities, or indeed threats, to the firm. As Hancké et al. summarize:

> The notions of 'complementarities' and 'system coordination' define the core of the VoC approach. Institutional subsystems (which govern capital, labour, and product markets) shape the evolution of political economies and often mutually reinforce each other. The presence of several 'correctly calibrated' subsystems increases the performance of the system as a whole, while producing specific adjustment paths in response to pressures for change. (Hancké et al. 2007, 3)

What implications might all this have for the MNE? At a fundamental level, these institutional subsystems directly influence firm-level attributes such as corporate governance, scope, competitive advantage and capacity for innovation (Carney et al. 2009). Hall and Gingerich (2004, 29) suggest that growth rates are higher where the political economy facilitates higher levels of market or strategic coordination, in comparison to a political economy with more variation or incoherence in types of coordination. Extrapolating from this, one might argue that MNEs are more likely to be attracted to countries that offer more attractive rates of growth. Wilkins (2010) also reflects on the notion of institutional heterogeneity which the VoC emphasizes. So, for example, she argues that it is the persistence of variations in, and the path-dependency of, national economies which explains why the presence of an MNE in a host country does not necessarily lead to international homogeneity in capitalist systems, even though expectations of FDI spillovers would logically lead to such a trend. MNEs adapt to different institutional imperatives, but not too much as this might prejudice the internal basis of their competitive advantage. Institutional diversity and levels of coordination have implications for the MNE and the host country in terms of their respective abilities to absorb ideas, adapt and learn from each other. If one views this aspect from the perspective of threats contained in the institutional domain, this means that when corruption is highly pervasive in the institutional environment, it in effect becomes another environmental dimension to be navigated by the MNE (Doh et al. 2003). Consequently, should the institutional system be coordinated by corruption and the subsystems reinforce corrupt activities across a range of institutional actors, this will lead to a particular set of 'path adjustments'.

It is possible also to differentiate not simply in terms of the institutional diversity of the political economy as typified by the VoC paradigm, but also in terms of the level of economic development of a country. One such typology distinguishes between developed, advanced emerging, secondary emerging and frontier markets (FTSE 2010). Levels of economic development can impact upon international business not least because they can be synonymous with weaker institutional development more broadly (Treisman 2000). Stronger institutions are likely to be associated with more secure property rights. The more robust legal and political institutions are, the lower are the risks associated with, and the costs of, enforcing contractual obligations agreed by business organizations. Empirically, contract enforcement in developing countries has been found to have a significant impact upon MNEs' FDI decisions (Alqhuist and Prakash 2010). North articulates this dynamic conceptually by juxtaposing Third World countries with advanced industrial nations as follows:

> The institutional infrastructure in the Third World lacks the formal structure (and enforcement) that underpins efficient markets. However, frequently there will exist in Third World countries informal sectors (in effect underground economies) that attempt to provide a structure for exchange. Such structure comes at high costs, however, because the lack of formal property right safeguards restricts activity to personalized exchange systems that can provide self-enforcing types of contracts. (North 1990, 67)

Implicit in North's reference to 'informal structures and underground economies' is corruption. Corrupt practices characterize the informal institutions which fill the void created by ill-functioning formal institutional infrastructure (Puffer et al. 2010). Over time, these informal structures create their own path-dependency. This has led some to argue that corruption can actually provide benefits to business by lowering transaction costs (Huntington 1968). Such an argument appears to fly in the face of received wisdom regarding the distortionary impact of corruption upon the efficient market exchanges. Moreover, it raises important questions about the nature of corruption itself, and how its related informal institutions, actors and activities impact upon the MNE. We shall now explore some of these issues.

11.3.3   Corruption: Sanding or Greasing the Wheels of Business?

In 1996, the President of the World Bank spoke of the need to tackle the 'cancer of corruption', clearly stating the view that corruption hinders the smooth running of business because 'corruption diverts resources from the poor to the rich, increases the cost of running businesses, distorts public expenditures, and deters foreign investors' (Wolfensohn 1996). Corruption has been found to be a significant variable in FDI decision-making (Busse and Hefeker 2007; Pfeffermann and Kisunko 1999). But what exactly do we mean by corruption?

It is useful to state, for the purposes of clarity, that we define corruption as the abuse (or misuse) of public power for private benefit (Collier 2002; Rodriguez et al. 2005; Treisman 2000; Uhlenbruck et al. 2006). Government corruption creates a whole range of direct costs to the MNE in the form of bribes, red tape, avoidance, the foregoing of market supporting institutions and engagement with organized crime. There are also general indirect costs such as reduced investment, distorted public expenditure, macroeconomic weakness and instability, weak infrastructure, squandered entrepreneurial talent and socio-economic failure which can impact upon business (Doh et al. 2003). Lack of transparency may also mean that these direct and indirect costs can be difficult for the MNE to judge or quantify (Calhoun 2002). Within corruption, it is possible to distinguish between two dimensions – pervasiveness and arbitrariness (Doh et al. 2003; Rodriguez et al. 2005). This is an important distinction to make, as these variables can exert significantly different influences upon FDI decision-making. They may also reflect particular dynamics across the different dimensions of institutional infrastructure, and specifically the relational elements which affect the MNE (Dunning and Lundan 2008; Hall and Soskice 2001b; Scott 2008).

Pervasiveness

Pervasiveness is 'the average firm's likelihood of encountering corruption in its normal transaction with state officials' (Rodriguez et al. 2005, 385) and it reflects 'the degree to which corruption is dispersed broadly throughout the public sector in a country' (Uhlenbruck et al. 2006, 403). The more pervasive, but centralized, is the corruption, the more clearly it can be seen by all parties. This has important implications for the MNE in terms of reducing the unpredictability of exchanges and associated transaction costs (Lee and Oh 2007). In effect, it may help to create a level playing field for competition. Although corruption is inherently secret, endemic corruption can lift this veil to a degree that firms can accurately incorporate this variable into transaction cost analysis. This is not to say that pervasive corruption has no meaningful effect. There are data to show that whilst corruption is beneficial for economic growth at low levels of incidence, it is detrimental at high levels of incidence (Méndez and Sepúlveda 2006). Furthermore, Zhao et al. (2003) found that corruption negatively affected FDI flows, disproportionately so when high levels of corruption were combined with a lack of transparency.

It is also possible to understand the dimension of pervasiveness from a social capital perspective (complementary to the VoC approach outlined previously). Revisiting North's (1990) work, we find that he identifies different types of exchanges: personalized, impersonal and impersonal with third-party enforcement. The first is typified by 'repeat dealing, cultural homogeneity (that is a common set of values), and a lack of third-party enforcement (and indeed little need for it)'; the second by constraints of institutional constructs such as kinship ties and bonding; and the third by coercive third-party enforcement. North argues that it is this final third-party enforced exchange that is a crucial fundamental of successful modern economies as it facilitates the complexity of exchanges and contracting synonymous with modern economic growth (North 1990, 34–35). The final form of exchange emphasizes the import of formal robust regulative infrastructure in developed economies, whilst the first two are predicated upon informal normative and cultural-cognitive dimensions in the context of less developed economies.

From this standpoint, it is easier to understand the basis and operation of embedded practices of *blat* and *guanxi*. These represent long-standing informal institutions based upon social networks of trust, expectation, kinship and reciprocity without requirements of enforcement (Tonoyan et al. 2010). Hsu (2005) argues that *guanxi* and *blat* came about because of the need to negotiate systemic scarcity and unresponsive institutions, that is, to fill institutional voids. Historically, such practices may have been perceived to be at the margins of abuse and their operation a mechanism for greasing the wheels of business (Hung 2008). More recently, these practices have become clearly perceived to be associated with corruption and, as such, impediments to efficient business exchanges (Fan 2002a; Hung 2008; Luo 2008). The MNE, lacking the network of local ties that may be available to host-country competitors, is at a significant disadvantage as these networks of bribery, reciprocity and nepotism may be less visible to a foreigner than other aspects of pervasive corruption. At worst, it seeks to enter a 'closed shop'; at best, entry is subject to unfamiliar and hard-to-calculate additional charges and/or exclusion from favourable contract terms, thereby reducing exchange efficiency.

Practices such as *guanxi* (Fan 2002b), *blat* (Ledeneva 2008; Rehn and Taalas 2004) and *wasta* (El-Said and Harrigan 2009; Loewe et al. 2008) are rooted within the informal normative and cultural-cognitive dimensions of particular paradigms of political economy, and thus are problematic to eradicate without sustained regulative focus and enforcement. It has been argued that they are more likely to dissipate as these less developed economies advance (Fan 2002b), and this reflects the move towards the more regulatively predicated, and coercively enforced, form of exchanges described as typical of modern economies by North.

Facing pervasive corruption, the MNE may find itself further constrained in its response by other institutional factors such as by ethical considerations (Rose-Ackerman 2002) which often reflect normative influences emanating from its home environment. Potentially, it is also subject to formal legal imperatives through home-country anti-corruption legislation such as the 1977 US Foreign Corrupt Practices Act or the more recent 2010 UK Bribery Act as well as transnational agreements such as the Organisation for Economic Co-operation and Development (OECD) Convention on Combating Bribery of Foreign Public Officials in International Business Transactions. These regulative instruments create risks of further, punitive, transaction costs for the MNE. Indeed there is evidence to indicate that laws against bribery abroad do act as a deterrent for organizations to engage in corruption in host domains (Cuervo-Cazurra 2008, 2006).

Arbitrariness
Differentiating a second dimension of corruption in terms of arbitrariness indicates the degree of uncertainty and capriciousness associated with public sector corruption (Uhlenbruck et al. 2006, 403). Government officials across the board charge, through the extraction of bribes, for goods which are officially owned by the state (Shleifer and Vishny 1998, 1993) either in a 'helping-hand' model where bureaucrats are corrupt but corruption is relatively limited and organized, or in a 'grabbing hand' model with large number of substantially independent bureaucrats pursuing their own agendas, including taking bribes (Frye and Shleifer 1997; Shleifer and Vishny 1998). The latter manifestation has much greater potential for unpredictability than the former. Rodriguez et al. (2005) argue that in situations of highly arbitrary corruption, transactions with government officials are riven with uncertainty as to the amount, target and number of corrupt payments necessary to obtain permissions, and therefore they

impede efficient transactions. High levels of arbitrariness also constrain the ability of organizations to learn what 'the rules of the game are' over time, as these are inconsistent and subject to the caprice of individual institutional agents. In turn, this has the potential to mitigate against increasing commitment to the host country through a process of experiential learning (Johanson and Vahlne 1990, 1977; Johanson and Wiedersheim-Paul 1975). Where arbitrariness is low, that is, corruption is pervasive but centralized, the margins of payment are clear and the services purchased through bribery can be expected to be delivered, bribery can be seen analogous to a form of taxation for business. It greases the wheels of industry and the mechanisms for payment are easily learnt. Conversely, highly arbitrary corruption sands the wheels, as unpredictability increases with respect to the amount of payment, to whom this is to be paid, and whether this shall result in the delivery of services (Lee and Oh 2007).

We can see then that in evaluating the impact of corruption upon the MNE, we must consider this in the context of the level of uncertainty that different forms of corruption might create for the organization. Effective institutions can be central to reducing MNE perceptions of environmental uncertainty (Demirbag et al. 2010). The higher the level of institutional instability and arbitrariness of corrupt practices, the greater the potential for additional transaction costs to be misjudged or ignored (Doh et al. 2003). Transparency can allay organizational disquiet, particularly in the form, stability and function of regulative infrastructures. In terms of paradigms of government, democracy has been found to improve the rule of law (Rigobon and Rodrik 2004). Part of the democratic paradigm includes independent institutions such the media and the courts. For example, an independent media can be a deterrent to corruption but a weak or colluding media can undermine attempts to deter corruption (Vaidya 2005). Most importantly, the rule of law underpins the enforcement of contracts and therefore property rights.

Writing about ex post costs of contract, Williamson (1985, 20) critiqued legal centralist assumptions that 'efficacious rules of law regarding contract disputes are in place and are applied by the courts in an informed, sophisticated, and low-cost way'. A similar argument is offered by North:

> A good deal of literature on transaction costs takes enforcement as a given, assuming either that it is perfect or that it is constantly imperfect. In fact, enforcement is seldom either, and the structure of enforcement mechanisms and the frequency and severity of imperfection play a major role in the costs of transacting and in the forms that contracts take. (North 1990, 154)

In reality, the existence of formal rules of law vary in form, structure and enforcement across different territories. The rule of law includes factors such as regulatory efficiency, public ethics and the effectiveness of dispute settlement procedures (Mia et al. 2007). For the MNE, robust legal infrastructure is of great importance, not least because the rule of law is a central device in securing property rights. For knowledge-intensive organizations, this may be of particular concern with respect to the protection of intellectual property rights. Evidence shows that reform of intellectual property rights has a positive effect on FDI flows (Branstetter et al. 2007; Khoury and Peng 2011). From this perspective, it is not surprising to see Hennart (2003) highlight the significance of the high costs of using the market when property rights are imperfectly defined and enforced. He argues that this factor is central to understanding the development of the MNE as an organizational form. In this respect, he suggests the MNE deviates from the traditional transaction cost explanation of the firm which emphasizes the centrality of asset specificity (Williamson 2005, 1981; Williamson and Winter 1991). However, it is perhaps more accurate to argue that the most successful MNEs are those which foster asset and transactional ownership advantages, and are most adept at capitalizing upon these (Dunning 1988, 3). These advantages may be negated by the existence of corruption which impedes contract enforcement. Legal enforceability increases the use of contract over relational reliability (Zhou and Poppo 2010). This allows the MNE greater flexibility in its choice of business partners which, in turn, means that this choice can be based upon exchange efficiencies rather than prior experience.

11.3.4   Corruption, Institutional Distance and Liability of Foreignness

Our discussion thus far has shown that institutions matter to the MNE because they provide the context within which transactions take place. When there is institutional failure, voids can arise which are filled by corrupt practices, resulting in uncertainty regarding transactions costs. This impacts upon the competitive position of the MNE. However, for the MNE, it is not simply a question of engagement with one country's institutional frameworks; instead the MNE finds itself navigating institutional imperatives in multiple territories. This adds a level of complexity in following the rules of the game because of differences across domains. The institutional domain of the host county is important for the MNE because of its unfamiliarity with the structures, culture and mores of the host country within which it is operating. Corruption is the reification of these structures, culture and mores. Institutional distance, that is, the degree to which there is significant difference between the institutional domain of the home and host country, potentially disadvantages the MNE vis-à-vis local incumbents (Eden and Miller 2004; Orr and Scott 2008). Due to its multiple embeddedness (Meyer et al. 2011), the MNE has to determine the rules of many different games and reconcile these with its organizational imperatives. As Eden and Miller observe (2004), 'distance matters'. It matters because it creates a liability of foreignness (LOF) for the MNE, and indeed a primary focus for LOF research is in finding effective mechanisms that can address these disadvantages faced by the MNE (Luo et al. 2002). However, the degree of LOF is not equally distributed across all types of MNE. It may vary according to the rationale underpinning the FDI decision, that is, whether FDI was market-seeking, resource-seeking, efficiency-seeking or strategic asset-seeking (Birkinshaw and Hood 1998; Dunning 2003).

LOF perspectives suggest that corruption is a powerful deterrent to FDI. Indeed, there is evidence to show that it impacts less upon local direct investment than FDI (Habib and Zuravicki 2002, 2001). However this may not always be the case. In the event that the business's home country is endemically corrupt, corruption in the host country may not be perceived as negative, and indeed the organization may actively seek to invest in host countries with prevalent corruption (Cuervo-Cazurra 2006). This suggests the significance of normative and cultural-cognitive institutional dimensions. Both psychic distance and experience can affect perceptions of uncertainty relating to corruption. Whilst often closely related to cultural distance, psychic distance does differ from it in that psychic distance reflects the perceiver's knowledge, familiarity and sense of understanding of a foreign country (Håkanson and Ambos 2010). Arguably this is a more useful instrument for making determinations regarding corruption distance (Duanmu 2011) than established cultural distance models such as Hofstede's model of national culture. Although widely utilized by researchers because of 'its clarity, parsimony, and resonance with managers' (Kirkman et al. 2006, 286), Hofstede's model does have certain limitations, which include: culture may be heterogeneous within a country; national culture is changeable; and the dimensions specified are overly simplistic (Sivakumar and Nakata 2001). Research on corruption distance indicates that FDI flows are much less from less corrupt to more corrupt counties, than they are between domains of similar high levels of corruption (Duanmu 2011; Wu 2006).

11.4   CONCLUSION

In this chapter we have shown the central role of institutions in the form and functioning of the MNE. A key challenge in understanding the relationship between the MNE and its institutional context arises from the diversity of the institutional domains within which it operates and the concomitant complex combinations of particular institutional factors (Pajunen 2008).

Countries with weaker institutions tend to be more corrupt than those with robust institutions. Increased corruption is a significant indicator of institutional inefficiency (Calhoun 2002), because weaker institutions lead to institutional voids which are filled by corrupt practices. This spans regulative, normative and cultural-cognitive dimensions. Robust regulative institutions such as government, policy and the rule of law are vital in enforcing contracts and protecting MNE property rights. Developed economies with established and effective regulatory mechanisms are less corrupt than emerging or transition economies. Paradigms of government, such as democracy, influence the effectiveness of institutional infrastructure. However, the process of modernization can actually lead to increases in corruption (Huntington 1968; Shleifer and Vishny 1998). Transition economies and emerging economies have been identified as particular examples (Puffer et al. 2010), and Russia (Rodriguez et al. 2005) and China (Hsu 2005) have been investigated as economies which are characterized by both pervasive and arbitrary corruption. These dangers reflect the instability arising from the dis-embedding and re-embedding of institutional infrastructure that such modernization involves. Consequently, whilst economic transition from poor to rich strongly reduces corruption, there may be a time lag during the modernization process which actually results in increases in corruption. In similar vein, it can be seen that instability and uncertainty associated with high inflation increases corruption (Paldam 2002). Research also shows that political stability is a key consideration for MNEs operating in developing countries (Vaaler 2008). This was manifested by elevated levels of risk as right-wing (or left-wing) incumbents looked likely to be replaced by left-wing (right-wing) challengers. As perceptions of risk increase, so the number of investment projects was found to decrease. This supports other data which indicates that managerial perceptions of uncertainty with respect to macroeconomic, political and government policy are crucial in determining FDI decisions because higher levels of uncertainty mean lower levels of predictability with respect to organizational performance (Miller 1993, 1992).

This chapter has highlighted key dynamics in the influence of institutions upon the MNE, which include: the difference between the formal and informal institutional structures between the home country (territory in which the MNE is headquartered) and the host (additional territory in which the MNE is operating); the additional costs that the MNE may incur due to institutional variation in the host environment; and the ability of the MNE to adapt effectively to institutional variation. We have utilized corruption as a vehicle for elucidating these variables of distance, transaction costs, and knowledge and experience because it 'warps' the rules of the game (Rodriguez et al. 2005). The study of corruption is an apposite focal point for considering the kaleidoscope of interacting and interlinked formal and informal structures and actors which comprise this rich and intricate mosaic of relationships. Equally importantly, the examination of corruption provides meaningful insights into efficiency and cost implications for the MNE arising from institutional failure.

REFERENCES

Akbar, Y.H. and J.B. McBride (2004), 'Multinational enterprise strategy, foreign direct investment and economic development: the case of the Hungarian banking industry', *Journal of World Business*, **39** (1), 89–106.

Alqhuist, J.S. and A. Prakash (2010), 'FDI and the costs of contract enforcement in developing countries', *Policy Sciences*, **43**, 181–200.

Barney, J.B. (1991), 'Firm resources and sustained competitive advantage', *Journal of Management*, **17** (1), 99–120.

Birkinshaw, J. and N. Hood (1998), 'Multinational subsidiary evolution: capability and charter change in foreign-owned subsidiary companies', *Academy of Management Review*, **23** (4), 773–95.

Blomström, M. and A. Kokko (1998), 'Multinational corporations and spillovers', *Journal of Economic Surveys*, **12** (3), 247–277.

Blomström, M. and F. Sjöholm (1999), 'Technology transfer and spillovers: does local participation with multinationals matter?' *European Economic Review*, **43** (4–6), 915–923.

Branstetter, L., R. Fisman, F. Foley and K. Saggi (2007), *Intellectual Property Rights, Imitation, and Foreign Direct Investment: Theory and Evidence*, Cambridge MA: National Bureau of Economic Research.

Brewer, T.L. (1993), 'Government policies, market imperfections, and foreign direct investment', *Journal of International Business Studies*, **24** (1), 101–120.

Buckley, P.J. and R. Strange (2011), 'The governance of the multinational enterprise: insights from internalization theory', *Journal of Management Studies*, **48** (2), 460–470.

Busse, M. and C. Hefeker (2007), 'Political risk, institutions and foreign direct investment', *European Journal of Political Economy*, **23** (2), 397–415.

Calhoun, M.A. (2002), 'Unpacking liability of foreignness: identifying culturally driven external and internal sources of liability for the foreign subsidiary', *Journal of International Management*, **8** (3), 301–321.

Carney, M., E. Gedajlovic and X. Yang (2009), 'Varieties of Asian capitalism: toward an institutional theory of Asian enterprise', *Asia Pacific Journal of Management*, **26** (3), 361–380.

Collier, M.W. (2002), 'Explaining corruption: an institutional choice approach', *Crime, Law and Social Change*, **38** (1), 1–32.

Cuervo-Cazurra, A. (2006), 'Who cares about corruption?' *Journal of International Business Studies*, **37** (6), 807–822.

Cuervo-Cazurra, A. (2008), 'The effectiveness of laws against bribery abroad', *Journal of International Business Studies*, **39** (4), 634–651.

Demirbag, M., M. McGuinness and H. Altay (2010), 'Perceptions of institutional environment and entry mode: FDI from an emerging country', *Management International Review*, **50** (2), 207–240.

Doh, J.P., P. Rodriguez, K. Uhlenbruck, J. Collins and L. Eden (2003), 'Coping with corruption in foreign markets', *Academy of Management Executive*, **17** (3), 114–127.

Duanmu, J.-L. (2011), 'The effect of corruption distance and market orientation on the ownership choice of MNEs: evidence from China', *Journal of International Management*, **17** (2), 162–174.

Dunning, J.H. (1980a), 'Explaining changing patterns of international production: in defense of the eclectic theory', *Oxford Bulletin of Economics and Statistics*, **41** (4), 269–295.

Dunning, J.H. (1980b), 'Toward an eclectic theory of international production: some empirical tests', *Journal of International Business Studies*, **11** (1), 9–31.

Dunning, J.H. (1988), 'The eclectic paradigm of international production: a restatement and some possible extensions', *Journal of International Business Studies*, **19** (1), 1–31.

Dunning, J.H. (2000), 'The impact of the completion of the European internal market on FDI', in J.H. Dunning (ed), *Regions, Globalization, And the Knowledge-Based Economy*, Oxford: Oxford University Press, pp. 131–169.

Dunning, J.H. (2003), 'The key literature on IB activities: 1960–2000', in A.M. Rugman and T.L. Brewer, (eds), *The Oxford Handbook of International Business*, Oxford: Oxford University Press, pp. 36–68.

Dunning, J.H. (2006), 'Towards a new paradigm of development: implications for the determinants of international business', *Transnational Corporations*, **15** (1), 173–227.

Dunning, J.H. and S. Lundan (2008), 'Institutions and the OLI paradigm of the multinational enterprise', *Asia Pacific Journal of Management*, **25** (4), 573–594.

Dunning, J.H. and A.M. Rugman (1985), 'The influence of Hymer's dissertation on the theory of foreign direct investment', *American Economic Review*, **75** (2), 228–232.

Durnev, A., V. Errunza and A. Molchanov (2010), 'Property rights protection, corporate transparency, and growth', *Journal of International Business Studies*, **40**, 1533–1562.

Eden, L., E. Levitas and R.J. Martinez (1997), 'The production, transfer and spillover of technology: comparing large and small multinationals as technology producers', *Small Business Economics*, **9** (1), 53–66.

Eden, L. and S.R. Miller (2004), 'Distance matters: liability of foreignness, institutional distance and ownership strategy', in M.A. Hitt and J.L.C. Cheng (eds), *Theories of the Multinational Enterprise: Diversity, Complexity and Relevance. Advances in International Management*, Oxford: Elsevier, pp. 187–221.

El-Said, H. and J. Harrigan (2009), '"You reap what you plant": social networks in the Arab world – the Hashemite Kingdom of Jordan', *World Development*, **37** (7), 1235–1249.

Fan, Y. (2002a), 'Ganxi's consequences: personal gains at social cost', *Journal of Business Ethics*, **38** (4), 371–380.

Fan, Y. (2002b), 'Questioning guanxi: definition, classification and implications', *International Business Review*, **11** (5), 543–561.

Frye, T. and A. Shleifer (1997), 'The invisible hand and the grabbing hand', *American Economic Review*, **87** (2), 354–358.

FTSE (2010), FTSE Global Equity Index Series Country Classification.

Ghemawat, P. (2007), *Redefining Global Strategy: Crossing Borders in a World Where Differences Still Matter*, Boston, MA: Harvard Business School Press.

Ghoshal, S. and C.A. Bartlett (1990), 'The multinational corporation as an interorganizational network', *Academy of Management Review*, **15** (4), 603–625.

Habib, M. and L. Zuravicki (2001), 'Country-level investments and the effect of corruption – some empirical evidence', *International Business Review*, **10** (6), 687–700.

Habib, M. and L. Zuravicki (2002), 'Corruption and foreign direct investment', *Journal of International Business Studies*, **33** (2), 291–307.

Håkanson, L. and B. Ambos (2010), 'The antecedents of psychic distance', *Journal of International Management*, **16** (3), 195–210.

Hall, P.A. and D. Gingerich (2004), *Varieties of Capitalism and Institutional Complementarities in the Macroeconomy: An Empirical Analysis*, Köln: Max Planck Institute for Study of Societies.

Hall, P.A. and D. Soskice (2001a), 'An introduction to varieties of capitalism', in P.A. Hall and D. Soskice (eds), 'Varieties of Capitalism', *The Institutional Foundations of Comparative Advantage*, Oxford: Oxford University Press, pp. 1–68.

Hall, P.A. and D. Soskice (eds) (2001b), *Varieties of Capitalism: The Institutional Foundations of Comparative Advantage*, Oxford: Oxford University Press.

Hamel, G. and C.K. Prahalad (1993), 'Strategy as stretch and leverage', *Harvard Business Review*, **71** (2), 76–85.

Hamel, G. and C.K. Prahalad (1996), *Competing For The Future*, Boston, MA: Harvard Business School Press.

Hancké, B., M. Rhodes and M. Thatcher (2007), 'Introduction: beyond varieties of capitalism', in B. Hancké, M. Rhodes and M. Thatcher (eds), *Beyond Varieties of Capitalism: Conflict, Contradictions, and Complementarities in the European Economy*, Oxford: Oxford University Press, pp. 1–38.

Hennart, J.-F. (2003), 'Theories of the multinational enterprise', in A.M. Rugman and T.L. Brewer (eds), *The Oxford Handbook of International Business*, Oxford: Oxford University Press, pp. 127–149.

Hoskisson, R.E., L. Eden, C.M. Lau and M. Wright (2000), 'Strategy in emerging economies', *Academy of Management Journal*, **43** (3), 249–258.

Hsu, C.L. (2005), 'Capitalism without contracts versus capitalists without capitalism: comparing the influence of Chinese guanxi and Russian blat on marketization', *Communist and Post-Communist Studies*, **38** (3), 309–327.

Hung, H. (2008), 'Normalized collective corruption in a transitional economy: small treasuries in large Chinese enterprises', *Journal of Business Ethics*, **79** (1–2), 69–83.

Huntington, S.P. (1968), *Political order in Changing Societies*, New Haven, CT: Yale University Press.

Hymer, S.H. (1976), *The International Operations of National Firms: A Study of Direct Foreign Investment*, Cambridge, MA: MIT Press.

Johanson, J. and J.-E. Vahlne (1977), 'The internationalization process of the firm: a model of knowledge development on increasing foreign commitments', *Journal of International Business Studies*, **8** (1), 23–32.

Johanson, J. and J. Vahlne (1990), 'The mechanism of internationalisation', *International Marketing Review*, **7** (4), 11–24.

Johanson, J. and F. Wiedersheim-Paul (1975), 'The internationalization of the firm – four Swedish cases', *Journal of Management Studies*, **12** (3), 305–322.

Khoury, T.A. and M.W. Peng (2011), 'Does institutional reform of intellectual property rights lead to more inbound FDI? Evidence from Latin America and the Caribbean', *Journal of World Business*, **46** (3), 337–345.

Kirkman, B.L., K.B. Lowe and C.B. Gibson (2006), 'A quarter century of "culture's consequences": a review of empirical research incorporating Hofstede's cultural values framework', *Journal of International Business Studies*, **37** (3), 285–320.

Kobrin, S.J. (1976), 'The environmental determinants of foreign direct manufacturing investment: an ex post empirical analysis', *Journal of International Business Studies*, **7** (2), 29–42.

Kobrin, S.J. (1982), *Managing Political Risk Assessments: Strategic Response To Environmental Change*, Berkeley, CA: University of California Press.

Kogut, B. and U. Zander (1993), 'Knowledge of the firm and the evolutionary theory of the multinational corporation', *Journal of International Business Studies*, **24** (4), 625–645.

Kolstad, I. and E. Villanger (2008), 'Determinants of foreign direct investment in services', *European Journal of Political Economy*, **24** (2), 518–533.

Ledeneva, A. (2008), 'Blat and guanxi: informal practices in Russia and China', *Comparative Studies in Society and History*, **50** (1), 118–144.

Lee, S.-H. and K. Oh (2007), 'Corruption in Asia: pervasiveness and arbitrariness', *Asia Pacific Journal of Management*, **24** (1), 97–114.

Loewe, M., J. Blume and J. Speer (2008), 'How favoritism affects the business climate: empirical evidence from Jordan', *Middle East Journal*, **62** (2), 259–276.

Luo, Y. (2008), 'The changing Chinese culture and business behavior: the perspective of intertwinement between guanxi and corruption', *International Business Review*, **17** (2), 188–193.

Luo, Y., O. Shenkar and M.K. Nyaw (2002), 'Mitigating liabilities of foreignness: defensive versus offensive approaches', *Journal of International Management*, **8** (3), 283–300.

Makino, S., P.W. Beamish and N.B. Zhao (2004), 'The characteristics and performance of Japanese FDI in less developed and developed countries', *Journal of World Business*, **39** (4), 377–392.

Méndez, F. and F. Sepúlveda (2006), 'Corruption, growth and political regimes: cross country evidence', *European Journal of Political Economy*, **22** (1), 82–98.

Meyer, J.W. and B. Rowan (1977), 'Institutionalized organizations: formal structure as myth and ceremony', *American Journal of Sociology*, **83** (2), 340–363.

Meyer, K.E., R. Mudambi and R. Narula (2011), 'Multinational enterprises and local contexts: the opportunities and challenges of multiple embeddedness', *Journal of Management Studies*, **48** (2), 235–252.

Meyer, K.E. and E. Sinani (2009), 'When and where does foreign direct investment generate positive spillovers? A meta-analysis', *Journal of International Busines Studies*, **40**, 1075–1094.

Mia, I., J. Estrada and T. Geiger (2007), *Benchmarking National Attractiveness for Private Investment in Latin American Infrastructure*, Geneva: World Economic Forum.

Miller, K.D. (1992), 'A framework for integrated risk management in international business', *Journal of International Business Studies*, **23** (2), 311–331.

Miller, K.D. (1993), 'Industry and country effects on managers' perceptions of environmental uncertainties', *Journal of International Business Studies*, **24** (4), 693–714.

Mmieh, F. and N. Owusu-Frimpong (2004), 'State policies and the challenges in attracting foreign direct investment: a review of the Ghana experience', *Thunderbird International Business Review*, **46** (5), 575–600.

Nelson, D.R., W.N. Adger and K. Brown (2007), 'Adaptation to environmental change: Contributions of a resilience framework', *Annual Review of Environment and Resources*, **32**, 395–419.

North, D.C. (1981), *Structure and Change in Economic History*, New York: W.W. Norton & Co.

North, D.C. (1990), *Institutions, Institutional Change And Economic Performance*, Cambridge: Cambridge University Press.

North, D.C. (1991), 'Institutions', *Journal of Economic Perspectives*, **5** (1), 97–112.

Orr, R.J. and W.R. Scott (2008), 'Institutional exceptions on global projects: a process model', *Journal of International Business Studies*, **39** (4), 562–588.

Ozawa, T. (2009), 'The role of multinationals in sparking industrialization: from "infant industry protection" to "FDI-led industrial take-off"', *Columbia FDI Perspectives*, **39**, http://www.vcc.columbia.edu/files/vale/print/Ozawa_FINAL.pdf.

Pajunen, K. (2008), 'Institutions and inflows of foreign direct investment: a fuzzy-set analysis', *Journal of International Business Studies*, **39** (4), 652–669.

Paldam, M. (2002), 'The cross-country pattern of corruption: economics, culture and the seesaw dynamics', *European Journal of Political Economy*, **18** (2), 215–240.

Pfeffermann, G. and G. Kisunko (1999), *Perceived Obstacles to Doing Business: Worldwide Survey Results*, Washington, DC: International Finance Corporation/World Bank Group.

Porter, M.E. (1980), *Competitive Strategy*, New York: FreePress.

Porter, M.E. (1981), 'The contributions of industrial organization to strategic management', *Academy of Management Review*, **6** (4), 609–620.

Puffer, S.M., D.J. McCarthy and M. Boisot (2010), 'Entrepreneurship in Russia and China: the impact of formal institutional voids', *Entrepreneurship Theory and Practice*, **34** (3), 441–467.

Rehn, A. and S. Taalas (2004), '"Znakomstva I Svyazi" – (Acquaintances and connections) – Blat, the Soviet Union, and mundane entrepreneurship', *Entrepreneurship and Regional Development*, **16** (3), 235–250.

Rigobon, R. and D. Rodrik (2004), 'Rule of law, democracy, openess, and income: estimating the interrelationships', Cambridge, MA: National Bureau of Economic Research.

Rodriguez, P., K. Uhlenbruck and L. Eden (2005), 'Government corruption and the entry strategies of multinationals', *Academy of Management Review*, **30** (2), 383–396.

Rose-Ackerman, S. (2002), '"Grand" corruption and the ethics of global business', *Journal of Banking and Finance*, **26** (9), 1889–1918.

Scott, W.R. (1992), *Organizations: Rational, Natural and Open Systems*, 3rd edn, Englewood Cliffs, NJ: Prentice Hall.

Scott, W.R. (2008), *Institutions and Organizations*, 3rd edn, Los Angeles, CA: Sage Publications.

Shleifer, A. and R.W. Vishny (1993), 'Corruption', *Quarterly Journal of Economics*, **108** (3), 599–617.

Shleifer, A. and R.W. Vishny (1998), *The Grabbing Hand: Government Pathologies and Their Cures*, Boston, MA: Harvard University Press.

Sivakumar, K. and C. Nakata (2001), 'The stampede toward Hofstede's framework: avoiding the sample design pit in cross-cultural research', *Journal of International Business Studies*, **32** (3), 555–574.

Stoian, C. and F. Filippaios (2008), 'Dunning's eclectic paradigm: a holistic, yet context specific framework for analysing the determinants of outward FDI. Evidence from international Greek investments', *International Business Review*, **17** (3), 349–367.

Teece, D.J. (1998), 'Capturing value from knowledge assets: the New Economy, markets for know-how, and intangible assets', *California Management Review*, **40**, 55–79.

Teece, D.J., G. Pisano and A.S. Shuen (1997), 'Dynamic capabilities and strategic management', *Strategic Management Journal*, **18** (7), 509–533.

Tonoyan, V., R. Strohmeyer, M. Habib and M. Perlitz (2010), 'Corruption and entrepreneurship: how formal and informal institutions shape small firm behavior in transition and mature market economies', *Entrepreneurship Theory and Practice*, **34** (5), 803–832.

Treisman, D. (2000), 'The causes of corruption: a cross-national study', *Journal of Public Economics*, **76** (3), 399–457.

Uhlenbruck, K., P. Rodriguez, J. Doh and L. Eden (2006), 'The impact of corruption on entry strategy: evidence from telecommunication projects in emerging economies', *Organization Science*, **17** (3), 402–414.

UNCTAD (1998), *World Investment Report 1998: Trends and Determinants*, New York, USA and Geneva, Switzerland: United Nations.

UNCTAD (2010), *World Investment Report: Investing in a Low Carbon Economy*, New York: UNCTAD.

Vaaler, P.M. (2008), 'How do MNCs vote in developing country elections?' *Academy of Management Journal*, **51** (1), 21–43.

Vaidya, S. (2005), 'Corruption in the media's gaze', *European Journal of Political Economy*, **21** (3), 667–687.

Vernon, R. (1966), 'International investment and international trade in the product cycle', *Quarterly Journal of Economics*, **80** (2), 190–207.

Wernerfelt, B. (1984), 'A resource-based view of the firm', *Strategic Management Journal*, **5**, 171–180.

Westney, D.E. and S. Zaheer (2003), 'The multinational entreprise as an organization', in A.M. Rugman and T.L. Brewer (eds), *The Oxford Handbook of International Business*, Oxford: Oxford University Press, pp. 349–379.

Wilkins, M. (2010), 'Multinational enterprises and the varieties of capitalism', *Business History Review*, **84** (4), 638–645.

Williamson, O.E. (1979), 'Transaction-cost economics: the governance of contractual relations', *Journal of Law and Economics*, **22** (2), 233–261.

Williamson, O.E. (1981), 'The economics of organization: the transaction cost approach', *American Journal of Sociology*, **87**(3), 548–577

Williamson, O.E. (1985), *The Economic Institutions Of Capitalism*, London: Collier Macmillan.

Williamson, O.E. (2005), 'The economics of governance', *American Economic Review*, **95** (2), 1–18.

Williamson, O.E. and S.G. Winter (eds). (1991), *The Nature of the Firm*, Oxford: Oxford University Press.

Wolfensohn, J.W. (1996), Speech to the World Bank/IMF annual meeting, 1 October.

Wu, S.Y. (2006), 'Corruption and cross-border investment by multinational firms', *Journal of Comparative Economics*, **34** (4), 839–856.

Zaheer, S. (1995), 'Overcoming the liability of foreignness', *Academy of Management Journal*, **38** (2), 341–363.

Zaheer, S. (2002), 'The liability of foreignness, redux: a commentary', *Journal of International Management*, **8** (3), 351–358.

Zhao, H.H., S.H. Kim and J. Du (2003), 'The impact of corruption and transparency on foreign direct investment: an empirical analysis', *Management International Review*, **43** (1), 41–62.

Zhou, K.Z. and L. Poppo (2010), 'Exchange hazards, relational reliability, and contracts in China: the contingent role of legal enforceability', *Journal of International Business Studies*, **41** (5), 861–881.

PART II

INSTITUTIONS AND CONTEXT: DEVELOPED ECONOMIES

12 The role of the MNE headquarters in subsidiary innovation: an institutional perspective
Kieran M. Conroy and David G. Collings

12.1 INTRODUCTION

In the dynamic and turbulent environment which characterizes the modern business world, the capability to identify innovations within the multinational enterprise (MNE) and transfer these across its international operations is considered central to the competitive positioning of the MNE (Gammelgaard et al. 2004; Gupta and Govindarajan 1991). As Taylor et al. (2007, 337) note: 'leveraging internal knowledge and innovation enables the firm to take advantage of its worldwide access to information, learning and creativity to improve its competitive offerings in products or services'. A key question that emerges in this regard however concerns the relationship between the multinational headquarters (HQ) and the focal subsidiary in the subsidiary innovation process. More specifically, what is the role of the HQ in subsidiary innovation processes? This question has heretofore not been a major concern in mainstream theories of the MNE (Ciabuschi et al. 2011). This chapter engages with this important question, drawing insights largely from the institutional perspective.

It is now commonly recognized that MNE innovation processes are largely context-specific, diversified activities carried out by different units in distinct institutional environments (Almeida and Phene 2004, 2008; Andersson et al. 2007; Asakawa 2001; Birkinshaw and Hood 1998; Doz and Prahalad 1981; Frost 2001; Ghoshal and Bartlett 1988; Hedlund 1986; Mudambi and Navarra 2004; Rugman and Verbeke 2001). In order for value creation to take place through subsidiary innovation we argue that knowledge absorbed from the subsidiary's local host environment must be combined or balanced with knowledge leveraged from within the MNE (Kogut and Zander 1992). This argument resonates with recent developments in the study of the MNE subsidiary environment through the institutional lens (Kostova and Zaheer 1999; Kostova and Roth 2002). Institutional theory highlights that MNE subsidiaries operate in dual institutional contexts where they face pressures to conform to the rules, laws, values and norms in both the host and home countries, regardless of efficiency effects (Forsgren 2008; Rosenzweig and Singh 1991). However there is a growing realization that if a balance is not achieved between these conflicting pressures then the subsidiary will not be able to act effectively as a knowledge bridge between the two distinct institutional environments, meaning that its potential for innovation will be significantly reduced. After all, as Schumpeter suggests, innovation takes place by 'carrying out new combinations' (1934, 65). Therefore, recent years have seen the burgeoning of empirical research into subsidiary roles and inter-unit knowledge transfer in the MNE, while at the same time scholarly interest in the role that the HQ plays in subsidiary innovation has decreased (Barner-Rasmussen et al. 2010). The subsidiary's external environment has more recently been portrayed as a far more powerful explanatory variable for the transfer of subsidiary knowledge within the MNE than the shared values between the subsidiary and HQ. This has led some scholars to question the role of the HQ in subsidiary innovation processes, arguing that they could have a negative rather than a positive effect on these developments (Ciabuschi et al. 2011).

Through an institutional lens, the most important determinant of subsidiary innovation in the differentiated MNE is the role that the subsidiary plays in balancing 'bringing the environment back in' (Pfeffer 1981) while simultaneously bringing 'HQ management back out' (Andersson et al. 2002). Because of the spatial and operational diversity of the MNE, this bridging role is especially relevant for the future development of innovation studies in the MNE (Andersson et al. 2002). Some scholars have argued that this balancing role is what constitutes the most relevant aspect of the 'multinational advantage' (Almeida and Phene 2008; Andersson et al. 2002; Barner-Rasmussen et al. 2010). Therefore the central argument of this chapter is that the most unique characteristic of the subsidiary innovation process is the maintenance of a dual position in two 'knowledge communities' (Davis and Meyer 2004; Frost 2001), with the effective balancing of the institutional pressures of this duality central to the success of the innovation process.

The chapter begins by briefly discussing how the evolution of thinking on MNE innovation has been driven by a number of emerging perspectives, resulting in an increased emphasis on the way in which the MNE subsidiary innovates in its local host environment. Subsequently, the business network approach to MNE innovation has allowed for the emergence of other theories that place more emphasis on the distinctive nature of the MNE subsidiary's institutional environments. This chapter will chronicle the application of institutional theory to the MNE and highlight its usefulness as a lens to broaden our conceptualizations of MNE subsidiary innovation. It will show how the increased focus on the MNE subsidiary environment has led to a diminishing view of the role of the HQ in subsidiary innovation processes. It concludes with the argument that subsidiary innovativeness can be improved by the subsidiary playing a bridging role between its dual institutional contexts.

12.2 EVOLUTION OF PERSPECTIVES ON THE MNE

Innovation can be 'an idea, practice or object that is perceived as new by an individual or other unit' (Rogers 2003, 12). Subsidiary innovativeness can be measured by the number of innovations it adopts or the pace at which these new innovations are developed (Damanpour and Gopalakrishnan 2001). The nature of the MNE's structural relationship with its subsidiaries has been the subject of considerable debate and empirical study over recent decades (Barner-Rasmussen et al. 2010; Birkinshaw 1995; Birkinshaw and Hood 2001). Conventionally, innovation in multinational firms has been understood as the domain of the parent organization located in the home base of the firm (Porter 1990; Vernon 1966). The MNE headquarters has been regarded as the 'brain of the firm' (Hedlund 1986, 19) or the 'commander-in-chief' (Forsgren et al. 2005, 185) which directs operations, assigns subsidiary roles, controls the transfer of innovations and steers the organization in a paternalistic fashion (Birkinshaw and Hood 2001). This perspective emphasizes the fit between corporate strategy, organizational design and the external environment, and has also been referred to as 'rationalistic' (Morgan and Kristensen 2006) or 'mainstream' (Dorrenbacher and Geppert 2006). This perspective very much resonates with the ethnocentric (Perlmutter 1969) or global (Bartlett and Ghoshal 1998) MNEs where HQ knowledge and approaches were perceived to be superior.

In the early 1970s and 1980s the business network perspective introduced a form of 'expansionism' (Birkinshaw and Hood 2001), which looked beyond the control that the internal MNE had over its different units and incorporated the influence that the subsidiary's external business environment had over it, mainly in the form of its business networks in local host countries (Andersson et al. 2002, 2007; Frost 2001). Further changes in the structure of the global economy combined with an apparent trend towards internationalization of the research and development (R&D) function within the MNE motivated researchers to treat more seriously the possibility that the different units within the MNE could play an important role as sources of innovations (Asakawa 2001; Bartlett and Ghoshal 1989; Hedlund 1986). As a result these emerging perspectives began to challenge the outdated design view and its notion of the MNE as a unitary rational actor, masterminded by the grand organizational plan of the headquarters (Barner-Rasmussen et al. 2010; Ciabuschi et al. 2010). It became apparent that the competitive advantage of the MNE as a whole was to a large extent dependent on the innovative activities of its geographically dispersed subsidiaries (Almeida and Phene 2008). Headquarters' role was recast to optimize communication channels and cooperation whilst maximizing the number of co-located activities and minimizing the costs of distance between interdependent subsidiaries. A number of different terms were utilized to portray the focus on the differentiated nature of the MNE's diversified operations: heterarchy (Hedlund 1981, 1986), diversified (Prahalad and Doz 1987) and transnational (Bartlett and Ghoshal 1989) and horizontal (Porter 1990). These perspectives developed largely through the lens of a business network approach to the MNE, which focused on the importance of business networks in the subsidiary's host-country environment. Ultimately, within this perspective, the perception of innovation in the MNE shifted dramatically from a dyadic, hierarchical view to an outlook consisting of a 'web of diverse, differentiated inter and intra-firm relationships' (O'Donnell 2000, 526).

More recently, the institutional lens has been applied to the study of the MNE (Kostova and Zaheer 1999; Kostova and Roth 2002; Morgan and Kristensen 2006; Rosenzweig and Singh 1991; Xu and Shenkar 2002). In comparison to the business network approach the institutional approach is viewed as a more valuable all-encompassing approach to the study of the MNE (Forsgren 2008). It goes beyond the notion of innovation through focusing solely on business networks, and instead incorporates the entire host country, viewing it as an institution in itself, representing markets and business opportunities, legal systems, political contexts, labour and financial markets, business systems and values (Forsgren 2008). In this way applying institutional theory to the study of the MNE provides a rich theoretical foundation for examining a wide range of critical issues and allows for theorizing at multiple levels of analysis, which is essential for MNE research (Cantwell et al. 2010; Edwards and Hayden 2001; Geppert and Matten 2006; Ghoshal and Westney 1993; Hillman and Wan 2005; Kostova and Zaheer 1999; Kostova et al. 2008; Kostova and Roth 2002; Lu and Xu 2006; Morgan and Kristensen 2006; Rosenzweig and Singh 1991; Tregaskis 2003; Westney 2003; Westney and Zaheer 2001; Xu and Shenkar 2002).

Perhaps the main contribution of the institutional perspective to the MNE is that it provides a powerful way of viewing the relationship between the MNE and the environment (Meyer and Scott 1983; Pfeffer and Salancik 1978). Here the environment is not only external to the organization but it also 'enters the organization' (Westney 1993, 56). The environment influences the beliefs and actions of individuals within the organization, while at the same time organizations are carriers of their national environments. As Anthony Ferner and others have argued (Ferner et al. 2005), MNEs do not become detached from their home environments when they internationalize but rather bring elements of their home institutional baggage with them which influences the nature of subsidiary operations. Barner-Rasmussen et al. (2010) show how this strong focus on subsidiary–environment interaction simultaneously entails that the subsidiary–headquarters relationship is treated more implicitly in this perspective.

Institutional theory suggests that the MNE headquarters suffers from radical uncertainty in the sense that knowledge is much more socially embedded and therefore not controlled by anyone in its entirety (Bjorkman 2006; Ferner et al. 2005; Ghoshal and Westney 2005; Kostova 1999; Rosenzweig and Singh 1991). Therefore, within the institutional perspective the role of the MNE in subsidiary innovation processes has been more critically viewed due to its relative lack of control and knowledge of its subsidiary's local institutional environment (Ciabuschi et al. 2011). On the other hand the HQ should not be viewed as being totally insignificant, and a more important contribution of the institutional perspective lies in the way it portrays the subsidiary being caught between conformity with its local host environment and loyalty to the HQ (Kostova and Zaheer 1999), referred to as 'institutional duality' (Kostova and Roth 2002). We argue that rather than focusing on a dichotomous either–or situation subsidiary managers should be proactive in responding to the institutional pressures of their distinct institutional environments in order to act as a knowledge bridge in their dual institutional contexts. In order to appreciate fully the complexity that is associated with the management of subsidiary innovation in its dual institutional context, we will firstly consider the ways in which institutional theory has been more generally applied to the MNE.

12.2.1   Institutional Theory in the MNE Context

Institutional theory has until recently been more concerned about the relationship between the organization and its environment rather than constructing a specific theory of the MNE (Barner-Rasmussen et al. 2010). Institutionalism in the MNE environment is broadly characterized by a diverse set of approaches, but Jackson and Degg (2008) distinguish between two broad forms, namely the 'thin' variable-based approach and the 'thick' case-based approach. The former is commonly applied to international business research and the latter is practised more in the literature on national innovation systems (NISs) (Coriat and Weinstein 2002). Within the latter domain some scholars have argued that the main benefit of the institutional approach to subsidiary innovation is to indicate clearly the existence of national innovation trajectories, that are largely determined by the institutional context in which the various MNE subsidiaries operate (Coriat and Weinstein 2002; Westney 1993). The NIS approach suggests that countries develop relatively stable and distinct trajectories of technological specialization. Thus the knowledge that the MNE possesses is likely to be different from the knowledge within the host country (Almeida and Phene 2008). The references to institutions are to be found in most studies related to innovation systems (Edquist 1997), and the importance of the role of local institutions in the dynamics of innovation is widely acknowledged in this perspective.

The former of Jackson and Degg's (2008) conceptualizations, namely the 'thin' variable-based or the 'organizational institutionalism' (Morgan and Kristensen 2006) approach was originally pioneered by Ghoshal and Westney (1993) and Kostova and colleagues (Kostova 1999; Kostova and Zaheer 1999; Kostova and Roth 2002; Kostova et al. 2008). Their advancements apply key tenets of neo-institutionalism originating from North American sociology (DiMaggio and Powell 1983; Meyer and Rowan 1977; Meyer and Scott 1983). Seen through this lens the MNE is 'characterized by substantial heterogeneity and complexity' (Roth and Kostova 2003, 888).

The point of departure is that MNEs like all organizations are socially embedded, meaning that their behaviour is explained with more reference to the social practices that surround them than the economic factors. Firms will therefore adopt practices and structures not just due to technical or efficiency reasons but also because they are commonly accepted 'rules of the game' in a certain society or country (Zimmerman and Zeitz 2002). These rules apply pressures to firms, pressures to be accepted by a given society. DiMaggio and Powell (1983) have shown how these pressures can arise from three distinct sources: coercive pressures, cognitive biases, or normative factors (Scott 2008). For instance, in an MNE environment coercive pressures may result from the necessity to apply for a licence for a joint venture when entering a certain foreign country. Cognitive pressures may arise when a firm enters a foreign market and has to enter into agreement with a trade union, because there may be a taken for granted belief that firms in a certain industry, in certain countries, are more credible when associated with trade unions. Finally, normative pressures require that companies entering into a foreign country demonstrate that its social values are congruent with those surrounding that society. Therefore, these institutional pressures add considerable complexity to the way in which a subsidiary operates, let alone attempts to innovate, in a host-country environment.

More importantly, in an institutional domain, it is widely acknowledged that each subsidiary of the MNE faces tension between, on the one hand, isomorphic pressures to adapt to these institutional pressures in the host country in which it operates and, on the other hand, similar pressures for consistency with other parts of the MNE, including the HQ (Kostova and Roth 2002; Rosenzweig and Singh 1991). Therefore, this position of institutional duality means that 'each foreign subsidiary is confronted with two distinct sets of isomorphic pressures emanating from host as well as home country' (Kostova and Roth 2002, 216), meaning that they must be able to balance cognitive, normative and coercive pressures that arise from each environment (DiMaggio and Powell 1983; Kostova and Zaheer 1999). This conceptualization of the MNE subsidiary is one of the most powerful insights that institutional theory offers us in the study of the MNE, thus it seems necessary to consider how it will impact on the subsidiary's innovativeness.

12.2.2   Dual Institutional Context of Subsidiary Innovation

It is widely acknowledged that a subsidiary's innovativeness is determined by the degree of knowledge it shares with both its external and internal institutional environments (Almeida and Phene 2004, 2008; Frost 2001; Gupta and Govindarajan 1991, 2000). Rather than being passive recipients of centrally developed innovations, subsidiaries undertake their own innovation and technological development, and as a result some of them acquire more important strategic roles within the MNE, such as centres of excellence (Frost et al. 2002) or global innovators (Gupta and Govindarajan 1991). Besides knowledge flow from the centre to the periphery, reverse flows from local subsidiaries to the HQ (Ghoshal 1987; Mudambi 2002) and flows between MNE subsidiaries (Ghoshal and Bartlett 1988; Gupta and Govindarajan 1991, 2000) can also be noted. Through their localization in diverse environments, subsidiaries can serve as listening posts by tapping into localized knowledge (Cantwell 1995; Porter 1990). Therefore, in order to understand the way in which a subsidiary's dual institutional context can affect its innovativeness, we first consider some of the studies that have looked at subsidiary innovation in the local host institutional environment, while also taking into account the way in which the headquarters' role in these processes is viewed through an institutional perspective.

12.3   MNE SUBSIDIARY'S LOCAL INSTITUTIONAL ENVIRONMENT

As with the view of the MNE the view of the host country has changed in more recent literature in international strategy (Almeida and Phene 2004). Although we emphasize the intra-organizational role of the subsidiary which is based on knowledge sharing with both internal and external institutions, there has been an empirical tendency for studies to concentrate on the subsidiary's host institutional environment as an important source of innovation because it is this source, above all, that makes subsidiaries differ from one another (Andersson et al. 2002, 2007; Frost 2001). While host countries were originally seen primarily as markets or sources of cheap labour for the MNE, increasingly they are seen as potential sources of subsidiary innovation (Almeida and Phene 2004, 2008; Andersson et al. 2002, 2007; Frost 2001). For example, Doz and Prahalad (1981) observed that headquarters–subsidiary relationships within the MNE cannot be understood without conducting an explicit analysis of the relationships held with institutions such as major customers and governmental authorities in the countries in which the specific subsidiary operates. Frost (2001) found that the greater the innovative scale of the subsidiary, the greater the likelihood that its innovations will draw upon technical ideas originating in the host institutional environment, indicating a logic of exploration rather the exploitation. Almeida and Phene (2004, 2008) established that although subsidiaries had slightly more linkages to the MNE than the host country, these linkages were less likely to result in innovations, concluding that it is linkages to host-country institutions that provide the best inputs for subsidiary innovation. They showed that in the subsidiary's host-country institutional environment the most innovative subsidiaries can have greater knowledge exchanges with the host-country institutions and are located in more diverse host environments (Almeida and Phene 2008). Further to this, Andersson et al. (2007) discovered that the strategic importance or competitiveness of the host country may or may not be important, depending on the nature of the subsidiary's relationships. It is the closeness of these institutional relationships that has a strong impact on the extent to which these environments can function as a platform for subsidiary innovation.

12.3.1   Institutional Embeddedness

The innovativeness of a subsidiary can be more specifically explained by its degree of embeddedness in any given institutional environment (Andersson et al. 2002, 2007; Dellestrand 2011; Forsgren et al. 2000; Frost

2001; Hakanson and Nobel 2001). Embeddedness defines how the development of innovations is not an isolated activity but occurs in a context of embedded relationships with institutions internal to the MNE, and also interaction with institutions external to the MNE (Andersson et al. 2001; Forsgren et al. 2005). There are a number of different ways to disaggregate the concept of embeddedness (Zukin and DiMaggio 1990) but there are two fundamental reasons as to the significance of embeddedness in the process of subsidiary innovation. Firstly, closeness in relationships with specific external counterparts improves the subsidiary's ability to absorb new knowledge from its institutional environments and hence improve its innovativeness (Hansen 1999), that is, 'relational embeddedness' (Andersson et al. 2002). Secondly, innovative behaviour is something that is as significant within relationships in the external environment as within firms (Von Hippel 1988), that is, 'structural embeddedness' (Andersson et al. 2002). The difference being that relational embeddedness is defined by learning in individual relationships rather than through positions in a system of relationships (Andersson et al. 2002, 2007). Most scholars have looked at relational embeddedness in an MNE environment due to the fact that they are coming from a business network perspective (Dellestrand 2011).

Frost (2001) also argues that a subsidiary's ability to gain access to local knowledge sources is likely to be dependent upon its embeddedness in the host-country context. The ability of the subsidiary to identify new technologies in its external environment and then to assimilate them is heavily dependent on the closeness of the subsidiary's institutional relationships (Andersson et al. 2007). Therefore, a high degree of institutional embeddedness is conducive to the subsidiary's ability to assimilate new technology from the environment, but also to develop new technology through close interaction with local institutions (Andersson et al. 2007). Some subsidiaries will inevitably be more innovative than others, or they might have access to particular technologies giving them a more pronounced role as givers rather than receivers within the MNE (Gupta and Govindarajan 1991). Therefore givers of technology will by definition be more innovative than receivers of technology (Andersson et al. 2007).

On the other hand, there have been studies that have portrayed subsidiary embeddedness as leading to technological isolation, because the complex, idiosyncratic interaction process between the subsidiary and its local institutions creates technologies that cannot easily be used in sister subsidiary business contexts (Asakawa 2001). The possibility that the subsidiary may be too embedded and the external relationship too tightly structured has also been noted by several scholars (Hakansson and Snehota 1995; Uzzi 1997). These studies highlight that when subsidiary embeddedness is positively related to the development of subsidiary inno-vations, there is a trade-off between embeddedness and the possibility to transfer knowledge internally. Ultimately the MNE HQ is always con-fronted with a dilemma whereby externally embedded subsidiaries give potential access to a variety of knowledge sources, but where increasing institutional embeddedness may also lead to a reduced interest in con-tributing to the MNE's overall innovative performance (Mudambi and Navarra 2004). Thus the subsidiary must also be cautious of isolating itself from the MNE as it could risk being totally separated from the HQ and other subsidiaries, retarding internal knowledge sharing. Going further, Dellestrand (2011) found that the internal and external embeddedness of a subsidiary with an innovation development project influenced the involve-ment of the HQ in transferring that project. Therefore, balancing its inter-nal and external institutional embeddedness can be an important factor for both the subsidiary, in the innovation development stage, and the HQ, in the transfer process of that innovation. With this increased focus on the local institutional environment of the subsidiary it is also important to consider the role of the MNE HQ in subsidiaries' innovative processes through an institutional lens.

12.3.2   Diminishing Role of MNE Headquarters in an Institutional Context?

When MNE subsidiaries are viewed as being highly embedded in their external institutional environments, this makes the MNE HQ extremely distributed when it comes to knowledge and control of its different units (Mudambi and Navarra 2004). In this view the HQ is always seen as having a limited possibility to understand, let alone control, innovation processes at the subsidiary level (Ciabuschi et al. 2011). The MNE HQ is only one source of institutional pressure on subsidiaries, and their position is continually being challenged from other institutional influences (Barner-Rasmussen et al. 2010). The higher the degree of subsidiary embedded-ness in the external environment then the more difficult it is for the HQ to exert influence over the subsidiary (Forsgren et al. 2005). Forsgren et al. (2005) question whether the headquarters actually does take the main role in coordinating knowledge transfer within the MNE, as it can be con-strained by the fact that it does not share the critical knowledge that the subsidiary gains from its external network. Institutional theory states that the HQ is likely to be 'groping in the darkness' when it comes to manag-ing the innovation processes at the subsidiary level (Ciabuschi et al. 2011). In this sense, the headquarters has become an 'outsider' (Forsgren et al. 2005) vis-à-vis the operational context of each subsidiary, or a 'player among others' (Andersson et al. 2007), fundamentally lacking the means to assess what expertise is needed, and possibly in possession of valuable expertise of which it is unaware (Ciabuschi et al. 2011). In other words the 'grand designer of old is now much more circumscribed in terms of the possibilities available to it' (Barner-Rasmussen et al. 2010, 95) due to its fundamental ignorance of the context in which the different units operate (Ciabuschi et al. 2011).

Other scholars have argued that the main problem is not the lack of information on the part of the HQ about the subsidiaries' innovation processes, but rather the fact that the HQ is often unaware of what its subsidiaries are doing (Birkinshaw et al. 2000; Taggart 1997). More specifically, Ciabuschi et al. (2011) conceptualize the role of the HQ in the form of the 'knowledge situation', arguing that the HQ will sometimes intervene in subsidiary innovation processes despite its lack of knowledge rather than because of its possession of relevant knowledge, an approach they term the 'sheer ignorance perspective'. Ciabuschi et al. imply that the HQ has limited capability to determine what information to collect, let alone to decide what role to play in its subsidiaries' innovation processes. Ultimately they argue that direct involvement of the HQ will make the innovation process at subsidiary level less likely to benefit from existing routines since the HQ is unlikely to have as much specific knowledge of the subsidiary's local institutional context. Hence, there is a gap between the reality of the local institutional context in which the innovation processes are carried out, and HQ knowledge of that institutional context.

Kristensen and Zeitlin (2001) have argued that according to local rationalities HQ 'decisions often simply appear stupid and wrong' (2001, 188). In other words, corporate management is seen as being too far removed from the operational realities that dominate daily experiences at the subsidiary level. The role of the HQ is instead reduced to constructing likely accounts for institutional investors in the stock market (Barner-Rasmussen et al. 2010). The metaphor Kristensen and Zeitlin use for the HQ is that of an 'absentee landlord' (2005, 234) who is not only ignorant, but who destroys rather than creates value, pointing to the potential dysfunctional relationships between the HQ and its subsidiaries. They also state that in such an organization fragmentation is more likely than unitary action: a state or 'warring fiefdoms' is more likely than an 'integrated network' (2005, 193). With this view, there is a danger that subsidiary-level operations and corporate-level strategy risk disconnection, potentially undermining any advantages of 'multinationality' (Barner-Rasmussen et al. 2010).

These arguments do not however spell the end for HQ involvement in innovation processes at subsidiary level but suggest that the HQ has to learn over time how much and in what way to intervene, if at all (Ciabuschi et al. 2011). More recently there have been a few studies that have attempted to refocus the role of the HQ in innovation transfer projects (Dellestrand and Kapen 2011). These authors view the MNE HQ as an orchestrator, where orchestration can be understood as the deliberate and purposeful actions undertaken in order to create or extract value from the subsidiary (Dhanaraj and Parkhe 2006). Dellestrand (2011) argues that one way for the HQ to orchestrate and add value to the innovation process of its subsidiaries is to involve itself in the transfer of innovations between subsidiaries. Andersson et al. (2007) argue that if the HQ possesses a sufficiently deep knowledge of its subsidiary's most important business relationships; it will be in a stronger position to evaluate the significance of these relationships in the subsidiary innovation process. This is crucial for the HQ if it wishes to have a say in the innovative processes of its subsidiaries.

It is clear from these arguments that the role of the HQ must be investigated further in order to search for new ways of understanding its position in the innovative processes of the different units within the MNE. The increasing complexity of the modern MNE has put great demands on the headquarters' function and traditional perspectives may no longer be sufficient to grasp fully the different roles the headquarters is expected to play, to the extent that there may be reason to question the concept of the 'headquarters' as a noun (Barner-Rasmussen et al. 2010). Perhaps the focus for future studies in this area could be for scholars to imagine a new role for the MNE HQ in the process of subsidiary innovation, one that is less of a hierarchical entity and more a participant collaborator. Some of the avenues where the complexity of the MNE's dual institutional context has been more prominently applied will be outlined below.

12.4   KNOWLEDGE SHARING IN A DUAL INSTITUTIONAL CONTEXT

Empirically, institutional theory has been most effectively applied to the study of cross-national transfer of policies and practices in an MNE context (Collings et al. 2010; Ferner et al. 2005; Kostova 1999; Kostova and Roth 2002). Similarly, firms that try to transfer innovation projects internationally to their different units can be faced with barriers and problems located in the institutional environment. More specifically these barriers arise due to the differences between the institutions of the country of origin and the receiving subsidiary's country. This is known as institutional distance, the differences in coercive, cognitive and normative institutions between the subsidiary's home and host country (Xu and Shenkar 2002). The larger the institutional distance the more difficult it will be to share knowledge or transfer an innovative project horizontally from the parent to the subsidiary or laterally from subsidiary to subsidiary. Liability of foreignness is another institutional factor that can affect the subsidiary in the transfer of innovations and knowledge sharing with its local host institutional environment. Doing business abroad results in substantial costs which arise from the unfamiliarity of the environment's institutional makeup, from cultural, political and economic differences (Zaheer and Mosakowski 1998).

Additionally the transfer of these innovation projects through the sharing of knowledge is further complicated when we introduce the notion of institutional duality. There is a realization that if the adaptation to the local institutional environment is given too great a prominence then the MNE is at risk of falling apart (Forsgren 2008). Alternatively if conformity to the corporate system is prioritized too strongly then the multinational will risk losing its legitimacy in the different institutional environments, resulting in less knowledge being shared (Kostova and Zaheer 1999; Rosenzweig and Singh 1991). The problem then becomes more complex when one realizes that there are conflicting institutional pressures not only on every subsidiary, but also on every function and process within the MNE (Rosenzweig and Singh 1991). In this sense it can be said that the transfer of knowledge or innovation projects between subsidiaries and their environments suffers from these conflicting institutional pressures, as highlighted earlier in the form of the subsidiary's dual institutional context. In order for subsidiaries to manage effectively the knowledge sharing that is so crucial to their innovativeness they must be able to balance the institutional pressures that arise from their unique position in this dual institutional context.

Therefore it seems that institutional theory can been most effectively applied to the study of the MNE subsidiary through the transfer of practices and policies. In going forward it seems logical to investigate the transfer of knowledge and innovation projects through an institutional lens. In doing so this will also allow for more consideration of the HQ's role in the innovative processes of subsidiaries. What is key here is the way in which the subsidiary balances its dual institutional pressures for conformity in order to act as a knowledge-bridge between its host and home environments, 'bringing the environment back in' (Pfeffer 1981) while simultaneously bringing 'HQ management back out' (Andersson et al. 2002).

12.5   INFLUENCING KNOWLEDGE-SHARING RELATIONSHIPS IN A DUAL INSTITUTIONAL CONTEXT

While knowledge sourcing from both contexts is critical to innovation, the utilization of this knowledge is dependent on the way in which the subsidiary is able to use this knowledge through the resources available to it (Birkinshaw and Hood 1998). Some scholars have looked at absorptive capacity, the firm's ability to recognize, assimilate and exploit new external information (Cohen and Leventhal 1990), in order to examine this domain. However, when looked at more closely, institutional theory suggests that managers can use resources from their institutional environment in order to influence their relationships with institutions in their dual institutional contexts. Institutional theory offers tools with which to evaluate the impact of the institutional environment on the behaviour of the MNE, as well as the way the MNE affects the institutional environment (Forsgren 2008). Therefore the interplay between the firm and its institutional environment is twofold, as not only do firms adapt to the society, but the society also adapts to large and powerful firms (Forsgren 2008).

Institutional theory therefore goes beyond the notion of embeddedness and incorporates how subsidiaries can influence the relationships they have with their institutional environments in that the subsidiary is not just reactive to the laws, norms and values of its institutional environment, but it can also be notoriously proactive (Dorrenbacher and Gammelgaard 2006; Forsgren 2008; Oliver 1991; Zimmerman and Zeitz 2002; Zott and Huy 2007). Most of these arguments resonate with earlier foundations that criticized institutional theory for a lack of explicit attention to the strategic behaviours that organizations employ in direct response to institutional processes and the role of agency (DiMaggio and Powell 1991; Greenwood and Suddaby 2006; Lawrence 1999, 2004; Oliver 1991, 1992). These arguments are closely aligned to what is commonly termed institutional entrepreneurship (DiMaggio 1988; Eisenstadt 1980; Greenwood and Suddaby 2006; Lounsbury and Glynn 2001; McGuire et al. 2004). Here the MNE subsidiary can be seen as an active player, not a passive pawn, capable of strategically influencing the behaviour of its HQ and its local host environment's institutions in the transfer of knowledge or innovations (Lawrence and Suddaby 2006; Scott 2008).

This emerging strand of institutional theory provides us with a way in which to investigate further the tools that subsidiary managers can use in influencing the way knowledge is shared in their dual institutional contexts. Effectively balancing the knowledge absorbed from these environments is key for the subsidiary in creating value through innovation. In this way the MNE has become to be defined as 'a contested social space in which subsidiaries and headquarters engage in negotiation and conflict over a multiplicity of possible future forms, directions and destinations' (Morgan and Kristensen 2006, 1471). The concept of space suggests a geographical terrain, which is occupied and fought over by individual actors representing different subsidiaries. Forsgren et al. (2005, 184) similarly state that the MNE is a 'heterogeneous, loosely coupled organization' in which 'bargaining and conflicts are natural ingredients' (2005, 99). Conflicts are inevitable because of the heterogeneous resources and interests of each individual subsidiary.

In this regard, HQ–subsidiary relationships are conflictual and potentially dysfunctional because the central argument, as suggested earlier, is that HQ is not in control. Within this contested social space the sharing or transfer of knowledge or innovations should be viewed as a process of negotiation rather than a dichotomous either–or one, in which transfers are debated and modified due to the growing recognition that subsidiaries are in a position to mobilize resources, giving them the power to negotiate the terms of the transfer (Forsgren 2008). To a large extent these resources emanate from their knowledge of their local institutional environment where the new policy is due to be implemented. Therefore subsidiary managers' roles as 'interpreters' of the local institutional environment gives them power to negotiate the terms of any potential transfer, particularly with the HQ (Forsgren 2008). These negotiations between the subsidiary and corporate managers will help also shed more light on the HQ's role in subsidiary innovation projects.

These views are still being explored and are consequently at an early stage of development in the study of an MNE context. In order for future studies in the area of the MNE subsidiary innovation to fully comprehend the way in which they can incorporate all the factors affecting their innovativeness, the pressures of its dual institutional environments need to be considered. Additionally, looking at the way in which subsidiary managers can use their institutional environments to influence their knowledge-sharing relationships will be one direction that should be explored more comprehensively in future studies.

12.6   CONCLUSION

This chapter highlights the utility of the institutional lens in the study of the subsidiary innovation process. Institutional theory provides us with a unique lens to examine subsidiary innovation as it goes beyond some of the theoretical developments in the popular business network approach. It does not restrict itself to looking solely at business networks but instead takes into account all institutions that can have an effect on a subsidiary's innovativeness. New approaches in this area are also starting to show how subsidiaries can use their institutional environments in order to alter their degree of influence in the knowledge shared with contributing institutions. More importantly the chapter highlights how subsidiary management can play a balancing role between their dual institutional contexts of knowledge communities, a combination that will ultimately increase their innovative capacity. Some questions that resonate from a review of the literature in this area include: what now is the role of the HQ in the process of subsidiary innovation? Do subsidiaries with a high degree of embeddedness in their host institutional environments still need to include the HQ in their innovation processes? Does the HQ create or destroy value in subsidiary innovative processes due to their lack of knowledge about the subsidiary host environment? Or should the key to effective subsidiary innovation be explained by the way it manages its institutional dualities in competing institutional environments? Can subsidiary managers utilize resources from their conflicting institutional environments to influence their knowledge-sharing relationships?

This chapter shows how new approaches to conceptualizing the MNE have recently surfaced that clearly break with previously dominant paradigms about the role of the MNE headquarters in subsidiary innovation. These new approaches are not yet fully understood, but their emergence is beginning to challenge the structure and conventionality of the MNE as an organization. More specifically this chapter has shown how, despite the apparent difficulties associated with applying these theories to the MNE, they are also providing us with opportunities to deepen our conceptualizations of the way in which the MNE headquarters should behave in order for it to add value to its diversified subsidiaries' innovative processes. From an institutional perspective subsidiaries are embedded in a dual institutional context where they must play a balancing role in order to bring HQ management back out and the environment back in, in order to be a more innovative knowledge bridge.

REFERENCES

Almeida, P. and A. Phene (2004), 'Subsidiaries and knowledge creation: The influence of the MNC and host country on innovation', *Strategic Management Journal*, **25** (8–9), 847–864.

Almeida, P. and A. Phene (2008), 'Innovation in multinational subsidiaries: the role of knowledge assimilation and subsidiary capabilities', *Academy of International Business*, **39**, 901–919.

Andersson, U., M. Forsgren and U. Holm (2001), 'Subsidiary embeddedness and competence development in MNCs a multi-level analysis', *Organization Studies*, **22** (6), 1013–1034.

Andersson, U., M. Forsgren and U. Holm (2002), 'The strategic impact of external networks: subsidiary performance and competence development in the multinational corporation', *Strategic Management Journal*, **23** (11), 979–996.

Andersson, U., M. Forsgren and U. Holm (2007), 'Balancing subsidiary influence in the federative MNC: a business network view', *Journal of International Business Studies*, **38** (5), 802–818.

Asakawa, K. (2001), 'Organizational tension in international R&D management: the case of Japanese firms', *Research Policy*, **30** (5), 735–757.

Barner-Rasmussen, W., R. Piekkari, J. Scott-Kennel and C. Welch (2010), 'Commander-in-chief or absentee landlord? Key perspectives on headquarters in multinational corporations', in U. Andersson (ed.), *Managing the Contemporary Multinational: The Role of Headquarters*, Cheltenham, UK and Northampton, MA, USA: Edward Elgar Publishing, pp. 85–105.

Bartlett, C.A. and S. Ghoshal (1989), *Managing Across Borders: The Transnational Solution*, Boston, MA: Harvard Business School Press.

Bartlett, C.A. and S. Ghoshal (1998), 'Beyond strategic planning to organization learning: Lifeblood of the individualized corporation', *Strategy and Leadership*, **26** (1), 34–39.

Birkinshaw, J. (1995), 'Taking the initiative', *Business Quarterly*, **59** (4), 97–102.

Birkinshaw, J., U. Holm, P. Thilenius and N. Arvidsson (2000), 'Consequences of perception gaps in the headquarters-subsidiary relationship', *International Business Review*, **9** (3), 321–344.

Birkinshaw, J. and N. Hood (1998), 'Multinational subsidiary evolution: capability and charter change in foreign-owned subsidiary companies', *Academy of Management Review*, **23** (4), 773–795.

Birkinshaw, J. and N. Hood (2001), 'Unleash innovation in foreign subsidiaries', *Harvard Business Review*, **79** (3), 131–137.

Bjorkman, I. (2006), 'International human resource management research and institutional theory', in G.K. Stahl and I. Bjorkman (eds), *Handbook of Research in International Human Resource Management*, Cheltenham, UK and Northampton, MA, USA: Edward Elgar, pp. 463–474.

Cantwell, J. (1995), 'The globalization of technology: what remains of the product cycle model?', *Cambridge Journal of Economics*, **19** (1), 155–174.

Cantwell, J., J.H. Dunning and S.M. Lundan (2010), 'An evolutionary approach to understanding international business activity: the co-evolution of MNEs and the institutional environment', *Journal of International Business Studies*, **41** (4), 567–586.

Ciabuschi, F., M. Forsgren and O. Martin Martin (2011), 'Rationality vs ignorance: The role of MNE headquarters in subsidiaries innovation processes', *Journal of International Business Studies*, http://dx.doi.org/10.1016/j.ibusrev.2011.02.003.

Ciabuschi, F., O. Martin and B. Stahl (2010), 'Headquarters' influence on knowledge transfer performance', *Management International Review*, **50** (4), 471–491.

Cohen, W.M. and D.A. Levinthal (1990), 'Absorptive capacity: a new perspective on learning and innovation', *Administrative Science Quarterly*, **35** (1), 128–152.

Collings, D.G., A. McDonnell, P. Gunnigle and J. Lavelle (2010), 'Swimming against the tide: outward staffing flows from multinational subsidiaries', *Human Resource Management*, **49** (4), 575–598.

Coriat, B. and O. Weinstein (2002), 'Organizations, firms and institutions in the generation of innovation', *Research Policy*, **31** (2), 273–290.

Damanpour, F. and S. Gopalakrishnan (2001), 'The dynamics of the adoption of product and process innovations in organizations', *Journal of Management Studies*, **38** (1), 45–65.

Davis, L.N. and K.E. Meyer (2004), 'Subsidiary research and development, and the local environment', *International Business Review*, **13** (3), 359–382.

Dellestrand, H. (2011), 'Subsidiary embeddedness as a determinant of divisional headquarters involvement in innovation transfer processes', *International Journal of Management*, http://dx.doi.org/10.1016/j.intman.2011.05.005.

Dellestrand, H. and P. Kappen (2011), 'Headquarters allocation of resources to innovation transfer projects within the multinational enterprise', *Journal of International Management*, http://dx.doi.org/10.1016/j.intman.2011.02.001.

Dhanaraj, C. and A. Parkhe (2006), Orchestrating innovation networks, *Academy of Management Review*, **31** (1), 659–669.

DiMaggio, P.J. (1988), 'Interest and agency in institutional theory', in L.G. Zucker (ed.), *Institutional Patterns and Organizations: Culture and Environment*, Cambridge, MA: Ballinger, pp. 3–21.

DiMaggio, P. and W. Powell (1983), 'The iron cage revisited: Institutional isomorphism and collective rationality in organizational fields', *American Sociological Review*, **48** (2), 147–160.

DiMaggio, P.J. and W.W. Powell (1991), 'Introduction', in P.J. DiMaggio and W.W. Powell (eds), *New Institutionalism in Organizational Analysis*, Chicago, IL: University of Chicago Press, pp. 1–38.

Dorrenbacher, C. and J. Gammelgaard (2006), 'Subsidiary role development: the effect of micro-political headquarters-subsidiary negotiations on the product, market and value-added scope of foreign-owned subsidiaries', *Journal of International Management*, **12** (3), 266–283.

Dorrenbacher, C. and M. Geppert (2006), 'Micro-politics and conflicts in multinational corporations: current debates, re-framing, and contributions of this special issue', *Journal of International Management*, **12** (3), 251–265.

Doz, Y.L. and C.K. Prahalad (1981), 'Headquarters influence and strategic control in MNCs', *Sloan Management Review*, **23** (1), 15–29.

Edquist, C. (1997), *Systems of Innovation. Technologies Institutions and Organizations*, London: Routledge.

Edwards, T. and A. Hayden (2001), 'The erosion of the country of origin effect: a case study of a Swedish multinational company', *Industrial Relations*, **56** (1), 116–140.

Eisenstadt, S.N. (1980), 'Cultural orientations, institutional entrepreneurs, and social change: comparative analysis of traditional civilizations', *American Journal of Sociology*, **85**, 840–869.

Ferner, A., P. Almond and T. Colling (2005), 'Institutional theory and the cross-national transfer of employment policy: the case of workforce diversity in US multinationals', *Journal of International Business Studies*, **36** (3), 304–321.

Forsgren, M. (2008), *Theories of the Multinational Firm: A Multidimensional Creature in the Global Economy*, Cheltenham, UK and Northampton, MA, USA: Edward Elgar.

Forsgren, M., U. Holm and J. Johanson (2005), *Managing the Embedded Multinational: A Business Network View*, Cheltenham, UK and Northampton, MA, USA: Edward Elgar.

Forsgren, M., J. Johanson and D. Sharma (2000), 'Development of MNC centres of excellence', in U. Holm and T. Pedersen (eds), *The Emergence and Impact of MNC Centres of Excellence*, London: Macmillan, pp. 45–67.

Frost, T.S. (2001), 'The geographic sources of foreign subsidiaries' innovations', *Strategic Management Journal*, **22** (2), 101–123.

Frost, T.S., J.M. Birkinshaw and P.C. Ensign (2002), 'Centers of excellence in multinational corporations', *Strategic Management Journal*, **23** (11), 997–1018.

Gammelgaard, J., U. Holm and T. Pedersen (2004), 'The dilemmas of MNC subsidiary transfer of knowledge', in V. Mahnke and T. Pedersen (eds), *Knowledge Flows, Governance and the Multinational Enterprise: Frontiers in International Management Research*, Basingstoke: Palgrave, pp. 195–207.

Geppert, M. and D. Matten (2006), 'Institutional influences on manufacturing organization in multinational corporations: the cherry picking approach', *Organization Studies*, **27** (4), 491–516.

Ghoshal, S. (1987), 'Global strategy: an organizing framework', *Strategic Management Journal*, **8** (5), 425–440.

Ghoshal, S. and C.A. Bartlett (1988), 'Creation, adoption, and diffusion of innovations by subsidiaries of multinational corporations', *Journal of International Business Studies*, **19** (3), 365–388.

Ghoshal, S. and D. Westney (1993), *Organization theory and the multinational Corporation*, New York: St Martin's Press.

Ghoshal, S. and D.E. Westney, (2005), *Organization Theory and the Multinational Corporation*, London: Palgrave Macmillan.

Greenwood, R. and R. Suddaby (2006), 'Institutional entrepreneurship in mature fields: the big five accounting firms', *Academy of Management Journal*, **49** (1), 27–48.

Gupta, A.K. and V. Govindarajan (1991), 'Knowledge flows and the structure of control within multinational corporations', *Academy of Management Review*, **16** (4), 768–792.

Gupta, A.K. and V. Govindarajan (2000), 'Knowledge flows within multinational corporations', *Strategic Management Journal*, **21** (4), 473–496.

Hakanson, L. and R. Nobel (2001), 'Organizational characteristics and reverse technology transfer', *Management International Review*, **41** (4), 395–420.

Hakansson, H. and I. Snehota (1995), *Developing Relationships in Business Networks*, London: Routledge.

Hansen, M. (1999), 'The search–transfer problem: the role of weak ties in sharing knowledge across organizational subunits', *Administrative Science Quarterly*, **44**, 82–111.

Hedlund, G. (1981), 'Autonomy of subsidiaries and formalisation of headquarters–subsidiary relationships in Swedish MNCs', in L. Otterbeck (ed.), *The Management of Headquarters-Subsidiary Relationships in Multinational Corporations*, New York: St Martins Press, pp. 25–78.

Hedlund, G. (1986), 'The hypermodern MNC – a heterarchy?', *Human Resource Management*, **25** (1), 9–35.

Hillman, A.J. and W.P. Wan (2005), 'The determinants of MNE subsidiaries' political strategies: evidence of institutional duality', *Journal of International Business Studies*, **36** (3), 322–340.

Jackson, G. and R. Degg (2008), 'Comparing capitalisms: understanding institutional diversity and its implications for international business', *Journal of international Business Studies*, **39**, 540–561.

Kogut, B. and U. Zander (1992), 'Knowledge of the firm, combinative capabilities and the replication of technology', *Organization Science*, **3** (3), 383–396.

Kostova, T. (1999), 'Transnational transfer of strategic organizational practices: a contextual perspective', *Academy of Management Review*, **24** (2), 308–324.

Kostova, T. and K. Roth (2002), 'Adoption of an organizational practice by subsidiaries of multinational corporations: Institutional and relational effects', *Academy of Management Journal*, **45** (1), 215–233.

Kostova, T., K. Roth and M.T. Dacin (2008), 'Institutional theory in the study of multinational corporations: a critique and new directions', *Academy of Management Review*, **33** (4), 994–1006.

Kostova, T. and S. Zaheer (1999), 'Organizational legitimacy under conditions of complexity: the case of the multinational enterprise', *Academy of Management Review*, **24** (1), 64–81.

Kristensen, P.H. and J. Zeitlin (2001), 'The making of a global firm: local pathways to multinational enterprise', in G. Morgan, P.H. Kristensen and R. Whitley (eds), *The Multinational Firm: Organizing across Institutional and National Divides*, Oxford: Oxford University Press, pp. 172–195.

Kristensen, P.H. and J. Zeitlin (2005), *Local Players in Global Games: The Strategic Constitution of a Multinational Corporation*, New York: Oxford University Press.

Lawrence, T.B (1999), 'Institutional strategy', *Journal of Management*, **25** (2), 161–188.

Lawrence, T.B. (2004), 'Rituals and resistance: membership dynamics in professional fields', *Human Relations*, **57** (2), 115–143.

Lawrence, T.B. and R. Suddaby (2006), 'Institutions and institutional work', in S.R. Clegg, C. Hardy, T.B. Lawrence and W.R. Nord (eds), *The Sage Handbook of Organization Studies*, London: Sage Publications, pp. 11–59.

Lounsbury, M. and M.A. Glynn (2001), 'Cultural entrepreneurship: stories, legitimacy, and the acquisition of resources', *Strategic Management Journal*, **22** (6), 545–564.

Lu, J.W. and D. Xu (2006), 'Growth and survival of international joint ventures: an external–internal legitimacy perspective', *Journal of Management*, **32** (3), 426–448.

McGuire, S., C. Hardy and T.B. Lawrence (2004), 'Institutional entrepreneurship in emerging fields: HIV/AIDS treatment advocacy in Canada', *Academy of Management Journal*, **47** (5), 657–679.

Meyer, J. and B. Rowan (1977), 'Institutionalized organizations: formal structure as myth and ceremony', *American Journal of Sociology*, **83** (2), 340–363.

Meyer, J.W. and W.R. Scott (1983), 'Centralization and the legitimacy problems of local government', in J.W. Meyer and W.R. Scott (eds), *Organizational Environments: Ritual and Rationality*, London: Sage, pp. 199–215.

Morgan, G. and P.H. Kristensen (2006), 'The contested space of multinationals: varieties of institutionalism, varieties of capitalism', *Human Relations*, **59** (11), 1467–1490.

Mudambi, R. (2002), 'Knowledge management in multinational firms', *Journal of International Management*, **8** (1), 1–9.

Mudambi, R. and P. Navarra (2004), 'Is knowledge power? Knowledge flows, subsidiary power and rent seeking within MNCs', *Journal of International Business Studies*, **35**, 385–406.

O'Donnell, S.W. (2000), 'Managing foreign subsidiaries: agents of headquarters, or an interdependent network?', *Strategic Management Journal*, **21** (5), 525–548.

Oliver, C. (1991), 'Strategic responses to institutional processes', *Academy of Management Review*, **16** (1), 145–179.

Oliver, C. (1992), 'The antecedents of deinstitutionalization', *Organization Studies*, **13** (4), 563.

Perlmutter, H.V. (1969), 'The tortuous evolution of the multinational corporation', *Columbia Journal of World Business*, **4**, 9–18.

Pfeffer, J. (1981), 'Management as symbolic action: the creation and maintenance of organizational paradigms', *Research in Organizational Behavior*, **3** (1), 1–52.

Pfeffer, J.S. and G. Salancik (1978), *The External Control of Organizations: A Resource Dependence Perspective*, New York: St Martins Press.

Porter, M.E. (1990), *The Competitive Advantage of Nations*, New York: Free Press.

Prahalad, C.K. and Y. Doz (1987), *The Multinational Mission: Balancing Local Demands and Global Vision*, New York: Free Press.

Rogers, E. (2003), *Diffusion of Innovations*, New York: Free Press.

Rosenzweig, P.M. and J.V. Singh (1991), 'Organizational environments and the multinational enterprise', *Academy of Management Review*, **16** (2), 340–361.

Roth, K. and T. Kostova (2003), 'The use of the multinational corporation as a research context', *Journal of Management*, **29** (6), 883–902.

Rugman, A. and A. Verbeke (2001), 'Subsidiary specific advantages in multinational enterprises', *Strategic Management Journal*, **22**, 237–250.

Schumpeter, J. (1934), *The Theory of Economic Development*, Cambridge, MA: Harvard University Press.

Scott, W.R. (2008), *Institutions and Organizations: Ideas and Interests*, London: Sage Publications.

Taggart, J.H. (1997), 'Autonomy and procedural justice: a framework for evaluating subsidiary strategy', *Journal of International Business Studies*, **28** (1), 51–76.

Taylor, S. (2007), 'Creating social capital in MNCs: the international human resource management challenge', *Human Resource Management Journal*, **17** (4), 336–354.

Taylor, S., S. Beechler and N. Napier (1996), 'Towards an integrative model of strategic international human resource management', *Academy of Management Review*, **21**, 959–985.

Tregaskis, O. (2003), 'Learning networks, power and legitimacy in multinational subsidiaries', *International Journal of Human Resource Management*, **14** (3), 431–447.

Uzzi, B. (1997), 'Social structure and competition in intrafirm networks: the paradox of embeddedness', *Administrative Science Quarterly*, **42** (1) 35–67.

Vernon, R. (1966), 'International investment and international trade in the product cycle', *Quarterly Journal of Economics*, **80** (2), 190–207.

Von Hippel, E. (1988), *The Sources of Innovation*, Oxford: Oxford University Press.

Westney, E. (1993), 'Institutionalization theory and the multinational corporation', in S.W.E. Ghoshal (ed.), *Organization Theory and The Multinational Corporation*, New York: St Martin's Press, pp. 53–76.

Westney, E. (2003),'Geography as a design variable', In J. Birkinshaw, S. Ghoshal, C. Markides, J. Stopford and G. Yip (eds), *The Future of the Multinational Company*, London: Wiley Publications, pp. 128–142.

Westney, E. and S. Zaheer (2001), 'The multinational enterprise as an organization', in Alan M.Rugman and T.L. Brewer (eds), *The Oxford Handbook of International Business*, New York: Oxford University Press, pp. 349–380.

Xu, D. and O. Shenkar (2002), 'Institutional distance and the multinational enterprise', *Academy of Management Review*, **27** (4), 608–618.

Zaheer, S. and E. Mosakowski (1998), 'The dynamics of the liability of foreignness: a global study of survival in financial services', *Strategic Management Journal*, **18** (6), 439–463.

Zimmerman, M.A. and G.J. Zeitz (2002), 'Beyond survival: achieving new venture growth by building legitimacy', *Academy of Management Review*, **27** (3), 414–431.

Zott, C. and Q.N. Huy (2007), 'How entrepreneurs use symbolic management to acquire resources', *Administrative Science Quarterly*, **52** (1), 70–105.

Zukin, S. and P. DiMaggio (1990), 'Introduction', in S. Zukin and P. DiMaggio (eds), *Structures of Capital: The Social Organization of the Economy*, Cambridge: Cambridge University Press, pp. 1–56.

13 Partial or full acquisition: influences of institutional pressures on acquisition entry strategy of multinational enterprises*

Ahmad Arslan and Jorma Larimo

13.1 INTRODUCTION

Foreign market entry mode decisions are an important research topic in the field of international business (IB) studies (Brouthers and Hennart 2007; Slangen and Hennart 2008). Foreign market entry mode decisions of multinational enterprises (MNEs) are commonly segmented into equity-based and non-equity-based modes (e.g. Pan and Tse 2000). The equity-based entry modes involve foreign direct investment (FDI) made by the MNEs (Dunning and Lundan 2008; Demirbag et al. 2008) and are considerably inflexible and irreversible in nature (e.g. Elango and Sambharya 2004). Therefore, the choice of FDI mode involves detailed analyses of trade-offs between control and investment risk as well as conformance to the institutional requirements of host countries (e.g. Luo 2001; Xu and Shenkar 2002; Gaur and Lu 2007). MNEs face two important decisions when they wish to enter new international markets using the FDI mode: the level of equity control in a subsidiary (formation of wholly owned subsidiary or a joint venture with local partner), and whether to acquire an existing enterprise (acquisition) or build a new start-up (greenfield investment) (Brouthers and Brouthers 2000; Dikova and van Witteloostuijn 2007; Slangen and Hennart 2008).

IB scholars have analyzed these FDI decisions of MNEs using different approaches. Some past studies have addressed the ownership mode choice of MNEs by studying the choice between a joint venture (JV) and full ownership (e.g. Anderson and Gatignon 1986; Luo 2002; Xu et al. 2004; Brouthers and Hennart 2007; Jung et al. 2008). Other IB scholars have concentrated more on the choice by MNEs between greenfield investment and acquisition entry by the MNEs (e.g. Hennart and Park 1993; Brouthers and Brouthers 2000; Datta et al. 2002; Larimo 2003; Shimizu et al. 2004; Slangen and Hennart 2008; Demirbag et al. 2008). Finally, some IB studies have also attempted to perform an in-depth analysis of equity entry mode choice by addressing

320

the choice between joint ventures, acquisitions and greenfield investments by the MNEs (e.g. Kogut and Singh 1988; Chang and Rosenzweig 2001; Elango and Sambharya 2004). However, the literature review reveals that very few studies have analyzed the choice of acquisition entry mode by MNEs in depth by addressing the choice between full acquisition and partial acquisition, in cases where the MNE decides to acquire a local firm at time of market entry. Although, some previous studies mention that acquisitions can be difficult to manage compared to greenfield investments (e.g. Hennart et al. 1998; Barkema and Vermeulen 1998), but acquisitions have also been found to suffer less from liability of foreignness and newness than the green-field subsidiaries (e.g. Pablo and Javidan 2004). Therefore, acquisitions can emerge as a preferred entry mode choice by investing MNEs in order to gain foothold faster in the local market, as well as to avoid problems associated with liability of foreignness and newness.

According to Chen and Hennart (2004), the lack of studies differentiating between full and partial acquisition in the past explains the variance in findings of studies addressing establishment and ownership mode choices of MNEs. Moreover, by putting full and partial acquisitions together in past studies, whether they addressed the choice between greenfield and acquisition, or joint venture or wholly owned subsidiary, important features of different types of acquisition entry have been ignored (Chen and Hennart 2004). Hence, the present study aims to fill this gap by specifically analyzing the choice between full and partial acquisitions by MNEs in their international markets. This study contributes to the application of the institution-based view of IB strategy (Peng 2002, 2003; Peng and Khoury 2009) in the studies on the use of the FDI mode in foreign market entry by MNEs. Our study is one of the first of its type to study the influences of institutional pressures on the choice between full or partial acquisitions of MNEs. This chapter is one of few studies to address the impacts of institutional pressures from host-country institutions using North's (1990) typology of formal and informal institutions. This study is also expected to contribute empirically to the use of the institution-based view in foreign market entry studies, as it is one of the first to develop measures for formal and informal institutional pressures in selected host countries in selected emerging economies, in the context of acquisitions made by Finnish MNEs.

13.2 THEORETICAL BACKGROUND AND STUDY HYPOTHESES

For MNEs, each new host country represents a different institutional environment, which can influence their choices and strategies substantially

(Henisz 2004; Estrin et al. 2009). As a result, MNEs entering new international markets are confronted with hurdles from both formal and informal aspects of institutional environments (Delios and Henisz 2003; Dikova et al. 2010). Previous literature also mentions that the frequency, motivation and type of acquisitions activity taking place across countries are strongly influenced by various institutional characteristics of the national business systems (Hall and Soskice 2001; Goergen et al. 2005). In the case of acquisition of local firms by MNEs, the formal institutions in any country can pressurize MNEs by establishing the permissible range of ownership for foreign firms in their local subsidiaries (Delios and Beamish 1999; Meyer et al. 2009; Arslan 2010). Therefore, partial acquisitions may emerge as the only option available for the investing MNEs in cases when there are legal restrictions on full ownership of foreign firms.

Informal aspects of institutions are often tacit in nature and understanding them requires intensive cross-cultural communication by the foreign firms (e.g. Peng 2003; Estrin et al. 2009). Therefore, the management of partial acquisitions may prove difficult for MNEs, especially if the MNEs seek to transfer organizational practices to the subsidiary. In this case, full acquisition can be a good option if there are no legal restrictions imposed by the host-country government. However, the choice between partial and full acquisitions by the MNEs has not been addressed specifically in the IB literature so far using the concept of pressures from formal and informal institutional pressures. Therefore, this study is expected to be one of the first to enrich IB and foreign market entry studies theoretically and empirically by using institutional perspective rooted in new institutional economics to study the acquisitions entry strategy of MNEs. This study addresses institutional pressures using North's (1990) metaphor of formal and informal institutions, as opposed to many past studies that used Scott's (1995) categorization of institutions which has been criticized for overlaps in the boundaries of its institutional dimensions, especially the normative and cognitive pillars (e.g. Peng et al. 2008; Peng and Khoury 2009). North's (1990) view of institutions and economic behavior in societies emphasizes the critical interaction between institutions and organizations. Hence, in the case of the acquisitions entry strategy of MNEs, the choice of full or partial acquisitions is dependent not only on the organizational skills and strategies, but also on the broader economic and social requirements represented by formal and informal institutional pressures in a host country.

In this study, we address the impacts of institutions on choice between full or partial acquisitions by analyzing the impacts of pressures exerted by the host-country's formal and informal institutions on these choices of MNEs. Previous literature mentions that firms entering new markets respond strategically to the opportunities and constraints presented by the institutional frameworks of their host countries (Peng et al. 2008; Meyer et al. 2009). FDI decisions of MNEs have been shown to be influenced greatly by the pressures and influences from the formal and informal institutions of host countries. Therefore, an increase in IB studies addressing the impacts of these unique institutional contexts of different host countries on strategies of MNEs can be observed in recent years (e.g. Peng 2003; Peng et al. 2008; Meyer and Tran 2006; Meyer et al. 2009; Estrin et al. 2009; Demirbag et al. 2010). Previous IB studies have also found that especially in emerging economies, FDI strategies of MNEs are significantly influenced by the fact that the market economy's legal, social and professional institutions are in the process of development (e.g. Globerman and Shapiro 2003; Meyer and Tran 2006; Flores and Aguilera 2007; Demirbag et al. 2008, 2010). These formal and informal institutions of emerging economies that are in the process of development can exert more pressures on MNEs to conform to the requirements set by them. Therefore, we aim to analyze how the MNEs respond to formal and informal institutional pressures from host-country institutions, especially in the case of acquisition entry strategy decisions.

13.2.1 Formal Institutional Pressures

Formal institutions refer to the legal bodies, laws and regulations of the host country (North 1990; Gaur and Lu 2007; Estrin et al. 2009). The coercive influences and pressures on organizational actions by the formal institutions have been addressed in some past studies, and the regulatory demands of a country's institutions are a major source of such pressures (e.g. Bada et al. 2004; Arslan 2010). The formal institutions are an important part of the governance structure of any country, and ensure freedom and security of business activities through a legal process (Globerman and Shapiro 2003). However, the host-country governments can also use their regulative and legal powers directly to restrict the behavior of enterprises, or provide incentives and guidance to influence their behavior (e.g. Henisz 2000; Rossi and Volpin 2003). Some studies have shown that governments can possibly directly intervene in the entry mode decision of foreign investors by imposing ownership restrictions or financial constraints so as to increase or decrease the expected returns of a specific entry mode (e.g. Brouthers 2002; Henisz 2004). Therefore, the formal institutions of a host country can exert pressures due to the fact that organizational deviance from legal rules can result in financial penalties on the foreign firms. These institutional pressures from formal institutions can also force firms to follow certain organizational strategies and restrict the behavior of the firm according to the desires of the host government (Henisz 2000).

It has been pointed out in past studies that acquisitions activity is higher in those economies where investor protection is greater, reflected by shareholder rights and good accounting standards (Baums 1993; Pagano and Volpin 2005). Full acquisitions can emerge as a suitable strategy by MNEs in host countries with concentrated ownership, since transfers of control may be easier (Dietrich 1994; Burkhart and Panunzi 2006). Moreover, in those host countries where legal protection for employment is low, full acquisitions emerge as an attractive option for MNEs (Pagano and Volpin 2005; Jackson 2005), as it offers flexibility for MNEs in restructuring the acquired firms. MNEs face problems in the emerging and developing economies of Central and Eastern Europe (CEE), Asia and Latin America because the regulative and legal frameworks required for a well-functioning market economy are in the process of development (Khanna 2005; Meyer et al. 2009). Hence, MNEs are expected to face more pressures from formal institutions when they are in the process of development because they can put restrictions on operations and strategies of foreign firms (MNEs).

MNEs entering these emerging markets may need to rely on networking and relationships with local governmental authorities (e.g. Henisz 2000; Henisz and Zelner 2005), which can be achieved through partial acquisition of an already established local firm. Similarly, Meyer (2002) suggests that partial acquisitions offer the opportunity to align the interests of an MNE and the host government in acquisitions, especially in relation to the privatization of state enterprises. Therefore, it can be expected that in those emerging economies where formal institutions are in the process of development and exert more pressures on MNEs, partial acquisitions are preferred rather than full acquisitions at the time of market entry. Based on the above discussion, it is hypothesized that:

Hypothesis 1: Partial acquisitions are preferred by the MNEs in response to high formal institutional pressures from the host-country institutions.

13.2.2   Informal Institutional Pressures

Informal institutions are embedded in the shared norms, values and beliefs of a particular society (North 1990). Informal institutions are significantly less observable to outsiders, and hence prove to be more difficult to understand for foreign firms (Peng 2003; Xu et al. 2004). The impacts of informal institutions arise from both values and norms prevalent in a society (Kostova and Roth 2002; Scott 2008). In some past management studies, professional norms and culture have also been shown to influence the firm's strategies (e.g. Singh et al. 1986; Dacin 1997). The informal institutional environment has been found to influence the transfer of organizational practices to the MNE subsidiaries, the management of subsidiaries, human resource practices in subsidiaries, and adaptation to the local professional environment (e.g. Kostova 1999; Kostova and Zaheer 1999; Kostova and Roth 2002; Gaur et al. 2007). It has also been found that the strategic behavior of firms can be significantly affected by these informal institutions because of the firm's constant interaction with the social and cultural environment of the country it operates in (e.g. Peng et al. 2008).

Previous IB studies have referred to joint ventures as a preferred entry mode choice by MNEs, when uncertainty and ambiguity are high due to pressures from informal aspects of the institutional environments of host countries (Delios and Beamish 1999; Guillen 2003; Arslan 2010). Therefore, it can be argued that firms entering new host countries using the acquisition entry mode may prefer partial acquisitions due to the uncertainty associated with pressures from informal institutions. This option would offer MNEs opportunities to use the local partner's contacts with local suppliers, distributors and authorities (e.g. Lu and Xu 2006), and the local partner is also expected to help the MNE in dealing with key informal institutions. Moreover, in an environment with high informal institutional pressures, partial acquisitions are also expected to offer the advantage to MNEs of low costs and resource commitments (Anderson and Gatignon 1986; Hill et al. 1990), which in turn can increase flexibility in strategy and operations for the MNEs (Hill et al. 1990; Brouthers and Brouthers 2001). The choice of partial acquisitions in response to high informal pressures can also help the MNEs in solving the information problem in emerging economies especially (e.g. problems such as biased financial reporting and deficient disclosure) (Ali and Hwang 2000). Moreover, the local partner, the acquired subsidiary, is also expected to help the MNE in understanding the requirements of local informal institutions (professional bodies and so on) and conforming to them. Hence, we hypothesize that:

Hypothesis 2a: Partial acquisitions are preferred by the MNEs in response to high informal institutional pressures from the host-country institutions.

However, it should be noted that the choice of partial acquisitions in response to high informal pressures is not always supported from previous studies that addressed similar issues. The literature also refers specifically to the role of governments and legal authorities in the choice of partial acquisitions by the MNEs, as they tend to place limits on the permissible level of ownership for foreign firms (Brouthers 2002), as well as permitting only partial acquisitions, only in certain industries, during privatization (Jakobsen and Meyer 2008). Moreover, for the MNEs, it can be difficult to work with partners in partial acquisitions that come from very different informal institutional backgrounds as they typically have different organizational structures (e.g. Kogut and Singh 1988), communication and management styles (e.g. Hennart and Zeng 2002), and may respond to the strategic issues differently and have workforces with different preferences and expectations (Schneider and De Meyer 1991; Park and Ungson 1997). Thus, although external uncertainty may be reduced through a partial acquisition, the internal inconsistency associated with equity collaborative ventures with partners from very different backgrounds (Dhanaraj and Beamish 2004; Slangen and Tulder 2009) can result in different operational and strategic difficulties for MNEs.

Although full acquisitions may also be subject to internal misunderstandings and conflicts caused by informal differences among employees, such misunderstandings and conflicts are less likely to be a source of internal inconsistency at organizational level (Tsang 1994; Dhanaraj and Beamish 2004). Moreover, as most employees in acquired firms are local, full acquisitions can also bring local culture-specific knowledge and work practices to the acquiring MNEs. Based on this discussion, we also hypothesize that:

Hypothesis 2b: Full acquisitions are preferred by the MNEs in response to high informal institutional pressures from the host-country institutions.

13.3   RESEARCH METHODS

13.3.1   Data Collection and Sample Description

The empirical data for the study are based on an internal databank of foreign investments (both greenfield and acquisitions) made by Finnish firms in their international markets in both developed and emerging economies. This databank has been developed and continuously updated during the past two decades by one of the authors. The data are drawn mainly from annual reports and press releases of the investing Finnish firms, and are supplemented with data gathered through direct contact with these firms. The sample for this study consists of 166 acquisitions of local firms made by Finnish MNEs at time of market entry in selected emerging economies of CEE, Asia and Latin America during the time period 1990–2006. The main aspects of the study sample are summarized in Table 13.1.

Table 13.1 Characteristics of the study sample

Sample characteristic	Description
Acquisition mode choice	Full acquisition (80), Partial acquisitions (86)
International experience of investing firms	Minimum (no experience), Maximum (74 foreign investments)
Host-country experience of investing firms	Minimum (no experience), Maximum (17 years in the host country)
Number of acquisitions in a particular year	1990 (10), 1991 (12), 1992 (7), 1993 (7), 1994 (8), 1995 (11), 1996 (10), 1997 (14), 1998 (11), 1999 (11), 2000 (12), 2001 (11), 2002 (6), 2003 (4), 2004 (4), 2005 (14), 2006 (14)
Number of acquisitions in a particular host region	Central and Eastern Europe (68), Asia (88), Latin America (10)

13.3.2 Measurement of Institutional Pressures

We calculate the scores for formal institutional pressures and informal institutional pressures using country-level indicators of institutional environments from various editions of the Economic Freedom of the World Annual Reports (for formal institutional pressures) published by the Economic Freedom Network, and World Competitiveness Yearbooks (for informal institutional pressures) published by the International Institute for Management Development (IMD), Lausanne, Switzerland.

Economic Freedom of the World Annual Reports measure countries' openness to international business and trade by measuring and ranking them along five major pillars: size of government; legal structure and security of property rights; access to sound money; freedom to trade internationally; and regulations of credit, labor and business. These pillars are further divided into different categories, and finally each country's summary ratings (1–10) are developed. Economic Freedom of the World reports use data from the World Economic Forum, World Bank, International Monetary Fund, United Nations and World Trade Organization to measure these variables (Economic Freedom Network 2008). The higher country score represents openness of the economy to international business, presence of strong market institutions, ease of business for foreign firms and sound financial and fiscal policies. This data source has been used broadly in studies in the field of international and institutional economics (see e.g. Dawson 1998; Ali 2003; Dreher and Rupprecht 2007) and political economy studies (e.g. Bengoa and Sanchez-Robles 2003; Boockmann and Dreher 2003). Lately DiRienzo

Table 13.2   Operationalization of formal institutional pressure

Indicator	Economic Freedom of the World Annual Reports
Legal structure and security of property rights	Scores 1–10.
Formal institutional pressures	10 (highest score) minus host-country score in the item 'Legal structure and security of property rights'

et al. (2007) have also used this source to study the impact of corruption in the context of international business studies. Therefore, it can be said that the use of data from Economic Freedom of the World Annual Reports for operationalization of the formal institutional pressures in this study is reliable.

Formal institutions refer to the legal institutions, laws and regulations of the host country and home country of the foreign-investing firm (North 1990). According to Globerman and Shapiro (2003, 19); 'the rule of law in a country is codified by its governance infrastructure, which represents attributes of legislation, regulation, and legal systems that condition freedom of transacting, security of property rights, and transparency of government and legal process'. This study uses the country scores in the category of legal structure and security of property rights from Economic Freedom of the World Annual Reports. This category includes the aspects of judicial independence, impartial courts, protection of property rights, military interference, integrity of legal system and legal enforcement of contracts. Therefore, it can be said that this category addresses most of the attributes of formal institutions as described by North (1990). The operationalization of formal institutional pressures is shown in Table 13.2.

Since 1989, the IMD has analyzed the ability of nations to create and maintain an institutional environment which is suitable for organizations operating there (IMD 2010). The World Competitiveness Yearbooks provide information about the competitiveness of 58 countries on criteria based on 327 factors. The IMD uses an annual survey of business executives to quantify different aspects of institutional environments in countries. These annual surveys are crafted and employed in collaboration with 54 partner institutes worldwide and sent to business executives in top and middle management position in 58 countries. These executives represent firms of various sizes, and different industrial sectors and national backgrounds, and the results of this survey do not have a single country or industry respondent bias, which makes it a reliable data source for country-level institutional comparison studies.

World Competitiveness Yearbooks have also been used by many past IB studies addressing the influences of business and institutional environments of countries on the strategies of firms (e.g. Delios and Beamish 1999; Gaur et al. 2007; Gaur and Lu 2007). Informal institutions are humanly devised constraints that are embedded in the shared norms, values and beliefs in a society (North 1990, 2005; Estrin et al. 2009). This study uses two survey categories from IMD executive opinion surveys from World Competitiveness Yearbooks (1995–2006): corruption, and national culture, which address key aspects of the informal institutional environment. Corruption or acceptance of corruption in a society has been referred to as an example of informal (normative) institutions in some previous studies (e.g. El Said and McDonald 2002; Tonoyan 2003; Peng et al. 2008). Therefore, one of the elements of informal institutional distance in this study is country scores in corruption from the World Competitiveness Yearbooks in the year of investment or in the nearest available year. Cultural distance has been used in some past studies to address the informal (normative and cognitive) institutional distance or institutional environment (e.g. Yiu and Makino 2002; Estrin et al. 2009). However, we argue that the society's openness to foreign ideas captured by the national culture category in this study addresses the informal attitude to foreign firms in these societies. North (2005) also referred to the importance of cognition in the informal behaviors of the society. This societal cognition impacts the openness of a society to foreign ideas, which has been referred to as one of the important characteristics of societies that have developed and achieved economic competitiveness (e.g. North and Thomas 1973; North 1981). We argue that this approach to operationalize the cultural component of informal institutions that is specific to the acceptance of foreign ideas and consequently the acceptance of operations of foreign firms in host countries is more relevant to the theme of the current study. Hence, we use this approach for the operationalization rather than using cultural distance index (Kogut and Singh 1988) based on Hofstede's (1980, 2001) work as done in many past IB studies (e.g. Yiu and Makino 2002). Informal institutional pressures in this study are calculated by difference in the average of the country scores in two elements of executive opinion survey from World Competitiveness Yearbooks from the highest score (10) as shown in Table 13.3.

13.3.3 Variables Description

The dependent variable of the study is acquisition mode choice, which is coded 1 for partial acquisitions and 0 for full acquisitions. This study

Table 13.3   Operationalization of informal institutional pressures

Indicator	Survey item from World Competitiveness Reports (1995–2006)
Corruption	Bribing and corruption do not exist (scores 1–10)
National culture	The national culture is open to foreign ideas (scores 1–10)
Informal institutional score	Host-country score in (Corruption + National Culture)/2
Informal institutional pressure	10 (highest score) minus informal institutional score of the host country

uses a number of control variables that have been found to be important for entry mode decisions (especially acquisitions) in past IB studies. It is expected that the use of these control variables will enhance the validity of the results. The details of operationalization of study variables along with relevant references are provided in Table 13.4.

13.3.4   Statistical Method

We have used a binomial logistic regression to test our hypotheses because the dependent variable is dichotomous. The binomial logistic regression model is formally expressed as:

$$P(y_i=1) = 1 / 1 + \exp(-a - X_i B)$$

where y_i is the dependent variable, X_i is the vector of independent variables for the ith observation, a is the intercept parameter and B is the vector of regression coefficients. The statistical software PASW Statistics 18 is used for the binomial regression analysis in this study. The dependent variable has value 1 if the MNEs chose partial acquisition at the time of market entry; hence, a positive regression coefficient indicates that a specific control or independent variable increases the probability of choice of partial acquisition entry by MNEs. Table 13.5 shows the descriptive statistics and correlations of the variables used in the study.

We conduct the analysis of variance inflation factor (VIF) test as suggested by Belsley et al. (1980) in order to observe whether potential collinearity among variables is going to influence the regression results of study or not. According to Belsley et al. (1980), in those regression models where the highly correlated variables are associated with the same

Table 13.4   Variables operationalization

Variables	Operationalization
Acquisition mode	0 = full acquisition, 1 = partial acquisition.
Formal institutional pressure	10 (highest score) minus host-country score in the item 'Legal structure and security of property rights' (Source: Economic Freedom of the World Annual Reports).
Informal institutional pressure	The average of difference in host-country score from the highest score (10) in the following items in the year of investment / scores in nearest available year (Source: World Competitiveness Yearbooks 1995–2006). 1. National culture is open to foreign ideas (scores 1–10) 2. Bribing and corruption do not exist (scores 1–10)
Parent MNE size	Natural log of global sales of the parent MNE in the year preceding the year of investment changed to euros (e.g. Hennart and Park 1993, Larimo 1997, 2003) (Source: internal databank).
International experience of MNE	The number of earlier manufacturing FDIs made by the MNE (Larimo 1993, 1997, 2003) (Source: internal databank).
Host-country experience of MNE	MNE's length of earlier manufacturing experience in host country (no. of years) (e.g. Hennart and Park 1993; Cho and Padmanabhan 1995; Larimo 2003) (Source: internal databank).
Economic growth	The annual growth of GDP in the host country, in the year of investment (e.g. Brouthers and Brouthers 2000) (Source: UNCTAD).
Host-country risk	The host-country risk in the year preceding the investment based on euro money country risk ratings (e.g. Cosset and Roy 1991; Larimo 2003) (Source: euro money country risk ratings).
BRIC dummy	1 for acquisitions in BRIC (Brazil, Russia, India and China) countries, 0 for other countries (Source: internal databank).
Timing	1 for acquisitions during 1990s. 0 for FDIs in 2000s (Source: internal databank).
CEE dummy	1 for acquisitions in host countries in CEE region and 0 for acquisitions in other regions (Source: internal databank).

condition index, the VIF value should not exceed 10. The VIF values of all the variables are much below 10, and hence it could be expected that the potential collinearity among variables is not going to impact the results of regression analysis of this study.

Table 13.5   Descriptive statistics and Pearson correlations

Variables	Mean	Std.Dv.	1	2	3	4	5	6	7	8	9	10	11
1. Acquisition mode	0.52	0.501	1										
2. Log parent MNE size	5.977	2.126	-.014	1									
3. International experience	23.73	23.657	0.082	0.643*	1								
4. Host-country experience	1.22	2.761	-0.117	0.211*	0.279*	1							
5. Host-country risk	59.945	14.602	0.197*	0.136	0.027	0.044	1						
6. Economic growth	4.498	6.377	-0.051	0.093	-0.023	0.137	0.621*	1					
7. BRIC dummy	0.60	0.491	-0.143	-0.063	-0.069	0.091	-0.216*	0.108	1				
8. Timing	0.61	0.490	0.387*	0.070	0.214*	-0.210*	-0.030	-0.249*	-0.425*	1			
9. CEE dummy	0.41	0.493	-0.128	-0.081	-0.019	0.014	-0.541*	-0.636*	-0.274*	0.116	1		
10. Formal institutional pressures	5.771	0.936	0.051	0.151	-0.035	0.118	0.744*	0.625*	-0.264*	-0.253*	-0.495*	1	
11. Informal institutional pressures	5.308	0.876	-0.226*	-0.103	-0.056	0.091	-0.484*	-0.222*	0.528*	-0.188*	0.350*	-0.498*	1

Note: * Correlations significant at 0.01 level (two-tailed test).

13.4   RESULTS AND DISCUSSION

Table 13.6 displays the results of binomial regression analysis of the study. The explanatory power of all the statistical models of the study is good, as their chi-square values are significant at the p < 0.01 level. Moreover, the predictive ability of the statistical models can be assessed by the correct classification rate. All the three statistical models of the study have a higher correct classification rate than the chance rate of 50 percent, which is calculated using the proportional chance criterion which is $a^2 + (1-a)^2$, where a is the proportion of partial acquisitions (52 percent) in the study sample. The logistic regression models show the correct classification rate of 72.3 percent to 77.1 percent. Hair et al. (1995, 204) suggest that the classification rate should be at least 25 percent greater than the chance rate, which is achieved in this case. Hence, it can be said that models offer sufficient predictive accuracy. Finally, good Nagelkerke R^2 (0.327, 0.364 and 0.365) values also depict significant predictive capability of all three models.

Table 13.6   Binomial logistic regression results (partial acquisition = 1)

Variables	Model 1: Control variables	Model 2: Formal institutional pressures	Model 3: Informal institutional pressures
Parent MNE size	−0.175	−0.157	−0.163
International experience	0.011	0.012	0.012
Host-country experience	−0.012	−0.034	−0.038
Host-country risk	0.073***	0.059**	0.059**
Economic growth in host country	−0.143***	−0.109**	−0.108**
BRIC dummy	0.423	0.193	0.70
Timing dummy	1.694***	1.456***	1.381***
CEE dummy	−0.798	0.022	−0.158
Formal institutional pressures		0.104**	
Informal institutional pressures			−0.126**
N (Partial acquisitions)	166 (86)	166 (86)	166 (86)
Model Chi-square	46.663***	53.085***	52.926***
−2 Log likelihood	183.245	176.823	176.982
Nagelkerke R^2	0.327	0.365	0.364
Correctly classified (%)	72.3%	77.1%	77.1%

Note: Levels of significance: * $p < 0.1$, ** $p < 0.05$, *** $p < 0.01$.

In Table 13.6, Model 1 presents the results of the binary logistic regression depicting the impact of control variables on the choice of partial or full acquisitions of Finnish MNEs. It can be observed that out of eight control variables, three variables – host-country risk, economic growth in the host country and timing of investment – are highly significant ($p < 0.01$ level) for the acquisition entry strategy of Finnish MNEs. The regression coefficients reveal that high host-country risk lead to the choice of partial acquisition, while high host-country economic growth leads to the choice of full acquisitions by the Finnish MNEs. Further, it can be observed that investments made during the 1990s tended to be partial acquisitions, as revealed by the significance of the timing dummy and positive regression coefficient. The choice of full acquisitions in the host countries with high economic growth can be explained by referring to the fact that high market potential and business opportunities offered by those markets motivated Finnish firms to acquire local firms fully whenever it was possible. This full acquisition of local firms offered the opportunities to use their existing resources and networks, as well as gain a strong foothold sooner in an attractive market. The choice of partial acquisition in cases of high host-country risk can be explained by referring to the previous studies, where it has been mentioned that firms tend to prefer joint ventures in countries with high risk, so that they can share it with a local partner (e.g. Kim and Hwang 1992; Mutinelli and Piscitello 1998; Pan and Tse 2000). We argue that the same logic can be applied in cases where the MNEs decide to enter the market using the acquisition mode, and therefore the choice of partial acquisition appears to be more appropriate in high-risk environments.

The significance of timing in choices of partial acquisition (that is, the preference of partial acquisition in investments made in 1990s) can be explained by referring to the specific host countries' characteristics of the sample, as well as the transition from planned to market economy taking place in host countries in the CEE region and China, and the gradual opening up of the market for FDI by other sample emerging economies. Meyer (2002) also found that partial acquisitions may be a means to align the interests of an investing MNE and the host government in acquisitions related to the privatization of state enterprises. Governmental agencies often have indirect means to influence the prosperity of a business. As the privatization of state-owned enterprises was one of the key economic characteristics of 1990s in most of the sample emerging economies, the choice of partial acquisition offered foreign investors an opportunity to align their interests with the those of host-country governments. This helped them to gain a foothold in the new host countries with institutions in the process of development, and to reduce the likelihood of surprise adverse interference by the state authorities.

Model 2 in Table 13.6 shows the impacts of formal institutional pressures on the acquisition strategy of Finnish MNEs. The regression coefficient shows that formal institutional pressures are significant at the $p <$ 0.05 level and high formal pressures result in the choice of partial acquisitions, which agrees with hypothesis 1 of the study. Therefore, hypothesis 1 is accepted. As discussed earlier, better investor protection reflected by shareholder rights and good accounting standards results in increased acquisition activity in those host countries (Baums 1993; Pagano and Volpin 2005). Therefore, in the emerging economies of CEE, Asia and Latin America where market economy institutions are in the process of development and strengthening, the choice of partial acquisitions by Finnish MNEs in cases of high formal pressures and restrictions is understandable. Moreover, the choice of partial acquisitions in host countries with high formal institutional pressures also offer the investing MNEs opportunities of good relationships with local authorities by using the existing networks, as well as sharing risks and costs with an established local partner firm.

Model 3 in Table 13.6 shows the impacts of informal institutional pressures on the acquisition strategy of Finnish MNEs. The regression results reveal that the informal institutional pressures are significant at the $p <$ 0.05 level; however the regression coefficient shows that high informal pressures lead to the choice of full acquisitions rather than partial acquisitions. This finding agrees with hypothesis 2b of the study and consequently hypothesis 2b is accepted. We would like to explain this finding by referring to previous IB studies that addressed the problems of working with a partner from a different informal (including cultural and organizational) background (e.g. Gomes-Casseres 1990; Estrin et al. 2009). Previous IB literature also mentions the important role of the regulative powers of state authorities in the choice of partial acquisitions by the MNEs, as they permit only partial acquisitions in some industries during privatization (Meyer 2002) by establishing a limit on the allowable level of ownership by foreign MNEs (Brouthers 2002; Yiu and Makino 2002). It is important to mention that for MNEs, it can be difficult to work with partners in a partial acquisition that come from a very different informal institutional background as they typically have different organizational structures (e.g. Kogut and Singh 1988) and communication and management styles (e.g. Hennart and Zeng 2002).

It has been found in past studies that a firm's strategic decisions are also influenced by the cognitive categories their decision-makers construct as they make sense of their environment (Douglas 1986; Singh et al. 1986). Consequently, partial acquisition partners from different informal institutional backgrounds can face problems such as different approaches to strategic decision-making and differences in expectations regarding the firm's strategies (Schneider and De Meyer 1991; Park and Ungson 1997). These inter-partner differences resulting from the informal institutional background can also result in conflicts and hinder the transfer of organizational practices from the MNE's headquarters to the foreign subsidiaries. Moreover, although full acquisitions may also be subject to internal misunderstandings and conflicts caused by informal differences among employees, such misunderstandings and conflicts are less likely to be a source of internal inconsistency at organizational level (Tsang 1994; Dhanaraj and Beamish 2004) than is expected in the case of a partial acquisition. The host countries in the sample consist of emerging economies representing very different informal institutions compared to Finland. It has also been found that partial acquisitions have been preferred in transition economies (Meyer and Tran 2006; Jakobsen and Meyer 2008) due to the role played by the governments in private business affairs in order to serve perceived public interests.

It is also important to mention the specific characteristics of the study sample, as most countries in the CEE region (except Russia) and to an extent certain Asian countries have successfully implemented market economy reforms. Hence, in cases where formal pressures are not higher, then the choice of full acquisitions despite high informal institutional pressures is understandable on the part of the Finnish MNEs entering emerging economies in CEE, Asia and Latin America. Finally, as the majority of employees of fully acquired firms are local, the acquiring MNE can use the practices, routines and organizational structures of the acquired firms (Barkema and Vermeulen 1998; Anand and Delios 2002) that fit well in the local informal context. Hence, despite full acquisition, it can be expected that investing MNEs can exhibit a certain level of local responsiveness and achieve their goals in the host country.

13.5   IMPLICATIONS, LIMITATIONS AND FUTURE RESEARCH DIRECTIONS

The purpose of this study was to examine the impacts of formal and institutional pressures on acquisition entry strategy (that is, the choice between full and partial acquisitions) of Finnish MNEs in emerging economies. We performed the analysis of our study hypotheses using a dataset of 166 acquisitions by Finnish firms in CEE, Asian and Latin American countries during the time period of 1990–2006. This study contributes to the application of the institution-based view of IB strategy in the foreign market entry literature by being one of the first specifically to address the choice between full and partial acquisitions by MNEs, using the concepts of formal and informal institutional pressures. The empirical context of Finnish FDI in emerging economies of CEE, Asia and Latin America has also revealed useful insights due to the different institutional environments as well as institutional development taking place in the host countries. This study is also one of the first specifically to address the acquisitions strategy of MNEs by using the concepts of formal and informal institutional pressures, rather than by addressing either establishment or ownership mode choice as done in most past IB studies.

The study results reveal that investments in host countries with high risk, and investments made during the 1990s by the Finnish MNEs, tended to be partial acquisitions. It was further found that in high-growth emerging economies, full acquisitions were preferred by Finnish firms; while in high-risk host economies, partial acquisitions were preferred. We further found that high formal institutional pressures in the host country result in a preference for partial acquisitions, while informal institutional pressures lead Finnish MNEs to prefer full acquisitions rather than partial acquisitions in the sample emerging economies. We explain this finding by referring to problems associated with working with equity partners with different informal characteristics and backgrounds, high informal differences from Finland of many host economies, and possibilities of exhibiting local responsiveness despite full acquisition by using existing the local organizational practices and strategies as well as retaining experienced local employees.

The findings of the study offer some guidelines for the managers of firms from the Nordic region aiming to use the acquisition mode to enter the emerging economies of CEE, Asia and Latin America. We found that high formal institutional pressures and high host-country risk lead to the choice of partial acquisitions of Finnish MNEs, while high host-country growth and high informal institutional pressures result in the choice of full acquisitions. It is advised that MNE managers of Nordic firms need to consider that in the host countries with high informal institutional pressures, some of the practices of acquired subsidiaries could be very useful, as they are aligned with the requirements of local informal institutions. Therefore, they should grant a certain level of autonomy to those subsidiaries as this would allow local responsiveness despite being a wholly owned subsidiary. Finally, the choice of full acquisitions despite high informal institutional pressures has some implications for the use of expatriates in the human resource strategy of the investing firms. Full acquisitions despite high informal institutional pressures also have implications for the human resource management strategy of MNEs, as they can use more local managers and train them, rather than using more expatriates in those subsidiaries. In this way, the firm would be able to mitigate some of the pressures resulting from ignorance of the local informal institutional context.

This study also has certain limitations. Our study uses MNEs from only one home country (Finland). However, still the study provides interesting insights to a relatively unexplored research area of acquisitions strategy from perspective of MNEs from Nordic regions, as well as representing small and open economies. For future research, it is suggested to expand the sample size by also including FDI made by MNEs from other Nordic countries as well as small and open economies such as the Netherlands, Belgium and New Zealand, and to study the impacts of institutional pressures on acquisition strategy. This would allow a comprehensive understanding of the impacts of institutional pressures on acquisitions strategy and would help in generalizing findings from a Nordic as well as small and open economy perspective. It is also suggested to study the impacts of institutional pressures on entry mode strategies of MNEs more in depth by analyzing the impacts of individual dimensions of pressures, as well as their joint effects. Finally, future research has the potential to test the impacts of institutional pressures on MNEs' greenfield entry strategy (wholly owned or collaborative), as well as joint venture strategy (minority, 50–50 and majority), as these specific modes have not been addressed in depth in past IB studies.

NOTE

*   This chapter is part of Academy of Finland financial project no. 250613, entitled 'Value Creation in International Growth: Focus on Acquisitions and Joint Ventures'.

REFERENCES

Ali, A.M. (2003), 'Institutional differences as sources of growth differences', *Atlantic Economic Journal*, **31** (4), 348–362.

Ali, A. and L. Hwang (2000), 'Country-specific factors related to financial reporting and the value relevance of accounting data', *Journal of Accounting Research*, **38** (1), 1–21.

Anand, J. and A. Delios (2002), 'Absolute and relative resources as determinants of international acquisitions', *Strategic Management Journal*, **23** (2), 119–134.

Anderson, E. and H. Gatignon (1986), 'Modes of foreign entry: a transaction cost analysis and propositions', *Journal of International Business Studies*, **17** (3), 1–26.

Arslan, A. (2010), 'Impacts of institutional pressures and the strength of market supporting institutions in the host country on the ownership strategy of multinational enterprises: theoretical discussion and propositions', *Journal of Management and Governance* (online first articles).

Bada, A.O., M.C. Aniebonam and V. Owei (2004), 'Institutional pressures as sources of improvisations: a case study from a developing country context', *Journal of Global Information Technology Management*, **7** (3), 27–44.

Barkema, H.G. and F. Vermeulen (1998), 'International expansion through start-up or acquisition: a learning perspective', *Academy of Management Journal*, **41** (1), 7–26.

Baums, T. (1993), 'Takeovers versus institutions in corporate governance in Germany', in D.D. Prentice and P.R.J. Holland (eds), *Contemporary Issues in Corporate Governance*, Oxford: Clarendon Press, pp. 151–183.

Belsley, D.A., E. Kuh and R.E. Welsch (1980), *Regression Diagnostics: Identifying Influential Data and Sources of Collinearity*, New York: Wiley.

Bengoa, M. and B. Sanchez-Robles (2003), 'FDI, economic freedom and growth: new evidence from Latin America', *European Journal of Political Economy*, **19** (3), 529–545.

Boockmann, B. and A. Dreher (2003), 'The contribution of the IMF and the World Bank to economic freedom', *European Journal of Political Economy*, **19** (3), 633−649.

Brouthers, K.D. (2002), 'Institutional, cultural and transaction cost influences on entry mode choice and performance', *Journal of International Business Studies*, **33** (2), 203–221.

Brouthers, K.D. and L.E. Brouthers (2000), 'Acquisition or greenfield start-up? Institutional, cultural and transaction cost influences', *Strategic Management Journal*, **21** (1), 89–97.

Brouthers, K.D. and L.E. Brouthers (2001), 'Explaining the national cultural distance paradox', *Journal of International Business Studies*, **32** (1), 177–189.

Brouthers, K. and J.F. Hennart (2007), 'Boundaries of the firm: Insights from international entry mode research', *Journal of Management*, **33** (3), 395–425.

Burkhart, M. and F. Panunzi (2006), 'Agency conflicts, ownership concentration and legal shareholder protection', *Journal of Financial Intermediation*, **15** (1), 1−31.

Chang, S.J. and P.M. Rosenzweig (2001), 'The choice of entry mode in sequential foreign direct investment', *Strategic Management Journal*, **22** (8), 747–776.

Chen, S-F. and J.F. Hennart (2004), 'A hostage theory of joint ventures: why do Japanese investors choose partial over full acquisitions to enter the United States?' *Journal of Business Research*, **57** (10), 1126–1134.

Cho, K.R. and P. Padmanabhan (1995), 'Acquisition versus new venture: the choice of foreign establishment mode by Japanese firms', *Journal of International Management*, **1** (3), 255–285.

Cosset, J.C. and R. Roy (1991), 'The determinants of country risk ratings', *Journal of International Business Studies*, **22** (1), 135–142.

Dacin, T.M. (1997), 'Isomorphism in context: the power and prescription of institutional norms', *Academy of Management Journal*, **40** (1), 46–81.

Datta, D.K., P. Herrmann and A. Rasheed (2002), 'Choice of foreign market entry mode: critical review and future directions' in M.A. Hitt and J.L.C. Cheng (eds), *Managing Transnational Firms: Resources, Market Entry and Strategic Alliances. Advances in International Management, Vol. 14*, Amsterdam: JAI Press, pp. 85–153.

Dawson, J.W. (1998), 'Institutions, investment, and growth: new cross-country and panel data evidence', *Economic Inquiry*, **36** (October), 603–619.

Delios, A. and P. W. Beamish (1999), 'Ownership strategy of Japanese firms: transactional, institutional and experience influences', *Strategic Management Journal*, **20** (8), 711–727.

Delios, A. and W.J. Henisz (2003), 'Political hazards and the sequence of entry by Japanese firms, 1980–1998', *Journal of International Business Studies*, **34** (3), 227–241.

Demirbag, M., E. Tatoglou and K.W. Glaister (2008), 'Factors affecting perceptions of the choice between acquisition and greenfield entry: the case of Western FDI in emerging markets', *Management International Review*, **48** (1), 5–38.

Demirbag, M., E. Tatoglou and K.W. Glaister (2010), 'Institutional and transaction cost influences on the partnership structure of foreign affiliates', *Management International Review*, **50** (6), 709–745.

Dhanaraj, C. and P.W. Beamish (2004), 'Effect of equity ownership on survival of international joint ventures', *Strategic Management Journal*, **25** (3), 295–305.

Dietrich, M. (1994), 'National patterns of corporate restructuring: mergers and joint ventures in the European community', in Robert Delorme and Kurt Dopfer (eds), *The*

Political Economy of Diversity. Evolutionary Perspectives on Economic Order and Disorder, Cheltenham, UK and Northampton, MA, USA: Edward Elgar, pp. 149–165.

Dikova, D., S.P. Rao and A. van Witteloostuijn (2010), 'Cross-border acquisition abandonment and completion: the effect of institutional differences and organizational learning in the international business service industry, 1981–2001', *Journal of International Business Studies*, **41** (2), 223–245.

Dikova, D. and A. van Witteloostuijn (2007), 'Foreign direct investment mode choice: entry and establishment modes in transition economies', *Journal of International Business Studies*, **38** (6), 1013–1033.

DiRienzo, C.E., D. Jayoti, K.T. Cort and J. Burbridge (2007), 'Corruption and the role of information', *Journal of International Business Studies*, **38** (3), 320–332.

Douglas, M. (1986), *How Institutions Think*, Syracuse, NY: Syracuse University Press.

Dreher, A. and S. Rupprecht (2007), 'IMF programs and reform – inhibition or encouragement?' *Economics Letters*, **95** (3), 320−326.

Dunning, J.H. and S. Lundan (2008), *Multinational Enterprises and the Global Economy*, 2nd edn, Cheltenham, UK and Northampton, MA, USA: Edward Elgar.

Economic Freedom Network (2008), *Economic Freedom of the World* (Annual Report), http://www.freetheworld.com/release_2008.html.

El Said, H. and F. McDonald (2002), 'Institutional reform and entry mode by foreign firms: the case of Jordan', *Journal for Institutional Innovation, Development and Transition*, **6** (1), 76–88.

Elango, B. and R.B. Sambharya (2004), 'The influence of industry structure on the entry mode choice of overseas entrants in manufacturing industries', *Journal of International Management*, **10** (1), 107–124.

Estrin, S., D. Baghdasaryan and K.E. Meyer (2009), 'The impact of institutional and human resource distance on international entry strategies', *Journal of Management Studies*, **46** (7), 1171–1196.

Flores, R.G. and R.V. Aguilera (2007), 'Globalization and location choice: an analysis of US multinational firms in 1980 and 2000', *Journal of International Business Studies*, **38** (7), 1187–1210.

Gaur, A.S., A. Delios and K. Singh (2007), 'Institutional environments, staffing strategies and subsidiary performance', *Journal of Management*, **33** (4), 611–636.

Gaur, A.S. and W. Lu (2007), 'Ownership strategies and survival of foreign subsidiaries: impacts of institutional distance and experience', *Journal of Management*, **33** (1), 84–110.

Globerman, S. and D. Shapiro (2003), 'Governance infrastructure and US foreign direct investment', *Journal of International Business Studies*, **34** (1), 19–39.

Goergen, M., M. Martynova and L. Renneboog (2005), 'Corporate governance convergence: evidence from takeover regulation reforms in Europe', Utrecht School of Economics, Discussion Paper Series 05-19.

Gomes-Casseres, B. (1990), 'Firm ownership preferences and host government restrictions: an integrated approach', *Journal of International Business Studies*, **21** (1), 1–22.

Guillen, M.F. (2003), 'Experience, imitation, and the sequence of foreign entry: wholly owned and joint venture manufacturing by South Korean firms and business groups in China, 1987–1995', *Journal of International Business Studies*, **34** (2), 185–198.

Hair, J.F., Jr, R.E. Anderson, R.L. Tatham and W.C. Black (1995), *Multivariate Data Analysis*, 4th edn, Upper Saddle River, NJ: Prentice Hall.

Hall, P.A. and D. Soskice (2001), *Varieties of Capitalism: The Institutional Foundations of Comparative Advantage*, New York: Oxford University Press.

Henisz, W.J. (2000), 'The institutional environment for multinational investment', *Journal of Law, Economics and Organization*, **16** (2), 334–364.

Henisz, W.J. (2004), 'The institutional environment for international business?' in P.J. Buckley (ed.), *What is International Business?* New York: Palgrave Macmillan, pp. 85–109.

Henisz, W.J. and B.A. Zelner (2005), 'Legitimacy, interest group pressures, and change in emergent institutions: the case of foreign investors and host country governments', *Academy of Management Journal*, **30** (2), 361–382.

Hennart, J.F., D.J. Kim and M. Zeng (1998), 'The impact of joint venture status on the longevity of Japanese stakes in US manufacturing affiliates', *Organization Science*, **9** (3), 382–395.

Hennart, J.F. and Y.R. Park (1993), 'Greenfield vs. acquisition: the strategy of Japanese investors in the United States', *Management Science*, **39** (9), 1054–1070.

Hennart, J.F. and M. Zeng (2002), 'Cross-cultural differences and joint venture longevity', *Journal of International Business Studies*, **33** (4), 699−716.

Hill, C.W.L., P. Hwang and W.C. Kim (1990), 'An eclectic theory of the choice of international market entry mode', *Strategic Management Journal*, **11** (2), 117−128.

Hofstede, G. (1980), *Culture's Consequences: International Differences in Work Related Values*, Newbury Park, CA: Sage.

Hofstede, G. (2001), *Cultures and Organizations: Software of Mind*, 2nd edn, New York: McGraw Hill.

IMD (2010), *World Competitiveness Yearbook 2010 and CD*, Lausanne.

IMD (annual editions, 1995–2006), *World Competitiveness Yearbook*, Lausanne: IMD World Competitiveness Center.

Jackson, G. (2005), 'Toward a comparative perspective on corporate and labour management: enterprise coalitions and national trajectories', in Howard Gospel and Andrew Pendleton (eds), *Corporate Governance and Labour Management: An International Comparison*, Oxford: Oxford University Press, pp. 284–309.

Jakobsen, K. and K.E. Meyer (2008), 'Partial acquisition: the overlooked entry mode', in J.H. Dunning and P. Gugler (eds), *Progress in International Business Research 2*, New York: Oxford University Press Inc, pp. 203–226.

Jung, J.C., P.W. Beamish and A. Goerzen (2008), 'FDI ownership strategy: a Japanese–US MNE comparison', *Management International Review*, **48** (5), 491–524.

Khanna, T. (2005), 'Strategies that fit emerging markets', *Harvard Business Review*, **83** (6), 63–76.

Kim, W.C. and P. Hwang (1992), 'Global strategy and multinationals' entry mode choice', *Journal of International Business Studies*, **23** (1), 29–54.

Kogut, B. and H. Singh (1988), 'The effect of national culture on the choice of entry mode', *Journal of International Business Studies*, **19** (3), 411–432.

Kostova, T. (1999), 'Transnational transfer of strategic organizational practices: a contextual perspective', *Academy of Management Review*, **24** (2), 308–324.

Kostova, T. and K. Roth (2002), 'Adoption of an organizational practice by subsidiaries of multinational corporations: institutional and relational effects', *Academy of Management Journal*, **45** (1), 215–233.

Kostova, T. and S. Zaheer (1999), 'Organizational legitimacy under conditions of complexity: the case of the multinational enterprise', *Academy of Management Review*, **24** (3), 64–81.

Larimo J. (1993), 'Foreign direct investment behaviour and performance. An analysis of Finnish direct manufacturing investments in OECD countries', Acta Wasaensia No. 32, Vaasa, Finland: University of Vaasa.

Larimo J. (1997), 'Mode of entry in foreign direct investments: behaviour of Finnish firms in OECD markets', Proceedings of the University of Vaasa, Discussion Papers, vol. 232, Vaasa, Finland: University of Vaasa.

Larimo, J. (2003), 'Form of investment by Nordic firms in world markets', *Journal of Business Research*, **56** (10), 791–803.

Lu, J.W. and D. Xu (2006), 'Growth and survival of international joint ventures: an external–internal legitimacy perspective', *Journal of Management*, **32** (3), 426–448.

Luo, Y. (2001), 'Determinants of entry in an emerging economy: a multilevel approach', *Journal of Management Studies*, **38** (3), 443–472.

Luo, Y. (2002), *Multinational Enterprises in Emerging Markets*, Copenhagen: Copenhagen Business School Press.

Meyer, K.E. (2002), 'Management challenges in privatization acquisitions in transition economies', *Journal of World Business*, **37** (4), 266–276.

Meyer, K.E., S. Estrin, S.K. Bhaumik and M.W. Peng (2009), 'Institutions, resources, and entry strategies in emerging economies', *Strategic Management Journal*, **30** (1), 61–80.

Meyer, K.E. and Y.T.T. Tran (2006), 'Market penetration and acquisition strategies for emerging economies', *Long Range Planning*, **39** (2), 177–197.

Mutinelli, M. and L. Piscitello (1998), 'The entry mode choice of MNEs: an evolutionary approach', *Research Policy*, **27** (5), 491–506.

North, D.C. (1981), *Structure and Change in Economic History*, New York: Norton.

North, D.C. (1990), *Institutions, Institutional Change and Economic Performance*, New York: Cambridge University Press.

North, D.C. (2005), *Understanding the Process of Economic Change*, Princeton, NJ: Princeton University Press.

North, D.C. and R.P. Thomas (1973), *The Rise of the Western World: A New Economic History*, Cambridge: Cambridge University Press.

Pablo, A.L. and M. Javidan (2004), 'Introduction', in A. Pablo and M. Javidan (eds), *Mergers and Acquisitions: Creating Integrative Knowledge,* Malden, MA, USA and Oxford, UK: Blackwell Publishing, pp. xiv–xviii.

Pagano, M. and P. Volpin (2005), 'The political economy of corporate governance', *American Economic Review*, **95** (4), 1105–1130.

Pan, Y. and D.K. Tse (2000), 'The hierarchical model of market entry modes', *Journal of International Business Studies*, **31** (4), 535–554.

Park, S.H. and G.R. Ungson (1997), 'The effect of national culture, organizational complementarity, and economic motivation on joint venture dissolution', *Academy of Management Journal*, **40** (2), 279–307.

Peng, M. (2002), 'Towards an institution-based view of business strategy', *Asia Pacific Journal of Management*, **19** (2–3), 251–266.

Peng, M.W. (2003), 'Institutional transitions and strategic choices', *Academy of Management Review*, **28** (2), 275–296.

Peng, M. and T.A. Khoury (2009), 'Unbundling the institution based view of international business strategy', in A. Rugman (ed.), *The Oxford Handbook of International Business*, 2nd edn, New York: Oxford University Press, pp. 256–268.

Peng, M., D. Wang and Y. Jiang (2008), 'An institution-based view of international business strategy: a focus on emerging economies', *Journal of International Business Studies*, **39** (5), 920–936.

Rossi, S. and P. Volpin (2003), 'Cross-country determinants of mergers and acquisitions', London: Centre for Economic Policy Research, Discussion Paper No. 3889.

Schneider, S.C. and A. De Meyer (1991), 'Interpreting and responding to strategic issues: the impact of national culture', *Strategic Management Journal*, **12** (4), 307–320.

Scott, W.R. (1995), *Institutions and Organizations,* Thousand Oaks, CA: Sage Publications.

Scott, W.R. (2008), *Institutions and Organizations: Ideas and Interests*, 3rd edn, Thousand Oaks, CA: Sage Publications.

Shimizu, K., M.A. Hitt, D. Vaidyanath and V. Pisano (2004), 'Theoretical foundations of cross-border mergers and acquisitions: a review of current research and recommendations for the future', *Journal of International Management*, **10** (3), 307–353.

Singh, J.V., D.J. Tucker and R.J. House (1986), 'Organization legitimacy and the liability of newness', *Administrative Science Quarterly*, **31**, 171–193.

Slangen, A.H. and J.F. Hennart (2008), 'Do multinationals really prefer to enter culturally distant countries through greenfields rather than through acquisitions? The role of parent experience and subsidiary autonomy', *Journal of International Business Studies*, **39** (3), 472–490.

Slangen, A.H.L. and R.J.M. van Tulder (2009), 'Cultural distance, political risk, or governance quality? Towards a more accurate conceptualization and measurement of external uncertainty in foreign entry mode research', *International Business Review*, **18** (3), 276–291.

Tonoyan, V. (2003), 'Entrepreneurship and corruption: integrating institutions, rationality and social norms', "Grüne Reihe" Nr. 54 des Instituts für Mitteltastandsforschung (ifm) der Universität Mannheim, S.35.

Tsang, E.W.K. (1994), 'Human resource management problems in Sino-foreign joint ventures', *International Journal of Manpower*, **15** (9–10), 4–21.

Xu, D., Y. Pan and P.W. Beamish (2004), 'The effect of regulative and normative distances on MNE ownership and expatriate strategies', *Management International Review*, **44** (3), 85–307.

Xu, D. and O. Shenkar (2002), 'Institutional distance and multinational enterprise', *Academy of Management Review*, **27** (4), 608–618.

Yiu, D. and S. Makino (2002), 'The choice between joint venture and wholly owned subsidiary: an institutional perspective', *Organization Science*, **13** (6), 667–683.

14 Managing improvisational practice: the tension between structure and creative difference

Holly Patrick, Gail Greig and Nic Beech

14.1 INTRODUCTION

Improvisation has traditionally been part of many creative practices including writing, music, art and drama. More recently it has been recognized as an important part of managerial practice and lessons have been drawn from jazz music in particular (Weick 1998) which conclude that management ought to be more flexible, exploratory and accepting of diversity (Montuouri 2003). However, improvisation does not entail a complete absence of structure but operates with 'minimal structures' (Kamoche and Cunha 2001) in which there are creative tensions between genre rules and the freedom of the performer. Indeed, improvisation can develop subgenre rules which result in performers adopting patterns of behaviour that may be less diverse than is immediately apparent. This can be observed in, for example, improvisational comedy where there are informal rules concerning the treatment of subjects such as race and gender, or in jazz where players develop identifiable styles of extemporization. Hence, improvisation is a creative practice (Townley et al. 2009) that occurs in a place of interaction between freedom–structure and diversity–consistency. Therefore, we would see improvisation as an example of bounded diversity and understanding it better can help develop our concept of the relationship between novel action and established ways of doing things.

In this chapter we explore the practice of theatrical improvisation (Vera and Crossan 2004) which is relatively under-researched compared to musical improvisation (Kamoche et al. 2003). In particular we are interested in improvisation as it occurs in the outreach activities of a theatre company in the UK which we will refer to as the Northern Theatre. Part of the purpose of the Northern Theatre is to engage with local communities and to bring theatre to sections of the population that would not normally access theatrical productions. In addition, there is an aim to contribute to the social development of communities, and part of the funding that the Northern Theatre receives relies on effective outreach and community development. As a result the Northern Theatre has a programme of activities in which members of the company go out to schools and local communities and collaborate with social and health services. During these outreach activities, improvisation plays a significant role, and we will explore how it operated in three settings. Before we do so, we will introduce some concepts of improvisational theory and activity theory that we will use to analyse the empirical examples. Our aim is to develop insights into improvisation as an organizational practice that spans both creative freedom and social structures.

The notion of bounded diversity is a feature of ongoing social science debates. It highlights the diversity of specific local practices in the face of the apparently homogenizing effects of institutional rules as they appear to spread across settings; but it also points to the limited extent to which such diversity flourishes within recognizable institutional frameworks of rules and norms indicative of broad social and cultural processes (Lane and Wood 2009; Lounsbury and Ventresca 2003). If both diversity in local practice and institutional rules and structures are discernable, this implies the presence of some means of enabling local practices and institutional rules and norms to 'hang together' (Schatzki 1996, cited in Dreier 2008). Bounded diversity is such a concept, concerning the relations between the general and the specific, between idiosyncratic and institutional practices, which encapsulate varying degrees of simultaneous convergence and divergence (Sorge 2005). The simultaneous presence of rules and norms and variation from these norms raises questions about the complex relationship of balance or tension between them (Sorge 2005). For example, how might institutional logics and apparently routinized patterns of practice be understood such that we can account for the diversity evident in local practices and the unpredictable nature of outcomes (Lane and Wood 2009)?

We adopt cultural historical activity theory (Engestrom et al. 1999a; Blackler 1993) in our empirical analysis of theatrical improvisation in order to explore its relational nature as an example of bounded diversity. In the next section, we provide a brief overview of the literature concerning improvisation in organization studies and theatrical practice.

14.2   IMPROVISATION

Improvisation has been used extensively as a metaphor to generate insights into boundary-crossing activities in organizations. For example, Brown and Eisenhardt (1998) incorporate improvisation into their conceptualization of strategic process as 'competing on the edge', and Hatch (1998) has argued that organizations which have to be highly responsive to changing environments can benefit from the loose boundaries and minimal hierarchies that can be observed in the practice of jazz improvisation. Improvisation is concerned with creating something new in the moment of performance, and Rehn and de Cock (2008) have argued that attempts to codify and predict such creative moments are paradoxical because systematizing the new entails it being already known (which renders it not new). Hence, when improvisation is creative it is a step into the unknown and unsystematized. However, improvisation does not exist without rules and hence a degree of systematic organization. For example, Kamoche et al. (2003), following Bailey (1992), distinguish between non-idiomatic improvisation, which is regarded as 'free' and without a specific identity; and idiomatic improvisation, which has the identity of, and expresses, a particular idiom such as swing or flamenco. Zack (2000) has mapped a range of types of jazz improvisation, some being quite highly structured (e.g. in traditional jazz), others entailing very little structure (e.g. in bebop and postbop). In the more structured varieties repeated use is made of melodies and riffs, the patterns of play between foreground solo instruments and supporting band are rehearsed, and keys and time signatures tend to remain consistent throughout an improvisation. In the less structured varieties passages of play can become atonal, keys and rhythms be deviated from, and players can do quite unexpected and unplanned things.

The concept of minimal structure (Kamoche and Cunha 2001) has been used to shed light on these different forms of improvisation. Three components of minimal structure are identified, including social structure, technical structure and repertoire. The social structure includes the norms, accepted forms of communication and shared understandings of the practising community. These provide a supportive culture for the risk-taking and trust involved in live improvisation. The technical structure is the knowledge of music theory, instrumentation and definition of keys, chord progressions and song structure that enable shared understanding and action. The repertoire is the base of songs and riffs that can be used as a basis for improvising. For example, improvisational performance can develop a new version of an old song, use snippets from an existing song in a new improvised composition, or use existing songs and performances as models for improvising a new solo. Whilst these resources provide a basis for performing an improvisation they do not specify what to do. The improvisation remains a relatively 'open space' (Hatch 1999) in which an indefinite variety of performances is possible (Donald et al. 2010).

Minimal structures are regarded as relevant to management practices as they relate to the use of resources in order to achieve hoped-for ends that cannot be firmly predicted, and the need to respond in real time and recognize patterns in action as they unfold. Hence, links can be made to emergent strategizing, organizational learning and creative practices (Cunha et al. 1999). Equally, organizational change can be associated with moments 'in between' structure (Beech 2010), as different practices come into close contact and produce competition, synthesis or dialogue (Van de Ven and Poole 2005).

Improvisation and minimal structures have also been researched in drama and theatre (Frost and Yarrow 1990) where some performances are highly scripted and directed, whilst others are based on a greater freedom for actors to express a character. In some forms of theatre, there is a great degree of improvisational freedom, whereas in others everything including the style of delivery and interpretation is carefully pre-planned. It has been argued that lessons from theatrical improvisation are applicable to managing and organizing because the resources that are drawn upon are more similar (speech, gestures and movement) to those that people are used to improvising in everyday conversations both inside and outside organizations (Vera and Crossan 2004). Lessons from theatrical improvisation emphasize the equivocal and unpredictable outcomes of the performance. Vera and Crossan (2004) draw attention to the idea that improvisation is not intrinsically good. Rather, improvisations can be of variable quality, depending in part of the perspective of the audience. In Vera and Crossan's view, the quality of improvisations is higher where there is a greater focus on the process than the outcome. That is, where the concern is for the development and use of resources of language and movement, the interactional nature of performance and the different roles played. This is held in contrast to an approach to improvising that is mainly focused on achieving an outcome (e.g. getting a message across, or linking between two pre-planned scenes).

Theatrical improvisations entail position-taking (Eikhof 2010), such as performer, producer or audience member. Within the different positions, diverse ways of making sense and setting priorities exist. For example, what might be important within a community of performers and hence important to a particular performer as he or she improvises, may be insignificant to some audience members and undesirably uncommercial to a producer (Eikhof and Haunschild 2007). In some situations there are tensions between these different positions, whilst in others different interests can produce creative outcomes. Sometimes positions are regarded as structural and relatively fixed; however an alternative view is that identity positions are always in the process of construction and negotiation (Ybema et al. 2009). In such cases, the (re)construction of identity positions occurs as an individual reflects on their own being within social structures (Watson 2009). As transitions through different roles occur, the person becomes aware that others perceive them differently (Sims 2005) and they can be stimulated to claim a different identity (Sveningsson and Alvesson 2003). If this constructionist perspective is adopted, attention is drawn not to the strong boundaries between positions, but to the mobility of people across boundaries. For example, in producing an improvised performance, an actor may also be a 'consumer' of plays that have inspired them, and of the performances of other actors that they regard as exemplary. In seeking to build a career, it is important for actors to be able to deliver work of a good artistic quality that is also commercially viable, and so the divisions between producers or investors and actors are not always as distinct and definite as might be imagined.

Thus, the literature on improvisation in general, and theatrical improvisation in particular, draws attention to the impact of minimal structures which incorporate elements of social, technical and repertoire structures, but which enable a variable degree of creative freedom. Whilst there might be genre and subgenre rules of performance and aesthetic judgement, these do not specify what the actor should actually do and hence practice-in-the-moment is a combination of semi-structured context and the immediacy of improvised action. Different positions can be adopted and to some extent these positions bring with them logics or patterns of sense-making that give priority to certain actions. However, the constructionist perspective is that there is also dynamism in these positions and that in order to understand improvisation as an activity at the boundary of minimal structures we should pay attention to the dynamic interactions in and around improvisations. In order to do this we will apply activity theory to observations of improvisations, and the next section will introduce the aspects of activity theory that will be used in our analysis.

14.3 ACTIVITY THEORY

Cultural historical activity theory, hereafter referred to as activity theory, takes a dialectical approach towards the study of social practices and focuses on the activities which comprise social practices (Chaiklin 2010; Lounsbury and Crumley 2007). An activity is purposeful, goal-oriented and enacted by actors who are held together by a mutual aim within the 'object of activity' which bears their collective motivation (Leont'ev 1974; Axel 1997). The object of activity is the focus of practice within activity systems. Activity systems form the basic unit of analysis (Engestrom 1987) and incorporate collective acting upon a shared object through a variety of mediating means in an organized way. That is, people collectively participate in practices towards a desired end that is meaningful to them using language and tools to do so. This occurs within a set of rules which are established and recognized by the practising community. Within the community there is a division of labour and particular actors become established as enacting specific parts of the overall practice. Hence, activity theory is interested in how practising communities develop shared meanings through which they develop foci on particular 'objects' and ways of practising.

Objects of activity are complex, future-oriented, partially given and partially created (Engestrom and Blackler 2005; Miettinen and Virkkunen 2005). They are partially given in that they do not occur in a social vacuum but are part of an interacting system of practice. However, they are partially created in that actors are not regarded as predetermined automata in what they do. Rather, they exercise a degree of interpretation and choice in acting, which is reflected in the intentions they have for their activity (Blackler and Regan 2009; Nardi 1996). These may change in light of various pressures and countervailing demands in the system of activity (Engestrom 1987). The object of activity may be the production of material objects, but this is not necessarily the case. It could equally involve the production of services, performances, ideas or other experiential or psychological objects. For example, studies have been conducted of health care provision and information technology (IT) call centres where advice and guidance is given. In these settings patient care or user advice are the objects of activity. There is a shared intention (to provide good care or advice) and the practitioners have developed an understanding of what it means to provide good care or advice. Although they bear a mutual overall aim or purpose, objects of activity are typically contested and negotiated (Blackler et al. 1999). For example, in theatrical practice the object of activity may be enacting a performance. But different actors may interpret the object of activity differently: the director may be concerned with the overall performance to ensure that all aspects come together smoothly to produce the play on stage; the actors may be motivated by the need to give convincing portrayals of their characters; the theatre manager may be concerned to see a critical appreciation of a demanding piece because of their belief in staging challenging work. These different foci are held together by the mutual object of activity of performing a play at the theatre. However, they exemplify the contested nature of objects of activity, as some actors might want to spend more rehearsal time on exploring character whilst others are concerned to develop narrative flow incorporating a range of characters, or some might be concerned with making the work accessible whilst others might pursue strict adherence to the script.

These conflicts are termed contradictions in activity theory: when the tensions between these simultaneously present but contradictory aspects of activity become too great, they may give rise to a change in aspects of the activity (Engestrom 1999). This may concern the nature of the object of activity itself, which may be more or less durable or changeable over time (Engestrom and Blackler 2005). The way that tensions or contradictions are coped with becomes a source of future learning for the actors. It is through managing such challenges that the practitioner community develops new rules (or minimal structures) that enable them to manage better in the future. Yesterday's way of coping becomes tomorrow's guideline.

The fluid and dynamic nature of activity means that contradictions arise and may stimulate coping actions. These can give rise to changes in the way in which the activity is organized, the division of labour amongst the practicing community, meanings associated with the object of activity, and the definition and application of rules of practice (Blackler and Regan 2006). Therefore, activity theory provides an approach to analysing theatrical improvisation as an example of bounded diversity within an activity system. The analysis of our data is based on exploring the construction and contestation of the object of activity, the division of labour amongst actors and the activities that constitute the practice of theatrical improvisation. Our aim is to develop insights into improvisation as an organizational practice that spans both creative freedom and social structure.

In the next section we present three illustrations of activities undertaken by the Northern Theatre. In each example, members of the theatre are facilitating improvisations as part of their outreach activities. The illustrations occur in three social settings: adults with learning difficulties, children with learning difficulties and children with behavioural difficulties, It is common to use improvisation with groups such as these in order to emphasize creativity and involvement. There are various actors involved in the examples including the theatre employees (the facilitators), the improvisation participants and their carers. A member of the research team observed each case and interviewed the actors to discuss their intentions and perceptions of what happened.

14.3.1   Example One: Exploring Objects of Activity

The first example of improvisation is drawn from an ongoing community engagement project run by the Northern Theatre in the local area. The activity occurs in weekly sessions in a day centre for adults with learning difficulties and is run by two actors from the theatre (the facilitators). On the occasion documented below, the theatre members were running a rehearsal of a Christmas play, based around a central theme incorporating improvised mime, to be performed the following week by a group of 15 participants.

When the facilitators arrived at the centre the group had just finished lunch, and were making their way through to the day room where the rehearsals were held. The two facilitators went into the room to prepare the materials for the rehearsal, greeting and being enthusiastically greeted by the group. As they were welcomed by the group and arranged the materials they had brought, the carers employed by the day centre continued to bring the participants into the day room and get organized for the activity. Whilst most of the group seemed very excited and enthusiastic for the rehearsal to begin, a small number were reluctant to take their places and one refused to join the rest of the group. While the carers attempted to encourage the remainder to join in, the facilitators engaged with the participants who were ready and waiting to begin the rehearsal. The carers appeared to be primarily concerned with getting the participants arranged in an orderly manner, whereas the facilitators actively encouraged the participants to choose their own seating arrangements. Following a short negotiation, the group sat in a rough circle and each participant was asked to relate an interesting thing that had happened to them since the previous week's rehearsal. By the time this activity had concluded, the carers had managed to assemble the remaining participants and had taken a visible step back (with most leaving the room for a break and two talking with each other at the other end of the room), allowing the facilitators to lead the session.

The play being rehearsed was a Christmas play, based around mime and audience engagement. The participants each had a clearly defined role within the play and the central scene involved the removal of an 'invisible present' from a box. The participants were then supposed to mime their present so that the audience would be able to guess what the present was. During the rehearsal the remaining carers were seated apart from the group and charged with being the audience. The facilitators removed themselves from a directive role in the improvisation session, allowing the group to negotiate the play themselves with facilitation from the sidelines. Fairly regularly, the participants would become distracted, and the facilitators encouraged the group to get the performance back on track themselves, only stepping in when they

. became unruly or very disorganized. However, the participants often got a bit lost in the process, leading to humorous reactions within the group, for example, when one participant mimed a present which was supposed to be mimed by someone else later in the performance. This kind of occurrence became more regular as the rehearsal progressed, with the participants becoming tired, and at this stage the audience were called upon to become more active. Thus they were often told the present in advance so that the correct mimes would be rewarded with applause, allowing the actors to realize when they were following the 'script' correctly. There were differences in the way this information was used by the audience, with the carers more often choosing to tell the performers what the present was, while the facilitators preferred to drop hints through mimes both to the performer and to the performing group as a whole.

This example illustrates the diversity of angles encapsulated by a collective object of activity; in this case, the collective object of activity being the rehearsal of the play. The activities of the carers – such as ensuring an orderly seating arrangement, using the rehearsal as an opportunity for a break, and directly offering stage instructions to the performers – show that their object of activity was focussed around generating an orderly and scripted theatrical performance. In contrast, the activities of the facilitators – such as their informal demeanour and arrangements and their reticence to become overly directive in the performance itself – indicate that their object of activity was focussed around engagement rather than a tightly scripted performance.

The session cast each of the participant groups into several roles, which mediate the relationship between their object of activity and their activities. The facilitators oscillated between the roles of friend (when they welcomed the participants and asked them to relate an interesting episode from the week), director (when they controlled the session through running through the rehearsal), 'audience' (when they allowed the participant group to self-direct the performance) and actor (when they joined in the rehearsal to facilitate). The participants played the roles of friend (when they welcomed the facilitators), dependant (when they needed to be encouraged into participating fully) and actor (when they were actively participating and engaging with the audience). Lastly, the carers employed by the day centre played the roles of carer (when they organized the participants before the session), audience (when they stepped back from the production and engaged as interested observers of a 'play'), director (when they told the participants what present they should be miming) and bystander (when the facilitators took over responsibility for the participants).

14.3.2   Example Two: Roles in Maintaining Collective Objects of Activity

The second example comes from a session run by a theatre member who was a dance specialist (the facilitator). The activity was based in a school specializing in teaching children with learning difficulties and engaged with a group of ten children between the ages of 7 and 12 in rehearsing a dance sequence to be performed as part of a larger group on the theatre stage.

The activity took place in a large hall which also functioned as a corridor between two separate areas of the school, meaning that the sessions were often interrupted by students and teachers making their way between classes. The facilitator arrived shortly before the rehearsal was due to begin and began to warm up accompanied by a stereo which was playing music featured in the performance. The students were escorted into the hall while the facilitator was completing her warm-up and they watched her moving around the hall, some copying the moves and commenting on her dancing. Once the children had been escorted in, one of the teachers spoke separately to the facilitator to inform her of the difficulties one of the children had been having throughout the week that might hamper the rehearsal. The facilitator thanked her for the information and said she would continue with the session and attempt to engage the child; the teacher said she would stay in case the child was difficult to engage or disruptive.

The facilitator proceeded with the session, getting the children chatting to one another and warming up. The children engaged in the activity to varying degrees and in different ways, depending on their physical and emotional impairments. After warming up the facilitator switched the music to the rehearsal accompaniment and set out some seats for the teachers to watch the performance before running through the sequence with the children. As one of the children was more energetic and playful than the others, the facilitator asked him to lead the group in the part of the performance which involved an improvised 'domino' dance sequence. During the run-through of the rehearsal the facilitator remained at the edge of the stage, giving encouragement, while the teachers applauded the performance. The performance was disrupted on two occasions, firstly when the aforementioned child became upset and the facilitator chose to dance beside him until he wanted to rejoin the group. Secondly, the performance was disrupted, and the sequence became fragmented, when the rehearsal area was being used as a corridor between classes, resulting in a more public performance than the performers were expecting. In the second instance one of the teachers in the original audience asked the passing group to continue on their journey whilst the facilitator was engaged in refocussing the performance.

In this situation each of the participants adopted several roles in relation to the collective object of activity, which is rehearsing a dance sequence for a performance. The facilitator was in the role of performer when the children arrived, casting them into the roles of audience and, in some cases, co-performer and critic. The members of school staff accompanying the pupils were originally cast as teachers through their responsibility for bringing the children and imparting information about their condition, to being audience when the rehearsal began. The children taking part in the rehearsal went from being audience upon arrival, to being led as participants during the warm-up to eventually being cast in the role of performer as they developed their dance and the facilitator became director.

Furthermore, we can see that the hall (which also functions as a corridor) was a means of mediating the different roles of participants within their object of activity. When the hall is used as a hall, it becomes a private rehearsal space in which the facilitator takes the role of director with the children as performers and the teachers as audience. However, when the hall is used as a corridor, the private rehearsal space becomes part of the larger school environment and the teachers are once more cast in an active role as teacher.

14.3.3   Example Three: Improvising to Maintain Collective Activity

The third situation is a session for children with behavioural difficulties from schools across the area and took place within a specially designated rehearsal room within the theatre. The session was run by an actor trained and experienced in dealing with children with behavioural difficulties (the facilitator) and was attended by eight children and two educational carers. This situation differs from the previous examples because although the collective object of activity could be seen to be a productive or successful session, opinions of what such a session would entail could be seen to differ greatly between the children, the facilitator and the carers. It also differs somewhat because the carers were involved in the activities along with the children, and were thus often cast into the same roles.

Inside the rehearsal room the facilitator immediately began the session, to avoid the children becoming unruly, with a game that involved passing a ball whilst standing in a large circle. As the game continued, some of the children played the game properly and seemed to be enjoying themselves; however a growing number of the children had begun hitting the ball out of the circle and were visibly bored. The carers tried to encourage the children to behave through positive affirmation but with limited success, as the children seemed to find the disruption more enjoyable than the game. Seeing this occurring, the facilitator finished the ball game and introduced an activity which involved the group, in teams of two, acting out an interview with a famous person, with one taking the role of an interviewer and the other taking the role of the celebrity. The identity of each celebrity (chosen by each pair acting out the interview) was to be kept a secret and the audience would be required to guess the identity through the questions asked by the 'interviewer'. The facilitator provided a microphone and a 'staged' seating arrangement as well as asking the carers to join in to draw the children into the activity.

The activity began as planned, with the groups who were not currently presenting being the audience as the first group (the carers) took their turn to act out the interview, managing to incite the audience into guessing correctly. The children rapidly began to treat the activity as a performance, and as a competition to see who could elicit the most laughter from the audience as part of the interview setting. The pair who had been relatively disruptive in the previous activity were due to begin the activity and asked whether they could leave the rehearsal room and enter through the doors and come down the staircase 'like Jonathan Ross' before beginning the interview. After instructing the children not to move away from the door whilst waiting to make their entrance the facilitator allowed the children to proceed, and the later groups followed their lead in incorporating this into the interview. However, after taking their turn to interview the disruptive pair soon became bored of being in the audience and began to make loud comments and move about the audience area. When the next group exited the room in preparation for their entrance one of the disruptive pair motioned for the audience to keep quiet, ran up to the door and locked it from the inside to prevent the 'interviewer' from re-entering the room. The children thought this was hilarious and laughed loudly, especially when the 'celebrity' emerged from the other door to find out why they had not been introduced yet.

While the carers seemed to be keen to get the door unlocked rapidly and reprimand the disruptive child, the facilitator called for the interviewer to go along the corridor and enter through the other door. After the interviewer had emerged the facilitator told the disruptive child that while locking the door had been a funny thing to do, they should now continue with the activity so that they would be able to guess who the latest celebrity was. After this incident the disruptive child engaged fully with the activity, shouting out suggestions and laughing along with the group and, although he joked about it, did not make an effort to disrupt the activity again.

The object of activity encapsulates the different foci of the three participant groups in this example. The carers, through their attention to ensuring that the session ran smoothly, can be seen to be primarily interested in encouraging good discipline in the children's behaviour. The children, through their eagerness first to disrupt the ball game then to escalate the theatricality of the interview game, can be seen to be primarily interested in engaging the attention and activity of other participants on their own terms. Finally, the facilitator, through their handling of the children's disruptions, can be seen to be primarily concerned with engaging the children, and thus maintaining discipline (object of carers) and ensuring an audience (object of children) through collective engagement in enjoyable activities.

Once in the rehearsal room, the facilitator adopted the leading role of director and, through incorporating the carers into the activity, cast them as co-performers with the children. When the second activity began the entire group were cast as audience, taking the role of performer only when it was their turn to play out the interview. However, one of the children disrupted the system by choosing to play the role of active author/performer at a time when he was designated as audience by the activity (by locking the door to humorous effect). This disruption caused the carers to attempt to assume the role of leader to reprimand the child, but they were cast as audience by the facilitator assuming the role of director and addressing the child as a humorous performer, rather than as a disruptive audience member. Through addressing the disruption as a performance, the facilitator improvised within the situation to ensure that the object of activity of the disruptor (to gain attention) remained aligned with the collective object of activity (to engage the children in a productive, collective activity).

A final interesting feature of this situation is the instance in which the performers improvised in their role, through borrowing from an established interviewing practice (that of Jonathan Ross), in order to enhance their role in relation to their perceived object of activity. Through incorporating the stairs into their routine they succeeded in becoming more entertaining and thus received more attention – their object of activity – whilst occupying the role of performer.

14.4. AN ACTIVITY THEORY PERSPECTIVE ON IMPROVISATION

Activity theory draws attention to tensions and contradictions within objects of activity and the construction of identities as they impact on the division of labour around the activities. Theatrical improvisation is a practice that operates on the boundary between structure and innovative practice. The situations we examined were structured in that they had purposes, expected roles and pre-planned practices that were expected to lead to particular outcomes. The purposes were to engage participants in developmental opportunities including self-expression through improvisation; the expected roles were of participants, facilitators and carers-as-audience; the pre-planned practices were structured activities that enabled participants to warm up, practise their skills and rehearse for performance; and the ultimate outcome was a performance. The workshops occurred within contexts that carried genre rules of appropriate behaviour. First, theatrical improvisation, in the way practised here, entails taking a role and enacting it without a script (or with very minimal script, such as the expectation of a particular present in the first example). The genre rules are largely unstated, but become obvious when deviated from or broken. For example, in the third example when a child locked the door he introduced a level of humour beyond that expected in the improvisation. Interviews with celebrities can clearly entail verbal humour, but the physical humour was a deliberate deviation from the genre. However, this deviation is more emphatic when viewed from the second context, which is of social care. In this context, the genre rules incorporate a scale of variability of behaviour by the participants, but not as extensive as that expected in theatrical improvisation. Hence, when a child acts in such a way as to alter the activity, to the facilitator there is a need to modify the behaviour a little, but there is an appreciation of the humour. In contrast, for the carers there is a more pressing need to contain the behaviour which is cast as too disruptive in a social care setting.

The counterpoint to structure is innovative practice. Improvisation is focused on creating something new in the moment of performance. As there is no script and quite a degree of interpretive space within the roles, the performer has to create as they perform. Equally, the other performers have to be spontaneously creative in their reaction to the performance they 'receive'. In the examples we explored, innovative practices are exemplified by the various roles, and interpretations of roles, that people adopted, and the variation in roles was not restricted to participants. Some variations occurred over time. For instance, in the second example the facilitator accidentally embodied the role of performer when her warm-up overran and carried on in front of the participants. This role was not created by the facilitator/performer alone, but occurred because the workshop participants undertook the role of audience. It was also significant that the role of performer was one that the facilitator lived for much of her professional life, and hence it was an easy role to fall into. Similarly, in the third example, the carers moved from audience back to carers when the 'misbehaving' child evoked their normal roles. Such movements, forwards and backwards, between normal and assumed roles can provide a source of creativity and innovation. They are fundamental to humour in much theatrical improvisation and to 'working across' genre rules. However, it is not that there are no rules, but rather that the rules allow sufficient freedom for surprises and humour to happen. People interpret and shift roles, but they do have roles. The scripts are created in the moment, but they cannot go in absolutely any direction. Indeed, when actions entail too much of a rescripting, such as the incident in the third example, or when participants in example one mime someone else's present, they are brought back into line with the expectations for the sessions.

From an activity theory perspective, the tension between structure and freedom can be understood as different objects of activity. The objects of activity are realized through meaningful patterns of activity undertaken by practising communities. In our case, different actors had different foci within objects of activity. The participants were interested both in the improvisational performance and in having time away from their routines, as exemplified by the clowning in example three and the adoption of the audience role in example two. The facilitators were seeking to enable the participants to create a good performance, and in order to do this they also aimed to keep sufficient order in order to make the session work, as they do in example one. For the carers the object of activity was partly the participants producing a performance that was rewarding for them and their families, but it was also about the participants being taken care of for an afternoon, and in this regard another activity could have been just as good as theatrical improvisation.

14.5   CONCLUSION

The theatrical improvisations discussed here are part of outreach activities by a professional theatre company, and as such they entail a number of objects of activity. The improvisations can be judged as having greater or lesser aesthetic value, as enabling developmental self-expression by participants, and as fulfilling part of the requirements of the funding of the Northern Theatre. This is at variance with much of the improvisation literature (e.g. Hatch 1998; Vera and Crossan 2004) where the data have indicated much less diversity of intention and meaning in the activity. However, we did not find that there was complete ambiguity and diversity of meaning. Although objects of activity varied over time and between groups, if there had been no shared meaning it would have been very difficult to conduct sessions without more sustained use of controlling influence. Different practising communities arrived at the events but there was a sufficient complementarity of practice between them to enable the improvisations to proceed.

Kamoch and Cunha (2001) have emphasized the role of minimal structures in improvisation and we saw evidence of this in our examples. There was a structuring of the events that framed the improvisations, and these structures drew on well-established social understandings. This was the case in example one with the idea of present-giving at Christmas, the idea of dominoes impacting on each other in example two and the idea of chat-shows in example three. Pre-existing roles (such as Jonathan Ross as chat show host) were drawn upon as resources in the creative activities. Hence, the improvisations did not come out of nothing, but the social structures and resources did not predetermine what would happen.

Facilitators, carers and participants were able to draw upon different discursive resources in order to project different aspects of their identities (Ybema et al. 2009). These identity dynamics occurred in dialogue with each other (Beech 2010) as participants produced role performances that elicited corresponding reactions in others. In the traditional literature on improvisation the main focus on interaction is within the band or performing company. In our case, however, although this was true in example one when participants improvised someone else's present and in example three when the door-locking activity emphasized the participants as an in-group, there were also cases of between-group identity dialogues. This occurred, for instance, in example three when the door-locking behaviour elicited a move from audience back to carer role for the carers. This was a noticeable and dramatic change, but in the everyday experience of these practices the dynamics were more subtle shifts in emphasis through which one aspect of identity (e.g. facilitator/ director) would come to the fore. It was not that there was complete freedom for any role or identity to be taken, but each participant had a restricted range that they could occupy before others in the group would react to influence them back into another (more acceptable) aspect of their identity.

Thus, we would regard these improvisatory practices as an example of the simultaneous presence of structure and variation. Traditional perspectives on improvisation see it as a practice of freedom and creativity, whilst subsequent studies (Kamoche and Cunha 2001) have emphasized some restrictions on freedom in the shape of minimal structures. The minimal structures were regarded as agreements in patterns of practice. We have chosen to examine more contested examples of improvisatory practice and have applied the ideas of objects of activity and the role-taking aspects of identity from activity theory (Blackler and Regan 2009) and as a result we have seen far greater tensions and disagreement in the practices. This is not to say that these examples are in some sense more negative that those of Vera and Crossan (2004) in theatre or the prior jazz improvisation examples (Weick 1998; Hatch 1998). Rather, we would see tensions within objects of activity and dynamics in the dialogical construction of identity as being potential sources of productive change and variation which counteract pressures towards conformity in improvisatory practice.

REFERENCES

Axel, Eric (1997), 'One developmental line in European activity theories', in M. Cole, Y. Engestrom and O. Vasquez (eds), *Mind, Culture and Activity: Seminal Papers from the Laboratory of Comparative Human Cognition*, Cambridge: Cambridge University Press, pp. 128–146.
Bailey, Derek (1992), *Improvization: Its Nature and Practice in Music*, New York: Da Capo Press.
Beech, N. (2010), 'Liminality and the practices of identity reconstruction', *Human Relations*, **64** (2), 285–302.
Blackler, F. (1993), 'Knowledge and the theory of organizations: organizations as activity systems and the reframing of management', *Journal of Management Studies*, **30** (6), 863–884.
Blackler, Frank, Alan Kennedy and Michael Reed (1999), 'Organizing for incompatible priorities', in Sue Dopson and Annabelle Mark (eds), *Organizational Behaviour in Health Care: The Research Agenda*, London: Macmillan, pp. 223–242.

Blackler, F. and S. Regan (2006), 'Institutional reform and the reorganization of family support services', *Organization Studies*, **27** (12), 1843–1861.

Blackler, F. and S. Regan (2009), 'Intentionality, agency, change: practice theory and management', *Management Learning*, **40** (2), 161–176.

Brown, Shona and Kathleen Eisenhardt (1998), *Competing on the Edge: Strategy as Structured Chaos*. Boston, MA: Harvard Business School Press.

Chaiklin, Seth (2010), 'The role of "practice" in cultural-historical science', in Michalis Kontopodis, Christoph Wulf and Bernd Fichtner (eds), *Children, Culture and Education*, New York: Springer, pp. 227–246.

Cunha, M.P., J.V. Cunha and K. Kamoche (1999), 'Organizational Improvization: what, when, how and why', *International Journal of Management Reviews*, **1** (3), 299–341.

Donald, Jane, Louise Mitchell and Nic Beech (2010), 'Organizing creativity in a music festival in Barbara', in Barbara Townley and Nic Beech (eds), *Managing Creativity: Exploring the Paradox*, Cambridge: Cambridge University Press, pp. 260–279.

Dreier, Ole (2008), *Psychotherapy in Everyday Life*, Cambridge: Cambridge University Press.

Eikhof, Doris (2010), 'The logics of art: analysing theatre as a cultural field', in Barbara Townley and Nic Beech (eds), *Managing Creativity: Exploring the Paradox*, Cambridge: Cambridge University Press, pp. 106–124.

Eikhof, D.R. and A. Haunschild (2007), 'For art's sake! Managing artistic and economic logics in creative production', *Journal of Organizational Behaviour*, **28** (5), 523–538.

Engestrom, Y. (1987), 'Learning by expanding: an activity theoretical approach to developmental research', Helsinki: Orienta-Konsultit, available at http://communication.ucsd.edu/MCA/Paper/Engestrom/expanding/toc.htm (accessed 3 March 2007).

Engestrom, Yrjo (1999), 'Innovative learning in work teams: analysing cycles of knowledge creation in work teams', in Y. Engestrom, R. Miettinen and R.L. Punamäki (eds), *Perspectives on Activity Theory*, Cambridge, Cambridge University Press.

Engestrom, Y. and F. Blackler (2005), 'On the life of the object', *Organization*, **12** (3), 307–330.

Engestrom, Yrjo, Reijo Miettinen and R. Raija-Leena Punamaki, (1999), *Perspectives on Activity Theory*, Cambridge: Cambridge University Press.

Frost, Anthony and Ralph Yarrow (1990), *Improvization in Drama*, New York: St Martin's Press.

Hatch, M.J. (1998), 'Jazz as a metaphor for organizing in the 21st century', *Organization Science*, **9** (5), 556–577.

Hatch, M.J. (1999), 'Exploring the empty spaces of organizing: How improvizational jazz helps redescribe organizational structure', *Organization Studies*, **20** (1), 75–100.

Kamoche, K. and M.P. Cunha (2001), 'Minimal structures: from jazz improvization to product innovation', *Organization Studies*, **22** (5), 733–764.

Kamoche, K., M.P. Cunha and J.V. Cunha (2003), 'Towards a theory of organizational improvization: looking beyond the jazz metaphor', *Journal of Management Studies*, **40** (8), 2023–2051.

Lane, C. and G. Wood (2009), 'Capitalist diversity and diversity within capitalism', *Economy and Society*, **38** (4), 531–551.

Leont'ev, A.N. (1974), 'The problem of activity in psychology', *Soviet Psychology*, **13** (2), 4–33.

Lounsbury, M. and E.T. Crumley (2007), 'New practice creation: an institutional perspective on innovation', *Organization Studies*, **28** (7), 993–1012.

Lounsbury, M. and M. Ventresca (2003), 'The new structuralism in organizational theory', *Organization*, **10** (3), 457–480.

Miettinen, R. and J. Virkkunen (2005), 'Epistemic objects, artefacts and organizational change" *Organization*, **12** (3), 437–456.

Montuouri, A. (2003), 'The complexity of improvization and the improvization of complexity: social science, art and creativity', *Human Relations*, **56** (2), 237–255.

Nardi, Bonnie A. (1996), 'Studying context: a comparison of activity theory, situated action models, and distributed cognition', in Bonnie A. Nardi (ed.), *Context and Consciousness:*

Activity Theory and Human–Computer Interaction, Cambridge, MA, USA and London, UK: MIT Press, pp. 69–102.

Rehn, Alf and Christian de Cock (2008), 'Deconstructing creativity', in Tudor Rickards, Mark Runco and Sue Moger (eds), *The Routledge Companion to Creativity*, London: Routledge.

Schatzki, Theodore R. (1996) *Social Practices: A Wittgensteinian Approach to Human Activity and the Social*, Cambridge: Cambridge University Press.

Sims, D. (2005), 'You bastard: a narrative exploration of the experience of indignation within organizations', *Organization Studies*, **26**, 1625–1640.

Sorge, A. (2005), *The Global and the Local: Understanding the Dialectics of Business Systems*, Oxford: Oxford University Press.

Sveningsson, S. and M. Alvesson (2003), 'Managing managerial identities: organizational fragmentation, discourse and identity struggle', *Human Relations*, **56** (10), 1163–1193.

Townley, B., N. Beech and A. McKinlay (2009), 'Managing in the creative industries: managing the motley crew', *Human Relations*, **62** (7), 939–962.

Van de Ven, A.H. and M.S. Poole (2005), 'Alternative approaches for studying organizational change', *Organization Studies*, **26** (9), 1377–1404.

Vera, D. and M. Crossan (2004), 'Theatrical improvization: lessons for organizations', *Organization Studies*, **25** (5), 727–749.

Watson, T. (2009), 'Narrative, life story and manager identity', *Human Relations*, **63** (3), 425–452.

Weick, K.E. (1998), 'Improvization as a mindset for organizational analysis', *Organization Science*, **9** (5), 543–555.

Ybema, S., T. Keenoy, C. Oswick, A. Beverungen, N. Ellis and I. Sabelis (2009), 'Articulating identities', *Human Relations*, **63** (3), 299–322.

Zack, M. (2000), 'Jazz improvization and organizing: once more from the top', *Organization Science*, **11**, 227–234.

PART III

INSTITUTIONS AND CONTEXT: EMERGING AND DEVELOPING ECONOMIES

15 South–South foreign direct investment: key role of institutions and future prospects

Axèle Giroud, Hafiz Mirza and Kee Hwee Wee

15.1 INTRODUCTION

Foreign direct investment (FDI) from developing countries has raised much academic interest in the early 2000s (for instance see, among others, Special Issues from the *Journal of International Business Studies* **38** (4), 2007; the *Journal of International Management* **13** (3), 2007; the *Multinational Business Review* **17** (2), 2009; the *Journal of International Management* **16** (2), 2010; the *Management International Review* forthcoming). It can be put forward that *the novelty has become the norm* (*The Economist* 20 January 2011). This is reflected by the continuous rise during the 1990s and 2000s of FDI flows from emerging countries, which in comparison with world FDI flows have reached a record level of $296 billion in 2008, while outward FDI from South-East Europe and the Commonwealth of Independent States (CIS) more than doubled in the late 2000s to reach $60 billion in 2008 (UNCTAD 2010). Undoubtedly, the rise in business of transnational corporations (TNCs) activity from 'what is traditionally considered the periphery of global commerce is shaping the structure of international business' (Gammeltoft et al. 2010). This claim is understandable considering the fact that the developing-country share of outward FDI stocks nearly doubled in the 1990s, rising among 8 per cent of the world total in 1990 to 14.2 per cent by 2000, and maintaining this level with 14.1 per cent in 2009.

FDI from emerging countries started to rise among a small number of countries in the 1970s, and companies from these countries were referred to as third world multinationals (Kumar and McLeod 1981; Kumar 1982). In the 1980s as well as today, authors suggested that there was a distinct path to internationalization by emerging TNCs (Wells 1983; Lall 1983; Dunning et al. 1997; Mirza 2000; Gao 2005; Goldstein 2006; Luo and Tung 2007; Wee 2007; Kalotay 2008), explained by cheaper factors of production, lack of skilled managers and lower levels of technological capabilities, in parallel with the factor endowments of the home and host developing economies, access to low-cost raw

materials locally and enhanced understanding of the market requirements of developing hosts.

We would argue that with the rapid globalization of the world economy,
enhanced communication and transportation means, liberalization of
government policies, and the ease with which emerging TNCs can access
technological knowledge by acquiring firms in the developed world, some
of these arguments do not seem as relevant to the twenty-first century.
Many emerging TNCs are large, and highly internationalized, thus not
conforming any longer to the small-scale advantage put forward by Lall
(1983) as one of the key competitive advantages facilitating flexibility.
Secondly, there is increasing evidence that the large share of FDI from
developing economies is directed to other developing countries; yet, there
remains a lack of a comprehensive framework demonstrating the context
of such South–South FDI (Kang and Jiang, 2012).

Researchers have focused on strategies adopted by emerging TNCs (see
for instance, Casanova 2004; Carney 2008), often emphasizing the need to
catch up (Young et al. 1996; Mathews 2006; Yeung 2007). More recently,
the home-country factors have been considered as important explanations
behind the international success of emerging TNCs. South–South FDI,
however, presents added challenges as both home and host are developing (Cuervo-Cazurra and Genc 2008; Ghauri and Yamin 2009). Emerging
TNCs have distinct FDI determinants (Buckley et al. 2007) and corporate
governance features, and developing economies have distinct locational
factors, some related to the unique institutional characteristics of these
environments (Yiu et al. 2007; Dunning and Lundan 2008b; Aulakh and
Kotabe 2008), examples being the transition process (Mirza and Freeman
2007) or the regionalization advantage (Mirza and Giroud 2004). Thus,
the institutional context of South–South FDI is expected to influence
significantly the potential for current and future investment prospects
(Cuervo-Cazurra and Genc 2008; Buckley et al. 2008; Mirza et al. 2011).

In this chapter, we wish first to grasp the rising importance of South
FDI and TNCs, before analysing South–South FDI specifically. Due to a
severe lack of detailed data, it is difficult to assess the South–South dimension of FDI from developing economies, and a variety of sources are used
here. We focus on the drivers and motives of South–South FDI, as well
as the challenges and obstacles to understanding the potential for further
consolidation of this trend. Thirdly, building on the recent literature
emphasizing the key role of institutions in both home and host developing economies, we analyse the support and constraints of the institutional
environment, economic liberalization and gradual institutional transition
that influence South–South FDI. Finally, a model emphasizing the factors
influencing future trends in South–South FDI is presented.

15.2 SOUTH–SOUTH FDI

The role of TNCs from the South in international markets has increased (Mirza 2000; Sauvant 2005; UNCTAD 2006, 2007; Khanna and Palepu 2006; Luo and Tung 2007; Mirza et al. 2011). A number of studies have investigated the specific nature of drivers and motives of TNCs from the South. These studies find some clear similarities between the rationale for internationalization when compared to developed countries' TNCs (Beausang 2003), yet it is undeniable that differences occur, particularly when TNCs from the South invest in developed countries, where they face challenges of being late movers (Young et al. 1996; Mathews 2006).

Developing and transition countries have increased their share in the world's outward FDI flows from just 8 per cent in 1990 to 20.8 per cent in 2009. Asia and Oceania is the largest source region of outward foreign direct investment (OFDI) among developing countries, followed by Latin America and the Caribbean.

As recently as 1990, only six developing and transition economies reported outward FDI stocks of more than $5 billion. By 2009, ten countries (if we do not include the British Virgin Islands and the Cayman Islands due to the unique nature of FDI transactions going through these countries) had outward stocks exceeding $50 billion, namely (in order of importance) Hong Kong, the Russian Federation, China, Singapore, Taiwan, Brazil, South Korea, Malaysia, South Africa and Mexico (UNCTAD 2010). The value of the stock of FDI from developing and transition economies was estimated at $2.69 trillion in 2009, or 14.1 per cent of the world total. Some distinctions in terms of the success by region and country can be identified.

South–South FDI is not easy to assess, given difficulties in recording investment flows to and from developing countries. Indirect estimates suggest that more than a third of FDI inflows in developing countries originate from the South (Aykut and Ratha 2003). South–South FDI increased throughout the 1990s and early 2000s, following the sharp rise in FDI from developing, emerging and transition economies. Given the lack of a comprehensive dataset showing direction of FDI by groups of countries, we selected 13 developing economies for which detailed data on outward FDI stock by destination was available, namely Brazil, Chile, China, Croatia, Hong Kong, Kazakhstan, Malaysia, Morocco, the Republic of Korea, Singapore, South Africa, Thailand and Turkey (analysis from ITC FDI Database). This enables us to illustrate the levels and key trends of South–South investment. In some cases, part of the OFDI is unspecified (indeed, these estimates of South–South investment suffer from serious inaccuracies), but the data available show interesting trends.

For each country and for the purpose of this chapter, investment destination is separated between regional investment, investment to developed economies and investment to other developing economies.

First, the direction of investment to developed or developing economies varies depending on the region where the investor is located. Latin American countries (Brazil and Chile), Croatia, South Africa and Turkey have largest investment stocks in developed economies. In contrast, Asian economies invest primarily in other developing countries. FDI stocks from Asian economies are the largest within the same region (East, South and South-East Asia), but stocks are also very high in other developing countries. China, for instance, has substantial investment in Africa, such as in Zambia and South Africa, in the West Asia in Saudi Arabia and the United Arab Emirates (UAE), as well as in transition economies (in the Russian Federation, Kazakhstan and Kyrgystan). The Republic of Korea has large stocks in Algeria, Egypt, South Africa and Sudan. In Latin America, Brazil, Argentina, Chile, Uruguay and Venezuela also attract South–South investment.

Second, smaller developing investors such as Croatia, Kazakhstan and Morocco have large stocks in countries that are close geographically. Morocco has large investments in North Africa (namely Egypt) but also across Africa (in countries such as Burkina Faso, Gabon and Mauritania). Croatia has investments in Bosnia & Herzegovina, Serbia and Montenegro.

Third, there is a tendency for Asian countries to invest primarily within their region. It is particularly noticeable that the largest stocks for Singapore, Malaysia and Thailand are found in other Association of South East Asian Nations (ASEAN) countries. The regional orientation is confirmed when looking at intra-regional OFDI data. Data on ASEAN and Mercosur in terms of overall OFDI flows, or ASEAN for intra-regional investment, suggest that being part of a regional grouping significantly influences FDI patterns. This could explain why African investment potential remains low. In their study of emerging TNCs in SSA, Henley et al. (2008) argue that one of the preconditions to strengthen existing export-oriented FDI in the region would be the development of efficient regional markets across Africa.

From a host-country perspective, South–South FDI has become a key source of investment in the 2000s (Dunning et al. 1997; Mirza 2000; UNCTAD 2006, 2007; Cuervo-Cazurra and Genc 2008). Developing countries with the highest dependence on FDI from developing and transition economies include China, Kyrgyzstan, Paraguay and Thailand, and least-developed countries (LDCs) such as Bangladesh, Ethiopia, the Lao People's Democratic Republic, Myanmar and the United Republic of

Tanzania. Indeed, FDI from developing countries accounts for well over 40 per cent of the total inward FDI of a number of LDCs (UNCTAD 2007). For example, in Africa, South Africa is a particularly important source of FDI; it accounts for more than 50 per cent of all FDI inflows into Botswana, the Democratic Republic of the Congo, Lesotho, Malawi and Swaziland. Moreover, the level of FDI from developing and transition economies to many LDCs may well be understated in official FDI data, as a significant proportion of such investment goes to their informal sector, which is not included in government statistics.

15.3 HOME AND HOST INSTITUTIONS AND SOUTH–SOUTH FDI PROSPECTS

Institution theory suggests that it is institutions that guide behaviour in a society and influence organizations' conduct by signalling acceptable actions (North 1990). Institutions affect the capacity of firms to interact and therefore the relative transaction and coordination costs of production and innovation (Mudambi and Navarra 2002, 636). The impact of formal and informal institutions has been widely studied in the context of how these institutions influence the growth of firms within the country. In transition economies, for instance, investors have responded positively to encouragement by government policy promoting both exploitation and expansion of own resources and capabilities (Meyer and Peng 2005).

Institutions have also been studied in the context of their impact on international activities. The institutional difference between the home and host country is used as a predictor for the difficulty faced by a foreign investor in understanding and responding to a new environment. Institutional differences may enhance the liability of foreignness, and the lack of familiarity with the foreign environment in which the TNC has operations, creating relational hazards (Eden and Miller 2004). The difference may lead to varying levels of international transfer of routines (Kostova 1999), notably resulting from difficulties in coordination across markets. Examining the case of emerging FDI in China, Li and Yao (2010, 145) note that little is known about the means through which institutional environments shape the patterns of international expansion by TNCs. Focusing on least-developed countries, Cuervo-Cazurra and Genc (2008) suggest that developing-country TNCs are more prevalent in environments with worse institutional conditions, because managers can more easily understand and adapt given their prior experiences in home countries.

In this chapter, we suggest that home institutions influence the type, structure and strategy of TNCs, while host institutions and the institutional gap between home and host institutions influence the location choices, investment motivations and conduct of TNCs in foreign markets.

15.3.1   Home and Host Countries' Institutions

In this section, we focus on key ways through which home- and host-countries' policies and institutional development influence South–South FDI. Much of the activities conducted by emerging TNCs are related to ownership-specific advantages created at home that can be internalized and exploited in other developing economies. TNCs respond to changes in the institutional environment by adapting their strategies (Peng et al. 2008; Hermelo and Vassolo 2010). As such: 'the institutional framework is critical in devising and implementing the formal and informal rules and incentives that guide the process of how knowledge generation and transfer are formed and implemented' (Dunning and Lundan 2008a, 577). In the context of developing economies, institutions are often closely linked to the potential for economic development, to the internationalization of local firms and to the attractiveness of the country to emerging TNCs.

Perhaps the most salient feature behind South–South FDI resides in the market liberalization programmes conducted by governments, in an effort to improve the competitive environment in which local and foreign firms operate. Liberalization programmes have resulted either from local governments' schemes towards economic development (this would be the case for many Asian home and host economies), from the transition process to market economies, or from the initiatives of international organizations, such as the International Monetary Fund (IMF), the World Trade Organization (WTO) or the World Bank-led liberalization programmes across many Latin American and African economies. Liberalization programmes have generally focused on enhancing competition within the marketplace, as well as on targeting TNCs. The focus on enhancing competition has often led governments in developing and transition countries to engage in privatization programmes (as in the case of Eastern Europe or African countries), partial privatization (such as in China), or the deregulation of numerous sectors in the economy (as witnessed in selected Latin American countries). Focusing on eight Turkish home TNCs, Erdilek (2008, 746) finds that liberalization of the home regulatory environment ranked as a powerful driver to overseas investment. This can be explained by the liberalization of the foreign exchange regime, of foreign exchange controls and of the Turkish foreign trade regime which allowed greater competition from imports.

Numerous emerging host economies' governments have focused on the promotion of inwards FDI via liberalization programmes, as illustrated by the high number of investment facilitation measures implemented during the first half of 2011, such as the release of 'Circular 1 of 2011' in India to consolidate FDI policy (UNCTAD 2011). Institutional support has also come through active OFDI promotion, such as offering fiscal incentives, providing insurance against political risk, providing assistance through government agencies to support private firms, or helping home TNCs deal with a host-country's governmental or legislative institution at the collective level in the case of Chinese TNCs (Luo et al. 2010, 69).

Developing-country governments have also influenced FDI through state-owned enterprises (SOEs). SOEs are frequently found in the infrastructure industry, with companies being created with government support in line with the economic development objectives of the country. Key examples include PSA in Singapore, and Senai Airport Terminal Services in Malaysia. There are no up-to-date systematic data on these firms, and therefore it is difficult to assess their impact on home and host developing markets, but it is clear that these governments, and China in particular, encourage their SOEs to expand abroad (Gökgür 2011).

It is to be noted that developing-country governments have often promoted other local business groups (as in the case of the South Korean *chaebols*, the Turkish *families*, Latin American and Spanish *grupos*, Indian groups) and their international expansion programmes. Governments frequently supported initial development of these groups, strengthening their competitive advantages by means of information asymmetries, favourable access to contracts or facilitated financial support. In addition, such business groups have acquired enhanced ability to adapt to disruptive international environments because of their familiarity with home instability, and through benefiting from economic liberalization in other developing countries (Aulakh and Kotabe 2008).

It is precisely the institutional void that provides an essential explanation behind the rise of business groups in developing economies (Yiu et al. 2007). This results from the fact that different groups were able to create value, utilizing various types of resources and capabilities available in their respective home-country contexts.

15.3.2   Home–Host Distance

The geographical and psychic distance between the home and host countries also play a role in explaining South–South FDI. A firm that invests abroad because its home market size is limited often favours foreign markets that are geographically close and that present similarities in terms of consumption patterns and institutions. This would apply to Russian TNCs investing in nearby Eastern European host economies (Kalotay

2008; Deloitte 2008). In a study of Chinese FDI in East and South-East Asia, Kang and Jiang (2012) find that four of the five institution indicators are significant in explaining Chinese firms' FDI location. The authors differentiate between regulative, normative and cognitive institutions, comparing the distance between the home Chinese environment and the host environment. They find that Chinese firms favour locating their FDI in countries with a smaller cultural distance, with a higher intensity of business transaction (indicating that bilaterial trade impacts upon the mindset of Chinese managers) and with a higher level of economic freedom, but countries that demonstrate a small difference in their political and legal regulative regimes as compared to China. Chinese firms are comfortable to invest in high-risk countries, often because they operate in a politically unstable and risky environment in their home market. This indicates that they can more easily gain institutional legitimacy in similar developing-country environments.

In some cases, institutional distance is related to geographical proximity, and can, for instance, explain large FDI from Hong Kong or Taiwanese TNCs in China, and intra-regional ASEAN FDI. Geographic proximity can also be linked to favourable regional policies easing regional FDI, as exemplified by favourable investment conditions for intra-ASEAN investment. In the case of Asian investment in Asia, ethnic Chinese networks have contributed to South–South FDI, and to the familiarity of these managers between home and host countries. Gao (2005) suggests that more than two-thirds of China's inward foreign direct investment (IFDI) originates from developing Asia. Family businesses and long-established relational networks contribute to this trend.

Linked to institutional factors, FDI motivations also explain South–South FDI. Many emerging TNCs can benefit from lower factor cost advantages when investing in other emerging markets, or may invest for strategic considerations, such as FDI by competitors, the need to maintain cost competitiveness or to upgrade capabilities – leading to mergers and acquisitions (M&A) amongst and between emerging TNCs. Competitive considerations provide opportunities for both home and host developing-country firms. 'Intra-regional investment in Asia, for instance, acts as a vehicle for technology diffusion, *recycling* of comparative advantages and competitive enhancement. It has been instrumental in the sequential upgrading of industries, across countries at various stages of development' (UNCTAD 2010, xx). But there is no guarantee that overseas expansion will lead to a positive impact on the firm's competitiveness. In the case of Thai TNCs, this is dependent upon the FDI motive, the corporate strategy, the capacity of the firm and the extent of synergy created by the outward FDI activities for the group as a whole (Wee 2007).

15.3.3   Supranational Institutional Framework

South–South FDI is increasingly important on governments' agenda in developing countries. This can be explained by the predominance of South–South investment in TNCs' strategies from the South. A study conducted by UNCTAD (2004) demonstrated the wave of South–South international investment agreements, with 653 bilateral investment agreements, 312 double taxation treaties, and 49 preferential trade and investment agreements among developing countries.

Still, specific support remains patchy, and is often linked to trade promotion and bilateral agreements. Examples include Indian special treatment to investments destined for other developing countries, Singapore's Regionalization 2000 programme and the Malaysian South–South Corporation Berhad (MASSCORP). In Brazil, PIBAC (Programa de Incentivo aos Investimentos Brasileiros na America Central e no Caribe) was created in 2005 with the aim of encouraging Brazilian investment in Central America.

Sometimes these efforts occur through regional groupings. For instance, a study found that India and ASEAN economies' economic structures were largely complementary, pointing to significant potential opportunities in terms of trade and investment (Sen et al. 2004), thus supporting the argument for further cooperation between India and ASEAN.

To date, however, there is little evidence about the success of these programmes. In this section, we will focus on cross-border initiatives in the South and on the regional institutions that influence inward and outward South–South FDI.

Cross-border initiatives and participation in the global institutional framework contribute to the support provided by home governments to their TNCs, and to improve the attractiveness of host developing locations. First, by joining the WTO, countries engage in a series of further liberalization and harmonization programmes that benefit local TNCs. This has been particularly important in the case of China and Vietnam. Secondly, governments engage in bilateral agreements, for trade and investment, which contribute to the ease of firms to engage in economic activities with partner countries. Governments are particularly proactive in terms of protection of their TNCs' foreign assets. In the South–South investment context, numerous new agreements are being signed. For instance, China's investment guarantee agreement with the Republic of Korea has been signed. Also, the Mainland and Hong Kong Closer Economic Partnership Arrangement was implemented in 2008 and has opened 11 sectors to investors from Hong Kong in China. In other cases, double taxation agreements were signed between Singapore and China, the Republic of Korea and Saudi Arabia. Altogether, Asian countries have signed a total of 12 new bilateral investment treaties (BITs) in 2008.

Finally, governments facilitate inward and outward FDI within their regional contexts. The effects of such cross-border policy agreements are felt by investors from outside the region, or in some cases solely by investors from within the region. For South-East Asian nations, agreements are often signed by the ASEAN Secretariat, but affect all countries and investors from the region. As an example, ASEAN has initiated negotiations for new bilateral trade and investment agreements with the EU since 2007. ASEAN is also negotiating an investment agreement to facilitate intra-regional FDI, and other agreements to promote South–South investments (such as the agreement for trade in services with the Republic of Korea signed in 2007).

Key regional agreements in the developing world include the Andean Community, CACM, CARICOM and Mercosur in Latin America; MENA, CEMAC, SADC and ECOWAS for Africa and the Middle East; the Asia-Pacific Economic Cooperation (APEC) and ASEAN for Asia. Regional economic integration can facilitate South–South investment, particularly when new BITs exist. Existing trading blocs across Asia, Africa and Latin America have implications for regional investments. Regional agreements influence investment, first, by integrating national economies (an increased regional market renders the region more attractive to market-seeking investment); and second, by facilitating trade and investment with reduced barriers (enhancing efficiency-seeking investment). It is to be noted that the trade effect is dominant, given that many regional agreement do not cover FDI. Hence their effect varies widely from one region to another. For instance, the beneficial effect of the agreement can only be maximized if appropriate infrastructure is in place to connect the production and trade systems. Thus, the impact of regional instruments on South–South FDI depends upon the political and economic context of individual agreements. It will also depend upon whether the regional investment agreement (RIA) occurs between hegemons such as ASEAN, or non-hegemons such as Mercusor (Mercado Camun del sur) or APEC (for a discussion on the impact of regional integration agreements and inward and outward FDI, see Balasubramanuam et al. 2002).

ASEAN has made the most progress towards the promotion of regional investment with specific investment related initiatives. The Andean Group has a provision for South–South FDI, focusing on favourable treatments for TNCs in which investors from two or more Andean countries own more than 60 per cent of the equity capital (UNCTAD 2006, 230). In the case of Caribbean Community and Common Market (CARICOM) countries, one article mentions that preferential treatment should be given to investors from CARICOM countries. Mercosur has worked towards regulating intra-regional FDI in the Colonia Protocol, but this Protocol is yet to be signed by member countries. The Common Market for Eastern and Southern Africa (COMESA) recognizes the support for regional investment, and member countries are in the process of negotiating a Common Investment Area.

Other considerations

The combination of factors and drivers for outward FDI differs by region and country. The key drivers of Asian FDI, for instance, are the growing capabilities of Asian firms, strong export orientation, and a need to access technology, brand names and strategic assets abroad. Some Asian governments are also actively encouraging their firms to become transnational. The growing number of regional free trade agreements, particularly between economies in North-East and South-East Asia, is also increasing investor interest in the region. In Latin America and the Caribbean, most outward investment is intra-regional. As illustrated by Brazil, which is the largest investor from this region, a large part of outward FDI has been undertaken for financial rather than production reasons (to avoid taxes and undertake currency transactions). FDI is negligible in primary activities and low in manufacturing. An exception is Mexico, from which relatively more outward FDI has been in manufacturing. The ultimate selection of host locations by TNCs from the South is based on considerations such as the market size of the host economy, production or transportation costs, skills, supply chains, infrastructure and technology support, as well as, in some cases, tax considerations.

15.4 INSTITUTIONAL CHALLENGES AND OBSTACLES TO SOUTH–SOUTH FDI

Emerging TNCs face issues and problems related to the regulatory treatment of foreign investors in emerging host environments. Concerns include taxation and rules of the nationalization of foreign ownership, legal and administrative restrictions in selected sectors, restrictions on ownership shares, restrictions in access to licences for natural resources and other sensitive business areas, and procedures of investment dispute resolutions.

Additional obstacles arise from the unfamiliarity of emerging TNCs with the local emerging host in terms of economic, administrative, legal and cultural features. To overcome these difficulties, Lukoil has opted for joint ventures with major companies in host countries to conduct specific business activities (particularly in Indonesia, Iran, Venezuela and Algeria), and also pays attention to requirements related to the size of share capital and share of local partners in the case of Kazakhstan. Lukoil is cautious about political risks, particularly in Venezuela and Iran.

In developing countries, foreign operations can be affected when a change of government occurs. Cemex (Mexico) decided to cease operations in Indonesia after the new government prohibited the full acquisition of the operations. Similarly, UC Rusal (Russia) came under threat in Guinea when a new government came in power in 2007 (Deloitte 2008). The company was asked to pay more for assets already held for two years, under threat of nationalization.

Another challenge arises when host governments revert to protectionist trends. Such obstacles are faced by Russian TNCs in Eastern Europe and the Baltic countries, because of a feared resurgence of the Russian dominance. In some extreme cases, emerging TNCs suffer from an image problem as they are often viewed as remnants of or surrogates for state-owned enterprises (Yeung 2007). Elsewhere, the fear of foreign dominance can be the result of managerial behaviour. In a study of 22 companies in Nigeria, South Africans were accused of being patronizing, bringing in local partners, ignoring their advice, and undermining local goods and services (Games 2004). Such criticism illustrates challenges faced by emerging TNCs in other developing countries, but also raises the issue of attitudes and strategies implemented in those host economies.

Obstacles related to home environments

Some obstacles to OFDI from the South are related to the home-country environment of the TNC. Firstly, some home-country governments maintain policies restricting investment in selected sectors or countries. Secondly, emerging TNCs suffer from their home country's negative business climate. This can result from poor economic performance at home, or other political factors inhibiting the competitive development potential of these firms in their home market. Erdilek (2008) finds that home-country factors significantly hinder the chance of Turkey achieving as high levels of OFDI (and IFDI) as other developing countries. Similar factors were used to explain why Egypt is still not achieving its full OFDI potential, particularly in terms of poor investment climate and prevailing geopolitical issues (Goldstein and Bonaglia 2006).

From a managerial perspective, the home country also plays a role. This was illustrated in the case of Malaysian South–South FDI. Jomo (2002) particularly questioned cronyism in some controversial investments in Cambodia, South Africa and Tanzania. This factor may not limit South–South FDI directly, but has a negative impact on the image of emerging TNCs in neighbouring developing economies.

Emerging TNCs still need to improve their organizational skills, and enhance the capacity of the parent to coordinate and control foreign operations as well as to ensure efficient interaction inside the international production network. Deloitte (2008, 37) identifies several firm-related issues for Russian TNCs. First, they need to formulate a foreign investment and international production development strategy. Second, they need to create an effective organizational mechanism to manage the international network.

Third, TNCs must integrate foreign production entities into corporate management and governance systems. Finally, emerging TNCs face specific strategic concerns related to family succession and political-economic alliances (particularly for the firms listed on stock exchanges in home emerging countries), as significant distractions from shareholder concerns may occur.

15.5   CONCLUDING REMARKS

The objective of this chapter was to address an increasingly important effect of the globalization process: the rising role and position of emerging TNCs, notably in other developing economies. Outward FDI from emerging economies remains concentrated within a small number of countries of origin, but the number of home developing economies has diversified during the 1990s and 2000s, and there are increasing numbers of globally competitive TNCs from the emerging world. This confirms a new phase of emerging TNCs' integration into the global economy, and the expected continuous strengthening of their position. South–South FDI is crucial because many emerging TNCs invest primarily in neighbouring or other developing hosts, and because inward FDI from emerging countries represents a powerful means for development for developing hosts. Figure 15.1 illustrates the issues that have been presented in this chapter, listing the drivers and challenges, to provide a framework for analysis of future trends in South–South FDI. In particular, the key role of the institutional framework was emphasized and investigated in depth.

Given the diversity of comparative advantages, political systems and levels of economic development (with related competitive environment and existing capabilities at firm and individual levels) and geographical features (in terms of climate or proximity to other markets), we acknowledge that there is no one-size-fits-all framework when we wish to explain future South–South prospects. Our framework however points to the dominant role of institutions, at both the national and international levels. Thus, we posit that South–South FDI will continue to increase if governments persevere

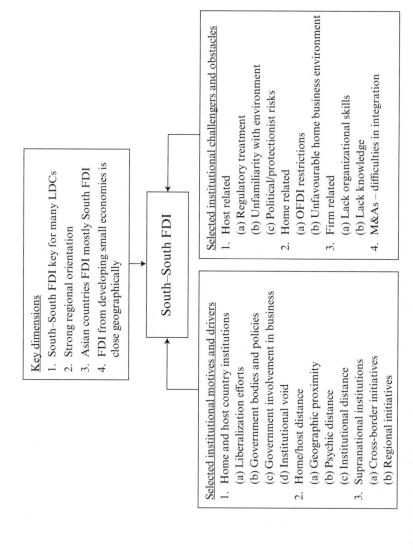

Figure 15.1   Institutional considerations and South–South FDI

in supporting the competitive advantages and internationalization strategies of indigenous firms, opening up their doors to TNCs and strengthening South–South cross-border initiatives. FDI flows are also dependent upon the success of countries in the economic development goals.

Data show the strong regional orientation of South–South FDI. FDI does not necessarily take place within regional groupings, but it is often directed (although not always, as demonstrated in this chapter) to neighbouring economies. Thus, in addition to creating bigger markets, developing countries ought to consider regional policies that can further support such regional cross-investments in order to facilitate the mutual development of countries. We would also suggest that a future increase in FDI from emerging TNCs is likely to generate growing demand from their business communities for greater protection of their overseas investments. As a consequence, in addition to using international investment agreements as a means to promote inward FDI, some developing-country governments will increasingly consider using international investment agreements to protect and facilitate outward investments.

South–South FDI is closely related to the potential for economic development of both home and host countries. The role of institutions does and will continue to influence inward and outward South–South FDI. As a final remark, we would therefore like to encourage future research on South–South FDI. Such FDI contributes to economic development in the developing world, and in turns this creates opportunities for developed countries.

REFERENCES

Aulakh, P.S. and M. Kotabe (2008), 'Institutional changes and organizational transformation in developing economies', *Journal of International Management*, **14**, 209–216.

Aykut, D. and D. Ratha (2003), 'South–south FDI flows: how big are they?' *Transnational Corporations*, **13** (1), 149–176.

Balasubramanuam V.N., David Sapsford and David Griffiths (2002), 'Regional integration agreements and foreign direct investment: theory and preliminary evidence', *Manchester School*, **70** (3), 460–482.

Beausang, F. (2003), *Third World Multinationals: Engine of Competitiveness or New Form of Dependency?* London: Palgrave Macmillan.

Buckley, P.J., J.L. Clegg, A.R. Cross, X. Liu, H. Voss and P. Zheng (2007), 'The determinants of Chinese outward foreign direct investment', *Journal of International Business Studies*, **38** (4), 499.

Buckley, P.J., J.L. Clegg, A.R. Cross, X. Liu, H. Voss and P. Zheng (2008), 'Explaining China's outward FDI: an institutional perspective', in K.P. Sauvant (ed.), *The Rise of Transnational Corporations from Emerging Markets: Threat or Opportunity?* Cheltenham, UK and Northampton, MA, USA: Edward Elgar, pp. 107–146.

Carney, M. (2008), 'The many futures of Asian business groups', *Asia Pacific Journal of Management*, **35**, 595–613.

Casanova, L. (2004), 'East Asian, European, and North American multinational firm strategies in Latin America', *Business and Politics*, **6** (1), 1–40.

Cuervo-Cazurra, A. and M. Genc (2008), 'Transforming disadvantages into advantages: developing-country MNEs in the least developed countries', *Journal of International Business Studies*, **39**, 957–979.

Deloitte (2008), 'Russian multinationals: new plays in the global economy', Moscow.

Dunning, J.H., R.V. Hoesel and R. Narula (1997), 'Third world multinationals revisited: new developments and theoretical implications', in John H. Dunning (ed.), *Globalization, Trade, and Foreign Direct Investment*, New York: Elsevier, pp. 255–286.

Dunning, J.H. and S.M. Lundan (2008a), *Multinational Enterprises and the Global Economy*, 2nd edn, Cheltenham, UK and Northampton, MA, USA: Edward Elgar.

Dunning, J.H. and S.M. Lundan (2008b), 'Institutions and the OLI paradigm of the multinational enterprise', *Asia Pacific Journal of Management*, **25**, 573–593.

Eden, L. and S.R. Miller (2004), 'Distance matters: liability of foreignness, institutional distance and ownership strategy', Bush School Working Paper # 404, Texas A&M University.

Erdilek, A. (2008), 'Internationalization of Turkish MNEs', *Journal of Management Development*, **27** (7), 744–760.

Games, D. (2004), *An Oil Giant Reforms: The Experience of South African Firms Doing Business in Nigeria*, Braamfontein, South Africa: South African Institute of International Affairs.

Gammeltoft, P., H. Barnard and A. Madhok (2010), 'Emerging multinationals, emerging theory: macro- and micro-level perspectives', *Journal of International Management*, **16** (2), 95–101.

Gao, T. (2005), 'Foreign direct investment from developing Asia: some distinctive features', *Economics Letters*, **86** (1), 29–35.

Ghauri, P.N. and M. Yamin (2009), 'Revisiting the impact of multinational enterprises on economic development', *Journal of World Business*, **44** (2), 105–107.

Goldstein, A. (ed.) (2006), *Emerging Multinationals in the Global Economy*, Basingstoke, UK and New York, USA: Palgrave.

Goldstein, A. and F. Bonaglia (2006), 'Outward foreign investment from Egypt', *International Journal of Emerging Markets*, **1** (2), 107–127.

Gökgür, N. (2011), 'Are resurging state-owned enterprises impeding competition overseas?' Columbia FDI Perspectives, N. 36.

Henley, J., S. Kratzsh, M. Külür and T. Tandogan (2008), 'Foreign direct investment from China, India and South Africa in sub-Saharan Africa: a new or old phenomenon?' Research Paper No. 2008/24, United Nations University, UNU-WIDER World Investitute for Development Economics Research.

Hermelo, F.D. and R. Vassolo (2010), 'Institutional development and hypercompetition in emerging economies', *Strategic Management Journal*, **31** (13), 1457–1473.

Jomo, K.S. (2002), 'Ugly Malaysians? South–South investments abused', Durban, South Africa: Institute for Black Research.

Kalotay, K. (2008), 'Russian transnationals and international investment paradigms', *Research in International Business and Finance*, **22**, 85–107.

Kang, Y. and F. Jiang (2012), 'FDI location choice of Chinese multinationals in East and Southeast Asia: traditional economic factors and institutional perspective', *Journal of World Business*, **47** (1), 45–53.

Khanna, T. and K.G. Palepu (2006), 'Emerging giants: building world-class companies in emerging markets', *Harvard Business Review*, **84** (10), 60–69.

Kostova, T. (1999), 'Transnational transfer of strategic organizational practices: a contextual perspective', *Academy of Management Review*, **24** (2), 306–324.

Kumar, K. (1982), 'Third world multinationals: a growing force in international relations', *International Studies Quarterly*, **26** (3).

Kumar, K. and M.G. McLeod (eds) (1981), *Multinationals from Developing Countries*, Lexington, DC: Heath.

Lall, S. (1983), *Third World Multinationals*, Chichester: John Wiley.

Li, J. and F.K. Yao (2010), 'The role of reference groups in international investment decisions by firms from emerging economies', *Journal of International Management*, **16** (2), 143–153.

Luo, Y. and R.L. Tung (2007), 'International expansion of emerging market enterprises: a springboard perspective', *Journal of International Business Studies*, **38** (4), 481–498.

Luo, Y., Q. Xue and B. Han (2010), 'How emerging market governments promote outward FDI: experience from China', *Journal of World Business*, **45** (1), 68–79.

Mathews, J.A. (2006), 'Dragon multinationals: new players in 21st century globalization', *Asia Pacific Journal of Management*, **31** (1), 5–27.

Meyer, K. and M. Peng (2005), 'Probing theoretically into Central and Eastern Europe: transactions, resources, and institutions', *Journal of International Business Studies*, **36** (6), 600–621.

Mirza, Hafiz (2000), 'The globalization of business and East Asian developing-country multinationals', in N. Hood and Stephen Young (eds), *The Globalization of Multinational Enterprise Activity and Economic Development*, Basingstoke: Macmillan.

Mirza, H. and N.J. Freeman (2007), 'Foreign direct investment in East Asia's transitional economies: perspectives on development and transition', *International Business Review*, **16** (2), 169–141.

Mirza, H. and A. Giroud (2004), 'Regionalisation, FDI and Vietnam: lessons from other ASEAN countries', *Journal of the Asia Pacific Economy*, **16** (2), 169–41.

Mirza H., A. Giroud and H.K. Wee (2011), 'Emerging multinational enterprises', in Brennan Louis (eds), *The Emergence of Southern Multinationals: Their Impact on Europe*, Basingstoke: Palgrave Macmillan, pp. 13–41.

Mudambi, R. and R. Navarra (2002), 'Institutions and international business: a theoretical overview', *International Business Review*, **11** (6), 635–646.

North, D.C. (1990), *Institutions, Institutional Change and Economic Performance*, Cambridge: Cambridge University Press.

Peng, M.W., D.Y. Wang and Y. Jiang (2008), 'An institution-based view of international business strategy: a focus on emerging economies'. *Journal of International Business Studies*, **39** (5), 920–936.

Sauvant, Karl P. (2005), 'New sources of FDI: the BRICs. Outward FDI from Brazil, Russia, India and China', *Journal of World Investment and Trade*, **6**, 640–709.

Sen, Rahul, M. Asher and R. Rajan (2004), 'ASEAN–India economic relations: current status and future prospects', *Economic and Political Weekly*, 17 July, pp. 3296–3307.

UNCTAD (2004), 'South–South investment agreements proliferating', Press release, UNCTAD/PRESS/PR/2004/036, 23 November.

UNCTAD (2006), *World Investment Report 2006: FDI from Developing and Transition Economies: Implications for Development*, New York and Geneva: United Nations, United Nations publication.

UNCTAD (2007), 'Global Players from Emerging Markets: Strengthening Enterprise Competitiveness through Outward Investment', New York and Geneva: United Nations.

UNCTAD (2010), 'World Investment Report 2010: investing in a law carbon economy', New York and Geneva: United Nations Publication.

UNCTAD (2011), 'Investment Policy Monitor', N.5, New York and Geneva: United Nations, UNCTAD/WEB/DIAE/IA/2011/5.

Wee, K.H. (2007), 'Outward foreign direct investment by enterprises from Thailand', *Transnational Corporations*, **16** (1), 86–116.

Wells, Louis T., Jr. (1983), *Third World Multinationals: The Role of Foreign Direct Investment from Developing Countries*, Cambridge, MA: MIT Press.

Yeung, H.Y.-C (2007), 'From followers to market leaders: Asian electronics firms in the global economy', *Asia Pacific Viewpoint*, **48** (1), 1–30.

Yiu, Daphne W., Lau Chung Ming and Garry D. Bruton (2007), 'International venturing by emerging economic firms: the effects of firm capabilities, home country networks, and corporate entrepreneurship', *Journal of International Business Studies*, **38**, 519–540.

Young, S., C.-H. Huang and M. McDermont (1996), 'Internationalization and competitive catch-up processes: case study evidence on Chinese multinational enterprises', *Management International Review*, **36** (4), 295–314.

16 Internationalization, institutions and economic growth: a fuzzy-set analysis of the new EU member states

Matthew M.C. Allen and Maria L. Aldred

16.1 INTRODUCTION

Within the international business literature, the importance of locational differences has recently come to the fore in many studies (Dunning 2009; Meyer et al. 2011; Mudambi and Navarra 2002; Rugman et al. 2011). However, in contrast to studies that are underpinned by a more comparative sociological perspective, many of these analyses within the international business literature adopt a relatively narrow definition of 'institutions' when examining the consequences for commercial activities of any locational differences. For instance, within the international business literature, many studies focus on a relatively narrow range of formal, regulatory institutions that shape arm's-length, impersonal exchange (Henisz 2003; Khanna and Rivkin 2001; Meyer et al. 2011; Young et al. 2008). This definition of institutions is favoured over broader ones that can encompass a greater range of regulation-based ones as well as more informal or, indeed, para-public institutions (Jackson and Deeg 2008). A corollary of this conceptualization of institutions is that several prominent studies in the international business literature refer to 'institutional voids' (Khanna and Palepu 2006; Kim et al. 2010; Tan and Meyer 2010; cf. Peng et al. 2008). By this, such analysts mean the lack of strong legal rules that can be enforced, for example to uphold the terms of a contract (Khanna and Palepu 2006, 62; Tan and Meyer 2010).

However, in studies that adopt a more sociological – or, perhaps better, organizational sociological – perspective that is common within the 'comparative capitalisms' literature, a term such as 'institutional void' would be anathema, as other institutions or 'rules of the game' that are enforceable either legally (Streeck and Thelen 2005) or in some other way (Crouch 2005; Culpepper 2001; Sako 1992; Thelen 2004; Whitley 1999) would be present. Whilst this latter approach does not preclude the possibility that the rule of law is so weak that the only people you can trust in business are family members or those with whom you have close personal ties, it does take into consideration a more wide-ranging set of institutions that can potentially influence firm behaviour. In short, in analyses of the ways in which locational differences, including institutional ones, influence the ways in which firms internationalize, international business scholars are likely to privilege regulatory institutions surrounding impersonal commercial exchange, whilst those who adopt a more sociologically informed perspective are likely to encompass a broader range of institutions, such as dominant patterns of corporate financing, labour market systems and interfirm networks, in their assessments (Allen and Aldred 2011; Casper and Matraves 2003; Hall and Soskice 2001; Liu and Tylecote 2009; Whitley 1999, 2007).

This difference between the two perspectives is important for three main reasons. Firstly, as will be discussed in greater detail below, international business scholars tend to downplay the influence that other institutions may have on firm behaviour, including the ways in which – and extent to which – they internationalize. In other words, and simplifying greatly, within the international business literature there is a tendency to assume that the only institutional resource that all firms need to rely on to help their competitiveness is the rule of law that is strictly upheld. By contrast, analyses within the comparative capitalisms literature encompass a broader set of institutional resources in their explanations of how firms compete (Allen and Aldred 2011; Liu and Tylecote 2009). Secondly, and consequently, in contrast to the international business literature the comparative capitalisms perspective seeks to explain how the organizational capabilities that are required by firms in different sectors of the economy if companies are to be competitive are created and maintained (Allen and Whitley 2012; Casper and Matraves 2003; Casper and Whitley 2004; Tylecote and Ramirez 2005; cf. Peng and Meyer 2011). In short, the comparative capitalisms literature, on the whole, pays greater attention to the specific capabilities that firms create and develop in their efforts to gain a competitive advantage over their rivals.

It is this emphasis on organizational capabilities in the comparative capitalisms literature that leads to a broader definition of institutions in that perspective compared to international business ones: the creation and development of organizational capabilities, which can vary in the degree to which, for instance, knowledgeable venture capital or employees with firm-specific skills are needed by firms to be competitive, will be helped or hindered by a number of institutions including, inter alia, labour market systems, corporate financing and interfirm networks (Amable 2003; Hall and Soskice 2001; Jackson and Deeg 2008; Lane 2007; Whitley 1999, 2007). In short, the comparative capitalisms perspective does not just focus on the rule of law to explain firm behaviour, but takes into consideration a broader set of institutional factors to assess the conditions under which firms from different institutional regimes are able to become and remain competitive.

Ultimately, then, these differences lead to a third key variation in the analytical foci of the two perspectives. In the international business literature, a corollary of the emphasis on the rule of law is that there is a proclivity to emphasize a convergence on this privileged institutional dimension in different countries, if firms located there are to be successful and, indeed, if countries are to attract foreign firms to invest there. For instance, as Meyer et al. (2011, 237–239; see also Globerman and Shapiro 2003) have written:

> To a considerable extent, as local institutions affect the location choices of firms, competition arises between institutional systems. There is mounting evidence that countries with more open and transparent systems have been more successful in achieving growth, and more MNEs are setting up local operations there. Laggard countries are beginning to selectively emulate the institutions of the successful countries, both to attract more foreign direct investment (FDI) and to accelerate economic growth.

In contrast, the comparative capitalisms literature assesses the conditions under which countries are likely to continue to have divergent sets of institutions, as there is no one institutional regime that is associated with superior firm – and, hence, country – performance across all sectors of the economy and across all measures (Allen and Aldred 2011; Allen et al. 2006; Amable 2003; Hall and Soskice 2001; Lane and Wood 2011; Whitley 1999, 2007).

It is this issue of divergence and convergence that this chapter assesses. Drawing on country-level data, it analyses the extent to which there is any one set of institutions that is clearly associated with superior macroeconomic performance. From the perspective of the international business literature, it can be expected that a strong legal framework will consistently and primarily be associated with superior macroeconomic performance. By contrast, the comparative capitalism perspective leads to expectations that there are likely to be a number of clusters that lead to good macroeconomic performance. Whilst the rule of law is also expected to be of significance from a comparative capitalisms perspective, it will be one institutional factor amongst many.

The next section sets out the theoretical differences between the two perspectives examined here. This is followed by sections on the research design, data and variable calibration, methodology, and results. The chapter concludes with a discussion of the results, and draws out some of the study's implications for future research.

16.2   THEORETICAL BACKGROUND

In examining the differences between the international business literature and that of the comparative capitalisms approach, this section will focus on how the two perspectives tend to assess the ways in which institutions impact upon firm behaviour. Within the international business literature the dominant approach is one that, as noted above, tends to privilege formal regulations that impact upon arm's-length, impersonal commercial exchange. As a result, analyses within the international business literature have, for instance, sought to explain the most appropriate entry mode to those foreign markets (see, for instance, Brouthers 2002; Meyer 2001). The focus of such studies is to examine the ways in which a relatively narrow range of formal institutions shape the type of commercial entities that firms establish and operate in foreign markets. In such analyses, the discussion of the role(s) that the subsidiaries will be carrying out – in terms of the types of activities that the foreign establishment will be conducting, and the integration of such activities into the firm's value chain – is relatively 'thin' (cf. Erramilli et al. 2002). Consequently, in-depth assessments of the ways in which the necessary organizational competencies and capabilities will be created and developed within the subsidiaries are also downplayed.

In addition, those studies within the international business literature that do take into consideration the ways in which home-country institutions shape the development of firm capabilities tend to treat institutions in a relatively limited way that emphasizes narrow, market-related regulations. As a result of inefficient or 'missing' institutions, domestic firms, if they are to be successful, will have to develop managerial capabilities to overcome these deficiencies (see, for example, Cuervo-Cazurra and Genc 2008; Peng et al. 2005). In short, ownership control or managers' personal networks are often regarded in the international business literature as substitutes for a relatively narrow set of 'inadequate' market-related institutions (Jackson and Deeg 2008). Such institutions are not assessed in terms of their influence over the firm's capabilities and, hence, competitiveness.

What is lacking from the international business literature, therefore, is a detailed treatment of the ways in which institutional diversity across a number of areas can impact upon either the types of organizational capabilities, which underpin firms' attempts to be competitive, that companies can successfully develop, or the dominant forms that innovation within companies is likely to take as a result of the institutional context within which they operate (Jackson and Deeg 2008). It is these areas that form a key part of the analytical focus within the comparative capitalisms literature (Allen and Aldred 2011; Allen et al. 2011; Casper 2009; Crouch and

Voelzkow 2009; Hall and Soskice 2001; Hollingsworth and Boyer 1997; Liu and Tylecote 2009; Whitley 1999, 2007). Within this perspective, the development of organizational capabilities is strongly shaped – but not determined – by the institutional regime within which companies operate. So, for instance, if a company is seeking to introduce a disruptive innovation, it is likely to find it easier to do so if knowledgeable venture capital is available, employees are willing to move readily between companies, and financial backers have a straightforward means to capitalize on any increase in the value of their investment (Allen and Whitley 2012; Casper and Matraves 2003; Tylecote and Ramirez 2005). A corollary of this emphasis is that sectoral characteristics in relation to competitiveness, such as the development of new technologies and the incremental upgrading of the firm's existing competencies, and attendant organizational capabilities become part of the analytical focus (Allen and Whitley 2012; Allen et al. 2011; Casper and Whitley 2004; Keizer 2005; Tylecote et al. 2010; Wright and Dwyer 2006).

In the comparative capitalisms approach, the inclusion of a wider set of institutions in the analysis, together with a theoretical framework that specifies the ways in which those institutions are likely to shape decision-making within companies and other organizations, arguably leads to a richer explanation of how and why firms carry out the activities that they do. For instance, if banks are the primary source of corporate finance within an economy, companies are likely to be monitored more closely by their backers across a range of measures rather than merely on short-term profitability, which is likely to be the case if firms have a dispersed ownership structure and there is a market for corporate control. Whilst financial backing from banks may make it more difficult for companies to move rapidly from one market to another, it is likely to be a boon if the company needs to adopt a long-term approach to build or maintain its competitive advantage. As a result, the comparative capitalism literature pays closer attention to the particular institutional context within which firms operate (Allen 2004; Crouch and Voelzkow 2009; Keune et al. 2009; Lane and Wood 2009, 2011; Lange 2009; Schneiberg 2007) as well as the ways in which firms may attempt to overcome domestic institutional constraints by accessing structurally conditioned resources that are based abroad (Allen and Whitley 2012; Casper 2009; Lange 2009).

An important theme within the comparative capitalism literature – and one that further differentiates it from much of the international business literature – is 'institutional complementarity' (Crouch 2005; Crouch et al. 2005; Hall and Soskice 2001). Although there has been much discussion over the meaning of this term, it will be defined here to mean that the presence of one institution increases the efficiency of another. This highlights the ways in which individual institutions may interact with one another to reinforce pressures on senior managers and others within firms to take particular decisions. For instance, the presence of relatively strict employment laws that make it difficult for employers to lay off workers may be viewed by companies as 'beneficial constraints' (Streeck 1997) that encourage firms to invest in the skills of their workers to a greater extent than might otherwise be the case (Harcourt and Wood 2007). If these employment regulations are coupled with a financial system that is characterized by long-term backing by banks, companies may find it easier to pursue strategies that require a focus on medium- to long-term growth at the potential expense of increases in short-term profitability. This, in turn, is likely to lead to firm success in those sectors of the economy that exhibit such characteristics (Casper and Whitley 2004; Hall and Soskice 2001).

16.3   RESEARCH DESIGN

The new member states of the European Union (EU) in Central and Eastern Europe (CEE) provide a strong basis upon which to assess the possibility that, for countries to grow economically, they need to conform to high standards in terms of the legal basis for, and enforcement of, impersonal commercial exchange. Indeed, they offer prime cases to study the extent to which these systems are likely to converge around a common model. The reasons for this are threefold. Firstly, the new member states are highly dependent upon foreign direct investment (FDI) (Bohle and Greskovits 2006; Lane and Myant 2007; Nölke and Vliegenthart 2009). Secondly, the competition between the new member states for such investment is likely to lead to pressures to create regulations that foreign firms find most attractive and, hence, that are likely to impose fewer constraints on business and institutional entrepreneurs than might otherwise be the case (Hansmann and Kraakman 2000; Lane 2007; McCahery et al. 2004; Walgenbach and Meyer 2008). Finally, the collapse of communism in the region created an opportunity to implement changes at a time when restrictions on the extent to which change could occur may have been reduced (Vaughan-Whitehead 2003).

This chapter examines the pressures for convergence by assessing the links between a broad range of institutions and gross domestic product (GDP) growth rates. If it can be shown that higher GDP growth rates are consistently and primarily associated with regulations that facilitate impersonal commercial exchange, this would suggest that countries in the region need to adopt a relatively standard set of measures if they wish to attract foreign investors and grow. Indeed, for international business scholars the main expectation is that narrow, market-promoting institutions are likely to be the primary influence behind higher GDP growth rates in CEE. For comparative capitalisms scholars, there is likely to be an expectation of greater diversity between countries as well as an anticipation that a number of institutions will shape GDP growth rates in the region.

This chapter assesses these divergent expectations by using fuzzy-set qualitative comparative analysis (fsQCA) (Ragin 2000, 2006, 2008), which is increasingly being used in related studies to identify the complex institutional configurations of both sufficient and necessary causes of various outcomes (Allen and Aldred 2011; Boyer 2004; Jackson 2005; Pajunen 2008; Schneider et al. 2009). The use of fuzzy sets has several advantages. Firstly, the technique enables the identification of any potential patterns in both necessary and sufficient causal conditions that promote higher GDP growth rates. This, in turn, will help to establish the extent to which institutional regimes are likely to converge across the region to a common model that includes regulations that lower the transaction costs of doing business. In addition, if a common institutional pattern is found for those countries that have higher GDP growth rates, this could point to policies that others could seek to emulate. Alternatively, if no common institutional configuration is found that can explain strong GDP growth rates, this will illustrate that diversity within the region will persist, as there will be more than one way to achieve success in this important area. Secondly, fuzzy sets are particularly appropriate for research designs that are limited to a relatively small number of observations, which is often the case with cross-country analyses (Jackson 2005). Finally, fuzzy sets facilitate a more nuanced examination of 'causal complexity', to put it one way (Ragin 2008), or 'institutional complementarities', as others have put it (Hall and Soskice 2001; Whitley 2007). This facilitates the assessment of combinations of factors, which is important as the issue of complementarity within the institutionalist literature has been scrutinized extensively (see, for example, Crouch 2005; Crouch et al. 2005; Morgan 2005).

Building on the arguments presented above, it is necessary to include issues of corporate governance in the analysis. Within the comparative capitalisms literature, the issue of corporate governance is a central one, and it has been ascribed an important role in capitalism in CEE (Bohle and Greskovits 2006; Hall and Soskice 2001; King 2007; Nölke and Vliegenthart 2009; Whitley 2007). As a result of the large amount of foreign investment in CEE, and as a result of formerly state-owned enterprises being privatized and then taken over by overseas companies, it has been argued that there have been important changes to the corporate governance systems of enterprises in the region (see, for instance, Czaban and

Henderson 2003). In particular, Nölke and Vliegenthart (2009, 682–683) contend that:

> major corporate decisions are not negotiated between managers and sharehold-
> ers, but rather between managers of the [East Central Europe] subsidiary and
> Western headquarters . . . As a result, corporate managers of [East Central
> Europe] subsidiaries are responsible to internal supervisors in other countries.

It is, therefore, the greater prevalence of foreign ownership that distinguishes firms in CEE from many of those in Western countries (King 2007;
Lane 2007).

The influence of those outside the countries of CEE does not stop
there: the corporate governance codes of the region have been strongly
shaped by transnational entities (Nölke and Vliegenthart 2009). In addition, foreign organizations may shape the capabilities of firms in CEE in
other – potentially less direct – ways. For instance, banks in CEE are often
foreign-owned (Bohle and Greskovits 2006) and overseas investors own a
large proportion of equities that are listed on the region's stock markets
(Allen and Aldred 2009). If foreign investors wish to have a more direct
influence over CEE companies, they will own their overseas subsidiaries
outright. This, in turn, will mean that they are not listed on local stock
markets and, hence, will not have to adhere to the relevant host-country
regulations. Consequently, host-country stock markets will be of little relevance to them (Lane 2007; Myant 2007; Mykhnenko 2007). Additionally,
wholly owned subsidiaries may be less likely to be reliant on banks in
the region for funding. If FDI is, indeed, the preferred route for foreign
companies to coordinate and control their subsidiaries in CEE, then those
countries that attract the most FDI may be the ones to post the strongest
GDP growth rates. By implication, if this is the main route to higher economic growth levels, then domestic banks and stock markets are likely to
play a less important role.

Another key element of analyses within the comparative capitalisms literature is the employment system, which covers various forms of employment regulations, such as employment protection, wage bargaining and
workplace representation. This is an area where there is a clear distinction between the two perspectives covered here, as the analytical focus
is narrower in the international business literature than it is within the
comparative capitalisms approach. In some countries, employment regulations provide employee representatives with relatively powerful means
to convey the views of workers to managers at the establishment level.
Indeed, in some areas employee representatives must give their consent to
proposed changes. Similarly, the importance of sectoral bargaining varies
between countries. These two institutions can promote the provision of

firm-specific skills (Hall and Soskice 2001; Whitley 2007); attempts to create such skills can be reinforced if the company relies on banks for equity rather than predominantly equity markets, as the former can help to foster commitment between employers and employees (Casper and Matraves 2003; Hall and Soskice 2001).

Whilst in some areas, such as collective bargaining, there are similarities between the new member states in CEE, in general there is a considerable amount of variation in employee relations in CEE. In terms of collective bargaining, for instance, much of it takes place at the company level in the new member states, with the exceptions of Slovenia, where the national level is important, and Bulgaria and Slovakia, where the sector plays a key role (Knell and Srholec 2007; Myant 2007; Neumann 2002; Nölke and Vliegenthart 2009). This is not, however, to suggest that employee relations in most of the new EU member states resemble relatively deregulated capitalist models. For example, Buchen (2007) and Feldmann (2006) have argued that employee relations in Estonia largely conform to the deregulated model, whilst those in Slovenia are more regulated (see also, for Estonia, Kallaste et al. 2008). Myant (2007) has noted that trade unions are in decline in the Czech Republic. However, in the Czech Republic and Slovakia legislation enables works councils to be established in organizations, although in both countries their powers are much less than they are in Germany (Majtan 2005; see also Stasek 2005). In Poland, trade unions have been described as being relatively weak, and employee relations as consensual (Mykhnenko 2007). In Hungary, workplace representation has been portrayed as informal and paternalistic (Richbell et al. 2010).

Regulations surrounding impersonal commercial exchange are deemed to be of great significance in many analyses within the international business literature in assessments of firms' overseas expansion, as it can, for example, alter transaction costs (Meyer 2001; Meyer and Peng 2005). The inclusion of this factor is important as, given the emerging nature of the economies in CEE, overseas investors which are considering establishing subsidiaries in a foreign country may be deterred from doing so if that country is deemed to place too great a burden on the companies that operate there. This may be the case even if employment regulations are viewed favourably by those potential investors. The inclusion of a variable that measures the ease of doing business in a country is an appropriate way to capture these more general aspects of a country's business environment.

Another factor that is likely to increase GDP growth rates is the availability of well-educated employees. In order to capture this possibility, this research includes the percentage of the labour force that has successfully completed a tertiary-level qualification. Tertiary education covers university undergraduate degrees. The inclusion of this variable is in line with related studies (see, for instance, Schneider et al. 2009). It will also help to shed light on the extent to which this factor is important to foreign investors and, hence, the extent to which states in CEE will not only have to promote the establishment of markets, but also increase workforce skills by, for instance, increasing the numbers of those going to university.

16.4 DATA AND VARIABLE CALIBRATION

In order to assess the extent to which the desire to increase GDP growth rates is likely to create pressures for economies in CEE to converge around a model that privileges strong regulations that facilitate commercial transaction, all ten countries from CEE that joined the EU in either 2004 or 2007 have been included in the analysis. In order to ensure that the results are not biased by, for instance, large one-off investments by foreign firms, mean annual values for the five-year period (2005 until 2009, inclusive) have been used for most of the variables in this study. The year 2009 is the latest for which most measures are available. The data on employment and business regulations are only available for one year; these values do not, however, suffer from large annual variations.

The outcome variable is GDP growth rates. Data for this factor along with those for six of the causal conditions were collected from the World Bank's World Development Indicators dataset, which itself draws on a number of sources; data for the seventh on 'participation' are from the European Trade Union Institute (ETUI). These data are for 2006; once again, this measure is not subject to significant fluctuations. The raw data for all of the variables used in this analysis are shown in Table 16.1; the sources and definitions for that data are set out in Table 16.2.

In order to use the data as part of a fuzzy-set analysis, the figures had to be transformed. To establish the set membership values, three anchor points need to be determined: two extreme points defining full membership and full non-membership, and a crossover point at which the country is neither in nor outside the set (Ragin 2000, 158–159). These anchors are assigned set membership values of 1, 0 and 0.5, respectively. A value of 1 was assigned to the country with the highest GDP growth rate; 0 to the country with the lowest. The crossover point was calculated as the arithmetic mean for all of the countries. Given these three anchor points, the set membership values for all cases were calculated by using the log odds method described by Ragin (2008). Using this measure, five countries are members of the 'high GDP growth rate' set (Bulgaria, the Czech Republic,

Table 16.1 Data used in the analysis prior to transformation

Country	GDP	FDI	Domcred	Stockmkt	Labforce	Diffbus	Diffcontract	Emprigidity	Participation
Bulgaria	4.1	19.6	59.2	26.4	24.1	51	87	19	0.08
Czech Republic	3.5	4.7	46.8	31.5	13.9	63	82	11	0.44
Estonia	1.8	12.3	91.0	22.3	33.3	17	49	51	0.06
Hungary	0.6	24.1	61.8	27.0	19.9	46	14	22	0.40
Latvia	2.0	5.0	88.4	10.4	21.8	24	15	43	0.06
Lithuania	2.6	4.0	56.9	22.2	28.9	23	17	38	0.04
Poland	4.7	4.2	40.9	34.4	18.8	70	75	25	0.25
Romania	3.8	6.5	34.8	20.6	12.2	56	55	46	0.43
Slovak Republic	5.1	3.4	40.2	6.8	14.4	41	61	22	0.44
Slovenia	2.6	1.8	60.4	33.6	20.5	42	60	54	0.57
Mean	3.1	8.6	58.0	23.5	20.8	43.3	51.5	33.1	0.28

Notes: All data are the annual averages for the five-year period 2005–2009 (inclusive), except 'domcred' for the Slovak Republic, for which the four-year mean from 2005 until 2008 has been used because of missing data; 'labforce', for which the five-year mean from 2003 until 2007 has been used because of missing data; and the data for 'diffcontr' and 'emprigid' which are for 2010 only.

Table 16.2   Causal conditions: definitions and sources

Variable	Definition	Source
GDP	GDP growth (annual %)	World Bank national accounts data, and OECD National Accounts data files. The five-year mean (2005–2009, inclusive) has been used.
Corporate Governance		
FDI	Foreign direct investment, net inflows (% of GDP)	International Monetary Fund, International Financial Statistics and Balance of Payments databases, World Bank, Global Development Finance, and World Bank and OECD data. The five-year mean (2005–2009, inclusive) has been used.
Domcred	Domestic credit to private sector (% of GDP)	International Monetary Fund, International Financial Statistics and data files, and World Bank and OECD data. The five-year mean (2005–2009, inclusive) has been used, except for Slovakia as data for 2009 are missing.
Stock	Market capitalization of indigenous listed companies (% of GDP)	Standard & Poor's, Emerging Stock Markets Factbook and supplemental S&P data. The five-year mean (2005–2009, inclusive) has been used.
Labour Market		
Emprigidity	Rigidity of employment index (0 = less rigid to 100 = more rigid)	World Bank, Doing Business project (http://www.doingbusiness.org/). Data are for 2010.
Participation	European Participation Index, measuring employees' plant-level, board-level, collective bargaining coverage, and trade union density (1 = highest level; 0 = lowest level)	European Trade Union Institute (ETUI), http://www.worker-participation.eu/About-WP/European-Participation-Index-EPI. Data are for 2006.
Labforce	Labour force with tertiary education (% of total)	International Labour Organization. The five-year mean for the latest available years (2003–2007, inclusive) has been used, except for Estonia, Romania and Slovenia (four-year mean, as data are missing).

Table 16.2   (continued)

Variable	Definition	Source
Business Regulation		
Diffbus	Ease of doing business index (1 = most business-friendly regulations)	World Bank, Doing Business project (http://www.doingbusiness.org/). Data are for 2010.
Diffcontract	Ease of enforcing contracts (rank; a higher value denotes greater difficulties)	World Bank, Doing Business project (http://www.doingbusiness.org/). Data are for 2010.

Poland, Romania and the Slovak Republic). The same procedure that was used to calculate the set membership for high GDP growth rates was used for all of the causal conditions. This results in countries having varying membership for each institutional variable.

The first measure of corporate governance is FDI, which is assessed on the basis of net FDI inflows as a percentage of GDP. The second measure of corporate governance, domestic credit, captures the credit provided by, primarily, banks in one country to companies in the same country as a percentage of GDP. It therefore indicates the prevalence of domestic banks in funding economic activities. If economies in CEE are to grow based upon domestic companies with strong competitive competencies, domestic sources of funding are likely to be important. The third and final measure of corporate governance, broadly defined, is stock market capitalization, which is proxied by the market capitalization of indigenous companies as a percentage of GDP. Similar to the arguments put forward on domestic credit, if domestic firms can create capabilities that allow them to grow and succeed internationally, there is likely to be a causal connection between high levels of stock market capitalization and strong GDP growth rates.

In order to measure labour market factors, two measures are included in the analysis. The 'employment rigidity' index captures general employment legislation, whilst the European Participation Index measures workplace and board-level employee representation, collective bargaining coverage rates and trade union density. The general regulatory environment is captured by the Ease of Doing Business Index – expressed in the analysis as the rigidity of doing business in order to aid the interpretation of the results. The ease with which legal agreements between corporations can be upheld in the courts is measured by the ability to enforce contracts.

16.5 METHODOLOGY

Developed by Ragin (2000) and drawing on Boolean algebra, fuzzy-set qualitative comparative analysis (fsQCA) provides a means to assess the relationship between combinations of 'causal conditions' and the outcome in question. In short, fsQCA examines how the membership of cases in the set of causal conditions is linked to membership in the outcome set. Like conventional statistical methods, fsQCA enables researchers to examine a higher number of cases than might be possible using many qualitative methods. However, unlike conventional statistical analytical techniques, such as multivariate analysis, fsQCA is based on the logic of set relations. This means that cases are considered differently in the two methods (Braumoeller and Goertz 2000; Ragin 2000, 2008). For instance, conventional statistical techniques would assess, in various ways, the correlation between two variables. However, the logic behind such a technique would lead to certain values being considered as errors (Ragin 2006). Yet fsQCA, precisely because it is based on set-theoretic reasoning, considers the cases, at least in some instances, to be causally linked (Ragin 2000, 2006).

An advantage of using fsQCA here is that it enables potential clusters of institutional configurations and, hence, countries to be identified. If any such clusters are found, this would potentially reveal strong convergence tendencies amongst countries in the region. If, on the other hand, there are no clusters of either necessary or sufficient causal conditions, such tendencies will be less. An additional advantage of the fsQCA approach is that it allows for the possibility that more than one combination of causal conditions may be found to be linked to the same outcome. In other words, there may be more than one way for countries to achieve high GDP growth rates. Hence, fsQCA captures the idea of equifinality or functional equivalents (Fiss 2007). This enables an assessment of the extent to which various institutional combinations can explain higher GDP growth rates.

Finally, unlike conventional statistical techniques which are based on examinations of sufficiency (Ragin 2000, 2006), fsQCA can examine the links between various combinations of causal conditions and the outcome as both necessary and sufficient conditions. This is important here, as it is yet to be established whether certain institutional features are either necessary and/or sufficient for countries in CEE to achieve strong GDP growth rates. The use of fsQCA means that causal conditions that are necessary and sufficient can be explored. These findings may, in turn, lead to clearer policy implications than would be the case from an analysis of the marginal effects obtained from regression analyses (Fiss 2007, 1195; Schneider et al. 2009).

16.6   RESULTS

16.6.1   Necessary Conditions and Functional Equivalents

The analysis begins by examining whether any of the causal conditions can be considered 'necessary' for the outcome. A necessary causal condition is one for which the instances of the outcome constitute a subset of the instances of the causal condition (Ragin 2006, 297). In other words, a necessary cause, as Ragin (2000, 91) has noted, is one that 'must be present for the outcome in question to occur'. Its presence does not, however, automatically lead to the outcome. This means that, for each case, the values of the set membership for the outcome will be lower than the values for the set membership for the necessary cause. However, as the data do not normally conform to that specification, fsQCA draws on consistency measures, which are calculated using probabilities, to enable assessments of the degree to which observations meet the requirement of necessity. Following the consistency rule suggested by Ragin (2006, 296–297), the analysis views near misses favourably, but views negatively those cases in which the scores for the causal membership greatly exceed those for the outcome membership.

A consistency score of 1 denotes that the causal condition or combination of causal conditions meets the necessity rule across all cases. Consequently, values closer to 0 indicate that many cases fail to conform to that rule and/or that there are a large proportion of cases that are a long way from meeting that rule. If a causal condition or a combination of them has a consistency score of 0.9 or above, this is conventionally deemed to be a 'necessary' or 'almost always necessary' condition. Table 16.3 shows the results of the analysis of causal conditions for all eight of the factors included here. Following convention, conditions that are written in lower case denote 'non-membership' of that set; those in upper case represent membership. Individually, no causal condition exceeds the threshold of 0.9. In other words, not one of the causal conditions countries examined here creates the necessary conditions for high GDP growth rates. This, as is discussed below, is an important finding, as it suggests that there is no single factor that countries in the region can change in order to promote higher GDP growth rates.

16.6.2   Sufficient Conditions

The analysis of sufficient conditions is based on the set-theoretic reasoning that a sufficient cause is one that, in a strict interpretation, leads to the outcome if for all cases the fuzzy-set membership value of the causal

Table 16.3   Analysis of necessary conditions

Condition tested	Consistency	Coverage
domcred	0.878	0.801
DIFFCONTRACT	0.856	0.780
DIFFBUS	0.796	0.783
fdi	0.774	0.586
labforce	0.749	0.702
emprigidity	0.741	0.760
STOCKMKT	0.660	0.582
PARTICIPATION	0.622	0.616
stockmkt	0.434	0.535
participation	0.402	0.430
LABFORCE	0.325	0.369
EMPRIGIDITY	0.322	0.331
diffbus	0.282	0.304
FDI	0.281	0.449
DOMCRED	0.235	0.276
diffcontract	0.224	0.264

Notes: Outcome variable is GDP. The use of upper case denotes the presence of a condition; lower case denotes its absence.

condition does not exceed the fuzzy membership value of the outcome (Ragin 2006). Combinations of factors can be considered in the same way and are denoted by a logical 'AND' (*). As individual cases or combinations of them are unlikely to satisfy the strict criterion for sufficiency across all cases, a consistency measure, as specified in Ragin (2006), is needed.

Those causal combinations that exceed a certain consistency score are categorized as sufficient. This leads to such cases being assigned a value of 1 in the truth table for the outcome (GDP). Those causal combinations that have a consistency score below the cut-off point are not deemed to be sufficient, and they receive a score of 0 for the outcome. Using 0.80 as the cut-off point for sufficiency leads to the combinations of causal conditions and outcome shown in Table 16.4. Out of the 258 possible logical combinations of causal factors, ten are observed. The fact that there are not fewer observed combinations suggests that there is little complementarity between the various institutions. In other words, having higher levels of, for instance, stock market capitalization does not mean that, say, employee participation levels will be comparatively strong or weak. This evidence indicates that there has been little convergence around any particular institutional model or models amongst the CEE countries.

In order to examine the sufficiency of the causes for strong GDP growth

Table 16.4 *Truth table and assignment of countries to institutional configurations (logical remainders not listed)*

Country	fdi	domcred	stockmkt	labforce	diffbus	diffcontract	emprigidity	participation	GDP	consist
Poland	0	0	1	0	1	1	0	0	1	0.998
Romania	0	0	0	0	1	1	1	1	1	0.998
Slovak Republic	0	0	0	0	0	1	0	1	1	0.997
Bulgaria	1	1	1	1	1	1	0	0	1	0.995
Czech Republic	0	0	1	0	1	1	0	1	1	0.861
Lithuania	0	0	0	1	0	0	1	0	0	0.465
Slovenia	0	1	1	0	0	1	1	0	0	0.418
Latvia	0	1	0	1	0	0	1	0	0	0.295
Estonia	1	1	0	1	0	0	1	0	0	0.168
Hungary	1	1	1	0	1	0	0	1	0	0.074

Table 16.5 *Sufficient combinations of conditions for high GDP growth rates*

Intermediate solution	Raw coverage	Unique coverage	Consist.
emprigidity*DIFFCONTRACT* DIFFBUS*labforce*STOCKMKT* domcred*fdi	0.310	0.293	0.894
PARTICIPATION*emprigidity* DIFFCONTRACT*diffbus*labforce* stockmkt*domcred*fdi	0.129	0.108	0.997
PARTICIPATION*EMPRIGIDITY* DIFFCONTRACT*DIFFBUS*labforce* stockmkt*domcred*fdi	0.140	0.119	0.998
participation*emprigidity* DIFFCONTRACT*DIFFBUS* LABFORCE*STOCKMKT* DOMCRED*FDI	0.120	0.107	0.995

Notes:
solution coverage: 0.654
solution consistency: 0.947
*: Presence of both conditions.
Calculation with fsQCA 2.0 software (www.fsqca.com).
The use of upper case denotes the presence of a condition; lower case denotes its absence.

rates, a truth-table algorithm is applied. The 'intermediate' solution is shown, which is recommended by Ragin (2008, 160–175) for interpretation. Each line in Table 16.5 represents a combination of sufficient conditions that lead to the outcome. As can be seen, all sufficient causes consist of more than one condition. In short, there is no one condition that is, by itself, sufficient to account for high GDP growth rates.

Four ways to achieve high GDP growth rates emerge from the sufficiency analysis. The scores for 'raw coverage' and 'unique coverage' that are shown in the table help to assess the empirical importance of these four routes to success in advanced technology markets (Ragin 2006). Raw coverage refers to the extent of the overlap between the causal combination set and the outcome set relative to the size of the outcome set (Ragin 2006, 301). The measure for unique coverage controls for overlapping explanations by drawing on the raw coverage data. For any particular causal combinations, it is calculated by subtracting the raw coverage score for all the other causal combinations (excluding the one of interest) from the raw coverage score for all causal combinations (including the one of interest). As there are four causal combinations that explain strong GDP growth rates, the unique coverage score for each combination is relatively modest. This indicates a relatively high degree of diversity amongst those CEE countries that have strong economic growth records.

The four sufficient combinations of conditions have one factor in common. That factor is, from a comparative capitalisms perspective and, *a fortiori*, from an international business perspective somewhat surprisingly, the difficulty in enforcing contracts. In other words, the more onerous it is to ensure compliance with the terms and conditions of a legal agreement between two companies, the higher the GDP growth rate is likely to be. In addition, the general difficulty in doing business in a country is, in three of the four combinations, a factor that helps to explain higher GDP growth rates. This does not conform to many of the expectations within the international business literature. The finding that, in three of the four combinations of conditions, more deregulated employment standards promote higher levels of economic growth, is more in line with the expectations of the international business literature.

The lack of consistency in the combinations of sufficient causes is at odds with some of the arguments within the comparative capitalisms perspective: if institutions do complement one another, this will reduce the number of combinations of causal conditions that explain higher GDP growth rates (Hall and Gingerich 2009; cf. Kenworthy 2006). However, the fact that a wide range of causal conditions are needed to explain stronger economic growth rates is more in keeping with the expectations of the comparative capitalisms literature than those of the international business literature. This is because greater emphasis is attached to the creation and development of organizational capabilities and, hence, the ways in which these are institutionally structured in the former perspective compared to the latter.

16.7   DISCUSSION AND IMPLICATIONS FOR FUTURE RESEARCH

One of the important findings of this research is that there is a great deal of institutional diversity within the new EU member states in CEE. As the results show, there are no clusters of countries around a specific variety of capitalism or an economic model that, in order to attract foreign investment, must adopt neoliberal characteristics. This, in turn, suggests that the pressures for convergence are not as great as some have argued (Globerman and Shapiro 2003; Meyer et al. 2011). Indeed, the differences between the empirically important causal combinations of factors that are sufficient to explain stronger GDP growth rates have important implications for the prospects of institutional convergence in CEE. This is clearly apparent in some of the labour market institutions: low levels of employee participation, for instance, are not universally sufficient to explain higher economic growth levels. In two of the four combinations of sufficient conditions that explain higher GDP growth rates, employee participation levels are above average. In the other two, they have below-average values. Although in three of the four combinations, relatively low employment regulations help to explain better economic growth levels, in the fourth combination, it takes an above-average value. These results, which indicate the importance of diversity, are also corroborated by the findings that relate to necessary conditions, as low employee participation levels and employment protection regulations were not consistently associated with higher economic growth levels. This acts as a warning against arguments to dismantle employment protection and forms of employee representation in companies (Harcourt and Wood 2007). A reduction in these factors will not – in terms of either necessity or sufficiency – lead to stronger GDP growth rates. Indeed, if changes were to be made this could have a detrimental effect on existing comparative advantages.

The findings from this research also have implications for those relatively pessimistic assessments of the future of CEE countries. As relatively high levels of FDI can, in some instances, help to explain stronger GDP growth rates, this contradicts some predictions that the ability of countries in CEE that depend heavily on inward FDI are unlikely to be able to forge their own, independent ways to economic growth (Bohle and Greskovits 2007; Nölke and Vliegenthart 2009). Those contentions implicitly assume that large amounts of FDI are likely to decrease the ability of domestic companies to compete. However, it has been shown here that strong GDP growth rates can be explained by the combination of large amounts of inward FDI together with comparatively high domestic stock market capitalization levels and above-average rates of domestic credit being made available to companies. In other words, FDI does not substitute for commercial activities by domestic firms. Indeed, FDI can be complemented by a vibrant domestic commercial sector, characterized by large stock markets and lending by banks, to explain higher GDP growth rates.

However, the combination of high levels of inward FDI, domestic credit to companies and stock market capitalization are, by themselves, insufficient to explain stronger GDP growth rates, as the examples of Bulgaria and Hungary show. Whilst these two countries share these characteristics, it is only Bulgaria that has an above-average GDP growth rate for the period assessed here. Hungary does not. This illustrates two key points. Firstly, the ways in which various institutions interact with one another is a highly complex issue. It is one that tends to be downplayed within the international business literature. Within that literature, the analysis focuses on a relatively narrow range of institutions. Even within the comparative capitalisms perspective, there has been a tendency to overlook the impact that the absence of key institutions can have on outcomes (Allen 2004). Yet, as this chapter has shown, variation between countries on a couple of key institutions may have a significant impact on a country's ability to outperform its peers.

Secondly, this variation between countries along a relatively small number of institutions calls into question the ability to group countries together in a meaningful way. Whilst categorizations that seek to group countries together will, by their very nature, reduce complexity, the purpose of such classifications – if they are used to contend that countries within any one group will exhibit similar tendencies – will be impugned, as relatively small within-group variations may lead to substantially different outcomes. In other words, what might appear to be relatively minor variations in institutional regimes can lead to widely divergent outcomes.

This second point draws attention to arguments concerning the degree to which countries' economic frameworks need to be complementary (or coherent) if firms within them are to be successful. In particular, it suggests that arguments that link greater coherence to heightened success should be reassessed (Hall and Gingerich 2009; Hall and Soskice 2001; cf. Kenworthy 2006; Lane and Wood 2009). The results for Bulgaria and Hungary could be construed to mean that because Hungary differs from Bulgaria on one key element, it somehow lacks coherence. However, this interpretation is undermined by some of the other findings: there is a relatively high degree of variation amongst those countries that exhibit above-average GDP growth rates. Although the institutional frameworks of the Czech Republic and Poland are very similar, there is still a major difference between them in terms of employee participation: the Czech institutional setting affords employees more influence than the Polish one does. This difference also highlights the fact that low levels of employee participation do not have to be coupled with relatively weak employment protection measures, as is contended by Hall and Gingerich (2009) and Hall and Soskice (2001), for countries to have higher than average GDP growth rates. Similarly, if the stock market plays an important role in the financing of companies in an economy, this may or may not be coupled with banks providing capital to companies, as the examples of the Czech Republic and Poland, on the one hand, and Bulgaria, on the other, demonstrate. It also does not preclude banks providing capital to companies, as the examples of Poland and Bulgaria demonstrate.

The results here, furthermore, indicate that the impact of institutions may not be as straightforward as some theoretical frameworks expect;

this is especially true for some of the international business analyses. For instance, one of the differences between Bulgaria and Hungary is that contracts are appreciably more difficult to enforce in Bulgaria than they are in Hungary; yet the former country has a superior record on economic growth during the period covered than the latter. In contrast to theoretical expectations, then, the more difficult it is to enforce contracts, the higher the levels of GDP growth are likely to be. Indeed, this is the only causal condition that is present in all four combinations of factors that explain the outcome. This poses a significant challenge to the international business literature, as the presence of 'institutional voids' – that is, the lack of a strong legal framework that facilitates impersonal exchange – is, in that perspective, generally associated with lower levels of economic growth.

This research has been able to map that diversity as well as examine, in a sophisticated way, both the necessary and sufficient causal combinations that account for higher levels of GDP growth. This research could be complemented by internationally comparative analysis at the micro or establishment level. This would help to uncover the complex interplay between, on the one hand, institutions and domestic and foreign strategic actors and, on the other, organizational capabilities and commercial specialization (Drahokoupil 2009). This, in turn, would then provide a basis upon which to make assessments about the specific ways in which countries' economies grow. Such studies would add to the emerging literature that attempts to link broader institutional frameworks to particular firms in order to examine the specific ways in which companies access these potential resources to enhance their competitiveness. In addition, such research would reveal intra-country diversity, as the particular institutional settings of firms or industries are likely to differ substantially from national-level depictions. This theme is attracting much interest within the comparative capitalisms literature in particular (Lane and Wood 2009, 2011).

REFERENCES

Allen, M.M.C. (2004), 'The varieties of capitalism paradigm: not enough variety?' *Socio-Economic Review*, **2** (1), 87–107.

Allen, M.M.C. and M.L. Aldred (2009), 'Varieties of capitalism, varieties of innovation? A comparison of old and new EU member states', *Journal of Contemporary European Research*, **5** (4), 581–596.

Allen, M.M.C. and M.L. Aldred (2011), 'Varieties of capitalism, governance, and high-tech export performance: a fuzzy-set analysis of the new EU Member States', *Employee Relations*, **33** (4), 334–355.

Allen, M.M.C., L. Funk and H.-J. Tüselmann (2006), 'Can variation in public policies account for differences in comparative advantage?' *Journal of Public Policy*, **26** (1), 1–19.

Allen, M.M.C., H.-J. Tüselmann and M.L. Aldred (2011), 'Institutional frameworks and radical innovation: an analysis of high- and medium-high-technology industries in Germany', *International Journal of Public Policy*, **7** (4–6), 265–281.

Allen, M.M.C. and R. Whitley (2012), 'Internationalization and sectoral diversity: the roles of organizational capabilities and dominant institutions in structuring firms' responses to semiglobalization', in Christel Lane and Geoffrey T. Wood (eds), *Capitalist Diversity and Diversity within Capitalism*, London: Routledge, pp. 97–120.

Amable, B. (2003), *The Diversity of Modern Capitalism*, Oxford: Oxford University Press.

Bohle, D. and B. Greskovits (2006), 'Capitalism without compromise: strong business and weak labor in Eastern Europe's new transnational industries', *Studies in Comparative International Development*, **41** (1), 3–25.

Bohle, D. and B. Greskovits (2007), 'The state, internationalization, and capitalist diversity in Eastern Europe', *Competition and Change*, **11** (2), 89–115.

Boyer, R. (2004), 'New growth regimes, but still institutional diversity', *Socio-Economic Review*, **2** (1), 1–32.

Braumoeller, B.F. and G. Goertz (2000), 'The methodology of necessary conditions', *American Journal of Political Science*, **44** (4), 844–858.

Brouthers, K.D. (2002), 'Institutional, cultural and transaction cost influences on entry mode choice and performance', *Journal of International Business Studies*, **33** (2), 203–221.

Buchen, C. (2007), 'Estonia and Slovenia as antipodes', in David Lane and Martin Myant (eds), *Varieties of Capitalism in Post-Communist Countries*, London: Palgrave Macmillan, pp. 65–89.

Casper, S. (2009), 'Can new technology firms succeed in coordinated market economies? A response to Herrmann and Lange', *Socio-Economic Review*, **7** (2), 209–215.

Casper, S. and C. Matraves (2003), 'Institutional frameworks and innovation in the German and UK pharmaceutical industry', *Research Policy*, **32** (10), 1865–1879.

Casper, S. and R. Whitley (2004), 'Managing competences in entrepreneurial technology firms: a comparative institutional analysis of Germany, Sweden, and the UK', *Research Policy*, **33** (1), 89–106.

Crouch, Colin (2005), *Capitalist Diversity and Change: Recombinant Governance and Institutional Entrepreneurs*, Oxford: Oxford University Press.

Crouch, C., W. Streeck, R. Boyer, B. Amable, P.A. Hall and G. Jackson (2005), 'Dialogue on "institutional complementarity and political economy"', *Socio-Economic Review*, **3** (2), 359–382.

Crouch, Colin and Helmut Voelzkow (eds) (2009), *Innovation in Local Economies: Germany in Comparative Context*, Oxford: Oxford University Press.

Cuervo-Cazurra, A. and M. Genc (2008), 'Transforming disadvantages into advantages: developing-country MNEs in the least developed countries, *Journal of International Business Studies*, **39** (6), 957–979.

Culpepper, P.D. (2001), 'Employers' associations, public policy, and the politics of decentralized cooperation in Germany and France', in Peter A. Hall and David Soskice (eds), *Varieties of Capitalism: The Institutional Foundations of Comparative Advantage*, Oxford, UK and New York, USA: Oxford University Press, pp. 275–306.

Czaban, L. and J. Henderson (2003), 'Commodity chains, foreign investment, and labour issues in Eastern Europe', *Global Networks*, **3** (2), 171–196.

Drahokoupil, J. (2009), 'After transition: varieties of political-economic development in Eastern Europe and the former Soviet Union', *Comparative European Politics*, **7** (2), 279–298.

Dunning, J.H. (2009), 'Location and the multinational enterprise', *Journal of International Business Studies*, **40** (1), 20–34.

Erramilli, M.K., S. Agarwal and C.S. Dev (2002), 'Choice between non-equity entry modes: an organizational capability perspective', *Journal of International Business Studies*, **33** (2), 223–242.

Feldmann, M. (2006), 'Emerging varieties of capitalism in transition countries: industrial relations and wage bargaining in Estonia and Slovenia', *Comparative Political Studies*, **39** (7), 829–854.

Fiss, P.C. (2007), 'A set-theoretic approach to organizational configurations', *Academy of Management Review*, **32** (4), 1190–1198.

Globerman, S. and D. Shapiro (2003), 'Governance infrastructure and foreign direct investment', *Journal of International Business Studies*, **34** (1), 19–39.

Hall, P.A. and D.W. Gingerich (2009), 'Varieties of capitalism and institutional complementarities in the political economy: an empirical analysis', *British Journal of Political Science*, **39** (3), 449–482.

Hall, P.A. and D. Soskice (2001), 'Introduction', in Peter A Hall and David Soskice (eds), *Varieties of Capitalism: The Institutional Foundations of Comparative Advantage*, Oxford: Oxford University Press, pp. 1–68.

Hansmann, H. and R. Kraakman (2000), 'The end of history for corporate law', *Georgetown Law Journal*, **89**, 439–468.

Harcourt, M. and G. Wood (2007), 'The importance of employment protection for skill development in coordinated market economies', *European Journal of Industrial Relations*, **13** (2), 141–159.

Henisz, W.J. (2003), 'The power of the Buckley and Casson thesis: the ability to manage institutional idiosyncrasies', *Journal of International Business Studies*, **34** (2), 173–184.

Hollingsworth, J. Rogers and Robert Boyer (eds) (1997), *Contemporary Capitalism: The Embeddedness of Institutions*, Cambridge: Cambridge University Press.

Jackson, G. (2005), 'Employee representation in the board compared: a fuzzy sets analysis of corporate governance, unionism and political institutions', *Industrielle Beziehungen*, **12** (3), 252–279.

Jackson, G. and R. Deeg (2008), 'Comparing capitalisms: understanding institutional diversity and its implications for international business', *Journal of International Business Studies*, **39** (4), 540–561.

Kallaste, E., K. Jaakson and R. Eamets (2008), 'Two representatives but no representation: cases from Estonia', *Employee Relations*, **30** (1), 86–97.

Keizer, Arjan B. (2005), *The Changing Logic of Japanese Employment Practices, A Firm-level Analysis of Four Industries*, Rotterdam: Erasmus Research Institute of Management.

Kenworthy, L. (2006), 'Institutional coherence and macroeconomic performance', *Socio-Economic Review*, **4** (1), 69–92.

Keune, M., G. Piotti, A. Tóth and C. Crouch (2009), 'Testing the West German model in East Germany and Hungary: the motor industry in Zwickau and Győr', in Colin Crouch and Helmut Voelzkow (eds), *Innovation in Local Economies: Germany in Comparative Context*, Oxford: Oxford University Press, pp. 91–120.

Khanna, T. and K.G. Palepu (2006), 'Emerging giants: building world-class companies in developing countries', *Harvard Business Review*, **84** (10), 60–69.

Khanna, T. and J.W. Rivkin (2001), 'Estimating the performance effects of business groups in emerging markets', *Strategic Management Journal*, **22** (1), 45–74.

Kim, H., H. Kim, and R.E. Hoskisson (2010), 'Does market-oriented institutional change in an emerging economy make business-group-affiliated multinationals perform better? An institution-based view', *Journal of International Business Studies*, **41** (7), 1141–1160.

King, L.P. (2007), 'Central European capitalism in comparative perspective', in Bob Hancké, Martin Rhodes and Mark Thatcher (eds), *Beyond Varieties of Capitalism: Conflict, Contradictions, and Complementarities in the European Economy*, Oxford: Oxford University Press, pp. 307–327.

Knell, M. and M. Srholec (2007), 'Diverging pathways in central and eastern Europe', in David Lane and Martin Myant (eds), *Varieties of Capitalism in Post-Communist Countries*, London: Palgrave Macmillan, pp. 40–62.

Lane, D. (2007), 'Post-state socialism: a diversity of capitalisms?' in David Lane and Martin Myant (eds), *Varieties of Capitalism in Post-Communist Countries*, London: Palgrave Macmillan, pp. 13–39.

Lane, David and Martin Myant (eds) (2007), *Varieties of Capitalism in Post-Communist Countries*, London: Palgrave Macmillan.

Lane, C. and G. Wood (2009), 'Capitalist diversity and diversity within capitalism', *Economy and Society*, **38** (4), 531–551.

Lane, C. and G. Wood (eds) (2011), *Capitalist Diversity and Diversity within Capitalism*, London: Routledge.

Lange, K. (2009), 'Institutional embeddedness and the strategic leeway of actors, the case of the German therapeutical biotech industry', *Socio-Economic Review*, **7** (2), 181–207.

Liu, J. and A. Tylecote (2009), 'Corporate governance and technological capability development: three case studies in the Chinese Auto industry', *Industry and Innovation*, **16** (4), 525–544.

Majtan, B. (2005), 'The Labour Code in the Republic of Slovakia', *Employee Relations*, **27** (6), 603–612.

McCahery, J.A., L. Renneboog, P. Ritter and S. Haller (2004), 'The economics of the proposed European Takeover Directive', in Guido Ferrarini, Klaus J. Hopt, Jaap Winter and Eddy Wymeersch (eds), *Reforming Company and Takeover Law in Europe*, Oxford: Oxford University Press, pp. 575–646.

Meyer, K.E. (2001), 'Institutions, transaction costs, and entry mode choice in Eastern Europe', *Journal of International Business Studies*, **32** (2), 357–367.

Meyer, K.E., R. Mudambi and R. Narula (2011), 'Multinational enterprises and local contexts: the opportunities and challenges of multiple embeddedness', *Journal of Management Studies*, **48** (2), 235–252.

Meyer, K.E. and M.W. Peng (2005), 'Probing theoretically into Central and Eastern Europe, transactions, resources, and institutions', *Journal of International Business Studies*, **36** (6), 600–621.

Morgan, G. (2005), 'Institutional complementarities, path dependency, and the dynamics of firms', in Glenn Morgan, Richard Whitley and Eli Moen (eds), *Changing Capitalisms? Internationalization, Institutional Change, and Systems of Economic Organization*, Oxford: Oxford University Press, pp. 415–446.

Mudambi, R. and P. Navarra (2002), 'Institutions and international business: a theoretical overview', *International Business Review*, **11** (6), 635–646.

Myant, M. (2007), 'The Czech Republic: from "Czech" capitalism to "European" capitalism', in David Lane and Martin Myant (eds), *Varieties of Capitalism in Post-Communist Countries*, London: Palgrave Macmillan, pp. 105–123.

Mykhnenko, V. (2007), 'Strengths and weaknesses of "weak" coordination: economic institutions, revealed comparative advantages, and socio-economic performance of mixed market economies in Poland and Ukraine', in Bob Hancké, Martin Rhodes and Mark Thatcher (eds), *Beyond Varieties of Capitalism: Conflict, Contradictions, and Complementarities in the European Economy*, Oxford: Oxford University Press, pp. 351–378.

Neumann, L. (2002), 'Does decentralized collective bargaining have an impact on the labour market in Hungary?' *European Journal of Industrial Relations*, **8** (1), 11–31.

Nölke, A. and A. Vliegenthart (2009), 'Enlarging the varieties of capitalism: the emergence of dependent market economies in east central Europe', *World Politics*, **61** (4), 670–702.

Pajunen, K. (2008), 'Institutions and inflows of foreign direct investment: a fuzzy-set analysis', *Journal of International Business Studies*, **39** (4), 652–669.

Peng, M.W., S.-H. Lee and D.Y.L. Wang (2005), 'What determines the scope of the firm over time? A Focus on Institutional Relatedness', *Academy of Management Review*, **30** (3), 622–633.

Peng, Mike W. and Klaus E. Meyer (2011), *International Business*, London: Cengage Learning.

Peng, M.W., D. Wang and Y. Jiang (2008), 'An institution-based view of international business strategy: a focus on emerging economies', *Journal of International Business Studies*, **39** (5), 920–936.

Ragin, C.C. (2000), *Fuzzy-Set Social Science*, Chicago, IL: Chicago University Press.

Ragin, C.C. (2006), 'Set relations in social research: evaluating their consistency and coverage', *Political Analysis*, **14** (3), 291–310.

Ragin, C.C. (2008), *Redesigning Social Inquiry, Fuzzy Sets and Beyond*, Chicago, IL: University of Chicago Press.

Richbell, S., L. Szerb and Z. Vitai (2010), 'HRM in the Hungarian SME Sector', *Employee Relations*, **32** (3), 262–280.

Rugman, A., A. Verbeke and W. Yuan (2011), 'Re-conceptualizing Bartlett and Ghoshal's classification of national subsidiary roles in the multinational enterprise', *Journal of Management Studies*, **48** (2), 253–277.

Sako, M. (1992), *Prices, Quality and Trust*, Cambridge: Cambridge University Press.

Schneiberg, M. (2007), 'What's on the path? Path dependence, organizational diversity, and the problem of institutional change in the US economy, 1900–1950', *Socio-Economic Review*, **5** (1), 47–80.

Schneider, M.R., C. Schulze-Bentrop and M. Paunescu (2009), 'Mapping the institutional capital of high-tech firms: a fuzzy-set analysis of capitalist variety and export performance', *Journal of International Business Studies*, **41** (2), 246–266.

Stasek, F. (2005), 'Employee relations in the Czech Republic – past, present and future', *Employee Relations*, **27** (6), 581–591.

Streeck, W. (1997), 'Beneficial constraints: on the economic limits of rational voluntarism', in J. Rogers Hollingsworth and Robert Boyer (eds), *Contemporary Capitalism: The Embeddedness of Institutions*, Cambridge: Cambridge University Press, pp. 197–219.

Streeck, Wolfgang and Kathleen Thelen (eds) (2005), *Beyond Continuity: Institutional Change in Advanced Political Economies*, Oxford: Oxford University Press.

Tan, D. and K.E. Meyer (2010), 'Business groups' outward FDI: a managerial resources perspective, *Journal of International Management*, **16** (2), 154–164.

Thelen, K. (2004), *How Institutions Evolve: the Political Economy of Skills in Germany, Britain, the United States and Japan*, Cambridge: Cambridge University Press.

Tylecote, A., J. Cai and J. Liu (2010), 'Why is mainland China rising in some sectors and failing in others? A critical view of the Chinese system of innovation', *International Journal of Learning and Intellectual Capital*, **7** (2), 123–144.

Tylecote, A. and P. Ramirez (2005), 'Corporate governance and innovation, the UK compared with the US and "insider" economies', *Research Policy*, **35** (1), 160–180.

Vaughan-Whitehead, Daniel (2003), *EU Enlargement versus Social Europe? The Uncertain Future of the European Social Model*, Cheltenham, UK and Northampton, MA, USA: Edward Elgar.

Walgenbach, P. and R.E. Meyer (2008), 'Institutional entrepreneurship and the structuring of organizations and markets', in Alexander Ebner and Nikolaus Beck (eds), *The Institutions of the Market, Organizations, Social Systems, and Governance*, Oxford: Oxford University Press, pp. 180–201.

Whitley, Richard (1999), *Divergent Capitalisms: The Social Structuring and Change of Business Systems*, Oxford: Oxford University Press.

Whitley, Richard (2007), *Business Systems and Organizational Capabilities: The Institutional Structuring of Competitive Competences*, Oxford: Oxford University Press.

Wright, E.O. and R. Dwyer (2006), 'The American jobs machine', in Geoffrey Wood and Phil James (eds), *Institutions and Working Life*, Oxford: Oxford University Press, pp. 275–314.

Young, M.N., M.W. Peng, D. Ahlstrom, G.D. Bruton and Y. Jiang (2008), 'Corporate governance in emerging economies: a review of the principal–principal perspective', *Journal of Management Studies*, **45** (1), 196–220.

17 Financial system and equity culture development in Central and Eastern European countries: the effect of institutional environment

Zita Stone, Fragkiskos Filippaios and Carmen Stoian

17.1 INTRODUCTION

The recent economic crisis (that is, the global financial crisis of 2008–2009) has confirmed that without adequate access to capital, firms in all types of economies suffer. The fact that the financial sector has been unable to provide adequate financing for many firms since 2008–2009 has resulted in corporate standstill or even declared insolvency of some formerly well-performing firms. As a result, most financial analysts and economists agree that the ultimate challenge for any economy at the time of such a serious economic crisis is to restore financial confidence and stability among all financial sector participants (the firms, investors, government and financial institutions), to enable the adequate flow of capital and to facilitate the efficient functioning of different financial systems.

Capital finance is essential for firm growth and, by implication, for economic growth (Stoian and Filippaios 2007). This leads to the question of how firms can best finance themselves and what types of financial systems are likely to be formed in the future. This is particularly relevant for countries with historically weak and underdeveloped financial systems, such as the transition countries of Central and Eastern Europe (hereafter CEECs). Limited availability of capital, poor access to finance and low-quality financial institutions form the characteristics of weak financial systems present in the majority of transition countries (Hermes and Lensink 2000). It is clear that without access to stable and adequate financial markets these countries' ultimate goal of catching up with their more developed counterparts is unachievable.

The current chapter investigates the financial systems of the CEECs which until the 1990s were operating under a state socialist system. In any political establishment, whether democratic or socialist, progress can only be achieved if there is economic growth (Kolodko 2000). In the late 1980s, the socialist economies of Central and Eastern Europe were experiencing serious economic, financial, social and, ultimately, political difficulties (Stiglitz 1995). This resulted in the region's inability to expand, satisfy its population's social needs, attract investment and boost productivity, and ultimately resulted in the need to change the existing centralized political and economic regime.

Today, two decades after the start of their transition process from centrally planned to market-oriented economies, the CEECs still have to face many challenges in order to catch up with the developed systems of their Western European counterparts and other developed nations worldwide. The creation and enhancement of an efficient and sustainable financial system is without a doubt one of the key challenges (EBRD 2006). Indeed, the underdeveloped banking system (overwhelmed with low capital, large volumes of non-performing loans to state enterprises, small branch networks, inexperienced staff and management, limited competition, and so on) and an even less developed capital markets system (with weak legal infrastructure, non-existent institutional investors, and so on) (Morelli 2010), both legacies of the previous political regime, have impeded the financial liberalization process and thus also the CEECs' growth and development potential.

Unlike the CEECs, more advanced economies have successfully adopted one of, or the combination of, two financial system models (bank-based or equity-based) and have accordingly created corporate governance structures, established financial institutions and legislative systems which function in support of each individual system (Amable 2003; Morelli 2009). In an effectively and efficiently functioning bank-based system there is a significant presence of banking tradition in a country, with strong historical roots and embedded trust within the banking sector (Levine 2002; Detragiache et al. 2006; Levine and Zervos 1998; Beck and Levine 2004). On the other hand, the equity-based model requires the presence of a strong and developed equity culture in a country (Kim and Kenny 2007; Bekaert et al. 2001; Li 2007; Bekaert et al. 2002; Smith 2003). A number of scholars point out that in advanced forms of financial systems bank financing is often at some stage followed by equity financing (Pagano 1993; Geschenkron 1962). Indeed, Smith (2003) observes that bank lending and government-determined allocation of capital are currently giving way to private equity financing in many advanced economies.

The institutional environment affects the financing decision-making of firms and the direction of financial system development overall (Peng 2004). Scientific research (Kim and Kenny 2007; Bakker and Gross 2004)

further confirms that the institutional environments of the banking oriented financial systems differ from the institutional environments of the
equity-oriented systems. An equity-based financing system requires an
institutional system characterized by low corruption, high accountability,
policies protecting investor rights and an efficient bureaucracy-free system
(Smith 2003; Bekaert et al. 2001). Although transparency is also important
in the banking system it does not have the same imperative role as we see in
the equity-based models. This is mainly because the private nature of most
bank-financed firms and the traditional bank–client relationships based
on trust are less transparency-centred (Beck and Levine 2004; Levine
and Zervos 1998). These institutional differences point to the existence
of the German–Japanese banking-oriented and the Anglo-Saxon equity-
oriented institutional systems.

The key aim of this chapter is to explore the effect of institutional
environment on financial system development and, more specifically, on
equity culture development in the CEECs. To achieve our aim we provide
a thorough literature review of the financial system development, the
creation of equity culture and the effect of the institutional environment
on both, to conceptualize the relationship. We then proceed empirically
by adopting a new methodology that allows us to display graphically the
differences of institutions in the ten CEECs and then compare them with
four benchmarks – the United Kingdom (UK) and the United States of
America (USA) on one hand, and Germany and Japan on the other –
discussed above. We provide evidence not only with regard to the institutional factors that influence the development of the financial system in the
CEECs but also highlight those factors that bring specific CEECs closer
to the Anglo-Saxon (UK and USA) model with a well-developed equity
culture, or closer to the German and Japanese model that relies more on
bank financing.

The remainder of this chapter is organized as follows. Section 17.2 provides an in-depth literature review discussing the key institutional factors
that influence financial system development and equity culture creation.
Section 17.3 provides the main characteristics of our sample and briefly
describes the key attributes. The following, section 17.4, justifies the
methodological approach of this study and discusses the Co-Plot method
applied. Section 17.5 presents the empirical evidence of our analysis whilst
section 17.6 concludes the chapter with some policy implications and
suggestions for future research.

17.2   FINANCIAL DEVELOPMENT, EQUITY CULTURE AND INSTITUTIONS: A REVIEW OF THE LITERATURE

17.2.1   The Role of Institutions in Financial System Development

The link between financial system development and economic growth was established early in the twentieth century (Schumpeter 1911). More recently, a number of financial analysts have empirically confirmed that a more developed financial system has a positive impact on economic growth, both at the macroeconomic level (Beck et al. 2000; King and Levine 1993; Rajan and Zingales 2003a) and at the microeconomic level (Beck et al. 2005; La Porta et al. 1997), as financial constraints stemming from a less developed financial system can negatively affect growth. Despite the popularity of the topic of financial system development in discussions of economic growth, there is still little agreement on how to define it and measure it (Levine 2002). For the purpose of this study we adopt a definition of a financial system development as developed by the World Economic Forum (WEF). It defines financial development as the 'factors, policies and institutions that lead to effective financial intermediation and markets, and deep and broad access to capital and financial markets' (WEF 2008, 3). The process of financial development depends, among other factors, on how the financial system's supporting mechanisms in a particular country are designed and established (Hermes and Lensink 2000). This includes the type and role of financial institutions, the design of the regulatory and supervisory system, and the role of government policies that are related to controlling that particular system (Levine and Zervos 1998; Rajan and Zingales 2003b).

The efficiency factors that contribute to the development of an advanced financial system are of a political, economic and institutional nature. Although the role of government as a financial service provider or financial regulatory body has been disputed (Beck 2006), its role and contribution to a financial system development has been commented on by many (e.g. La Porta et al. 1999; Strange 1995). This is because financial system development can only progress to an advanced level if political forces support and do not go against the economic and institutional reforms necessary for such progress. This viewpoint is in line with Rajan and Zingales's (2003a) findings who point out that a favourable (or unfavourable) political outlook on financial development is the main reason for cross-country differences in the quality of financial development. In fact, it is believed that in some less developed countries financial system development has been prevented by special country interests

(Hermes and Lensink 2000). Scholtens (2000) takes the view that local politics shapes the economic and institutional conditions in a country, and through these influences the type of financial intermediaries that are able to develop and the level of efficiency they can function at. In a more recent assessment of financial systems and their functionalities, Purda (2008) calls for a compatibility between economic policies and the existing political economy in a country, which encompasses the areas of institutional quality, politics and economics. In our study, we follow the view of Scholtens (2000) and account for the political influences through institutional indicators.

Institutional quality, pointing both to legal efficiency and competent corporate governance, is a crucial pillar of an effective financial system. The certainty of legal rights of borrowers, creditors and other investors can only be secured through an enforcement of contracts and their adherence to these. Importantly, the significance of creating a sound legislative framework before considering the set-up of a particular financial system (bank-based or market-based) is, according to some scholars, (e.g. Kaufmann et al. 2000; Levine 2002; Monks and Minow 2001) essential at the early stages of a country's financial system development. Countries with good investor protection laws, competition laws and proper disclosure of information have financial systems represented by larger and broader financial markets, which means better accessibility to external finance for individual firms (La Porta et al. 1997; Pagano and Volpin 2005). Moreover, good governance practices in the financial and corporate sectors are critical for the development of an effective financial system (Kaufmann et al. 2000; La Porta et al. 1999). The studies of Klapper and Love (2003) and Francis et al. (2005) find that the quality of corporate governance is positively related to growth opportunities of firms and their need for external financing. Simply put, governance provides assurance that the market is honest, that investors make decisions based on reliable information and that management is running the enterprise for the stakeholders' benefit (Monks and Minow 2001). Committing to better corporate practices might not be easy in less developed economies and in countries with poor state investor protection, as the mechanisms to do so might not be present or are too expensive (Doidge et al. 2007). Firms that have access to foreign markets are less dependent on the progression of their domestic financial systems and often if they pursue better corporate practices, it may be because of the foreign country governance requirements. Drawing on the earlier literature we consider the nature of an institutional system to be an essential determinant for the type of financial system developed in a country.

17.2.2   Equity Culture and Transition Economies

For the development of an equity-based financial system it is necessary that an equity culture is created (Myners 2001). It can be said that an equity culture develops alongside an equity-based financial system. The existing literature offers several definitions of the phenomenon of an equity culture. Some claim that an equity culture denotes a culture of shared ownership adopted by firms and stock company formation (Bekaert et al. 2002). Others suggests that a solid equity culture means that firms are able to finance their business activities through financial assets of which share investments account for a significant proportion (Beck and Levine 2004). Equity culture is also defined as 'the route to a wider shareholder democracy' (Myners 2001) or is even seen as an expansion of share ownership by individuals (Bilias et al. 2009). Claessens (1995) in his earlier work states that equity culture means a market economy that has a corporate sector in which individuals are enabled to participate. In some works, however, an exact definition of equity culture is missing and authors refer to a bundle of definitions. For instance, Smith (2003) first defines equity culture as the culture of stock markets themselves. Then he implies that equity culture actually represents public willingness to invest in stocks. This confuses the reader. To avoid confusion, for the purpose of this study we draw on these earlier works yet offer our own definition, as we see equity culture as a financing culture adopted by a country's corporate sector implying its preference for equity-based financing (built on the principle of wealth creation through shared ownership) subject to feasible market conditions.

Transition economies are characterized by their bank-based financial systems (Gehrke and Knell 1992). The fact that equity financing has not been extremely successful as a source of capital acquirement in transition countries is not surprising. The former centrally planned systems embedded constraints and simply did not allow for the development of equity financing. It is believed that the development of equity financing as an equal form to debt financing has been hindered due to special country interests (Stiglitz 1999). Indeed, equity culture development supporters have had to overcome massive obstacles, such as mistrust of stock exchanges, nationalistic aversion to adopting 'Anglo-Saxon' financial techniques, and resistance to sound corporate practices on which a viable public equity market depends (Smith 2003).

Specifically, in the transition economies of Central and Eastern Europe, the former communist regimes opposed the development of stock markets, the primary financial intermediaries of equity-based financing, and thus their level of development in 1989 was comparable to that of the British stock markets in the nineteenth century (Hermes and Lensink 2000).

Indeed, only a small part of corporate investments was financed by equity (Kornai 2006). As a result of the narrow scope of financial markets in Central and Eastern Europe, capital providers have associated firm financing in these transition countries with higher risk than in other more developed economies (Wyplozs 2002). The disregard for transparency, medium to high levels of bankruptcy, and lack of adequate business expertise and experience have been identified as the main reasons for this (Bakker and Gross 2004). Despite considerable advances over the 2000s, existing European financial markets are still functioning below their potential (EBRD 2006). As a result, particularly the transition EU economies have been losing out on jobs and growth. Economists agree that the main reason for this is the fragmentation of these markets which is driven by domestic bias, inefficient regulation and risk-averse culture. This results in the inability of many funds to become sufficiently specialized and to achieve critical mass within a (short) timescale (that is attracting large number of companies and investors). Therefore, the majority of firms in the CEECs have preferred traditional ways of financing such as debt financing, leasing and renting.

However, recent views point out that a combination of global and region-specific factors gives an indication that there may be a realistic potential for equity culture development in transition economies (Segal 2009). Firstly, the recent financial crisis highlighted a number of 'cracks' in the current banking sector and the issues related to the corporate sector's overdependence on it. Secondly, the economic improvement demonstrated in the majority of transition economies prior to the financial crisis (e.g. removed restrictions on foreign ownership, improved accounting and information standards), and in many cases the transition countries' ability to limit the negative consequences caused by the financial crisis, have been identified as reasons to believe that the promotion of equity financing as a direct competitor to debt could be plausible (Djankov and Murrell 2002). Cumulatively, these events could be seen as potential catalysts for the development of an equity culture in transition economies.

In the case of the transition economies of Central and Eastern Europe the following have to be noted. Firstly, the reform process in the CEECs is still ongoing. Although the CEECs succeeded in complying with the economic requirements imposed upon them by the European Union (EU), the financial liberalization process is far from being finished (EBRD 2009). This provides an opportunity for correct economic policy shaping which could be potentially geared towards supporting an equity culture in these countries. Secondly, events such as privatization of formerly state-owned businesses, the establishment of the euro currency, and the shift in the pension systems from state-owned to individual retirement accounts and defined contribution pension plans (just to name a few) have prompted the 'equity culture' supporters to raise their hopes. Thirdly, the substitution of top-down corporate governance systems based on central planning with corporate governance systems that react to and base their decisions upon market signals is seen by many as a signal for the change of direction of these countries' financial systems (Djankov and Murrell 2002). Fourthly, the increased interest of foreign investors in the CEE region has a significant impact, as 'equity culture' emerges where a strong investor base is. The increased interest of the foreign investors has been prompted by the downturn in the mature equity markets. Investors are therefore looking for new and exciting markets with substantial growth and potential. The CEECs might not be the centre of their investment activities (with the BRIC – Brazil, Russia, India, China – countries being the centre of investors' activities) but the spillover effect may have an economic policy-changing impact. Lastly, but perhaps most importantly, the majority of the corporate sector in the CEECs are dissatisfied with the financing services that their financial systems offer (EBRD 2008b). Indeed, a strong increase in the demand for sophisticated financial services in the rapidly expanding economies of Central and Eastern Europe has been noted (EBRD 2006). Many firms in the CEECs feel that the limited availability of finance is the major constraint to their growth and development, as many have their bank loan applications declined or receive only part of what they request (Scholtens 2000). Furthermore, due to limited competition at the local level, banks are able to overcharge for their capital-raising services, with the effect of locking companies into long-term relationships. The banking sector also has started to require an increased amount of information on business propositions before granting loans. This trend could remove an advantage of bank finance (because it was quick and easy to arrange). Klapper et al. (2002) find that the main sources of dissatisfaction firms express are red tape, poor services, excessive bank charges and the inappropriateness of solutions offered.

From the research perspective, international authorities (e.g. the World Bank, The European Bank for Reconstruction and Development, EBRD) have recognized that transition economies as new democratic economies have high growth potential and, therefore, have called for more scientific work on the transition type of economy (OECD 2009). Indeed, since the transition process started, financial systems in these countries have started to be analysed, transition processes in individual countries have been evaluated and some downfalls of the existing systems rooted in the inherited legacy of the previous regime have been identified (Bakker and Gross 2004; Doyle and Walsh 2005; Underhill 1995). However, a number of authors have identified more areas that need further clarification and gaps that require additional research.

For instance, Purda (2008) points out that there is a need for further research on transition countries (e.g. transition economies of the CEECs) as 'caution should be used in extending the results from research on financial systems of developed economies with well-functioning financial markets to the context of transition and post-transition countries'. Bekaert and Harvey (2002) stress the requirement for a better understanding of the combination of factors (macroeconomic and institutional) influencing financial system reforms in transition markets; and Klapper and Love (2003) emphasize the need to refocus the research in transition economies from country level to firm level, or a combination of these two levels. Pinkowitz et al. (2002) highlight the need to analyse corporate governance mechanisms when assessing financing choices of firms, in particular equity capital, in transition economies. Fisher et al. (1997), and later on Kornai (2006), add that at the corporate level the motivations behind firm financing choices should be more closely examined. Bakker and Gross (2004) call for more attention specifically to the transition economies of Central and Eastern Europe as 'these markets are particularly interesting since they provide us with a number of comparable, yet in many interesting respects, different cases'. Also, the need to provide empirical knowledge on factors affecting the CEECs' future financial systems' developments and direction has been accentuated by many (e.g. Hermes and Lensink 2000; Nord 2000), with some particularly stressing the importance of an assessment from the equity financing perspective (EBRD 1998; Smith 2003). However, to our knowledge, in the case of the transition literature, the attention to equity culture as a phenomenon coexisting in a financial system with a strong capital market sector, the effect of its limited existence in the transition economies, and viable suggestions for its possible development have been neglected.

17.3   DATA AND SAMPLE DESCRIPTION

In our research to identify the relationship between financial system and equity culture development and the institutional environment, we adopt a quantitative approach and use data selected from various secondary sources. To investigate institutional environments of individual countries we use data from the International Country Risk Guide (ICRG), a valuable source of data on institutional quality. Then, to investigate the institutional environments in the CEECs even deeper we examine the EBRD transition indicators database. The aim of this section is to provide an overview of our sample and create CEECs' profiles on the status of their financial system developments with the focus on equity culture creation.

We then apply in the next section a relatively new clustering method – the Co-Plot method (Gilady et al. 1996; Raveh 2000a; Talby et al. 1999), which enables us to observe the positioning of individual CEECs in relation to each other and to four benchmarks (Germany, Japan, the UK and USA) on a two-dimensional scale.

As discussed in detail in the literature review, the institutional environment facilitates, or not, the development of a specific financial system. While equity-based systems require institutional systems which guarantee the protection of individual shareholders, efficient bureaucracy and low corruption leading towards high transparency, the bank-based models necessitate the presence of institutional reforms and policies geared towards coordination within the banking sector and its regulation. To assess the institutional quality in our sample countries, as we mentioned above, we examine two sets of data. Firstly, we employ the political risk components of ICRG institutional data, which enables us to assess the institutional quality of both the CEECs and the benchmarks. Secondly, to consider the institutional progress specifically in the transition countries, we include a smaller set of EBRD transition indicators in our analysis.

The first set of variables (government stability, socio-economic conditions and investment profile) can have a minimum number of 0 points assigned and a maximum of 12, whereas the remaining variables can have a minimum number of 0 points assigned but a maximum of 6. In every case the lower the risk point total, the higher the risk; and the higher the risk point total, the lower the risk. 'Government stability' is a measure of a government's unity, legislative strength and popular support. 'Socio-economic conditions' evaluates socio-economic pressures at work (in particular unemployment, consumer confidence and poverty) that could constrain government action or lead to social dissatisfaction. 'Investment profile' assesses factors affecting the risks to investment that are not covered by other political social or financial risk components (in particular contract viability, profits repatriation and payment delays). Corruption measures a political threat to investment as it can distort economic and financial environments, reduce the efficiency of a government and businesses, and introduce instability into the organizational processes. 'Law and order' comprises two subcomponents: 'law' and 'order'. While the former assesses the strength and impartiality of a country's legal system, the latter is concerned with the application of law and effective sanctioning. 'Democratic accountability' reflects on the type of governance employed in each country. The ICRG identifies five different types of governance (alternating democracy, dominated democracy, de facto one-party state, the jury one-party state, autarchy) and assigns the highest number of risk points to alternating democracies (low risk) and the lowest number of risk points to autarchies (high risk). 'Bureaucracy quality' is another indicator of a country's institutional strength. Countries demonstrating high points on this variable run bureaucracy systems independent from political pressures with established effective bureaucratic mechanisms.

For the assessment of the institutional quality in the transition economies we also apply transition indicators from the EBRD as follows: 'large-scale privatization' (an indicator on the process of transferring state ownership of large firms into private hands); 'small-scale privatization' (an indicator on the process of transferring state ownership of small firms into private hands); 'banking reform and interest rate liberalization' (an indicator on the progress of banking laws and regulation); 'securities markets and non-bank financial institutions' (an indicator on the progress of securities laws and regulation); 'governance and enterprise restructuring' (an indicator on the progress of corporate governance). Individual scores indicate the following: a score lower than 1.5 means a country has undergone only a few reforms (achieved limited progress); a score between 1.5 and 2.5 means a country has improved its position moderately (achieved moderate progress); a score between 2.5 and 3.5 means a country has demonstrated some significant actions (achieved significant progress); a score between 3.5 and 4.5 means a country has experienced a substantial improvement (achieved substantial progress); a score higher than 4.5 means a country has reached the level of advanced economies (achieved a progress comparable to advanced economies).

As a first step we apply analysis of variance (ANOVA) to assess the variance of institutional data for the CEECs and our four benchmarks. We find that in the case of the CEECs all groups have a probability level at 1 per cent level which suggests that data differ substantially among individual countries for the period under examination (1996–2008). The same significance level is present in most observations for the benchmarks' group with three exceptions: government stability, investment profile and bureaucracy quality.

The ANOVA table (Table 17.1) displays very similar levels for the developed countries, with the UK and USA performing slightly better on the indicators of law and order, corruption and bureaucracy quality. The CEECs' group institutional quality indicators are on average lower than those of our four benchmarks, with Bulgaria and Romania displaying the lowest values in most cases. Interestingly, Estonia scores on average lower on the variable of investment profile than most other CEECs, however its value is close to that of the UK.

The ANOVA table (Table 17.2) of the transition institutional indicators indicates that there are significant differences among the CEECs as all indicators are significant at the 1 per cent level. While the Czech Republic,

Table 17.1 *ANOVA table: indicators of institutional quality*

Institutional Quality (Indicators)		Government Stability	Socioeconomic Conditions	Investment Profile	Corruption	Law and Order	Democratic Accountability	Bureaucracy Quality
No.	Country	Mean	Mean	Mean	Mean	Mean	Mean	Mean
1	Bulgaria	8.36	3.81	10.29	2.71	3.85	5.24	2.00
2	Czech Rep	7.37	7.18	10.18	3.21	5.15	5.29	3.00
3	Estonia	8.92	6.87	9.93	3.54	4.00	5.08	2.61
5	Hungary	8.33	6.19	10.49	3.78	4.64	5.88	3.59
7	Latvia	8.76	5.85	10.01	2.28	4.92	5.00	2.38
8	Lithuania	7.91	6.51	10.01	2.51	4.00	5.30	2.38
9	Poland	7.89	5.38	10.46	3.08	4.41	5.88	3.05
10	Romania	8.34	4.40	8.33	2.67	4.24	5.78	1.00
11	Slovakia	8.07	6.86	9.97	3.00	4.38	5.56	3.06
12	Slovenia	9.63	6.51	10.47	3.28	4.67	5.05	3.00
	Total	8.36	5.96	10.01	3.01	4.43	5.41	2.61
	F statistics	3.49	15.27	2.65	5.2	10.20	10.00	200.43
	Prob > F	0.0007	0.0000	0.0077	0.0000	0.0000	0.0000	0.0000
4	Germany	8.94	9.98	11.14	4.21	5.36	5.30	3.97
6	Japan	8.89	8.88	10.82	3.33	5.31	5.10	3.97
13	UK	9.12	7.51	9.67	4.59	5.83	5.84	4.23
14	USA	9.39	8.17	10.53	4.67	5.48	5.82	4.00
	Total	9.09	8.63	10.54	4.20	5.50	5.52	3.99
	F statistics	0.32	12.60	1.64	17.02	3.57	15.74	1.6
	Prob > F	0.8099	0.0000	0.1918	0.0000	0.0207	0.0000	0.202

Source: ICRG (2001) and author's ANOVA performed in STATA.

419

Table 17.2   ANOVA table: transition indicators of institutional quality

Institutional Quality Indicators (II)	Large scale privati- zation	Small scale privati- zation	Banking reform & interest rate liberalization	Securities markets & non- bank financial institutions	Governance and Enterprise restructuring
No. Country	Mean	Mean	Mean	Mean	Mean
1 Bulgaria	3.51	3.57	3.16	2.28	2.46
2 Czech Rep	4.00	3.23	3.92	2.85	4.30
3 Estonia	4.00	4.33	3.69	3.18	3.31
5 Hungary	4.00	4.30	3.18	3.64	3.38
7 Latvia	3.33	4.23	3.41	2.67	2.85
8 Lithuania	3.49	4.25	3.26	2.59	2.87
9 Poland	3.30	4.33	3.38	3.54	3.31
10 Romania	3.23	3.57	2.85	2.23	2.18
11 Slovakia	3.92	4.33	3.23	3.05	3.23
12 Slovenia	2.97	4.33	3.25	2.70	2.85
Total	3.58	4.05	3.33	2.87	3.07
F statistics	19.34	88.04	9.28	28.41	75.40
Prob > F	0.0000	0.0000	0.0000	0.0000	0.0000

Source: EBRD (2008a) and author's ANOVA performed in STATA.

Estonia, Hungary and Slovakia's average values for the institutional data are the highest, indicating a substantial improvement of the institutional indicators, Bulgaria, Romania and Slovenia are the worst-performing countries in the group. In particular, the Czech Republic, Estonia and Hungary perform the best on the indicator of large-scale privatization, and Estonia, Poland, Slovakia and Slovenia show the highest values on the indicator of small-scale privatization. In terms of banking reform we observe that the Czech Republic, Estonia and Latvia demonstrate a proactive reform approach. On the other hand, the indicator of the presence of securities markets and non-bank financial institutions shows on average higher values in the cases of Estonia, Hungary, Poland and Slovakia.

17.4   METHODOLOGY

Proceeding a step further into examining the relationship between institutional environment and financial system and equity culture development, we apply a Co-Plot methodology. Classical multivariate statistical analysis methods, such as principal component analysis (PCA), correspondence analysis (CA) or multidimensional scaling (MDS), analyse variables and observations separately (Talby et al. 1999). However, a relatively new clustering method designed for multi-criteria analysis – the Co-Plot method, has the advantage of analysing variables and observations simultaneously and in a simple manner (Raveh 2000a, 2000b; Segev et al. 1990). The method produces three results. Firstly, it shows similarity among data (that is, decision-making units – DMUs) by the composite of all criteria (variables) involved; secondly, it gives the structure of correlations among the variables; and thirdly, it provides mutual relationships between the data and the variables (Raveh 2000a).

The Co-Plot method has been applied widely: in an exploratory study of national versus corporate cultural fit in mergers and acquisitions (Weber et al. 1996), in an analysis of 1980–1990 computers (Gilady et al. 1996), in a car selection problem analysis (Raveh 2000a), in a comparative study of the Greek banking system (Raveh 2000b), and as an exploratory study for suggesting a methodology for presenting data envelopment analysis (DEA) graphically (Adler and Raveh 2008). The application of the Co-Plot method for the analysis of the structure of MBA programmes in the UK and the USA (Paucar-Caceres and Thorpe 2005; Segev et al. 1990) has been recently criticized by Mar-Molinero and Mingers (2007). Their findings point out that the Co-Plot method is inappropriate for zero–one type (that is, dichotomous) variables. Our study does not contain such variables and therefore, we deem the Co-Plot method viable for our considerations.

The Co-Plot is a graphical display technique useful for visual inspection of data matrices such as $X_{n \times k}$. The data – the DMUs – are displayed as n points and the variables are shown as k arrows relative to the same axis and origin. Co-Plot records the observations in a manner such that similar DMUs are positioned closely on the map. DMUs belonging to the same group (cluster) possess similar characteristics and behave similarly. The Co-Plot technique enables the simultaneous study of DMUs and variables by sequentially superimposing two graphs – one for points (DMUs) and the other for arrows (variables) (Adler and Raveh 2008). The further an observation is located along a particular arrow, the more efficient the DMU is with respect to that ratio. In addition, Co-Plot also identifies extreme outliers. Raveh (2000a) points out that these can be a sign of data measurement errors or lack of homogeneity amongst observations, or they can be used to identify unnecessary variables.

Co-Plot has four stages: two preliminary treatments of the data matrix $X_{n \times k}$ – the standardization of data and the measurement of distance between cases; and two subsequent stages – the production of a two-dimensional representation of the data and the drawing of the variables into the space of the observations. A brief methodological explanation follows.[1]

The Standardization of Data

In order for the variables to be treated equally, $X_{n \times k}$ is normalized into $Z_{n \times k}$. The elements of $Z_{n \times k}$ are deviations from column means $(\bar{x}..j)$ divided by their standard deviations (S_j):

$$Z_{ij} = (x_{ij} - \bar{x}_{j)}) / S_j$$

The Measurement of Distance between Cases

In this stage a measure of dissimilarity $D_{il} \geq 0$ between each pair of observations (rows of $Z_{n \times k}$) is chosen. A symmetrical $n \times n$ matrix (D_{il}) is produced from all the different pairs of observations. The city-block distance (i.e. the sum of absolute deviations) is used as a measure of dissimilarity:

$$D_{il} = \sum_{j=1}^{k} |Z_{ij} - Z_{lj}|$$

The Creation of a Two-Dimensional Representation of the Data using the MDS Method

The matrix D_{il} is recorded using the multidimensional scaling (MDS) method. The algorithm produced by this method plots the matrix D_{il} into Euclidean space in such a way that similar observations (that is, observations with a small dissimilarity between them) are close to each other on the Co-Plot, and the dissimilar observations are distant from each other on the Co-Plot map.

Co-Plot uses Guttman's (1968) smallest space analysis (SSA) out of the group of MDS methods. SSA uses the coefficient of alienation θ as a measure of goodness of fit. The coefficient of alienation determines the quality of the two-dimensional Co-Plot map. The smaller the coefficient, the better the output; and all values under 0.15 are deemed good (Adler and Raveh 2008).

The Presentation of Variables into the Space of Observations

In the last stage of the Co-Plot method, variables k are displayed on the Euclidean space obtained in stage 3. Talby et al. (1999) state that this is the most interesting part of Co-Plot. Here, each variable k is represented by an arrow j. The arrows emerge from the centre of gravity of the n points. The maximal correlation between the actual values of the variables and their projections on the arrow determine the direction of the arrow. The length of the arrows is undefined. Arrows associated with highly correlated variables will point in the same or a similar direction. Furthermore, individual observations with a high value in a particular variable will be positioned around the space that the arrow points to, while observations with low value in that particular variable will be at the other side of the Co-Plot map.

Furthermore, in this stage, k individual goodness-of-fit measures are obtained for each of the k variables separately. These are the magnitudes of the k maximal correlations. The gained correlations suggest whether to keep or eliminate certain variables, as variables with low correlations do not fit into the graphical display, and therefore have to be removed. Raveh (2000a) states that the higher the variable's correlation, the better the variable's arrow represents the direction and the order for the projections of the n points along the rotated axis. This also points to the high explanatory power of such variables if they are used together to form a cluster.

17.5   EMPIRICAL ANALYSIS

This section benchmarks and clusters the CEECs with regard to their financial system development. We focus on the examination of conditions that contribute to the development of an equity culture. We apply a relatively new clustering method, discussed in detail in the previous section, the Co-Plot method (Gilady et al. 1996; Raveh 2000a; Talby et al. 1999), which enables us to observe on a two-dimensional scale the positioning of individual CEECs in relation to each other and four benchmarks – Germany, Japan, the UK and USA. This method enables us to observe the process of development of various institutional factors affecting equity culture in the CEECs as we examine several years in the 1996–2008 period.

In order to present the evolution of clusters in a robust yet reader-friendly way for a continuous period of 12 years, we pick only four years: 1996, 2000, 2004 and 2008. The justification for the selection of these specific years is the following. Firstly, 1996 is the first year of our research period. The transition literature (Brown 1999; Lavigne 1999; Stiglitz 1997) suggests that despite the fact that the political transition took place in the early 1990s, institutional transformation and system democratization was considered to be still in its early days in 1996. Secondly, 2000, marks a transitional decade when CEECs were actively preparing to join the EU by increasing the transparency of their economic policy-making and financial institutions, and strengthening their financial systems overall (Nord 2000). In the aftermath of the 1999 Helsinki European Council all CEECs were confirmed as to join the EU in the future, and therefore they were making efforts to progress towards reforms. Djankov and Murrell (2002) also point out that 2000 was a year of increased trade activity as foreign direct investment (FDI) levels went up across the Central and Eastern European (hereafter CEE) region. Thirdly, 2004 was the year of the EU's enlargement eastwards. Eight CEECs joined the EU and two more were actively preparing to enter in the three coming years. Lastly, 2008 is the last year of our research period. By 2008 all CEECs had become EU members and accomplished all the major transition reforms as directed by the EU (Schwab and Porter 2008). In this year, the Czech Republic – as the first CEEC – was taken off the list of transition countries and was awarded the status of a developed European economy. This is also the last year for which we have consistent data available.

17.5.1   Quality of the Institutional Environment

We examine data on institutional quality in the CEECs and the four benchmarks. From the ICRG database we select seven institutional variables that we see to be relevant in evaluating financial system development and an equity culture creation. We expect these variables to demonstrate institutional differences between those that support the existence of an equity-based system, and those that facilitate the functioning of bank-based financial systems. We choose the indicators of government stability – an indicator on the ability to carry out programmes and ability to stay in office ($i1$); socio-economic conditions – an indicator on public satisfaction/dissatisfaction on public policies ($i2$); investment profile – an indicator on the attitude toward investment: expropriation/contract viability, taxation, repatriation, labour costs ($i3$); corruption – an indicator on the legal abidance to law ($i4$); law and order – an indicator on the strength and imparity of legal system ($i5$); democratic accountability – an indicator on government's legal responsiveness to people ($i6$); bureaucracy quality – an indicator on institutional strength and quality of bureaucracy ($i7$) to distinguish between different types of institutional environments, with the liberal market institutional environment and coordinated market institutional environments being the two differentiating institutional prototypes.

We evaluate the total set of $n = 14$ countries with measurements on $i = 7$ variables for each individual year of the 1996–2008 period (Figures 17.1, 17.2, 17.3 and 17.4 respectively). The raw data, a $X_{14 \times 7}$ matrix is submitted

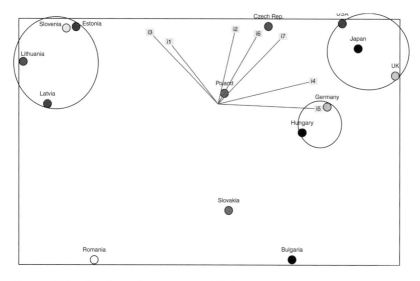

Figure 17.1   Quality of institutions, 1996

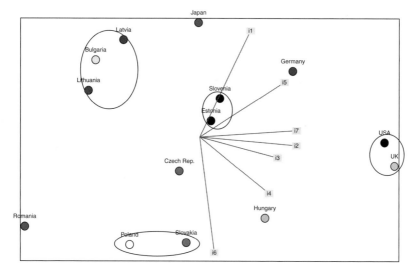

Figure 17.2   Quality of institutions, 2000

to Co-Plot. With all 14 countries the coefficient of alienation is 0.14 for 1996, 2000 and 2008, and 0.15 for 2004, indicating a reliability of 85 per cent and above. The average of the correlations is 0.79 which signals a positive contribution of all seven variables.

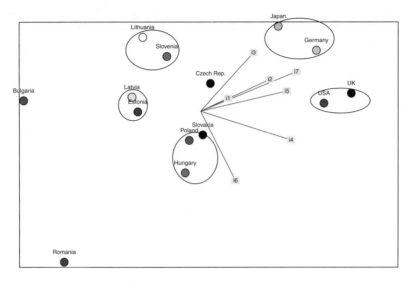

Figure 17.3   Quality of institutions, 2004

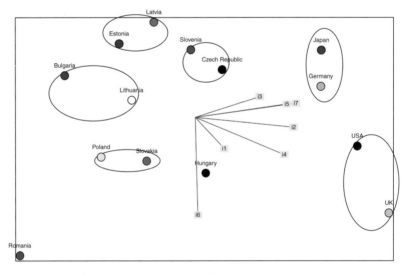

Figure 17.4   Quality of institutions, 2008

We find that Co-Plots exhibit several clusters for the 1996–2008 period. Although our four benchmarks are positioned in every year of observation on the same side of the graphical display, in no time observation do they form a single cluster. This is what we expected, as it is proof of the presence of differing institutional systems in the benchmark countries. The UK and the USA are grouped together and this cluster exhibits high values for law and order, corruption and bureaucracy quality – three prerequisites of institutional transparency. Germany and Japan display slightly lower values on the same attributes and form a cluster on their own. Furthermore, the second cluster of Germany and Japan also performs better on variables displaying better socio-economic conditions and a higher investment profile. This is consistent with the identification of institutional characteristics in the 'varieties of capitalism' theory.

Within the CEECs' group there are variations not only in terms of the overall quality of their institutional environments but also relating to which group of benchmarks (UK and USA, or Germany and Japan) individual CEECs follow. Firstly, the Czech Republic is in 1996 the best performer on institutional variables in comparison to the other CEECs. The values on democratic accountability and bureaucracy quality are especially high. The investment profile indicator also remains one of the strongest among the CEECs for the rest of the research period. Similarly, Hungary in 1996 displays the presence of a reputable legal system; by 2000 the corruption levels improve and by 2004 democratic accountability achieves higher values. By 2008, due to its improvement in corruption and the increased levels of democratic accountability, Hungary secures a position of one of the better institutionally performing CEECs. From the institutional quality perspective the ascending trend in these two CEECs suggests the presence of an institutional environment feasible for the development of an advanced financial system. However, while the Czech Republic seems to follow the path of Germany in terms of its institutional characteristics, Hungary's positioning closer to the UK suggests a different trend of institutional development.

Secondly, despite the fact that in 1996 Slovakia and Poland are far from being co-members of one cluster (Poland displays average values for the majority of institutional variables while Slovakia was an underperformer), by 2000 these two countries join the same cluster characterized by high to above-average values for democratic accountability. By 2008, however, the position of this cluster moves closer to the centre of gravity, suggesting the presence of more average values across all chosen institutional variables. Although the indicators of democratic accountability and corruption suggest an improvement of the institutional environment, and position these two CEECs in the direction of the UK's institutional system, the low quality of bureaucracy and average levels for the law and order indicator do not support their positioning as close to this benchmark as we saw in the case of Hungary.

Thirdly, Estonia, Latvia, Lithuania and Slovenia are interchangeably joining and leaving mutual clusters. Co-Plot adjusted to examine the CEECs without direct comparison to the benchmarks reveals a closer position of two countries in particular: Estonia and Slovenia. According to the graphical display corruption levels are lower compared to Latvia and Lithuania, and bureaucracy quality has scored better when compared to the same two countries. This suggests an improvement of institutional quality in Estonia and Slovenia, and institutional stagnation in Latvia and Lithuania. Therefore, from the institutional perspective point of view, Estonia and Slovenia appear to have an institutional advantage over Latvia and Lithuania. The same graphical display suggests that Estonia is following a path similar to Slovakia, Poland and Hungary (benchmarks UK and USA) and Slovenia is following the path of the Czech Republic (benchmarks Germany and Japan).

Fourthly, Bulgaria and Romania are the weakest performers on institutional indicators. This suggests a limited improvement of the institutional environment in these countries. Firms seeking equity financing in these two countries face high transaction costs due to the low institutional quality. Therefore, advanced sources of financing such as equity seem to be an unfeasible option to most Bulgarian and Romanian firms.

17.5.2   Transition Data on the Quality of Institutions

In this section more institutional data related to the transition process are examined to supplement the institutional environment analysis performed above. The EBRD transition data on the progress of the institutional advancement of the CEECs provides information on: large-scale privatization ($i8$); small-scale privatization ($i9$); banking reform and interest rate liberalization ($i10$); securities markets and non-bank financial institutions ($i11$); governance and enterprise restructuring ($i12$). Privatization, FDI, financial liberalization and corporate governance factors vastly shape the characteristics of an institutional environment in transition economies (Choi and Jeon 2007) and therefore play a vital role in our assessment of the quality of the institutional environment in the CEECs. These EBRD institutional indicators enrich our discussion on the different varieties of institutional systems that are the reason for, and continue developing alongside, bank-based and equity-based financial systems.

In this case we evaluate the total set of $n = 10$ CEECs (as there are no relevant data available for our four benchmarks) with measurements on $i = 5$ transition variables for each individual year (Figures 17.5, 17.6, 17.7 and 17.8). The raw data, an $X_{10 \times 5}$ matrix, is submitted to Co-Plot. With all

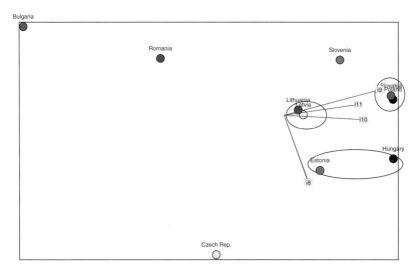

Figure 17.5   Quality of institutions (Transition data), 1996

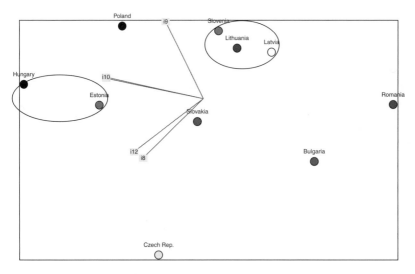

Figure 17.6   Quality of institutions (Transition data), 2000

ten countries the coefficient of alienation is 0.11 for 1996 and 2008, 0.07 for 2000 and 0.13 for 2004, indicating a reliability of 87 per cent and above. The average of the correlations is 0.85 which indicates a positive contribution of all four variables.

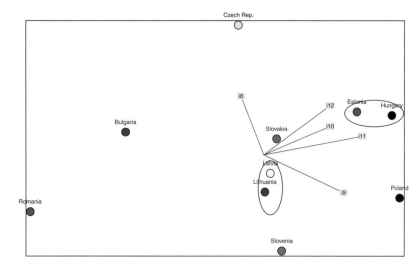

Figure 17.7   Quality of institutions (Transition data), 2004

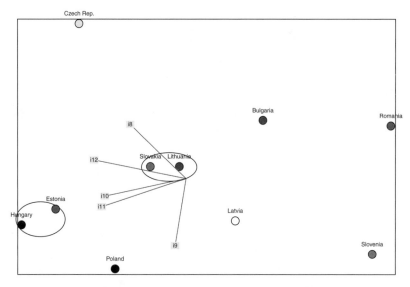

Figure 17.8   Quality of institutions (Transition data), 2008

The Co-Plot display confirms that the Czech Republic, Hungary, Estonia and Poland are the strongest performers on transitional-institutional indicators. The Czech Republic and Poland do not belong to the same cluster as Hungary and Estonia. While the former exhibits a higher proportion of large-scale privatization in all time observations than any other of these four CEECs and also scores high on the governance and enterprise restructuring indicator, the latter performs extremely well on the small-scale indicator in 1996, but other indicators start performing better after 2000. In the case of Hungary and Estonia small-scale privatization is prevalent and a steady performance of all the other indicators is present since 1996.

The Czech Republic's large-scale privatization efforts result in a performance typical of advanced industrial economies where more than 75 per cent of enterprise assets are in private hands with effectively functioning corporate governance (EBRD 2008b). If these private hands have a foreign nature, the Czech government statistical data (Czech Republic Statistical Office 2008) states that they come from Germany, Italy, Austria, the USA and France (the biggest FDI source is listed first). Hungary, Estonia and Poland, on the other hand, perform better on small-scale privatization. In these countries the privatization of small companies with tradable ownership rights was complete by 1996 and there was no state ownership of state enterprises by 2000. By the end of the same year, more than 50 per cent of state-owned enterprises were in private hands and there was also an improvement in corporate governance. Furthermore, by 2004 prudential supervision and regulation are in place, with significant lending to private businesses and significant presence of private banks. By 2008 substantial financial deepening is also noted (EBRD 2008b).

Based on the above information we can deduce that the Czech Republic, Hungary, Estonia and Poland progressed better in their transition process in terms of their institutional environments than other CEECs from our research sample. Growing institutional support for the banking sector together with a prevalent source of FDI from host countries known for their bank-oriented financial systems (e.g. Germany, Austria, Italy) can be identified as partial reasons for the bank-oriented systems in these CEECs. However, in the case of Hungary and Estonia a strong presence of non-bank financial institutions could be a sign of a growing demand for other than bank financing, and thus the sound banking sector could be seen just as a preparation for the entry of a more advanced form of corporate financing – equity financing. Therefore, at this stage, we maintain that the developed stage of the institutional sectors in the Czech Republic, Hungary and Estonia serves as a predisposition for sound financial systems development, whether bank- or equity-oriented.

Although the other four CEECs – Latvia, Lithuania, Slovakia and Slovenia – do not form one single cluster in any observations, they interchangeably become cluster co-members in different years and remain in a close position on the graphical display. These countries share the characteristics of advanced small-scale privatization with privatized firms possessing individual ownership rights (EBRD 2008b). By 2000 all four countries had made substantial progress in the establishment of bank solvency and in the framework for prudential supervision and regulation. In this year the differences in institutional transition became more visible between these four countries. While Slovenia stagnated in the transition and displayed the same levels achieved in 2000 until 2008, Latvia, Lithuania and Slovakia made better progress. While these three countries improved on the banking reform and interest rate liberalization indicator by achieving full interest rate liberalization and significant bank lending to private enterprises, two of them also performed better in another way. In Lithuania and Slovakia, in addition to a growing regulatory framework for bank financing, the non-bank financial institutions, such as investment funds and private insurance companies started emerging and an associated regulatory framework was formed.

Latvia, Lithuania, Slovakia and Slovenia exhibit a good effort in small-scale privatization. However, large-scale privatization forces major unresolved issues regarding corporate governance. The transition process of institutional conditions necessary for the development of a sound financial system is in place, but with some limitations. With the exception of Lithuania and Slovakia, it seems that these CEECs have to first overcome corporate governance issues such as weak to moderate bankruptcy legislation, moderate to high bureaucracy quality and the lack of tight credit and subsidy policies. Once this is accomplished, firms seeking equity financing have a better chance of experiencing lower, and therefore more acceptable, transaction costs.

The last two CEECs, Bulgaria and Romania, confirm their position of laggards in terms of the transition toward an institutional environment supportive of a sound banking system and possibly equity-oriented financial system. By 2008, when the best-performing CEE countries have achieved institutional conditions comparable to other developed industrialized economies, Bulgaria and Romania have a comprehensive programme for implementation of privatization in place but not all their enterprises are privatized, they struggle to strengthen competition and corporate governance, and lack a regulatory system necessary for the functioning of non-bank financial institutions. Unless these conditions improve, equity culture development is not feasible as high transaction costs are an obstacle for firms diverting from the usual sources of financing to a riskier alternative – equity financing.

17.6   CONCLUSIONS

This chapter serves as a conceptual discussion of equity culture and its creation mechanism. We believe that the conceptualization itself can be regarded as a valuable theoretical contribution in its field. Equity culture is a less popular source of finance in the CEECs but nevertheless, it is developed in a number of economically advanced economies. The way these economies (that is, CEECs) will proceed is a dynamic and challenging issue to observe.

We graphically displayed ten CEECs from our research sample and four benchmarks in terms of their institutional characteristics and thus cumulatively, we believe, portrayed the status of their financial system developments and equity culture creation. The Co-Plot applied to create the exhibits enabled us, firstly, to identify indicators leading to debt financing and equity financing; and secondly, to place individual CEECs not only in terms of their general financial system development credibility but also in relation to equity culture creation.

Evidence from business-related publications (e.g. LSE 2006; World Bank 2002) as well as our personal observations from the world of finance suggest that financial system development in Central and Eastern Europe and, specifically, the subject of equity culture are important current issues. The question of which CEECs have the best potential to develop and adopt an equity culture requires attention so that correct and suitable policy implications can be proposed.

Domestic governments in both the CEECs and also the European Commission are concerned with improving economic growth rates of European member states. Our research identifies those countries which are lagging behind in terms of equity culture development and, further, suggests causes of this. This research should give an impetus to countries to continue with the reforms necessary.

Organizations such as the International Monetary Fund (IMF), the World Bank and regional development banks such as the Asian Development Bank (ADB) and Intra-American Development Bank (IADB) are concerned with the economic development of transition economies. Our study identifies key factors in the development of an equity culture in the CEECs which may be applied to other groups of transition countries. We believe that our research and methodology will be of considerable interest to this group of international finance and development institutions.

The presence of an efficient bureaucratic system and an institutional system with low corruption levels is a necessary condition. This is to say that transition countries which do not satisfy the institutional conditions of efficient bureaucracy and low corruption can still have certain firms demanding equity finance. However, in such institutional conditions only a small proportion of firms will move towards developing an equity culture. Therefore, if a country wants to start building an equity culture at all levels of its corporate sector, improved quality of the bureaucratic system and low levels of corruption may enable it to achieve that.

Now that the conceptualization is in place, the main external forces which affect equity culture development have been identified, the conditions which have to be satisfied so that equity culture can develop have been named, and certain policy-making recommendations for the development of an equity culture have been proposed, the research focus can change from the macro-level to the micro-level, and utilize further quantitative methods to provide a more holistic approach to the phenomenon.

NOTE

1. For a detailed Co-Plot methodology see Raveh (2000a), Raveh (2000b) and Adler and Raveh (2008).

REFERENCES

Adler, N. and A. Raveh (2008), 'Presenting DEA graphically', *International Journal of Management Science*, **36**, 715–729.

Amable, B. (2003), *The Diversity of Modern Capitalism*, Oxford: Oxford University Press.

Bakker, M.-R. and A. Gross (2004), *Development of Non-bank Financial Institutions and Capital Markets in European Union Accession Countries*, Washinghton, DC: World Bank.

Beck, T. (2006), 'Creating an efficient financial system: challenges in a global economy', World Bank Research Working Paper, Washington, DC: World Bank.

Beck, T., A. Demirgüç-Kunt and V. Maksimovic (2005), 'Financial and legal constraints to firm growth: does firm size matter?' *Journal of Finance*, **60**, 137–177.

Beck, T. and R. Levine (2004), 'Stock markets, banks, and growth: panel evidence', *Journal of Banking and Finance*, **28**, 423–442.

Beck, T., R. Levine and N. Loayza (2000), 'Finance and sources of growth', *Journal of Financial Economics*, **58**, 261–300.

Bekaert, G. and C.R. Harvey (2002), 'Research in emerging markets finance: looking to the future', *Emerging Markets Review*, **3**, 429–448.

Bekaert, G., C.R. Harvey and R. Lumsdaine (2002), 'Dating the integration of world equity markets', *Journal of Financial Economics*, **65**, 203–248.

Bekaert, G., C.R. Harvey and C. Lundblad (2001), 'Emerging equity markets and economic development', *Journal of Development Economics*, **66**, 465–504.

Bilias, Y., D. Georgarakos and M. Haliass (2009), 'Equity culture and the distribution of wealth', NETSPAR working paper, NETSPAR.

Brown, A. (ed.) (1999), 'When is Transition Over?' Upjohn Institure for Employment Research.

Choi, J.J. and B.N. Jeon (2007), 'Financial factors in foreign direct investments: a dynamic analysis of international data', *Research in international business and finance*, **21**, 1–18.

Claessens, S. (1995), 'The emergence of equity investment', *World Bank Economic Review*, **9**, 1–17.

Detragiache, E., P. Gupta and T. Tressel (2006), 'Foreign banks in poor countries: theory and evidence', Working paper 06/18, Washington, DC: International Monetary Fund.

Djankov, S. and P. Murrell (2002), 'Enterprise restructuring in transition: a quantitative survey', *Journal of Economic Literature*, **40**, 739–792.

Doidge, C., G.A. Karolyi and R.M. Stulz (2007), 'Why do countries matter so much for corporate governance?' *Journal of Financial Economics*, **86**, 1–39.

Doyle, O. and P.P. Walsh (2005), 'Did political constraints bind during transition? Evidence from Czech elections, 1990–2002', in O. Doyle and P.P. Walsh (eds), *Corporate Governance, Corporate Restructuring and Corporate Finance in Transition Economies*, London: Blackwell, pp. 575–601.

EBRD (1998), 'Transition Report 1998: financial sector in transition', Transition Reports, London: European Bank for Reconstruction and Development.

EBRD (2006), 'Transition Report 2006: finance in transition', Transition Reports, London: European Bank for Reconstruction and Development.

EBRD (2008a), 'Transition Indicators', European Bank for Reconstruction and Development.

EBRD (2008b), 'Transition Report 2008: growth in transition', Transition Reports, London: European Bank for Reconstruction and Development.

EBRD (2009), 'Transition Report 2009: transition in crisis?' Transition Reports, London: European Bank for Reconstruction and Development.

Fisher, S., R. Sahay and C.A. Vegh (1997), 'From transition to market: evidence and growth prospects', in S. Zecchini (ed.), *Lessons from the Economic Transition: Central and Eastern Europe in the 1990's*, Dordrecht: Kluwer Academic Publishers, pp. 79–103.

Francis, J., I. Khurana and R. Perreira (2005), 'Disclosure incentives and effects on cost of captial around the world', *Accounting Review*, **80**, 1125–1162.

Gehrke, C. and M. Knell (1992), 'Transitions from centrally planned to market economy', in M. Knell and C. Rider (eds), *Socialist Economies in Transition: Appraisals of the Market Mechanisms*, Aldershot, UK and Brookfield, UT, USA: Edward Elgar Publishing, pp. 43–65.

Geschenkron, A. (1962), *Economic Backwardness in Historical Perspective: A Book of Essays*, Cambridge, MA: Belknap Press of Harvard University Press.

Gilady, T., Y. Spectator and A. Raveh (1996), 'Multidimensional scale: an analysis of 1980–1990 computers', *European Journal of Operational Research*, **95**, 439–450.

Guttman, L. (1968), 'A general non-metric technique for finding the smallest space for a configuration of points', *Psychometria*, **33**, 479–506.

Hermes, N. and R. Lensink (2000), 'Financial system development in transition economies', *Journal of Banking and Finance*, **24**, 507–524.

ICRG (2001), *International Country Risk Guide*, Stockholm: PRS Group (The Political Risk Services Group).

Kaufmann, D., A. Kraay and P. Zoido-Lobaton (2000), 'Governance matters: from measurement to action', *Journal of Financial Development*, **37**, 10–13.

Kim, B. and L.W. Kenny (2007), 'Explaining when developing countries liberalize their financial equity markets', *Journal of International Financial Markets, Institutions and Money*, **17**, 387–402.

King, R.G. and R. Levine (1993), 'Finance, entrepreneurship and growth: theory and evidence', *Journal of Monetary Economics*, **32**, 513–542.

Klapper, L. and I. Love (2003), 'Corporate governance, investor protection and performance in emerging markets', *Journal of Corporate Finance*, **195**, 1–26.

Klapper, L.F., V. Sarria-Allende and V. Sulla (2002), 'Small- and medium-size enterprise financing in Eastern Europe', World Bank Policy Research Working Paper, Washington, DC: World Bank.

Kolodko, G.W. (2000), *From Shock to Therapy. The Political Economy of Postsocialist Transformation*, Helsinki, Finland and Oxford, UK: UNU/Wider and Oxford University Press.

Kornai, J. (2006), 'The great transformation of Central Eastern Europe', *Economics of Transition*, **14**, 207–244.

La Porta, R., F. Lopez-De-Silanes, A. Shleifer and R. Vishny (1997), 'Legal determinants of external finance', *Journal of Finance*, **52**, 1131–1150.

La Porta, R., F. Lopez-De-Silanes, A. Shleifer and R. Vishny (1999), 'The quality of governments', *Journal of Law, Economics and Organization*, **15**, 222–279.

Lavigne, M. (1999), *The Economics of Transition, From Social Economy to Market Economy*, London, UK and New York, USA: Macmillan and St Martin's Press.

Levine, R. (2002), 'Bank-based or market-based financial systems: which is better?' Working paper No. 9138, National Bureau of Economic Research.

Levine, R. and S. Zervos (1998), 'Stock markets, banks, and economic growth', *American Economic Review*, **88**, 537–558.

Li, K. (2007), 'The growth in equity market size and trading activity: an international study', *Journal of Empirical Finance*, **14**, 59–90.

LSE (2006), 'AIM – Europe update', in LSE (ed.), London: London School of Economics.

Mar-Molinero, C. and J. Mingers (2007), 'An evaluation of the limitations of, and alternatives to, the co-plot methodology', *Journal of the Operational Research Society*, **58**, 874–886.

Monks, R.A. and N. Minow (2001), *Corporate Governance*, Oxford: Blackwell.

Morelli, D.A. (2009), 'Capital market integration: evidence from the G7 countries', *Applied Financial Economics*, **19**, 1043–1057.

Morelli, D.A. (2010), 'European capital market integration: an empirical study based on an European asset pricing model', *Journal of International Financial Markets, Institutions and Money*, **20** (4), 363–375.

Myners, P. (2001), *Review of Institutional Investment in the UK*, London: HM Treasury.

Nord, R. (2000), 'Central and Eastern Europe and the new financial architecture', *Finance and Development, IMF*, **37**, 32–35.

OECD (2009), 'Organisation for Economic Co-operation and Development', www.oecd.org, accessed September 2009.

Pagano, M. (1993), 'Financial markets and growth: an overview', *European Economic Review*, **37**, 613–622.

Pagano, M. and P. Volpin (2005), 'Shareholder protection, stock market development, and politics', ECGI Finance working paper, 105.

Paucar-Caceres, A. and R. Thorpe (2005), 'Mapping the structure of MBA programmes: a comparative study of the structure of accredited AMBA programmes in the United Kingdom', *Journal of Operational Research Society*, **56**, 25–38.

Peng, M.W. (2004), 'Institutional transitions and strategic choices', *Academy of Management Review*, **28**, 1–26.

Pinkowitz, L., R.M. Stulz and R. Williamson (2002), *Corporate Governance and the Home Bias*, Columbus, Ohio: Ohio State University.

Purda, L.D. (2008), 'Risk perception and the financial system', *Journal of International Business Studies*, **39**, 1178–1196.

Rajan, R.G. and L. Zingales (2003a), 'The great reversals: the politics of financial development in the 20th century', *Journal of Financial Economics*, **69**, 5–50.

Rajan, R.G. and L. Zingales (2003b), 'Financial dependence and growth', *American Economic Review*, **88**, 559–586.

Raveh, A. (2000a), 'Co-plot: a graphic display method for geometrical representations of MCDM', *European Journal of Operational Research*, **125**, 670–678.

Raveh, A. (2000b), 'The Greek banking system: reanalysis of performance', *European Journal of Operational Research*, **120**, 525–534.

Scholtens, B. (2000), 'Financial regulation and financial system architecture in Central Europe', *Journal of Banking and Finance*, **24**, 525–553.

Schumpeter, J. (1911), *The Theory of Economic Development*, Cambridge, MA: Harvard University Press.

Schwab, K. and M. Porter (2008), *The Global Competitiveness Report 2008–2009*, Geneva: World Economic Forum.

Segal, J. (2009), 'The equity culture loses its bloom', *Institutional Investor Magazine*, April, pp. 1–4.

Segev, A., A. Raveh and M. Farjoun (1990), 'Conceptual maps of leading MBA programmes in the United States: core courses, concentration areas, and the rankings of the school', *Strategic Management Journal*, **20**, 549–565.

Smith, B.M. (2003), *The Equity Culture: The Story of the Global Stock Market*, New York: Farrar, Strauss & Giroux.

Stiglitz, J. (1995), 'The theory of international public goods and the architecture of international organisations', United Nations Background Paper 7, New York: UN, Department for Economic and Social Information and Policy Analysis.

Stiglitz, J. (1997), 'Transition economy is still a well-defined category', Transition. *World Bank*, **8** (2), 1–3.

Stiglitz, J. (1999), 'Whither reform? Ten years of the transition', *Annual Bank Conference on Development Economics*, Washington, DC: World Bank.

Stoian, C.R. and F. Filippaios (2007), 'Foreign direct investment and aid: engines for growth in transition economies', Kent Business School Working Papers Series, Canterbury: University of Kent.

Strange, S. (1995), *States and Markets*, London: Printer Publishers.

Talby, D., D.G. Feitelson and A. Raveh (1999), 'Comparing logs and models of parallel workloads using the co-plot method', in D.G. Feitelson and L. Randolph (eds), *Job Scheduling Strategies in Parallel Processing*, Berlin: Springer-Verlag, pp. 43–66.

Underhill, G.R.D. (1995), *Global Capital Markets and EU Financial Integration*, Coventry: University of Warwick, Department of Politics and International Studies.

Weber, Y., O. Shenkar and A. Raveh (1996), 'Natural versus cultural fit in mergers and acquisitions: an exploratory study', *Management Science*, **42**, 1215–1227.

WEF (2008), *The Financial Development Report*, Geneva: World Economic Forum.

World Bank (2002), 'Building institutions for markets', *World Development Report*, Washington, DC: World Bank.

Wyplozs, C. (2002), 'How risky is financial liberalization in the developing countries?' *Comparative Economic Studies*, **44**, 1–26.

18 Between welfare and bargaining: union heterogeneity in Europe's 'Far East'
Richard Croucher and Claudio Morrison

18.1 INTRODUCTION: INSTITUTIONAL THEORY AND UNIONS

Institutional theory has only recently begun to extend beyond the developed, relatively stable societies of Western Europe and the USA; recognition of heterogeneity in union functions is likely to constitute a prerequisite for its further extension within post-socialist Europe. This chapter identifies the sources and nature of union functional diversity in Moldova. We illustrate that this type of internal diversity, in part a product of external influences and incoherent reform, is greater than in much of the rest of Europe where unions' key industrial function is collective bargaining. Trade union functions, as we illustrate, may not be assumed or derived from Central and East European (CEE) countries (for a helpful institutionalist analysis of CEE countries see Noelke and Vliegenhart 2009), still less from West European or American models.

Neoliberal-based discussions of institutions have contributed to the study of post-Communist societies (Meyer 2001; Meyer and Peng 2005). They have assumed a union-free world and to this extent have seriously distorted socio-economic reality. This influential analytic tradition is concerned with those institutions assumed to be required by neoclassical economics for markets to function effectively such as privatization, enterprise restructuring, banking reform, securities markets, commercial law and financial regulation (North 1990). These institutions as social norms, as North persistently underlined, are held to constitute the essential impersonal rules of the game for development. In Moldova, as elsewhere, many of the institutional reforms undertaken to promote them have had negative effects on trade unions but have reshaped rather than destroyed them. The strand has been combined with a second neoliberal stream of analysis which complements it: transaction cost economics (TCE). The importance of transactions was initially demonstrated by the institutional economist J.R. Commons, who emphasized the importance of institutions including trade unions in structuring outcomes, and viewed their contribution to employee welfare positively. Williamson (1975), a founder of 'new institutional economics', built on but in this respect inverted Commons's framework, condemning unions *a fortiori* as imposing additional burdens on firms. More recent research on post-Communist Europe within this broad tradition (Meyer 2001; Meyer and Peng 2005), simply ignores industrial relations institutions despite conclusive evidence that their nature influences firm behaviour including decisions to invest directly (Cook 1997; Bognanno et al. 2005).

The theoretical bases of such analyses were strongly challenged by Moran and Ghoshal (1999), who argued that an excessive focus on external rule-making was fundamentally inadequate and that internal rule-making within the firm could both raise efficiency and aid development more widely. This approach represents an advance but is also problematic in that it excludes consideration of employee voice mechanisms, ascribing rule-making power solely to management and failing to acknowledge the possibility of negotiated outcomes at firm level. Nevertheless, it restored management if not worker agency to a previously arid 'institutional' terrain. This is highly relevant to our case, because the trade unions in question here are essentially workplace-based organizations.

Institutionalist analyses within the 'varieties of capitalism' tradition have on the other hand attempted to integrate trade unionism into their frameworks. Yet these are also fundamentally unsatisfactory. Thus, analyses of the European economies characterized by Lane and Myant (2007) as 'consolidated market economies' (Estonia, Slovenia, the Czech Republic, Poland, Ukraine), as 'hybrid economies' (Russia, Kazakhstan, the Western Balkans) or 'statist market economies' (Belarus, China) operate within implicit frameworks that assume Western forms of unionism. Thus, Mykhnenko (2007), in a comparative analysis of Ukraine and Poland, adopts Organisation for Economic Co-operation and Development (OECD) criteria including collective agreement coverage to estimate the state of manager–employee relations. Yet the extent to which collective agreements in Ukraine show these relations, since they are often the result of management decisions, is both questionable and undocumented (Croucher 2004). Similarly, in her analysis of Belarus, Korosteleva (2007, 229) argues that unions were reduced to irrelevance 'in the system of wage determination' by political authoritarianism. This assumes that wage determination was previously a central function of local unions, when this is at best questionable (Danilovich and Croucher 2011). Moreover, while Belarus demonstrates extreme political authoritarianism even by the region's standards, the conclusion may not be drawn that unions enjoy no leverage in relation to management since unions derive power from their state regulation enforcement functions

(Danilovich and Croucher 2011). Thus, unions in Ukraine, Belarus and Moldova have historically sticky functions that are quite different from the Western models implicitly used in analysis (Croucher 2000, 2004; Danilovich and Croucher 2011). Not only are the assumed functions inadequately specified, but they are also generalized to the national level without qualification when in reality there is considerable heterogeneity at the firm level.

Prior to examining these unions' functions and how they have evolved in different trajectories at workplace level, we sketch the national context within which they are embedded. The remainder of the chapter is structured as follows. First, we outline an 'ideal type' of the 'unreformed' trade union in order to establish a baseline for our analysis of heterogeneity, and advance some explanations for its continued resilience. We then provide an account of the evolution of Moldovan trade unionism during the 'protracted transition' of the last two decades, showing how interactions between local drivers for change interacted with foreign interventions to move some workplace unions towards reform.

Major state intervention in union affairs has attracted international attention on trade union rights grounds. This might be presumed to have created homogenized unions, but we show that this has not eliminated the variation in their functions. To demonstrate this empirically we examine three unions until recently affiliated to the state-favoured union confederation operating within the clothing sector, and characterize the form of trade unionism within them. Finally, we draw out some implications for institutional theory.

We draw on two main sources for our empirical account of union activity. The first is one of the authors' extensive notes on his work in intensive educational programmes conducted on behalf of several Global Union Federations in Moldova between 1999 and 2006, an involvement prefaced by a period of formal visits to union offices, workplace visits and interviews. The second is the other author's longitudinal research into three case study workplaces between 2004 and 2011. In each workplace, extensive interviews were held with union officials, workplace union representatives, managers and employees. Both authors have remained in contact with respondents up to the time of writing in 2011.

18.2   THE MOLDOVAN CONTEXT

It has been observed that post-socialism represents an exceptionally favourable site for large-scale social experimentation and it has been suggested that differentiation of organizational forms might be one of the most significant outcomes (Soulsby and Clark 2007). Moldova, one of Europe's smallest and poorest countries, has been subjected to radical reforms with dramatic consequences; it therefore reveals the contradictions of the transformation process in extreme forms. Its geopolitical location means that it has endured divergent and sometimes contradictory influences. The Communist Party, in power for the last decade, pursued a route to Europe while relying on traditional soviet practices at home. In industrial relations, it has embraced 'social partnership' but translated it into paternalism. Liberalization has progressed steadily – the most recent concession to foreign capital by the Communist government was the abolition of centrally drafted pay scales essential for unions to claim a minimum wage. It has also left unions their material assets and tried to manipulate rather than annihilate them.

Moldova lacks strong internal centripetal forces, leaving it in a state of flux and encouraging multiple organizational forms. The state is strongly affected by external forces and this represents a major obstacle to achieving coherence in institutional reform. Ambiguity in state policies leaves greater space for the exercise of discretion by local actors. Low levels of law enforcement and widespread general mistrust of the state have increased the discretion of peripheral state administrators and foreign investors.

The role of the latter is ambivalent. Foreign direct investment (FDI), as elsewhere, has shown mixed results and is not contributing to Europeanization (Meardi 2007; Tholen 2007). Foreign ownership has generated change in management approaches but investors have also been inclined to seize upon systemic informality, lawlessness, corruption and paternalism to maximize cost advantages. High labour turnover, migration and skills shortages result, and indicate that the present configuration is unstable and imposes costs on investors as well as employees.

18.3 THE 'UNREFORMED' TRADE UNION

Union structures, practices, cultures and functions in Moldova and more widely in South East Europe continue to be stamped by their historical inheritance, bringing renewed calls for their 'modernization' after 20 years of transition (Feicht 2010). All of their trajectories under 'transition' begin with the classical soviet form of unionism. As we describe in the following section, many have made strenuous efforts to break out of this mould, but its marks remain even on those unions that have undertaken reform. We create an 'ideal type' both for analytic purposes and to describe the form of trade unionism promoted by the Communist government at the beginning of the twenty-first century.

Soviet unions were designed to transmit party policies, and operated as mechanistic bureaucracies, which eliminated or marginalized non-approved forms of self-activity. National and regional officers were party appointees. At the workplace, the union and its committee (*Profkom*) was essentially the personnel arm of management, and managers were often elected to union positions. Workers' problems, if touched on, were dealt with as legal and administrative issues. The workplace 'collective agreements' which formed the basis of workers' terms and conditions were simply agreed between unions and the rest of management; no meaningful bargaining occurred. The union's functions were to act as a legal watchdog and, most importantly, to distribute welfare in the form of payments to members in difficulties. Finally and vitally, unions allocated recreational and other benefits (sometimes including housing) to workers.

By the end of the soviet system, unions were strongly enterprise-based and had highly decentralized finances, contradicting the principle of 'centralized finance' which the Webbs (Webb and Webb 1897) saw as essential to union strategy and cohesion. The great majority of subscription income was (and is still) retained at workplace level with only small amounts being remitted to regional and national bodies; few services therefore flowed down to support workplace unions. 'Lower' committees were seen as responsible to their 'higher' counterparts rather than to members. Reporting was upwards, from the workplace to the regional and federal levels. With the collapse of Communism, this translated into very weak articulation between different levels, since the very varied fate of enterprise unions gave rise to a very wide range of large-scale problems that overwhelmed the small number of extra-workplace officials. In the classical soviet trade union, intra-union hierarchies were strict and team-working between different levels and regions was entirely absent.

During 'transition', workplace activists became increasingly dissatisfied with national and regional organizations. Many personnel remain from before 1989, and there is therefore an ageing body of paid officers, all party appointees. Workplace unions continue therefore to resist persistent attempts to have them pay higher subscriptions to the regional and national levels, and jealously guard their autonomy. Many, since Thirkell et al. (1998), have asserted (see for example Croucher 2004) that the old ways of working survive even in those unions where structures have changed, indicating the durability of soviet union culture. The International Confederation of Free Trade Unions (ICFTU) (now the International Trade Union Confederation, ITUC) and the International

Trade Secretariats (now the Global Union Federations, GUFs) did not initially regard these unions as independent organizations. Only in the late 1990s were they considered eligible for membership, and then only as unions formally committed to reforming themselves (Croucher and Cotton 2009). Yet the international union bodies had no effective means of ensuring that they did in fact reform.

Despite their formal commitments to change, many workplace unions in Moldova, Ukraine and more widely in South East Europe remain locked into these structures and ways of working; in all cases, the welfare functions persist even where supplemented by others. There are two sets of reasons for this continued attachment to the welfare model of unionism. The first is derived from ideology and habitus. At the political level, no tradition of social democratic independent or militant trade unionism existed or was initiated that could support alternative visions of union purpose, identity and tactics. Habitus is also important. The general tendency in organizations is to retain established ways of working, a tendency that is especially marked in trade unions with deeply ingrained collective cultures (Hannigan 2005). A second cluster of reasons is more material: the weakness of employees in the employment relationship is particularly pronounced in 'transition' countries (Bohle and Greskovits 2006). This also means that mobilization, either as a basis for campaigning in relation to the state or, especially, for direct action against the employer, is difficult for unions to achieve. Moreover, unions are fearful that mobilizing and bargaining styles of unionism may bring powerful employer countermeasures, threatening the status quo in terms of their bureaucracies' assets and privileges. There is also a basis for the welfare emphasis in worker expectations. State welfare safety nets are poor and weakly developed; Moldova is Europe's poorest country. Therefore, easy-to-access welfare benefits administered within the workplace community can play a crucial role in workers' domestic economies and provide a vital supplement or alternative to state provision. Employee demand is therefore a factor in preserving these functions.

Thus, the 'method of mutual insurance' referred to by Webb and Webb (1897) as a key tool of trade unionism remains central in Moldova and more widely, even if in many cases employers are dispensing at least part of the insurance benefits. It provides a continuous activity within which other necessarily more sporadic actions may be located. It is therefore a fundament within the hybrid welfare–bargaining–campaigning forms of unionism that have developed. This in turn may constitute one reason for the 'labour quiescence' in evidence during the protracted and socially damaging transition process.

18.4 THE TRAJECTORY OF MOLDOVAN TRADE UNIONISM, 1990–2010

18.4.1 1990–2000: Uneven and Contested Reform

Two possible strategic lines of development for trade unions in the post-socialist sphere were proposed by a Bulgarian expert in the late 1990s. Unions of the classical soviet type, it was argued, should firstly transform themselves into collective bargaining institutions along Western lines on the one hand, and secondly, develop outside of the 'industrial relations' sphere and into community activism on the other. It was suggested that the emphasis should increasingly be on collective bargaining and campaigning at the political level through unions' implantation in civil society (Petkov 1998).

The CSRM Moldovan trade union confederation is a direct descendant of its predecessor under Communism. Alternative views of how trade unionism should develop, similar to those of Petkov (1998), developed widely in the Moldovan unions.

If we now take the example of Moldova's largest union, it is simply because of its prominence. This union, the agricultural and food processing workers' organization Agroindsynd, adopted both of the orientations advocated above. The reasons derived largely from its leadership's politics but simultaneously corresponded to the needs of the union's different membership bases. The leaders were 'Reform Communists' already active in urging reform under Communism. They identified one cause of the collapse of Communism to be a failure of trade unions to act as democratic, mobilizing bodies that could extract concessions from the ruling elite. If and when full-blown capitalism arrived, there would be even more of a need for a new form of trade unionism that made reality of the Communist unions' formal *raison d'être*, namely 'defence of the workers' interests'. Three major and related problems were perceived that induced them to drive change: acute disarticulation between different union levels, an increasingly hostile state and the arrival of foreign employers.

Agroindsynd's strategy throughout the two decades since the end of Communism was to maintain workplace unions' welfare functions but also to develop the workplace union organizations as bargaining and campaigning agents. Its orientation was not shared by other similar unions in the adjacent countries. In the Ukraine, the equivalent union (the massive Agroindustrial Complex Workers Industrial Union) initially centred its strategy on defending its residual but still sizeable role in administering the state welfare system. The political strategy failed, as the role was finally abolished at the beginning of the twenty-first century. Internal reform was delayed by this dead-end strategy and it was only after that point that the union's leadership took major measures to push internal change.

Trade union education was identified by Agroindsynd's leadership as a cost-effective tool for developing activists whilst raising the levels of membership involvement and internal discussion. Well-trained cadres close to the membership could provide a crucial first line of services at the workplace. In pragmatic terms, by building local capacities and confidence, pressure could be taken off a diminishing body of national salaried employees. The traditional inactivity of members could potentially be overcome, shoring up union defences against membership loss. Agroindsynd's second national congress in 1995 passed resolutions that initiated major developments in the union's education system. The key resolution designated 5 per cent of all subscriptions collected from workplace unions to be used for educational purposes. Finance could also be drawn from cultural and sporting budgets, although revealingly this (since it concerned a function considered central) was the subject of heated controversy. The resolution made funds available and raised the profile of education within the union.

The subjects of Agroindsynd's representative education are both significant. One course was at the centre of its work: 'The Union Yesterday, Today and Tomorrow'. The first course that all representatives were encouraged to attend, it aimed to bring participants to understand the need to define their union activity against that of the past, and help them develop a vision of the union in the future. The other two main courses are on negotiating skills and trade union management. The accent in terms of content is therefore primarily on bargaining, and union organization to that end. The union made these materials available to other Moldovan unions (Centrul Didactico-Metodic al Syndicatelor din Moldova 1998).

The educational methods used are designed to encourage activity from below, and reflect one of the long-standing traditions in European workers' education: that of self-activity (Feidel-Mertz 1964). This was important, given the cultural legacy of soviet-style trade unionism, with its top-down approach; a new form of activity was being modelled. Methods were therefore 'student-centred' with participants collectively approaching tasks and discussing practical problems from the workplace, rather than receiving lectures from external experts as in soviet times. These methods encouraged the unlocking of tacit knowledge within the organization, built intra-union activist networks, and raised the level of union participation both inside and outside of the classroom.

The developments in Agroindsynd were rapidly generalized more widely, through the intervention of the global union movement, the European Union and the national union education centre. Thus, the development of the trade unions was largely funded and supported from external sources. The ICFTU helped the Moldovan Confederation access European Union funds in 1996–1997 to train 17 tutors in these methods. The Global Union Federations (GUFs) were also drawn into providing assistance. Agroindsynd's GUF, the International Union of Food, Agricultural, Hotel, Restaurant, Catering, Tobacco and Allied Workers' Associations (IUF), approached its partner GUF, the International Federation of Chemical, Energy, Mine and General Workers' Unions (ICEM), and they jointly launched a programme of education aimed at their Moldovan and Ukrainian affiliates (Barbaneagre 1999). The national union education academy, despite limited resources, then played an important role in generalizing these initiatives beyond their original bases to the Moldovan unions more widely (Kiriyak 1999).

Tangible outcomes ensued in both the campaigning and workplace bargaining spheres. The Moldovan unions organized nationwide actions on wage arrears, mobilizing tens of thousands of members in December 1998 and June 1999. Respondents suggested that the groundwork for these mobilizations was, at least in part, the result of the building of social capital through the education programmes. The processes and results of the GUF's two-year educational project for Moldovan and Ukrainian unions have been described elsewhere, and include cases of mobilization and collective bargaining at workplace level (Croucher 2000, 2004). Collective bargaining occurred in the first instance to expand resources for education. Moldovan employers are legally obliged to earmark funds for vocational training. These are frequently underutilized and unions expanded their use of these funds through clauses in workplace collective agreements. In a round of interviews held in 2003, union leaders claimed that about half of their workplace unions were engaging more widely in some form of meaningful bargaining over workplace collective agreements. Sogge (2004) reported that in 2003, local unions affiliated to the national union Syndlukas bargained 48 collective agreements at workplace level, mostly for three-year periods, where none had previously been in any sense negotiated.

The process described above had strict limits. First, it was 'top-down' and small scale. Many of the large number of workplace unions (Agroindsynd had over 1400 in 2000) therefore remained untouched or uninfluenced by it. Second, it was a political initiative driven by a 'Reform Communist' vision not shared by all union leaderships, including at least one of those involved in the educational programmes. Reservations were in some unions linked to a perception of 'foreignness' since the programmes were funded from outside the nation and linked to a 'Western' conception of trade unionism. Therefore, the programme did not simply reinforce one strategy but rather crystallized the main options. The processes under way evoked alarm within the influential Communist Party, but its limits also suggested a stratagem for arresting it.

18.4.2   2000–2010: National-Level Backlash

In 2000, the Communist Party was elected to government and a breakaway from the CSRM was created, Solidaritatea, based on national unions prepared to signal their acceptance of the welfarist form of unionism (Borisov and Clarke 2006). Two entire federations, the Federation of Unions of the Chemical Industry and Energy Workers and the 'Moldsyndcoopcomerc' Federation left the CSRM to join Solidaritatea. In 2003, the Communist Party openly took over the breakaway confederation. At that point, the CSRM claimed over 500 000 members and Solidaritatea some 400 000. In a sustained campaign, the Communist government attacked the CSRM, and Agroindsynd in particular, and sought to have workplace unions transfer their allegiances from one federation to the other.

The ITUC, in its annual report on violations of trade union rights, described in detail how pressure was exerted on workplace unions:

> Syndlukas, the commerce, HORECA and service trade unions, became a target of the government's campaign to force CSRM-affiliated trade unions to switch their affiliation to the Solidaritatea confederation. In May Mr Vladimir Nirka, the head of the commerce, service and catering department of the Chisinau municipality, instructed the enterprise directors to arrange the transfer of the Syndlukas enterprise-level organizations to a trade union affiliated to Solidaritatea. The heads of the Chisinau enterprises that sold non-food products received similar instructions. In the second half of 2006 the department officials organized a number of meetings with the heads of state, municipal and private enterprises, where private entrepreneurs were warned their licences would be cancelled and their activities obstructed should they fail to influence the unions.
>
> The campaign was successful in a number of workplaces. For example, workers at the school catering company 'Adolescencea' voted for transfer of affiliation, under duress. The deputy director of another school catering company, 'Liceist', Ms. Lydia Sarandi, collected workers' signatures without clearly explaining what the signatures were for. Trade union leaders were not informed of the campaign. Later it became apparent that the signatures were needed to draft the 'minutes' of a trade union meeting that 'decided' to withdraw from Syndlukas. The management used these forged minutes to stop transferring union dues to the Syndlukas bank account. Similar tactics were used at the 'Bukurina El' school catering company.
>
> Syndlukas lost nine big company-level organizations, totalling more than 1000 members, as a result of this campaign. (ITUC 2007)

Despite these setbacks, the CSRM continued its educational and bargaining activities, winning clauses in collective agreements such as that in the

Drokiya district whereby employers allocated substantial funds for worker and union activist training. In other collective agreements, employers agreed to pay for workers to attend sanatoria, traditionally a union function. In August 2005, after long and difficult negotiations, the workplace union at the large and important Tiraspolsky bakery concluded a collective agreement with the private management containing clauses on wage payments, health and safety, working hours and rest time, job security, trade union facilities and social activities (Teosa et al. 2007). Solidaritatea affiliates also carried out serious collective bargaining, concluding an agreement with the private company Inkonarm in 2005 after long negotiations throughout 2004.

The extensive and detailed report on Moldovan unions by Teosa et al., completed in 2007, concluded that there was a tendency in both union confederations towards growing articulation between the different levels of union organization, as extra-workplace levels made increased efforts to support workplace unions. This was a response to increasing centrifugal tendencies within the unions whereby workplace unions 'go it alone', as workplace unions did in the Solidaritatea-affiliated metalworkers' federation. Workplace unions continue to retain large subscription funds and are on occasions prepared to cede from national confederations when the level of services is perceived as inadequate. Improved articulation started from a very low level and workplace unions remain insulated from national- and regional-level influences, severely constraining attempts by confederations to induce them to work in particular ways.

Hence, government attempts to shape trade unionism had real but bounded success. Having shifted the balance between the two confederations, the government pushed them towards merger, which has now been completed. This might lead us to expect a more homogenous approach from workplace unions in the future, but our evidence indicates that workplace unions continue to show considerable heterogeneity.

We now analyse three workplaces in the immediate pre-confederation merger period to examine how and why union functions in this industry either remained close to the Communist ideal type, or moved in the 'reform' direction.

18.5   CASE STUDIES: EMPLOYMENT RELATIONS BETWEEN CONFLICT AND COLLABORATION

18.5.1   Introduction

The three case studies are all privatized former state enterprises in the clothing industry. Two belong to foreign investors, and one is owned by former managers. The industry has been mostly privatized to foreign capital and is divided between larger establishments and informal sweat-shops. The union has retained a presence only in the former, so the cases represent a representative cross-section of the unionized sector. Foreign presence has changed perceptions of industry. As one unionist put it: 'our industry does not belong to the Moldovan economy: the owner, materials and the market are all foreign' (interview with union leader, Stalag 2, summer 2006). Hence the cases also reflect more general tendencies in this globalized sector delocalizing eastward in Europe.

The national union, an affiliate of the Solidaritatea confederation, formally pursues 'social dialogue' with employers in line with government policies and foreign recommendations. This is not represented as a simple matter, as a union official points out: 'relations between owners and labour collectives were characterised by open conflict but gradually they have found a common language on at least a number of issues' (interview, 2005). Attempts by union officials to protect workers' rights and conduct bargaining encounter hostility: 'they do not grant unions access to enterprises . . . if a trade union leader is an honest independent person they try to force him into submission' (ibid.). However, the union rejects open confrontation ('going to the streets never achieved anything', ibid.) attempting at best to rely on the state (trade unions 'ought to build trust with the Ministry of Labour', ibid.) and to seek justice though the courts ('we are often involved in law suits to reinstate people in their jobs or to have wages paid', ibid.). The reality of a hostile environment and the rhetoric of dialogue coexist, albeit uneasily. This reflects contradictory pressures from more powerful stakeholders on the one hand, and on the other, a base of semi-autonomous enterprise union leaders whose demands represent diverse and increasingly divergent industrial relations contexts.

The case study enterprises are all deemed good employers, yet in industrial relations terms they are all problematic: at Manifactura 'they work as a single team . . . it is difficult to understand where the director and the enterprise union are . . . they should be separate things'; Stalag 1 'is a good example of partnership, yet even there we have problems with Italian investors'; at Stalag 2 'wages and conditions are normal' but the director is engaged in a long-running court case which he brought against the union, causing uproar. A brief account of the case studies will allow exploration of the nature and origins of the three different forms of unionism.

18.5.2 Case Study 1: Manifactura: Restructuring in Continuity

The company is a single-factory manufacturer of classic outdoor wear. Both organizationally and technologically it has changed little since

1989–1990, largely because of its particular route to privatization as an insider-owned managerially controlled enterprise. A common feature in Russian privatization outcomes, this is unusual in Moldova. The enterprise is well known and prides itself for being a 'people's enterprise' (Morrison 2007a). The position of the union and specifically of its leader, Anna, is intimately related to this context.

Unlike in other enterprises, management took a controlling stake in order to hold on to the company and continue production. The director, an authoritative female figure, is held by Anna to be the company's saviour ('when privatisation came we fought; the factory was privatised to the labour collective' 2006). The labour collective represents the solidaristic community which the soviet trade union was intended to nurture and sustain materially. Such rhetoric is a crucial aspect of enterprise policy, and the union's views at this site are very much in line with the paternalism of the previous Communist government. In reality it overstates continuity with the past while understating the conflicts of interest implicit in the new context.

Entering Manifactura reminded one of the authors of his experience in negotiating his status in Russian factories (Morrison 2007b). Anna would escort Morrison through the gates and stroll down the managerial quarters in the office block. Once in her office she would administer presents and permissions to obsequious workers. Tanya, on the other hand, had to smuggle him into her office after the owners declared any foreigner an unwelcome guest. Once acquaintance was established with her, local managers would volunteer to be interviewed.

The enterprise only survived through painful lay-offs and applying low wages and management's speeding up work rate to a new workforce of young recruits from the provinces. As union confederation sources point out: 'some managers bought it and called it a people's place . . . but then they came to face the same problems [as other companies], they too work for foreign customers' (interview with union official, 2005). Anna herself participated in the process and has become a member of the board of directors. She started as a cadre in production and then became personnel manager. Rumours within the union claim that she became a union leader thanks to her support for the company leadership ('the director chose Anna informally', interview with union leader, 2006). In the words of a union official: 'the director and the union work as a single team . . . this is not a good thing' (interview with union official, 2005).

Anna is therefore an integral part of management. She argues: 'the trade union [confederation] colludes with power. The communists [the party in power till 2009] raised pensions at the expense of wages . . . it is not convenient for us' (2006). She openly challenges the confederation's authority and unilaterally reduces the transfer of dues to the centre, as critically reported by the union leader at Stalag 1. She has built a minority group which made various attempts at overthrowing the union's current 'centrist' leadership.

The job of the union at the enterprise consists primarily in administering corporate welfare. In her own words: 'I am in the middle between the director and shop representatives. Union funds are used to sustain enterprise welfare: holidays, competitions, bonuses. We use corporate channels to communicate with workers. The rationale is to provide an incentive to those who work here' (ibid.).

Critically, yet with a touch of envy, the union leader at Stalag 1 highlights how Anna operates: 'she is good [Anna]. If she needs something the director approves. In the workers' eyes she is good. The director takes care of things: they have a health centre, a resort, a factory shop, a canteen and (proper) lavatories' (ibid. 2006). Welfare is sustained and administered by the union in full accordance with management's wishes.

Despite retaining soviet welfare arrangements, Manifactura is particularly affected by high turnover. It pays low wages and enforces harsh discipline as suggested by workers who later moved to Stalag 1. Union confederation officials went as far as suggesting we approach its workers in the street because of the climate of fear reigning in the factory. Anna admits that 'work has intensified' but her primary concern is the retention of cadres using welfare as a lever.

Accounts provided in interviews with workers and cadres confirm a lack of career prospects, favouritism and suspicion (interviews with selected employees, 2006). Cadres admit a deterioration of relations with subordinates: 'work is quite distressing, always arguing with workers' (respondent 9, foreman). Younger cadres are cynical or dismissive of union welfare: 'I'd prefer they gave less to trade unions and we got higher wages' (respondent 12, economist).

The union continues to attract enthusiastic support from older cadres: 'I've been involved all my life in social activities . . . life in the collective is easier and more interesting' (respondent 2, TU shop leader/pensioner). These workers appreciate the union's work as a terrain for social engagement: 'as soon as I get home I feel like coming back' (respondent 3, TU shop leader/pattern maker). Alleviating the heavy duties of family life, welfare serves the female collective. It is aimed not simply at providing material incentives but also at achieving socialization in a non-conflictual environment.

Other workers' attitudes to this union orientation are lukewarm. A young seamstress confesses: 'I am dead tired because we have to work fast and with quality . . . I do not take part in social life but always go on holiday trips' (respondent 18). Welfare is welcome but the union otherwise does nothing to alleviate taxing working conditions. Anna herself shows awareness of the nature and limitations of her role: 'our main task is administering welfare; what will happen if it is cut further or wages go up too much, will we still be needed?'

The union at Manifactura continues to organize, perform and legitimize itself around a function established in soviet times. Yet it cannot be described simply as arising from the habitus of the agents, very limited restructuring or inertia. The enterprise union's integration into management reflects its adaptation to the circumstances of capitalism in the post-soviet context (Clarke 2007). Nevertheless, the fragility of this form of 'unreformed' unionism is clear.

18.5.3   Case Study 2: Stalag 1: 'Mixed' Unionism

Stalag 1 was once unrivalled for its welfare provisions. This multi-site knitting company previously employed 5000 and followed a different privatization path, with mismanagement leading it to bankruptcy. In about 2001 a small business developed, led by an Italian investor. Recruiting a handful of cadres and skilled workers from the disbanded collective, it has grown into a successful enterprise, cutting and sewing knitted articles for leading European brands. Soaring profits and productivity followed increases in employment, from 250 to the current 800 employees, after a peak of 1000-plus before the crisis. The business now has a new owner, an Italian entrepreneur aiming to create his own brand. Here the old union has survived by coming to terms with 'third Italy' family management, combining ruthless efficiency, quality and paternalism.

Bankruptcy had literally expelled the union from the site. As Tanya, the union representative recollects, the union's reinstatement required thorny negotiations: 'at first they [the first investor] threw boxes at me . . . they said in Italy we have no trade unions, then they understood I am not people's enemy' (2005). In 2009, she greeted the new owner's family as they treated her to an inaugural party, assuring continuity in 'social partnership'. A strong element of continuity with soviet practices was offered by the old management: 'the shop chiefs are all acquaintances from the old enterprise'. This included, until recently, the managing director: 'if I need to fund a trip she will find the money' (2006).

Tanya operates by lobbying the owner and using personal relations. In making her case, she relies on legal provisions: 'according to the law the owner should pay for the union representative'. A novel aspect is represented by clients' ethical concerns as some require a functioning union on site before placing orders. Her approach to members is pervaded by the solidaristic ethos of the collective: ('I empathize with all my colleagues') and charitable aims ('I try to help as much as I can'). Yet, unlike Anna, Tanya admits that wage bargaining is an issue: 'when I ask for wage rises he [the owner] says "I haven't seen any profit yet" but if he didn't he wouldn't be still here'. This prompts her to argue: 'foreign investors are satisfied: good workmanship and cheap labour; they keep us in misery as long as possible' (ibid.). Working conditions are also high on the agenda. Tanya complains of a lack of lavatories, a canteen, ventilation etcetera. She sustains her arguments by reference to the owner's 'interests' and health and safety regulations: 'I told them it is required by the law'.

The limitations of this approach have prompted workers to take things into their own hands, albeit in an uncoordinated fashion. Nadya, a veteran worker, tells of continuous pressure on Tanya and the director about wages ('I have been asking the enterprise more than once to raise wages', summer 2006) and working conditions ('We went to Tanya asking the trade union to act on poor ventilation', ibid.). The union headquarters confirm that workers wrote a petition to the authorities: 'A crisis broke out when ninety workers filed a complaint this summer about bad working conditions' (interview with union official, 2005).

Management responded by opening a direct channel of communication: 'People can voice their demands: we have set up a suggestion box in the changing rooms' (interview with chief economist, summer 2006). Tanya reports engaging workers to 'bring them to reason' and head off their 'fantastic' demands: 'I explain to them where revenues go, that it is not just about wages . . . that is not possible to make extravagant demands . . . the young ones . . . are easy to manipulate' (ibid.).

The union focuses not on such matters but on welfare issues. Tanya's own account of her work and interests revolves essentially around the organization and funding of holiday trips, sport and entertainment events: 'I organize going to operas . . . and other venues for workers.' She even shamelessly admits enjoying free holiday trips on travel agents' accounts. This is also an area where the owner shows a more sympathetic face: 'he gives money for concerts and holidays by the sea' (winter 2005–2006).

Like Anna she believes this to be her primary duty to union members: 'I have been re-elected for twenty years: workers are happy to have holidays with me' (ibid.). Workers themselves, including the young, understand this as the primary union function: 'the trade union is that woman who gives holiday packages' (respondents 4 and 5, seamstresses, summer 2006). On the shop floor, workers are left to their own devices to conduct individual resistance and bargaining: 'here everyone stands up for herself' (ibid.). However, Tanya lacks the human resources required for full-scale soviet-type 'social work': unlike Manifactura, 'there are not many staff employees left' (ibid.). Work organization has also altered the collective's structure: '[in the past] the brigade leader was a father and a mother for the brigade. Now people change work station all the time' (ibid.). Shop management is now directly involved in production and tightly coordinated.

Stalag represents a particular form of departure from established models of unionism. Unlike in Manifactura the union is not part of management yet it continues to rely heavily on their support. Negotiation is the normal way of engagement but, without organizing and mobilizing, it is limited to lobbying and ultimately depends on the owner's good will. Reliance on the law, and ultimately the state, also reflects the traditional union function of legal watchdog and has regained ground as a negotiating tool. Welfare remains the major function of the union but is not aimed at reproducing the soviet labour collective, but rather at guaranteeing minimal cohesion in the face of constant, destabilizing innovation. We can therefore identify a 'mixed' form as the evolutionary trajectory of this union displays distinctive elements of both old and new.

18.5.4   Case Study 3: Stalag 2: Mobilizing Unionism

Stalag 2 was successfully privatized to the old management. As with Stalag 1, it ended in foreign hands in 1998 after initial joint-venture collaboration. The company has thrived; it now supplies branded lines for women in 45 countries. Foreign investors were not saviours of an ailing business. This was a state-brokered hostile takeover followed by bitter confrontation between the union, representing the collective, and the management, mostly aligned with the new German parent company. The presence of open conflict makes it a special, albeit not a unique, case of mobilizing unionism. We chose to carry out in-depth research here to find out whether this was more than a case of mismanagement or clash of personalities as rumoured at the union confederation's headquarters: 'the director and the union leader are both lawyers' (interview with union official, 2006).

The new owners refused from the beginning to comply with both customary and legal rules on pay, grading, working time and the like. The state labour inspectorate called in by the union discovered that the new work scheduling and layout rearrangements were all unlawfully introduced and had led to a doubling of workforce morbidity. Nikita, the union leader, reacted firmly: 'I was told that what they were looking for were low wages and weak trade unions; I resolved: "I will show you *weak* trade unions!"' (summer 2006). The arguments and the legal watchdog role are similar to the previous case but their strategic use is different. They are situated within a wider policy of worker mobilization, open confrontation, appealing to the press and state authorities, and seeking public support. They are therefore clearly novel.

The company retaliated by stopping collection of dues, effectively calling the union's existence into question. Nikita did not limit herself to lobbying ('I went to the Director to ask on what grounds he did so', ibid.) but mobilized members ('we had everyone sign and collected the dues in cash: in three months we re-established the union', ibid.). Such a pattern of action, relying on workers' mobilization, was to be repeated on a larger scale and has become a significant feature for this union, very much unlike the previous cases.

The union began to assume a militant character with Nikita's appointment (focus group with union activists, winter 2006–2007): 'when there is a leader, then people start raising their heads' (shop leader/finisher); this resulted from dissatisfaction with the then incumbent: 'that union leader was the director's "right hand"' (group leader/skilled seamstress). The difference with leaders in previous cases is striking. Moreover the union at Stalag 2 is not a one-woman business, nor is it relying on management and old connections for its operations. A helping hand was offered by the owners themselves as they pressed managers to withdraw from the union; as a result, Nikita explains: 'in soviet times committee members were foremen and brigade leaders – as it is now at Manifactura – this would be pointless now because shop management represents the company's interests'. Unlike confederation officials, Nikita is unconcerned 'because abroad managerial staff are not in the unions' (ibid.). Her lengthy and detailed explanations of meetings, routines and organizational issues are a convincing argument in favour of describing this as a disciplined and well-organized workers' union.

The organization's internal coherence grew over time and with experience. A painstaking series of negotiating rounds, and the daily experience of managing individual and collective grievances, has reinforced solidarities among workers and with the union to create a new ethos: 'Some come to our factory and say that we have strong unions that know how to defend people. They will not defeat us!' (respondent 4, focus group ibid.).

In 2002, the union began to press for negotiations over piece-rate prices, lay-offs and working conditions. A stoppage was planned to support grievances but failed due to a lack of coordination and constant pressure from management. In 2005 similar circumstances recurred. The union manoeuvred carefully, first building up a legal case, and then agitating among workers at general meetings where demands were hammered out in open discussion. In the face of management's obduracy an action was planned in secrecy which defied management expectations of passivity ('Production chiefs . . . did not know what to do', respondent 4, ibid.).

In Nikita's words the action was carried out 'wonderfully, thanks to the quality of the collective'. The aftermath was a legal battle begun by the director over the alleged 'strike' (the right to strike is seriously restricted in Moldova), which ultimately reinforced collective bonds among employees in relation to management.

The union has over the years extended its agenda to issues such as holidays, extra work and unfair dismissals, attempting systematically to bring these areas out of the soviet customary sphere, that is, the discretion of production management. Equally minor disputes over piece-rates, sick leave and the like are not left to personal relations in the shops: 'Every day I [Nikita] take a walk in the shops. Often we solve controversies' (ibid.). This is a long way from Anna and Tanya sitting in their offices waiting to rubber-stamp workers' requests scrutinized by their superiors.

The union has not renounced welfare and customary 'social events'. They remain very much in demand and are on the union agenda (respondent 2, 'New Year gifts, when to organize evening entertainment', ibid.). Now they are used by the union to reinforce bonds between its members. On the ideational terrain, Nikita, in common with other union leaders, frequently sustains her arguments by reference to working mothers' specific needs ('the administration refuses to recognise we are a collective of women', Complaint to the state labour inspector 14 March 2006).

The case demonstrates a long journey of transformation towards a members' union. The union's primary function and main source of legitimacy rests on bargaining on a range of subjects. It has severed its links with management and openly contests issues in the shops. Old functions and ideas have not evaporated; rather, they have been transformed. Overall this represents a substantial departure from soviet unionism. For these reasons we can denominate this a 'reformed' union.

18.6   CONCLUSION

FDI generates real contradictions and sharply contrasting tendencies in state action and 'social dialogue'. Therefore, consolidation of a coherent set of institutions in industrial relations, contributing to a stable, regulated political economy as envisaged by institutionalists in 'varieties of capitalism' (VoC) models, currently appears unlikely. In this respect, North makes a relevant point in asserting the importance of 'rules of the game', singularly lacking in our context. Regulationist accounts, it has been noted by others, tend to overstate coherence and to overlook contradictions (Gambino 2003; Thompson 2003). The lack of coherence evident in the post-Communist context shows acute forms of these wider issues. Current institutional arrangements are particularly unstable, dysfunctional, fragile and heterogenous, since the key interests impinging on them exist outside of the (primarily national) institutional framework. As we have seen, these contradictions are especially evident in the trade union case.

Our cases are taken from unions affiliated to the 'pro-Communist' federation rather than from the federation which earlier undertook the most serious reform efforts. The case study enterprise unions nevertheless display quite different evolutionary paths. Workplace-level bargaining is emerging as one significant function as welfare declines, although the latter still plays a considerable role; the legal watchdog function is reviving. In political terms, unions call upon the state to protect local employees against abusive investors, fuelling the rhetoric if not the practice of positing local stakeholders' interests against those of foreign capital. The state has continued its deregulation of labour law, reducing the possibilities for unions to influence management. This in turn limits prospects for union renewal through these traditional methods, but simultaneously suggests alternative, more direct forms of action which, as we have seen, have already been used.

If the prospects of union renewal are limited by continuing liberalization of labour markets, the current regulatory paradigm also threatens to increase certain costs on employers. Employers face a restricted labour supply due to extensive exit in the forms of turnover and migration. They may also encounter intensified problems such as employee theft identified as an issue by other researchers (Morrison 2003; Sacchetto 2011). These are symptoms of low levels of employer–employee interdependence, associated with low-trust relations that reduce employee willingness to engage in internal entrepreneurship or socialize tacit knowledge (Whitley 1999). This in turn imposes certain costs on Moldova more widely since it increases the likelihood of FDI industries being effectively locked into the lowest-value-added forms of work in the international division of labour, thereby restricting development possibilities.

REFERENCES

Barbaneagre, V. (1999), 'Invatamantul a trezit interesul activului syndical', in FGSRM, *Conferinta practico-scientifica 'Problemele invatamantului syndical la etapa actuala'*, Chisinau: FGSRM, pp. 59–65.
Bognanno, M.F., M.P. Keane and D. Yang (2005), 'The influence of wages and industrial relations environments on the production location decisions of US multi-national corporations', *Industrial and Labor Relations Review*, **58**, 171–200.
Bohle, D. and B. Greskovits (2006), 'Capitalism without compromise: strong business and weak labour in Eastern Europe's new transnational industries', *Studies in Comparative International Development*, **41** (1), 3–25.

Borisov, V. and S. Clarke (2006), 'The rise and fall of social partnership in postsocialist Europe: the commonwealth of independent states', *Industrial Relations Journal*, **37** (6), 607–629.

Centrul Didactico-Metodic al Syndicatelor din Moldova (1998), *Negocierea Contractului Colectiv de Munca*, Chisinau: CDMSM.

Clarke, Simon (2007), *The Development of Russian Capitalism*, London: Routledge.

Cook, W. (1997), 'The influence of industrial relations factors on US direct investment abroad', *Industrial and Labor Relations Review*, **51**, 3–17.

Croucher, R. (2000), 'Trade union education and union strategy: renewing agricultural unions in Moldova, the Ukraine and Russia', *South East Europe Review*, **3** (1), 157–169.

Croucher, R. (2004), 'The impact of trade union education: experience from three countries in Eastern Europe', *European Journal of Industrial Relations*, **10** (1), 90–109.

Croucher, Richard and Elizabeth Cotton (2009), *Global Unions, Global Business. Global Union Federations and International Business*, London: Middlesex University Press.

Danilovich, H. and R. Croucher (2011), 'Labour management in Belarus: transcendent retrogression', *Journal of Communist Studies and Transition Politics*, **27** (2), 241–262.

Feicht, Roland (2010), *Aktuelle Entwicklungen in Südosteuropa: Wirtschaftskrise, politische Lage und Herausforderungen für die Gewerkschaften*, Berlin: Friedrich Ebert Stiftung, Referat Mittel- und Osteuropa.

Feidel-Mertz, H. (1964), *Zur Ideologie der Arbeiterbildung*, Frankfurt am Main: Europäische Verlaganstalt.

Gambino, Ferruccio (2003), 'A critique of the Fordism of the regulation school', in Werner Bonefeld (ed.), *Revolutionary Writing: Common Sense Essays In Post-Political Politics Writing*, New York: Autonomedia.

Hannigan, T.A. (2005), *Managing Tomorrow's High-Performance Trade Unions*, Hartford, CT: Information Age Publishing.

ITUC (2007), *Annual Survey of Violations of Trade Union Rights*, Brussels: ITUC.

Kiriyak, P. (1999), 'Instruirea trebuie sa contribuie la consolidarea miscarii syndicale', in FGSRM (ed.), *Conferinta practico-scientifica 'Problemele invatamantului syndical le etapa actuala'*, Chisinau: FGRSM, pp. 9–23.

Korosteleva, Julia (2007), 'Belarus: heading towards state capitalism?' in David Lane and Martin Myant (eds), *Varieties of Capitalism in Post-Communist Countries*, Basingstoke: Palgrave Macmillan, pp. 221–238.

Lane, David and Martin Myant (eds) (2007), *Varieties of Capitalism in Post-Communist Countries*, Basingstoke: Palgrave Macmillan.

Meardi, G. (2007), 'Multinationals in the new EU member states and the revitalisation of trade unions', *Debatte: Journal of Contemporary Central and Eastern Europe*, **15** (2), 177–193.

Meyer, K.E. (2001), 'Institutions, transaction costs, and entry mode choice in Eastern Europe', *Journal of International Business Studies*, **32**, 357–367.

Meyer, K.E. and M.W. Peng (2005), 'Probing theoretically into Central and Eastern Europe: transactions, resources and institutions', *Journal of International Business Studies*, **36**, 600–621.

Moran, P. and S. Ghoshal (1999), 'Markets, firms and the process of economic development', *Academy of Management Review*, **24** (3), 390–412.

Morrison, C. (2003), 'Labour and technological discipline: chaos and order in a Russian textile company', *Research in Economic Anthropology*, **22**, 71–197.

Morrison, C. (2007a), 'Ownership and management in holding companies and the future of Russian textiles', *Post-Communist Economies*, **19** (2), 167–186.

Morrison, C. (2007b), *A Russian Factory Enters the Market Economy*, London: Routledge.

Mykhnenko, Vlad (2007), 'Poland and Ukraine: institutional structures and economic performance', in David Lane and Martin Myant (eds), *Varieties of Capitalism in Post-Communist Countries*, Basingstoke: Palgrave Macmillan, pp. 124–148.

Noelke, A. and A. Vliegenhart (2009), 'Enlarging the varieties of capitalism: the emergence of dependent market economies in East Central Europe', *World Politics*, **61**, 670–702.

North, Douglass (1990), *Institutions, Institutional Change and Economic Performance*, Cambridge: Cambridge University Press.

Petkov, K. (1998), 'Globalization and the syndicates from the Central and East Europe', paper presented to regional seminar for workers' organizations on Globalization and Trade Unions in Central and Eastern Europe, Budapest.

Sacchetto, Devi (ed.) (2011), *Ai Margini dell'Unione Europea, Spostamenti e insediamenti a Oriente*, Roma: Carocci.

Sogge, D. (2004), 'Turning the problem around: FNV Mondiaal in Eastern Europe and the Soviet Unions', Amsterdam: Report for the Netherlands Ministry for Foreign Affairs and FNV Mondiaal.

Soulsby, A. and E. Clark (2007), 'Organization theory and the post-socialist transformation: contributions to organizational knowledge', *Human Relations*, **60** (10), 1419–1442.

Teosa, V., V. Moshnyaga and E. Babare (2007), 'Trade Unions of the Republic of Moldova', INTAS Project Report.

Thirkell, J.E.M., J. Petkov and S. Vickerstaff (1998), *The Transformation of Labour Relations: Restructuring and Privatization in Eastern Europe and Russia*, Oxford: Oxford University Press.

Tholen, Jochen (2007), *Labour Relations in Central Europe: The Impact of Multinational's Money*, Aldershot: Ashgate.

Thompson, P. (2003), 'Disconnected capitalism: or why employers can't keep their side of the bargain', *Work, Employment and Society*, **17** (2), 359–378.

Webb, Sydney and Beatrice Webb (1897), *Industrial Democracy*, New York: Longmans, Green & Co.

Whitley, Richard (1999), *Divergent Capitalisms: Social Structure and Change of Business Systems*, Oxford: Oxford University Press.

Williamson, O.E. (1975), *Markets and Hierarchies, Analysis and Antitrust Implications: A Study in the Economics of Internal Organization*, New York: Free Press.

19 Explaining persistence of dysfunctionality in post-Communist transformation

Martin Upchurch

19.1 INTRODUCTION

Spatial and socio-political variants continue to exist within post-Communist transformation states. Marketization, privatization and liberalization have sometimes stalled or been delayed, and in some transformation countries the role of the state in maintaining control over the production and distribution of goods and services remains strong. Most importantly, two key aspects of market failure are evident across the transformation states. First, predictions from orthodox economists of economic convergence with the West have failed to materialize. Second, crime, corruption and informal working persist and in many cases have become more prominent in both absolute and relative measurement. As such the market appears 'dysfunctional', exhibiting continuing inefficiencies. Dysfunctionality, and its persistence, is thus characterized by inefficient forms of market regulation, the lack of regard for the rule of law, together with continuing problems of crime, corruption and state capture models of governance. It is argued in this chapter that the persistence of dysfunction is a consequence of the adoption of a particular model of labour exploitation. The associated poor business ethics and weak standards of corporate governance are a consequence of the combination of market liberalization, dependence on labour exploitation for comparative advantage, and the abandonment of one-party authority over control of industrial production. This chemistry of events allowed rapacious rent-seeking by individuals well placed to benefit from the newly deregulated regime (Filatov 1994). In turn, this has created political and economic space for the informal economy to grow and mafia crime and corruption to flourish.

The chapter reviews evidence of the persistence of both economic divergence and informal working and 'crony' or 'wild' capitalism within these states. Orthodox explanations of the persistence of market failure and dysfunction are reviewed, and alternative heterodox explanations are presented. The chapter concludes that 'dysfunctional' capitalist activity is a product of both path-dependent and path-shaping activity, and that persistence may be explained by the process of uneven and combined development, in which old practices sit side by side with new. In effect, 'dysfunctional' practices are themselves embedded.

19.2 THE LACK OF ECONOMIC CONVERGENCE

In order to understand the persistence of dysfunctionality we need first to consider the economic model of transformation. The dominant economic model, revealed in neoliberal prescriptions applied by governments, international financial institutions and their advisors, was that of the establishment of comparative advantage through trade integration, capital shift and equalization of marginal profit rates. This Heckscher–Ohlin–Samuelson international free trade model would anticipate the development of comparative advantage in national production regimes, reinforced by capital transfers and foreign direct investment in the cheaper labour economies of the East, complemented by labour migration in the opposite direction (Dunford and Smith 2004). The technology gap between East and West would be bridged by the process of investment and this would in turn lead to a closure of the productivity gap. This would then act to equalize marginal profit rates as labour costs and rates of return on capital investment converged. Shock therapy was designed to act as an enabling vehicle of this process, by clearing the post-Communist market of labour rigidities, and allowing investment opportunities in both privatized formerly state-owned industries and greenfield industry. The opening of markets, aided in some states by accession to the European Union (EU), would also act as a spur for convergence. However, after 20 years and more of post-Communist transformation, while there is clear evidence of trade integration, the evidence on convergence is weak. On trade integration the World Bank finds:

> Trade integration in the transition (formerly centrally planned) ECA countries – measured by the sum of merchandise exports and imports as a share of GDP in purchasing power parity – rose from 20 percent in 1994 to around 50 percent in 2008, about 10–15 percentage points higher than in developing East Asia and Latin America. Turkey saw an increase from 10 percent to 30 percent over the same period. The averages mask substantial variation across subregions – the ratio ranged from a median value of around 35 percent in the South Caucasus, Central Asia and Moldova, where exports are generally intensive in natural resources and unskilled labor, to nearly 85 percent in the new member states of the European Union and Croatia, where exports are intensive in capital and skilled labor. (World Bank 2010, 1)

Indeed, the process of integration into the world economy was associated with and led by export-led development in transformation countries, alongside credit expansion designed to help build domestic capital formation and consumer demand (EBRD 2010, v). However, this growth did not lead to convergence. Evidence of convergence (or lack of convergence) has been monitored by international financial institutions (IFIs) such as the European Bank for Reconstruction and Development (EBRD), the International Monetary Fund (IMF) and the World Bank. The World Bank, for example, has produced two reports, ten years and 20 years on from 1989 (World Bank 2002, 2010). Three key areas are identified by the IFIs for measurement where lack of convergence can be observed, as described below.

19.2.1 Low Rates of Growth of Production

The recovery of individual economies from the initial shock of the fall of the command economy has been both slow and extremely uneven. Gross domestic product (GDP) growth rates over the last 20 years has reached 3 per cent in Poland, has peaked at no more than 0.8 per cent in Romania and Bulgaria, while that of the Baltic States has hardly grown at all. Poland was the first country to recover to 1989 levels of production, which it achieved in 1995, followed by Slovenia (1998) and Hungary (2000). For many other transformation states production levels have still not reached their 1989 levels. Serbia and Ukraine, for example, are still at about 70 per cent of 1989 levels of production, while Latvia is languishing with production levels in 2010 only 56 per cent of 1989 levels:[1]

> At the beginning of the new millennium, a profound divide lies between Central and Southeastern Europe (SEE) and the Baltics (CSB) and the Commonwealth of Independent States (CIS). In the CSB, officially measured gross domestic product (GDP) bounced back from a transition recession, recovered to its 1990 level by 1998, and exceeded that level by 6 percent in 2000. However, in the CIS GDP in 2000 stood at only 63 percent of its 1990 level. While GDP in Poland, the most populous country in the CSB, increased by more than 40 percent between 1990 and 1999, it shrank by 40 percent during the same period in the Russian Federation, the most populous country in the CIS. (World Bank 2002)

19.2.2 Unevenness and Disparity

The difficult return to 1989 production levels also has a geo-economic dimension. Those states geographically closest to the European Union generally have higher totals of production relative to 1989, and higher income per capita. Those former Communist states which have become full members of the EU have also fared better than later members, or non-members. Both Slovenia and the Czech Republic, for example, record income levels per capita closest to the EU-15 median at approximately 75 per cent in 2008 (measured in purchasing power parity – PPP). However, most CIS states are between 5 and 10 per cent, and the majority of EU accession states are at about 50 per cent (World Bank 2010, 26). There is evidence of convergence of incomes since 1998, but this is often from a very low starting point measured in PPP. Nominal wage levels remain much smaller than in the West. The convergence that has taken place is largely explained by a growth of real wages from 2003 to the financial crash of 2008. This growth followed a major fall in real wage growth in the immediate period after 1989, and in some countries, such as Bulgaria and Lithuania, the recent growth is still not enough to bring real wages back to the levels of 1989 (Onaran 2010).

19.2.3 More Informal Working

There is a continuation of a heavy presence of informal working within the post-Communist states. Data on informal working are difficult to assemble both because of lack of data officially assembled at government level, and because of the difficulties of definition, and as a consequence are generally measured by independent surveys. Schneider (2003, 26) estimates, with figures from a variety of sources, 'that the average size (measured as proportion of GDP) of the shadow economy in the nine CEE Transition Countries has increased from 23.4 percent for the years 1990–1993 to 29.2 percent in 2000–2001'. Within the countries of the former Soviet Union the average size of the informal economy reached 44.8 per cent in 2001, an increase from an estimated 35.7 per cent estimated for 1990–1993 by Johnson et al. (1997). While informal working has also been growing in the states of the EU-15, it has grown at a lower overall level and not by as fast a rate as in the post-Communist states. This is supported by evidence collected by Galgóczi and Mermet (2003) on wage share. Estimates were that the share of wages in the GDP of the ten Central and Eastern European countries is 40.5 per cent on average, while the value for the EU-15 member states is 59 per cent. Rather than falling as a share of all wages, informal working seems still to be growing.

The phenomena of 'jobless growth' is apparent across the region, at a scale larger than is evident in the countries of the EU-15 (Boeri and Garibaldi 2006). Employment levels are depressed and decreasing in total, while unemployment levels increase. Furthermore the evidence would suggest that the 2008 financial crisis has generally had more severe effects in the post-Communist states than in most of Western Europe. Hungary, Latvia and Romania have resorted to IMF credit, but the associated level of austerity introduced as part of the package is more intense than

Western European comparisons, including that of the 'peripheral' states of Portugal, Ireland, Greece and Spain (Onaran 2010). In Latvia, for example, public sector wages have been cut by 35 per cent and pensions by 10 per cent, while VAT has been increased from 18 to 21 per cent. In other countries, such as Estonia and Lithuania, deep cuts of 20 per cent have also been enforced as part of austerity measures (Gligorov et al. 2009). But although the net result of the persistence of the above features has been a miserable one for the mass of working people, it has been a lucrative one for the elite. Inequality has increased markedly. Pre-transition Gini coefficients were around the 0.25 mark across the region, but had increased to levels approaching 0.36 by 2005 (AMECO database). The average coefficient for the EU-15 in 2005 was 0.31,[2] so only in the area of inequality has convergence taken place.

19.3   'WILD' OR 'CRONY CAPITALISM'

A second, and undoubtedly associated problem of transformation has been the persistence of non-regulated or poorly regulated forms of economic behaviour. The existence of large informal, black or grey economies, for example, appears inextricably linked to crony capitalism and crime and the wider problems of what may be termed 'wild' capitalism whereby non-documented working is encouraged as illegal working. Indeed, corruption and bribery remain endemic in ex-Soviet, Central East and South East Europe (SEE) states. A recent survey indicates that 31 per cent of survey respondents claim to have failed to win a contract because of a competitor's bribes to the purchaser (Gosztonyi and Bray 2009). The 2010 Transition Report from the European Bank for Reconstruction and Development finds that corruption 'is the top concern for businesses in eight of the transition countries, and among the top three in another third of them' (EBRD 2010, 83). Transformation states also score at the more 'corrupt' end of the Transparency International's Corruption Perceptions Index. Serbia, for example, stands alongside Albania and Bosnia Herzogovina as the least transparent states in Europe, while Russia and the states of the CIS score even lower on transparency.[3]

Such 'wild' capitalism has a number of distinct associated features. There is a weakening of social solidarity and fair income distribution as social safety nets are downscaled or withdrawn in an effort to 'roll back' the scope and content of responsibility of government. This decline of the salience of social solidarity is accompanied by an ideological emphasis on individualism as the mantra of the free market pervades everyday discourse and practice. In Gramscian terms, some commentators have noted a process of *trasformismo*, whereby a revolution in ideology takes place 'from above' as elite discourse freezes out political space and opportunity for alternatives 'from below' (Morton 2007; Simon 2010). Such ideological restructuring, at least in the immediate years following the upheavals of 1989, was aided and abetted by political elites, management consultants and some academics from Western business schools (for a critique of this process in Serbia see Cicmil and Upchurch 2006). The downgrading of the protective labour codes has also enabled the process of informalization whereby regulations on dismissals and redundancies as well as pension provision have been loosened in an effort to clear labour market 'rigidities'. Indeed, such downgrading of labour protection has been a major focus of IFI conditionality in the granting of loans and grants (Forteza and Rama 2001; Upchurch 2009).

A concomitant absence of rules and regulations, or sometimes deliberate ignoring of regulations governing the behaviour of corporations and corporate elites within wider society and the market, can also be discerned (Aglietta and Rebérioux 2005). This is partly engendered by states wishing to create favourable conditions for foreign direct investment, partly by the collapse of party authority and command planning, and partly by delayed societal adjustment to new regimes of practice. There is also a preponderance of weak and underdeveloped agencies within 'civil society' (Howard 2003), which might otherwise have been able to keep selfish corporate and individual interests in check. This 'weak' civil society in most cases sits side by side with a strong state, containing many authoritarian features of the past. However, such a strong state may contain dominant traits of administrative corruption based on asymmetry of information between politicians and civil servants whereby 'benevolent politicians (if any) are just not informed about misdemeanour of their subordinates' (Begović 2005, 3). Notable by their absence may be, as Lane Bruner (2002, 180) suggests in the case of Russia, 'Public education, strong and independent judiciaries, a free press, federal oversight through security exchange commissions, the rule of law, enforceable private contracts, and numerous other institutions and the values that support them must be in place'.

Political, economic and social space is thus created whereby norms of expected behaviour within society are formed which emphasize personal rent-seeking at the expense of 'ethical' business behaviour. The informal 'rules of the game' thus sit side by side with efforts to regulate behaviour in terms of Western 'best practice'. Most crucially, wild capitalism, and its crony variant, is recognizable by the continuance of the control of regime 'insiders', who have often bought up privatized concerns to maintain and enhance their wealth and privilege. Woods (2006, 121), for example, reports on the process in Russia whereby Yeltsin's loans-for-shares programme of privatization 'left controlling stakes in the newly privatised companies firmly in the hands of newly established financial institutions' and in so doing 'conferred enormous power on the oligarchs or financial-industrial groups'. The process of insider acquisition of economic power also expands into the political arena. In Serbia, for example, many privatized concerns passed directly into the hands of key members of political parties. As Pesic (2007, 16) records:

> The 17 biggest companies founded by the government of Serbia are managed by the parties that comprise the ruling coalition at the national level – the managing boards, presidents and directors – are compiled and by a quota-system are divided up among each of the parties of the ruling coalition which appoint the management positions as if the companies were their own property. All other public companies – about 500 – are in the hands of the ruling coalitions at the local levels.

In such a scenario the door is opened for 'state capture' models of political process, whereby competing elites jostle for privilege and position while having a collective vested interest in preserving oligarchical and clientelist systems of governance. In these 'capture economies' oligarchs and captor firms do not pressure states to regulate through institutions, rather they seek to enhance their property rights by directly purchasing advantages from the state (Hellman et al. 2000).

The very nature of 'transformation', its speed of application and the deliberative mechanisms engendered by the state, thus militate against any easy formation of 'new entrant' entrepreneurs from within the mass of population. The existing minority ruling elite attached to the old Communist Parties were in a position of power, they held the necessary networks and resources, and controlled production of goods and services as a distinct interest group or class. They seized the chance to become the new economic power elite under market capitalism. Of course, such an elite will need to socially reproduce itself if the current structure of power is not to be destabilised. As Hankiss (1990) and Haynes and Husan (2002) suggest, the old *nomenklatura* simply moved sideways from command to market economy in an orgy of personal asset accumulation and insider dealing as privatization of state assets gathered pace. The dominant political aspiration under transformation may have been social democracy, but there remained a persistence of practice characterized by authoritarianism, state patronage and clientelism.

Wild capitalism clearly produces inefficiencies within the economic and political system. The high income inequality generated by wild capitalism militates against the creation of efficient distribution of disposable income necessary for effective consumer demand. It creates a low aggregate propensity for tax collection which in turn reduces aggregate state revenue and subsequent infrastructure development. Capital and financial markets remain underdeveloped or starved of sufficient funds, further exacerbating problems for potential new entrants into the business arena. The weak or non-existent business ethics, gangsterism and corruption are barriers to outsider and institutional investors seeking a safe home for their investment. Money made in the country leaves the country. Assets of the elite have been 'tunnelled' into offshore accounts, and dynasties are created as a result. Cronyism and corruption are breeding grounds for the (legal) process of 'tunnelling' whereby private individuals are 'paid' in shares in the company which are then cashed in overseas bank accounts:

> They were also unable to contain tunneling, the expropriation of assets and income belonging to minority shareholders, and theft through either rule of law or administrative control. Though many of these countries did encourage new entry early in the transition, the capture of the state by a narrow set of vested enterprises – old enterprises and well-connected early entrants – discouraged further entry and created a poor investment climate, resulting in a pattern of protection and selective encouragement. (World Bank 2002, xvii)

The process of tunnelling and private acquisition of funds and assets was clearly exacerbated and encouraged by the credit boom within many post-Communist countries. Latvia provides an example *in extremis* whereby 'destructive rent seeking' fed by external credit led to a boom in real estate prices at the expense of productive investment (Sommers and Bērziņš 2011, 137).

Such problems are recognized by international agencies as they attempt to encourage transformation states to tackle corruption and economic crime. Most especially the United Nations Development Programme (UNDP) has developed an Anti-Corruption Practitioners Network. There is special focus on the Commonwealth of Independent States (CIS) and post-conflict transformation countries such as Serbia and Bosnia & Herzogovina. However, prospects for reform do not look favourable. For example in the Serbian case, the government has created a range of anti-corruption measures and institutions including an internal anti-corruption task force, and measures to depoliticize the civil service. But action on the ground appears slow and constrained by lack of resources. An independent report on progress commissioned by the UNDP in 2007 concluded that: 'Although there have been major improvements in a range of development areas in recent years, progress in respect to mitigating corruption has been partial and slow' (UNDP 2007, 5). In addition the resources, both technical and in terms of manpower, available to the police force to investigate corruption were found by the report to be 'not sufficient' (ibid:, 23). Indeed, Serbia was still ranked 97th out of 169 countries in the Transparency International Corruption Perception Index[4] in 2007.

Of course, channelling of corporate profits into personal accounts of shareholders is not unique to post-Communist states, it is a practice common (and often legal) among Western elites as well. Bribery associated with crime and corruption is also an international phenomenon, and as Transparency International reports: 'just four of 36 countries party to the OECD Anti-Bribery Convention are active enforcers. There is moderate enforcement in 11 and little to no enforcement in the 21 remaining countries. Such performance throws into question governments' commitments and threatens to destabilise the definitive legal instrument to fight international bribery' (Transparency International, 2009, 6). Corruption may be endemic in all market-based systems; the phrase 'there ain't no such thing as a free lunch' (TANSTAAFL), for example, has its origins in 1930s America, in a country also associated with 'pork barrel' politics. We are mindful of Habermas's (1987 [1981]) theoretical construct of the 'lifeworld'. This allows us to imagine the possibility of self-deceptive norms of behaviour continuing, despite the tendency of external norms to 'colonize' under the power and authority of external agencies such as the international financial institutions or the EU.

19.4   ORTHODOX EXPLANATIONS OF PERSISTENCE

Orthodox economic explanations for the lack of convergence focus on a number of explanations. These explanations include claims *inter alia* that in terms of production statistics, the pre-transformation states had falsely calculated totals for production (Åslund 2001) and that the 'fall' in production post-transformation is exaggerated as a result. However, even given the likelihood of such false calculation the falls in output have been excessive, and over a 20-year period consistency in statistical production has been achieved. Other commentators point to the impact of external trade shocks, a mismatch in aggregate demand and supply of goods and services, or simply policy mistakes as the cause of falls in output (see Turley and Luke 2011, 242–243 for a review of these arguments). Some also point to a 'theory of disorganization' as an explanatory factor whereby existing supply chains under the command economy have been broken by the turn to the market, and new supply chains have not yet developed in response (Blanchard and Kremer 1997; Roland and Verdier 1999).

More salient are the possible hypotheses presented by Lucas (1990) in addressing the problem of why capital generally does not flow from rich to poor countries. He suggests, in respect to underdeveloped economies, that human capital effects, political risk and barriers to entry in profitable sectors are better explanatory factors for the lack of convergence than theories which depend on capital mobility. But most transformation states had high levels of human capital, skills, literacy and education. This would make their potential experience different from the underdeveloped countries alluded to within Lucas's argument.

The above explanations, which all may have some validity in the short term, begin to appear unsatisfactory given the extended period of more than 20 years of transition, in which output levels, while sometimes growing have struggled in both relative and absolute terms. Neither do they necessarily explain lack of convergence in other indicators, such as labour market participation, or give reasons to explain the relative increase in informal working.

The persistence of wild capitalism is explained in orthodox accounts primarily by agency factors linked to blockages to reforms. Such 'blockage', it is suggested, is engendered by corrupt insiders with vested interests (Gustafson 1999; Bruner 2002; Peev 2002; Harper 2006). For proponents of neoliberal restructuring the key question is then how such features of blocked reform can be overcome (e.g. Havrylyshyn and Odling-Smee 2000). The World Bank also adopts the position in its working papers that many of the features of wild capitalism, including cronyism, crime and corruption, are temporary features that can be overcome by further institutional reform. In its 2002 report on transition the Bank focuses attention on removing obstacles to 'new entrants' into the business system who may rise and challenge 'oligarchs and insiders' (World Bank 2002, xxii). The report (2002, 106) also attempts to contextualize the problem of lack of reform by reference to the competitiveness (or not) of the individual political systems within each state. 'Concentrated' political regimes (e.g. Croatia, Bulgaria, Russia), it is argued, are more open to 'state capture' and reform blockage than 'competitive' regimes (e.g. Poland, Slovenia, Hungary). The 2010 report focuses (almost impenetrably to non-specialists) on the 'reforms' thought necessary in the financial sector in order to smooth the operation of financial markets in the region (World Bank 2010). The necessity of tackling the 'vested interests' within post-Communist states is also a recurring theme within IMF documents. Such vested interests, it is argued, might be overcome 'through the emergence of a strong leader willing to take on the vested interests, or from the political clout of a growing middle class, or pressure from foreign competitors and international financial institutions' (IMF 2000).

Other commentators offer cultural and historical explanations for the persistence of bribery and corruption. In particular, the (relative) lack of corruption in Western countries is explained by religious tradition, whereby countries which have a background of British colonial rule, with Protestant origins and a long exposure to 'democracy' are less likely to experience corruption than poorer, non-English-speaking, non-Protestant countries (see, for example La Porta et al. 1999; Treisman 2000). One culturalist argument put forward to explain continuing corruption comes from the 'Slavic' tradition depicted in Serbia. That is to say that within Serbian popular tradition it is considered perfectly acceptable to bribe someone in order to oil the wheels of business. Commercial bribery becomes acceptable when local or national public authorities remain impassive to the problem, or engage in corruption on a widespread basis themselves. Thus: 'Popular tradition tacitly approves and has great understanding for an individual who by bribery expedites or receives certain decisions or settlement, because it knows that the state administration or authorities, or state employees who are representatives of the authorities, can always find an excuse for not issuing a ruling'(Antonić et al. n.d., 26).

However, it would be mendacious, as in the above examples, to explain the high incidence of corruption, cronyism and 'wild' capitalism purely by ethno-pathology. Structural factors must also be considered. For example, 'Anglo-Saxon', Protestant countries have long held a dominant position in the world economy, and would have accessed and controlled markets through the exercise of power relations which reflected their dominance. Many British ex-colonies also now score badly on indices of corruption. Corruption may also be more nuanced and subtle in advanced Western democracies, manifesting itself in informal networks and given as contractual favours rather than as hard bribes. Tunnelling of share options, corporate raiding and management buy-ins are common features of 'Western' capitalism, and are perfectly legal practices which embed excess and personal gain. Reward systems of shares and bonus payments also operate on a mimetic basis, reinforcing excess by benchmarking 'median' rates determined by uncontested remuneration committees. In reality, there is an interplay between structural and agency factors which offers a more reliable explanation of corruption. In transformation states this interplay is spurred by opportunities created by privatization of state assets and deregulation of labour markets.

19.5   GRADUALISM AND SOCIAL CAPITAL?

Joseph Stiglitz and other liberal critics of the IFIs have adopted an institutionalist perspective on reform and have argued against the 'shock therapy' position. Stiglitz does not reject the privatization and reform process but argues for 'gradualization', recognizing institutional differences between countries, and supporting the need for institutional preconditions which include the building up of social and political capital to enable the necessary reforms (Stiglitz 1999). The International Monetary Fund has recognized the problem alluded to by Stiglitz in its 'Second Generation Reforms' in terms of the lack of social capital which might act as a check to the power and authority of dominant and sometimes corrupt elites. In addressing the IMF on the necessity of social capital development in post-Communist regimes, Fukuyama argues that: 'the economic function of social capital is to reduce the transaction costs associated with formal coordination mechanisms like contracts, hierarchies, bureaucratic rules, and the like' (Fukuyama 1999). Indeed, the IMF, in its Operational Guidelines (2006, para.7), has included trade unions in its description of civil society organizations which may be included in its rubric of 'social capital'. The guidelines state that: 'Staff should encourage the authorities to engage in a transparent participatory process . . . and be prepared to assist the authorities . . . by meeting with various interest or political groups (that is) parliamentary committees, trade unions, business groups etc.' Such an approach is also endorsed by the World Bank in a report published in 2008 by its Social Development Department (World Bank 2008). It advocates policy based on 'political economy' because:

> Development practitioners engaged in policy dialogue often have in-depth knowledge about the political economy of the contexts where they work, but their expertise tends to remain 'hidden' due to the sensitivity of such issues in an ostensibly technical relationship with the client government. (World Bank 2008, i)

In developing the approach of practitioner engagement, 'political economy' and participation the World Bank has also highlighted the positive role of trade unions and collective bargaining in reducing relative poverty. The Bank collected evidence to show that:

> union density . . . appears to have little or no impact on comparative labour market performance . . . there is, however, one significant exception . . . high union density is associated with compression of wage distribution and a reduction of earnings inequality. (World Bank 2003)

However, the reliance on contextual framework, participatory approaches and 'political economy' remains problematic for the IFIs if fundamental divisions within societies under scrutiny are denied, obscured or obfuscated. Trade unions, to take a key example, are always likely to prove an obstacle to IFI conditionality and policy prescription because so much of the agenda of the IFIs adversely affect workers' collective interest. Trade unions inevitably address issues of class-based division within society which may prove uncomfortable to IFI policy based on establishing national business competiveness. Trade union interest representation, in contrast to many other agents within civil society, directly challenges existing power relationships between capital and labour, and is likely to be more disruptive of 'consensus' than may otherwise be the case with many civil society organizations.

Discussion papers commissioned by the World Bank do in fact begin to address this problem (Mosse 2004), by differentiating participation as a vehicle for empowerment by which poorer groups can have the power to do things, against those for which empowerment allows them to have power over things or people within the context of a struggle for resources (Nelson and Wright 1994). This conundrum between power over and power to do poses problems for policy which relies on the development of social capital for its theoretical and practical base. Policy solutions will remain elusive so long as social capital is considered a class- 'neutral' transformative vehicle. This is because, as Das (2006) has observed, social capital can lubricate the capitalist production regime, as in a partnership orientation, or obstruct it as in a class conflict orientation. Such tensions within a framework of social capital posed by the role of trade unions are apparent in the discourse of the IFIs in offering explanations of dysfunction. Most often the 'problem' is presented as one of ambiguity and complexity, rather than one of class-differentiated interests. Thus, in its 2008 report the World Bank refers to 'the experience of operational teams that work in complex political economies' (2008, i). In respect of this conundrum of 'complexity' and 'ambiguity', Upchurch and Weltman (2008) have argued through textual analysis that the IFI approach is little more than a form of 'utopian liberalism . . . (whereby) a false *harmony of interests* is presumed between capital and labour that in reality cannot be bridged'.

Given this obfuscation of reality it may not be so surprising that the World Bank and other agencies continue to struggle to explain dysfunction by simply addressing the problem through the lens of further market tampering. To take the analysis further we may need to view wild capitalism not as a temporary deflection from normative market efficiency, but rather as a permanent or embedded feature of transformation. Alternative explanations of the persistence of 'dysfunctionality' are necessary which avoid the utopianism of liberal economic normative thought.

19.6   SOME ALTERNATIVE AND CRITICAL EXPLANATIONS

While neoliberal prescription promulgates the argument that blockages to progress are simply a product of delayed 'reform' a variety of theories offer more nuanced explanations. These explanations revolve around the dimensions and combinations of path-dependency, path-contingency and path-shaping. The emphasis on path-dependency follows from the early work of Veblen and Myrdal whereby development is seen as a product of culture and history. Thus variance in experience within post-Communist transformation can be explained by variance in historical development of institutional practice. 'State-led' models (e.g. Amsden et al. 1994) place alternative emphasis on the difference between Western market-based capitalism and that which might be appropriate for transformation from command to market economy. Endogenous rather than exogeneous pressures are emphasized, leading to an alternative prescriptive model of the 'gradualist' development of a Western-style social democratic, corporatist order.

Contemporary analysts within the varieties of capitalism (VoC) approach may also emphasize the embeddedness of institutional complementarities. Such accounts generally locate post-Communist transformation within a liberal market economy paradigm (Feldmann 2006; Buchen 2007), with the exceptional case of Slovenia as a coordinated market economy. However, the VoC approach proves unsatisfactory when it comes to explaining wild capitalism, cronyism and generally 'dysfunctional' market-based behaviour. The ideal ' types' of liberal or coordinated market economies are presented as bundles of institutional complementarities designed to promote efficient market capitalism. Wild capitalism is characterized by chaotic and rule evasive behaviour which denies complementarity or efficiency. As Jackson and Deeg (2006, 571) highlight, 'existing typologies are too focused on economic co-ordination rather than distributional outcomes, the politics of class compromise are often missing, and consequently . . . the (VoC) literature has failed to understand the dynamics of change in contemporary capitalism'. Once again, it is precisely through such ignored 'distributional outcomes' that we can see a failure of convergence in GDP per capita, the persistence of an increasing gap in income equality, and a persistence of high unemployment.

The dominance of neoliberal practice has also been explained in path-dependent terms by the trajectory of economic restructuring within the region. Indeed, a focus on exploitative relationships can be discerned in some critical Marxist interpretations of transformation. In this scenario the entry of the post-Communist economies into the world market was predicated on a state strategy of encouraging and promoting production regimes based on labour rather than capital intensity. For some, this was an elite-driven process whereby state restructuring in post-Communist states was linked to the interests of Western-based transnational capital (van der Pijl 1993; Shields 2008). Gowan (1995) similarly argued that West European capital sought eastward expansion precisely to exploit cheaper labour and expand markets. Such extensive labour exploitation, achieved through poor working conditions and relatively low pay, was necessary both for capital accumulation in the East and profit maximization of Western-based capital expanding to the East. Neoliberal marketization may then have fulfilled the objectives of Western capital by opening up new production opportunities in geographical spaces unfettered by restraints on profit maximization. Indeed, models of exploitation might explain the denial of the 'factor-price equalization' model to operate and go some way to explaining non-convergence. Neoliberalism, in such accounts, is thus subject to its own contradictory forces and produces a paradox of low consumption demand in the East which holds back pressure for higher rates of wage growth, pro-ductivity increase and factor equalization. Data collected by Onaran (2008) suggests that wage growth has generally not kept pace with productivity growth (GDP per employee) in the region, especially in manufacturing. Unit labour costs would therefore have fallen in relative terms, confirm-ing the exploitation 'model'. Furthermore, in terms of general political economy, there is little room for the institutions of social democratic models of corporatism and associated 'good' governance to develop within this model as they did in post-war Western Europe, not least because the con-ditions of mass consumerism and Keynesian welfareism are absent in the post-Communist states (Bohle and Greskovits 2004; Bohle 2006).

But how might the persistence of the features of wild capitalism be explained in these models of exploitation? David Harvey (2003, 145–147) offers a potential explanation by suggesting that capitalism post- 'golden age' has developed specific dominant features, most notably a tendency for 'accumulation by dispossession' similar to the 'primitive' stage of accu-mulation as defined by Marx. Harvey's model postulates the reduction of whole populations to 'debt peonage' as the power of chief executive offic-ers (CEOs) is increased and the finance sector dispossesses assets by credit and stock manipulation. This model of contemporary capitalism assumes the development of rapacious activity under a new neoliberal version of capitalism driven by a distinct class of capitalists who seek to expand their own profits at the expense of other capitalists. This 'dispossession' thesis would assume that the dispossessors are agents of Western capital conducting a raid on the assets of the post-Communist states. The process would be mediated through the agency of financiers.

However, while there is credibility in Harvey's conclusions the central proposition of finance-driven dispossession does not help explain why 'indigenous' asset-stripping and personal enrichment has taken place within these states by an 'insider' elite. Harvey's analysis has also been refuted by Harman (2007) on logistical grounds. Harman argues that such dispossession is not valid as it cannot enable the capitalist class as a whole to accumulate. Furthermore, Harvey may be wrong in claiming that the officious process of 'primitive' accumulation which he associates with contemporary 'dispossession' had ever gone away in the 'golden age' and beyond. Primitive accumulation certainly existed in the post-war colonies, and has arguably been a feature of the period of rapid industrialization in both the Soviet states and post-1978 China. Thus corruption may be integral to the dynamic of capitalism in general, rather than specific to a certain variant.

19.7   TOWARDS A SYNTHESIS: UNEVEN AND COMBINED DEVELOPMENT?

To summarize the analysis so far, we have seen that levels of production, income and employment still lag behind 20 plus years after 1989. There is unevenness in the record, with those states geographically closer to the West and the EU faring better than those further away. The convergence predicted by the neoliberal tableau has not occurred, and there is a persistence of features of wild capitalism such as cronyism, corruption, crime, and informal and illegal working. Neoliberal prescription, aided and abetted by the financial institutions, tells us that insiders who profit from such malfeasance are barriers to reform, and therefore new entrants must be encouraged by more of the same reforms to break the mould. Wild capitalism, and the resultant lack of convergence, is then presented as a temporary dysfunction on way to the nirvana of the invisible hand. A harmony of interests is assumed whereby social capital and institution building is presented as a necessary precondition to barrier erosion. It is suggested in this chapter that such a harmony of interests is an illusion, founded on obscuration of class division and interests and manifested as a form of utopian liberalism. It is possible, however, to offer explanations for the lack of convergence and the continued lag of growth and production. This may be rooted in a model of exploitation whereby the driving force of development is grounded in the search for low unit labour costs and profit maximization, rather than factor-price equalization and convergence. As such, the neoliberal model is hoist on a petard of its own contradictions. What is more difficult to explain is the continuation of wild capitalism as a distinct and common feature across transformation states. In this respect, rather than adopt a purely path-dependent, institutionalist approach to the analysis it is more appropriate to adopt a 'critical' institutionalist approach that marries the dialectic of both path-dependency and path-shaping in helping our understanding (see, for example, Nielsen et al. 1995).

As an aid to developing such an approach we might see that the process of transformation, and its outcomes, is governed by both uneven and combined development of the social forces of production. Such theories of uneven and combined development have a long history, and were applied most trenchantly to analyses of the form and content of the 1917 Russian Revolution, most notably in Trotsky's *History of the Russian Revolution* (1977 [1932]) and more recently by Novack (1980). More recently, uneven and combined development has become a substudy in disciplines as diverse as evolutionary biology, archaeology, anthropology and international relations theory, with research centres devoted to its study. An ongoing debate has developed about whether or not the theoretical framework can be applied trans-historically (Rosenberg 2006) or can be only limited to study of capitalist regimes of production (Ashman 2009). Given the globalizing period of capital expansion which embraced the 1989 revolutions, such theories are trenchant as the post-Communist economies enter the world market order on an 'unfettered' basis (see Dale 2011 for a more detailed exposition of this theoretical position). As these economies entered the world market they were subsumed into a generalizing tendency to equalize the rate of profit under the weight of the law of value, in that product competition became governed by the necessity to produce with the minimum amount of labour time (see Hardy 2009). However, as Barker (2006) suggests, it is this very process of creating evenness in the rate of profit that exposes unevenness in the productive capacity of enterprises within transformation states:

> The interaction of capitals, through the circuit of production and circulation, involves unevenly advantaged capitals which differentially invest in new means of production, thus tending to cheapen commodities at the point of sale. They act in this way because of competition between them, and because, in any case, technical change does not occur evenly. (Barker 2006, 81)

Where unevenness exists it is exposed in the final price of goods and services with the consequence of enterprise collapse and industrial restructuring. Evenness, in the case of neoliberal prescriptive methods under transformation, may only be achieved on an exploitative labour-price model and (combined) 'Western' forms of work organization and technological input. In such a model the extraction of value is either achieved through extensive forms of exploitation (lower pay, longer working hours and so on) or intensive exploitation (technological inputs). However, the reliance on an exploitative model further highlights unevenness, not only between East and West, but also within and between post-Communist states themselves. Unevenness is thus a combination of both backwardness in technique, productivity and innovation as well as forwardness by which the backward nations skip whole phases of development by adopting the most advanced techniques of production and industrial organization. Unevenness between the post-Communist states described in the opening section therefore reflects different combinations of (relative) backwardness and processes of 'skipping over' to more advanced stages within states' own unique place in the world economy. The combined aspect of development follows on from the unevenness, in that the most modern and technologically efficient modes of production sit side by side with 'pre-existing modes' of organization (Burawoy 1985, 99). As such, work organization expressed as extensive exploitation of cheap labour and low cost may be found alongside 'cathedrals in the desert' where advanced technical processes are applied to extract value through intensive means (Hardy 2009).

As Davidson (2010) suggests, uneven and combined development affects not just the economy but society in general, its norms of behaviour, and patterns of authority and control. So there emerges a direct linkage between the material base of the production process and the continuation and adaptation of behavioural practice. One can thus discern in post-Communist states a continuation of many of the ways and means of the 'old order' combined with the new. This is especially important when we consider two important aspects of the organization of working life, that of informal and illegal working. Unevenness produced by the predatory nature of neoliberalism provides an explanation not only for the persistence of lagged production growth but also for the increasing informalization of the economy (Woolfson 2007).

In terms of informal working, Williams and Round (2007) provide sound evidence that informal working had always been a feature of the economy under the command economy and is now carried over post-transformation as custom and practice. Informal working may under the old order have supplemented formal employment, have been utilized as 'off-the-books' payment in 'brown envelope' bonuses, or simply paid as favours akin to forms of mutual aid between individuals and households. We must also consider, as Clarke (2002) reminds us, that under the command economy a large range of services (e.g. painting and decorating, TV and radio repair, care of elderly) were not provided by state-owned enterprises. 'Informal' working, when depicted by such tasks, was integral to the system. Informal working, as Williams and Round (2007, 2326) suggest, may thus be considered as a 'core means of livelihood for a significant proportion of households' that has since been carried over into the new order. Rather than being discouraged by a state's entry into the world economy, the legacies of past practices of informal working are encouraged to expand. Round et al. (2008), in their study of employment practices for Ukrainian graduates, for example, find that informal methods of recruitment and selection predominate alongside the growth of informal working. Most notably, bribery and corruption are *de rigeur* within this subset of employment practices. Furthermore, while the Ukrainian government have taken steps to counter bribery and corruption, it has little effect other than driving up the price of bribes in reflection of the higher risks (see Jain 2001). A related feature is that under Communism the black market economy created and sustained a market for shortfall products within the system. The black economy was by definition 'off the books', and more often than not involved in trading goods and services illegally.

There emerges a distinct interplay between informal working and illegal working, between the grey economy of informal working and the black economy of illegal working. The operators of the black market under transformation conditions were well placed to take the economic and political opportunity to expand their trading relationships with the clientelist groups associated with the new ruling elites. The old *nomenklatura* and the *penumbra* mafia operators of the black market thus have a vested interest in blocking any 'reform' of the economy constructed in regulatory form. The two social forces combined to preserve their position within the new market-based economy. Their complicity with, and sometimes integration, into the state machinery regularizes irregularity, and ensures the continuation of old habits alongside attempts to introduce new regulatory regimes based on the Western ideal. In conclusion, we can begin to appreciate that rather than being a temporary dysfunction, wild capitalism emerges as the normal *modus operandi* of post-Communist transformation. Orthodox prescriptions merely exacerbate the problems of wild capitalism by opening further the doors of irregular market behaviour and blocking the possibility of economic convergence. Most importantly, in terms of structure, the process of transformation remains inextricably linked to a particular model of labour exploitation that feeds more general economic asymmetries between East and West.

NOTES

1. http://www.databasece.com/en/industrial-output-during-transition.
2. http://www.eurofound.europa.eu/areas/qualityoflife/eurlife/index.php?template=3&radi oindic=158&idDomain=3, accessed 5th April 2011. The Gini co-efficient actually varies

considerably within the EU-15, with the lowest ratio recorded by Sweden (0.23) and the highest by Portugal (0.41).
3. See http://www.transparency.org/policy_research/surveys_indices/cpi/2010 for results.
4. http://transparency.org/policy_research/surveys_indices/cpi.

REFERENCES

Aglietta, Michel and Antoine Rebérioux (2005), *Corporate Governance Adrift: A Critique of Shareholder Value*, Cheltenham, UK and Northampton, MA, USA: Edward Elgar.

Amsden, Alice, Jacik Kochanowicz and Lance Taylor (1994), *The Market Meets its Match: Restructuring the Economies of Eastern Europe*, Boston, MA: Harvard University Press.

Antonić, D., A. Babović, B. Hiber, Z. Ivavević, D. Kavran, B. Mijatović, B. Stovanović, Z. Vacić, M. Vasović and S. Vuković (n.d.), 'Corruption in Serbia', Belgrade, Center for Liberal Democratic Studies.

Ashman, S. (2009), 'Capitalism, uneven and combined development and the transhistoric', *Cambridge Review of International Affairs*, **22** (1), 29–46

Åslund, A. (2001), 'The myth of output collapse after Communism', Carnegie Endowment for International Peace Working Paper No. 18, Washington, DC.

Barker, Colin (2006), 'Beyond Trotsky: extending combined and uneven development', in Bill Dunn and Hugh Radice (eds), *100 Years of Permanent Revolution*, London: Pluto pp. 72–87.

Begović, B. (2005), 'Corruption in Serbia: causes and remedies', Policy Brief 27, William Davidson Institute, University of Michigan, USA.

Blanchard, O. and M. Kremer (1997), 'Disorganisation', *Quarterly Journal of Economics*, **112** (4), 1091–1126.

Boeri, T. and P. Garibaldi (2006), 'Are labour markets in the new member states sufficiently flexible for EMU?' *Journal of Banking and Finance*, **30** (5), 1393–1407.

Bohle, D. (2006), 'Neo-liberal hegemony, transnational capital and the terms of the EU's eastward expansion', *Capital and Class*, **88**, 56–86.

Bohle, D. and B. Greskovits (2004), 'Capital, labor and the prospects of the European social model in the East Central and Eastern European', Working Paper No. 58, Centre for European Studies, Harvard University.

Bruner, M. Lane (2002), 'Taming "wild" capitalism', *Discourse and Society*, **13** (2), 167–184.

Buchen, Clements (2007), 'East European Antipodes: varieties of capitalism in Estonia and Slovenia', in David Lane and Martin Myant (eds), *Varieties of Capitalism in Post-communist Countries*, London: Palgrave Macmillan, pp. 60–95.

Burawoy, Michael (1985), *The Politics of Production: Factory Regimes under Capitalism and Socialism*, London: Verso.

Cicmil, S. and M. Upchurch (2006), 'Transferring management knowledge from the west to the Balkans: dilemmas, diversity, and the need for congruence', *International Journal of Diversity in Organisations, Communities and Nations*, **5** (1), 165–180.

Clarke, Simon (2002), *Making Ends Meet in Contemporary Russia: Secondary Employment, Subsidiary Agriculture and Social Networks*, Cheltenham, UK and Northampton, MA, USA: Edward Elgar.

Dale, Gareth (ed.) (2011), *First the Transition, then the Crash: Eastern Europe in the 2000s*, London: Pluto.

Das, R. (2006), 'Putting social capital in its place', *Capital and Class*, **90**, 65–92.

Davidson, N. (2010), 'From deflected permanent revolution to the law of uneven and combined development', *International Socialism*, **128**, 167–202.

Dunford, Mick and Adrian Smith (2004), 'Economic restructuring and employment change', in Michael Bradshaw and Alison Stenning (eds), *East Central Europe and the Former Soviet Union*, Harlow: Pearson, pp. 33–58.

EBRD (2010), *Recovery and Reform, Transition Report 2010*, London: European Bank for Reconstruction and Development.

Feldmann, M. (2006), 'Emerging varieties of capitalism in transition countries: industrial relations and wage bargaining in Estonia and Slovenia', *Comparative Political Studies*, **39**, 829–854.

Filatov, A. (1994), 'Unethical business behavior in post-Communist Russia: origins and trends', *Business Ethics Quarterly*, **4** (1), pp. 165–180.

Forteza, A. and M. Rama (2001), 'Labour market "rigidity" and the success of economic reforms across more than one hundred countries', World Bank Working Papers – Governance No. 2521, Washington, DC: World Bank.

Fukuyama, F. (1999), 'Social capital and civil society', Paper presented to the IMF Conference on Second Generation Reforms, George Mason University, 1 October, available at https://www.imf.org/external/pubs/ft/seminar/1999/reforms/fukuyama.htm#II.

Galgóczi, B. and E. Mermet (2003), 'Wage developments in candidate countries', *Transfer*, **9** (1), 50–63.

Gligorov V., J. Pöschl and S. Richter (2009), 'Where have all the shooting stars gone?' Vienna Institute for International Economic Studies, Current Analyses and Forecasts 4.

Gosztonyi, K. and J. Bray (2009), 'Business, corruption and economic crime in Central and South-East Europe', *Control Risks*, 2009, p. 3.

Gowan, P. (1995), 'Neo-Liberal theory and practice for Eastern Europe', *New Left Review*, **213**, 3–60.

Gustafson, G. (1999), *Capitalism Russian Style*, Cambridge: Cambridge University Press.

Habermas, Jurgen (1987), *Lifeworld and System: A Critique of Functionalist Reason*, Volume 2 of *The Theory of Communicative Action*, English transl. by Thomas McCarthy, Boston, MA: Beacon Press (first published in German, 1981).

Hankiss, Elemer (1990), *East European Alternatives*, Oxford: Clarendon Press.

Hardy, Jane (2009), *Poland's New Capitalism*, London: Pluto Press.

Harman, C. (2007), 'Theorising neo-liberalism', *International Socialism*, available at http://www.isj.org.uk/index.php4?s=contents&issue=117.

Harper, Krista (2006), *Wild Capitalism: Environmental Activists and Post-Socialist Ecology in Hungary*, Boulder, CO: East European Monographs.

Harvey, David (2003), *The New Imperialism*, Oxford: Oxford University Press.

Havrylyshyn, O. and J. Odling-Smee (2000), 'Political economy of stalled reforms', *Finance and Development*, **37** (3), 7–11.

Haynes, M. and R. Husan (2002), 'Market failure, state failure, institutions and historical constraints in the east European transition', *Journal of European Area Studies*, **10** (1), 105–129.

Hellman, J., G. Jones and D. Kaufman (2000), 'Seize the State, seize the day: an empirical analysis of state capture, corruption and influence in transition', World Bank Policy Research Paper No 2444, Washington, DC: World Bank.

Howard, Marc (2003), *The Weakness of Civil Society in Post-Communist Europe*, Cambridge: Cambridge University Press.

IMF (2000), 'Transition economies: an IMF perspective on progress and prospects', Issue Brief 00/08, November, available at http://www.imf.org/external/np/exr/ib/2000/110300.htm#III.

IMF (2006), 'Operational Guidance to IMF staff on the 2002 Conditionality Guidelines', Washington DC.

Jackson, G. and R. Deeg (2006), 'Comparing capitalism: recent debates' (Book review), *British Journal of Industrial Relations*, **44** (3), 569–575.

Jain, A. (2001), 'Corruption: a review', *Journal of Economic Surveys*, **15** (4), 71–121.

Johnson, S., D. Kaufmann and A. Shleifer (1997), 'The unofficial economy in transition', Brookings Papers on Economic Activity, Fall: Washington, DC: Brookings Institute.

La Porta, R., F. Lopez-de-Silanes, A. Shleifer and R. Vishny (1999), 'The quality of government', *Journal of Law, Economics, and Organizations*, **15** (1), 222–279.

Lucas, R. (1990), 'Why doesn't capital flow from rich to poor countries?' *American Economic Review*, **80** (2), 92–96.

Morton, Adam (2007), *Unravelling Gramsci: Hegemony and Passive Revolution in the Global Political Economy*, London: Pluto.

Mosse, David (2004), 'Power relations and poverty reduction', in Ruth Alsop (ed.), *Power, Rights and Poverty: Concepts and Connections*, London: DFID/World Bank, pp. 51–67.

Nelson, Nici and Susan Wright (1994), *Power and Participation*, London: Intermediate Technology Publications.

Nielsen, Klaus, Bob Jessop and Jerzy Hausner (1995), 'Institutional change in post-socialism', in Jerzy Hausner, Bob Jessop and Klaus Nielsen (eds), *Strategic Choice and Path Dependency in Post Socialism*, Aldershot, UK and Brookfield, VT, USA: Edward Elgar, pp. 3–45.

Novack, George (1980), *Understanding History: Marxist Essays*, New York: Pathfinder Press.

Onaran, Ö. (2008), 'Jobless growth in the Central and Eastern European Countries: a country specific panel data analysis for the manufacturing industry', *Eastern European Economics*, **46** (4), 97–122.

Onaran, Ö. (2010), 'From transition crisis to the global crisis: labour in the Central and Eastern EU new member states', Discussion Paper Number 135, Department of Economics and Statistics, Middlesex University Business School.

Peev, E. (2002), 'Ownership and control structures in transition to "crony capitalism": the case of Bulgaria', *Eastern European Economics*, **40** (5), 73–91.

Pesic, V. (2007), 'State capture and widespread corruption in Serbia', CEPS Working Document, 262, Brussels, Centre for European Policy Studies.

Roland, G. and T. Verdier (1999), 'Transition and the output fall', *Economics of Transition*, **7** (1), 1–28.

Rosenberg, J. (2006), 'Why is there no international historical sociology?' *European Journal of International Relations*, **12** (3), 307–340.

Round, J., C. Williams and P. Rodgers (2008), 'Corruption in the post-Soviet workplace: the experiences of recent graduates in contemporary Ukraine', *Work, Employment and Society*, **22** (1), 149–166.

Schneider, Friedrich (2003), 'The size and development of the shadow economies and shadow economy labor force of 22 transition and 21 OECD countries: what do we really know?' in Boyan Belev (ed.), *The Informal Economy in the EU Accession Countries*, Sofia: Centre for the Study of Democracy, pp. 121–139.

Shields, S. (2008), 'How the East was won: transnational social forces and the neoliberalisation of Poland's post-communist transition', *Global Society*, **22** (4), 445–468.

Simon, R. (2010), 'Passive revolution, perestroika, and the emergence of the new Russia', *Capital and Class*, **34** (3), 429–448.

Sommers, Jeff and Janis Bērziņš (2011), 'Twenty years lost: Latvia's failed development in the post Soviet world', in Gareth Dale (ed.), *First the Transition, then the Crash*, London: Pluto, pp. 119–142.

Stiglitz, J. (1999), 'Whither reform? Ten years of the transition', Keynote address to the World Bank's Annual Bank Conference on Development Economics, April.

Transparency International (2009), *OECD Anti Bribery Convention: Progress Report*, Berlin: Transparency International.

Treisman, D. (2000), 'The causes of corruption: a cross national study', *Journal of Public Economics*, **76** (3), 399–457.

Trotsky, Leo (1977 [1932]), *History of the Russian Revolution*, London: Pluto.

Turley, Gerard and Peter Luke (2011), *Transition Economics: Two Decades On*, London: Routledge.

UNDP (2007), *The Fight against Corruption in Serbia: An Institutional Framework Overview*, Geneva: United Nations Development Programme.

Upchurch, M. (2009), 'The IFIs and labour reform in post communist economies', *Globalizations*, **6** (2), 297–316.

Upchurch, M. and D. Weltman (2008), 'International financial institutions and post communist labour reform: a case of utopian liberalism?' *Debatte*, **16** (3), 309–330.

van der Pijl, Kees (1993), 'Soviet socialism and passive revolution', in Stephen Gill (ed.),

Gramsci, Historical Materialism and International Relations, Cambridge: Cambridge University Press.

Williams, C. and J. Round (2007), 'Beyond negative depictions of informal employment: some lessons from Moscow', *Urban Studies*, **44** (12), 2321–2338.

Woods, Ngaire (2006), *The Globalizers: The IMF, the World Bank and Their Borrowers*, Ithaca, NY, USA and London, UK: Cornell University Press.

Woolfson, C. (2007), 'Pushing the envelope: the "informalization" of labour in post-communist new EU member states', *Work, Employment and Society*, **21** (3), 551–564.

World Bank (2002), *Transition, The First Ten Years: Analysis and Lessons for Eastern Europe and the Former Soviet Union*, Washington, DC: World Bank.

World Bank (2003), *Unions and Collective Bargaining: Economic Effects in a Global Environment*, Washington, DC: World Bank.

World Bank (2008), 'The political economy of policy reform: issues and implications for policy dialogue and development operations', Report No. 4428–GLB. Washington, DC: World Bank Social Development Department.

World Bank (2010), *Turmoil at Twenty: Recession, Recovery and Reform in Central and Eastern Europe and the Former Soviet Union*, Washington, DC: World Bank.

20 The co-evolution of the institutional environments and internationalization experiences of Turkish internationalizing firms

*Bahattin Karademir and Attila Yaprak**

20.1 INTRODUCTION

As emerging markets have become significant economic entities in the new world economy, the evolution and composition of economic institutions in them has inspired a rich literature in the organizational sciences. Among the institutions that have received some attention are the large, diversified conglomerates and networks of closely affiliated businesses (Ramamurti and Singh 2009; Khanna and Palepu 2010). Given their increasing importance, these groups have attracted scholarly attention from a variety of theoretical perspectives. For example, researchers have focused on institutional environments (Chung 2001, 2004; Carney and Gedajlovic 2002; Maman 2002; Tsui-Auch and Lee 2003), markets (Khanna and Palepu 1997, 1999a, 1999b 2000a, 2000b; Khanna and Rivkin 2001) and organizational capabilities (Amsden and Hikino 1994; Kock and Guillen 2001) as drivers of the organizational strategies and structural configurations of these groups operating in many emerging markets (EMs). Even with this increased attention, however, we still know very little about how firm capabilities and organizational strategies and the particular environments in which these emerge co-evolve over time and reflect the changes that underscore the nature of their institutional environments (Teece et al. 1997; Kock and Guillen 2001; Khanna and Palepu 2006).

Among the questions that require exploration are at least the following. How do the reciprocal interactions between firms and environmental institutions affect organizational renewal, adaptation, and selection? How do organizational, institutional and market mechanisms shape, and how are they in turn shaped by, their economic, social and political environments, independently and in concert? How do institutional isomorphism, interdependence and path-dependence create an environment of mutual and reciprocal influence between institutional change and organizational action? How do the institutional context and the internationalization of firms interact; that is, are there any path-dependencies in the internationalization of EM firms? Do these differ from those of developed country internationalizing firms? What roles do endogenous factors, such as managerial intent, knowledge and willingness to internationalize, and exogenous variables such as the nature of markets and institutions, affect internationalization patterns? How do the reciprocal interactions among these happen? For example, how have increased liberalization of international trade and investment regimes and the opening of markets that were once passionately protected by EM governments changed these firms' capabilities? What are the motivating forces that have driven EM multinationals out of their markets to date? Are these forces changing, and if so, how? What are the internationalization paths that EM firms have chosen to follow in light of these institutional transformations and market drivers? How different are these from those that have been followed by internationalizing firms from the developed Western economies in the latter part of the last century?

While these questions have been explored in the literature to some extent (see, e.g., Carney and Gedajlovic 2002; Peng 2002, 2006; Rodrigues and Child 2003; Dieleman and Sachs 2006; Madhok Liu 2006; Yang et al. 2009), our knowledge of the answers to them remains shallow, evidenced by a recent Boston Consulting Group report (2010) which underscores this void in the literature.

Yet, it seems natural that we can learn a lot about these issues from studies that consider the historical, cultural and evolutionary antecedents of firm behavior in these markets and their institutional contexts as co-evolutionary frameworks. We address this issue in this chapter by showing how Turkish internationalizing firms have evolved and function in the distinctive institutional environment of Turkey in which they are embedded today, and how they have been propelling themselves into international markets during the recent past. While our work is exploratory and is based on our study of internationalizing firms in only one EM, Turkey, we believe that it is worthy of inspiring significant questions and future work on this interface in other EMs. Extending earlier work in this area (Kock and Guillen 2001; Carney and Gedajlovic 2002), we show how the institutional environments and organizational strategies of Turkish firms have co-evolved during the past nine decades (1923–2012) and that this co-evolution was complex and dynamic, yet interdependent.

Our study draws from earlier work on business group (BG) behavior in EMs (Khanna and Yafeh 2007) and from work on Turkish BGs (Goksen and Usdiken 2001; Karademir et al. 2005; Yaprak and Karademir 2010, 2011). As that research stream shows, Turkish BGs share many common features with highly diversified BGs found in other emerging markets (see, e.g., Chang and Hong 2000; Maman 2002), but also reflect the unique characteristics of Turkish society and its social and political history (Bugra 1994a; Karademir and Danisman 2007). The study of Turkish internationalizing firms is interesting also because they are in some ways similar to multinational corporations (MNCs) operating in multiple countries around the globe, yet are different from them and from state-owned enterprises (SOEs) operating in Turkey and elsewhere (Boston Consulting Group 2010). Like these other organizational forms in other EMs, Turkish firms' internationalization efforts appear to be sourced in system dynamism and improved economic performance in some periods during their evolution, yet a source of system inflexibility in other periods.

The remainder of our chapter is organized as follows. We review the institutional and co-evolutionary explanations that underline the inter-nationalization of Turkish internationalizing firms. We then show how the institutional environments and organizational strategies of these firms have co-evolved over time in Turkey as the Turkish economy has evolved from humble beginnings to liberalization, and now to post-liberalization. We then focus on the internationalization patterns that Turkish firms have followed during the past three decades or so (1980–2012). We conclude by offering questions for future research.

20.2 RELEVANT LITERATURE

20.2.1 The Institutional Approach to Internationalization

Peng (2002) suggests that the strategic choices firms make are not only driven by industry conditions and firm resources, but also reflect the insti-tutional and cultural context in which the firm is embedded. That is, the firm's strategic choices, such as whether and the extent to which to inter-nationalize, reflect the formal and informal constraints of national insti-tutional contexts that firm managers confront; and these contexts should be considered, in addition to firm resources and industry conditions, in understanding how firm strategies are shaped and how these shape the contexts in which they are embedded. Peng et al. (2008) underscore this view when they argue that the international dimension of business strat-egy is inherently driven by the local and global institutional, industry and resource considerations that internationalizing firms face, as do Yang et al. (2009), who suggest that this framework is useful in explaining the dif-ferences and the similarities of international expansion of economic actors embedded in diverse institutional, market and resource settings.

Khanna's work indicates that EM internationalizing firms evolve in the wider range of the unique sociological and cultural factors that define these markets (Khanna and Rivkin 2001; Khanna and Yafeh 2007). Their institutional environment frames the emerging organizational arrangements, practices and structures with which these firms operate; that is, converging values and norms in organizational settings that move these organizations in the same institutional setting to become homogeneous, but different from those in other contexts (Baum and Oliver 1991; Oliver 1991; Haveman 1993; Holm 1995). Organizations adopt similar organizational arrangements and practices which reflect the values of their institutional contexts (Meyer and Rowan 1977; Meyer et al. 1983; Zucker 1987). Recent work by Maman (2002) illustrates, for example, that deliberate, intended state economic policies and protection of local entrepreneurship in their home environments, and not dependence on MNCs for inward foreign direct investment (FDI), gave rise to internationalizing firms from Israel and South Korea to expand abroad. The institutional approach also provides an illustrative venue for understanding the dynamics of national economic change. Tsui-Auch and Lee (2003) and Chung (2001) show that patterns of internationalization in Singapore and South Korea and Taiwan, respectively, are functions of these markets' institutional environments.

An interesting extension of this research stream is that in entrepreneurship, especially in the context of the rapidly internationalizing firms in EMs (Knight and Cavusgil 2004). These studies show how institutional settings influence the context that leads to the emergence and development of entrepreneurship in markets. Bruton et al. (2010) suggest that institutional theory provides a useful theoretical lens through which researchers can identify and examine such issues as culture, legal and regulatory environment, tradition and history in an industry economic incentives' impact on industry and, in turn, entrepreneurial success.

20.2.2   The Co-Evolutionary Perspective[1]

One of the derivatives of the institutional view on internationalization is the co-evolutionary perspective. This perspective offers us the opportunity to understand better the dynamic nature of organizations and their environments from a co-evolutionary perspective (e.g. Baum 1999; Lewin and Volberda 1999; Lewin et al. 1999; Tan and Tan 2004). Co-evolution – the joint outcome of managerial intentionality, the environment and institutional effects (Lewin and Volberda 1999) – argues that patterns of organizational attributes and relationships are formed by environmental determinants and/or managerial adaptation and are interdependent. In this view, the dynamic nature of organizational change and renewal are accounted for by the concurrent operation of adaptation and selection

(Flier et al. 2003); adaptation and selection are interrelated and co-evolving, and organizational and environmental dynamics are forged from their reciprocal interactions (Levinthal and Myatt 1994; Rosenkopf and Tushman 1994). Thus, causes and effects of interaction among organizations and their environments help explain the changes that occur in organizations that interact (Baum and Singh 1994).

The co-evolutionary framework indicates that organizational forms and practices have their genesis in particular sets of social and political circumstances forged from the interaction of both exogenous and endogenous influences (Carney and Gedajlovic 2002). These involve varying levels of analysis, ranging from the micro to the macro level, but reciprocal interactions are the focal point. While micro co-evolution refers to co-evolution within firms, macro co-evolution takes place between firms and their markets (McKelvey 1997). Interactions between these different levels in the firm's institutional environment, its competitive environment and its bundle of resources generate the unique mechanisms that drive specific co-evolutionary patterns (Lewin and Volderba 1999; Flier et al. 2003). In sum, the co-evolutionary perspective describes the dynamic interrelationships between organizations and their environments, and how these lead to a continuous spiral of the shaping of organizational forms and actions and the reshaping of environments (Baum and Singh 1994).

Carney and Gedajlovic (2002) argue that the co-evolutionary framework incorporates notions of not only interdependence, but also path-dependence, and system openness (the system is open to endogenous and exogenous forces on itself); they claim that in addition to underlining mutual and reciprocal influence between institutional environments and organizational action, this perspective helps create new organizational forms. According to them, as environmental conditions are reshaped, reciprocal adjustments are made by both established and emergent firms; emergent firms adapt to the adaptations of established firms while new organizational forms with novel business practices arise that alter the competitive landscape of established firms which provides the impetus for further adaptive behavior by established firms. These adjustments create endogenous forces for environmental change in the next period which, after interacting with the exogenous forces in that period shape new environmental conditions in the next period. Carney and Gedajlovic (2002) view interdependence as the fundamental fulcrum of this perspective; that is, they contend that it is strategies of mutual adjustment, reciprocation and accommodation among a community of actors that bring about significant institutional change. Path-dependence is also important in this effort since it is this dependence on historical patterns of firm–environment interdependence that organizational strategies and institutional environments co-evolve. Firms reflect the institutional conditions in which they emerge. Firms and their human actors, in turn, shape that environment both directly through their resource allocation patterns and their strategies, and indirectly as infrastructure and other institutional structures develop to support their needs. Carney and Gedajlovic's work (2002) is significant in its emphasis on the processes by which organizational forms emerge, become institutionalized for a period, then become de-institutionalized in their particular environments, such as EM contexts.

Rodrigues and Child's work (2003) points to the virtues of combining a firm's strategic choices with a simultaneous focus on the isomorphic effects of institutional constraints. They contend that the nature of the environment in co-evolution requires not only macro and micro considerations, but also sector (meso) concerns where the interactions between the institutional regimes and the firm's actions give rise to isomorphic effects (conditions that affect the performance of the sector are shared by its member firms). The co-evolutionary cycle at the micro level is seen to be partly stimulated by environmental changes and partly by internal developments including managers' mental models and strategic actions. At the macro level, it is important for the firm to be able to adapt, augment and renew its resource bundles and capabilities over time as its policies, identity and form unfold with changes in its institutional construction and deconstruction.

Rodrigues and Child's work (2003) also points to the capacity of management to shape its environment. In their view, tight social networks extending across different system levels, such as micro and meso, are important as are management's degree of embeddedness in the macro system and its capacity to work that system. According to them, a high level of institutionalization in the system is not necessarily dysfunctional; new forms can arise as a result of changes within the organizational community and in the power and legitimacy of social groups and the business models they espouse, since the capabilities one builds up during a certain period do not necessarily guarantee survival as an independent entity in later periods. That is, managerial intentionality matters in co-evolution: by their insertion into circuits of power, actors can make critical interventions to introduce new visions and innovative practices into organizations. Mutations arising from new institutional closures and openings around market ideologies create new organizational practices, and the evolution of successful new practices under this ideology, in turn, lends credibility to the emerging ideology.

A parallel view is offered by Dieleman and Sachs (2006). They contend that as institutional transitions intensify in EMs – that is, as institutions modernize – the basis for competition in the environment moves from relationship-based to market-based, oscillating between these forms, but with irregular dynamics caused by both external (that is, exogenous) and internal (that is, endogenous) influences.

Yang et al. (2009) and Madhok and Liu (2006) extend these generic arguments to the internationalization arena. Focusing on inward and outward FDI (IFDI and OFDI) in China and Japan, Yang et al. (2009) contend that internationalization may be a response to the institutional developments of the firm in its home market. In each case, there may have been institutional, industry and resource drivers that may have led firms in one direction or the other; that is, OFDI preceding IFDI in Japan, IFDI preceding OFDI in China. The size and sophistication of the home versus host markets, the infusion and presence of foreign capital in the market, regulatory incentives and barriers, and internal capabilities of the firm itself may all have influenced the internationalization trajectories of the Chinese versus the Japanese internationalizing firms.

Madhok and Liu (2006) argue that the multinational enterprise (MNE) provides a suitable venue through which the merits of co-evolutionary theory can be assessed. They contend that the MNE should be viewed as an internal knowledge subeconomy, where different levels of absorption of knowledge by the MNE's different affiliates can lead to desynchronization in knowledge absorption. Constructively managing this tension – that is, between the macro and the micro aspects of this co-evolution – can lead to direct implications for competitive advantage configurations for the MNE. That is, macro and micro actors and activities in the MNE's environment jointly influence its competitive advantage configurations and, by extension, its co-evolution. These then help the MNE chart its internationalization course, that is, how it should balance its internationalization effort, what forms of ownership it should prefer in various markets and what strategies it should employ as it expands.

This review of the institutional and co-evolutionary approaches to internationalization underscores the value in viewing the firm's international expansion through the lenses of organizational action and environmental dynamism. In the next section, we present one example of this interaction in one EM context, Turkey, to illustrate the lessons that can be learned from viewing the impact of environmental dynamics on firm strategy.

20.3 THE EVOLUTION OF THE INSTITUTIONAL ENVIRONMENT OF TURKISH INTERNATIONALIZING FIRMS[2]

The unique institutional context with which Turkish internationalizing firms have co-evolved can be partitioned into five distinct periods:

recovery to nationhood (1923–1930), state-centered development (1930–1950), democratic development (1950–1960), planned development (1960–1980), and export-promotion-oriented liberalization (1980 to the early 2000s). We analyze the institutional context, the market environment, the firms themselves and the interactions among these in each period. Although these periods differ somewhat from each other, they also share economic, social and political common denominators that mark a late industrializing country. These include an inadequate marketing infrastructure, lack of regulatory discipline, market failures, and chronic political and economic instability (Arnold and Quelch 1998; Khanna and Palepu 2010).

20.3.1   A Brief Look at the Pre-Nationhood Period

The capital accumulation in the Ottoman Empire started in the nineteenth century. Trade concessions attracted foreign capital inflow to the country. The business class was mostly composed of ethnic minorities and foreign investors, and commercial activity was centered in and around Istanbul and involved interactions among these actors. Keyder (1994a) identifies three groups of manufacturers in this century: small handicrafts, modern manufactures undertaken by the state and privately owned urban manufactures of recent origin. Small handicrafts manufacturing employed low-capital, labor-intensive technology, and the traditionally-organized labor. State enterprises employed industrial technology and were larger in scale when compared to small handicrafts manufacturing. They employed imported machinery and inputs and a significant number of foreign managers and workers. A great number of these enterprises failed as they suffered from high worker turnover, improper management and competition from imported products. The emergent urban manufacturers were owned by ethnic minorities, foreign investors and the modernizing segments of the Muslim population. They were small, but were organized in a capitalistic fashion. They benefited from port city trade. Prior to the First World War, political reformists realized that the survival of the state was dependent upon the adoption of a market economy and the development of an indigenous business class. They used economic incentives and state contracts to stimulate industrialization and greater nationalization of the economy. The Ottoman economy suffered during the long First World War years, however. Many of the factories were destroyed or failed, and the flight of ethnic minorities from Istanbul after the war led to the loss of skilled craftsmen and the merchant class (Keyder 1994a, 1994b).

20.3.2 The Recovery to Nationhood Period (1923–1930)

The Izmir National Economic Congress of 1923 set the stage for establishing a national economy. Four interrelated objectives were identified at this congress to begin establishing a national economy: creating an indigenous business class, encouraging industrialization, protecting domestic industry and the formation of a property rights regime. These objectives were to be achieved within the following internal context: a limited number of small, ill-equipped and mechanized factories providing the production base; small numbers of businesspersons and skilled craftsmen to actualize commerce; and emigration of skilled ethnic minorities to other countries. These endogenous influences were paralleled by a major exogenous influence: reparations and restraints outlined in the Lausanne Treaty (1923) overshadowed the drive to develop a protectionist economy during this period. This treaty required the implementation of the old trade regime, and payment of foreign debts inherited during the old regime. To meet these obligations, the state nationalized some private businesses and enacted new taxes to generate the necessary funds for meeting the requirements of that treaty (Ahmad 1981; Hale 1981). Turkey experienced budget deficits matched with exceptionally high inflation. By the late 1920s, the world economic crisis increased doubts about the viability of the market economy; thus, a radical shift toward a state-run economic model and policy orientation followed (Bugra 1994a, 98–101). The political context of the country during this period helped determine the social profile of the business class. The state encouraged former government employees, merchants and professionals to become entrepreneurs.

The national economy evolved through the joint efforts of state-owned enterprises and privately owned urban manufacturers during this period (Keyder 1994b). Many of these enterprises failed as they suffered from high worker turnover, improper management and competition from imported products. The economic agenda focused on building a market economy and building an indigenous private business class while keeping secularism intact. The state-supported capital accumulation in the private sector led to the emergence of a new merchant class, exemplified by the Koc and the Karamehmet families. This determined policy orientation encouraging private enterprise led to the emergence and earlier development of some of the largest business groups in Turkey. Internationalization was rare for these firms, however, as they lacked the managerial, financial, labor and marketing resources with which they would compete abroad. Internationalization was limited to trade, with state support for the indigenous business class to accelerate inward international trade. These businesspersons, who were connected to the state, sold imported economic inputs to state-owned enterprises and local consumers. Internationalization and organizational development, both limited in scope and context, co-evolved in this manner during this period. See Table 20.1.

20.3.3   The State-Centered Development Period (1930–1950)

This period was marked by: (1) the aftermath of the Great Depression in the Western world (exogenous); and (2) the increasing role of the state in charting economic, political and social transformation in Turkey (endogenous). The Great Depression helped reduce export opportunities for fledgling Turkish enterprises; while state-led industrialization, with the objective of creating a mixed economy where state and the private business activity would be harmonized, helped focus Turkish businesses' attention on the developing domestic market (Boratav 1981). While private business grew slowly, incoming foreign direct investment was insufficient to achieve the desired levels of economic growth. Economic planning through five-year development plans began in this period which led to the establishment of SOEs in textiles, iron and steel, ceramics and glass, paper and artificial fibers, and chemical and mining industries. State banks were created to finance and control expanding state economic activity. These plans also introduced price controls, new regulations for the international trade regime and new taxes. The state centralized the allocation of foreign currency and institutionalized the international capital movements in order to maintain a stable exchange rate and a balanced budget (Bugra 1994b). This increased state role led to rising uncertainty, however, exacerbated by the onset of the Second World War. This inspired the emerging business class to search for a more market-oriented economic policy. This was realized in the immediate aftermath of the war when the state returned to a more liberal economy emphasizing private enterprise development supported by Western economic aid (Bugra 1994a).

While the span of industries populated by SOEs increased during this period, private enterprises using domestic inputs also rose, benefiting from protectionist trade regimes, incentives, government contracts, inexpensive inputs provided by SOEs, government price controls and buy-domestic policies. Export-oriented private business could not flourish, however, as the state concentrated its economic focus on enhancing the productivity of its SOEs, partially at the expense of the growing private business class. A disappointing dimension of this period is the implementation of the Wealth Tax, a capital gains tax placed on speculative gains that was applied unfairly on ethnic minority businesses. This application could

Table 20.1   The recovery to nationhood period (1923–1930)

Exogenous influences	Endogenous influences	Established firms	Emerging firms	Co-evolutionary patterns of internationalization
The Lausanne Treaty (1923) required implementation of the old free trade regime and payment of the debts inherited from the Ottoman period.	The single party regime has an authoritarian modernization approach. Economic agenda stresses: (i) creating a national economy and an indigenous business class; (ii) industrialization; and (iii) formation of a property rights regime.	A limited number of small size and ill-equipped mechanized factories exist in the beginning of the period. Limited number of businessmen and craftsmen exist due to the coincidence of skilled ethnic minority emigration and lack of an indigenous business class.	State-backed former bureaucrats, merchants, and professionals emerge as businessmen. Their contact capabilities with the state are vital in order to emerge as businessmen and survive and prosper.	Free trade coincides with state support for the indigenous businessmen and accelerates inward internationalization. State-backed businessmen import to sell both to the state-owned enterprises (SOEs) and local consumers.

have led to the departure of at least some of these businesses from Turkey, hampering internationalization efforts of Turkish businesses, since many of these businesses were involved in international trade. In sum, both inward and outward internationalization suffered from domestic-oriented, protectionist economic policies. Only those who had established relationships with the state flourished in the international context during this period. See Table 20.2.

20.3.4   The Democratic Development Period (1950–1960)

This period was marked by: (1) the arrival of the multiparty system and the ensuing shift in the economic agenda from state to liberal capitalism; and (2) the arrival of a Westernization orientation exemplified by North Atlantic Treaty Organization (NATO) membership, which led to inflows of Western aid, such as through the Marshall Plan. The government sought to increase agricultural output as a mechanism to stimulate consumer purchasing power and, by extension, increased demand for consumer and industrial goods. This intent was realized: escalating incomes did fuel industrial production and consumer goods manufacturing, increasingly by the private sector, and led to rural-to-urban migration. As investment growth in the private sector was slowed by political uncertainties toward the end of this decade and the demographics were shifting more rapidly, however, increased government spending and enlarged trade deficits led to an inflationary economy, and liberalization of the trade regime was short-lived. These were exacerbated by the introduction of protectionist trade measures by the middle of the decade, and foreign currency shortages by the late 1950s. These developments fueled debate about the need for a planned economic system (Bugra 1994a).

This dynamic context of enterprise capitalism along with still-active state engagement in economic development led to a meaningful structural transformation in the business environment. While private enterprises remained too small to achieve true economic efficiency, and suffered to some extent from unplanned growth and undercapitalization, a new entrepreneurial class, exemplified by the second wave of family businesses, began emerging during this period (e.g., the Sabanci and the Eczacibasi family businesses). The state participated in this transformation by extending preferential credits, government contracts and foreign exchange allocations, especially to import businesses to stimulate capital accumulation and business growth. Speculative behavior increased as a consequence of increasing regulations and restrictions, and private business suffered from ever-changing regulations. The emerging business class remained dependent on the state for economic leadership and SOEs for productive input

Table 20.2   The state-centered development period (1930–1950)

Exogenous influences	Endogenous influences	Established firms	Emerging firms	Co-evolutionary patterns of internationalization
Great Depression turns out to be a worldwide economic crisis. The Second World War (WWII) has devastating effects on the world economy, and by extension, the Turkish economy.	The single party regime shifts to a relatively more authoritarian approach. Mixed economic approach sets the economic agenda; (i) planned efforts for industrialization through integrated SOEs; (ii) protectionist trade policies; (iii) state interventions through price controls, foreign currency allocation, and control of international capital movements; (iv) restrictions for preventing war time speculation; and (v) excessive and discriminatory taxes. In the immediate aftermath of WWII economic policy orientation shifts in order to become one of the beneficiaries of the Western Aid.	State's involvement in business creates business uncertainty and risks. Large size private companies: find state support at the expense of SMEs but not as much as SOEs. Large size private manufacturing companies become highly dependent on the state since buying centrally allocated foreign exchange and import licenses become vital for them. Large companies become heavily involved in and profit from trade at the expense of industrial production. Established ethnic minority businesses suffer from the Wealth Tax of 1942. Some are sold, acquired or nationalized by the state while others barely survive.	SMEs suffer from economic policies which give priority to large enterprises.	Local market oriented firms using domestic inputs benefit from: (i) the protectionist trade regime; (ii) incentives; (iii) government contracts; (iv) cheap inputs provided by SOEs; (v) price controls; and (vi) policies enforcing employees buying domestic products. Both inward and outward inter-nationalization suffers from protectionist trade policies. Contacts with economic policy-makers and bureaucrats become significant.

(Bugra 1994a). Inward FDI was insufficient; lack of managerial and financial prowess in the private sector made the desired privatizations of economically inefficient SOEs difficult; and the overvalued national currency hampered efforts at exports by private businesses. In sum, various internal and external forces facilitated the development of a dynamically changing market context which co-evolved with business organizations which oscillated between prosperity (earlier in the period) and hardship (later in the period). Internationalization was limited primarily to importing by a select group of firms, while exporting was limited to agriculture-related industries, such as textiles, foodstuffs and cereals. See Table 20.3.

20.3.5   The Planned Development Period (1960–1980)

This period was marked by: (1) three military interventions (1960, 1971 and 1980) and the subsequent three transitions to civilian political power (that is, constitutional changes, successive coalition governments and political instability) and centralized economic planning to implement rapid industrialization through import substitution policies (endogenous); and (2) integrating Europe, to which Turkey applied for membership in 1963 and became an associate member in 1964; the Cyprus conflict in 1974 that isolated Turkey from the community of Western nations; and social movements for greater freedoms and human rights, in both Turkey and abroad (exogenous).

Internally, five-year development plans were reactivated to stimulate industrialization and rejuvenation of private business growth through economic incentives, state credits and legal modifications. Despite shifting governmental policy and uneven enforcement, these economic measures generally supported capital accumulation in the private sector. Labor and agricultural incomes also increased, in turn increasing aggregate market demand. The protectionist trade regime eliminated competition in the internal market, and planned industrialization efforts created a market that was attractive to private business. Thus, private capital-intensive manufacturing enterprises producing consumer goods increased rapidly. The still small number of actors in capital-intensive manufacturing began forming partnerships with foreign firms, often in the form of licensing and/ or distribution arrangements or in assembly manufacturing, and a service industry led by increasing tourism began to emerge (Pamuk 1981). Legal modifications helped growing businesses to reorganize themselves into holding company structures and their contacts with various government entities and contributions to industrial policy increased (Karademir 2004; Karademir et al. 2005).

This period was rife with political instability, however, marked by

Table 20.3 The democratic development period (1950–1960)

Exogenous influences	Endogenous influences	Established firms	Emerging firms	Co-evolutionary patterns of internationalization
Opening up to international commerce through external aid, i.e. the Marshall Plan and NATO membership.	The multiparty regime era begins. Economic agenda stresses: (i) transforming into a market economy; (ii) increasing agricultural output and stimulating consumer purchasing power; (iii) increasing demand for industrial and consumer goods; and (iv) liberalizing of the international trade regime. The economy grows and consumer purchasing power increases. Yet, increases in government spending and chronic budget deficits result in high inflation and foreign exchange shortages. Government unwillingly introduces protectionist trade measures in 1954. Foreign currency shortage and crisis in 1957. Military coup in 1960.	While private enterprises remain small to achieve economic efficiency, they suffer from unplanned growth and under-capitalization. Investment growth in the private sector slows due to political uncertainties toward the end of this period.	The emerging business class remains dependent on the state for economic leadership and SOEs for productive input; the second wave of family businesses emerges during this period. The emerging business class remains dependent on the state for economic leadership and SOEs for productive input.	Various internal and external forces facilitate the development of a dynamically changing market context which co-evolves with business organizations which oscillate between prosperity (earlier in the period) and hardship (later in the period). Internationalization is limited to importing by a select group of firms, while exporting is limited to agriculture-related industries, such as textiles, foodstuffs, and cereals.

successive coalition governments and three military takeovers. The emerging business class suffered tremendously from these disruptions. Economic instability paralleled these interruptions as the country found itself with deepening balance-of-payments deficits, spiraling inflation and chronic unemployment (Senses 1988; Bugra 1994b). Still protected by blatant import substitution policies, the now growing conglomerates began diversifying into unrelated business areas, often rapidly into sectors in manufacturing and services. Imperfections in the markets for labor, resources and technologies and the consumers' voracious appetite for consumers' goods and services, in parallel with a revolution of rising consumer expectations, accelerated this trend. The Turkish business context had arrived at the cusp of becoming a consumption society ripe for entrepreneurial initiative and opportunity (Bugra 1994a). The protected market in this period allowed for the emerging holding companies to develop export capacity which was to follow in the next period and the flow of inward FDI began growing. Some SMEs began growing as suppliers to the holding companies and their affiliated firms which were primarily serving the expanding domestic market. This helped to prepare them for the challenge of increasingly global competition that was to follow in the next period. As this discussion indicates, the market context helped organizations, both large and small, to enhance their organizational capabilities, though they were often troubled by the political uncertainties and commercial hardships they faced. Thus, this environmental dynamism helped shape the forms and actions of Turkish firms as they co-evolved with it during this period. See Table 20.4.

20.3.6   The Liberalization Period (1980–2000s)

This period was marked by: (1) increasing liberalization of the economy following an export expansion orientation and currency liberalization to support such expansion; increasing liberalization of financial markets, including expansion of capital accounts and the convertibility of the Turkish lira; orthodox stabilization programs under the auspices of the International Monetary Fund (IMF); and increasing investments into SMEs through authorizing legislation and subsidy support for exports (endogenous); and (2) the confluence of increasing globalization and technological advances, including the emergence of internet-based communication, the implosion of the Soviet system and expansion of market opportunities abroad (exogenous).

In the first of these decades (1980–1990), the Turkish economic context was hampered by: (1) runaway inflation and the IMF programs that followed aimed at correcting inflationary and balance-of-payments problems

Table 20.4 The planned development period (1960–1980)

Exogenous influences	Endogenous influences	Established firms	Emerging firms	Co-evolutionary patterns of internationalization
The Cold War intensifies. US and Soviet interests conflict, increasing instability in the country. Turkey's European integration journey begins with the Association Agreement signed in 1963; the Cyprus conflict erupts in 1974 that isolates Turkey from the community of Western nations; and social movements for greater freedoms and human rights, strengthen in both Turkey and abroad.	Three military interventions (1960, 1971 and 1980) and the subsequent transitions to civilian political power; centralized economic planning to implement rapid industrialization through import substitution policies. Coalition governments are reluctant to implement the planned approach due to their differing political perspectives and the planned approach's rigid nature.	The small number of actors in capital-intensive manufacturing begin forming partnerships with foreign firms, often in the form of licensing and/or distribution arrangements or in assembly manufacturing and a service industry led by increasing tourism begins to emerge. Legal modifications help growing businesses to reorganize themselves into holding company structures and their contacts with various government entities and contributions to industrial policy increase. The emerging business class suffers from political and economic disruptions. Protected by import substitution, the now-growing conglomerates begin diversifying into unrelated business areas, i.e. in manufacturing and services.	Some SMEs begin growing as suppliers to the holding companies and their affiliated firms who serve primarily the expanding domestic market. This helps prepare them for the challenges of increasingly global competition that follows in the next period.	The market context helps organizations, both large and small, to enhance their organizational capabilities, though they are often troubled by the political uncertainties and commercial hardships they face. The protected market allows for the emerging holding companies to expand their export capacity which helps prepare them for international competition in the next period.

and maintaining undistorted price mechanisms; (2) liberalizing international trade as a part of export-oriented industrialization; and (3) privatizing underperforming SOEs. These initiatives yielded impressive export growth, significant progress on the liberalization of the import regime and liberalization in the financial markets (Inselbag and Gultekin 1988). Export promotion was fostered by tax rebates, preferential export credits and a friendly exchange rate system, but this increased inflationary pressures and placed a heavy debt burden on the economy (Balkir 1993). Unemployment followed as a major problem paralleled by increasing internal and external debt. Instability became a major ingredient in the business environment (Nas 1988). While foreign FDI increased, this was primarily in the industries entered during the import substitution period.

The transformation from an import-substituting to an export-promoting policy orientation triggered many changes in the organizational structures and strategies of firms in private industry. Firms that had become accustomed to producing behind protective walls were encouraged to become exporters; some were not able to make this transformation, but those who were, became stronger for it. This turned out to be a mixed blessing, however, as those who achieved success in the export sector did so to some extent at the expense of manufacturing. Output growth and productivity in the private sector increased for most, but not for all, firms (Karademir et al. 2005). A significant development was the creation of foreign trade capital companies as a response to government incentives. Some of these were established by the largest conglomerates; later supported by government incentives, many succeeded in the export sector (Ilkin 1991; Onis 1991).

In the second of these decades (1990–2000), coalition governments led to political instability, rising terrorism became a major political and economic problem for the country, and successive domestic economic crises in 1994 and 2001 destroyed the business environment and eroded earlier gains (Akat 2000; Akyüz and Boratav 2003; Dibooglu and Kibritcioglu 2004). Externally, while the implosion of the Soviet system and the subsequent liberalization of the former Soviet republics opened up many opportunities for Turkish internationalizing firms, especially in the Turkic republics of Central Asia, the 1997 East Asian and the 1999 Russian currency crises eroded these opportunities very quickly. Capital inflows from abroad that were experienced during the 1995–1997 period slowed by the 1999 crisis, and the 1997 and the 1999 earthquakes contributed to a significant downturn to the domestic economy (Uygur 2001; Akyüz and Borotav 2003).

A positive development was Turkey's connection to the European Union (EU) through its Customs Union Agreement with the EU in 1996. While this event hit Turkish firms hard initially, as they were relatively less able to compete internationally, they soon became experienced in overcoming the challenges of global competition and sometimes outperformed their foreign rivals in the domestic market. For example Arcelik not only outperformed its foreign counterparts in the Turkish market, it soon was able to expand abroad, and establish sizable market shares through brand building in some European markets such as the United Kingdom (UK). In automotive components, textiles, foodstuffs and construction, firms such as Temsa, the Zorlu group, Enka and Vestel internationalized rapidly and succeeded in this effort during this period. In addition, the second-wave (or rapidly internationalizing) entrepreneurial firms began expanding abroad with government initiatives favoring not only their outward expansion but also their partnerships with inward FDI investors as partners in the domestic market. While they were typically less sophisticated in this regard than their first-wave counterparts, they were more nimble and possessed greater entrepreneurial skills which made them more attractive potential partners. Both the first-wave and the second-wave internationalizers provided opportunities for foreign investors to invest in third-country markets about which these firms had gained valuable market knowledge and experience (Yaprak and Karademir 2011).

In the early 2000s, Turkey was already recovering from the 2001 economic crisis through IMF and self-imposed austerity measures and was establishing conservative bank and financial system regulations. The single-party rule achieved in the 2002 elections brought stability to the political arena and the pro-business expansion approach adopted by the ruling party opened up international opportunities for Turkish firms. This was supported by Turkey's new foreign policy diversifying Turkey's political, economic and social influence and favoring its neighbors at the expense of some of its former major markets. Turkish firms were expanding abroad with greater regularity and were establishing new beachheads in many parts of the world, including Africa and Latin America, but solidifying established market shares in Asia, Europe and North America through acquisitions, mergers, joint ventures and other partnerships. The internationalization of Turkish firms was well under way during this period, having been helped by the co-evolution of the Turkish market environment with Turkish firms' own organizational strategies. See Table 20.5.

20.4 INTERNATIONALIZATION OF TURKISH FIRMS IN PERSPECTIVE

Turkish firms' internationalization strategies have been influenced substantially by their co-evolution with their unique institutional environment; we

Table 20.5 The liberalization period (1980–2000s)

Exogenous influences	Endogenous influences	Established firms	Emerging firms	Co-evolutionary patterns of internationalization
The confluence of increasing globalization and technological advances, including the emergence of internet-based communication, the implosion of the soviet system and expansion of market opportunities abroad collectively create internationalization, and by extension, market diversification opportunities.	In the 1980s, increasing economic liberalization following an export-expansion orientation and currency liberalization; increasing liberalization of financial markets and the convertibility of the Turkish lira; orthodox IMF stabilization programs; increasing investments into SMEs through legislation and subsidy support for exports; expansion of inward FDI, beginning of outward FDI.	Organizational change in response to the change from an import-substituting to an export-promoting policy orientation. Increasing output growth and productivity in the private sector. Creation of foreign trade capital companies as a response to government incentives.	Increasing internationalization of second-wave firms, both large and small, through exports and high-tech licensing and through partnerships, primarily for the domestic market; expansion into European and Asian markets; OEM manufacturing; increasing managerial and technological	Globalization and technological change and their own growth and maturity led the established firms to institutionalize Western managerial standards; they began enhancing their organizational capabilities through alliances and partnerships, learning, and leveraging competencies to other EM contexts; emergence of the established firms as regional MNEs

| In the 1990s, Customs Union agreement with the European Union; Asian and Russian currency crises. | In the 1990s, battling runaway inflation and IMF austerity programs; privatizing SOEs; export promotion; high unemployment; increasing internal and external debt; increased political and economic instability; terrorism. In the 2000s, political and economic stability with a pro-market approach; new foreign policy decreasing international conflicts with the neighbors and diversifying political, economic, and social relations. | Increasing internationalization of established firms and groups of firms through acquisitions, mergers, and partnerships; expansion into central Asia, Middle East and Eastern Europe, later into Africa and Latin America. | sophistication; begin investing in brand building through FDI (later in the period); integration of European corporate norms through partnerships with European firms; facilitating the expansion of foreign partners into other EM contexts based on experience in the Turkish market. | and the emerging firms as contending players in trade and beginning players in FDI; development of SMEs' managerial capabilities, i.e. brand building, supplying OEMs in automotive, textiles, and foodstuffs; emergence of industrial clusters, i.e. in automotive in Bursa; Turkish firms becoming increasingly competitive in world markets in response to government incentives. |

present three as examples, the Koc Group, the Sabanci Group and the Zorlu Group's international expansion, in the Appendix. In general, while many firms are becoming more internationally involved and experienced, they still lack the globalization success of some EM groups and conglomerates, such as those from South Korea, India and China. This is a function, at least partially, of several periods of uncertainty and turbulence in the economic and political environment in which they have evolved, but also a function of overdiversification and overprotection for a longer period of time than in those countries. In this context, while the government has, with fidelity, encouraged and even fostered the development and high performance of these firms and groups through various incentive programs, these measures have sometimes distorted the very market mechanisms they were created to ease, and created the basis for rent-seeking opportunities for these firms. In their highly uncertain and turbulent environment, it was only natural for these groups to choose to diversify through unrelated diversification (Yaprak et al. 2007).

It is possible that the IMF-imposed stabilization programs actually yielded conflicting objectives for the government: both to boost exports and to support free markets (Onis 1991). Although the incentive systems were very influential in attracting investments into particular sectors, they distorted the more general market forces that were being supported by the government. Business groups that possessed strong political affiliations took advantage of the circumstances and diversified into promising sectors through these connections. During the liberalization period, these groups invested into high-growth-promising industries such as tourism, finance, retailing, textiles, clothing, food, transportation equipment and technology. They also diversified by participating in the privatization programs of the government (Karademir et al. 2005).

Aguiar et al. (Boston Consulting Group Report 2010) suggest that EM firms and groups internationalize through any one, or a combination of, six low-cost-based, outward-oriented globalization models: (1) taking their brands global; (2) turning EM engineering into global innovation; (3) assuming global category leadership; (4) monetizing EM natural resources; (5) rolling out new business models to multiple markets; and (6) acquiring natural resources.

Most Turkish firms and groups have typically internationalized through exports and serving as alliance partners to foreign firms in the form of inward-oriented joint ventures (Goksen and Usdiken 2001). They have learned to compete against foreign competitors in internal markets, but only recently have they become truly competent in competing against foreign rivals in foreign markets. For example, Arcelik of the Koc Group was able to internationalize through exports to Western Europe, followed by competing for category leadership in table-top refrigerators in the UK market where it reached a 17 percent market share by 2010. Others have more aggressively sought foreign alliance partners for outward expansion. The main reasons for partnership formation for these groups were gaining access to foreign technology and management know-how; product and market portfolio diversification; and maintaining financial stamina – in addition to gaining access to the partner's foreign markets. These firms and groups often had difficulty in coordinating their entrepreneurial style and local orientation into their MNC partner's organizational culture in these partnerships.

From the perspective of the foreign firm, while the larger, more established groups continue to be promising partners for increased local and regional (or even global) market expansion from the local market, emerging groups offer opportunities for external expansion springing from economic scale advantages. These groups' foci on niche opportunities that capitalize on their existing (typically cost-based) strengths have made them attractive partners in outward expansion (Khanna and Palepu 2006).

20.5   DISCUSSION AND SUGGESTIONS FOR FUTURE RESEARCH

During the past two decades or so, the Turkish economy has undergone a profound transformation, changing from a state-planning-led, protected growth environment to a liberalized, international trade and investment-oriented system, paralleling similar growth patterns in other EMs, like Brazil, China, India and Mexico. As a function of this transformation, the fittest of the firms and groups in Turkey have had to shape up, restructure their business and market portfolios, and pursue growth opportunities abroad, sometimes in partnership with developed-country MNCs. These initiatives have often led to improved financial and market performance.

As Khanna and Palepu (2006) suggest, Turkish firms' success was to some extent a function of their excellent knowledge of the local market; sometimes this resulted from their adept exploitation of their knowledge of local talent and capital markets, serving customers at both home and abroad in a cost-effective manner. At other times, it was a function of their ability to exploit institutional voids to generate excessive rents from their operations. In still other circumstances, Turkish firms were able to develop and exploit inimitable and rare competencies and capabilities, especially in local market-based processes and procedures, such as working through intermediaries and government contacts that gave them a competitive advantage in competing against both domestic and foreign rivals in both their home as well as in foreign markets. They have been able to build on their familiarity with local resource markets, take advantage of institutional voids by treating these as business opportunities, and score gains with near excellent execution and increasingly transparent governance (Khanna and Palepu 2006). In essence, their co-evolution with their environmental dynamics has made them what they are today.

Today, Turkish firms still face a wide range of issues, however, that can be expressed in the following dilemmas identified by Spyckerelle and Hampden-Turner (2001). The first is family succession versus public ownership. While many have made significant inroads in becoming more public, many others are still trying. The second dilemma revolves around withstanding the competitive pressures of global rivals, at home and abroad, while maintaining strong national and regional loyalties. Here, too, many appear to be overcoming this challenge with leaner operations and better focus on profitable sectors and markets, but some appear to be slowly achieving this balance. Third, finding the right balance between thriving in a country that may remain primarily a Middle Eastern state versus a country that can become a center of exploding commercial activity and a platform from which to spring to markets in Asia, the Middle East, and Eastern Europe, will continue to be a difficult challenge. Finally, overcoming success inertia (especially in the local market) versus finding new directions (particularly in foreign markets) remains a formidable task. For example, success in original equipment manufacturing (OEM) continues to hold back global branding efforts of some firms and groups. All things considered, however, Turkish firms have learned that they will have to overcome these dilemmas and outgrow their organizational, structural and cultural limitations to continue to play the economically formative role they have been playing so effectively during the evolution of their unique institutional context, and to build on and leverage the competencies they have been able to develop as a function of that context.

Yet, many questions still remain for scholars of firms and their co-evolution in EMs to address. These include, at least, the following. Is it better for EM firms to internationalize? Will their internationalization breed improved performance at home and abroad, whether financial, market or otherwise? When they do go international, are they more likely to follow the incremental (stages) model of internationalization or the embedded multinational network model discussed earlier in this chapter? What internal and external factors should trigger their internationalization? When they engage in globalization through partnerships, what scale and scope goals should they pursue? How and when along the partnership curve will their bargaining advantages change? How can these be resolved? What trade-off portfolios (market access versus learning opportunities versus technology transfer versus capability development, and so on) should they pursue? How will the interface with their institutional environment affect their internationalization growth in the future? What institutional transformations will trigger which type of international involvement, and in what kinds of markets? As Turkish firms become early movers to markets in certain regions of the world and develop their own networks, such as in Africa and Latin America, how will they embed others, such as subsidiaries of MNCs with whom they partner, into these networks? These are only a few of the many fascinating questions that remain unanswered in our knowledge about co-evolution of firms in EMs. We hope that our chapter will contribute to this important and fascinating inquiry.

NOTES

*   The authors thank Professors Richard N. Osborn and Huseyin Ozgen for their contribution to an earlier version of this chapter that was presented at the 21st Colloquium of European Group for Organizational Studies (Berlin).
1.   The section on co-evolutionary theory draws partly from Karademir and Danisman (2007).
2.   The section on the evolution of the institutional environment of Turkish internationalizing firms draws partly from Karademir (2004).

REFERENCES

Ahmad, F. (1981), 'The political economy of Kemalism', in A. Kazancigil and E. Ozbudun (eds), *Ataturk: Founder of a Modern State*, London: Hurst, pp. 145–163.
Akat, A. (2000), 'The political economy of Turkish inflation', *Journal of International Affairs*, **54** (1), 265–282.
Akyüz, Y. and K. Boratav (2003), 'The making of the Turkish financial crises', *World Development*, **31** (9), 1549–1566.
Amsden, A.H. and T. Hikino (1994), 'Project execution capabilities, organizational know-how and conglomerate corporate growth in late industrialization', *Industrial and Corporate Change*, **3** (1), 111–147.
Arnold, D.J. and J.A. Quelch (1998), 'New strategies in emerging markets', *Sloan Management Review*, **40** (1), 7–20.
Balkir, C. (1993), 'Trade strategy in the 1980s', in A. Eralp, M. Tunay and B. Yesilada (eds), *The Political and Socioeconomic Transformation of Turkey*, London: Praeger Publishers, pp. 51–68.
Baum, J.A.C. (1999), 'Whole-part coevolutionary competition in organizations', in J.A.C. Baum and B. McKelvey (eds), *Variations in Organization Science: In Honor of Donald T. Campbell*, London: Sage, pp. 113–136.
Baum, J. and C. Oliver, (1991), 'Institutional linkages and organizational mortality', *Administrative Science Quarterly*, **36**, 187–218.
Baum, J.A.C. and J.V. Singh (1994), 'Organization–environment coevolution', in J.A.C. Baum and J.V. Singh (eds), *Evolutionary Dynamics of Organizations*, New York: Oxford University Press, pp. 379–402.

Boratav, K. (1981), 'Kemalist economic policies and etatism', in A. Kazancigil and E. Ozbudun (eds), *Ataturk: Founder of a Modern State*, Hamden, CT: Archon Books, pp. 165–191.

Boston Consulting Group (2010), 'Companies on the move: rising stars from rapidly developing economies are reshaping global industries', Boston Consulting Group, Boston, MA.

Bruton, G.D., D. Ahlstrom, and H. Li (2010), 'Institutional theory and entrepreneurship: where are we now and where do we need to move in the future?' *Entrepreneurship Theory and Practice*, **94** (3), 421–440.

Bugra, A. (1994a), *State and Business in Modern Turkey*, New York: State University of New York Press.

Bugra, A. (1994b), 'Political and institutional context of business activity in Turkey', in A. Oncu, C. Keyder and S.E. Ibrahim (eds), *Developmentalism and Beyond: Society and Politics in Egypt and Turkey*, Cairo: American University in Cairo Press, pp. 231–257.

Carney, M. and E. Gedajlovic, (2002), 'The co-evolution of institutional environments and organizational strategies: the rise of family business groups in the ASEAN region', *Organization Studies*, **23** (1), 1–29.

Cavusgil, S.T. (1980), 'On the internationalization process of firms', *European Research*, **8**, 273–281.

Chang, S.J. and J. Hong (2000), 'Economic performance of group-affiliated companies in Korea: intragroup resource sharing and internal business transactions', *Academy of Management Journal*, **43** (3), 429–448.

Chung, C. (2001), 'Markets, culture and institutions: the emergence of large business groups in Taiwan, 1950s–1970s', *Journal of Management Studies*, **38** (5), 719–745.

Chung, C. (2004), 'Institutional transition and cultural inheritance', *International Sociology*, **19** (1), 25–50.

Dibooglu, S. and A. Kibritcioglu (2004), 'Inflation, output growth, and stabilization in Turkey, 1980–2002', *Journal of Economics and Business*, **56**, 43–61.

Dieleman, M. and W. Sachs (2006), 'Oscillating between a relationship-based and a market-based model: the Salim Group', *Asia Pacific Journal of Management*, **23** (4), 521–536.

Flier, B., F.A.J. Van Den Bosch and H.W. Volberda (2003), 'Co-evolution in strategic renewal behavior of British, Dutch and French financial incumbents: interaction of environmental selection, institutional effects and managerial intentionality', *Journal of Management Studies*, **40** (8), 2163–2187.

Forsgren, M., U. Holm and J. Johanson (2005), *Managing the Embedded Multinational: A Business Network View*, Cheltenham, UK and Northampton, MA, USA: Edward Elgar Publishing, pp. 379–392.

Goksen, N.S. and B. Usdiken (2001), 'Uniformity and diversity in Turkish business groups: effects of scale and time of founding', *British Journal of Management*, **12** (4), 325–340.

Hale, W.M. (1981), *The Political and Economic Development of Modern Turkey*, New York: St Martin's Press.

Haveman, H.A. (1993), 'Organizational size and change: diversification in the savings and loan industry after deregulation', *Administrative Science Quarterly*, **38** (1), 20–51.

Holm, P. (1995), 'The dynamics of institutionalization: transformation process in Norwegian Fisheries', *Administrative Science Quarterly*, **40** (3), 398–423.

Ilkin, S. (1991), 'Exporters: favoured dependency', in M. Heper (ed.), *Strong State and Economic Interest Groups: The Post 1980 Turkish Experience*, Berlin: de Gruyter, pp. 89–98.

Inselbag, I. and B. Gultekin (1988), 'Financial markets in Turkey', in T.F. Nas and M. Odekon (eds), *Liberalization and the Turkish Economy*, New York: Greenwood Press, pp. 131–139.

Johanson, J. and J.E. Vahlne (1977), 'The internationalization process of the firm – a model of knowledge development and increasing foreign market commitments', *Journal of International Business Studies*, **8** (1), 23–32.

Karademir, B. (2004), 'Institutional isomorphism, markets, firm resources, and business group corporate diversification in emerging economies: a study of Turkish business groups', unpublished doctoral dissertation, Cukurova University, Adana, Turkey.

Karademir, B. and A. Danisman (2007), 'Business groups and media in emerging economies: a co-evolutionary approach to their interrelationships in Turkey, 1960–2005', *Problems and Perspectives in Management*, **5** (3), 44–57.

Karademir, B., H. Ozgen, R.N. Osborn and A. Yaprak (2005), 'The co-evolution of institutional environments, markets, organizational capabilities, and organizational strategies: a comparative case study of Turkish family holdings', paper presented at the 21st Colloquium of European Group for Organizational Studies, Berlin.

Keyder, C. (1994a), 'The agrarian background and the origins of the Turkish bourgeoisie', in A. Oncu, C. Keyder and S.I. Ibrahim (eds), *Developmentalism and Beyond: Society And Politics in Egypt and Turkey*, Cairo: American University Press in Cairo, pp. 44–74.

Keyder, C. (1994b), 'Manufacturing in Turkey 1900–1950', in D. Quataert (ed.), *Manufacturing in the Ottoman Empire and Turkey*, Albany, NY: Suny Press, pp. 123–163.

Khanna, T. and K. Palepu (1997), 'Why focused strategies may be wrong for emerging markets?' *Harvard Business Review*, **75** (4), 41–51.

Khanna, T. and K. Palepu (1999a), 'Policy shocks, market intermediaries, and corporate strategy: the evolution of business groups in Chile and India', *Journal of Economics and Management Strategy*, **8** (2), 271–310.

Khanna, T. and K. Palepu (1999b), 'The right way to restructure conglomerates in emerging markets', *Harvard Business Review*, **77** (4), 125–134.

Khanna, T. and K. Palepu (2000a), 'Is group affiliation profitable in emerging markets? An analysis of diversified business groups', *Journal of Finance*, **55** (2), 867–891.

Khanna, T. and K. Palepu (2000b), 'The future of business groups in emerging markets: long-run evidence from Chile', *Academy of Management Journal*, **43** (3), 268–285.

Khanna, T. and K. Palepu (2006), 'Emerging giants: building world-class companies in developing countries', *Harvard Business Review*, **84** (10), 60–69.

Khanna, T. and K. Palepu (2010), *Winning in Emerging Markets: A Roadmap for Strategy and Execution*, Boston, MA: Harvard Business School Press.

Khanna, T. and J.W. Rivkin (2001), 'Estimating the performance effects of business groups in emerging economies', *Strategic Management Journal*, **22** (1), 45–74.

Khanna, T. and Y. Yafeh (2007), 'Business groups in emerging markets: paragons or parasites?' *Journal of Economic Literature*, **45** (2), 331–372.

Knight, G.A. and S.T. Cavusgil (2004). 'Innovation, organizational capabilities, and the born-global firm', *Journal of International Business Studies*, **35** (2), 124–141.

Kock, C.J. and M.F. Guillen (2001), 'Strategy and structure in developing countries: business groups as an evolutionary response to opportunities for unrelated diversification', *Industrial and Corporate Change*, **10** (1), 77–113.

Levinthal, D. and J. Myatt (1994), 'Co-evolution of capabilities and industry: the evolution of mutual fund processing', *Strategic Management Journal*, **15**, 45–62.

Lewin, A.Y., C.P. Long and T.N. Carroll (1999), 'The coevolution of new organizational forms', *Organization Science*, **10** (5), 535–550.

Lewin, A.Y. and H.W. Volberda (1999), 'Prolegomena on coevolution: a framework for research on strategy and new organizational forms', *Organization Science*, **10**, 519–535.

Madhok, A., and Liu, C. (2006), 'The coevolutionary theory of the multinational firm', *Journal of International Management*, **12** (1), 1–21.

Maman, D. (2002), 'The emergence of business groups: Israel and South Korea compared', *Organization Studies*, **23** (5), 737–758.

McKelvey, B. (1997), 'Quasi-natural organization science', *Organization Science*, **8**, 351–380.

Meyer, J.W. and. B. Rowan (1977), 'Institutionalized organizations: formal structure as a myth and ceremony', *American Journal of Sociology*, **83** (2), pp. 340–363.

Meyer, J.W., W.R. Scott and T.E. Deal (1983), 'Institutional and technical sources of organizational structure: explaining the structure of educational organizations', in J.W. Meyer and W.R. Scott (eds), *Organizational Environments: Ritual and Rationality*, Beverly Hills, CA: Sage, pp. 45–67.

Nas, T.F. (1988), 'Problems and prospects: a commentary', in T.F. Nas and M. Odekon (eds), *Liberalization and the Turkish Economy*, New York: Greenwood Press, pp. 185–200.

Oliver, C. (1991), 'Strategic responses to institutional processes', *Academy of Management Review*, **16** (1), 145–179.

Onis, Z. (1991), 'Political economy of Turkey in 1980s: anatomy of unorthodox liberalism', in M. Heper (ed.), *Strong State and Economic Interest Groups: The Post 1980 Turkish Experience*, Berlin: de Gruyter, pp. 27–40.

Pamuk, S. (1981), 'Political economy of industrialization in Turkey', *MERIP Reports*, No. 93, pp. 26–30.

Peng, M.W. (2002), 'Towards an institution-based view of business strategy', *Asia Pacific Journal of Management*, **19** (2–3), 251–267.

Peng, M.W. and A. Delios (2006), 'What determines the scope of the firm over time and around the world? An Asia Pacific perspective', *Asia Pacific Journal of Management*, **23**, 385–405.

Peng, M.W., D.Y.L. Wang and Y. Jiang (2008), 'An institution-based view of international business strategy: a focus on emerging economies', *Journal of International Business Studies*, **39** (5), 920–936.

Ramamurti, R. and J. Singh (2009), *Emerging Multinationals in Emerging Markets*, Cambridge: Cambridge University Press.

Rodrigues, S.R. and J. Child (2003), 'Co-evolution in an institutionalized environment', *Journal of Management Studies*, **40**, 2137–2162.

Rosenkopf, L. and M.L. Tushman (1994), 'The coevolution of technology and organization', in J.A.C. Baum and J.V. Singh (eds), *The Evolutionary Dynamics of Organizations*, New York: Oxford University Press, pp. 403–424.

Senses, F. (1988), 'An overview of recent Turkish experience with economic stabilization and liberalization', in T.F. Nas and M. Odekon (eds), *Liberalization and the Turkish Economy*, New York: Greenwood Press, pp. 9–27.

Spyckerelle, J. and C. Hampden-Turner (2001), 'Innovating the corporate dynasty: Rahmi M. Koc, the Koc Group', in F. Trompenaars and C. Hampden-Turner (eds), *21 Leaders For the 21st Century*, Blacklick, OH: McGraw-Hill, pp. 379–392.

Tan, J. and D. Tan (2004), 'Environment-strategy co-evolution and co-alignment: a staged model of Chinese SOEs under transition', *Strategic Management Journal*, **26**, 141–157.

Teece, D.J., G. Pisano and A. Shuen (1997), 'Dynamic capabilities and strategic management', *Strategic Management Journal*, **18** (7), 509–533.

Tsui-Auch, L.S. and Y. Lee (2003), 'The state matters: management models of Singaporean Chinese and Korean business groups', *Organization Studies*, **24** (4), 507–534.

Uygur, E. (2001), 'Krizden Krize Turkiye: 2000 Kasım ve 2001 Subat Krizleri' (From crisis to crisis: the crises of November 2000 and February 2001), Türkiye Ekonomisi: Tartışma Metni (Turkish Economy: Discussion paper), No. 2001/01.

Yang, X., Y. Jiang, R. Kang and Y. Ke (2009), 'A comparative analysis of internationalization of Chinese and Japanese firms', *Asia Pacific Journal of Management*, **26** (1), 141–162.

Yaprak, A. and B. Karademir (2010), 'The internationalization of emerging market business groups: an integrated literature review', *International Marketing Review*, **27** (2), 245–262.

Yaprak, A. and B. Karademir (2011), 'Emerging market multinationals' role in facilitating developed country multinationals' regional expansion: a critical review of the literature and Turkish MNC examples', *Journal of World Business*, **46** (4), 438–446.

Yaprak, A., B. Karademir and R.N. Osborn (2007), 'How do businesses groups function and evolve in emerging markets? The case of Turkish business groups', *Advances In International Marketing*, **17**, 275–294.

Zucker, L.G. (1987), 'Institutional theories of organization', *Annual Review of Sociology*, **13**, 443–464.

APPENDIX: THE INTERNATIONALIZATION PATTERNS OF THE KOC, SABANCI AND THE ZORLU BGS

A. The Koc Group's Internationalization

Founded in 1926 in very humble beginnings in Ankara, the Koc Group (KG) has grown to become the leading BG in Turkey and one of the largest conglomerates in the world. As of 2007, its international operations spanned 24 countries, with a sales volume of $39.5 billion, ranging from autos to white goods. What is remarkable is that the KG has been able to grow into one of the world's premier marketing companies in just seven decades. This astonishing growth aptly illustrates the co-evolution of institutions, markets and organizations in Turkey, each feeding off the development of the others as the national context moved from statehood building, through the rooting of democratic traditions, to market liberalization.

The KG's inward internationalization appears to have started with contractual agreements with foreign firms seeking entry into its home market (e.g. Ford Motor Company, General Electric). These have involved distributorships of the foreign firm's products in the Turkish market initially, followed by licensing of technology and joint ventures to manufacture or co-produce a product in Turkey, followed by looser alliances later to serve the home market, or jointly address selected host markets (e.g. the Fiat partnership).

Its outward internationalization seems to have begun with exports, often in the form of OEM production (e.g. production of refrigerators, washing machines, dryers and dishwashers for Whirlpool to be marketed in the United States under the Kenmore brand name of Sears) to the geographically and the culturally similar countries (e.g. the Balkans, North Africa and the Middle East), followed by investment entry into and expansion in aspirational markets (most major Western European markets), and marked finally by brand-building efforts in its previously entered markets and selected emerging economies, such as China and Russia (e.g. Beko in England, France, Germany, China and the Russian Federation). This internationalization pattern seems to fit the stages model of international involvement proposed by Johansson and Vahlne (1977) and Cavusgil (1980). More recently, however, KG's attention appears to have shifted to embedding itself in multinational networks through partnerships with foreign firms, in line with the embedded networking model proposed by Forsgren et al. (2005) (e.g. with the Fiat network around the globe).

Among the KG partners today are: LG Electronics (South Korea); Yamaha, Kagome, Sumitomo and Tokio Marine (Japan); Fiat Auto

Spa, Iveco Fiat and Unicredito (Italy); Allianz Kredit (Germany); B&Q and New Holland (England); and Ford Motor Company (the United States). Today, KG has a production and/or marketing presence, sometimes through solely owned subsidiaries but mostly through alliances with partners within networks in which KG is embedded in the following countries: Algeria, Austria, Azerbaijan, Bahrain, Bulgaria, China, Czech Republic, England, France, Germany, Holland, Hungary, Iraq, Ireland, Italy, Kazakhstan, Kyrgyzstan, Macedonia, Poland, Romania, Russia, Spain, the United States and Uzbekistan. Among its internationally marketed brands, Beko (white goods) is perhaps the most popular; it claims 17 percent of the refrigerator market in England, with lower market shares in France, Germany and Spain.

B. The Sabanci Group's Internationalization

Founded as a holding company in 1967 but its operations dating back to the 1930s, the Sabanci Group (SG) has grown to become a leading BG in Turkey and one of the largest conglomerates in the world. As of 2007, its international operations spanned 18 countries, with consolidated sales revenues of $13 billion, ranging from autos and auto parts to banking and financial services products, and from energy companies to retail partnerships with foreign firms. The SG's astonishing growth aptly illustrates the co-evolution of institutions, markets and organizations in Turkey, each feeding off the development of the others as the national context moved from statehood building, through the rooting of democratic traditions, to market liberalization.

The SG's inward internationalization appears to have started with contractual agreements with foreign firms seeking entry into its home market (e.g. International Paper). These have involved distributorships of the foreign firm's products in the Turkish market initially, followed by licensing of technology and joint ventures to manufacture or co-produce a product in Turkey (Cigna Insurance, Carrefour retailing), followed by looser alliances later to serve the home market, or jointly address selected host markets (e.g. the Toyota partnership).

Its outward internationalization seems to have begun much later, with exports of finished or semi-finished products (e.g. plastic pipes, tire cord fabric, synthetic yarns, cement by-products) to markets where the SG saw opportunities to exploit, followed by investment entry into and expansion from aspirational markets in North and Latin America. Brand-building is a very new phenomenon for the SG in foreign markets. This internationalization pattern seems to fit mostly the stages model of international involvement proposed by Johansson and Vahlne (1977) and Cavusgil

(1980). More recently, SG's attention appears to have been shifting to embedding itself in multinational networks through partnerships with foreign firms, in line with the embedded networking model proposed by Forsgren et al. (2005) (e.g. with the Toyota network around the globe).

Composed of 71 separate companies, SG's business network includes firms in financial services, automotive, tire and tire reinforcement materials, retail, cement and energy. The SG markets these products in country markets in Europe (e.g. Austria, Germany), the Middle East (e.g. Egypt), Asia (e.g. China, Japan), North America (e.g. United States), and Latin America (e.g. Brazil).

Among the SG's many international partners today are: Bridgestone Tires, Mitsubishi Motors, Toyota Motor Company and Yazaki of Japan; Carrefour Supermarkets and Danone Foods of France; Citigroup, DuPont, Hilton International, IBM, International Paper, Investa Group, Kraft Foods and Philip Morris of the United States; Dia, Heidelberg Cement, Hoechst and Verbund of Germany; and Arcadia of the United Kingdom. Today, the SG has a production and/or marketing presence, sometimes through solely owned subsidiaries but mostly through alliances with partners, in the following countries: Austria, China, England, France, Germany, Holland, Italy, Spain and the United States.

C.   The Zorlu Group's Internationalization

The world's leader in home-textiles production, the Zorlu group (ZG) was founded in Denizli, in Turkey's southwest Anatolian peninsula. Its operations date back to the 1930s in Denizli and Trabzon on the Black Sea coast. Today, exporting to 110 countries around the globe from its Vestel City, an electronics manufacturing and research and development (R&D) base in Turkey, the ZG entered the high-technology business sector with the acquisition of Vestel Electronics in 1994, and entered the energy production and distribution field in 1996. These were followed by entries into banking and finance in 1997, and foreign trade in 1998, among entries into other industries in the 2000s. As of 2007, the ZG's international marketing presence through its own retailing network and sales to foreign affiliates and partners spans 50 countries, in addition to the 110 countries to which it exports its products, ranging from consumer electronics and energy to financial services, home textile products, information technology services, real estate investments, tourism and white goods. For example, the ZG group has 21 textile manufacturing and marketing companies located in France, Germany, Macedonia, South Africa, the United Kingdom and the United States. The ZG group's textile products are exported to over 60 countries located on every continent, ranging from Algeria and

Belgium to the United Kingdom and the United States. The group's net sales revenue in 2005 was $5.2 billion, with total export revenue from all operations of $3.1 billion. The ZG group's astounding growth in the last four decades aptly illustrates the co-evolution of institutions, markets and organizations in Turkey, each feeding off the development of the others as the national context moved from statehood building, through the rooting of democratic traditions, to market liberalization.

The ZG's inward internationalization appears to have started in the 1990s with contractual agreements, such as licensing of technology, with foreign firms seeking entry into its home market (e.g. Bel-Air Industries). These have involved distributorships of the foreign firm's products in the Turkish market initially, followed by licensing of technology and joint ventures to manufacture or co-produce a product in Turkey (OEM production of consumer electronics or appliances for foreign brands such as Hitachi, Sharp, Sanyo, Toshiba, Whirlpool, Moulinex, Tefal, Rowenta, Samsung, Motorola), followed by looser alliances later to serve the home market, or jointly address selected foreign markets (e.g. partnerships with Benetton and Sisley).

Its outward internationalization seems to have involved exports of finished or semi-finished products (e.g. home textiles) from almost its very beginning to markets where the ZG saw opportunities to exploit, followed by investment entry into and expansion from aspirational markets in North America and Western Europe (e.g. Zorlu USA and Zorlu UK). For instance in 2005, 58 percent of all televisions exported from Turkey were manufactured by Vestel Electronics; it became Europe's largest TV manufacturer in 2005 supplying 26 percent of Europe's television receivers that year. Brand-building is a very new phenomenon for the ZG in foreign markets, but today, Vestel markets products through its own subsidiaries located in France, Germany, Holland, Hong Kong, Italy, Romania, Russia, Spain, Taiwan, the UK and the US. This internationalization pattern seems to fit mostly the embedded networking model proposed by Forsgren et al. 2005 (e.g. with the Bel-Air network around the globe). Composed of 22 separate companies, Vestel Electronics, the ZG's crown jewel consumer electronics network, is Turkey's export champion, with net sales of $3.3 billion and export sales of $2.4 billion in 2005.

21 Exploring Western and Chinese business relationship paradigms
Dorothy A. Yen and Bradley R. Barnes

21.1 INTRODUCTION

Along with globalization and rapid economic growth in the Far East, international buyer–seller relationships involving Western and Eastern counterparts are increasing in importance in both academic and practitioner discourse. This chapter aims to provide a comparative overview relating to the Western literature on business relationships and the Chinese notion of *guanxi*, translated as 'relationships' and 'connections' (Luo 1997a; Seligman 1999). Specifically, this chapter will compare Western theories on buyer–supplier relationships with the Chinese *guanxi* paradigm by highlighting their differences and similarities. The chapter will help to identify some gaps within the current literature so that future frameworks can be built for further examination on cross-cultural business relationships. In order to provide an in-depth discussion on the similarities and differences between the Western and Chinese literature, this chapter begins by providing a general overview on Western buyer–supplier relationships and the Chinese *guanxi* theory. Then, the two relationship paradigms will be compared in terms of their origins, concepts and area of focus. A discussion will follow, outlining some of the key constructs that are used in Western and Chinese literature. Finally, a brief conclusion will be presented to summarize our discussion and highlight further research that may be of interest to you and other readers.

21.2 WESTERN RELATIONSHIPS

Much of the early research on Western buyer–seller relationships tended to originate from North America and Europe. In Europe, the literature dates back to the early 1970s, when a group of researchers joined forces and came together to form the International (Industrial) Marketing & Purchasing Group (IMP Group). The group was formed by a number of researchers in Europe and Scandinavia who shared a similar interest and recognized both the significance and the complexity of buyer–seller relationships (Håkansson 1982). At around the same time, scholars in North America began looking at the developments of relational exchange between buyers and sellers and began to focus on the areas of channel management (Dwyer et al. 1987).

The European IMP literature stresses that relationships occur somewhat naturally between buyers and sellers (Håkansson and Snehota 2000), and because these relationships are connected they form part of an overall network. In their opinion, relationships can be developed and enhanced through the constant interplay between actor bonds, resource ties and activity links (Håkansson and Snehota 1995). A network therefore consists of a web of relationships where one actor is connected directly and indirectly to other actors through exchange relationships. These relationships may vary from weak to strong, depending on the connections between resources, the complementarities of activity structures and the bonds established between individual actors (Håkansson and Ford 2002).

In contrast, the North American literature discusses channel management, industrial relationships and buyer–seller relationships. Researchers in North America have helped to enhance the understanding of the differences between traditional transactional exchange and relational exchange (Dwyer et al. 1987). Through a developmental process from discrete transactions to relational exchange, Dwyer et al. (1987) explained that relational exchange transpires over time, so each transaction must be viewed in terms of its history and its anticipated future.

In addition to the conceptual discussions relating to the difference between transactions and relational exchange, researchers in North America have also developed and tested many empirical constructs that proved influential on buyer–seller relationships. For example, and influenced by social exchange theory, Wilson and Mummalaneni (1988) developed a social bonding model that examined relationships among social bonds, satisfaction, trust, commitment and investments. Morgan and Hunt (1994) further developed a relationship marketing model and highlighted the key mediating effects of trust and commitment.

Based upon discussions from both European and North American scholarly activity, a comparison is drawn here, followed by a discussion on the constructs that are used to evaluate the quality of relationships from both perspectives. Key differences do exist between the European and North American literature. For example, the North American literature has tended to emphasize more the interpersonal and personal constructs (that is, personal competence and relational selling behavior, and so on) and their influence on buyer–seller relationships, whereas the European research focuses more on economic attributes (that is, external, environmental, organizational and financial factors).

Moreover, during the 1990s in North America, whilst pioneering work by Morgan and Hunt (1994) was able to demonstrate trust and commitment as two key mediating variables, research in Europe focused on the sub-dimensions of trust (credibility and benevolence) and commitment (affective and calculative) in greater depth (Geyskens et al. 1996; Wetzels et al. 1998). In addition, whilst North American research tended to test models using national data, the European work, to some extent has focused more on international buyer–seller relationships, which may have wider implications in an international context (Havila et al. 2004).

In both sets of literature, relationship quality is of significance to business relationships, because a successful working relationship is likely to bring respective and significant benefits, including reduced uncertainty, exchange efficiency and social satisfaction that can also insulate the seller from price competition (Dwyer et al. 1987). Such working relationships have also been referred to as providing relationship value and partnership success (Mohr and Spekman 1994), collaborative exchange relationships (Jap 1999) and successful relationships (Naudé and Buttle 2000). The attribute of relationship quality is of significance to academics and practitioners because it is important for companies to be able to distinguish successful relationships from those that are unsuccessful (Naudé and Buttle 2000). In summary, it was found that the main attributes that can be used to measure relationship quality include trust, satisfaction, commitment, coordination, cooperation, communication, social bonds and investments.

Within the European literature, the early focus of business relationships was solely based upon dyadic relationships between buying and selling firms. Although the IMP Group has used the term 'actors' to describe individuals that are involved in relationships between two organizations (Håkansson and Snehota 1995), not much has been undertaken empirically to explore the possible influence of individuals and social bonds on interorganizational relationships between two companies (Brekke 2005). In comparison, and as alluded to earlier, the North American literature has focused more on the possible influence of sales managers' personal attributes (e.g. expertise and power) and their relationship-building ability (e.g. likability, similarity, frequent business and social contacts) on organizational relationships (Doney and Cannon 1997).

Despite some discussions on the interpersonal constructs and their impact on organizational buyer–seller relationships, more work is still needed to explore such constructs and their influence on business relationships further. For example, how exactly do these constructs influence the quality of buyer–seller relationships between the buying and selling firms? Moreover, to what extent in quantifiable terms can they influence buyer–seller relationships?

Furthermore, under the influence of globalization and international trade, companies will have to expand and establish their relationships or networks on cross-cultural or cross-national contexts (Williams et al. 1998). Because such interpersonal constructs might vary significantly in a different cultural context, this identifies a gap for further research to examine the extent of impact of these interpersonal constructs in business relationships in different cultural contexts (Ambler and Styles 2000; Rodrigez and Wilson 2002). Thus, the next part of the chapter will further explore the concept of buyer–seller relationships and the attributes of successful relationships in a Chinese context.

21.3   CHINESE *GUANXI* RELATIONSHIPS

Distinct from the Western literature on buyer–seller relationships, *guanxi* as a relationship concept has been embedded in Chinese culture for thousands of years (King 1991). It has been explained as a mutually correlated connection that implies the existence of a formalized and hierarchical relationship through a particular tie (Jacobs 1979), tight or close knit networks (Yeung and Tung 1996), as well as a concept of drawing on connections to secure favors in personal relations (Luo 1997a). *Guanxi* has been widely used by the Chinese to cultivate relationships. In the business context, *guanxi* is a concept that is practiced by Chinese businesses to secure better positions and competitive advantage (Standifird and Marshall, 2000). In particular, when resources are limited, *guanxi* may become a rescue strategy and a mode of survival (Tsang 1998).

Compared to the Western literature that focuses on relationships between and among organizations, *guanxi* places greater emphasis on personal relationships. In the Chinese context, a person can form various *guanxi* applications with different people, such as families, localities, kinships and co-workers (Chen 2001). Within a business context, *guanxi* emphasizes the interpersonal relationships between and among all the individual actors instead of the organizational relationships between and among companies. In contrast to the perspective of Western buyer–seller relationships, the Chinese *guanxi* literature stresses the use of close friends and associates (networks) as intermediaries in assisting with general business activities (Bruun 1993; Yeung and Tung 1996) and uses socializing as a means for developing and nurturing business connections on a long-term basis (Standifird and Marshall 2000; Wong and Leung 2001).

The quality of *guanxi* is reflected by three Chinese constructs. These are *ganqing*, *renqing* and *xinren*. *Ganqing* refers to the emotional attachment that exists among network members (Wang 2007). It denotes a sense of loyalty and solidarity, the willingness to take care of each other under all circumstances (Chen and Chen 2004). *Renqing* consists of two parts: reciprocity and empathy (Hwang 1987) and is practiced through the exchange of favors (Wong and Leung 2001). The more the exchange of favors, the closer two parties become.

Xinren represents 'trust' in the Chinese context (Chen and Chen 2004). *Xinren* takes time to establish and can be gradually developed through repeating activities of exchanging favors (Wong and Chan 1999). According to Chen and Chen (2004), trust underlines the differentiated order of one's *guanxi* network. However, instead of trust between organizations, *guanxi* stresses interpersonal trust between individuals (Chen 2001). The higher the level of trust between two parties, the better the *guanxi* quality will be. Through the interplay of these Chinese constructs, *guanxi* can be cultivated between two parties (Kipnis 1997).

In terms of networking, *guanxi* stresses key targets, which include local alliance partners, corporate executives from local firms and governmental officials (Lo and Everett 2001). Rather than looking at resources and activities, *guanxi* is more about the actors and their personal relationships. After all, it is an individual's connections that expand one's *guanxi* networks (Chen 2001). Considering the amount of time and effort that is required for establishing *guanxi*, it is extremely important for individuals to decide with whom they should further develop their connections (Jacobs 1979). Then, activities and resources such as visiting, socializing, exchanging favors and gift giving can be utilized by the actors as ways of enhancing *guanxi* (Kipnis 1997).

As discussed earlier, the concept of *guanxi* began via the teaching of Confucius and has been embedded in Chinese culture for thousands of years (Chen 2001). However, although it has been expanded and explored within a business context, research on *guanxi* is often more theoretical and conceptual (e.g. Luo 1997a; Chen 2001; Chen and Chen 2004). Less empirical research has been conducted, compared to the Western literature on buyer–seller relationships. This might be because *guanxi* is still relatively new to academics and therefore most research into *guanxi* has tended to be exploratory and qualitative (Ambler 1995; Kipnis 1997).

In the past, some researchers have attempted to compare the *guanxi*-related constructs to Western constructs of relationship quality (Yen et al. 2007), and to explain and measure the quality of *guanxi* using similar factors from the Western literature (Mavondo and Rodrigo 2001). However, *guanxi* is a Chinese construct and because Chinese is a high-context culture, *guanxi* and its attributes need to be explored further within the Chinese cultural context (Tsang 1998). This highlights a gap in the literature and more work is needed to examine and explain the *guanxi* constructs explicitly in their own context (Lee and Dawes 2005). Instead of using Western substitute measures, *guanxi* should be measured by its own attributes, such as *ganqing, renqing* and *xinren*. Moreover, as not much research has been undertaken to explore the constructs in detail, there is a need to examine and enhance such measures further (Yen et al. 2010).

Besides a lack of well-developed measurements for *guanxi* constructs, another gap in the current literature is the lack of exploration on the extent of *guanxi*'s influence on buyer–seller relationships. Although *guanxi*'s impact has been discussed in various business scenarios, such as overcoming hidden barriers (Davies et al. 1995), facilitating business negotiations (McGuiness et al. 1991) and as a marketing tool (Leung et al. 1996), very little research has examined the means by which *guanxi* can significantly influence buyer–seller relationships. For example, does *guanxi* influence relationship performance directly or indirectly?

Despite Luo (1997b) declaring *guanxi* has a strong impact on a firm's performance, his research did not really measure constructs of *guanxi*. Instead, his work suggests that *guanxi*'s influence on firm performance is reflected in the performance of sales force, marketing and credit-granting departments. In fact, *guanxi*'s influence on buyer–seller relationships and the construct of performance has not been examined. Therefore, further research is needed to explore the linkages between *guanxi* and performance and how *guanxi* actually affects buyer–seller relationships between Western suppliers and Chinese buyers. The next part of the chapter will further discuss the differences and similarities between Western and Chinese perspectives regarding business-to-business relationships, and highlight the opportunities for future research focus.

21.4 WESTERN BUYER–SELLER RELATIONSHIPS AND CHINESE *GUANXI*: A COMPARISON

Western buyer–seller relationships and Chinese *guanxi* relationships are derived from totally different backgrounds. Compared to the culturally oriented *guanxi* (Chen 2001), the pervasion of Western buyer–seller relationships came from increased competition among various industries, when both buyers and suppliers were searching for secure commitments in order to obtain increased competitive advantages in the marketplace (Håkansson 1982). In fact, the concept of buyer–seller relationships was not widely studied until the late 1970s in the West (Turnbull et al. 1996). By contrast, Chinese *guanxi* is a relatively old paradigm. It has been deeply entrenched within Chinese society for thousands of years under a network concept that was derived from the five traditional cardinal human relations of Confucius (Chan 1963; Fang 1999). Moreover, by practicing these five fundamental relations over generations, the concept of *guanxi* has influenced not only the Chinese way of thinking but also their approach to doing business (King 1991).

In addition to the cultural background, the environmental uncertainty in China during the past 200 years has also encouraged the pervasiveness of *guanxi* in Chinese society (Huang et al. 1994). Living in a country with a deprived financial system and eminent political risks, the Chinese have learned to use *guanxi* to acquire limited resources, secure their own safety and protect their families. This explains the heavy reliance on *guanxi* in Chinese society and the prevailing use of *guanxi* as a crucial approach for conducting business (Kipnis 1997).

In contrast, the development of Western buyer–seller relationships has flourished together with progress of the economy and marketing theories germinated from the Western developed countries. Rather than being used as a defensive strategy, the concept of relational exchange is proposed to assist Western companies in increasing their profits and competitive advantage (Dwyer et al. 1987). In short, dissimilar to Chinese *guanxi* that was mostly applied as a means of rescue, the concept of buyer–seller relationships was derived from the belief that successful relationships can help both buyers and sellers benefit from cost savings and added value (Ford 1980).

Besides the cultural and environmental backgrounds, the fundamental difference between Western buyer–seller relationships and the Chinese *guanxi* theory is their different emphasis on relationships. Whilst Western buyer–seller research studies tend to examine relationships between two organizations, Chinese *guanxi* focuses on the interpersonal relationships of the individuals (Chen 2001) and may be influenced by environmental uncertainties. Therefore, instead of focusing at the company level, within the context of buyer–seller relationships, *guanxi* is established at the personal level. Lee and Xu (2001) commented that if managers of a company have various connections and good networks, this company will have little problems in running a successful and smooth business in the Chinese market.

In contrast, Western buyer–seller studies stress relationships between firms. Although the construct of social bonds has been vaguely discussed, it is not a focal construct that emerges in the field of buyer–seller relationships within the Western literature (Wilson and Jantrania 1996; Mavondo and Rodrigo 2001). This may be due to the development of Western society, where institutionalized trust mechanisms have been fully developed to ensure strict contractual compliance. Such systems have therefore helped reduce people's need to rely on personal knowledge and trust in their business partners (Whitley 1994).

As well as focusing on different levels of relationships, the Western relationship and Chinese *guanxi* literature also have different views on networks, and apply dissimilar approaches in terms of the expansion of networks. While Cunningham and Homse (1986) proposed that dyadic relationships form the core of a relationship network in the West, Chen (2001) pointed out that a *guanxi* network is like a concentric circle, where every individual is the centre of their own *guanxi* network (Chen 2001). Therefore, the way to expand a *guanxi* network is to go through the intermediaries, who can act as bridges for people to meet new contacts and enlarge their *guanxi* networks (Wong and Leung 2001).

In contrast with the Chinese *guanxi* approach, Håkansson and Snehota (1995) suggested that firms within a dyadic relationship should further expand their network through the interplay of activity links, actors' bonds and resource ties. Rather than using individuals or an individual company as the core of a relationship network, the Western literature views dyadic interactions as the means for establishing a position in a wider network of relationships (Mattsson 1997; Håkansson and Snehota 2000).

Despite such differences, Western buyer–seller relationships and Chinese *guanxi* share a similar approach in terms of being selective of targets of relationships. Considering the amount of time and effort that is required for establishing *guanxi*, Lo and Everett (2001) suggest that firms should focus their energy on securing good *guanxi* with local alliance partners, corporate executives from local firms and governmental officials. As long as firms have established good *guanxi* with these key targets, they are able to obtain more accurate market information and to attain preferential treatment. This leads to smoother transactions, lower costs, better corporate performance and greater ability to cope with legal uncertainties (Arregle et al. 2000; Luo and Peng 2000; Lo and Everett 2001). Nevertheless, although these key targets are suggested in order for business to focus their *guanxi* effort in the first place, diversifying one's *guanxi* network is not discouraged. As *guanxi* can often be used in an emergency to rescue a situation, it is generally believed among the Chinese that the more *guanxi* the better. This is because a diverse *guanxi* network can help dilute the risk of losing any useful connections and therefore assure greater maneuverability (Chen 2001).

Similar to *guanxi*, Western buyer–seller relationships can also be exclusive. According to Turnbull et al. (1996), both buyers and suppliers in industrial markets may be extremely cautious in terms of who they have relationships with, as relationships bring costs as well as benefits. For example, a cooperative working relationship requires both parties to undertake a lot of formal and informal adaptations and investment, including management time, training and effort to coordinate resources and activities (Ford 1980). Moreover, the costs also include potential conflicts of interest between the parties and the possibility of missing out on opportunities with alternative companies (Anderson and Narus 1990).

In addition to being selective in terms of with whom to have relationships, the concept of continuity is also mutually shared in the Western and Chinese literature. Similar to *guanxi* that emphasizes relationships on a long-term basis (Chen 2001), Western buyer–seller relationships also focus on long-term interactions, and the financial returns that long-term relationships can bring (Storbacka et al. 1994). Nevertheless, the methods of facilitating long-term relationships are different in these two contexts. Wong and Leung (2001) explain that if the Chinese expect a relationship to continue in the long term, they will conduct more social interactions and exchange favors to maintain and improve *guanxi* between key personnel (e.g. the procurement manager and the sales representative). In contrast, rather than focusing on social interactions and the exchange of favors, the Western literature tends to emphasize the impact of trust, commitment and satisfaction on the continuity of relationships (Wilson and Mummalaneni 1988; Garbarino and Johnson 1999).

In short, Western buyer–seller relationships and Chinese *guanxi* are dissimilar in terms of their cultural and environmental backgrounds and their emphasis on different levels of relationships. For instance, while Chinese *guanxi* stresses interpersonal relationships, the Western literature puts more emphasis on buyer–seller relationship dyads at the organizational level. Moreover, because of their different focus, they have developed various perspectives regarding networks and the approaches that are used to expand networks. Nevertheless, both the Western and Chinese literature share similar views on relationship continuity and both suggest that firms should be selective with their relationship partners.

21.5 WESTERN AND CHINESE RELATIONSHIP CONSTRUCTS

In order to clarify further such similarities and differences between the Western and Chinese literature, this section explores some of the key relationship constructs that are used to assess the quality of the relationships and *guanxi*. It begins with a comparison of the key constructs of relationship quality highlighted in both literatures. Afterwards, a brief discussion is provided to explain the meaning of each key construct in both contexts.

Although various constructs have been used in different studies to assess the quality of relationships in Western discourse, the most popular and well-discussed constructs are trust, commitment, satisfaction, co-operation, coordination, communication, bonds and investments (Crosby

Table 21.1   Constructs of relationships and guanxi quality

Western relationship quality constructs		Chinese *guanxi* constructs
Trust	Credibility	*Xinren*
	Benevolence	
Commitment	Affective	*Ganqing*
	Calculative	*Renqing*
Satisfaction		
Coordination		
Cooperation		
Communication		
Bonds	Social Bonds	*Ganqing*
	Structural Bonds	
Investments		*Renqing*

et al. 1990; Morgan and Hunt 1994; Naudé and Buttle 2000). On the contrary, although the quality of *guanxi* has not been discussed as intensively as in the West, recent studies have started exploring the constructs that can be used to measure *guanxi* between two parties (Kipnis 1997; Wong and Leung 2001; Chen and Chen 2004; Yen et al. 2010). These key constructs include *ganqing* (affection, sentiment and emotion), *renqing* (human sympathy, favors and gift giving) and *xinren* (trust, belief and confidence).

As some of the constructs are shared between the two, Table 21.1 lists these constructs from the Western perspective and shows where the Chinese constructs appear to overlap. As shown, trust, commitment, social bonds and investments are the only Western constructs that correspond to *guanxi* constructs in the Chinese literature. However, this does not mean that the constructs of satisfaction, cooperation, coordination, communication and structural bonds are least important in the Chinese literature; instead, they are often used as either the antecedents or the consequences, rather than the attributes, of *guanxi*. In the following paragraphs, each construct will be discussed in more depth from both a Western and a Chinese perspective.

Trust is a construct that has been widely discussed in both the Western and Chinese literature – despite the fact that the Chinese construct *xinren* refers to trust at the interpersonal level, rather than the organizational level. In congruence with some Western beliefs, trust is regarded as a norm for facilitating exchange and has been identified as one of the key founda-tions on which relationships in China are based (Mavondo and Rodrigo 2001). As a Confucian value, trust influences the Chinese in many Asian countries and is a key component of successful *guanxi* (Tsang 1998). In Chinese culture, trust is taken as a basic social and business norm and it often eradicates the need for structural bonds, that is, formalized contracts, which in the West often act as a safeguard mechanism against opportun-istic behavior (Yen et al. 2007). Therefore, normally when Chinese people trust, there is belief that continued transactions will be facilitated, even in the absence of legal and contractual mechanisms (Luo 2001).

In parallel with the West, credibility is also acknowledged in the Chinese context (Yau et al. 2000). Because credibility takes time to accumulate, and instead of exchanging formalized contracts to facilitate business, the Chinese prefer to get to know their commercial counterparts initially, as there is a tendency not to do business with individuals they are unfa-miliar with (Luo 2001). In short, trust can enhance relational exchange among Western and ethnic Chinese business people, and should be taken as a central mechanism to help lubricate complex business net-works (Menkhoff 1993). For most Chinese business people, trust is often regarded with utmost priority, because if there is no trust, the formalized contract is meaningless (Ambler 1995).

Whilst to some degree a consensus may exist in Western and Chinese relational approaches regarding the fundamental characteristics of trust, Luo (2001) suggests that commitment may not necessarily imply the same thing for the two relational forms. Instead, it is related to two individual Chinese constructs, *ganqing* and *renqing*. As shown in Table 21.1, affective commitment overlaps with the emotional side of *guanxi* (*ganqing*); calcu-lative commitment meanwhile reflects more on materialistic obligations (*renqing*). Since affective commitment refers to a firm's loyal intention to remain in the relationship based upon their feelings and involvement with an exchange partner (Gilliland and Bello 2002), it is very similar to *ganqing*, that is, reflects on emotional understanding and connections, as well as a sense of loyalty and solidarity (Chen and Chen 2004).

In contrast, calculative commitment is based on the constant weigh-ing up of the benefits of a relationship with a partner against the costs of that relationship (Wetzels et al. 1998). When costs outweigh benefits, calculative commitment can cause a harmful impact on the continuity of relationships (Garbarino and Johnson 1999). This negative side of cal-culative commitment is in congruence to situations when the reciprocity rule of *renqing* is broken and *guanxi* between the two parties is damaged accordingly (Luo 2001).

Nevertheless, although affective and calculative commitment are similar to *ganqing* and *renqing* in the Chinese context, as with trust, commitment in a Chinese context should be considered more on a personal basis (Luo 2001). Thus, Mavondo and Rodrigo (2001) defined commitment as the dedication to a long-term interpersonal relationship of individual A (representing company A), with individual B (representing company B). This is considered to be highly applicable as it illustrates more the personal emphasis that is associated with Chinese commitment values (Yen et al. 2007).

As shown in Table 21.1, satisfaction is emphasized in the West as a construct of relationship quality. It is explained as a positive affective state resulting from the appraisal of all aspects of a working relationship relative to alternatives experienced or observed (Anderson and Narus 1984). This definition of satisfaction is in line with the meaning of satisfaction in the Chinese context. However, although satisfaction is recognized in the Chinese context, it is not necessarily viewed as an attribute that can reflect on the quality of *guanxi*. Instead, it is mostly used as an outcome of trust (Armstrong and Yee 2001), or good *guanxi* (Leung et al. 2005).

In the West, coordination is explained as the synchronization of activities and flows (Mohr and Nevin 1990) and can reflect on situations where parties work together to achieve mutual goals (Anderson and Narus 1990). Briefly speaking, there is no significant difference in terms of the meaning of coordination in the Chinese context. However, instead of being used as a key indicator of *guanxi*, coordination has been used as a consequence of trust (Sheu et al. 2006). In the Western context, Jap (1999) further explained that interpersonal trustworthiness is expected to be an important facilitator of dyadic coordination. Because individuals who trust each other are willing to share relevant ideas, exchange information and clarify goals and problems, then they tend to approach the relationship with a problem-solving orientation.

According to Cannon and Perreault (1999), cooperation is defined as the belief that both the supplier and reseller work jointly to achieve mutual and individual goals. It emphasizes joint problem-solving, which is also useful in conflict resolution (Mohr and Spekman 1994). Cooperation has been viewed as a consequence of trust and commitment (Morgan and Hunt 1994), a precursor for continued exchange (Möller and Wilson 1995) and a definite contributor to performance (Hewett and Bearden 2001). Although it has not been highlighted as a component that can be used to assess the quality of *guanxi*, in congruence with the Western literature, cooperation is often related to harmony and conflict-solving in a Chinese context. For example, whilst in the West, confrontation and disagreements are often openly aired as a strategy for integrating individuals with different perspectives (Hofstede 1980), conflict is not valued among the Chinese and aggressive confrontation is regarded as being rude and ill mannered (Yen et al. 2007). Chinese people are taught from a very early age that negative emotional displays are both unsociable and inconsequential for influencing outcomes. Therefore, should interorganizational conflict occur, Chinese managers often seek cooperative resolutions so that all parties involved can maintain an apparent harmony (Luo 2001).

To attain such a harmonized goal, Chinese people view communication as an opportunity for social interaction, where both parties can gain greater familiarity and a better understanding of their counterparts. Frequent communication (especially face-to-face communication) is therefore useful for nurturing relations (Kipnis 1997; Pearce and Robinson 2000). In the West, although communication has been suggested as an antecedent of trust, commitment, cooperation and satisfaction (Anderson and Narus 1990; Morgan and Hunt 1994; Mohr et al. 1996), the emphasis of communication is often seen more from a business perspective or as a form of activity link to coordinate activities and exchange facts or information (Håkansson and Snehota 1995). If the two parties fail to understand each other's communication styles, such differences may prove detrimental to the future evolvement of the exchange process (Beamer 1998). Moreover, Lin and Germain (1999) discovered that whilst being open and explicit characterized US culture, prudence and ambiguity more typified the Chinese, and such differences were a common problem in US–Chinese joint ventures.

In the West, relationship bonds are divided into structural and social bonds. Structural include contracts, mutual assets and specific investments that are made in new products, property and technology (Wilson and Jantrania 1996). Social bonds refer to the mutual friendship and liking that is shared by exchange partners (Wilson 1995). These bonds recognize the influence of personal or emotional elements on business relationships, which are similar to the Chinese construct, *ganqing* (Jacobs 1979; Chen and Chen 2004). According to Kipnis (1997), *ganqing* can be positively influenced through regular visits or meetings, exchanging favors, hosting or attending banquets and through providing gifts. Because it is often associated with *guanxi*, *ganqing* is frequently used as an attribute to assess the quality of *guanxi* in the Chinese context. In contrast, with the exception of contracts, other sorts of structural bonds appear to be less apparent in Chinese relationship discourse. Nevertheless, and as explained earlier, formal contracts are often replaced by trust, as rather than treating business as a binding legal process, the Chinese hold the view that a contract is a summary of discussion and a snapshot of the relationship, which is open to change (Chen 2001; Luo 2001).

As highlighted in Table 21.1, *renqing* may also correspond to investments in the West, as it shares similar characteristics which can be both tangible and intangible (Jap 1999). In terms of tangibility, it can relate to preferential treatment or the special allocation of resources. However, it can be intangible, as one could do a favor by providing particular know-how or a specific technology. According to Wong and Leung (2001), *renqing* implies the rule of a 'favor for a favor', and reflects the reciprocity emphasized in Confucius philosophy (Fang 1999; Chen 2001). Therefore, similar to the existence of investments, which often enable coordination and provide several important relationship-stabilizing properties (Jap 1999), *renqing* follows the obligation rule of reciprocity (Luo 2001).

However, reciprocation in Chinese relations is not expected to be equal, compared with investments in the West, and there is less hesitancy in being the first and greater beneficiary (Yen et al. 2007). Yau et al. (2000) explain that in Western circles there is a tendency to emphasize the symmetrical balance of reciprocity and repay what is owed as soon as possible in order to relieve tension. The Chinese believe that repayment need not be made immediately, because *renqing* can be saved and, like an insurance policy, one only wants to use it when there is really a need. However, it is very important to let the other party know that they appreciate and will repay at any time when needed. As the Chinese proverb says, 'If you honor me a linear foot, I should in return honor you ten feet'.

21.6   SUMMARY

In brief, we hope this chapter has successfully provided an overview relating to some of the research that has been undertaken in the West and China over the last 35 years or so in the area of business relationships. We have attempted to provide a brief synopsis relating to some of the work in both areas. At the same time, we have also provided a discussion relating to some of the similarities and differences associated with business relationships in these two distinct regions of the world. Overall, we would like to think that this chapter has stimulated the reader's appetite to read more, and we suggest looking at our work as further reading. We have therefore provided several references below.

FURTHER READING

Barnes, B.R., L.C. Leonidou, N.Y.M. Siu and C.N. Leonidou (2010), 'Opportunism as the inhibiting trigger for developing long-term oriented Western exporter–Hong Kong importer relationships', *Journal of International Marketing*, **18** (2), 35–63.
Barnes, B.R., D.A. Yen and L. Zhou (2010), 'Investigating guanxi dimensions and relationship outcomes: insights from Sino-Anglo business relationships', *Industrial Marketing Management*, **40** (10), 510–521.

Yen, D.A. and B.R. Barnes (2010), 'Analyzing stage and duration of Anglo-Chinese business-to-business relationships', *Industrial Marketing Management*, **40** (3), 346–357.

Yen, D.A., B.R. Barnes and C. Wang (2010), 'The measurement of Guanxi: introducing the GRX model', *Industrial Marketing Management*, **40** (1), 97–108.

Yen, D.A., Q. Yu and B.R. Barnes (2007), 'Focusing on relationship dimensions to improve the quality of Chinese–Western business-to-business exchanges', *Total Quality Management*, **18** (8), 1–11.

REFERENCES

Ambler, T. (1995), 'Reflections in China: re-orienting images of marketing', *Marketing Management*, **4** (1), 23–30.

Ambler, T. and C. Styles (2000), 'The future of relational research in international marketing: constructs and conduits', *International Marketing Review*, **17** (6), 492–503.

Anderson, J.C. and J.A. Narus (1984), 'A model of distributor's perspective of distributor–manufacturer working relationships', *Journal of Marketing*, **48** (1), 62–74.

Anderson, J.C. and J.A. Narus (1990), 'A model of manufacturer and distributor working partnerships', *Journal of Marketing*, **54** (1), 42–58.

Armstrong, R.W. and S.M. Yee (2001), 'Do Chinese trust Chinese? A study of Chinese buyers and sellers in Malaysia', *Journal of International Marketing*, **9** (3), 63–87.

Arregle, J.L., A. Borza, M.T. Dacin, M.A. Hitt and E. Levitas (2000), 'Partner selection in emerging and developing market contexts: resource-based and organizational learning perspectives', *Academy of Management Journal*, **43** (3), 449–467.

Beamer, L. (1998), 'Bridging business cultures', *China Business Review*, **25** (3), 54–58.

Brekke, A. (2005), 'How should you act?' 21st IMP Conference, Rotterdam.

Bruun, O. (1993), *Business and Bureaucracy in a Chinese City, Institute of East Asian Studies*, Berkeley, CA: University of California Press.

Cannon, J.P. and W.D. Perreault, Jr. (1999), 'Buyer–seller relationships in business markets', *Journal of Marketing Research*, **36** (4), 439–460.

Chan, W.T. (1963), *A Source Book in Chinese Philosophy*, Princeton, NJ: Princeton University Press.

Chen, M.J. (2001), *Inside Chinese Business*, Boston, MA: Harvard Business School Press.

Chen, X.P. and C.C. Chen (2004), 'On the intricacies of the Chinese guanxi: a process model of guanxi development', *Asia Pacific Journal of Management*, **21** (3), 305–324.

Crosby, L.A., R.E. Kenneth and D. Cowles (1990), 'Relationship quality in services selling: an interpersonal influence perspective', *Journal of Marketing*, **54** (3), 68–81.

Cunningham, M.T. and E. Homse (1986), 'Controlling the marketing–purchasing inter-face: resource development and organisational implications', *Industrial Marketing and Purchasing*, **1** (2), 3–27.

Davies, H., K.P. Leung, T.K. Luk and Y.H. Wang (1995), 'The benefits of guanxi: the value of relationships in developing the Chinese market', *Industrial Marketing Management*, **24** (3), 207–214.

Doney, P.M. and J.P. Cannon (1997), 'An examination of the nature of trust in buyer–seller relationships', *Journal of Marketing*, **61** (2), 35–51.

Dwyer, R.F., P.H. Schurr and S. Oh (1987), 'Developing buyer–seller relationships', *Journal of Marketing*, **51** (2), 11–27.

Fang, T. (1999), *Chinese Business Negotiating Style*, CA: Sage Publications.

Ford, D. (1980), 'The development of buyer–seller relationships in industrial markets', *European Journal of Marketing*, **14** (5–6), 339–354.

Garbarino, E. and M.S. Johnson (1999), 'The different roles of satisfaction, trust, and commitment in customer relationships', *Journal of Marketing*, **63** (2), 70–87.

Geyskens, I., J.B. Steenkamp, L.K. Scheer and N. Kumar (1996), 'The effects of trust and interdependence on relationship commitment: a trans-Atlantic study', *International Journal of Research in Marketing*, **13** (4), 303–318.

Gilliland, D.I. and D.C. Bello (2002), 'Two sides to attitudinal commitment: the effect of calculative and loyalty commitment on enforcement mechanisms in distribution channels', *Journal of the Academy of Marketing Science*, **30** (1), 24–43.

Håkansson, H. (ed.) (1982), *International Marketing and Purchasing of Industrial Goods: An Interaction Approach*, Chichester: John Wiley.

Håkansson, H. and D.T. Ford (2002), 'How should companies interact in business networks?' *Journal of Business Research*, **55** (2), 133–139.

Håkansson, H. and I. Snehota (1995), 'Analysing business relationships', in H. Håkansson and I. Snehota (eds), *Developing Relationships In Business Networks*, London: Routledge, pp. 24–46.

Håkansson, H. and I. Snehota (2000), 'The IMP perspective, assets and liabilities of relationships', in J. Sheth (ed.), *Handbook of Relationship Marketing*, Thousand Oaks, CA: Sage Publications, pp. 69–93.

Havila, V., J. Johanson and P. Thilenius (2004), 'International business-relationship triads', *International Marketing Review*, **21** (2), 172–186.

Hewett, K. and W.O. Bearden (2001), 'Dependence, trust and relational behavior on the part of foreign subsidiary marketing operations: implications for managing global marketing operations', *Journal of Marketing*, **65** (4), 51–56.

Hofstede, G.H. (1980), *Culture's Consequences: International Differences in Work-Related Values*, Beverly Hills, CA: Sage Publications.

Huang, Q., R.S. Andrulis and T. Chen (1994), *A Guide to Successful Business Relations with the Chinese: Opening the Great Wall's Gate*, New York: Binghamton.

Hwang, K.K. (1987), 'Face and favor, the Chinese power game', *American Journal of Sociology*, **92** (4), 944–974.

Jacobs, B.J. (1979), 'A preliminary model of particularistic ties in Chinese political alliances: Kan-ch'ing nad Kuan-his a Rual Taiwanese township', *China Quarterly*, **78**, 237–273.

Jap, S.D. (1999), 'Pie-expansion efforts: collaboration processes in buyer–supplier relationships', *Journal of Marketing Research*, **36** (4), 461–475.

King, A.Y.C. (1991), 'Kuan-his and net work building: a sociological interpretation', *Daedalus*, **120** (2), 63–84.

Kipnis, A.B. (1997), *Producing Guanxi: Sentiment, Self, and Subculture in a North China Village*, N.C.: Duke University Press.

Lee, D.Y. and P.L. Dawes (2005), '*Guanxi*, trust, and long-term orientation in Chinese business markets', *Journal of International Marketing*, **13** (2), 28–56.

Lee, M. and P. Xu (2001), *Doing Business in China: The Experience of Taiwanese Businessman in Various Place of China*, Taipei, Taiwan: Commercial Culture.

Leung, T.K.P., K.H. Lai, R.Y.K. Chan and Y.H. Wong (2005), 'The roles of xinyong and guanxi in Chinese relationship marketing', *European Journal of Marketing*, **39** (5–6), 528–565.

Leung, T.K.P., Y.H. Wong and S. Wong (1996), 'A study of Hong Kong businessmen's perceptions of the role of guanxi in the People's Republic of China', *Journal of Business Ethics*, **15** (7), 749–758.

Lin, X. and R. Germain (1999), 'Predicting international joint venture interaction frequency in US–Chinese ventures', *Journal of International Marketing*, **7** (2), 5–23.

Lo, W.C.W. and A.M. Everett (2001), 'Thriving in the regulatory environment of e-commerce in China: a guanxi strategy', *SAM Advanced Management Journal*, **66** (3), 17–24.

Luo, Y. (1997a), 'Guanxi: principles, philosophies, and implications', *Human Systems Management*, **16** (1), 43–51.

Luo, Y. (1997b), 'Guanxi and performance of foreign-invested enterprises in China: an empirical inquiry', *Management International Review*, **37** (1), 51–70.

Luo, Y. (2001), *Guanxi and Business*, Singapore: World Scientific Publishing.

Luo, Y. and M.W. Peng (2000), 'Managerial ties and firm performances in a transition economy: the nature of a micro-macro link', *Academy of Management Journal*, **43** (3), 486–501.

Mattsson, L.G. (1997), '"Relationship marketing" in a network perspective', in H.G. Gemunden, T. Ritter and A. Walter (eds), *Relationships and Networks in International Markets*, Oxford: Pergamon Press, pp. 37–47.

Mavondo, F.T. and E.M. Rodrigo (2001), 'The effect of relationship dimensions on interpersonal and interorganizational commitment in organizations conducting business between Australia and China', *Journal of Business Research*, **52** (2), 111–121.

McGuiness, N., N. Cambell and J. Leontiades (1991), 'Selling machinery to China: Chinese perceptions of strategies and relationships', *Journal of International Business Studies*, **22** (2), 187–207.

Menkhoff, T. (1993), *Trade Routes, Trust and Trading Networks: Chinese Small Enterprises in Singapore*, Saarbrücken: Breitenbach.

Mohr, J., R.J. Fisher and J.R. Nevin (1996), 'Collaborative communication in interfirm relationships: moderating effects of integration and control', *Journal of Marketing*, **60** (3), 103–115.

Mohr, J. and J.R. Nevin (1990), 'Communication strategies in marketing channels: a theoretical perspective', *Journal of Marketing*, **54** (4), 36–51.

Mohr, J. and R. Spekman (1994), 'Characteristics of partnership success: partnership attributes, communication behavior and conflict resolution techniques', *Strategic Management Journal*, **15** (2), 135–152.

Möller, K. and D.T. Wilson (1995), *Business Marketing: An Interaction and Network Perspective*, MA: Kluwer Academic Publishers.

Morgan, R.M. and S.D. Hunt (1994), 'The commitment-trust theory of relationship marketing', *Journal of Marketing*, **58** (3), 20–38.

Naudé, P. and F. Buttle (2000), 'Assessing relationship quality', *Industrial Marketing Management*, **29** (4), 351–361.

Pearce, J.A. and R.B. Robinson (2000), 'Cultivating guanxi as a foreign investor strategy', *Business Horizons*, **43** (1), 31–38.

Rodrigez, C.M. and David T. Wilson (2002), 'Relationship bonding and trust as a foundation for commitment in US–Mexican strategic alliances: a structural equation modelling approach', *Journal of International Marketing*, **10** (4), 53–76.

Seligman, S.D. (1999), *Chinese Business Etiquette*, New York: Warner Business Books.

Sheu, C., H.J.R. Yen and B. Chae (2006), 'Determinants of supplier–retailer collaboration: evidence from an international study', *International Journal of Operations and Production Management*, **26** (1–2), 24–47.

Standifird, S.S. and R.S. Marshall (2000), 'The transaction cost advantage of guanxi-based business practices', *Journal of World Business*, **35** (1), 21–42.

Storbacka, K., T. Strandvik and C. Grönroos (1994), 'Managing customer relationships for profit: the dynamics of relationship quality', *International Journal of Service Industry Management*, **5** (5), 21–38.

Tsang, E.W.K. (1998), 'Can guanxi be a source of sustained competitive advantage for doing business in China?' *Academy of Management Executive*, **12** (2), 64–73.

Turnbull, P., D. Ford and M. Cunningham (1996), 'Interaction, relationships and networks in business markets: an evolving perspective', *Journal of Business and Industrial Marketing*, **11** (3–4), 44–62.

Wang, C.L. (2007), 'Guanxi vs. relationship marketing, exploring underlying differences', *Industrial Marketing Management*, **36** (1), 81–86.

Wetzels, M., K. De Ruyter and M. Van Birgelen (1998), 'Marketing service relationships: the role of commitment', *Journal of Business and Industrial Marketing*, **13** (4–5), 406–423.

Whitley, R. (1994), *Business System in East Asia*, London: Sage Publications.

Williams, J.D., S.L. Han and W.J. Qualls (1998), 'A conceptual model and study of cross-cultural business relationships', *Journal of Business Research*, **42** (2), 135–143.

Wilson, D.T. (1995), 'An integrated model of buyer–seller relationships', *Journal of Academic Marketing Science*, **23** (4), 335–345.

Wilson, D.T. and S. Jantrania (1996), 'Understanding the value of a relationship', *Asia-Australia Marketing Journal*, **2** (1), 55–66.

Wilson, D.T. and V. Mummalaneni (1988), 'Modeling and measuring buyer–seller relationships', Unpublished working paper, Institute For The Study of Business Markets Report, Pennsylvania State University.

Wong, Y.H. and R.Y.K. Chan (1999), 'Relationship marketing in China: guanxi, favouritism and adaptation', *Journal of Business Ethics*, **22** (3), 107–108.

Wong, Y.H. and T.K.P. Leung (2001), *Guanxi Relationship Marketing in a Chinese Context*, New York: International Business Press.

Yau, O.H.M., J.S.Y. Lee, R.P.M. Chow, L.Y.M. Sin and A.C.B. Tse (2000), 'Relationship marketing the Chinese way', *Business Horizons*, **43** (1), 16–24.

Yen, D.A., B.R. Barnes and C. Wang (2010), 'The measurement of guanxi: introducing the GRX model', *Industrial Marketing Management*, **40** (1), 97–108.

Yen, D.A., Q. Yu and B.R. Barnes (2007), 'Focusing on relationship dimensions to improve the quality of Chinese–Western business-to-business exchanges', *Total Quality Management*, **18** (8), 1–11.

Yeung, I.Y.M. and R.L. Tung (1996), 'Achieving business success in Confucian societies: the importance of guanxi (connections)', *Organizational Dynamics*, **25** (2), 54–65.

22 Reforms in Russian corporate governance and evaluation of Russian boards of directors

Dilek Demirbas, Andrey Yukhanaev and Roman Stepanov

22.1 INTRODUCTION

All organizations around the world, regardless of either Western or Eastern origin, are currently undergoing significant changes. One of the major changes within these organizations is corporate governance, and these changes in corporate governance have become the focus of all related parties such as directors, investors, stakeholders and regulators. Indeed, Tricker (2000), considering the evolution of business environment and corporate development, postulated the following chronology: entrepreneurship as a nineteenth-century phenomenum, management prevalence as a catalytic force in the twentieth century and corporate governance as a leitmotif of modern times. The common conclusion of all parties involved is that companies across the world need to adopt commonly accepted corporate governance standards in order to attract foreign capital, to become internationally more competitive and to deal with corporate governance problems in today's economic environment.

With the intention of providing the best and most commonly accepted international corporate governance standards, in 1999 the Organisation for Economic Co-operation and Development (OECD) developed an international corporate governance code and global principles of 'good' governance. In 2004, the OECD revised its previous attempt, *Principles of Corporate Governance* and defined 'good corporate governance'. Since the date of first publication, the OECD *Principles* (1999, 2004) have gained substantial recognition worldwide as a framework for reforms and a reference point for corporate governance literature. Now, there is a positive tendency among company directors around the world to support reforms, partly as a result of increasing international pressures to harmonize corporate governance standards at the global level in accordance with the OECD *Principles*, and partly as a result of the positive guidance of governments on the legal system and the economy.

To maintain good corporate governance (CG), board of directors is seen as the key mechanism for achieving transparency, efficiency, independency and good communication within the organization. According to the OECD *Principles* (2004) boards of directors have to focus on transparency and fulfilment of the following functions and responsibilities through relevant board committees: (1) continuously review and guide corporate strategic development with special attention to risk management policies and divestitures, budgeting and investments, corporate performance objectives and business plans, as well as monitor the implementation process; (2) proactively oversee and audit the corporate governance practices aimed at effectiveness, integrity of accounting and financial reporting procedures; (3) rationally select, nominate, remunerate and replace the key corporate executives, ensuring the attainment of shareholder satisfaction together with conflict resolution between various groups of stakeholders; and (4) efficiently disclose and communicate processes which control conformity with the relevant laws as well as reputable conduct standards.

On the same lines as the OECD *Principles*, the UK Higgs Report (Higgs 2003) also underlines the importance of constant scrutiny and independent enquiry by the relevant board committees comprised of effective non-executive professionals, which in turn should be driven by:

- the highest ethical standards of integrity and probity;
- the highest CG standards and compliance with codes of reputable conduct;
- support of top managers in their leadership while monitoring their conduct;
- intelligent questioning, constructive debating and rigorous challenging;
- balanced views of others, inside and outside the board;
- trust and respect of other board members.

In the literature, Pettigrew and McNulty (1998), exploring intricacies of the directorship role, argue that corporate boards are extremely complex collectives and fascinating societal institutions comprised of highly influential individuals and differentiated by various power distribution mechanisms. Indeed:

> much is now known about the structure and composition of boards and about patterns of CEO succession and executive compensation, but we know much less about how boards work as institutions, the contributions made by various board members, and how those contributions are shaped by the balance of power in and around the boardroom. (Pettigrew and McNulty 1998, 198)

Of course this trend did not happen with the same speed and smoothness in many Eastern European countries – in particular, transition economies – as it happened in the Western countries. Some transition countries, such as Russia, are still in the process of reforms and have not completed the transformation even though they might be considered as moving in the right direction to do so. Russia exhibits a special case waiting to be examined.

In the 1990s, Russian communism had failed and the seeds of a market economy had been planted by rapidly privatizing the state-owned enterprises, creating stock markets and adopting corporate legal codes. However these rapid changes left Russia with extremely weak corporate governance in particular, throughout the privatization period. Furthermore, during the 2000s, the government significantly increased its presence in the economy through the nationalization of a number of large companies (see, for more detail, OECD 2006; Vernikov 2007) when corporate scandals, global competition and financial crises forced Russia to have a robust institutional environment (Stiglitz 1999; International Finance Corporation 2004; Perotti 2004). As a result, addressing some important calls such as introduction of international corporate govern-ance standards, financial statements and an independent board of direc-tors have become urgent issues for many Russian companies wishing to do business with other international companies and develop within the com-petitive environment (Puffer and McCarthy 2003; Yakovlev 2004). Since 2007 the Russian government has taken a number of measures to assure general improvement in the institution of corporate governance: the bank-ruptcy law was revised; the Joint Stock Companies Act was passed in the new version; the Code of Corporate Conduct was designed; the reform of the judicial system was launched; dissemination of best practices of corporate governance was promoted; and the law enforcement system was enhanced (Yakovlev 2006).

Even though adopting common standards and corporate governance attracted some scholars' attention, nevertheless, only a few studies have been conducted on the relationship between the boards of directors and corporate reforms in Russia from the perspective of reforms and the legal aspects. Among them, Bevan et al. (2001) find that companies whose boards of directors are controlled by 'outside' shareholders tend to be more willing to aspire to restructuring and management renewal than enterprises whose boards are dominated by insiders. Kapalyushnikow and Demina (2005) demonstrate that there is a positive relationship between the length of tenure of a board chairman and good corporate governance. Along the same lines, Goltsman (2000) also confirms the idea that high ownership of shares by managers and outsiders leads to a significant increase in the turnover frequency of board members. Moreover, Muravyev (2003) shows that insider director representation rights and appointed directors in Russia are negatively correlated with chief executive officer (CEO) turnover. Judge et al. (2003) also quantitatively confirm that an enterprise whose board of directors is virtually controlled by a CEO has a significant disadvantage regarding performance over enterprises that are compliant with provisions of the Joint Stock Companies Act, which prohibits one person from simultaneous holding of the offices of CEO and chairman of the board.

In addition, Black (2001) examines the relationship between corporate governance behaviour and market value for a sample of 21 Russian firms, and concludes that the correlation between the corporate governance and market value is statistically very strong, and that corporate governance has a powerful effect on company market value in a developing country where legal and cultural constraints on corporate behaviour are relatively fragile. On the other hand, the correlation between the corporate governance and market value is very weak in a country with a strong corporate governance system, such as the USA, due to the fact that a minimum quality of corporate governance is determined by securities law, corporate law, stock exchange rules and behavioural norms, and it is also accepted that almost no effect of corporate governance behaviour on company market value is observed. Black (2001) demonstrates that a country like Russia, with weaker rules and norms, offers more scope for interfirm variation and thus the potential for stronger results.

The main aim of this chapter is to review the structure of corporate governance in Russia and focus primarily on the Russian boards of directors, in detail. Namely, we will examine the legal aspects of the Russian corporate governance and pertinent institutional changes. The remainder of the chapter has the following structure. Section 22.2 considers the general aspects of corporate governance and recent reforms in Russia. Section 22.3 focuses on the Russian legal system and its implication for corporate governance and explores the evolution of Russian boards of directors. The chapter is concluded in section 22.4.

22.2   GENERAL ASPECTS OF CORPORATE GOVERNANCE AND HARMONIZATION PROCESS

Tricker (2000), reviewing the history of corporate governance, notes that the study of how power is exercised over corporate entities is less than a century old, while the phrase 'corporate governance' has been used only since the 1980s. Breton and Pesqueux (2006) concur that corporate governance affects many social, political and organizational aspects within societies, since it entails an intertwined network of collaborative relationships between different groups, communities and individuals. Similarly, Claessens (2003, 5) perceives corporate governance as 'the relationship between shareholders, creditors, and corporations; between financial markets, institutions, and corporations; and between employees and corporations. CG would also encompass the issue of corporate social responsibility, including such aspects as the dealings of the firm with respect to culture and the environment'.

After Berle and Means (1932) drew attention to the phenomenon of separation of power between salaried management and owners, it took nearly 40 years for boards and directors to come under academic and scholar study, with Mace (1971) pioneering the field 'of what directors really did'. Although the theoretical exploration of the subject (boards' roles and processes, in particular) is relatively mature, consensus still seems to be quite distant.

A much quoted report by the Cadbury Committee (Cadbury 1992) suggests a straightforward definition of corporate governance – 'the system by which companies are directed and controlled', where boards are appointed by shareholders and consist of two types of directors, executive and non-executive. The former are responsible for the company's strategy and operations, and report to the company shareholders. The latter are part-time outsiders, working as 'guardians', 'monitors', 'challengers', 'auditors', 'advisors', 'buffers' (Pass 2004), 'mentors' and 'ambassadors' (Heidrick & Struggles 2007).

In the modern days of globalization, market dynamics and rampant hypercompetition in many industries it is becoming impossible to remain competitive without progressive strategic guidance and competent leadership radiating from proficient corporate boardrooms. Boards of directors in Western corporate governance have a strategically important role, and shareholders have the power to elect the supervisory body to represent their interests. This body essentially provides strategic direction to and control over the company's managers. Managers are responsible to this supervisory body, and this body is accountable to shareholders through the General Meeting of Shareholders (GMS). It is normal to expect that a board of directors will provide attentive supervision of a company's management for the benefit of all its shareholders by finding ways to achieve the best possible balance between shareholders' interests and good managerial practices. For Melkumov (2009), effective boards of directors in most Western economies have been pivotal pillars in ensuring the appropriate maintenance of CG standards, conceptualization and systematic monitoring of strategic corporate development. Daily et al. (2003) perceive the boards as the central instrument of CG mechanics. Likewise, Adams and Ferreira (2007) concur that the board directors hold the legal power, decision-making authority and ultimate responsibilities for the future corporate development. Cadbury (1992) considers the boards of directors to be an indispensible link between shareholders, investors and executive management of the companies. In broader terms, Brennan (2006, 579), considering the boards' strategic involvement, assumes that: 'board performance of its monitoring duties is influenced by the effectiveness of the board, which in turn is influenced by factors such as board composition and quality, size of boards, duality of CEO/Chairman positions, board diversity, information asymmetries and board culture'.

Nevertheless, the role and importance of the corporate board of a private sector company have some contradictory assessments in both the academic literature and business society. Van den Berghe and Levrau (2004) point out that 50 years ago a Harvard Business School professor observed that too many boards of directors were passive and rather decorative. Since then, the situation has not seemed to change considerably for the better: contemporary definitions that have been given to the boards by academic scholars often vary widely. Drucker (1974) described boards as 'an impotent ceremonial and legal fiction'. Lorsch and MacIver (1989), investigating the American boards, find many of them acting 'like pawns of their CEOs'.

Corporate scandals of 1999–2001 put a new spotlight on the boards (Van den Berghe and Levrau 2004), and brought a new wave of discussion on how to improve their performance and to rebuild trust. Monks and Minow (2001) tag the board as the company's 'non-performing idle assets'. Bryne (2002) refers to them as 'mere ornaments on a corporate Christmas tree'. On the other hand, Romano (1996) defines the boards as 'the principal governance structure for shareholders in diffusely held firms'. Cadbury (1992) considers the boards of directors to be a bridge between the shareholders and the management. Daily et al. (2003) see the board as 'the most central internal governance mechanism'. Adams and Ferreira (2007) concur that the board is 'the ultimate legal authority with respect to decision making in the firm'. Brennan (2006) goes further, positioning the boards as 'the official first line of defence against managers'. Moreover, the academics' point of view is supported by Murphy (2006) of PricewaterhouseCoopers consultancy, who asserts that for companies it is fundamental to be headed by an effective board of directors which is collectively responsible for the success of the company.

The situation seems even more ambiguous when country and cultural peculiarities are brought under consideration. There are diversities of capitalism, for example the 'crony' approach in some parts of East Asia and Japan and the 'gangster capitalism' in Russia, discovered by Garratt (1999), as well as different corporate governance traditions such as the Anglo-Saxon 'market-oriented' model (Corbetta and Salvato 2004), the 'network-oriented' model of Japan, Latin American countries, Italy and France (Weimer and Pape 1999) and a social partnership model practised in Germany (Tricker 2000).

Although the current law on joint stock companies and additional Acts have been influenced by the Anglo-Saxon corporate model, it could never be a replica of already existing legal provisions in the developed countries. Despite the fact that such provisions have passed the test of time, their adoption in the Russian reality has been hindered by the underdeveloped capital markets, ineffective institutional and legal infrastructures and, more importantly, the absence of solid social traditions (Black 2001). The latter sheds some light on the reasons for placing a sometimes disproportionate emphasis on the trust-based arrangements with the authorities. These arrangements relate the issues arising from the allocation of private property prior to a substantial investment (BBC 2005). The task of changing social perception and aligning it with the 'capitalist way' could never be a straightforward one, and is unlikely to produce a similar legal infrastructure at least in the short- and medium-term future.

22.3   REFORMS ON RUSSIAN CORPORATE GOVERNANCE AND BOARDS OF DIRECTORS

Russia is a unique case study for the international CG literature, with numerous gaps to explore for researchers and policy-makers studying issues of good CG standards, international accounting standards, independent boards of directors and consistent corporate governance codes. Since the early 2000s the establishment of CG governance together with identification of good governance practices has become an increasingly important task for at least two reasons (Filatotchev 2006; Fox and Heller 2006; Tricker 2009). As a result of the significant government presence in the economy – which was expressed in the nationalization of a number of large companies through either back tax claims (see Yukos) or discounted acquisitions of controlling stakes in the privately owned companies by the state-owned enterprises (SOE) (see, for more detail, Stiglitz 1999; International Finance Corporation 2004; Perotti 2004; OECD 2006; Vernikov 2007) – the introduction of international corporate governance standards, financial statements and the independent board of directors have become urgent issues for many companies looking for ways to survive and develop in the context of such an environment (Puffer and McCarthy 2003; Yakovlev 2004).

Dissecting these grandiose aims into structural components, it is important to analyse the crucial role played by the efficient financial infrastructure in general and the sound CG system in particular within the Russian economy in realizing the expected modernization reforms. The main aim of this chapter is therefore to review the impacts and outcomes of those modernization reforms, together with their shortcomings.

22.3.1   Specifics of Russian Corporate Governance

Most Russian joint stock companies are owned and controlled by owner-managers (Jenkins 2002) who emerged from mass privatization in Russia in the early 1990s and combined the functions of ownership (over 80 per cent of shareholding in some companies) and sole management. They usually take position of either CEO or president or chairman in their groups.

Contemporarily, many large Russian joint stock companies have listed some small percentages (8–12 per cent) of their shares on Western stock exchanges and recruited non-executive directors to their boards, claiming to proceed in line with Western standards of corporate governance. But that hardly changes the main point: all those companies retain their family nature, with one man in charge of everything. This type of corporate governance is often referred to in terms of autocracy or authoritarianism (Bradford and Bernstain 2006), where decisions are taken within and by the undivided authority of an owner. In the view of some authors, such an ownership and control structure is highly unsustainable. For example, Adizes (2006), viewing management as 'a process realized by people to make their company efficient and effective in short and long term run', considers that it has nothing to do with such notions as control, supervision or guidance, and therefore team management is inevitable.

A medal of close control over Russian business has its reverse side, which seemingly affects its strategic vision and decision-making. Oleynik (2007) of Canadian Memorial University points out the 'conditional – not absolute – nature of ownership' in Russia. This conditionality is of a political character, that is, it depends upon the level of political relations between a businessman and governmental institutions (from local to federal level) and, hence, it is believed to be extremely unstable. In other words, the owners of big business in Russia can hardly be too confident in their future, and such an uncertainty has multiple negative effects including those over long-term investments and strategy.

22.3.2 Russian Legal System: Implications for Corporate Governance

Russia is a civil law country. However, the Supreme Court and the Supreme Arbitration Court have the authority to make rulings which become obligatory for the relevant lower-level courts (Bushev 2001). Moreover, according to article 15 of the Constitution of the Russian Federation, international law has precedence over the Constitution, international treaties and domestic law. This characteristic sometimes leads to inconsistencies in the Russian Code of Corporate Conduct (2002) and needs to be dealt with by means of establishing a clear hierarchy between codified and non-codified acts.

The Russian Code of Corporate Conduct (2002) divides legal entities into commercial and non-commercial organizations. Non-commercial organizations are outside the scope of this chapter and therefore a greater emphasis will be placed on the theoretical analysis of the legal provisions in relation to commercial entities. In Russia, commercial enterprises can be represented by general partnerships, limited partnerships, limited liability companies, additional liability companies and joint stock companies. The joint stock company is the most popular type of commercial enterprise among foreign businesses operating in Russia. The Russian Law on Joint Stock Companies is the legal underpinning for the open and closed joint stock companies. Therefore, the Russian Law on Joint Stock Companies is used as the prime point of reference for the theoretical analysis of the provisions therein. It has to be noted that there are a number of additional Acts which seek to regulate separate types of business activity, specific aspects of the status of commercial organizations (size, foreign participation, employee involvement, and so on) and certain areas of the activities of commercial organizations (Bushev 2001).

It has been suggested that the alternative systems produce varying degrees of investor protection (La Porta et al. 1997). The common law system is recognized to be more responsive to the changing needs of corporate governance, offering greater levels of investor protection. Here, judges have a free hand to apply provisions of constantly evolving principles of good governance directly in the form of a codified judicial Act. Therefore, the legal status of the main governance principles can be viewed as that of enforceable regulation. In contrast, in civil law countries it is unclear as to the legal status of the existing governance provisions. This is the case because judges cannot add to the law by means of precedent, but need to have the law developed through the parliament (Cuervo 2002) which is a lengthy and sometimes convoluted process. It could be argued that this system is less well equipped when it comes to dealing with the dynamic aspect of modern governance. There is an academic proposition that 'precedential regulation of social relations arises from the diversity of social life and the freedom of individual initiative' (Neshataeva 2003). Therefore adequate regulation solely through legislation is practically impossible. It is generally recognized that the civil law countries reject judicial practice as the source of law. However, it has to be mentioned that the precedential element in terms of the origin of law has always existed in Russia and within the continental European legal system in the form of analogy (Neshataeva 2003).

Despite the latter consideration, there is little doubt that the law of precedence is much more developed in common law countries for fundamental reasons stemming from the inherent legal system. Conversely, civil law countries are void of comprehensive case law and the associated responsiveness of court rulings. Because the specific legal characteristics of civil law countries are imbedded in the legal system itself, the prospect of developing case law in the form of precedents in countries like Russia is not seen as a viable option. The proposed solution with regard to the development of corporate governance lies in the call for more market control (Cuervo 2002). The pivotal role here is played by shareholders since they are regarded as the driving force of market control. Therefore, facilitation of shareholder involvement through greater participation and decision-making powers informed by quality information are considered as the prime focus of the required reforms. This fact has been recognized by the Russian government which developed and endorsed the Corporate Legislation Development Concept up to 2008.

The role of legislation
The primary role of corporate legislation in developed economies is to facilitate the business process. Here, company law and its reform are designed in such a way as to assist the decision-making process aimed at wealth maximization, which is indeed the principal goal of corporate legislation (Black and Kraakman 1996). The law attempts to act in unison with supporting institutions that oversee the management, and typically reacts to the anomaly of expropriation and/or management malfunction. This fact addresses deficiencies of the system while allowing a greater level of flexibility in the way a public organization is run. Ideally, good managers need complete decision-making freedom in their pursuit of wealth maximization, as some restrictions might prevent profitable deals from taking place. On the other hand, investors require a certain level of protection which will minimize the risk of misappropriation and bad practice. In the developed economies, this role of legislation is supported by the effects of competition, relatively efficient stock markets and a developed accounting profession, together with enforceable and clear rules against expropriation. This results in a sophisticated management culture which,

coupled with informed investor expectations, lead to a relatively healthy business environment. Furthermore, courts have a sufficient level of expertise and enforcement capabilities to apply the concept of fiduciary duty as a measure against blatant cases of managerial misconduct. Whatever is in the grey area is left for the markets to interpret. The process is facilitated by a number of mechanisms that seek to align the interests of shareholders (principals) and managers (agents). These mechanisms are board structure, internal control, external audits, disclosure and transparency requirements, remuneration and nomination procedures. In developed economies this structure, although not faultless, more often achieves the required balance of power to the mutual benefit of those who provide the finance and those who manage the business.

The corporate governance landscape in the developing economies such as Russia is different from that in the developed economies. Here, the primary role of legislation is the protection of investors' interests from the self-benefiting actions of insiders. The law on joint stock companies in Russia provides reassurance of the status and position of the company in the eyes of investors. This is a challenging task, particularly in the absence of the essential market institutions and the required social and management traditions and culture. The balance in favour of investor protection inevitably diminishes managerial freedom because it comes in the form of compulsory rules and prescribed practices. It diminishes managerial freedom because the business process is too complex and deals with too many uncertainties to be systematically consistent with categorical rules which need to be blindly adhered to. However, in the Russian context there is a lot of sense in sacrificing managerial freedom to act in the interests of shareholder rights. The argument here is that it is that same managerial freedom which is likely to lead to misappropriation of shareholder funds if deliberately misused by otherwise powerful insiders. Furthermore, an ownership structure where majority control typically belongs to insiders, and outside shareholders are in the minority, makes the governance structure in Russia even more vulnerable to expropriation practices. This ultimately leads to the negative political side-effect of growing public dissatisfaction with the concept of the market economy and property rights. This political pressure further emphasizes the protective role of legislation, and curtails managerial freedom.

Anglo-Saxon model versus continental model
The Anglo-Saxon model of corporate governance has been characterized by a dispersed ownership, sophisticated institutional investment mechanisms, active private equity market, active takeover and corporate control market, high degree of shareholder equality, high disclosure,

broadly aligned incentives and non-executive majority boards (Roberts 2004). These characteristics coupled with well-developed laws and effective enforcement mechanisms have produced the most developed capital markets. It has to be said that this system has its weaknesses. One of the weaknesses is a greater distance between ownership and control, leading to certain aspects of the agency problem (e.g. collective action problem) (Osugi 2000). Although the agency cost is inevitable in the modern corporate environment, the supporting market institutions and specific governance mechanisms can act in such a way as to minimize the cost of the agency problem. Although there is an ongoing debate as to which model is more effective at reducing the agency cost, the relative success of the Anglo-Saxon system has resulted in a general shift towards a more market-driven approach (Nooteboom 1999; Mintz 2005). However, dispersed ownership tends to favour exit as the main mechanism of corporate control. Here shareholders prefer to sell their shares rather than look for ways of protecting their interests through exerting positive influence over the company's management (Nooteboom 1999). This is an example of the fact that the pure market-driven system is not flawless (Shleifer and Vishny 1997) and might be one-sided in terms of setting corporate objectives and the ways of their attainment.

The Continental model is very different in terms of the adopted corporate governance characteristics. Concentrated ownership, long-term debt finance, close involvement of banks, importance of private funding, underdeveloped capital markets, limited takeover market, inadequate minority protection, limited disclosure, difficulties with aligning interests and insider domination are all prominent features of the Continental model. In Russia, the most dominant corporate characteristic is extremely concentrated ownership Radygin (2006). Although it could be argued that such an ownership pattern is a reaction to the dysfunctional formal institutions, the disproportionate dominance of a single shareholder leads to minority abuses. Hence, there is a need to concentrate on minority protection mechanisms. Furthermore, because significant stockholders have a greater capacity for exercising control, market-oriented mechanisms of control here tend to be less developed (Aguilera and Jackson 2003). Traditionally, firms following the Continental model have a greater level of reliance on trust-based arrangements because of the long-term nature of partnership between the influential stakeholders. Dissatisfaction of shareholders with the management's performance is typically resolved by means of a greater involvement on the part of the latter. Nooteboom (1999) refers to this phenomenon as the 'voice' strategy – the feature which has a fundamental influence over how intrinsic conflicts of interests are dealt with. This is reinforced by the popular opinion that post-communist Russia is a state with a rule of relationships, where informal networks and institutions are of particular importance (Estrin and Prevezer 2010). However, the latter point is rivalled by Pistor and Xu (2005) and Hendley (2006) who concluded that in modern-day Russia formal legal enforcement mechanisms are used much more extensively than in other transition economies such as, for example, China. Despite the latter consideration which reflects on the change rather than the state of affairs, it is recognized that informal networks are extremely important in today's corporate Russia.

22.3.3   Evolution of Russian Board of Directors

After the collapse of the communist regime Russia experienced confusion on the issues of political identification and future economic direction. Newly emerged democratic reformers made intensive efforts to find a unique formula for further national development, which led to a great deal of social and economic problems. Among the numerous unfortunate events of the modern Russian economic model appear to be the 'shock-therapy' approach to privatizing national wealth, and the iniquitous creation of a new breed of property and asset owners in the 1990s (Murrell 1993; Goldman 2008). Many believe that such an unprecedented level of socio-economic transformation and radical institutional changes resulted in ubiquitous civil rights violations, fraudulent asset-stripping, massive embezzlement of corporate funds, tax evasion and endemic corruption. However, the transitional movement from the controlled and centrally planned mode to the market-based economy initiated the necessary irreversible institutional reforms and structural organizational modernisation. Within the above-mentioned processes, much was revolutionized in the area of Russian corporate governance, which is considered, by a number of academic experts, to be one of the most important catalysts for the incremental economic growth and business development (McCarty and Puffer 2002).

The Russian Federation is a special case of international corporate governance with numerous gaps to explore for researchers and policy-makers studying issues of good corporate governance standards, international accounting standards, independent boards of directors and consistent corporate governance codes. Even though the most sophisticated theoretical and empirical works on corporate governance have mostly focused on advanced Western market economies, there is an urgent need to have more theoretical and empirical studies in order to improve the transparency, fairness, responsibility and accountability of Russian corporate governance and independent boards of directors.

In general, a key aspect of any well-functioning corporate governance model, as well as a healthy corporate and business environment, is to be able to attract long-term capital investments through international financial markets, and thus receive a wide range of significant economic and financial benefits. Overall, there is no single clear-cut recommendation, hence the debate continues over whether Russia needs to implement further structural changes within its corporate governance model, so as to converge toward the more conventional Anglo-Saxon, German or Asian models, or persist to develop its own unique trajectory based on national competencies coupled with legal, cultural and institutional discrepancies (McCarty and Puffer 2002; Buck 2003; Judge and Naoumova 2004). Regardless of the chosen option, Russian public companies are urged to meet the internationally accepted listing requirements such as: transparent ownership structure and clear information disclosure procedures; compliance with international accountancy standards; corporate social responsibility; presence of independent directors on boards and existence of special board committees (Tricker 2009). According to La Porta et al. (1997) there is an evident dependency of the external capital investments on the confidence in the legal environment, effective regulatory systems and transparent law enforcement procedures within the investment environment. The problems caused by the lack of aforementioned elements in the effective 'rule of law' infrastructure substantially influenced the method of corporate governance development and the framework of institutional transformation leading to unequal and unjust wealth distribution within Russian society (Black et al. 2000).

Under the soviet system, the government owned and controlled all large enterprises and therefore corporate governance did not exist in the traditional capitalist form. Accordingly, the roles, operational methods and performance objectives of governing bodies, so-called 'councils of directors', had been contemplated through a different set of ideological perspectives. After the soviet regime in Russia, the concept of boards of directors was first introduced with the country's transition to a market economy during the privatization period in the 1990s. It is surprising to know that such structure did not exist in state-owned enterprises during the Soviet Union. In terms of adopting the best model, recent analysis of the present-day CG arrangements and practices in Russia, despite the insufficient clarity of the stock market regulations and general implementation of the 'rule of law', have a relevant tendency towards the Anglo-Saxon model through the adaptation of a unitary board of directors structure and an increased role of 'outsiders', independent members of the supervisory boards. Therefore, the Russian Code of Corporate Conduct also sets certain conditions under which directors cannot be considered truly independent; they are as follows:

- There are issues with business reputation, ethical standards, leadership skills and business experience.
- There is no public declaration of independent status prior to election to the board.
- Direct or indirect ownership of equity stakes in the company, sufficient for self-nomination to the corporate board of directors.
- Received payments and rewards for consulting or any other services provided to the company beyond the board membership remuneration.
- Represented interests of consultants or parties affiliated with the company.

Even within this framework, top managers are often keen to find ways to underestimate the importance of this supervisory structure, and the role of a strong, vigilant and independent board of directors often remains unclear. Along the same lines, Peng et al. (2003, 356) identify four possible reasons for the ineffectiveness of corporate board members in Russia: (1) foreign investors are forced to initiate changes by fear of political reaction; (2) directors tend to display a collective mentality; (3) influence of unstable macroeconomic conditions; and (4) turbulent environmental dynamism.

Recently, Chen (2009) has argued that the prevalence of insider control structures is the reason for the possible malfunctioning of corporate governance mechanisms, since these structures fail to provide a sufficient degree of information disclosure and transparency to existing shareholders and other stakeholders. Previously, Estrin and Wright (1999) explained that one of the peculiar characteristics of the mass privatization of state enterprises implemented in 1992 was the achieved composition of the managerial insider control structure, which in turn established a widespread dominance of incumbent managers as majority shareholders. As a result, such inadequate separation between company management and controlling shareholders affected the subsequent development of the corporate governance system in the country. Nevertheless, in the last decade, several legislative endeavours have been undertaken in the domain of national corporate Acts in order to improve law enforcement practices concerning resolution of intra-corporate and inter-corporate disputes. Another significant feature of equity ownership rights in Russia, especially within the primary and secondary sectors of the economy, was the formation of consolidated financial industrial groups (FIGs): 'these groups represent large diversified holding companies owned by banks and trading companies, and sometimes they become simply a vehicle for creating pyramidal ownership structures' (Filatotchev 2006, 114).

For Melkumov (2009), effective boards of directors in Russia are important to ensure the appropriate maintenance of CG standards, conceptualization and systematic monitoring of strategic corporate development. Recent research conducted by Iwasaki (2008, 547) defines boards of directors in Russia as: 'a struggle for hegemony over corporate management between company managers and their countervailing parties represented by large shareholders, who seek to maximize their power and benefits'. He also finds that Russia's legal system has some influence on board composition. In this study, Iwasaki (2008) used a data set of 730 joint stock companies to study the determinants of corporate board composition in Russia, and came to the conclusion that a large number of Russian companies now appoint outsider directors to monitor top management. Iwasaki also finds that Russia's legal system has some influence on board composition. On the legal side, in particular, the Russian Joint Stock Companies Act is designed to secure a higher level of independence of the boards of directors than even those in the United States of America (USA) and the United Kingdom (UK) (Black and Kraakman 1996; Iwasaki 2003, 2004). However, on the practical side, the question whether Russian boards of directors are really independently supervising CEOs and others in the top management positions has led researchers to investigate the relationship between the ownership structure and board composition in Russia.

On the board independency issue, some scholars came to the conclusion that Russian board of directors are not really independent players (Lazareva et al. 2007). In fact, boards are mostly dominated by management, family members and large shareholders' representatives and not by independent directors (Standard & Poor's 2007). According to Lazareva and Rachinsky (2006) the fraction of insiders on boards is positively related to the share of small owners, due to the fact that many small owners in the Russian companies are actually employees. Kapalyushnikow and Demina (2005) show that there is a positive correlation between the length of tenure of a board chairman and good corporate governance. Along the same lines, Goltsman (2000) also confirms the idea that high ownership of shares by managers and outsiders leads to a significant increase in the turnover frequency of board members. Moreover, Muravyev (2003) shows that insider director representation rights and the appointed directors in Russia are negatively correlated with CEO turnover. Judge et al. (2003) also quantitatively confirm that an enterprise whose board of directors is virtually controlled by a CEO has a significant disadvantage regarding performance over enterprises that are compliant with provisions of the Joint Stock Companies Act, which prohibits one person from simultaneous holding of the offices of CEO and chairman of the board.

In addition, Black (2001) examines the relationship between CG behaviour and the market value for a sample of 21 Russian firms and concludes that the correlation between the CG and market value is statistically very strong, and CG has a powerful effect on company market value in a developing country where legal and cultural constraints on corporate behaviour are relatively fragile. Some other studies (Bevan et al. 2001; Black 2001; Filatotchev 2006) suggest that reforms to support good CG are beneficial for the accountability of directors, transparency of financial reporting, responsibility of management and fairness of shareholders' rights, therefore global principles of good CG should be developed on the rationale that common international standards of corporate governance are essential for the expansion of international institutional investment and for the closer integration of global financial markets.

In order to examine the roles and functions of boards of directors of listed companies on the Russian Trading System (RTS) Stock Exchange, Demirbas and Yukhanaev (2011) conducted a survey with 33 questions. There are 1414 listed companies on the RTS Stock Exchange, which is the first regulated stock market in Russia and is also the main benchmark for the Russian securities industry. The questions are analysed and presented in terms of 'more' significant to 'less' significant regarding to their mean, median and mode values. If the mean value of any question is closer to 1 and its standard value is lower, it reveals more significant answers. On the other hand if the mean value is closer to 4 and its standard value is low, it is less significant.

In parallel with these facts there is still some contrasting evidence that firms construct independent boards of directors and strengthen oversight of the managers. On the interrelationship between the ownership and board composition, Blasi and Schleifer (1996) and Dolgopyatova (2003) focus on the average number of board members in Russian enterprises and conclude that the number usually stands at seven. They find that this number has not altered significantly throughout the transition, but the number of board members has diversed according to the size of the company as there were many companies with more than seven directors. For example, Iwasaki (2007) reports the results of the survey conducted in 2001 on 56 large listed companies and conclude that the average number of board members for those companies was nine (4 per cent of those companies had from one to five board members, 77 per cent from six to ten directors, 15 per cent from 11 to 15 directors, and the remaining 4 per cent had 16 directors or more). To preserve core values such as transparency, responsibility, fairness and accountability within the corporate governance system, corporate boards of directors all over the world are now more cautious about the fact that they should maintain their independence in order to gain international acceptance.

22.4   CONCLUSION

The OECD *Principles* (2004) state that the corporate governance framework should ensure the strategic guidance of the company, the effective monitoring of management by the board, and the board's accountability to the company and the shareholders. To ensure an effective corporate governance framework, it is necessary that an appropriate and effective legal, regulatory and institutional foundation is established upon which all market participants can rely in establishing their private contractual relations (Judge et al. 2008; Judge 2011). The corporate governance framework should protect and facilitate the exercise of shareholders' rights.

Despite the fact that the Russian government undertook several measures to streamline the activities of SOEs and improve the institutional environment (e.g. the revision of the bankruptcy law and the Joint Stock Companies Act, the introduction of the Russian Code of Corporate Conduct and dissemination of best CG practices, implementing the change of the judicial and law enforcement system) Russian policy-makers should continue the structural reforms to enhance the legitimate corporate governance framework and have 'good' CG practices in place. These statements are supported by Demirbas and Yukhanaev's (2011) empirical findings in which they examined two assumptions about the attitudes of the Russian listed company directors. Firstly, that company directors in Russia view the board of directors as good corporate governance practice and support the improvements and government controls to maintain the independence of the board of directors. And secondly, that company directors desire corporate governance reforms in Russia, and emphasize the positive relationship between corporate governance reforms and corporate governance standards. From their investigation, they came to the conclusion that, as claimed in the first assumption, respondents recognize the board of directors as an important instrument of efficient and good corporate governance practice, and they strongly disagree with the statement that the board does not determine the quality of corporate governance.

In order to achieve further international recognition and better integration into the global markets, policy-makers should facilitate more independency and transparency of decision-making by the boards of directors, improve information disclosure and accountability to shareholders and, therefore, continue further implementation and convergence with international standards so as to attract more foreign capital investments.

REFERENCES

Adams, R.B. and D. Ferreira (2007), 'A theory of friendly boards', *Journal of Finance*, **62** (1), 217–242.

Adizes, I. (2006), 'Making management by teamwork', *Expert Business Weekly*, Interview by Daria Denisova, No 43, 20–26 November.

Aguilera, R. and G. Jackson (2003), 'The cross-national diversity of corporate governance: dimensions and determinants', *Academy of Management Review*, **28** (3), 447–485.

BBC (2005), 'Putin "halts" privatisation probe', BBC News, http://news.bbc.co.uk/go/pr/fr/-/2/hi/business/4379957.stm (accessed 18 April 2006).

Berle, A. and G. Means (1932), *The Modern Corporation and Private Property*, New York: Macmillan.

Bevan, A., S. Estrin, B. Kuznetsov, M.E. Schaffer, M. Angelucci, J. Fennema and G. Mangiarotti (2001), 'The determinants of privatized enterprise performance in Russia', Working Paper 452, Ann Arbor, MI: William Davidson Institute, University of Michigan Business School.

Black, B. (2001), 'The corporate governance behaviour and market value of Russian firms', *Emerging Market Review*, **2**, 89–108.

Black, B. and R. Kraakman (1996), 'A self enforcing model of corporate law', *Harvard Law Review*, **109** (8), 1911–1982.

Black, B., R. Kraakman and A. Tarassova (2000), 'Russian privatization and corporate governance: what went wrong?' *Stanford Law Review*, **52** (7), 1731–1808.

Blasi, J. and A. Schleifer (1996), 'Corporate governance in Russia: an initial look', in R. Frydman, C.W. Gray and A. Rapaczynski (ed.), *Corporate Governance in Central Europe and Russia, Insiders and the State*, Budapest: Central European University Press, pp. 78–108.

Bradford, L.D. and V. Bernstain (2006), 'Every team has its own currency exchange', Interview to the *Expert Business Weekly*, by Anastasia Matveyeva, **44**, November 27–December 3.

Brennan, N. (2006), 'Boards of directors and firm performance: is there an expectations gap?' *Corporate Governance*, **14** (6), 577–593.

Breton, G. and Y. Pesqueux (2006), 'Business in society or an integrated vision of governance', *Society and Business Review*, **1** (1), 7–27.

Bryne, J.A. (2002), 'Commentary: board room changes that could rebuild trust', *Business Week*, 17 June.

Buck, T. (2003), 'Modern Russian corporate governance: convergent forces or product of Russia's history?' *Journal of World Business*, **38**, 299–313.

Bushev, A. (2001), 'The theory and practice of corporate governance in Russia', *Review of Central and East European Law*, **1**, 71–91.

Cadbury, A. (1992), *Report of The Committee on The Financial Aspect of Corporate Governance*, London: Gee Publishing.

Chen, A. (2009), 'Corporate governance in Russia and some points of comparison with China', *Chinese Economy*, **42** (3), 41–59.

Claessens, S. (2003), *Corporate Governance and Development*, Global Corporate Governance Forum, Washington, DC: International Bank for Reconstruction and Development/The World Bank.

Corbetta, G. and C. Salvato (2004), 'The board of directors in family firms: one size fits all?' *Family Business Review*, **17** (2), 119–134.

Cuervo, A. (2002), 'Corporate governance mechanisms: a plea for less code of good governance and more market control', *Corporate Governance an International Review*, **10** (2), 84–93.

Daily, C.M., D.R. Dalton and A.A. Cannella, Jr (2003), 'Introduction to special topic forum – Corporate Governance: Decades of Dialogue and Data', *Academy of Management Review*, **28**, 371–382.

Demirbas, D. and A. Yukhanaev (2011), 'Independence of board of directors, employee relation and harmonisation of corporate governance', *Employee Relations*, **33** (4), 444–471.

Dolgopyatova, T. (2003), 'Ownership and corporate control structures as viewed by statistics and surveys', *Russian Economic Barometer*, **12** (3), 12–20.

Drucker, P. (1974), *Management: Tasks, Responsibilities, Practices*, Oxford: Butterworth-Heinemann.

Estrin, S. and M. Prevezer (2010), 'A survey on institutions and new firm entry: how and why do entry rates differ in emerging markets?' *Economic systems*, **34** (3), 289–308.

Estrin, S. and M. Wright (1999), 'Corporate governance in the former Soviet Union: an overview', *Journal of Comparative Economics*, **27**, 398–421.

Filatotchev, I. (2006), 'Corporate governance and business strategies in Russia', in Subhash C. Jain (ed.), *Emerging Economies and Transformation of International Business: Brazil, Russia, India and China*, Cheltenham, UK and Northampton, MA, USA: Edward Elgar, pp. 111–137.

Fox, M. and M. Heller (2006), *Corporate Governance Lessons from Transition Economy Reforms*, Princeton, NJ: Princeton University Press.

Garratt, B. (1999), 'Developing effective directors and building dynamic boards', *Long Range Planning*, **32**, 28–35.

Goldman, M. (2008), *Oilopoly: Putin, Power and the Rise of the New Russia*, Oxford: One World Publications.

Goltsman, M. (2000), 'Empirical analysis of managerial turnover in Russian firms', working paper BSP: 00/035, Moscow: New Economic School.

Heidrick & Struggles (2007), '"Independent foreigners" on the board of directors of a Russian company: importance of a successful overseas IPO', Moscow: Heidrick & Struggles International.

Hendley, K. (2006), 'Assessing the rule of law in Russia', *Cardozo Journal of International and Comparative Law*, **14** (2), 347–391.

Higgs, D. (2003), *Review of the Role and Effectiveness of Non-Executive Directors*, London: DTI.

International Finance Corporation (IFC) (2004), *The Russia Corporate Governance Manual*, International Finance Corporation, Washington, DC.

Iwasaki, I. (2003), 'The governance mechanism of Russian firms: its self enforcing nature and limitations', *Post Communist Economies*, **15** (4), 503–531.

Iwasaki, I. (2004), 'Corporate law and governance system in Russia', *Beyond Transition*, **15** (1), 1–11.

Iwasaki, I. (2007), 'Enterprise reform and corporate governance in Russia: a quantitative survey', *Journal of Economic Survey*, **21** (5), 849–902.

Iwasaki, I. (2008), 'The determinants of board composition in a transforming economy: evidence from Russia', *Journal of Corporate Finance*, **14**, 532–549.

Jenkins, M. (2002), 'Cognitive mapping management', in David Partington (ed.), *Essential Skills for Management Research*, London, UK; Thousand Oaks, CA, USA; New Delhi, India: Sage Publications.

Judge, W. (2011), 'What level of analysis is most salient for a global theory of corporate governance', *Corporate Governance: An International Review*, **19** (2), 97–98.

Judge, W., T.J. Douglas and A.M. Kutan (2008), 'Institutional antecedents and corporate governance legitimacy', *Journal of Management*, **34** (4), 765–785.

Judge, W. and I. Naoumova (2004), 'Corporate governance in Russia: what model will it follow?' *Corporate Governance*, **12** (3), 302–313.

Judge, W., I. Naoumova and N. Koutzevol (2003), 'Corporate governance and firm performance in Russia: an empirical study', *Journal of World Business*, **38** (4), 385–396.

Kapalyushnikov, R. and N. Demina (2005), 'Concentrated ownership and management turnover: the case of Russia', *Russian Economic Barometer*, **14** (1), 10–21.

La Porta, R., F. Lopez-de-Silanes, A. Shleifer and R. Vishny (1997), 'Legal determinants of external finance', *Journal of Finance*, **3**, 1131–1150.

Lazareva, O. and A. Rachinsky (2006), 'A study on Russian boards', working paper no.

107, Centre for Economic and Financial Research/New Economic School, CEFIR/NES, Moscow.

Lazareva, O., A. Rachinsky and S. Stepanov (2007), 'A survey of corporate governance in Russia', working paper No. 103, Centre for Economic and Financial Research at New Economic School, CEFIR/NES.

Lorsch, J.W. and E. MacIver (1989), *Pawns or Potentates: The Reality of Americas's Corporate Boards*, Boston, MA: Harvard University Graduate School of Business Administration.

Mace, M.L. (1971), *Directors – Myth and Reality*, Boston, MA: Graduate School of Business Administration, Harvard University.

McCarty, D. and S. Puffer (2002), 'Corporate governance in Russia: towards a European, US, or Russian model?' *European Management Journal*, **20** (6), 630–640.

Melkumov, D. (2009), 'Institutional background as a determinant of boards of directors', internal and external roles: the case of Russia', *Journal of World Business*, **44**, 94–103.

Mintz, S. (2005), 'Corporate governance in an international context: legal systems, financial patterns and cultural variables', *Corporate Governance: An International Review*, **13** (5), 582–597.

Monks, A. and N. Minow (2001), *Corporate Governance*, 2nd edn, Oxford: Blackwell Publishing.

Muravyev, A. (2003), 'Turnover of senior managers in Russian privatized firms'. *Comparative Economic Studies*, **45** (2), 148–172.

Murphy, R. (2006), 'Powers and duties of the non-executive director', *Accountancy Ireland*, **38** (6), 35–37.

Murrell, P. (1993), 'What is shock therapy? What did it do in Poland and Russia?' *Post-Soviet Affairs*, **9** (2), 111–140.

Neshataeva, T. (2003), 'International civil procedure in the Russian Federation: sources and issues', *Review of Central and East European Law*, **2**, 137–165.

Nooteboom, B. (1999), 'Voice- and exit-based forms of corporate control: Anglo-American, European, and Japanese', *Journal of Economic Issues*, **33** (4), 845–860.

OECD (1999), *OECD Principles of Corporate Governance*, Paris: Organisation for Economic Co-operation and Development (OECD).

OECD (2004), *OECD Principles of Corporate Governance*, Paris: Organisation for Economic Co-operation and Development (OECD).

OECD (2006), *Economic Survey of the Russian Federation*, Paris: Organisation for Economic Co-operation and Development (OECD).

Oleynik, A. (2007), 'The economical anatomy of the tragedy, the state and the business', *Vedomosty Daily Business Paper*, 30 May, No. 97, p. A4.

Osugi, K. (2000), *Enforcement of Minority Shareholders Rights: Shareholder Rights and Equitable Treatment*, Moscow: OECD/World Bank Corporate Governance Roundtable for Russia.

Pass, C. (2004), 'Corporate governance and the role of non-executive directors in large UK companies: an empirical study', *Corporate Governance: An International Review*, **4** (2), 52–63.

Peng, M., T. Buck and I. Filatotchev (2003), 'Do outside directors and new managers help improve firm performance? An exploratory study in Russian privatization', *Journal of World Business*, **38**, 348–360.

Perotti, E. (2004), 'State ownership: a residual role?' working paper No. 3407, World Bank Policy Research.

Pettigrew, A. and T. McNulty (1998), 'Sources and uses of power in the boardroom', *European Journal of Work and Organizational Psychology*, **7** (2), 197–214.

Pistor, K. and C. Xu (2005), 'Governing emerging stock markets: legal vs. administrative governance', *Corporate Governance an International Review*, **13** (1), 5–10.

Puffer, S.M. and D.J. McCarthy (2003), 'The emergence of corporate governance in Russia', *Journal of World Business*, **38** (4), 284–298.

Radygin, A. (2006), 'Corporate governance, integration and reorganization: the contemporary trends of Russian corporate groups', *Economic Change and Restructuring*, **39** (3), 261–323.

Roberts, G. (2004), 'Convergent capitalisms? The internationalization of financial markets and the 2002 Russian governance code', *Europe–Asia Studies*, **56** (8), 1235–48.

Romano, R. (1996), 'Corporate law and corporate governance', *Industrial and Corporate Change*, **5** (2), 277–339.

Russian Code of Corporate Conduct (2002), http://www.ecgi.org/codes/code.php?code_id=102 (accessed 15 March 2011).

Shleifer, A. and R. Vishny (1997), 'A survey of corporate governance', *Journal of Finance*, **52** (2), 737–783.

Standard & Poor's (2007), 'Portrait of Russian corporate boards mirrors their concentrated ownership structure and highlights hindrances to stronger governance', Russia: Standard & Poor's Governance Service.

Stiglitz, J. (1999), 'Whither reform? Ten years of the transition', Keynote address at Annual World Bank conference on Development Economics.

Tricker, B. (2000), 'Editorial: corporate governance – the subject whose time has come', *Corporate Governance: An International Review*, **8** (4), 289–296.

Tricker, B. (2009), *Corporate Governance: Principles, Policies, and Practices*, Oxford: Oxford University Press.

Van den Berghe, L.A.A. and A. Levrau (2004), 'Evaluating boards of directors: what constitutes a good corporate board?' *Corporate Governance: An International Review*, **12** (3), 461–478.

Vernikov, A. (2007), 'Corporate governance and control in Russian banks', Working Paper No. 78, SSEES Centre for the Study of Economic and Social Change in Europe.

Weimer, J. and J.C. Pape (1999), 'A taxonomy of systems of corporate governance', *Corporate Governance: An International Review*, **7** (2), 152–166.

Yakovlev, A. (2004), 'Evolution of corporate governance in Russia: government policy vs. real incentives of economic agents', *Post Communist Economies*, **16** (4), 387–403.

Yakovlev, A. (2006), 'The evolution of business state interaction in Russia: from state capture to business capture', *Europe-Asia Studies*, **58** (7), 1033–1056.

23 Firms, markets and the social regulation of capitalism in sub-Saharan Africa

Gilton Klerck

23.1 INTRODUCTION

This chapter explores the relevance of regulation theory to an understanding of the operation of firms and markets in sub-Saharan Africa. The challenges confronting the region are numerous, complex and daunting. A majority of the people in sub-Saharan Africa face a future in which 'not even bare survival is assured' (Leys 1994, 34). Out of a total population of about 800 million, nearly 400 million are living in abject poverty. Per capita incomes have been falling at over 2 per cent a year since 1980, world demand for what sub-Saharan Africa produces is growing slowly or even declining, while world supplies are constantly expanding and are produced much more efficiently elsewhere (Rankin et al. 2006). The decline in world trade in the early 1980s created systemic instability at the level of the global economy and a much less favourable international climate for the industrialization of developing countries. Attracting and retaining foreign investment became increasingly difficult at exactly the time when it was punted as a central pillar of economic growth.

In general, there is little prospect of industrial development solving the problems in most African countries. For a start, social and political conditions in much of Africa have reached a point where manufacturing investment no longer appears profitable. Many African countries have seen significant disinvestment by foreign companies since the 1990s. The level and share of manufacturing in the region remains extremely low compared with other parts of the developing world. There has also been minimal growth in manufactured exports from the region (Riddell 1993, 223). Furthermore, manufacturing based on current technologies will never absorb Africa's surplus population, while goods that are still produced by labour-intensive methods are less and less in demand. What is required is a 'fundamental restructuring' of African economies rather than a perpetuation of the 'neo-colonial monoculture export production system at a time when the external demand prospects are dismal' (Adedeji 1991, 781).

The emphasis on market forces in the prescriptions for economic reform imposed on Africa encourages a tendency to give markets the credit for effects generated or co-generated by other regulatory mechanisms. While markets provide signals to which producers and consumers can respond, 'there is no mechanism to reconcile the responses to people in their role as producers, where wages appear as a cost, and their role as consumers, where their wages appear as a source of revenue' (Sayer 1995, 137). This underscores the form that the necessary trade-off between keeping costs of production down and keeping consumption up assumes within market economies as well as the inadequacy of market mechanisms for resolving it. For regulationists, markets can only exist as a set of social practices characterized by social networks, collective norms, socially constructed identities and accepted forms of social interaction. The normative framework that gives particular markets their coherence and their functionality, and tempers the outright exercise of economic power, is best viewed as 'a form of micro-political regulation, as a social constitution' (Jones 1996, 127). In other words, the market is a socio-political and not exclusively economic institution. As a social institution, the market is dependent on state intervention; is differentially organized, regulated, embedded and influenced by contextual factors; and is characterized by an uneven distribution of information and power. Exposing society to the naked discipline of the market would precipitate social destruction. Some form of regulation is therefore necessary to ensure social reproduction over time. Markets can never be a complete alternative to planning and hierarchy, and certainly not to production (as implied by the market–hierarchy dualism).

Bureaucratic control is the norm for all firms if they are to cope with large throughputs of information and materials. Although no two firms can be expected to be governed in an identical manner, the regulation of an industry or region is largely systemic. While economic processes are essentially open-ended and unpredictable, regulatory processes are structured and largely path-dependent. Governments in sub-Saharan Africa have sought to establish institutional frameworks that are conducive to economic development, and to strengthen the channels through which business is conducted. These efforts focus on establishing a legislative, regulatory and institutional framework; introducing public promotion and incentive programmes; and creating intermediary structures to foster interaction between industries and firms. Since these activities depend on detailed microeconomic and social information, it does not automatically follow that government policy will be welfare improving. Given the ubiquity of imperfect information, bureaucratic inertia, pressure group activity and the like, inappropriate or misguided governmental interventions always remain a distinct possibility. While policy-makers may enjoy superior coordinating ability across a diverse range of institutions, there is no presumption that they have a superior understanding of market circumstances or technological information.

In Africa, as elsewhere, modes of regulation involve a complex of institutions, rules and practices through which economic relations are governed. With the transition from authoritarianism to democracy in many parts of the continent, governments hardly engaged in a process of complete institutional displacement or renewal. During the transition to democracy, old institutional frameworks do not simply dissolve, but rather remain entrenched in the new social order. In other words, social actors always transform existing structures. A key focus of the arguments in this chapter is the notion that there is a simple and direct correlation between labour market regulation and the proliferation of market-determined forms of employment. The relationship between regulation and flexibility is considered in light of shifts in the modalities of labour regulation and the growth of non-standard employment in post-independence Namibia. It is argued that regulatory changes involve distinct trade-offs between the various forms of flexibility and security rather than a simple process of substituting one for the other. Although the primary focus is on Namibia, an attempt will be made to draw out (some of) the broader relevance of this case for the sub-Saharan region.

23.2   REGULATIONIST ACCOUNTS OF 'PERIPHERAL' SOCIETIES

Regulation theorists sought to provide political and theoretical alternatives to the neoliberal vision of unregulated competition (that is, the separation of state and economy) by emphasizing the social regulation of market forces. The theoretical workhorse of orthodox development theories – evolutionary neoclassical economics – presents the capitalist system as a 'pure' economy in a 'natural' state of equilibrium maintained by 'perfect' competition. Regulation theorists deny the notion of an equilibrium position for a society or economy: periods of sustained or balanced growth are 'always relative, always partial and always provisional' (Jessop 1988, 151). They jettison the notion of 'general laws' based on an abstract price mechanism in favour of a view of the economic process as dependent on the structural forms, institutional mechanisms and cultural norms specific to each historical period. Each period has its own specific economic laws and regularities of behaviour, as crystallized in a given structural, normative and institutional framework. Market mechanisms cannot automatically affect, even in the long-term, these national specificities (Aglietta 1982, 6). There is thus no long-run trend towards uniformity in international relations through the homogenization of national economies and the equalization of growth rates.

23.2.1   Basic Contours of Regulation Theory

The central insight of regulation theory – that a discernable coherence in capitalist economic development is the product of the interplay of a whole series of regulatory mechanisms – highlights the recurring instabilities in the processes of valorization, rooted in antagonistic features of the employment relationship and expressed in imbalances between investment, production and consumption. For regulationists, the process of social regulation dampens and spreads over time, rather than eliminates, the imbalances that permanently arise from the processes of capital accumulation (Aglietta 1979). In short, it specifies the particular forms assumed in time and space by the institutionalization of class conflict. Boyer (1990, 20) defines regulation as: 'the conjunction of the mechanisms working together for social reproduction, with attention to the prevalent economic structures and social forms'. Regulation in this sense refers to a set of institutional mechanisms and patterns of behaviour through which the economic and social system is reproduced while at the same time maintaining its coherence and identity. The accumulation of capital is socially 'regulated' in the sense that a whole ensemble of social structures and practices (such as the law, state policy, collective bargaining, social security, behavioural norms, political practices, education and training systems) are formed to mitigate the contradictions inherent in capitalist accumulation. According to Jessop (2001, 12):

> an adequate account of regulation must not only consider the material preconditions of, and constraints upon, reproduction . . . but must also take account of the different modes of calculation and the orientations of the various social forces involved in economic and social regulation. An important theoretical development in this context would be a more explicit concern with the 'spatio-temporal fixes' within which capitalist reproduction and regularisation occur.

Regulation theory is concerned with how capitalism can survive when the capital relation in itself, and of necessity, generates social contradictions and crises that threaten the very accumulation process on which it is based. This involves attempts to explain the dynamics of long-term cycles of economic stability and change by studying the role of mechanisms of social mediation. The focus of research is therefore on concrete institutional forms, societal norms, values and the patterns of strategic human action that both express and regulate conflict until the inevitable tensions and divergences among the various regulatory forms reach a crisis point

(Lipietz 1987, 3–5). Regulation theory seeks to combine an appreciation of 'the generic features of capitalism (such as its appropriation of nature and human labour, its surplus-generating dynamics, its crisis-proneness) with an understanding of its specific (institutional) forms in time and space' (Peck 2000, 63). That is, the social regulation of capitalism cannot be properly understood without considering how modes of regulation modify and yet remain subject to the generic laws of capitalist accumulation. The general dynamics of capitalism define the 'basic tendencies and counter-tendencies, structural contradictions, strategic dilemmas, and overall constraints which inevitably shape modes of regulation, which find a provisional, partial and unstable resolution in the latter, and whose continued presence and even development eventually undermine any given institutional and organizational solutions' (Jessop 1992, 50). Capital accumulation is thus never a self-sustaining process but rather depends on (among others) an institutionalized compromise between contending classes and a contingent unity of the circuits of capital.

Regulation theory emphasizes 'the *improbability* of capitalist reproduction and [examines] the changing conditions which allowed production and consumption to be combined temporarily into a virtuous circle of accumulation' (Jessop 2001, 511). While they acknowledge the essentially anarchic role of market forces in mediating capitalist reproduction, regulationists highlight the complementary functions of other mechanisms – such as institutions, organizational forms, rules, norms, customs, conventions and patterns of conduct – in structuring, facilitating and guiding accumulation (Lipietz 1988). A mode of regulation does not denote a completed regulatory system; rather it signifies one in the process of formation, which does not accentuate stability and continuity at the expense of instability and change. Painter and Goodwin (1995) suggest that the notion of regulation as a process implies a temporal and spatial unevenness that is contingent on the interaction of various practices operating in and through particular sites and institutions. In other words, rather than being achieved, regulation is always emergent and tendential. Instead of searching for coherent regulatory modes, emphasis should be placed on:

> the ebb and flow of regulatory processes through time and space. At certain times and places, those processes will be more effective than at others. In our view, the process of regulation is the product of material and discursive practices that generate and are in turn conditioned by social and political institutions. (Painter and Goodwin 1995, 342)

Consumption, money, interfirm relations and forms of state intervention are especially important areas for institutional formation and mediation. These structures are not the spontaneous outcome of competition, but rather emanate from the creation of social institutions, legitimized by the collective values from which societies draw their cohesion. Regulation theory is associated, above all, with the claim that changing systems of capital accumulation engender complementary institutional arrangements, including patterns of urbanization, consumption norms and so on. In contrast to orthodox economics, regulation theory suggests that the market mechanism must be supplemented by collective action, expressed in institutional forms as social mediation (Aglietta 1998, 50). Regulation theory not only places great emphasis on the contingent, partial and unstable nature of socio-economic reproduction, but also explicitly rejects teleological accounts of economic development. It is neither prescriptive nor deterministic, and insists that the developmental trajectory of a particular society is open. This implies that 'no immanent destiny ordains a certain nation to hold a certain position in an international division of labour' (Lipietz 1986, 23). Regulationists stress the fact that the development of capitalism has always been mediated through spatio-temporally specific institutional forms, regulatory institutions and norms of behaviour. These include wage relations, forms of competition, capital flows, the state, monetary forms, international commercial and financial systems, and the various cultural aspects corresponding to such institutional forms and regulatory institutions.

23.2.2   'Bloody Taylorism' and 'Peripheral Fordism'

Distinct national growth paths are the product of 'a coherent and interlocking system of consumption, production and social reproduction' that forecloses certain paths of development by virtue of its embeddedness in a specific societal system (Rubery 1994, 347). Since the notion of a single, universal dynamic in capitalist development is rejected and causal powers are allocated to specific cultural and political forms, the peculiarities of national capitalisms take on a new significance. As such, regulation theory stimulates interest in:

> the unequal capacities of different capitalist nations to generate and assimilate new techno-economic systems and a major concern becomes the qualitatively different impact of the same techno-economic forces in time and space. Although major structural crises are seen as inevitably taking on international dimensions, it becomes of importance to track down the historically specific conditions under which the determinants of crisis have collided – the *conjuncture* of general and particular determinants of crisis and transformation. (Elam 1994, 57–58)

Marx's analysis of the 'circuits of capital' identified a unity between the spheres of production, distribution and exchange. On this view, the circuits of commodity capital (growth in world trade), money capital (expanding international financial markets) and productive capital (rise of multinational corporations) represent three different, yet interrelated, aspects of the same relation: the expanded reproduction of the capital relation. An exclusive focus on only one 'moment' in the internationalization of capital results in a reductionism that can at best yield a partial or one-sided account of reality. By emphasizing the growth of world markets and the transfer of surpluses to the 'centre', dependency theorists such as Wallerstein and Frank failed to consider the tendency of capitalism to expand by raising the productivity of labour. In fact, as Lipietz (1986, 30) points out, the proportion of exports of manufactured goods to the less developed countries in the mid-1960s accounted for only 2 per cent of the gross domestic product (GDP) for the European Economic Community and 0.8 per cent for the United States of America (USA). If the search for markets was the cause of underdevelopment in the 'periphery', the 'core' no longer needed a periphery. Dependency theory's exclusive concern with the sphere of exchange led to an emphasis on low wages in the 'world-market factories' as the major stimulus for the relocation of production (Fröbel et al. 1980). Developing countries were therefore presented as lacking any autonomous, internal dynamic and dedicated primarily to creating and maintaining reservoirs of cheap labour. State strategies aimed at attracting foreign investment and/or promoting production for export were thus either neglected or viewed as an accommodation to the needs of capital in the centre. Regulationists, by contrast, place great emphasis on the successful completion of the circuit of capitalist production: that is, all levels of the circuit are in need of regulation (Lipietz 1988, 24–28).

One response to the crisis of Atlantic Fordism, which emerged in early 1970s, was to develop a growing division of labour between the industrialized economies of the North and the developing countries in the South (Storper 1990). Fordism was the central concept in regulation theory's analysis of the dynamics of development in the South. First, regulationists explain the development of these countries in terms of the geographical expansion of 'central Fordism'. Lipietz (1987) argues that declining profits in metropolitan capitalism led multinational manufacturing firms and banks to seek higher profits by relocating and financing semi- and unskilled production processes in the peripheral economies of the South, especially in East Asia. The integration of these economies into the circuits of Fordism spurred the growth of 'global Fordism'. Second, the regime of accumulation that emerged in the South is itself analysed as a type of Fordism. Initially, this took the form of 'bloody Taylorism', which involves deregulated labour markets, repression of the labour force and a detailed division of semi-skilled labour (Lipietz 1982). The integration of developing economies into the international division of industrial labour entailed the adoption of 'export-substitution' strategies, which facilitated a shift in key exports from primary goods to cheap, mass-produced consumer goods. These strategies were also often associated with special concessions in defined export-processing zones and an extensive reliance on workers from rural areas, especially women, with no prior experience of the rigours of capitalist labour processes. This strategy, according to Lipietz (1984), achieved only limited success. Insofar as export advantage was premised on the super-exploitation of labour, it was politically unstable and entailed significant social costs. Moreover, since it was primarily export-orientated, the internal market remained underdeveloped.

The export penetration of bloody Taylorism prompted a protectionist response from developed countries (Lipietz 1984). This encouraged some developing countries in the 1970s to replace bloody Taylorism with 'peripheral Fordism', which is a mode of growth that incorporated some features of central Fordism. Subsequent monetarist attempts to resolve the crisis of central Fordism undermined the conditions for accumulation in the newly industrialized countries and precipitated a crisis of peripheral Fordism. The latter, in Lipietz's analysis, is therefore closely linked to the dynamics of global Fordism. In the absence of detailed studies of specific social formations in the South, this analysis tends to reduce the 'periphery' to an undifferentiated mass with no internal dynamics of its own. In reality, however, some developing countries assumed an increasingly important mass production role in the global division of labour, developed intensive regimes of accumulation and expanded domestic consumption of consumer durables. Nevertheless, as Table 23.1 indicates, there are significant differences between peripheral Fordism and central Fordism.

While regulation theory offers an alternative to market-centred or state-centred explanations of developing and newly industrializing countries, the work on peripheral Fordism was largely Eurocentric in the sense of relying too strongly on central Fordism as the baseline for comparison. While acknowledging the originality of Lipietz's account, Jessop and Sum (2006, 159–160) argue that it is problematic on four grounds. Firstly, he defines and interprets the periphery in terms of the dynamics of the centre, and consequently focuses on the Fordist rather than non-Fordist aspects of its labour process. Despite the fact that peripheral Fordism lacks key features of central Fordism, Lipietz is compelled to depict the periphery in Eurocentric terms as an incomplete or partially realized form of Fordism, thereby overlooking its diversity and distinctive modalities. Secondly, the notion of peripheral Fordism is premised on dichotomies such as centre–periphery and global–national, and reduces the internal dynamics of developing countries to their role in the global system. There

Table 23.1   Comparison between central and peripheral Fordism

Central Fordism	Peripheral Fordism
Autocentric logic of mass production and mass consumption	Mass production articulated to global circuits of capitalism
Mass production by assembly lines	Mass production based on assembly lines and Taylorist practices
Research-intensive and skilled production	Semi-skilled production processes with R&D, design, skilled labour and management located overseas
Production for domestic consumption	Production mainly for exports and the global market
Mass consumption by the working class	Consumption by urban middle class and weak working class
Responsible trade unionism	Emergent working class
Keynesian welfare state	Emerging international regulation and absence of welfare policies

Source: adapted from Jessop and Sum (2006, 158).

is a long-standing opposition to such functionalist and top-down, holistic explanations among regulation theorists. Thirdly, Lipietz identifies urban middle-class consumption as the key internal link in the virtuous circle of production–consumption in peripheral Fordism. However, he fails to provide any firm institutional grounding to this notion and neglects the key role of the articulation of internal–external dynamics in shaping the economic and social regulation of the periphery.

Lastly, Lipietz's view of peripheral Fordism is 'spatially unbound as well as temporally overbound' (Jessop and Sum 2006, 160). That is, his claim that peripheral Fordism is confined to countries where an expanding local market played a key role in the national system of accumulation renders the concept imprecise and equivocal. The distinctive development paths in Latin America, East Asia and Africa highlight the need for greater spatio-temporal specificity. To this end, Jessop and Sum (2006) suggest that Lipietz's 'bloody Taylorism' should be confined to the stage of primary export-orientated industrialization as peripheral enclaves became export-processing zones. Next, variants of peripheral Fordism characterize the secondary import substitution industrialization stage as an expanding urban middle class fuels the domestic market. A third form of integration into the world market emerges as a new form of export-orientated industrialization is superimposed on import substitution industrialization, as in East Asia after the 1970s. The latter is presented as a stylized model of 'exportism' that is analogous to, yet distinct from, Fordism. In the light of these shortcomings in the explanatory power of the notion of peripheral Fordism, Jessop and Sum (2006, 161) advise against the use of umbrella terms and propose 'a more historically contingent account' of the periphery 'as a "belated" (or "catchup") form of capitalism' that should be explained 'in non-Eurocentric terms'.

Recent studies have avoided the tendency to analyse the South in terms of concepts derived from a study of the North. There is a growing recognition that such concepts may only have limited traction in developing countries. The latest generation of regulationist studies explore 'the socially embedded, socially regularized nature of economies and the intertwining of the distinctive institutional logics of specific economies and political orders in specific social formations' (Jessop and Sum 2006, 152–153). An important inference drawn from these studies is that no single emerging pattern characterizes the integration of developing countries into the international division of labour. There is a whole variety of different modes of growth – a 'global mosaic of regions' in the words of Scott and Storper (1992) – both between and within various countries. By implication, it is necessary to conceptualize modes of growth not only in terms of successive phases of development, but also in terms of 'historically coexistent and competing local alternatives' (Peck 1996, 120). In contrast to the notion of 'dependent development', which assumes that capitalism can only successfully develop in the industrially advanced societies, contemporary regulation theory can account for the comparatively intensive industrialization of the countries in East Asia (e.g. South Korea), Africa (e.g. South Africa) and Latin America (e.g. Brazil). The development of 'peripheral' societies is not functionally related to that of the 'centre' and the development of capitalism in the South is seen as uneven, partial and unstable. This casts serious doubt on generalizations about the impact of the international division of labour on the developing world in general and Africa in particular, and raises the need for concrete analyses of specific social formations. One aspect of such an analysis is an explanation of the variegated patterns that characterize the social regulation of firms and markets.

23.2.3   Markets, Hierarchies and Social Regulation

Regulation theory has made a significant contribution to our understanding of the complex and contradictory relations between markets, hierarchies and social regulation. However, there is much to be gained from drawing on parallel developments in (among others) economic sociology, economic geography and heterodox economics. Sayer (1995,

100–102) draws a useful distinction between production and market 'optics'. Orthodox Marxist perspectives on the concept of 'markets' are characterized by a 'production optic', which treats production and capital as prior to exchange. Consequently, the role of exchange is limited to realizing the value of commodities and allocational effects are of little or no interest. Neoliberal perspectives are characterized by a 'market optic', which collapses production into exchange. The focus is on allocational effects, while production and its social relations are either ignored or conceived as a sphere of transactions or exchanges. In the market optic of orthodox economics, the whole economy becomes 'the market' – that is, markets are everywhere the state is not. This creates the illusion that markets actually produce things. Other forms of regulation that exist within most economies, as Sayer (1995, 84–85) points out, are often incorrectly seen as 'rivals' of markets. Likewise, markets are not an alternative to production or to firms or hierarchies, but a mode of coordination of the division of labour. The socially corrosive effects of commodification involve not the disappearance of social relations, but a shift to a different kind of social relation, which is selective and transient (Sayer 1995, 89). In some contexts, marketization can be a disguise for proletarianization. Imperialist powers in Southern Africa employed means such as taxes and the commodification of land to force self-sufficient producers onto the labour market.

In recent years, the ideological notion of latent or implicit markets, which only need freeing for economic benefits automatically to follow, has figured strongly in neoliberal discourse. The neoliberal tendency to see markets everywhere encourages the view that individual 'choice', rather than production or social regulation, is the organizing principle of economic behaviour. Orthodox views of the market marginalize the social relations of production and the processes of production and consumption on which supply and demand depend. Non-market exchanges are far more common, especially between firms, than orthodox economic theory would care to admit. The rationalist methodology of neoliberal economics contrasts strongly with the view, associated above all with Polanyi (1957), that markets are social constructions whose creation and evolution are problematic and require extensive regulation by the state and other institutions. Far from being unnecessary 'interventions' or 'distortions', the latter are a normal feature of real markets (Sayer 1995, 87). The orthodox view of markets is 'undersocialized' in the sense that they are viewed as operating in a social context that is of no consequence (Lazonick 2003). In reality, markets and exchange are always socially embedded (Granovetter 1985). Markets rely on wider social processes and relationships such as formal and tacit rules and conventions, social norms and accepted standards of behaviour (Sayer 1995, 114). The latter are a precondition for the existence of markets, and their coordinating effects extend beyond production and consumption.

Since markets are not a self-sufficient mode of regulation, they invariably require supplementing by other modes. For regulationists, markets are institutions, which rely on the state; are organized, regulated, embedded and influenced by context; information and power are unevenly distributed within them; and they can disempower as well as empower people. At an abstract level, all markets have certain essential features, whereas in concrete cases they can be developed in various ways and combined with other modes of regulation so that behaviour and outcomes can vary significantly (Sayer 1995, 94–95). In real markets, outcomes depend on the nature of products and technologies, forms of calculation used, legal and moral frameworks and strategic information possessed. Since markets are always embedded to some degree and since there are always other modes of regulation present even in the most marketized society, the actual behaviour of agents in concrete markets cannot be read off simply from the market structure (though it is constrained and enabled by markets) and hence cannot be predicted and judged purely a priori (Sayer 1995, 144).

In Williamson's (1985) dichotomous view of markets and hierarchies, the firm is hermetically sealed off from markets and, by extension, from the broader social context. The increasing involvement of firms in non-market arrangements with other firms and agencies contradicts the view of firms simply as 'islands of planned coordination in a sea of market relations'. Such involvement is highly dependent on the particular institutional, organizational and industrial conditions under which it occurs (Lazonick 2003, 35). The investment of social capital reduces transaction costs between firms and other organizations, notably search and information costs, bargaining and decision costs, and control and enforcement costs (Landry et al. 2002, 686). Transaction cost approaches, however, do acknowledge that 'transactions in the middle range' between hierarchy and markets are arranged within a continuum with market exchanges at one pole and hierarchies at the other (Williamson 1985, 83). Moving from the market towards the hierarchy pole, one encounters subcontracting arrangements, joint ventures, collaborative networks and the like. Explaining the existence of these intermediate forms of transactions usually involves cataloguing the deficiencies of integrated hierarchies and competitive markets, and then arguing that they 'solve' these problems (Grabher 1993, 6). The institutional set-up referred to as 'relational contracting' by Williamson (1985), or 'organized market' as Lundvall (1993, 55) prefers to call it, is a continuous process of exchange between users and suppliers of qualitative information. This information exchange involves a process of interactive learning that enhances the capability of the supplier as well as the competence of the user.

There are areas in which closely related activities can be coordinated directly through various blends of collaboration, negotiation and domination. Contrary to the fiction of markets as a self-contained mode of coordination needing only price information, actors cannot rely on merely 'going to the market' to see what is on offer and to see who will buy their wares. Groups with common interests, especially producers, need to share information, negotiate and build trust as a precondition of any successful ongoing economic relationship, form common views about the future and harmonize plans. In the literature on industrial restructuring, considerable emphasis is placed on the benefits of long-term collaborative relationships. This creates the impression that networks are beginning to supplant market relations and the price mechanism. They may be supplanting arm's-length market transactions to some degree, but the fact that the members of the network remain under separate ownership and still exchange most of their products as commodities shows that networks usually supplement rather than displace market exchange (Sayer and Walker 1992). Networks modify and regulate markets, but do so over restricted categories of activities within production chains. That is, networks entail the supplementation, not displacement, of markets and hierarchies by other forms of coordination (Sayer 1995). The empirical reality of socio-economic change reveals an overlapping, interpenetration and combination of market, authority and network relations (Ferlie and Pettigrew 1998, 215–217). Moreover, these relations are never constructed in a social vacuum: the various control mechanisms are 'grafted on to and leveraged off existing social structures' (Grabher 1993, 7). It is therefore wrong to assume that markets, hierarchies and networks are mutually exclusive forms of economic governance.

Network relations do not assume a single, universal form: firms can choose from a wide variety of organizational modes of cooperation depending on their circumstances. No single argument for or against a particular mode of coordination can override all the rest: trade-offs and compromises are unavoidable (Sayer 1995, 144). The interpenetration of markets and hierarchies associated with networking cannot be adequately addressed within a framework that examines the firm as an analytically distinct organizational unit. Networks are supposed to reduce the problems of opportunism and a lack of reciprocity and trust, but they often need the assistance of a body standing outside the competitors – such as the state, an industry association or an industrial council – to override individualistic pressures. Networks, like markets, are not self-sufficient but require support from other modes of regulation or coordination. Due to the inherent dynamic of network governance, a continuous process of reorganizing network structures takes place. The boundary separating the interior and exterior of an enterprise is constantly shifting because of changes in the interactions between members of a network. Consequently, network governance appears to be considerably less stable than governance by the market or hierarchy. Networks are, by their very nature, in imbalance and characterized by power relations so that a benefit for one party may well be a cost to another.

23.3   SUB-SAHARAN AFRICA: THE SOCIO-ECONOMIC AND POLITICAL CONTEXT

The developmental problems confronting sub-Saharan Africa are formidable. The industrial base of most African countries remains small, fragile and predominantly high cost (Riddell 1993, 219–220). Production is linked primarily to a limited processing of agricultural or mineral products and exports are dominated by low-value-added primary commodities (Kwasi Fosu et al. 2001). In 1988, industry contributed 25 per cent to GDP in sub-Saharan Africa, while the manufacturing share was only 10 per cent as compared to 24 per cent for all low-income countries (Riddell 1990, 5). In fact, sub-Saharan countries contributed only 3.6 per cent of total manufacturing value added in all developing countries (Riddell 1990, 11). None of the economies in the region has managed to overcome the restrictions on economic growth imposed during the era of colonial dependence. Industrial development is constrained by low degrees of interlinkage between manufacturing and other productive sectors of the economy, outdated machinery, a lack of skilled labour, poor management skills, low productivity and a small domestic market. The slowdown of economic growth in the 1980s – combined with the sharp rise in the price of imported capital goods, growing shortages of foreign exchange and declining levels of investment – exacerbated these constraints as capacity utilization levels plummeted, plant and equipment deteriorated, and processes of de-industrialization set in (Adedeji 1991; Riddell 1993; Mihyo and Schiphorst 2002). As Leys (1994, 45) puts it, it is not so much that Africa 'got off to a bad start' at independence, it is rather that:

> the timing of its original incorporation in the world capitalist system, combined with the extreme backwardness of its precolonial economies and the limitations of subsequent colonial policy, prevented most of the continent from

starting at all on the key transition to self-sustaining capital accumulation after independence.

When we consider the types and patterns of industrial growth in sub-Saharan Africa, the following features stand out: (1) the predominant source of growth in manufacturing has been domestic demand rather than either import-substitution or export growth; (2) the pace of growth in manufacturing output seems to have been critically determined by the dynamics of the wider domestic economy; (3) manufacturing growth has been dependent on access to sufficient amounts of foreign exchange (to finance plant, equipment and inputs) that the sector itself has in large measure been unable to earn; (4) substantial growth in manufacturing would be highly unlikely unless the leading productive sectors were also experiencing sustained growth and expansion; (5) the process of substituting for imports has tended to be rather haphazard – it has resulted in neither a very significant degree of linkage with other sectors of the economy nor a significant fall in the importation of even simple consumer goods; (6) the dominance of consumer rather than intermediate or capital-goods manufacture suggests not only that manufacturing is relatively simple in technique, but also that there has been little structural change in the post-independence period; (7) there is plenty of scope for further import substitution, placing in better perspective the view that future manufacturing policy should be dominated and determined by an expansion of domestic demand; and (8) success in import-substituting industrialization depended not so much on the dominance of one or other characteristic, but rather on the convergence of many supportive elements over a relatively long period of time (Riddell 1993).

The so-called Washington Consensus, which fundamentally shaped economic policies in Africa during the 1980s and early 1990s, endorsed a universal formula for development in the region: macroeconomic stabilization, deregulation, economic liberalization, elimination of trade and tariff barriers, privatization and market-driven institutional reforms. This myopic, neoliberal approach failed to deliver any meaningful economic development, let alone any significant reduction in poverty. The basic outline of a post-Washington Consensus, which emerged from the World Bank in the late 1990s and early 2000s, regards poverty reduction as a key goal of policy implementation, acknowledges that freeing markets and reducing the state do not constitute the sole basis for sustained growth, and reaffirms the belief that the private sector is the engine of economic development. In addition, greater emphasis is placed on the development of social and physical infrastructure, raising agricultural production, increasing trade in diversified products, the reduction of external debts, greater protection of rights to private property, easier access to credit, and more effective social protection in the form of pensions, grants and allowances, and access to basic services. To succeed, however, this strategy requires:

> not only the liberalizing measures of the Washington Consensus, but also embedding the market in a facilitative framework of reformed institutions, and providing safety nets to ensure that the losers from reform, together with the chronic poor, remain quiescent . . . the actions for release of [entrepreneurial] energies must originate in Africa and must start with much better governance . . . [A] revitalised private sector . . . [will require] improving the 'investment climate' . . . Poor governance must be rectified . . . [before] the state will play its designated role as 'enabling' an efficient and reliable market economy. (Sandbrook 2005, 1118–1119)

Given the fact that almost half of the population in sub-Saharan Africa lives in dire poverty, social protection measures need to offset the inequalities generated by the sway of market forces. These measures need to mediate the difficult trade-offs and contradictions that inevitably arise. In practice, however, there is insufficient linkage between macro-economic policies and microeconomic realities of African economies and society (Bhorat et al. 2006).The daily difficulties that African firms face in conducting business have been widely documented. These include major inefficiency at all stages of the value chain, inadequacy and inef-fectiveness of formal legal institutions, problems of contract enforce-ment, pervasiveness of delays and non-delivery by firms' suppliers, as well as the extraordinary lengths employers go to in order to avoid theft (Fafchamps 2004). Firms cope with these problems in a variety of different, often creative and largely informal ways. A report by the World Bank marvels at the capacity of Africans 'to operate through an apparent anarchy', identifying 'social networks' that, though 'invisible' to outsiders, 'create social capital', which is crucial to the survival of communities 'in the face of low incomes and few formal economy jobs' (cited in Sandbrook 2005, 1121). In Africa, the rationality that informs neoliberal prescriptions for economic development coexists with two other, contradictory rationalities in which neither land nor labour is regarded as a commodity:

> One is the rationality of mutual support systems, in which economic activity is, in effect, embedded in a community – an extended family, a clan, a village, or increasingly in contemporary Africa, a religious association. Here, a complex set of mutual obligations governs economic roles and the distribution of the product . . . The other rationality is that of redistribution, in which a surplus is channelled to a political centre and then redistributed according to some religious or political principle. (Sandbrook 2005, 1120)

The rationalities of the market, mutual support and redistribution are embedded in different institutional matrices with opposing logics of action, modes of calculation and methods of legitimation. A shift in the relative dominance of any of these rationalities will, of necessity, involve significant tensions in and disruptions to the prevailing social fabric. These tensions and disruptions stem from the fact that existing institutions reflect a particular constellation of power and distribution of resources in a society, the disruption of which is likely to be opposed by those with vested interests. Likewise, the integrative and coordinating functions of one rationality may be undermined by the rising prominence of another. For instance, the designation of land as a commodity by market rationality clashes with the principles of communal land tenure that maintain some degree of equality in rural areas and provide an important safety net. Moreover, given the sheer scale of poverty and deprivation, government-supported social protection schemes are unlikely to compensate the rural poor for a loss of access to communal land and the decline of the reciprocal ties of existing social networks.

In a contemporary form of redistribution – namely, neopatrimonialism – a central political elite appropriates resources from economic agents and redirects them to individuals and groups based on political allegiance. The latter, in turn, is often premised on pre-existing tribal or ethnic loyalties. Of particular importance is the role played by these loyalties in supplier networks, contract enforcement and information sharing. Sandbrook (2005) identifies an elective affinity between neopatrimonialism and the socio-economic conditions of many sub-Saharan countries, which accounts for the system's prevalence. Political elites are confronted with the daunting task of governing weakly integrated societies with a largely destitute rural population and a burgeoning urban informal sector characterized by a limited commodification of land and labour, respectively. While the patronage (such as taxes, duties, foreign aid, loans, revenues from state-owned corporations, tenders and appointments to the public sector) that oils the cogs of client–patron relations entails a significant brake on economic development, it nevertheless provides a fragile, yet partially effective, basis of rule. In the absence of immediately viable alternatives, a 'failed state' is an exceedingly likely outcome of attempts to dislocate precarious neopatrimonial systems. The social basis of the patrimonial state comprises poor rural communities under the control of traditional leaders, a small and fragmented working class as well as business classes and urban middle classes, which tend to be 'politically weak, as they are small in number, dependent on governmental largesse, and often poorly organised in representative associations' (Sandbrook 2005, 1122–1123). The costs of neopatrimonial rule are considerable: long-term market considerations (investment) are subordinated to short-term political expediency (personal power and privilege); officials continuously need to capture new resources to maintain the loyalty of cronies; rampant fraud and corruption remain unpunished; patronage appointments lead to incompetent and unqualified personnel; and resources are steered away from long-term investments.

The calls by the World Bank and other international agencies for improved governance, a revitalized and efficient public service, a vibrant and active civil society, reduced socio-economic inequalities and greater political freedoms are fundamentally at odds with the continuation of neopatrimonial rule. Neoliberal reforms are premised on a disembedding of the economy from society. However, as the implementation of structural adjustment programmes (which were integral to African governments' economic plans) amply demonstrated:

> the policies designed to reduce waste, corruption and 'mismanagement', to shrink the state bureaucracy, and to privatise money-losing state corporations undermined existing clientele networks. Subaltern patrons, cut off from resource flows from the centre, turned to freelancing in their pursuit of resources to distribute. (Sandbrook 2005, 1124)

Existing institutional, organizational and normative frameworks represent a distinct, prior set of possibilities and constraints for the establishment of new forms of regulation. Most post-colonial governments in Africa faced a common contradiction at independence: 'the conditions that had allowed international capital to realize large, even vast profits, and were expected to do so again, were in contradiction with those for constructing an equitable and civilized society for its people' (Saul and Leys1995, 196). Post-colonial governments had to balance the heightened expectations among the citizens following the process of decolonization with the need to attract foreign investment and maintain economic stability. This balancing act invariably led to a contradictory fusion of neoliberal and neopatrimonial forms of regulation. In Namibia, this combination of regulatory forms was overdetermined by the legacy of colonialism and apartheid capitalism.

23.4   NAMIBIA: PRODUCTION, REGULATION AND SEGMENTATION

23.4.1   Colonialism and Apartheid Capitalism

As a newly industrializing and recently democratized country, Namibia provides an instructive context for the study of changes in firms, markets and regulation. The two decades since independence has witnessed a deepening of the division in the Namibian economy between a relatively small, advanced 'formal' sector and a growing, impoverished 'informal' sector. This division is firmly rooted in settler colonialism and apartheid capitalism. It is revealed in the stark contrast between the relative wealth of the country and the high degrees of inequality and poverty. On the one hand, Namibia has the per capita income of a middle-income country and, on the other, a high degree of poverty. Namibia's ranking according to its per capita GDP is 79, while its rank according to the Human Development Index is 116 (Hansohm et al. 1998, 1). A World Bank study in 1992 reveals that the GDP per capita for the white population was US$12 839, for the black wage employment sector US$585, and for the rural ('subsistence') sector only US$55 (cited in MoL 1994, 11). The vast majority of black people in Namibia are considered poor and, with a Gini-coefficient of 0.7, inequality is among the highest in the world. About half of the Namibian population continues to live in conditions of extreme poverty in a country with a low population density that possesses some of the richest and most abundant natural resources in Africa.

The colonial character of the Namibian economy meant that the bulk of production was for export. This, in turn, meant that businesses did not rely on the local market and it therefore did not matter if most Namibians could not afford to buy their products. A report by the United Nations Institute for Namibia in 1977 described the country as a 'classic case of an economy which, in respect of goods, produces what it does not consume, and consumes what it does not produce' (cited in Herbstein and Evenson 1989, 132). Namibia's economy is dominated by foreign private investment and up to half of its GDP was estimated to be creamed off annually in the form of dividends and remittances sent abroad during the colonial era (Cronje and Cronje 1979, 7). Mining accounted for more than half of total exports and contributed an average of 40 to 50 per cent of government revenue. This extreme dependence on a few mining operations constituted a serious economic risk to the post-independence economy. Moreover, not only did the black majority benefit very little from mining's contribution to the colonial economy, but also the taxes that accrued from the mining sector helped to sustain South Africa's unlawful occupation of the territory and provided a significant incentive for its continuation. The largely foreign-owned mining industry also stands accused of tax evasion, transfer pricing and the payment of excessive dividends instead of reinvestment in the country.

An export share in GDP that is twice as high as for sub-Saharan Africa signals the high degree of openness of the Namibia economy. Namibia's economy is characterized by its export orientation, sensitivity to changes in external demand and reliance on the export of primary commodities. Through its structural dependence on South Africa and its highly uneven distribution of wealth, the colonial economic structure has attained a largely self-perpetuating dynamic. The pace of social transformation in post-independence Namibia is severely curtailed by an economy that was run as an enclave of transnational corporations. The most salient features of Namibia's inherited socio-economic structure include: an underdeveloped rural sector, especially in the populous north; a small industrial sector dominated by the production and export of a few primary products with minimal processing; a capital-intensive production structure that is not commensurate with the need for a labour-absorbing growth strategy; a severe shortage of skilled labour combined with high rates of illiteracy among the black population; a highly skewed distribution of income resulting in a small domestic market; a poorly integrated industrial structure with few vertical linkages; and a high degree of dependence on the South African economy. The vitally important diamond industry, for example, continues to be the most profitable and most foreign-owned sector of the Namibian economy.

Namibia's fragmented industrial structure with little or no links between the various sectors means that growth in one sector simply raises import demand rather than stimulating growth in other sectors. The lack of horizontal integration has resulted in the different sectors of the economy being more closely tied to outside interests than to each other. This renders the short-term potential for creating additional employment and expanding downstream operations negligible. Poorly developed interfirm linkages in the Namibian economy are reinforced by the fact that the largest and most profitable companies produce almost exclusively for export and consume very little of Namibian origin except labour, water and electricity. Likewise, the extensive reliance on imported basic consumer goods, such as food and clothing, means that few jobs and economic opportunities are created for Namibians. The dominant industries in Namibia are mainly mature, non-science-based sectors, benefiting either from local natural resources or from cheap labour. The capacity to innovate and lead technological development is severely limited, design and production methods are standardized, productivity growth is slow and the major form of competition is price competition, depending predominantly on labour costs.

The model of development in Namibia is inextricably tied to the historical evolution and deepening crisis of regulation in South Africa. Drawing on regulation theory, Gelb (1991) identified 'racial Fordism' as the nationally specific model of development in South Africa. The defining characteristic of this model is the post-war combination of apartheid and import-substitution industrialization. Like Fordism in the developed societies, accumulation in South Africa during the period 1948–1974 involved linking improvements in mass production to the expansion of mass consumption. But, unlike Fordism elsewhere, 'both production and consumption were racially structured' (Gelb 1991, 13). A confluence of mounting national, regional and international pressures during the late 1980s placed demands on the regulation of accumulation in South Africa, which its apartheid-based mode of regulation could not absorb. This compelled the apartheid regime to seek an internal negotiated settlement and to end its occupation of Namibia. When it became clear to the South African government that any political solution, which excludes the South West African People's Organisation (SWAPO), would lack legitimacy, the regime shifted its energies and resources towards a neocolonial outcome that would ensure the continued protection of South African interests under a future SWAPO government.

23.4.2   Neocolonialism, Neopatrimonialism and Neoliberalism

In 1990, the first democratically elected government in Namibia inherited an unstable and discredited political system rooted in discrimination and oppression; a fractured society scarred by a prolonged war and widespread deprivation; a distorted and dependent economy highly susceptible to climatic conditions and mineral prices; and an industrial relations system in which conflict and coercion were endemic (Wood 1991; Leys and Saul 1995a; Winterfeldt et al. 2002). The system of social and economic institutions inherited by the SWAPO government was designed to serve purposes very different from its own stated goal of combining efficiency and equality. As Wood (1991, 769) puts it:

> Successive South African government policies ensured that, on independence, the material base, core apparatus and ideological coherence of the new Namibia state remained weak. A lack of new financial resources, a legacy of ethnic fragmentation and the preponderance of populist and clientelist political relations inhibit what little the state can do to overcome the sharp social contradictions between rich and poor.

There are significant indications that the dualistic economic structure of the colonial era is being reproduced in a new form by the post-independence political order. The foundations for a black elite were laid during the 1980s and consolidated through (among others) a network of clientelism and an expansion of the public sector after 1990. The hegemonic position of this new elite, however, is dependent on real concessions to the subordinate classes. In a society where capitalist and subsistence modes of production interpenetrate, the extended family system that was preserved in the rural areas tended to mitigate the effects of growing class contradictions by reinforcing the legitimacy of elites. Under such circumstances, as Tapscott (1995, 166) explains:

> Kinship obligations and clientelism . . . serve to reduce tensions between the elite and subaltern classes by extending influence and, to a lesser extent, economic gains to subordinate groups. In Namibia, the reciprocities and obligations of the extended family system are such that the socio-economic standing of many rural households depends heavily on remittances from those in waged employment.

The neocolonial character of the Namibian economy – with its dependence on cheap black labour, the predominance of primary commodity exports and extensive resource shortages – renders it highly vulnerable to external economic shocks. Given the high costs of imported technologies, the preponderance of cost-based competitiveness and a narrow and racially differentiated market, sustained growth and the development of economies of scale are crucially dependent on increased exports and growing foreign investments. The overall picture, however, remains one of an economy dominated by a large non-tradable sector (government services) and an export-orientated primary sector (agriculture, fishing and mining). A small internal market, an inability to attract significant foreign direct investment (FDI), and a 'new world order' opposed to protectionist, state-driven economic policies ruled out a viable import-substituting industrialization strategy in post-independence Namibia. As Curry and Stoneman (1993, 42) argue, although Namibia had:

> experienced a thoroughgoing free market experience from its integration with South Africa, and has inherited a price structure completely unrelated to its own development needs, it has nevertheless joined most other countries in committing itself to adopting a world market price structure . . . that may be equally inappropriate for the needs of internal development. The observed outcome in Namibia of integration through a free market with a more advanced economy, is a structure of extreme distortions.

South African companies dominate diamond and other mineral mining as well as the construction, fishing, retail, hotel, banking and financial services sectors. Local companies are highly dependent on supply chains dominated by South African firms and, in the absence of protective barriers, South African companies exert monopoly control over the Namibian market through dumping, overpricing of intermediate inputs and restrictive purchasing policies. Since the bulk of their products are exported to South Africa and production is mainly small-scale, Namibian producers have little experience in or opportunities for competing on world markets.

South Africa's dominance within the Southern African Customs Union (SACU) also has a major impact on the conditions under which Namibian firms produce for the domestic market. Historically high levels of sub-sidization, together with economies of scale, have given South African exporters a distinct advantage over their counterparts in SACU.

In an attempt to promote business confidence, minimize potential political instability, and prevent the flight of skills and capital, the SWAPO government adopted conservative economic policies. SWAPO's policy of 'national reconciliation' – despite its political and eco-nomic expediency in light of experiences in Angola, Mozambique and Zimbabwe – reinforced and legitimized the colonial legacy by protecting the pre-independence gains of the white minority. A pragmatic decision to avoid alienating the white business and farming elites, according to Simon (2002, 172), favoured 'a relatively hands-off approach' to the economy. This is perhaps best exemplified by the emphasis placed on attracting FDI into a capital-scarce and labour-abundant economy. The equipment, training, transport and processing facilities necessary to reap greater rewards from the beneficiation of raw materials require the active participation of the (largely white and foreign-owned) private sector. The latter, however, is unlikely to succeed in stimulating a more diverse, integrated and higher value-added industrial sector in the absence of resolute government invention 'to counteract the underlying pattern established by market forces' (Curry and Stoneman 1993, 42). This will require, among others, the protection of nascent and strategic industries; the expansion of the small and medium-sized enterprise sector; the provi-sion of institutional and financial support to encourage greater invest-ment by local firms; the introduction of measures to foster backward and forward linkages within the economy; the development of tendering systems to increase local preference in government contracts; and the establishment of institutions to promote skills development (Isaksen and Shipoke 1992).

The success of an export-led growth path depends in large measure on an institutional framework capable of controlling costs, keeping wage growth in line with productivity and curtailing the excesses of market-based regulation. However, proponents of the 'new world order' stressed the unbridled role of market forces at precisely the time that Namibia required extensive state intervention to transform its apartheid-based mode of regulation and colonial regime of accumulation. The crux of the problem, as the president of the Chamber of Mines noted, is that:

> Namibia [is] a poor country eager to attract foreign investment. However, to succeed the government had to pass legislation that would protect both existing

and future investments and allow unrestricted dividend returns to investors. (cited in Kempton and Du Preez 1997, 599)

The new world order dictates that economic intervention by national governments should be limited to the creation of an 'investor-friendly' business environment. According to these prescriptions, the activities of the state need to be rolled back from areas that are best left to the market. That is, growth on business's own terms is regarded as the *sine qua non* of economic stability and competitiveness. The Namibian government believes that it was compelled by the force of circumstances to create a favourable climate for FDI by endorsing a market-driven process of economic reform. The Foreign Investment Act of 1990 amounts to a free-market investment code with considerable protection against state expropriation, extensive incentives for foreign firms, and no requirements for participation or shareholding by local firms in the operations of foreign enterprises. The objectives of this Act were reinforced by provisions in the Manufacturing Incentives of 1993 and Export Incentives of 1994. The Export Processing Zones Act of 1995 provides that any factory within Namibia may apply for export-processing zone status subject to certain conditions. After an initial flurry of investment, several export-processing zone companies went out of business, with those remaining providing only a few hundred, mainly low-wage, low-skill jobs (LaRRI 2000). The flagship of the export-processing zone programme at Walvis Bay soon became 'an enclave with little organic linkage to the rest of the economy' (Simon 2002, 183). Despite considerable opposition from the trade unions, the Export Processing Zone Act also suspended key elements of the Labour Act (such as the right to strike) within the export-processing zones. Former president Sam Nujoma suggested that 'the non-application of Namibia's [labour] code in the export processing zone regime is a delicate compromise which is necessary to achieve the larger goal of job creation' (*Namibian* 30 October 1995). As a result, the incentive-led export-processing zone strategy is associated with a regime of labour regulation characterized by jobs of variable quality with almost half of the workforce in non-standard employment; widespread union avoidance strategies by employers; the almost total absence of collective bargaining; low wages and minimal benefits; dangerous and unsafe working conditions; high rates of absenteeism and low levels of productivity (Simon 1998, 119–121; LaRRI 2001, 83–84).

The legacy of colonialism, combined with the pressures of globalization and the dictates of neoliberalism, seriously hampered the government's capacity to sustain a durable and redistributive trade-off between the imperatives of economic efficiency and the demands for greater social equality. Revisions to industrial policy remain firmly committed to market-driven solutions for the lack of competitiveness, diversification, integration, beneficiation, skills development, equal economic opportunities, small enterprise development and technology transfer (MTI 1999b). The government summarized its approach to industrial policy in the following terms:

> Government policies will be orientated at creating and maintaining markets. Specific interventions will operate through markets by providing the appropriate incentives and information . . . Government will strengthen its institutional capacity in order to increase its ability to implement flexible industrialisation strategies . . . As a small open economy, trade liberalisation represents a unique opportunity for the Namibian industrial sector to benefit from access to larger markets. (MTI 1999a, 4–6)

An 'inevitable complement' of a neocolonial economic structure, as Leys and Saul (1995b, 4) note, is a neocolonial politics that 'limits popular demands for radical social and economic policies'. In fact, the transition to democracy in Namibia was characterized by considerable restraints on the ability of labour and other organs of civil society to press their demands on the post-independence political structure. As Dobell (1998, 104) puts it: 'the nature of the transition process itself . . . served to institutionalize democratic political structures in Namibia, while simultaneously helping to construct perhaps insurmountable obstacles to the extension of political democracy to social and economic institutions'. The lack of effective tripartite structures at the level of the economy and industry means that there is no supportive institutional framework for cooperation in restructuring at the workplace level. Institutional arrangements play an important role in providing workers with employment security in the context of industrial restructuring, encouraging greater economic efficiency without increasing social inequalities and establishing sustainable, high-productivity coalitions in the workplace (Esping-Andersen and Regini 2000). A low-cost response to market pressures and changes appears to be most frequent in countries with weak institutions, low levels of unionization, decentralized bargaining structures and limited government intervention in the economy. In a country such as Namibia where these conditions prevail, there is a lack of significant moderating influences on the tendency of firms to adjust to competition by reducing and controlling labour costs.

23.4.3 Labour Markets, Managerial Control and Collective Regulation

The evolution of labour regulation highlights the complex and contradictory interaction between firms and markets. The forceful separation of production and reproduction by the systems of labour migration that evolved in most settler colonies in Southern Africa could only be sustained by extra-economic institutions. The dissolution of the production regime associated with colonial despotism facilitated a growing intervention of the state apparatuses in the processes of labour regulation. The rise of the post-colonial state was therefore accompanied by a greater interpenetration of production and state apparatuses. That is: since:

> the company state was fragmented and the new production apparatuses were weaker, less extensive, and more autonomous from management, the state itself intervened to narrow the scope of purely industrial struggle . . . [by introducing mechanisms] for the regulation and absorption of class struggle at the level of the firm. (Burawoy 1985, 245)

These mechanisms, however, tend to have establishing and exclusionary effects as well as protective and stabilizing effects. A key feature of the post-independence era in Namibia is the convergence of a strengthened legal and social safety net covering the standard employment relationship and a proliferation of non-standard employment relationships at the margins of this regulatory framework. To unravel the connections between changes in the employment relationship and the wider socio-economic context, we must start with the institutional framework that regulates the supply of and demand for labour (Peck 1996). Much of the interaction between the requirements of the labour process and the social context occurs through the local labour market.

The local adaptation of new methods of work organization has followed classic apartheid-colonial lines. The system of low-skill, low-wage and low-trust relations embedded in industrial and work organization in Namibia makes it very difficult for Namibian firms to realize the cooperative benefits of participatory forms of production such as quality circles. Most Namibian firms lack the market power and resources to move into higher-value-added batch production and lack the stability and levels of demand necessary to reap the benefits of economies of scale. In the lower-value-added segment of international trade, Namibia has to compete with low-wage economies like China. Much of the low productivity observed in different sectors arises as a direct consequence of the outdated forms of organization that pervade Namibian enterprises. This rendered most unionized firms highly vulnerable to changes in the regulatory framework. Comparatively high wages, combined with low labour productivity, act as a major brake on competitiveness. Although wages in Namibia are considerably lower than those in the industrialized countries, they remain high by comparison with many other developing countries, especially in Asia.

While the nature, extent and direction of change depend on a multiplicity of factors, they are patterned by the internal structures and dynamics of a firm. Strong internal labour markets provide incentives to employers to reduce costs and increase flexibility through casualization and outsourcing. Conversely, a weak internal labour market may provide sufficient sources of flexibility so that the benefits of non-standard employment do not offset their disadvantages. Unsurprisingly, therefore, medium to large firms tend to be the predominant employers of non-standard employees in Namibia. The selective functioning of coordinating regulations and institutional forces in the structuring of the labour market provides employers with the opportunity to reassert market-determined wages and employment conditions for some workers. Moreover, the increased uncertainty and volatility associated with globalization has reduced the incentives to invest and innovate, and reinforced the reliance on low pay and casualized employment as a vital means of survival. These initiatives add up to an emergent labour market strategy that places low-waged, poorly regulated labour at the forefront of attempts to improve competitiveness and reduce costs. Rising levels of urban unemployment, social marginalization and informal economic activity not only reflect the deepening of poverty, but also lay the foundations for 'the consolidation of a new underclass' (Tapscott 1995, 164). The redistributive effects associated with the consolidation of a black urban elite were simply not on the scale necessary to preclude the growth of such an 'underclass'. Consequently, the efforts to overcome discrimination, poverty and unemployment, while ensuring that the economy diversifies and becomes internationally competitive, generated distinct sets of winners and losers.

A growth in non-standard employment is all too readily implicated in a causal relationship with 'deregulatory' practices in the labour market. This view can be expressed in a simple equation: more market-based regulation = more flexibility = more growth and employment. The economic order underlying flexibility theories is essentially that of a 'free' market. In reality, however, market forces can only attain equilibrium under conditions – such as complete information and costless contracting – that rarely, if ever, obtain in the labour market.

Of particular significance is the extent to which there is an acceptance of the idea that regulation and flexibility are two poles on the same continuum. The increase in non-standard employment in countries such as Namibia and South Africa coincided with rising levels of state and trade union intervention in the employment relationship. This is evident in the introduction of new statutory-based minimum standards and the establishment of labour market institutions that place a premium on the collective regulation of employment policies and practices. We are in a sense confronted by a paradox: the rise of poorly regulated non-standard employment relationships in a context of expanding institutional and statutory regulation of the labour market. This paradox, however, is more apparent than real. There has been a consensus developing among policy-makers since the late-1980s that an overarching narrative of 'flexibility' can best explain changes in the regulatory framework of the employment relationship. As a result, the policy debate over labour market reform is posed 'in stark "either/or" terms . . . opposing regulation and rigidity to deregulation and flexibility' (Fudge and Vosko 2001, 329). In practice, however, regulatory changes involve distinct trade-offs between the various forms of flexibility and security rather than a simple process of substituting one for the other. In other words, the conjunction of an expanded regulation of the standard employment relationship and an increase in non-standard forms of employment presupposes the existence of distinct labour market segments with different modes of regulation. This implies that an expansion in non-standard employment is facilitated as much by its active promotion through policies of 'flexibility' as by a passive tolerance of silences and inconsistencies in the (expanding) protective functions of labour market institutions.

The co-existence of different forms of labour regulation is reflected in the distinct opportunities and constraints associated with the division between largely non-competing groups in the labour market. Distinct regulatory frameworks in the labour market reflect, in part, the manner in which a particular distribution of the costs and rewards of restructuring is institutionalized. In particular, 'flexible' employment policies tend to exacerbate inequalities in the labour market by removing protection from the weakest segments of the workforce and exposing them to greater levels of competition. The lack of coverage by legislation and/or collective bargaining means that the determination of wages and conditions for non-standard workers is subject largely to unilateral managerial decision-making and outdated common law contractual principles. The different forms of non-standard employment are subject to greater or lesser levels of formal control and generate variable patterns of flexibility. Non-standard employment tends be more prevalent in countries such as Namibia where standard employment contracts are tightly regulated and non-standard work is loosely coordinated and controlled. Legal regulation was intended to fulfil a secondary role of plugging the gaps left by collective bargaining by establishing a floor of statutory protection, especially for vulnerable and unorganized workers. In reality, as Dickens (1988, 139) argues, 'legal regulation has mirrored, rather than supplemented, social regulation and, consequently, those falling through the net of collective bargaining protection tend to fall through the legal regulation safety net as well'.

There is no simple or direct relationship between the nature of labour market regulation and the incidence of non-standard employment. Very rarely can changes in a regulatory regime be adequately understood as simply an extension or a restriction of the role of statutory or social regulation to the benefit or detriment of market mechanisms (Regini 2000, 23). Hence, it is wrong to anticipate a simple trade-off between markets (flexibility) and institutions (regulation). Deregulation does not involve the simple unleashing of pristine or unregulated market forces and a corresponding elimination of social regulation. As Peck (1996, 188) correctly notes, market forces are not simply 'out there' waiting to be freed, but are politically constructed and institutionally mediated. Even in circumstances such as the casualization of employment in which market forces might appear to reign supreme, employment contracts are inherently social and context-dependent. Labour market flexibility was generally pursued through a process of 'reregulation' (Deakin and Mückenberger 1992, 144) involving the replacement of direct and uniform substantive legal regulation by alternative regulatory regimes under procedures that still rest ultimately on legal sanction. Reference to the various forms or modes of labour regulation suggest the existence of both a variety of regulatory institutions and a variety of levels at which the employment relationship may be coordinated. Current regulatory change cannot be reduced to 'some unidirectional process of deregulation/marketization' (Peck 2000, 71). In some cases, a reform intended as a flexibility measure actually results in its opposite. MacKenzie's (2002, 599) research into subcontracting arrangements shows that, far from dismantling hierarchical employment structures and leading to greater exposure to market imperatives, the movement towards an increased reliance on external sources of labour reflect 'the reconfiguration of the bureaucratic organization of production'.

The non-standard employment contract not only limits the scope of collective regulation and facilitates a more detailed specification of employment conditions, but also allows for the enforcement of a highly disproportionate wage-effort bargain. The standard employment contract, by contrast, is generally silent on both the actual pace of work and the levels of wage and extra-wage compensation. These are determined largely through collective struggle and accommodation. A common assumption is that by turning a permanent employee into a subcontracted labourer, management replaces employment relations with commercial contracts (Bresnen et al. 1985; Mückenberger 1989; Fevre 1991). In fact, MacKenzie (2000, 709) suggests that the subcontracting of labour relocates 'the mediation of the firm's activities through a series of commercial contracts rather than via vertically integrated bureaucratic structures'. In reality, however, bureaucratic forms of control are supplemented rather than simply supplanted by market forces. As Rubery et al. correctly point out, ostensibly deregulated labour markets 'required a more frequent recourse to the law [and other social institutions] in order to regulate the system of industrial relations' (cited in Peck 1996, 74). All means to regulate labour require some degree of active management. Contractualization is therefore not self-sufficient, without contradictions or identical in all places. Non-standard work is a form of unprotected employment that has flourished within the gaps left by the limits in regulatory coverage. For workers falling outside the legal definition of an employment relationship, the managerial prerogative, custom and practice at the workplace and social conventions in the labour market tend to substitute for statutory and collective rights and obligations.

The proliferation of non-standard employment has occasioned a shift in, rather than the decomposition of, the established mechanisms through which the employment relationship is regulated. The exclusion of non-standard workers from collective bargaining and statutory protective measures relegates their terms and conditions of employment to the dictates of contract. To the extent that statutory and collective regulation was limited or rolled back, it gave way to the contract of employment. Far from revealing 'a state of *anomie*, [this] placed the law of the contract of employment in a new position of prominence . . . as a regulatory system in its own right' (Freedland 1995, 18). In the 'free' market solutions to the restructuring of the labour market, contractual regulation is regarded as the most efficient mechanism for the allocation of the rational preferences of utility-seeking individuals. The role of the law of contract is thus being redefined not just in relation to an enhanced freedom of contract, but also in terms of a rudimentary conception of contractual employment relationships. Non-standard jobs are premised on a selective decoupling of the employment relationship from statutory, and hence almost invariably also collective, protective measures. This grants employers considerable latitude in constructing the form and content of non-standard employment relationships to suit their needs. A more intensive contractual regulation of the employment relationship is a defining feature of most forms of non-standard employment. In fact, employment 'flexibility' is premised on a shift in both 'the form in which labour is contracted and the scope provided to management by the contract of employment for varying labour inputs' (Regini 2000, 15–16). By contrast, regulation of the standard employment relationship traditionally involved the introduction of legislation, which set limits on both the individual freedom to contract and the managerial prerogative. Within this framework:

> regulation means 'de-contractualisation' – i.e. institutionalisation of legal guarantees for workers which are not at the disposal of the parties to the individual

contract of employment. As opposed to that, deregulation means 're-contractualisation' – i.e. a process shifting back terms of employment to the contractual regime and thus to managerial prerogative. (Mückenberger 1989, 385)

The institutional determinants of prevailing standards of living are important elements in the analysis of changes in an employment system. Employers may seek to reduce or constrain the historical and moral element in wages by drawing on sources of labour whose social reproduction costs are borne partially by the state and/or family networks. Given the low inputs from the former in Namibia, the latter are particularly significant in further reducing wage levels at the bottom end of the casual labour market. In situations of high unemployment and discontinuous work, the division of labour in the family is central to social reproduction (Beneria and Roldan 1987). The pooling of a variety of sources of income from different labour markets, pensions, remittances and unemployment benefits increasingly becomes a necessary survival strategy for low-income families. This places the household at the centre of the social reproduction of labour.

Namibian employers (especially in smaller firms) were eager to minimize the impact of what they perceived to be a costly, burdensome and overly prescriptive regulatory framework. As a result, the institutionally and collectively regulated segment of the labour market is narrowly confined to the more skilled, better-paid and organized workers in the larger urban enterprises. The lack of statutory or collective disincentives to use non-standard workers in Namibia is reflected in the ease with which certain functions can be casualized or outsourced. The prominence of small firms in the outsourcing industry has exacerbated this lack of disincentives. Trade unions have encountered many obstacles in their attempts to enforce legal regulations and collective agreements in small firms (LaRRI 2002). A rise in the incidence of non-standard employment is seldom the product of a qualitative change in employment policies. Rather, it appears to be the result of an intensification of existing practices; a reaction to unfavourable economic conditions; the exploitation of inconsistencies and silences in the prevailing patterns of statutory and collective regulation; and an expansion of those industries that have always relied on a 'peripheral' or 'marginal' workforce. A long-standing reliance on large numbers of black migrant workers, combined with a burgeoning informal sector, have generated a labour market structure in Namibia that is characterized by significant variation in both the rules that govern employee conduct and the terms and conditions of employment on offer. The Namibian labour market has historically displayed a dual character. Firstly, the organized (urban) workforce with relatively high wages and considerable job security constitutes a protected primary labour market. Many unionized workers have gained substantially from the restructuring of employment in the formal sector. Secondly, workers on temporary and fixed-term contracts, those in the informal and subsistence economies and the underemployed comprise an exposed secondary labour market, which has experienced no meaningful improvements since independence.

The form that state intervention takes tends to have a significant impact on the regulation of non-standard employment relationships. In Namibia, the legal distinction between permanent and casual employment is clearly delineated. However, the commitment to voluntarism in industrial relations means that the inequalities inherent in the employment relationship are to be ameliorated primarily through social rather than legal regulation. This system of regulation seeks to limit the unilateral determination of terms and conditions of employment by the employer through legislative support for trade unionism and voluntary collective bargaining. The role of regulatory legislation in providing a minimum level of rights has therefore been limited in favour of the voluntarist goal of encouraging self-regulation by unions and employers. This emphasis on self-regulation introduces a latent deregulation into the system of labour regulation that achieves much of the same outcomes as an explicit focus on deregulation. Voluntarism in collective labour regulation has not only encouraged the development of disparate conditions at the local level, but also frustrated the attempts at transforming the labour market structures of Namibia.

The various types of non-standard labour are employed for a variety of different and interacting reasons, in different market circumstances and positions in the occupational hierarchy, and as a 'solution' to different regulatory dilemmas. The use of non-standard employment is not solely determined by the volatility or unpredictability of product markets as implied by flexibility theories; equally important are the functional divisions of a firm, the skill requirements of various stages of production, degrees of specialization, levels of job protection and labour-supply factors. In other words, the relationship between the industrial sector and the levels, forms and functions of non-standard employment is multifaceted and contingent on a whole host of factors. In stark contrast to the low levels of production subcontracting between large and small firms in Namibia, the subcontracting of labour is widespread. Non-standard employment in Namibia is not confined to cases of short-term employment to meet exceptional or irregular work demands in industries such as construction. Non-standard employment is found – in varying degrees and forms – in virtually all economic sectors. The significantly different experiences and conditions of temporary and part-time workers underscore the heterogeneity of the 'peripheral' workforce as well as the variegated patterns of market–firm relations.

23.5   CONCLUSION

A focus on labour market regulation is particularly effective in dispelling the myth of a 'free' market unconstrained by social rules. The pervasive importance of notions such as 'fairness' and 'equity' in the employment relationship can only be adequately accounted for in a conception of the labour market as a socially constructed, institutionally governed and politically mediated structure of conflict and accommodation (Peck 1996). Institutions in the labour market protect workers from destructive cost-cutting competition by providing a coordinating role that establishes labour standards, checks trends towards heterogeneity, introduces uniform rules and prices, and guarantees the social reproduction of labour (Rubery 1996). The national character of an industrial relations system derives from the vital role of the state in the domain of industrial and employment policy, the linguistic and cultural elements that bind the system together, and the other policies, laws and rules that shape a country's economy. These factors influence not only the timing and scale of labour market reforms, but also their pace and dynamics. The use of non-standard employment contracts is facilitated or obstructed (to varying degrees) by the nature of the regulatory framework surrounding the employment relationship and by the impact of labour market institutions. This social context provides 'a framework of entitlements and obligations, comprising a range of opportunities and constraints, that shape levels and forms of participation in employment' (Felstead and Jewson 1999, 9). The use of non-standard employment, therefore, does not entail a simple shift to market forces or the absence of institutional mechanisms. Utilizing labour from beyond the boundaries of the firm compelled employers to fill the regulatory gaps in the non-standard employment relationship in an attempt to guarantee the supply of labour and the reproduction of skills. Crucially, the alternative mechanisms of regulation that were developed:

> were beyond the influence of collectively bargaining structures and procedures, and therefore subject to unilateral management sovereignty . . . [T]hrough the development of these alternative mechanisms, the firm essentially had sought to address the problems experienced in association with the processes of deregulation, by appropriating the role of regulation wrested from, or surrendered by, traditional instruments and agents associated with [standard] employment. (MacKenzie 2000, 723)

There is a tension between the reliance on vulnerable and precarious sources of labour in the external labour market and the demands for a stable internal labour market. The same institutions that set constraints or impose burdens on employers may also provide them with resources and opportunities. Extensive job security, for instance, is not only a constraint on management's capacity for strategic action, but also a resource enabling employers to harness the commitment and malleability of labour. The incidence and distribution of non-standard employment reflect the need of managers for employment practices aimed at decreasing the impact of uncertainty in the market, increasing the stability of the permanent workforce and enhancing their power over the use and deployment of labour in the lower reaches of the occupational hierarchy. However, employers are constrained in their employment practices by prevailing social norms, labour laws, the power of organized labour, and so on. Labour market segmentation is therefore the complex outcome of resistance and accommodation between the different fractions of capital and labour. The different rules in the labour market for standard and non-standard employees underpin the growing differentiation between the regulation of standard employment relationships and non-standard employment relationships. As Sayer (1995, 142) points out, the tensions between strengthening labour and making firms more competitive need to be interpreted not only in terms of the 'vertical' relations of class and class struggle, but also in terms of the 'horizontal' relations between different workers and different production systems.

Regulation theory can be effectively deployed to explain firms, markets and governance in developing and newly industrializing countries. It highlights the mediating influences of cultural norms and institutionalized expectations, welfare and training systems, family structures and gender relations, divisions of class, ethnicity and age, and the like on the interaction between markets and firms. A regulatory system is more than the sum of its parts. It is in this context that the concept of a 'mode of regulation' assumes such importance and yields its most penetrating insights. Central to regulation theory is the idea of positive and negative feedback between different economic activities, the belief that social institutions matter in economic change, and the notions of cumulative causation and of virtuous and vicious cycles. The path-dependency of changes in regulatory systems means that regulatory solutions that are effective in one context may not be readily supplanted into others. Establishing a durable form of regulation is a contingent process dependent on experimentation, chance discoveries and the degree of resistance encountered by particular interventions. As such, the outcomes of regulation can be best characterized as contingent, emergent and indeterminate. There is an urgent need for a greater appreciation of the conditional, open-ended and complex nature of economic change. The interaction between production, distribution and consumption suggests that we should seek to understand the ways in which broader socio-economic, political and cultural processes are shaped in different industries and regions. The uneven nature of economic development raises the issues of contingency and particularity:

> If sweatshops and economic backwardness would result from industrial restructuring in one place, while technological innovation and the revival of craft might emerge in another, one challenge was [*sic*] to clearly understand the factors responsible for shaping different patterns of industrial change. Underlying this approach is the conviction that no superior logic dictates how the profile of industry *must* evolve. The process will always be contingent upon local, political, social and cultural forces that deserve to be placed at the centre of economic analysis. (Benton, cited in Lawson 1992, 12)

These forces are precisely the focus of attention in regulation theory. As such, it provides a conceptual framework whereby we can grasp variations between countries, and specifies a developmental dynamic that is not determinist, functionalist or teleological. The value of regulation theory lies in its emphasis on the historically specific ways in which economic and social processes articulate. The basic research programme of regulation theory enables us to: (1) appreciate more fully the complex and cyclical nature of accumulation by combining the openness and contingency of capitalist development with a continuing stress on the systematic nature of capitalism as a mode of production; (2) substitute the idea of history as a regular succession of events with a view that highlights the causal powers, which are generative of behaviour, possessed by social objects; (3) uncover the social relations that sustain different regimes of accumulation while retaining the centrality of class struggle in their development; (4) examine the reproduction of the capital relation from the standpoint of production, consumption and exchange as well as the relationships between demand, investment, productivity and growth; and (5) transcend the developmentalist problematic by rejecting any notion of universal stages of development and formulating a non-deterministic account of phases of capitalist evolution that leaves considerable scope for historical variation and national diversity.

REFERENCES

Adedeji, Adebayo (1991), 'Will Africa ever get out of its economic doldrums?', in Adebayo Adedeji, Owodunni Teriba and Patrick Bugembe (eds), *The Challenge of African Economic Recovery and Development*, London: Frank Cass, pp. 772–787.

Aglietta, Michel (1979), *A Theory of Capitalist Regulation: the US Experience*, London: New Left Books.

Aglietta, M. (1982), 'World capitalism in the eighties', *New Left Review*, **136**, 5–42.

Aglietta, M. (1998), 'Capitalism at the turn of the century: regulation theory and the challenge of social change', *New Left Review*, **232**, 41–90.

Beneria, Lourdes and Marta Roldan (1987), *The Crossroads of Class and Gender: Industrial Homework, Subcontracting and Household Dynamics in Mexico City*, Chicago, IL: University of Chicago Press.

Bhorat, H., S. Hanival and R. Kanbur (2006), 'Poverty, trade and growth in sub-Saharan Africa', *Journal of African Economies*, **15** (4), 505–509.

Boyer, Robert (1990), *The Regulation School: A Critical Introduction*, New York: Columbia University Press.

Bresnen, M.J., K. Wray, A. Bryman, A.D. Beardsworth, J.R. Ford and E.T. Keil (1985), 'The flexibility of recruitment in the construction industry: formalisation or re-casualisation?', *Sociology*, **19** (1), 108–124.

Burawoy, Michael (1985), *The Politics of Production. Factory Regimes under Capitalism and Socialism*, London: Verso.

Cronje, Gillian and Suzanne Cronje (1979), *The Workers of Namibia*, London: International Defence and Aid Fund.

Curry, S. and C. Stoneman (1993), 'Problems of industrial development and market integration in Namibia', *Journal of Southern African Studies*, **19** (1), 40–59.

Deakin, Simon and Ulrich Mückenberger (1992), ' Deregulation and European labour markets', in Alberto Castro, Phillippe Méhaut and Jill Rubery (eds), *International Integration and Labour Market Organisation*, London: Academic Press, pp. 135–149.

Dickens, L. (1988), 'Falling through the net: employment change and worker protection', *Industrial Relations Journal*, **19** (2), 139–153.

Dobell, Lauren (1998), *SWAPO's Struggle for Namibia, 1960–1991: War by Other Means*, Basel: P. Schlettwein Publishing.

Elam, Mark (1994), 'Puzzling out the post-Fordist debate: technology, markets and institutions', in Ash Amin (ed.), *Post-Fordism. A Reader*, Oxford: Blackwell, pp. 43–70.

Esping-Andersen, Gosta and Marino Regini (eds) (2000), *Why Deregulate Labour Markets?* Oxford: Oxford University Press.

Fafchamps, Marcel (2004), *Market Institutions in Sub-Saharan Africa*, Cambridge, MA: MIT Press.

Felstead, Alan and Nick Jewson (1999), 'Flexible labour and non-standard employment: an agenda of issues', in Alan Felstead and Nick Jewson (eds), *Global Trends in Flexible Labour*, London: Macmillan, pp. 1–20.

Ferlie, Ewan and Andrew Pettigrew (1998), 'Managing through networks', in Chris Mabey, Guy Salaman and John Storey (eds), *Strategic Human Resource Management*. London: Sage Publications, pp. 200–222.

Fevre, R. (1991), 'Emerging "alternatives" to full-time and permanent employment', in Philip Brown and Richard Scase (eds), *Poor Work: Disadvantage and the Division of Labour*, Milton Keynes: Open University Press, pp. 56–71.

Freedland, M. (1995), 'The role of the contract of employment in modern labour law', in Lammy Betten (ed.), *The Employment Contract in Transforming Labour Relations*, Deventer: Kluwer, pp. 17–27.

Fröbel, F., J. Heinrichs and O. Kreye (1980), *The New International Division of Labour*, Cambridge: Cambridge University Press.

Fudge, J. and L.F. Vosko (2001), 'By whose standards? Reregulating the Canadian labour market', *Economic and Industrial Democracy*, **22** (3), 327–356.

Gelb, Stephen (1991), 'South Africa's economic crisis: an overview', in Stephen Gelb (ed.), *South Africa's Economic Crisis*, Cape Town: David Philip, pp. 1–32.

Grabher, Gernot (1993), 'Rediscovering the social in the economics of interfirm relations', in Gernot Grabher (ed.), *The Embedded Firm: on the Socioeconomics of Industrial Networks*, London: Routledge, pp. 1–31.

Granovetter, M. (1985), 'Economic action and social structure: the problem of embeddedness', *American Journal of Sociology*, **91** (3), 481–510.

Hansohm, Dirk, Moono Mupotola-Sibongo and Daniel Motinga (1998), *Overview of the Namibian Economy*, Windhoek: Namibian Economic Policy Research Unit.

Herbstein, Denis and John Evenson (1989), *The Devils are Among Us: the War for Namibia*, London: Zed Books.

Isaksen, J. and P. Shipoke (1992), 'Some notes on an industrial policy for Namibia', Working Paper No. 11, Windhoek: Namibian Economic Policy Research Unit.

Jessop, B. (1988), 'Regulation theory, post Fordism and the state: more than a reply to Werner Bonefeld', *Capital and Class*, **34**, 147–168.

Jessop, Bob (1992), 'Fordism and post-Fordism: a critical reformulation', in Michael Storper and Alan Scott (eds), *Pathways to Industrialization and Regional Development*, London: Routledge, pp. 42–62.

Jessop, B. (2001), 'Capitalism, the regulation approach, and critical realism', Department of Sociology, Lancaster University, available at http://www.comp.lancs.ac.uk/sociology.

Jessop, Bob and Ngai-Ling Sum (2006), *Beyond the Regulation Approach: Putting Capitalist Economies in their Place*, Cheltenham, UK and Northampton, MA, USA: Edward Elgar.

Jones, Bryn (1996), 'The social constitution of labour markets: why skills cannot be commodities', in Rosemary Crompton, Duncan Gallie and Ken Purcell (eds), *Changing Forms of Employment. Organisations, Skills and Gender*, London: Routledge, pp. 109–132.

Kempton, D.R. and R.L. Du Preez (1997), 'Namibian–De Beers state–firm relations: cooperation and conflict', *Journal of Southern African Studies*, **23** (4), 585–613.

Kwasi Fosu, A., S. Nsouli and A. Varoudakis (eds) (2001), '*Policies to promote competitiveness in manufacturing in sub-Saharan Africa*', Development Centre Seminars, OECD available at www.oecd-ilibrary.org/policies-to-promote-competitiveness-in-manufacturing-in-sub-saharan-africa_9789264193772-en.

Labour Resource and Research Institute (LaRRI) (2000), *Export Processing Zones in Namibia: Taking a Closer Look*, Windhoek: LaRRI.

Labour Resource and Research Institute (LaRRI) (2001), *Playing the Globalisation Game: the Implications of Economic Liberalisation for Namibia*, Windhoek: LaRRI.

Labour Resource and Research Institute (LaRRI) (2002), *The Small and Micro Enterprise Sector in Namibia: Conditions of Employment and Income*, Windhoek: LaRRI.

Landry, R., N. Amara and M. Lamari (2002), 'Does social capital determine innovation? To what extent?' *Technological Forecasting and Social Change*, **69**, 681–701.

Lawson, V.A. (1992), 'Industrial subcontracting and employment forms in Latin America: a framework for contextual analysis', *Progress in Human Geography*, **16** (1), 1–23.

Lazonick, W. (2003), 'The theory of the market economy and the social foundations of innovative enterprise', *Economic and Industrial Democracy*, **24** (1), 9–44.

Leys, C. (1994), 'Confronting the African tragedy', *New Left Review*, **204**, 33–47.

Leys, Colin and John Saul (eds) (1995a), *Namibia's Liberation Struggle: the Two-edged Sword*, London: James Currey.

Leys, Colin and John Saul (1995b), 'Introduction', in C. Leys and J.S. Saul (eds) *Namibia's Liberation Struggle: the Two-edged Sword*, London: James Currey, pp. 1–18.

Lipietz, A. (1982), 'Towards global Fordism?' *New Left Review*, **132**, 33–47.

Lipietz, A. (1984), 'How monetarism has choked third world industrialization', *New Left Review*, **145**, 71–87.

Lipietz, Alain (1986), 'New tendencies in the international division of labour: regimes of accumulation and modes of regulation', in Alan Scott and Michael Storper (eds), *Production, Work, Territory*, Boston, MA: Allen & Unwin, pp. 16–40.

Lipietz, Alain (1987), *Mirages and Miracles: the Crisis of Global Fordism*, London: Verso.

Lipietz, A. (1988), 'Accumulation, crises, and ways out: some methodological reflections on the concept of "regulation"', *International Journal of Political Economy*, **18** (2), 10–43.

Lundvall, B. (1993), 'Explaining interfirm cooperation and innovation: limits of the transaction-cost approach', in G. Grabher (ed.), *The Embedded Firm: On the Socioeconomics of Industrial Networks*, London: Routledge, pp. 52–64.

MacKenzie, R. (2000), 'Subcontracting and the reregulation of the employment relationship: a case study from the telecommunications industry', *Work, Employment and Society*, **14** (4), 707–726.

MacKenzie, R. (2002), 'The migration of bureaucracy: contracting and the regulation of labour in the telecommunications industry', *Work, Employment and Society*, **16** (4), 599–616.

Mihyo, Paschal and Freek Schiphorst (2002), 'Africa: a context of sharp economic decline', in John Kelly (ed.), *Industrial Relations: Critical Perspectives on Business and Management – Volume I*, London: Routledge, pp. 410–428.

Ministry of Labour (MoL) (1994), *Country Report on Namibia*, Windhoek: National Preparatory Committee for the World Summit for Social Development.

Ministry of Trade and Industry (MTI) (1999a), *Industrial Policy Beyond 2000*, Windhoek: Ministry of Trade and Industry.

Ministry of Trade and Industry (MTI) (1999b), *Review of the 1992 White Paper on Industrial Development*, Windhoek: Ministry of Trade and Industry.

Mückenberger, U. (1989), 'Non-standard forms of work and the role of changes in labour and social security regulation', *International Journal of the Sociology of Law*, **17**, 381–402.

Painter, J. and M. Goodwin (1995), 'Local governance and concrete research: investigating the uneven development of regulation', *Economy and Society*, **24** (3), 334–356.

Peck, James (1996), *Work-Place: The Social Regulation of Labor Markets*, New York: Guilford Press.

Peck, James (2000), 'Doing regulation', in G.L. Clark, M.P. Feldman and M.S. Gertler (eds), *The Oxford Handbook of Economic Geography*, Oxford: Oxford University Press, pp. 61–80.

Polanyi, Karl (1957), *The Great Transformation*, Boston, MA: Beacon Press.

Rankin, N., M. Söderbom and F. Teal. (2006), 'Exporting from manufacturing firms in sub-Saharan Africa', *Journal of African Economies*, **15** (4), 671–687.

Regini, Marino (2000), 'The dilemmas of labour market regulation', in Gosta Esping-Andersen and Marino Regini (eds), *Why Deregulate Labour Markets?* Oxford: Oxford University Press, pp. 11–29.

Riddell, Roger (1990), *Manufacturing Africa: Performance and Prospects of Seven Countries in sub-Saharan Africa*, London: James Currey.

Riddell, Roger (1993), 'The future of the manufacturing sector in sub-Saharan Africa', in Thomas Callaghy and John Ravenhill (eds), *Hemmed In: Responses to Africa's Economic Decline*, New York: Columbia University Press, pp. 215–247.

Rubery, J. (1994), 'The British production regime: a societal-specific system?' *Economy and Society*, **23** (3), 335–354.

Rubery, J. (1996),'The labour market outlook and the outlook for labour market analysis', in R. Crompton, D. Gallie and K. Purcell (eds), *Changing Forms of Employment. Organisations, Skills and Gender*, London: Routledge, pp. 21–39.

Sandbrook, R. (2005), 'Africa's great transformation?' *Journal of Development Studies*, **41** (6), 1118–1125.

Saul, John and Colin Leys (1995), 'The legacy: an afterword' in C. Leys and J.S. Saul (eds), *Namibia's Liberation Struggle: the Two-edged Sword*, London: James Currey, pp. 196–206.

Sayer, Andrew (1995), *Radical Political Economy: a Critique*, Oxford: Blackwell.

Sayer, Andrew and Richard Walker (1992), *The New Social Economy: Reworking the Division of Labour*, Oxford: Blackwell.

Scott, Alan and Michael Storper (1992), 'Industrialization and regional development', Michael Storper and Alan Scott (eds), *Pathways to Industrialization and Regional Development*, London: Routledge, pp. 9–28.

Simon, David (1998), 'Desert enclave to regional gateway? Walvis Bay's reintegration into Namibia', in David Simon (ed.), *South Africa in Southern Africa: Reconfiguring the Region*, Cape Town: David Philip, pp. 103–128.

Simon, David (2002), 'Namibia's economy: from colonial chattel to postcolonial pragmatism', in Anthony Lemon and Christian Rogerson (eds), *Geography and Economy in South Africa and its Neighbours*, Aldershot: Ashgate, pp. 171–185.

Storper, M. (1990), 'Industrialization and the regional question in the third world: lessons of postimperialism; prospects of post-Fordism', *International Journal of Urban and Regional Research*, **14** (3), 423–444.

Tapscott, Chris (1995), 'War, peace and social classes', in Colin Leys and John Saul (eds), *Namibia's Liberation Struggle: the Two-edged Sword*, London: James Currey, pp. 153–170.

Williamson, Oliver E. (1985), *The Economic Institutions of Capitalism*, New York: Free Press.

Winterfeldt, Volker, Tom Fox and Pempalani Mufune (eds) (2002), *Namibia – Society – Sociology*, Windhoek: University of Namibia Press.

Wood, B. (1991), 'Preventing the vacuum: determinants of the Namibian settlement', *Journal of Southern African Studies*, **17** (4), 742–769.

Index